The Turkish Political Elite

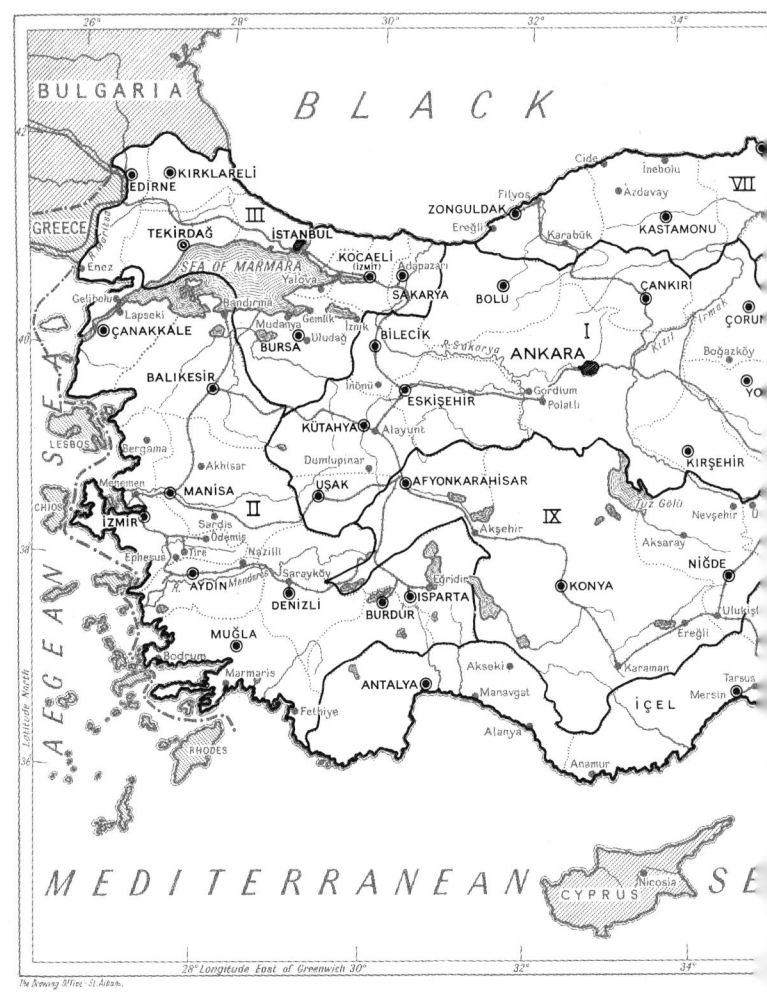

NOTE: The nine agricultural regions are indicated by Roman numerals and heavy lines. For a more detailed description, see Appendix B.

The Turkish Political Elite

Frederick W. Frey

The M. I. T. Press
*Massachusetts Institute of Technology
Cambridge, Massachusetts*

Copyright © 1965 by
The Massachusetts Institute of Technology
All Rights Reserved

Library of Congress Catalog Card Number: 65-13834
Printed in the United States of America

To J. D. H., G. R. H., and their daughter:
true communicants of Minerva

Foreword

HAROLD D. LASSWELL AND DANIEL LERNER

THE POLITICAL AFTERMATH of World War I exhibited the widest, and possibly deepest, transformations in the history of modern Europe. In a few short years the great imperial dynasties were gone or going. As the dynasties fell — Romanov, Habsburg, Hohenzollern — their powers were rapidly seized by a new breed of "revolutionary elites" never before seen at the governing councils of Eastern and Central Europe. They established their authority by ideology and assured their power by coercion. Even when they initiated their regimes under republican banners, the succession was soon claimed by the coercive ideologists.

The present volume deals with one such movement that shares some characteristics with the others, but exhibits an essential character of its own. Just as the Ottoman Turks were distinctive among the imperial dynasties, so the Republican Turks have been distinctive among the revolutionary elites. A clue of some import is the fact that late Ottoman Turkey was an *Asian* empire, with only the tiny Thracian hinterland of its Istanbul capital, across the Bosphorus, technically recognized as European. But Republican Turkey, with its Ankara capital deep in the Anatolian steppe, has obliged the United Nations to recognize it as a *European* nation. Republican Turkey thus became the only Islamic country in Europe — and the only country in the modern world — to have changed its continental identity.

Current Chinese polemics, which refuse to confer "Asian" status upon the U.S.S.R., remind us that Turkey's accomplishment is no mean feat and no mere legalism. The Turkish change of continental identity certified a deep sea-change in the Turkish polity. As a result,

Turkey can now be protected by the "Truman Doctrine" or apply to the European Common Market just as freely as Greece, the classic source of European culture. What is more, Turkey can be a full partner in NATO while uniquely carrying full partnership in CENTO as well. Republican Turkey thus has already won from the West the two-continent status that Soviet Russia still must seek to win from the East.

This achievement is due to the elite of the Turkish Republic. Born in the post-1918 demise of imperial dynasties and the subsequent upsurge of revolutionary elites, the Republican Turks have been both ideological and coercive — like their European contemporaries. But their ideology was liberal, and their coercion was minimal. Kemal Atatürk was the nearest approximation to a genius of modernization that any "emerging nation" had seen in this quarter-century. Kemalism was "ideological" — but it dealt with the behavior of persons (fez and language), not the attributes of social classes (proletarians and capitalists). Kemalism was "coercive" — but it diminished the terrifying *gendarmerie* and increased the power of the individual voter. The result was that Turkey, uniquely, turned out of office the party of the "revolutionary elite" — in the stunning election of 1950, in which Atatürk's own Republican People's Party was defeated. (Note that this *never* happened in Nazi Germany, Fascist Italy, or Falangist Spain — not to mention Communist Russia, which has now managed several major changes of regime under single-party control.)

Professor Frey's study of this remarkable elite provides the first comprehensive, empirical, and systematic account of its recruitment and composition. It is a welcome addition to the literature not only for the valuable body of information it makes available but for other reasons as well. The study is a model of conceptual and methodological sophistication in empirical research. It operates with equal effectiveness on both the quantitative and qualitative levels of analysis. Professor Frey has coded, counted, and tabulated his data; but he has also interviewed individuals, recorded and interpreted the information obtained from them. His numerical tables are thus enriched by specific incident and concrete example; his anecdotes are validated by objective measures of distribution and duration. Professor Frey's mastery of Turkish language and history interacts with his sure grasp of political theory and research method to produce a study that documents the proposition that the multidisciplinary skills required for political sociology can be effectively unified by an individual scholar.

Professor Frey's findings speak for themselves. We call attention here to only one conclusion that seems to us of capital importance. He writes that "all Turkish revolts to date, including the Young Turks, the Atatürk Revolution, and the 'Gentle Coup' of May 27, 1960, have been engineered by *intellectual* and *official* cadres! They were revolutions primarily to maintain or enhance the prestige of the state, not essentially to admit a rising new class to power or adjust a society to major economic or social changes." Professor Frey goes on to elaborate this statement in his chapter on education, which he shows to be a key factor in this Turkish tradition of "revolts from above."

We take special note of this finding because the role of educated men in the Turkish elite is an early instance of a relationship that has come to be more widely enacted and appreciated since World War II. The interaction between higher education and political power will be exhibited in many and diverse societal contexts in the volumes scheduled to appear in this series.

Professor Frey's account of the Turkish elite provides an invaluable summary of political changes that modified the shaping and sharing of power inside Turkey and among the prime political units in world politics. His study has the added merit of showing how the political leaders were able to consolidate an inner and outer position of strength by blending indigenous patterns with particular innovations selected from the capitalist and socialist systems in a geopolitical zone of continuing importance.

Preface

WHEN I began studying Turkish politics in 1956, I encountered many explanations of political phenomena in terms of the social backgrounds of the political elite. Various commentators opined that the country was run by the military, that early opposition to political modernization sprang mainly from the Muslim clergy, that medical doctors constituted a vital leadership element, that with the opening up of the tutelary system in 1950 a new wave of common men moved into the parliament, and so on. Nevertheless, I soon found that while regimes, parties, groups, and individuals were asserted to differ from one another in critical background characteristics (presumably with associated variations in political behavior), there actually existed no systematic study of the social backgrounds of the modern Turkish political elite. Nor was there, naturally, any analysis of the *changes* in elite background characteristics through time. Furthermore, the theoretical question of the relationship between the social backgrounds of political elites and the performance of political systems had not been fully explored. Hence, both for its intrinsic disciplinary interest and as an essential prolegomenon to future research in Turkey, I decided to undertake such an investigation myself. The present study of *The Turkish Political Elite* and a forthcoming theoretical work on social background analysis as a mode of political inquiry are the result. They are a response to their author's "felt needs." It is my obvious hope that they will also prove useful to other students of political behavior, of modernization processes, of the Near East, and of Turkey.

This study will have to speak for itself; I shall try to avoid the insidious temptation that a preface provides an author to review his own work. However, a few words explaining some of the idiosyncrasies of approach may not be amiss. I have tried throughout to quicken and deepen the statistical portrayal of elite social backgrounds by providing specific historic illustrations of how each given background characteristic has influenced an actor or an incident on the Turkish political scene. I have also attempted to provide succinct broader analyses of relevant institutions, key figures, and political trends as the context in which these social background data must be interpreted.

Although there are, inevitably, many tables and charts in such a work as this, it has seemed generally unnecessary to employ elaborate statistical tests of significance. In most instances the found differences between groups are, by the nature of the case, significant. No sample has been drawn, and there is no attempt to generalize to some larger population. An essentially complete enumeration has been secured. Hence, found differences *are* significant — do hold for the relevant population — though the reader must still always ascertain for himself the "impressiveness" of intergroup differences. I have occasionally considered the null hypothesis that differences between subgroups of deputies could have been obtained by chance from a random assignment, though only in a few instances where such a calculation seemed needed. In every case, however, I have tried to provide the interested reader with sufficient data to make such calculations for himself if he is so inclined. This study is intended to be a work of descriptive historical reference as well as political analysis.

I should have liked to consider several social background factors in addition to those examined — factors such as ethnicity, sectarian religious differences, wealth, sib position, etc. — but no appropriate data were available. Even more critically, the use of additional behavioral indicators to be run against social background factors would have been most desirable. But these data too were unfortunately unavailable, and their procurement would have necessitated a research effort beyond the resources of the author. All reasonably available information has, I hope, been exploited.

Finally, we come to that which makes preface-writing worth while — the opportunity publicly to thank a few of the people who have contributed unselfishly to another's work. Such people have been many. I can only mention a few. Dankwart Rustow, of Columbia University, not only gave me strong encouragement and sound advice but also fully shared his own hard-won data with me and spent hours in detailed checking of mine. His aid has been invaluable.

The other person without whose help this work could hardly have been written is Bedia Yağız, of the Secretariat of the Grand National Assembly in Ankara. With the noblest motive of all, simple friendship, she obtained many essential materials for me, spent weeks counting and tabulating voting records, and introduced me to other knowledgeable persons in the parliamentary Secretariat. There is no way adequately to express my gratitude to her, though I hope she can view this book as some real recompense for her selfless asistance.

Many are the Turks whom I have bedeviled with questions and to whom I owe a great deal of whatever insight into Turkish politics I possess. Mümtaz Soysal, Arif Payaslıoğlu, Cemal Mıhçıoğlu, Şerif Mardin, Turhan Feyzioğlu, Osman Okyar, Selâmi Erkut, Cevat Dursunoğlu, Şahap Tuza, Suphi Baykam, Hüseyin Nail Kubalı, Necat Erder, Evner Ergun, Orhan Sertel, Faruk Yağız, Nermin and Yavuz Abadan, Tahsin Bekir Balta, Bülent Ecevit, Şefik Uysal, Abdürrahman and Bedia Sanay, Mithat Enç, and many others have, in greater or lesser degree, imparted to me some of their understanding of their society. Even more, they have permitted me rashly to dispute with them on occasion. From all of them I have learned a great deal. The same can be said of George Harris and Bill Angell, two close American friends possessing deep knowledge of various aspects of Turkish life. I have profited greatly from many long discussions with both.

Though his influence is manifested less in this work than in others that are now in preparation, my personal and intellectual debt to Herbert Hyman is exceeded only by my affection for him; it is a pleasure, though hopefully unnecessary, to acknowledge both.

Lastly, in this all too slim list of my personal benefactors, I should like to thank my former secretary, Emmalyn Heed, who devotedly typed and retyped this ever-shortening but still bulky manuscript, and Nancy Callander who prepared the index.

Most of the field research on which this study is based was done under a Foreign Area Training Fellowship, granted by the Ford Foundation, to which I want to express my gratitude. And finally I should also like to indicate my appreciation of the support I have always received from my colleagues Daniel Lerner, Lucian Pye, Ithiel Pool, and others in the Political Science Section at M.I.T. and in the Center for International Studies who, despite much evidence to the contrary, maintained their confident belief that I would eventually finish this tome!

Obviously, though much needed aid has been received, the responsibilities of authorship and its meager royalties remain with me.

Wayland, Massachusetts FREDERICK W. FREY
September, 1964

Contents

Foreword *by Harold D. Lasswell and Daniel Lerner* ix

Preface xiii

PART ONE. INTRODUCTION

CHAPTER ONE

Turkey and the Grand National Assembly 3
 The Political Significance of Turkey 3
 The Grand National Assembly 6

CHAPTER TWO

The Methods of Research 16
 Sources of Background Information 16
 Tabulation and Verification of Data 21
 Analytic Technique 22

PART TWO. THE AGGREGATE VIEW

CHAPTER THREE

Education: The Hallmark of the Elite 29
 Development of the Turkish Educational System 32
 The Political Significance of Educational Developments 37
 Educational Level of the Turkish Population and of the Deputies 43
 The Political Significance of Educational Differences 46

Quantitative Data on the Significance of Formal
    Education   49
Summary   70

CHAPTER FOUR

Occupation: The Portal to Politics   73
    The Importance of Occupation in Turkish Society   74
    Occupational Profile of the Population and of the
        Deputies   78
    General Analysis: Broad Interoccupational Differences   84
    Localism   89
    Miscellaneous Characteristics of Vocational Groups   98

CHAPTER FIVE

Characteristics of Specific Occupations   111
    The Free Professions   111
    The Officials   114
    Economic Occupations   123
    Religion   126
    Journalism   127
    Summary   129

CHAPTER SIX

Fathers, Faiths, and Females   135
    The Fathers of the Deputies: Occupational Mobility   136
    Religious Orientation   143
    Women Deputies   147
    Summary   155

PART THREE.   ANALYSES OF CHANGE

CHAPTER SEVEN

The Ten Assemblies   161
    Parliamentary Service   163
    Age   168
    Marital and Parental Status   173
    Education   175
    Occupation   180
    Regionalism and Localism   184

Women Deputies 192
Summary 193

CHAPTER EIGHT

New Deputies and Cohort Groups 199
The Recruits 199
Cohort Analysis 212
Summary 222

CHAPTER NINE

Elites within an Elite: Levels of Formal Leadership 224
Establishment of Leadership Levels 225
Ratings of Posts and Committees 228
Formal Power Scores 242
Characteristics of Leadership Groups 246
Summary 264

CHAPTER TEN

Elites within an Elite: Cabinets and Ministries 269
The Cabinet 269
The Individual Ministries 284
Summary 297

CHAPTER ELEVEN

Political Parties: 1920–1946 301
The Role of Party in Turkish Politics 301
The First and Second Groups of the First Assembly 306
Speaking in the First Assembly 313
The Progressive Republican and the Republican People's Parties of the Second Assembly 323
The Liberal Republican Party of the Third Assembly 335
The Independent Group of the Republican People's Party 343

CHAPTER TWELVE

Political Parties: 1946–1957 348
The Eighth Assembly 350
Political Parties in the Ninth and Tenth Assemblies 356
The Voting Behavior of Deputies 360
Summary 375

PART FOUR. CONCLUSION

CHAPTER THIRTEEN

Emphases and Evaluations 387
    Comments on the Turkish Political System 387
    Some Hypotheses and Generalizations 393
    More Limited Hypotheses and Leads 397
    Power and Prestige 400
    Some Stages of Political Development 406

APPENDICES

APPENDIX A

Formal Requirements for Deputies 423
    The Electoral System 423
    Political Party Membership and Candidate Nomination 430

APPENDIX B

Official Number of Deputyships and Actual Number of Deputies by Region and Province 438

APPENDIX C

Analysis of Judges' Ratings of Assembly Posts and Committees: 1920–1957 443

APPENDIX D

Committee Rankings 445

APPENDIX E

The Number of Times Selected Prominent Deputies Spoke on the Floor of the Parliament during the First Assembly, by Faction 448

Select Bibliography 450

Index 475

List of Figures

Frontispiece	Map of Turkey	ii – iii
Figure 3.1	Educational Attainments of All Deputies, 1920–1957	44
Figure 3.2	Literacy of Turkish Population over Six Years of Age, by Sex and for Selected Years	45
Figure 3.3	Distribution of Turkish Youth Enrolled in Public Schools in the School Year 1957–1958	45
Figure 3.4	Percentage of Those Deputies with Higher Education and Knowledge of a Foreign Language Who Were Elected More than Once, by Number of Foreign Languages Known	56
Figure 3.5	Types of Higher Education: University-Educated Deputies (1920–1957) and All Male Turkish University Graduates (1938–1950)	64
Figure 4.1	Mean Number of Times Elected of All Deputies and Those Deputies First Elected at a By-Election, According to Major Occupations: Covering All Deputies, 1920–1957	105
Figure 7.1	Average Age and Average Age on First Election, by Assembly	172
Figure 7.2	Educational Levels of Deputies, by Assembly	176
Figure 7.3	Broad Occupational Classification of Deputies, by Assembly	184
Figure 7.4	Percentage of Deputies Born in Constituency Represented, by Assembly	188
Figure 8.1	Average Ages of New Deputies, Carryover Deputies, and All Deputies, by Assembly	201
Figure 8.2	Percentages of New Deputies and of All Deputies Born in the Marmara Region, by Assembly	204
Figure 8.3	Percentages of New Deputies, Carryover Deputies, and All Deputies Born in Province Represented, by Assembly	207
Figure 8.4	Occupational Distributions of New Deputies and All Deputies, by Assembly	211
Figure 8.5	"Quarter Life" and "Tenth Life" of Cohort Groups, by Assembly Intervals and Date of Entry into the Deputyship	216

xxii LIST OF FIGURES

Figure 9.1	Deputies Reelected to the Subsequent Assembly, by Leadership Level	246
Figure 9.2	Deputies with Previous Assembly Experience, by Leadership Level	247
Figure 9.3	Average Age on First Election, by Leadership Level	249
Figure 9.4	Average Age of Deputies, by Leadership Level	250
Figure 9.5	Deputies Born in the Marmara and Aegean Regions, by Leadership Level	252
Figure 9.6	Deputies with University-Level Education, by Leadership Level	253
Figure 9.7	Average Number of Foreign Languages Claimed per Deputy, by Leadership Level	254
Figure 9.8	Broad Occupational Categories of Deputies, by Leadership Level	257
Figure 9.9	Deputies with Legal and Medical Vocations, by Leadership Level	259
Figure 9.10	Deputies with Governmental, Military, and Educational Vocations, by Leadership Level	260
Figure 9.11	Deputies with "Trade" and Agricultural Vocations, by Leadership Level	262
Figure 9.12	Deputies Born in the Province They Represented in the Assembly, by Leadership Level	263
Figure 10.1	Official and Total Sizes of Cabinets: Ministers Serving a Complete Term in the Same Ministry, by Assembly	270
Figure 10.2	Birth in Province Represented, Cabinet Ministers and All Deputies, by Assembly	277
Figure 10.3	University-Level Education of Cabinet Ministers, Top Leaders, and All Deputies, by Assembly	279
Figure 10.4	Persons Claiming Knowledge of at Least One Foreign Language: Cabinet Ministers, Top Leaders, and All Deputies, by Assembly	280
Figure 11.1	Party Groupings in the First Assembly, by Leadership Levels	313
Figure 11.2	Average Age of Deputies, by Party Group and Amount of Speaking in the First Assembly	318
Figure 11.3	Previous Parliamentary Experience of Deputies, by Party Group and Amount of Speaking in the First Assembly	319
Figure 11.4	Percentage of Deputies Born in Province Represented, by Party Group and Amount of Speaking in the First Assembly	321
Figure 12.1	Broad Occupational Distribution of Deputies in the Eighth Assembly, by Party	352
Figure 12.2	Negative Voting on Governmental Proposals during the First Assembly, by Faction	363
Figure 12.3	Percentage of Deputies Born in Province Represented, by Voting Support of Governmental Proposals and Faction	365

Figure 12.4	Governmental Voting Support of Deputies with Military and Religious Occupational Backgrounds, by Faction	366
Figure 12.5	Average Age of Democratic Party Deputies in the Ninth and Tenth Assemblies, by Governmental Voting Support	373
Figure 13.1	Composite Representation of Social Background and Broad Political Changes, 1920–1960	389
Figure 13.2	Four Characteristic Power Structures during the Process of Political Development	412

List of Tables

Table 3.1	Parliamentary Experience by Educational Level (All Deputies)	51
Table 3.2	Parliamentary Experience by Educational Level and Knowledge of Foreign Language (Percentages)	53
Table 3.3	Parliamentary Experience of Those with University Education, by Knowledge of Foreign Languages and Publications	58
Table 3.4	Ages of All Deputies at First Election, by Educational Level	59
Table 3.5	Political Experience by Types of Higher Education	65
Table 3.6	Deputies Obtaining Higher Education in Various Western Countries, by Type of Faculty Attended	68
Table 4.1	Occupational Distribution of All Deputies, 1920–1957	80
Table 4.2	Occupations of Turkish Male Population, Fifteen Years of Age and Over, in Selected Years (Percentages)	81
Table 4.3	Occupations of Household Heads, 1955	83
Table 4.4	Mean Number of Times Elected, According to Occupation: All Deputies, 1920–1957	84
Table 4.5	First Election at a By-election, According to Occupation: All Deputies, 1920–1957	86
Table 4.6	Foreign Language Competence, Publication Record, and University Education of Deputies According to Occupation: All Deputies, 1920–1957	87
Table 4.7	Age at First Election According to Occupation: All Deputies, 1920–1957	88
Table 4.8	Percentages of Deputies Born in Turkey and Born in a Constituency Represented, According to Occupation: All Deputies, 1920–1957	93
Table 4.9	Mean Election Rates of Occupational Groups of Deputies by Birth in a Constituency Represented	96
Table 4.10	Listed Elective Local Government Experience According to Broad Occupational Groupings: All Deputies, 1920–1957	98

LIST OF TABLES   XXV

Table 4.11	Listed Membership in at Least One Voluntary Association According to Broad Occupational Groupings: All Deputies, 1920–1957	99
Table 4.12	Percentage of Deputies Elected More than Once but Representing Only One Constituency in Their Careers, According to Broad Occupational Groupings: All Deputies, 1920–1957	101
Table 4.13	Percentages of Deputies Born in Istanbul, According to Occupational Groupings: All Deputies, 1920–1957	104
Table 4.14	Foreign Languages of Deputies by Occupational Groups	107
Table 5.1	Highest Educational Levels Reached by Turkish Bureaucrats (1938) and Turkish Deputies with Bureaucratic Backgrounds (1920–1957) (Percentages)	116
Table 6.1	Deputies' Occupations Compared with Their Fathers' Occupations	141
Table 7.1	Parliamentary Service, Experience, and Reelection, by Assembly (Percentages)	163
Table 7.2	Average Age and Average Age at First Election of Deputies, by Assembly	170
Table 7.3	Marital and Parental Status of Deputies, by Assembly	174
Table 7.4	Foreign Language Claims of Deputies, by Assembly (Percentages)	178
Table 7.5	Occupations of Deputies, by Assembly (Percentages)	181
Table 7.6	Birthplaces of Deputies, by Region (Percentages)	185
Table 7.7	Deputies Born in Region of Constituency Represented (Percentages)	190
Table 8.1	Regional Birthplaces of All Deputies and Newly Elected Deputies, by Assembly (Percentages)	203
Table 8.2	Comparative Regional Recruitment of New Members in the Fifth and Tenth Assemblies	205
Table 8.3	Educational Levels of Newly Elected Deputies, by Assembly (Percentages)	208
Table 8.4	Occupations of Newly Elected Deputies, by Assembly (Percentages)	210
Table 8.5	Cohort Analysis: Percentage of Cohort Remaining at Successive Assemblies	213
Table 8.6	Rank Orderings of the Percentages of Each Cohort Remaining at Successive Assemblies	214
Table 8.7	Average Longevity Rankings of All Cohorts	215
Table 8.8	Cohort Analysis: Percentage Born in Constituency Represented, by Assembly Intervals	218
Table 8.9	Cohort Analysis: Percentage Representing Same Constituency as in Immediately Preceding Assembly, by Assembly Intervals	220
Table 8.10	Cohort Analysis: Percentage with University-Level Education, by Assembly Intervals	221

LIST OF TABLES

Table 9.1	Judges' Rankings of Top Political Posts for the Period 1920–1923	228
Table 9.2	Judges' Rankings of Top Political Posts for the Period 1923–1939	231
Table 9.3	Judges' Rankings of Top Political Posts for the Period 1939–1950	236
Table 9.4	Judges' Rankings of Top Political Posts for the Period 1950–1957	238
Table 9.5	Leadership Groups by Assembly (Percentages)	245
Table 9.6	Formal Power Ratings of Cohort Groups — Percentage of Top Leaders	248
Table 9.7	Occupational Categories of Deputies, by Leadership Levels and Assemblies (Percentages)	256
Table 10.1	Reelection, Parliamentary and Ministerial Experience of Ministers, by Assembly (Percentages)	272
Table 10.2	Regions of Birth of Cabinet Members, by Assemblies (Percentages)	274
Table 10.3	Regional Representation of Cabinet Members, by Assemblies (Percentages)	276
Table 10.4	Faculties Attended by Cabinet Ministers with Higher Education, by Assemblies (Percentages)	281
Table 10.5	Occupations of Cabinet Ministers, by Assemblies (Percentages)	283
Table 10.6	Various Characteristics of Ministers, 1923–1957	286
Table 11.1	Party Groupings in the First Assembly, by Occupation (Percentages)	311
Table 11.2	Party Groupings in the First Assembly, by Incidence of Speaking (Percentages)	315
Table 11.3	Party Groupings in the First Assembly, by Reelection and Incidence of Speaking (Percentages)	316
Table 11.4	Party Groupings in the First Assembly, by Amount of Speaking (Percentages)	317
Table 11.5	Party Groupings in the First Assembly, by Leadership Level and Amount of Speaking (Percentages)	320
Table 11.6	Party Groupings in the First Assembly, by Occupation and Amount of Speaking (Percentages)	322
Table 11.7	Progressive Republican and People's Parties, by Occupation (Percentages)	333
Table 12.1	Comparison of the People's Party Assembly Group of the Seventh and Eighth Assemblies with the Democratic Party Assembly Group of the Eighth Assembly along Selected Dimensions	353
Table 12.2	Occupations of Democratic and People's Party Deputies, Ninth and Tenth Assemblies (Percentages)	359
Table 12.3	Negative Voting on Government Proposals, by Assembly	362
Table 12.4	Average Number of Negative Votes Cast on Government Proposals, Per Deputy, by Region	368
Table 13.1	Number of Times Elected, All Deputies in France under the Third and Fourth Republics and in Turkey under the First Republic (Percentages)	395

Part One

Introduction

CHAPTER ONE

Turkey and the Grand National Assembly

THREE GREAT CRISES swirl over the world in the second half of the twentieth century. One is the conflict between communism and the "free world." The second is the transition into affluent "mass societies" of the major European powers — to be followed by Japan and then by other states. The third crisis is the struggle of the "emerging nations" to move from traditionalism to modernity.

THE POLITICAL SIGNIFICANCE OF TURKEY

Turkey is a stategic country with respect to the first and the third of these crises. Many of us are aware that this is militarily true, since Turkey guards the southern flank of the NATO defenses with what is possibly "... the most effective *land* force in continental non-Soviet Europe."[1] Today, as in the past centuries, her proximity to Russia and her control over the Dardanelles and the Bosphorus give her a pivotal geopolitical position. As the sole Near Eastern member of both NATO and CENTO, Turkey continues to act as a bridge between Europe and Asia.

Though these considerations are still critical, improvements in the technology of weapons and monitoring devices will probably reduce the purely military importance of Turkey in the not-too-distant future. Recognition of this prospect, however, does not lead to a lowered

---

[1] Richard D. Robinson, *The First Turkish Republic* (Cambridge: Harvard University Press, 1963), p. vii.

estimate of the international significance of Turkey. Already there has been a distorted inclination to regard her almost entirely in terms of her military role — the "unsinkable aircraft carrier" close to the Soviet Union. But aircraft carriers are becoming obsolete, except for limited war, while Turkey's political significance for both the policy maker and the political scientist is now greater than ever before.

The reason for this special political significance of Turkey is simply that Turkey is an "emerging" nation that has had, until quite recently, unique and exemplary success. Proceeding further and faster down the road to modernity than most other emerging states, she has, moreover, in the past few years careened off that road at a critical turning point which the others have not yet reached. Hence, her experiences are of particular interest to analysts of the developmental process.

Scores of nations, containing the bulk of world population, are currently in the throes of this developmental activity. The politics of transition is difficult, perilous, and complex. It is, in fact, still a moot point whether an underdeveloped nation *can* simultaneously sustain rapid movement toward economic modernity and toward political democracy. Some strong arguments can be offered in support of the view that the two goals are in fundamental conflict. Greatly accelerated economic development, from very meager beginnings, often seems to require a high concentration of power in the hands of the state, whereas democracy is frequently regarded as a political system under which power is widely shared. On the one side, mobilization and coordination are emphasized; on the other side, stress is given to dispersion and individualism.

One extremely common answer to this dilemma has been to conceive of "modernization" as ideally proceeding by distinct stages. In any given stage, attention is focused on a limited and mutually compatible set of subordinate goals (such as social reform or industrialization). These goals are to be achieved before moving on to other, possibly conflicting parts of the over-all objective. The "tutelary" approach to development is one such answer, which suggests that in the early stages of the process democratic goals can artfully be held in abeyance while the society concentrates on seemingly prerequisite social and economic reforms. Democracy can then be erected on suitable social and economic foundations as a second stage in the construction process.

Though the appeal of this tutelary approach has been great throughout the developing areas, against it there has always been leveled the grim argument that once the "tutors" are installed — once a dictatorship is established, even though benevolent — the later peaceful sharing of power is most unlikely. Power corrupts, and tutelary dictatorship leads to total dictatorship, not to democracy, in the view of the proponents of this argument.

In any event, modernization usually is led by a "modernizing cadre" that pushes through the early reforms and sets in motion the forces of self-conscious transition. Ultimately the profound problem of the transfer of power arises. The original modernizing cadre is confronted with pressures, perhaps of its own making, to surrender power to other groups, perhaps the products of its own reforms. Learning to negotiate the peaceful transfer of power to a freely organized opposition is a major milestone on the emerging nation's path to democracy.

Turkey is almost the only prominent emerging nation that has successfully and independently advanced through this crucial phase in the developmental process. After foreign invasion and a nationalistic War for Independence she moved into a near-model tutelary system. A benevolent dictatorship was established under the brilliant leadership of Mustafa Kemal Atatürk, and an energetic attempt was made to hammer the structure of the society into a different, more modern shape. Then in the face of mounting pressures, under the leadership of Kemal's comrade and political heir, Ismet Inönü, opposition was permitted to organize. That opposition won a free election, and the party of the tutelary years wisely and gracefully handed power to its successor.[2]

Of course, Turkey has floundered badly in the process of transferring this power back again the second time. The reason for this failure, however, is an involved and momentous question, which this study should help illumine. Nevertheless, in examining Turkey's experience, we have an opportunity to investigate a stage of political development through which other nations may yet pass — if they get so far. We have a chance to inspect a model tutelary movement, an earnest attempt to democratize such a system, and the apparently tragic impasse to which this most promising course has come. In addition, there is the basic interest that *any* political system, particu-

---

[2] Cf. John H. Herz, "The Problem of Successorship in Dictatorial Regimes: A Study in Comparative Law and Institutions," *Journal of Politics*, XIV (1952), p. 23, n. 3, where he says, speaking of contemporary Turkey, "... we have here the — probably unique — case of a dictatorship's 'voluntary' self-transformation into what comes near to a democracy or, at least, a more-than-one-party system." See also George Lenczowski, *The Middle East in World Affairs* (Ithaca: Cornell University Press, 2nd ed., 1956), p. 120, for a similar view of Turkey's political uniqueness. Outside of Latin America the obvious other case is that of the Philippines, whose connection with the United States was so intimate that the example seems less appropriate, and which, of course, never went through a real tutelary dictatorial period.

larly any non-Western system, has for the political scientist concerned with comparative politics.

The word "tragic" has been used here with deliberation, for if Turkey, with her many advantages of able leadership, discipline, and capacity for self-sacrifice, could not work out these problems, what other emerging nation can do so? The world urgently needs a visible example of a nation that is successfully developing economically, socially, and *politically* — a nation that is improving the welfare of her people and advancing democratically at the same time. Turkey long appeared to be among the best hopes for such an example or model. Analysis of her case — of what went right and what went wrong — therefore seems to carry special significance. The present study attempts to contribute in a clearly limited way to that end.

The Grand National Assembly

Three fundamental points must be emphasized: (1) the extreme importance of government in Turkish society (which is asserted but not documented here); (2) the highly integrated character of Turkish government during the period under investigation; and (3) the focal position of the Grand National Assembly in that governmental structure.

Because of this high degree of governmental integration, when one examines the social backgrounds of the deputies to the Grand National Assembly, one obtains, *ipso facto*, information on the backgrounds of all the cabinets and ministers, on the formal leadership of the Assembly, and on the top political party leaders as well. Hence, unlike an analysis of the American Congress and more like — but beyond — an analysis of the British House of Commons or French Assembly, we have a picture of the social characteristics of the formally dominant political elite in the nation. Impressionistic evidence further indicates that this group of men probably constituted a major portion of the wielders of disproportionate *real power*, not formal authority, in Turkish society. All signs are that national political life in Turkey revolved about these men. Not everybody was of equal importance, quite plainly. In addition to analysis of the whole group and of individual Assemblies, I shall concentrate on smaller, more important leadership groups such as the cabinet and the political parties. But even these leaders spent most of their political energies in the Assembly environment, reacting to it and trying to influence it. Thus description of the backgrounds of all the members of the institution is essential for full understanding even of its small group of top leaders. It is for these reasons that I decided to undertake an analysis of the deputies to the Grand National Assembly rather than of other actors on the Turkish political scene.

This investigation of the social backgrounds of the deputies to the Grand National Assembly (*Türkiye Büyük Millet Meclisi*) covers the period from 1920, when the Assembly was founded, to 1957. These thirty-seven years include the first ten Assemblies out of the eleven occurring before the military *coup d'état* of May 27, 1960, that resulted in a major revision of the Turkish Constitution and the termination of the First Turkish Republic. Thus the period comprises a marked epoch in the political history of modern Turkey. Along many dimensions the analysis will be extended to 1960, though the Eleventh Assembly (1957–1960) cannot be fully analyzed because all relevant materials are not yet available. Since this Assembly greatly resembled its predecessor, the Tenth, in social background, its complete inclusion would not alter the outlines of the picture I shall present.

The Grand National Assembly of Turkey was born of the National Struggle (*Millî Mücadele*) by the Turks to prevent Allied dismemberment of the Turkish core of the Ottoman Empire (Anatolia, Istanbul, and Eastern Thrace) after the severe Ottoman defeat in World War I. The Assembly was the central, authoritative organ symbolizing Turkish resistance to Allied pressures and to the Greek military invasion of Turkey, which was launched at Izmir on May 15, 1919. As a national legislature, it grew out of the various local Defense of Rights, Rejection of Annexation and Occupation, and other resistance organizations through which scattered Turkish elements spontaneously tried to preserve all or part of their society. In particular, it sprang from the Association for the Defense of Rights of Anatolia and Rumelia (*Anadolu ve Rumeli Müdafaai Hukuk Cemiyeti*), and from the Representative Committee (*Heyeti Temsiliye*), which emerged from the Erzurum and Sivas Congresses of the Defense of Rights Associations in 1919.[3]

---

[3] It is not my purpose to describe the history of these dramatic events. The general picture can be acquired from excellent brief surveys in English of modern Turkish history such as Bernard Lewis, *The Emergence of Modern Turkey* (London: Oxford University Press, 1961); "The United States and Turkey," by Lewis V. Thomas, in Lewis V. Thomas and Richard N. Frye, *The United States and Turkey and Iran,* (Cambridge, Mass.: Harvard University Press, 1951), pp. 3–172; and Geoffrey Lewis, *Turkey* (London: Ernest Benn Ltd., 1955). The official Turkish view is available in a French translation in *Histoire de la République Turque* (Istanbul: Devlet Basımevi, 1935), hereafter referred to as *Histoire....* Another indispensable source is Mustafa Kemal (Atatürk)'s famous six-day "Great Speech" (*Büyük Nutuk*), delivered as his apologia pro vita sua to the Second Grand Congress of his Republican People's Party in October 1927: Gazi Mustafa Kemal, *Nutuk (Speech)*, (Istanbul: Devlet Basımevi, 1938), or, in English translation, *A Speech Delivered by Ghazi Mustafa Kemal* (Leipzig: K. F. Koehler, 1929). On the assorted resistance organizations, their pro-

After the Allies had physically occupied Istanbul and arrested and deported to Malta many deputies to the Ottoman Assembly, the captive, timorous Sultan, Mehmet VI (Vahdeddin), dissolved the Ottoman Chamber of Deputies on April 11, 1920. Having foreseen these measures and having specifically warned the Istanbul deputies of them, Mustafa Kemal began, on the sixteenth of March, a few days after the occupation of Istanbul, to plan for the convening of a national legislature with "extraordinary authority" in Ankara.

Elected under provisions that will be explained in Appendix A, the Grand National Assembly met officially for the first time on April 23, 1920. Naturally, it immediately passed some temporary organizational regulations; but the first major organic act was the Law of Fundamental Organization (*Teşkilâtı Esasiye Kanunu*) of January 20, 1921. This law asserted that sovereignty belonged unconditionally to the nation, and that the sole rightful representative of that nation was the Grand National Assembly. Very interestingly, all executive *and* legislative powers were said to be concentrated in the Assembly, which was the supreme repository of governmental authority. There was no separation of powers. The government was labeled the "Government of the Grand National Assembly" (*Büyük Millet Meclisi Hukûmeti*) — an accurate description, since the Assembly not only elected its own President, who was authorized to sign for it, but also elected, *individually,* all members of the Council of Ministers (*Icra Vekilleri Heyeti*). In addition, the Council of Ministers elected from its own members a chairman.[4]

This was truly a *régime d'assemblée.* The great authority of the Assembly and the close integration of all top governmental organs, though subsequently modified, continued to be the *outstanding structural characteristics* of this highest level of Turkish government throughout the period being studied.

On October 29, 1923, the formal break with the six-hundred-year-old house of Osman occurred. The Turkish Republic was pro-

---

grams, and their structures, the invaluable major source is Tarık Z. Tunaya's compilation, *Türkiyede Siyasî Partiler (Political Parties in Turkey)*, (Istanbul: Doğan Kardeş Yayınları, 1952), Book III, pp. 472–539. Naturally, other references abound and are furnished in the bibliography. But these are minimally necessary and basic. For a good description of the atmosphere of the Erzurum Congress, cf. Cevat Dursunoğlu, *Millî Mücadelede Erzurum (Erzurum in the National Struggle)*, (Ankara: T. C. Ziraat Bankası Matbaası, 1946). A valuable survey and interpretation of developments during the entire period of our concern is R. D. Robinson, *The First Turkish Republic, op. cit.*

[4] Cf., for the text of the law, A. Şeref Gözübüyük and Suna Kili (eds.), *Türk Anayasa Metinleri (Turkish Constitutional Texts)*, (Ankara University Political Sciences Faculty, Administrative Sciences Institute Publication No. 2; Ankara: Ajans-Türk Matbaası, 1957), pp. 85–87.

claimed by the G.N.A. (Grand National Assembly). Shortly thereafter, discussions were begun regarding a new constitution, which was adopted by the G.N.A. on April 20, 1924.[5] This constitution, though subject to some modifications, remained the basic organic act of Turkish government throughout the remainder of our period (1924–1957, the Second through the Tenth Assemblies), and up to the military *coup d'état* of May 1960.

Article 4 of the 1924 Turkish Constitution stated that "only the Grand National Assembly of Turkey represents the Turkish nation and only it exercises the right of sovereignty in the Nation's name." Article 5 stipulated that "legislative authority and executive power are manifested and concentrated in the Grand National Assembly." Articles 6 and 7 added that the Assembly utilized its legislative authority directly and that it wielded its executive power through the President of the Republic elected by it and through a Council of Ministers *chosen by the President*.

The President of the Republic was elected by the Assembly *from its own members* for a term coincident with the duration of that Assembly, and he was eligible for reelection (Article 31). He was the formal head of state, presided over the Council of Ministers whenever he deemed it necessary, and had a legislative veto (except for constitutional and budgetary matters) that could be overridden by another normal passage of the bill (Articles 32, 35). All decrees promulgated by the President of the Republic had to be countersigned by the Prime Minister and the appropriate departmental minister (Article 39).

The Prime Minister was appointed by the President of the Republic *from among the members of the Grand National Assembly*. All other ministers were chosen by the Prime Minister *from among the members of the Assembly* and approved by the President of the Republic (Article 44).[6]

---

[5] For the text in modern script of these interesting debates, see A. Şeref Gözübüyük and Zekai Sezgin (eds.), *1924 Anayasası Hakkındaki Meclis Görüşmeleri (Assembly Debates Concerning the 1924 Constitution)*, (Ankara University Political Sciences Faculty, Administrative Sciences Institute Publication No. 3; Ankara: Balkanoğlu Matbaacılık, 1957). An introductory discussion of this work in English and Turkish is Edward C. Smith's "Debates on the Turkish Constitution of 1924," *Ankara Üniversitesi Siyasal Bilgiler Fakültesi Dergisi (Journal of the Faculty of Political Sciences of Ankara University)*, XIII (September 1958), pp. 82–130.

[6] For the text of this constitution in both the relatively archaic 1924 version and its official translation into more modern Turkish in 1945, cf. Gözübüyük and Kili, *op. cit.*, pp. 101–123. It is interesting to note that even the Turkish style used in the text of the constitution became something of a political football. In the early years of the Menderes-Bayar regime, a law was passed returning the text to the 1924 version and formally dropping the 1945 formulation (Law No. 5997, December 24, 1952). An official English translation of the

The G.N.A. elected for each yearly session, *from its own members,* its presiding officer, the President of the Assembly, and three Vice-Presidents of the Assembly, who presided in the President's absence (Article 24). These Assembly officers, together with three administrative officials and six clerks, also elected *from its own members* by the Assembly, constituted the Council of the Presidency of the Assembly (*Riyaset Divanı*), a body basically analogous in function to the Speakership and Deputy Speakerships of the British House of Commons (plus some of the functions there performed by the Clerk of the House), or to the Speaker and Speakers pro tem (and some clerks) of the U.S. House of Representatives. Since the Turkish President of the Assembly was often an active party politician as well as presiding officer, he probably more resembled the American than the British Speaker.[7]

Most of the permanent committees of the Assembly had three or four officers: a chairman, sometimes a vice-chairman, a *rapporteur,* and a secretary. Some of the financial committees also had a treasurer. These committee officials were elected for each session (roughly, annually) by the committee members from the personnel of the committee. After the Second Assembly (1923-1927), a deputy was not normally a member of more than one major, permanent committee and could not be a member of more than two permanent committees. Besides the housekeeping committees and the important Budget Com-

---

constitution is furnished in the brochure of the Turkish Information Office, *Government in Turkey* (New York: Turkish Information Office, n.d.), pp. 4–20, reprinted in Thomas and Frye, *op. cit.,* pp. 156–166; another English translation is available in Geoffrey Lewis, *op. cit.,* pp. 197–210.

[7] See, for the composition and duties of the Council of the Presidency, *T.B.M.M. Teşkilâtı Esasiye Kanunu Ve Dahilî Nizamname* (*G.N.A. Law of Fundamental Organization and Internal Regulations*) (Ankara: T.B.M.M. Matbaası, 1954–1958), Articles 5–7, pp. 198–211. As with the Turkish text of the constitution, the Turkish names for these offices vary according to the party in power. The Democrats preferred the older Turkish terms (e.g., *Vekil* for *Bakan* as "minister," *Reisicumhur* for *Cumhurbaşkanı* as "President of the Republic," etc.), while the People's Party supporters preferred the newer terms. I shall omit some of the Turkish titles rather than clutter the text with both. For the British Speaker's and Clerk's positions, see Sir Gilbert Campion, *An Introduction to the Procedure of the House of Commons* (London: Macmillan and Co., 1950), pp. 73–82, and for the American arrangement see, e.g., George B. Galloway, *The Legislative Process in Congress* (New York: Thomas Y. Crowell, 1953), pp. 346–350. A strong Turkish critique of the partisan activities of the President of the Assembly (who was also a member of the party General Executive Committee) under the Democratic regime is found in Turhan Feyzioğlu, *Demokrasiye ve Diktatörlüğe Dair* (*On Democracy and Dictatorship*) (Istanbul: Istanbul Matbaacılık T.A.O., 1957), pp. 93–94. Cf. also, on this point, Basri Savcı, "Mecliste Başkanlık Divanı Meseleleri" ("Problems of the Council of the Presidency in the Assembly"), *Ankara Üniversitesi Siyasal Bilgiler Fakültesi Dergisi,* XIII, No. 3 (September 1958), pp. 256–259.

mittee, there was normally a permanent committee for each ministry of the government.⁸

No constitutional court able to review the constitutionality of legislation passed by the G.N.A. existed. Individual ministerial acts could be declared *ultra vires*, but within the framework of the constitution, which contained no limitation on the legislative power of the G.N.A. (save that Article 1, declaring the Turkish state to be a republic, was entrenched by Article 102), the authority of the Assembly was absolute.⁹

Political Parties

For much of the period under examination only one legal political party existed in Turkey — the Republican People's Party (*Cumhuriyet Halk Partisi*), erected by Mustafa Kemal in 1923 on the foundations of the Association for the Defense of Rights of Anatolia and Rumelia. This party had a parliamentary group (*Meclis Grubu*) in the Grand National Assembly headed by an Executive Committee. Moreover, most of the high officials of the regular party organization and its General Executive Committee were deputies. As such, they figure in this analysis of the different levels of leadership among the deputies.

Though the People's Party dominated the scene for most of the thirty-seven-year period, there was actually some formal opposition. I shall examine several opposition groups in the Assembly. The first of these, chronologically, was the "Second Group" within the Defense of Rights organization in the First Assembly (1920–1923). In 1924 there followed the *Terakkiperver Cumhuriyet Fırkası* (Progressive Republican Party), and in 1930, the *Serbest Cumhuriyet Fırkası* (Liberal Republican Party).¹⁰ Finally, with the opening-up of political

---

⁸ *T.B.M.M. Teşkilâtı Esasiye Kanunu Ve Dahilî Nizamname, op. cit.*, Articles 22–26.

⁹ Article 26 of the Turkish Constitution specified generally the main functions of the Grand National Assembly: "The Grand National Assembly directly exercises such functions as enacting, modifying, interpreting and abrogating laws: concluding conventions and treaties of peace with foreign states; declaring war; examining and approving laws relative to the General Budget and Financial Accounts of the State, coining money, approving or annulling contracts and concessions involving monopolies and financial obligations; proclaiming partial or general amnesty; reducing or modifying sentences, postponing legal investigations and penalties and approving definitive death sentences pronounced by the courts."

¹⁰ On these parties, consult Tunaya, *Turkiyede Siyasî Partiler, op. cit.*, pp. 540–635, 646–689. A short official history of the People's Party (C.H.P.) is *C.H.P., 25 Yıl* (*Republican People's Party, 25 Years*), (Ankara: Ulus Basımevi, 1948). A fuller treatment of the Liberal Republican Party is found in Walter Weiker, "The Free Party of 1930 in Turkey, Loyal Opposition in a Rapidly

life, which began in the immediate postwar years (1945-1946) and culminated in the defeat at the polls and tumble from power in 1950 of the People's Party, there appeared a proliferation of political party organizations. I shall examine in detail the outstanding party among these, the Democratic Party (*Demokrat Parti*), which ruled Turkey from 1950 to 1960. I have the same information for it on the parliamentary group, its Executive Committee, and the General Executive Committee that I have for the People's Party.

Formal Qualifications of Deputies

Clearly, the legal provisions governing the qualifications of deputies, cabinet ministers, and other leading political figures may limit the possible variations in their social backgrounds. So also may the regulations of the political party organizations regarding candidate qualification and designation. Hence, we must look briefly into these formal controls on the characteristics of deputies so as not to ascribe to other processes social background patterns that are merely legally or organizationally induced. In addition, it is often intrinsically interesting to note the sort of formal social background stipulations that a given polity or party makes concerning its authoritative elite.

No adequate description of the provisions of Turkish electoral laws and party regulations regarding voter and candidate qualifications exists in English. Thus I have included this information in Appendix A. Here I shall simply summarize these descriptions so as to outline the range within which social background variations among deputies were formally possible.

The electoral system that prevailed in Turkey during the First Republic was, in most respects, a carry-over from the Ottoman system established in 1877 during the First Constitutional Period and reinvoked during the Second Constitutional Period in 1908. Its essential features were as follows: Deputies had to be over thirty years of age, male, and Turkish citizens. Those in the service of a foreign state, sentenced for various offenses against the law, under guardianship, deprived of their civil rights, and unable to read and write Turkish were excluded from legal candidacy. Also excluded were certain governmental and military officials unless they had resigned their official positions prior to the election. No additional social background requirements for cabinet posts or other offices of Assembly or party leadership existed.

Obviously, the crucial limitations were in terms of age, sex, and literacy. Those under thirty, female, and illiterate in Turkish were

---

Modernizing Nation" (unpublished Ph.D. dissertation, Department of Politics, Princeton University, 1962).

barred from the Assembly. The effect of these provisions, at any given time, was to deny candidacy to approximately 90 per cent of the population. On the other hand, there was no residential restriction at all; in fact, the Burkean conception of a national, rather than local, constituency for each deputy — even though he had actually been elected by the voters of one particular province — had long since been formally adopted.

Provisions similar to these were, of course, found in many other nations, and one of these provisions was itself relaxed during the period under discussion. In February 1934, the word "male" was dropped from the necessary qualifications of both electors and deputies. Eighteen females were elected to the Fifth Assembly in 1935.

Until 1946, the parliamentary electoral system was indirect. The ordinary voters chose secondary electors who, in turn, selected the actual deputies. Such a procedure made the system easier to control from above, and its abandonment was part of the opening-up of the political system after World War II.

There had previously been a major codification of electoral laws in 1942. One particularly revealing provision in that codification dealt with the manner in which the eligible Turkish citizen, desirous of becoming a deputy, was legally certified as a valid candidate. One of the three listed requirements for certification was the presentation of the would-be candidate's name to the Provincial Inspection Committee by "... *the* political party" (my emphasis). Since there was only one legal political party operating in the national elections of the Turkish Republic up to the election of 1946, this requirement gave that party, the Republican People's Party, legal control over the nomination of all candidates for the Grand National Assembly. In point of fact, this was merely the belated expression of a situation that existed in reality at least from 1927 on, with minor exceptions. In 1946, this provision was also changed to permit the aspiring candidate to offer *either* nomination by *a* political party *or* a petition signed by three hundred electors in order to secure certification.

Since political party support was so vital to candidacy and election as a deputy, it is necessary to ascertain whether party regulations regarding membership and nominations did not also act to restrict variations in the social backgrounds of deputies, even beyond the limitations enacted in the electoral laws. Again, I have furnished in Appendix A a rather full summary of the relevant political party stipulations regarding party nominations for deputyship to the Grand National Assembly. Here I shall give merely the most salient limitations.

In general, a nominee had to be a member of the party. There were a few illustrious persons nominated by the People's Party who were not party members, but they were exceptions. The additional restrictions arising from this requirement of party membership pertained more to psychological factors than to social background. Until 1946, when party structures were democratized, a member of the People's Party was usually supposed to be over eighteen years of age, not of bad repute, without conviction for criminal or dishonorable offense, free of the taint of having worked against the National Movement, and without a "negative political psychology." These provisions gave the party a legal justification for denying membership to those it found uncongenial. The prospective member also had to accept fully the goals of the party, furnish a written commitment to abide by its regulations and principles, and be endorsed by two party members.

Basic formal power to decide on the party's candidates for deputyships rested with the Council of the Presidency of the party. This body of three party leaders consisted of the General-President of the party, the General-Vice-President (appointed by the General-President), and the General-Secretary (appointed by the General-President from among the members of the General Executive Committee). As these formal arrangements suggest, basic power over the designation of People's Party candidates during the single-party years rested with the General-President of the party. However, considerable influences from strong provincial delegations, from the General-Secretary, and from other sources could not be and were not disregarded. At the same time, individuals sometimes found themselves nominated and then elected to a deputyship without ever having been personally consulted. For example, Ali Rıza Türel, who later became Minister of Justice, was asked by a reporter just how he first became a deputy. He replied: "I was Assistant Prosecutor in Izmir. I saw my name among the list of candidates which was published [in the newspaper], and so I learned." [11]

Conspicuous changes in the organization, structure, and nominating procedures of the People's Party came with the liberalization of political life after World War II. Candidates in all major parties now were predominantly selected by the provincial party organizations. In the feverish competition for votes, partly manifested in a race to see which party could most democratize its structure, the central organizations lost a great deal of formal and real power. Membership requirements were measurably eased, disciplinary control was softened, and local influences became generally decisive in candidate recruitment and nomination. Under highly competitive multi-party conditions, old restrictions designed to maintain central elite control were hard hit — so hard that the balance seems at times to have been

---

[11] Feyyaz Tokar, "Ali Rıza Türel'in Cevapları" ("The Answers of Ali Rıza Türel"), *Cumhuriyet*, December 7, 1959, pp. 1, 5.

tipped too far in the other direction. Parochialism, logrolling, and lack of coordination often appeared to be the replacements for elitist nationalism and rigidity. In any event, under post–World War II conditions, the formal membership and candidacy requirements of the political parties of Turkey no longer added in any pronounced way to the social background limitations on deputies contained in the electoral laws.

CHAPTER TWO

The Methods of Research

THIS ANALYSIS of the political leadership of modern Turkey focuses specifically on the social backgrounds of those men who reached the high position of deputy to Turkey's Grand National Assembly. I shall attempt to answer several questions: What sorts of persons reached this topmost level of formal power in Turkish society? What manner of men became backbenchers, cabinet ministers, party leaders, and the like, in the eventful years between 1920 and 1957, virtually the entire period of the First Turkish Republic? What difference did it make that persons of the found characteristics, rather than others, reached these positions of political leadership? Did politicians from divergent social backgrounds exhibit significantly different types of political behavior? Was there any clear association between the distinctive political styles of Turkish regimes and the social composition of their leading cadres, or between the nature of the party system and the social characteristics of the formal political elite?

SOURCES OF BACKGROUND INFORMATION

There were eight types of sources that provided the basic background information on the 2,210 deputies under observation. These eight sources were: governmental publications; political party publications and statements; school annuals and histories; biographical dictionaries and encyclopedias; standard biographies of famous figures; newspaper and magazine articles and obituaries; questionnaires from two (largely unsuccessful) attempts to get information directly from the deputies themselves; and personal interviews and correspondence with deputies, their relatives, officials of the parliamentary secretariat, journalists, academics, etc. I shall elaborate upon each of these sources to specify the factual foundations on which the analysis rests.

Governmental Publications

A study of this scope would prove practically impossible in many "emerging" nations. Fortunately for my purposes, from its very early days the Turkish government perspicaciously gathered basic information on the deputies to the Grand National Assembly. Elections to the permanent committees of that body were explicitly based in part on the vocational specialties of the deputies. For example, Article 228 of the *Internal Regulations (Nizamnamei Dahiliye)* of the Assembly stated the following:

> On the day of his joining the Assembly, a biographical questionnaire is given to each new member (deputy) by the General Secretariat. This questionnaire is completed and returned to the General Secretariat by the following day so that the lists which aid in the election of committees can be prepared.
> The questionnaire contains the following:
> I. The deputy's first and family names
> II. His father's and mother's names
> III. The date of his birth and the places of his birth and residence
> IV. His education, his foreign language, his expertise, his works [essentially, his publications, though the term — *eserleri* — is as vague in Turkish as is "works" in English], and his academic degrees
> V. His vocation and his occupational position [actually, the last post held before becoming a deputy]
> VI. His marital status and number of children, so that his traveling expenses can be estimated

Article 23 of the *Internal Regulations* further provided that: "At the first meeting of the session, in order to aid in the [permanent] committee elections, a list showing the specializations and vocations of the deputies, based on their brief biographical dossiers, is prepared by the Presidency of the Assembly, and distributed to each member and posted." [1]

Since 1928, the Secretariat of the Grand National Assembly has been publishing a parliamentary *Annual (Yıllık), Name List (Isim Defteri),* and *Album (Albüm)* with considerable regularity. A retrospective *Album* for the First Assembly (1920–1923) was published

---
[1] *T.B.M.M. Teşkilatı Esasiye Kanunu ve Dahilî Nizammame, op. cit.,* Article 228, pp. 85–86; Article 23, p. 9. Throughout this study, all translations, unless otherwise specified, are the author's. The titles of all Turkish works will normally be translated on the first citation in this book.

on its twenty-fifth anniversary in 1945.[2] These publications together not only contain the biographical information indicated above but also normally present information on, among other things: committee offices and assignments; the composition of the cabinet and Council of the Presidency of the Assembly; deaths, resignations, by-elections, and credential rejections; and the composition of the parliamentary parties and two of the highest permanent party organs (the General Executive Committee and the Parliamentary Group Executive Committee). Hence, the backbone of the material lies in these official publications.

To fill deficiencies in my information on certain organizational assignments, especially for the Second and Fourth Assemblies, I have had recourse mainly to the official parliamentary debates and gazette. From these official debate records I also obtained the data for voting and speechmaking measures.

Political Party Publications

The political party publications consulted for biographical material were primarily the reports and debates of party congresses containing information about the composition of party organs. For the last two Assemblies, the *Annual*s of the Assembly did not give the membership of the party General Executive Committees. Therefore, I have obtained this information directly from the party headquarters by telephone or in writing.[3] Naturally, with regard to nonbiographical matters of party organization, extensive reference has been made to various party regulations and programs.

School Publications

A valuable source of further information, particularly for the vocations of the fathers of the deputies and for secondary and primary educational backgrounds, has been that of school histories and an-

---

[2] *Türkiye Büyük Millet Meclisinin 25nci Yıl Dönümünü Anis Albümü (Grand National Assembly of Turkey's 25th Anniversary Commemorative Album)*, (Ankara: T.B.M.M. Basımevi, 1945). There are *Isim Defterleri* for all of the first ten Assemblies. There are *Yıllıklar,* with a few gaps, from the Third Assembly (1927–1931) on. The main lacuna is that of the Second Assembly (1923–1927), which I have filled, as best I can, by recourse to the *Assembly Debates (Zabit Ceridesi* or *Tutanak Dergisi),* the *Official Gazette (Resmi Gazete),* or other sources.

[3] I wish to express my appreciation to Turhan Feyzioğlu, Osman Okyar, Selâmi Erkut, and others at the Republican People's Party's Research Bureau *(Cumhuriyet Halk Partisi Araştırma Burosu)* for preparing detailed lists for me. Unfortunately, despite positive initial assurances from Basri Aktaş, the organizational secretary of the Democratic Party *(Demokrat Parti),* no real cooperation from that party was forthcoming. I was, however, able to get basic information on this topic, the composition of the General Executive Committee, by telephone from Democratic Party headquarters.

nuals. Outstanding among these is one dealing with the present Political Science Faculty, the former Civil Service School, entitled *The History of the Civil Service School and Its Graduates*.[4]

Biographical Encyclopedias and Biographies

Several biographical encyclopedias have been consulted in standard fashion. Most helpful were Gövsa's *Famous Turks,* the *Inönü* (now *Turkish*) *Encyclopedia,* and two volumes sketching the careers of illustrious Turkish lawyers and Turkish doctors.[5] Several regular biographies also furnished material on famous single individuals, and the intermediate-length biographical articles in *Living Histories* were rewarding.[6] As with all other sources, detailed references are given in the bibliography, and I am now merely indicating the most important contributions.

Obituaries

To bolster the information available on deputies serving in the earlier, less documented Assemblies, I selectively checked the obituary notices appearing in four Turkish newspapers since the introduction of Roman script in 1928. These papers were *Hâkimiyeti Milliye (National Sovereignty)* and its successor *Ulus (Nation)* — the official papers of the People's Party — checked from 1930 through 1946 and at specific times thereafter; the independent Istanbul daily, *Cumhuriyet (Republic),* checked from 1928 to 1959; and the Ankara organ of the Democratic Party, *Zafer (Victory),* checked for the period from 1950 to 1959. Though these labors were not nearly as rewarding as had been hoped, in the sense that much new information was not unearthed (owing to poor obituary coverage in the Turkish press), the effort did serve as a partial control on the accuracy of material garnered from official and other sources and did yield some interesting results. However, its value in corroborating data was not perfect, particularly for the minor figures for whom I most wanted information, since in many cases the obituaries for these figures were based on the official parliamentary *Annual*s and *Album*s.

---

[4] Ali Çankaya, *Mülkiye Tarihi Ve Mülkiyeliler* (Ankara: Örnek Matbaası, 1954), 3 vols.

[5] Ibrahim Alaettin Gövsa, *Türk Meşhurları Ansiklopedisi* (Istanbul: Yenigün Neşriyatı, 1946); Afşin Oktay and Kemal Bağlüm, *Biyografiler Ansiklopedisi 1959* (Ankara: n.p., 1959); *Resimli Türk ve Dünya Meşhurları Ansiklopedisi* (Istanbul: Altın Kitaplar, 1959); Osman Nebioğlu, *Kim Kimdir Ansiklopedisi* (Istanbul: Nebioğlu Yayınevi, 1961); Fethi Erden, *Türk Hekimleri Biyografisi* (Istanbul: Çituri Biraderler Basımevi, 1948); Hasan Basri Erk, *Meşhur Türk Hukukçuları* (Adana?: n.p., 1959).

[6] *Canlı Tarihler* (Istanbul: Türkiye Yayınevi, 1944–1947), 6 vols.

Direct Questionnaires

Detailed, highly worthwhile material for about forty to fifty deputies, usually backbenchers, came from two unsuccessful attempts at administering a direct questionnaire to all or some of the deputies of an Assembly. One attempt, made jointly four or five years previously by a distinguished American professor and a section of the Political Science Faculty of Ankara University, netted about thirty completed questionnaires (from four or five hundred deputies at the time). The other attempt, also highly disappointing in its few returns, was made by the author and the People's Party Research Bureau. It furnished details on a few more deputies. Though limited and unrepresentative, when used with care these questionnaires have been helpful in some areas — particularly that of vocations of deputies' fathers, partially correcting a known bias toward inclusion of too many famous figures in my sample.[7]

Personal Interviews and Correspondence

The final source, and in some ways the most useful for filling important holes in basic biographical material, was that of personal correspondence and interviews with people familiar with the life histories of many deputies. Some former deputies, or their close friends and relatives, retain much valuable information about a wide range of politicians.[8] This method has the additional virtue of giving the researcher a chance to probe more deeply into various individual conceptions of the social and personal significance of different social backgrounds. But since the method is most time-consuming and the marginal returns for effort expended are slight, as well as for other practical reasons, I have not exploited the personal-interview sources to the utmost.

---

[7] After hearing of the difficulties of officials of the Assembly Secretariat in getting replies to their officially sanctioned questionnaire, after encountering all sorts of problems in obtaining returns to a questionnaire sent to its own deputies by one of the two major political parties, and after observing the failure of a questionnaire sent to the deputies (though not really "pushed") by the Political Science Faculty of Ankara, I am dubious about the prospects of getting adequate coverage of this busy group through a self-administered questionnaire. Fortunately, other sources are adequate. But future attitudinal, sociometric, or deeper social background research on these deputies will probably have to proceed via the method of direct personal interviews.

[8] For example, the amazingly strong memory and wide contacts of Cevat Dursunoğlu, a prominent former deputy, have been significantly helpful. I also contacted several dozen deputies by letter and generally received useful replies.

Tabulation and Verification of Data

Material from all these sources was assembled onto some 4,387 index cards — one for each incumbency. In other words, if a deputy served in three separate Assemblies, say the Fourth, Fifth, and Sixth (1931-1943), he would have three cards, one for each Assembly in which he served. Since there were 2,210 deputies filling 4,387 incumbencies, the average length of service of each deputy was approximately two Assemblies (1.98+). Put another way, the average deputy was elected twice in all, or reelected once.

The information available about each deputy in sufficient scope for this analysis includes the following: birthplace, party, parliamentary experience, birth date, province represented, vocation, significant occupational positions held (subsample only), foreign language claimed, publications, Assembly committees and offices, ministerial experience and offices, party positions, listed memberships in other organizations, and tenure — that is, whether the deputy served a full or short term in the Assembly (whether he was elected at a by-election, was rejected, resigned, or died).

For many of these categories (e.g., vocation, age, education), I employed a classificatory scheme different from that used in my sources, so that a large amount of coding was done. The coding schemes used will be explained as the specific categories of material are presented. Since I did all the coding myself, problems of reliability are minimized, though the danger of consistent coding bias may be increased. One important internal check on coding reliability and on the accuracy and agreement of my sources existed in the process of index card collation. One reason for preparing separate cards for each deputy of each of the ten Assemblies was that this process acted as a limited coding and source control. Each deputy was classified anew for each of the Assemblies of which he was a member, without reference to his classification in any preceding or subsequent Assemblies. Then, at the end of the data-collecting process, all separate Assembly cards of each individual deputy were gathered together and critically compared. Differences in classification between cards could be due to any of three causes: (1) discrepancies between sources, such as a man's being listed as born in 1898 in the *Annual* for the Third Assembly and in 1900 in the *Annual* of the Fourth Assembly; (2) coding errors, such as coding a retired military man who had turned to farming as "military" in the Third Assembly and "agriculture" in the Fourth; or (3) an actual change in the characteristics of the deputy, such as getting married between sessions, or improving his education (e.g., Menderes) or his language ability (e.g., Inönü) while a deputy. Fortunately, except for usually trivial discrepancies in birth dates, largely as a result of Muslim-Christian calendrical confusions, these collations revealed a minimal level of coding and source errors. The total percentage of corrections on all items was much less than 1 per cent. For birth date, the most unreliable item, corrections ran about 5 per cent, with the preponderance of disagreements being only one year. This, obviously, is not to say that my data are totally accurate or that the coding is flawless. It is merely that various sources of data have been checked against one another and found to be in basic agreement, and that the coding, whatever its validity, is reliable throughout.

Analytic Technique

Very simply, the following are the main analytic techniques employed. Wherever possible, the social backgrounds of the deputies are compared with the relevant characteristics of Turkish society as a whole, and of large and germane subgroups therein, to answer the crucial question as to whether the deputies actually do differ in social background from these comparison groups and to ascertain where the *watershed of difference* lies. Because Turkey has been little studied, in this aspect of the research I offer less supporting evidence than I should like. But engaging in research in such a truly "underdeveloped" field is somewhat like attempting a "do-it-yourself" project in which one must first make his own saw, hammer, and other tools before he can even begin to tackle the main creation. Consequently, results are tardier and cruder than one may have wished or expected.

So far as possible, I have tried to avoid mere presentation of single items of social background, such as giving only the educational level of all deputies, then giving — again alone — their vocations, and so on. Instead, I have sought to cross-tabulate the various social background items as much as possible to learn which characteristics were regularly associated with each other. My aim is to uncover whatever *modal types* of social background existed.

When the social background material has been refined in this fashion, I then examine (1) the relationship between it and the deputy's *formal, structural position* in this top echelon of Turkish government, and (2) the relationship between his social background and some particular aspects of his *political behavior*, such as his voting and speechmaking. In one sense, the deputy's formal position at this level of Turkish government is itself a behavioral indicator, but not an individual one. It reflects the recruitment and promotional patterns of those segments of the political system which are influential in this respect. In other words, one sort of behavior displayed by the system as a whole, or by parts of the system, is that of selecting new recruits to the legislature itself, to the cabinet, to the Committee of the Presidency of the Assembly, to the highest party organs, to offices in the permanent committees of the Assembly, etc. To learn what sorts of people are selected may provide some insight into the processes of selection — the behavior of the selectors. Cecil Gibb, in his article on "Leadership," refers to these as "the phenomena of succession" and argues that:

> This power of incumbent leaders to determine their own succession and to influence future leadership cannot be overlooked. Commonly they compel the group to select their own kind, as when the Nazi regime set up machinery for inducting leaders of the same temperamental make-up as the incumbents themselves. At the very least it must certainly be true that where succession to leadership is determined by appointment from above the persons so chosen are perceived to meet the needs of the superior sponsoring group and to owe their primary obligations to higher echelons of control.[9]

As I shall show, throughout much of the period under investigation the Grand National Assembly followed the *co-optative* policies Gibb describes. Hence, the social characteristics of the personnel selected and differentially elevated provide a sort of inferential behavioral indicator for those doing the selecting. Furthermore, beginning about 1946, this co-optative process was greatly altered, and an increased dispersion of the power to recruit new legislators was found. Therefore, there is an opportunity to analyze the social background effects of two different recruitment processes, one virtually co-optative and the other a democratic electoral system. In general, I shall do this by examining the social composition of the Assembly as a whole and of the different, important subordinate units at this level of government that were predominantly or totally staffed by deputies. These units, of course, include the cabinet, party organs, parliamentary committees, and so on, previously mentioned. In addition, using the ratings of a "panel of experts," I shall attempt to combine these formal positions into an index of position-holding or formal authority for each deputy. Thus (with other criteria as well) it is possible to distinguish three or four basic levels of formal authority for each Assembly: the top leaders, the middle leaders, the backbenchers, and the inconsequentials. I shall inspect these authoritative groups to see if they differed from each other regularly in social background.

The analysis probably is weakest behaviorally. Three fundamental behavioral indicators are used: reelection rates, voting, and speechmaking. Reelection rates (the relative frequency of reelection of a deputy) actually are a mixture of the type of *group* behavioral indi-

[9] Cecil Gibb, "Leadership," in Gardner Lindzey (ed.), *Handbook of Social Psychology* (Cambridge: Addison-Wesley, 1954), II, p. 913.

cator just described and an individual indicator (that is, the deputy's desire or willingness to serve). The voting patterns of the deputy on legislative proposals and his speaking practices (number of speeches, length, topic, etc.) are more strictly individual indicators, though even they partake of both aspects. For instance, the party designates spokesmen on issues and awards speaking time; the President of the Assembly recognizes deputies. Voting behavior presents a special problem, since party discipline was usually extremely strong. As a result, I have examined primarily those instances or periods when party discipline happened to have been weakened, rather than futilely analyzing unbroken party divisions and repeatedly finding merely the social background differences that distinguish the parties from each other.

Other significant and reliable behavioral indicators are very hard to find. One can think of such items as the frequency of visiting the constituency, contact with interest groups, participation in party caucuses, and campaign style, all of which are of considerable potential interest. The problem is that no general information on these topics is available. One can also contemplate content-analyzing the speeches of every deputy, or even of calculating the attendance record for every deputy. In this case the problem is that of the impossible amount of work involved in these relatively simple and valuable tasks. Soon, perhaps, we shall have COMIT, General Inquirer, or other computer programs sufficiently developed and ordinary language computer input facilities sufficiently available so that parliamentary debates can be relatively quickly and cheaply content-analyzed. When that day comes, all our social background data should become much more significant. But it has not yet arrived.

The truth is that the political scientist's ability to handle behavioral analysis, as arbitrarily distinguished from attitudinal and formal structural analysis, is currently very limited. In the United States we have done much with roll-call votes. But voting is far less revealing under most circumstances in most other societies since party discipline obtrudes. When voting is omitted, the residual arsenal of techniques for the analysis of the behavior of politicians is meager indeed. In fact, we might generalize this to social science as a whole. Our present ability to deal with certain attitudinal phenomena (verbal manifestations of behavior under special conditions) far outstrips our ability to handle, with similar sophistication, other forms of behavior. Probably the greatest problem facing social background research, as well as many other forms of political inquiry, is the relatively feeble development of our techniques for discerning, obtaining, and analyzing data on nonverbal or partially verbal behavior and on informal and unstructured verbal material.

The last basic aspect of the methods of analysis that must be mentioned here is the attempt to utilize the extended time coverage in two ways. I shall present a *trend analysis* of the social background changes that occurred in the ten Assemblies and in their component organs. I shall also try to present the rough outlines of Turkish political and social developments for this same period to display in general the relationships between what was happening to the social characteristics of national political leaders and what was being done by the national government in the society.

As a further exploitation of the broad time coverage — in fact, as a subvariant of trend analysis — I shall offer a *cohort analysis* of the subjects. I shall take the incoming, neophyte deputies for each Assembly and trace what happened to them, in social background terms, with each successive Assembly. What were the characteristics of those first entering the legislature in the Third Assembly (1927)? How many were left by the Fourth, Fifth, Sixth, and other Assemblies? How did those remaining differ from those who departed? The cohort analysis will provide answers to these questions and some idea of basic legislative career patterns that typify deputies of different social characteristics. Moreover, it constitutes another way of looking at some of the information contained in the analysis of reelection rates and legislative turnover, and it may substantiate, correct, or clarify observations emanating from that analysis. It also gives us important data on the characteristics of the newly elected deputies over time.

I shall start to examine the social backgrounds of the deputies by looking at the aggregate of all 2,210 persons who served as deputy to the Grand National Assembly between 1920 and 1957. This procedure will furnish a broad panorama of the subject and will permit, because of the size of the group, certain more refined cross-tabulations than would be possible with any single Assembly. I shall first correlate one social background characteristic with another — searching for any basic *types* of background that characterized large groups of deputies. In this over-all inspection, I shall employ as the main behavioral indicator the *election rate* — or average number of times elected to a deputyship — of groups of deputies possessing similar social backgrounds. Later on, when I inspect the compositions of individual Assemblies, I shall use additional behavioral indicators.

The Aggregate View

CHAPTER THREE

Education: The Hallmark of the Elite

THROUGHOUT MOST of Turkey's modern history, the fundamental social distinction has been that based upon education. Both the more impressionistic writings of traditional scholarship and the few studies of modern social science are in agreement on this point. Writer after writer remarks the crucial chasm between the "intelligentsia" and the "peasantry," the "vast gulf between the uneducated masses and the educated few." [1] Careful observers, in discussing the political dominance of the country by a small segment of its population, almost invariably employ the following terms to describe the elite: "the intellectual group," "the educated cadres," "the enlightened elite," "the educated ruling minority," "the intellectual ruling class," etc.[2] Nor are

---

[1] The last phrase is Frank Tachau's description of the influential Turkish thinker Ziya Gökalp's view of Turkey's greatest difficulty: "To him [Gökalp], the greatest single problem for Turkey as a nation and a society was to bridge the vast gulf between the uneducated masses and the educated few." "The Face of Turkish Nationalism as Reflected in the Cyprus Dispute," *Middle East Journal,* XIII (Summer 1959), p. 272.

[2] Observers emphasizing this distinction include such respected but diverse writers as Halide Edib Adıvar, Fahir Iz, H. N. Kubalı, Bernard Lewis, Moshe Perlmann, Howard Reed, Wilfred Cantwell Smith, Lewis Thomas, and Arnold Toynbee, arbitrarily to name a few. Though not specifically referring to education, Kemal Karpat, in his valuable work, *Turkey's Politics: The Transition to a Multi-Party System* (Princeton: Princeton University Press, 1959), summarizes the studious comment on this subject by saying, "It is generally accepted that the structure of the Ottoman society was simple and undifferentiated and that it consisted of two layers: the Sultan and the ruling classes on top, and the masses at the bottom." (p. 77)

more detailed and explicit characterizations lacking. Donald Webster, for example, noted in the mid-thirties that "The masses just are not active in what is going on: they never have been and they probably will not be during the present generation. The *effective* majority, which is found among the educated portions of Turkish society — persons for the most part with no less than a junior high school training — is vocally and sincerely in support of the Kamâlist regime and its head."[3] Similarly, Turhan Oğuzkan, a Turk, writes (in the fifties): "The intellectual group, although small in number, has had the upper hand in directing the affairs of the nation since the beginning of the Republic."[4]

Two other illustrative items of evidence from quite diverse points of view are to be found in the able works of Mary Gough and Daniel Lerner. Mrs. Gough, a keen observer who has spent much time in Anatolia, focuses her attention in the following passage on that fulcrum of modern Turkey — the provincial town. This is the strategic point where the "enlightened" (*münneverler* or *aydınlar*) and the villagers or peasants (*köylüler*) truly meet. Moreover, Mrs. Gough looks at a vital institution in these towns — the Turkish coffeehouse — and tries to fathom the rather obvious social distinctions displayed there.

> The two terraces of the coffee-garden represent the two social strata of Mut. The top terrace is the common one; here foregather the farmers, peasants and artisans who live in the little town and, on Fridays, those who have come in from distant villages to shop and to go to the mosque. The lower terrace is the more exclusive; here is the Şehir Kulübü — the City Club, where the notables of the town are to be found; the civil servants, the doctors and the schoolmasters. It is hard accurately to define the exact qualifications which determine the terrace on which an inhabitant of Mut will drink his coffee. Money certainly does not come into it, as many a farmer on the upper terrace will be much wealthier than a struggling schoolmaster on the lower; nor is it birth. *Probably the best rough and ready criterion is that those on the lower terrace have had, at least, a secondary education.*[5]

Lerner arrives at a similar conclusion while utilizing some of the sophisticated techniques of modern social science. In a study of certain aspects of the communications behavior of Turkish people, he

---

[3] Donald Webster, *The Turkey of Atatürk* (Philadelphia: The American Academy of Political and Social Science, 1939), p. 287.

[4] Turhan Oğuzkan, *Adult Education in Turkey* (Educational Studies and Documents No. XIV; Paris: UNESCO, Education Clearing House, 1955), p. 10.

[5] Mary Gough, *The Plain and the Rough Places* (London: Chatto & Windus, 1954), p. 196. (My emphasis)

inspects individuals representing both the "modern" elite and the "transitional" and "traditional" masses. In this process, he gives perhaps the most graphic single-word description of the situation I am examining when he refers to a "bifurcated" Turkey. The main basis of the bifurcation — "the single most powerful discriminator between the types [of Turkish citizens, 'modern, transitional, and traditional']" — is revealed by a close examination of the latent structure analysis employed in Lerner's *The Passing of Traditional Society*. This basis, once again, is found to be *education*. Looking for larger implications, Lerner adds that "this reconfirms the critical function of education for modern and modernizing persons." [6]

A relevant generalized comment is made by another social scientist, Edward Shils, writing on the role of intellectuals in the political development of new states. He says, "The gestation, birth, and continuing life of the new states of Asia and Africa, through all their vicissitudes, are in large measure the work of intellectuals. In no state-formation in all of human history have intellectuals played such a role as they have in these events of the present century.... The intellectuals have created the political life of the underdeveloped countries; they have been its instigators, its leaders, and its executants." [7]

The importance of education in Turkish social stratification and a desire to check in at least one specific case the type of observation made by Shils led me to look initially at the educational qualifications of the 2,210 Turkish deputies. This I shall do after providing some further information about education in Turkey that will make the findings more meaningful.

Noting the basic bifurcation of Turkish society along educational lines should not beguile us into thinking that each of the resultant parts — the educated group and the uneducated — was internally homogeneous. Indeed, the nature of the internal subdivision *within* the enlightened elite provides a valuable key to an understanding of the modern political history of Turkey. This educated element was itself further bifurcated along educational lines, with a major political struggle running parallel to that educational division. The resolution of these educational schisms and the solutions developed for Turkey's outstanding political conflicts are but different facets of the same social process.

[6] Daniel Lerner, *The Passing of Traditional Society: Modernizing the Middle East* (Glencoe, Ill.: The Free Press, 1958), pp. 130, 442–443, 445. Lerner prefers to employ the attribute "literacy" rather than education. But the indicator actually used is that of level of formal education.

[7] Edward Shils, "The Intellectuals in the Political Development of the New States," *World Politics*, XII (April 1960), pp. 329–330.

Development of the Turkish Educational System

In the heyday of the Ottoman Empire, when a beleaguered Europe scrambled to hold off the pressing Janissaries, Ottoman education seems to have been as modern and effective as any offered in the West. The caliber of this educational system was reflected in Ottoman competence — from the level of artilleryman to ambassador. However, sometime after the reign of Süleyman the Magnificent, growth and progress in education appear to have ceased; the vitality of the institution ebbed, followed by inevitable deterioration and decay. The Turkish educator, Fahir Iz, sums it up well in the following words:

> Up to the end of the sixteenth century, the *Medreses* (the religious schools) in addition to theology taught mathematics, physics and medicine. Each of these subjects received serious attention and had special institutions devoted to them.... The Janissaries or professional troops of the Turkish Army received military training in special barracks. The more gifted among them were sent to the Palace School, where they were taught Muslim humanities, music and arts and crafts, and were promoted exclusively on merit.
>
> These educational institutions, which for centuries had trained first-class men who carried the empire to its zenith, had degenerated by the eighteenth century into centers of laziness, ignorance, and bigotry.[8]

Ottoman decline was ignored as long as possible by the Sublime Porte. After two centuries of dismaying defeat, however, some sort of corrective was essential for the very survival of the state. Since the technical military superiority of the West was unmistakable — and most painful — one of the early approaches to reform was to try to command some of that technical military skill. A leading step in the new direction occurred in 1795 with the opening of an artillery school that featured instruction by French officers. This was followed in the early nineteenth century by schools of military engineering, military medicine, and a War College. In these schools, an essentially secular education in the Western pattern was offered, and this was the

[8] Fahir Iz, *The Role of Education in the Westernization of Turkey* (25th Annual Sir John Adams Lecture; Los Angeles: University of California, 1959), p. 4. For the same point see, e.g., H. A. R. Gibb and Harold Bowen, *Islamic Society and the West,* Vol. I: *Islamic Society in the Eighteenth Century* (London: Oxford University Press, 1957), Part II, p. 150. On the Palace School, the classic source is Barnette Miller, *The Palace School of Muhammad the Conqueror* (Harvard Historical Monograph XVII; Cambridge, Mass.: Harvard University Press, 1941). Note also, e.g., the statement of Mustafa Kemal to a congress of teachers in Ankara on the eve of the great battle of Sakarya: "I am of the opinion that the principles of education and training which have been followed up to now are the most important factor in the decline in our nation's history." "Atatürk," *Islam Ansiklopedisi,* X (Istanbul: Milli Eğitim Basımevi, 1949), p. 778.

opening institutional wedge that ultimately split the Ottoman ruling elite beyond repair.

During the latter half of the nineteenth century, the secular educational movement spread to nonmilitary areas with the founding of the Civil Service School (*Mülkiye*) in 1859, the Law School in 1888, and even the American-sponsored Robert College in the 1860's. Istanbul University, though formally claiming 1453 as the date of its establishment, was opened in 1871, then closed for most of the repressive reign of Abdülhamit II, and finally reestablished in 1900. It was under the Young Turks, after the Revolution of 1908, that the University of Istanbul became truly active for the first time.

With the Atatürk Revolution, Turkey's important system of higher education began to take its adult shape. The University of Istanbul was reorganized. The University of Ankara was created, commencing with the formation of the Ankara law faculty in 1925, and continuing through the later additions of the faculty of language, history and geography, the medical faculty, a science faculty, etc. Two of the most vital professional schools in the country, the War College (*Harbiye*) for the training of the Turkish army's officers' corps and the School of Political Sciences (*Mülkiye*) for the training of bureaucrats, were moved from Istanbul to Ankara, the former remaining independent and the latter eventually becoming part of Ankara University. In addition, major new institutions, such as the Gazi Pedogogical Institute in Ankara and Istanbul Technical University, were created to meet rapidly growing needs for certain types of trained personnel.[9]

Less immediately important was a concomitant but weaker devel-

[9] Useful general works on the Turkish educational system are: Turkish Information Office, *Education in the New Turkey* (Turkey Today Series No. 5; New York: Turkish Information Office, n.d.); *Education in Turkey* (Turkey Today Series No. 2; New York: Turkish Information Office, n.d.); *L'Instruction Publique en Turquie Républicaine* (Ankara: Matbaat Umum Müdürlüğü, 1936); *Türkiye Cumhuriyeti Maarifi, 1923–1943* (Ankara: Maarif Matbaası, 1944); Osman Ergin, *Türkiye Maarif Tarihi*, 5 vols. (Istanbul: Osmanbey Matbaası, 1939–1943); Adnan Eseniş, *Education for Democracy in Turkey* (Ankara: Milli Eğitim Basımevi, 1950); Nafi Atuf (Kansu), *Türkiye Maarif Tarihi* (2nd. ed.; Istanbul: Milliyet Matbaası, 1932); M. de Salve, "Education in Turkey" *Circulars of Information of the Bureau of Education* (No. 3-1875; Washington, D.C.: U.S. Government Printing Office, 1875); Paul Monroe, "Education," in Eliot G. Mears (ed.), *Modern Turkey* (New York: Macmillan, 1924). For discussion of more political aspects, see Frederick W. Frey, "Education and Politics in Turkey," in Robert E. Ward and Dankwart A. Rustow (eds.), *Political Modernization in Japan and Turkey* (Princeton: Princeton University Press, 1964), pp. 205–235. See also Richard E. Maynard, *The Lise and Its Curriculum in the Turkish Educational System* (unpublished Ph.D. dissertation, Department of Education, University of Chicago, 1961); and Turkish National Commission on Education, *Report of the Turkish National Commission on Education* (Istanbul: American Board Publication Department, 1961).

opment of Turkish secondary and primary education in this same period. Although the origins of nonreligious public primary and secondary education are sometimes traced as far back as the *Tanzimat* (Reform) Era of the second quarter of the nineteenth century, and although a school law of 1869 nominally created a system of compulsory public education at this level over the entire country, it was not really until the advent of the Young Turk regime in 1908 that any extensive system was constructed. According to Paul Monroe, for example, there were apparently only eighty-one Turkish secondary schools in the entire empire in 1908.[10] As late as 1871, half of the annual appropriation for the Ministry of Public Instruction went toward paying the salaries of the minister, his secretary, and his counselors. Even with the astronomical graft of the time, this betrays an agency of dubious impact.[11] In short, then, the foundation of public education in Turkey was quite small and frail until well into the twentieth century. Not until roughly the middle of the Atatürk period could this system be described as having any true depth and scope.[12]

Until about 1924, alongside the primary- and secondary-level public schools there were local schools supported by philanthropic bequests and small fees and taught by an *imam* (cleric) of the neighborhood. The curriculum consisted essentially of memorizing the Koran through oral recitation. These schools, offering almost exclusively religious instruction, can be considered part of the *medrese* hierarchy, though of course students did veer from them into the higher secular institutions on occasion.[13] Contrasting them with the incipient system of secular public education, we see a lower-level reflection of that same dualism which divided higher education.

This quick survey of the history of the Turkish educational system would not be complete without some mention of the minority and foreign schools on the primary and secondary level. In the Ottoman

[10] Monroe, in Mears, *op. cit.*, p. 124. For some earlier figures on the schools opened, up to the exile of Mithat Paşa in 1881, see Yusuf Hikmet Bayur, *Türk Inkilabı Tarihi* (*History of the Turkish Revolution*) (Ankara: Türk Tarih Kurumu Basımevi, 1952) II, Part IV, p. 469.

[11] De Salve, *op. cit.*, p. 242.

[12] For example, the number of public secondary schools (*liseler*) increased between 1923 and 1933 from 23 to 62, with a corresponding rise in students from 513 to 1,827. See, for detailed figures of changes of this sort at all levels of the Turkish educational system in this period, the tables presented in *L'Instruction Publique en Turquie Républicaine, op. cit.*, pages and tables unnumbered. Even today, lycée-level facilities in Turkey are accessible primarily to urban youth. For the curricula of primary (*ilk*), middle (*orta*), and lyceum (*lise*) level schools in the mid-Atatürk period, see H. Malik Evrenol, *Revolutionary Turkey* (Ankara: Librairie Hachette, 1936), pp. 50–53.

[13] Cf. Howard A. Reed, "The Faculty of Divinity at Ankara," *Muslim World,* XLVII (October 1956), pp. 295–296; de Salve, *op. cit.*, p. 241.

Empire, just prior to World War I, if the available figures are to be trusted, approximately 22 per cent of all students at these levels were in minority and foreign schools.[14] Certainly it can be said that these institutions were a significant part of the total educational effort in the Ottoman state at that time.

There is evidence both from Turkey and from other nations that attendance at a distinctive secondary school may be the most influential educational experience of all for many types of subsequent political behavior. The major changes of adolescence occur at this time. A more discriminating and critical attitude toward the adult world develops, and one may first become aware of the fact that society is already assigning him to certain roles carrying with them very definite ranges of expected behavior. Friendships established in this period among one's schoolmates often seem to have a special bond, a deeper intimacy, than is possible after the crust of the adult personality is fully formed. Thus, it seems that those who are given secondary education at a prestigious, select school (usually, though not necessarily, private or wealthy) are frequently profoundly affected by this experience. It shapes their conception of the world and their place in it. It helps determine the circle of persons with whom they stay in close contact throughout the remainder of their lives.

Outstanding political examples of the importance of such educational experiences come readily to mind. Probably the most graphic is afforded by the former British Prime Minister, Lord Baldwin, who is represented as having said, "When the call came to me to form a government, one of my first thoughts was that it should be a government of which Harrow should not be ashamed."[15] Accordingly, Baldwin chose as his ministers the largest number of Harrovians ever collected in a single cabinet. On the other hand, Lord Balfour, who was educated at Eton, recruited almost half of his cabinet ministers from Etonians.[16] The American author C. Wright Mills, in his description of an alleged "Power Elite" in the United States, gives

---

[14] Monroe, in Mears, *op. cit.*, p. 135, presents a comparative table of schools and students in the pre-1914 Ottoman Empire. According to this table, there were 1,331,000 students in "Turkish" (government) schools, 184,568 students in "Greek" schools, and a total of 375,825 students in all the minority and foreign schools listed. Unfortunately, there is a confusion in the first two lines of this table. The "Turkish" and "Armenian" school figures are inverted, and the "Turkish" student figure is given as 133,100, though elsewhere in the text it is presented as 1,331,000. I have taken the latter figure as more plausible.

[15] S. Hazey, *Tory M.P.* (London: Gollancz, 1939), p. 180.

[16] Harold J. Laski, "The Personnel of the English Cabinet, 1901–1924," *American Political Science Review*, XXII (1928), p. 23. Sometimes it is argued that the specific internal traditions and practices of these schools, besides their general social positions, become important. Thus, according to Kingsley, Bertrand Russell views the "fag system" of the British "public school" as an im-

primary emphasis to prep school attendance, even as opposed to matriculation at an "Ivy League" college, on the grounds that the prior prep school credentials really determine, in most cases, which of the "two Harvards," for example, one attends.[17] And the modern novels of many countries are replete with examinations of the distinctive later lives of the particular national equivalent of our "St. Grottlesex" boy.

In Turkey, too, distinctions of this sort even within the relatively limited range of secondary education are important. The mutual contacts and the awareness of a common intellectual heritage typical of the *Galatasaraylılar*, the graduates of the Galatasaray Lycée — the old French-influenced Imperial School (*Mektebi Sultani*) — become clear after very much discussion of education in Turkey with leading Turkish politicians.[18] And though Galatasaray is the most famous

---

portant clue to the nature of British imperialism. It supposedly strengthened attitudes of obedience and command and increased the desire to govern sometimes to the point of the individual's becoming a *"fanatique du pouvoir."* Cf. J. Donald Kingsley, *Representative Bureaucracy* (Yellow Springs: Antioch Press, 1944), p. 154, and W. L. Guttsman, "Aristocracy and the Middle Class in the British Political Elite, 1886–1916," *British Journal of Sociology*, V (March 1954), pp. 16–17.

[17] C. Wright Mills, *The Power Elite* (New York: Oxford University Press, 1956), p. 67. "The one deep experience that distinquishes the social rich from the merely rich and those below is their schooling.... Accordingly, if one had to choose one clue to the national unity of the upper social classes in America today, it would best be the really exclusive boarding school for girls and prep school for boys." (pp.63–64)

[18] "The influence of the Galatasaray school on the rise of modern Turkey has been enormous. As the need for administrators, diplomats, and others with a Western education and a capacity to handle Western administrative apparatus became more and more pressing, the graduates of Galatasaray came to play a preponderant role in the politics and administration of the Ottoman Empire and, after it, of the Turkish Republic. The Imperial Ottoman Lycée had no playing fields, but not a few of the victories of modern Turkey were won in its classrooms." B. Lewis, *The Emergence of Modern Turkey, op. cit.*, p. 120. Also on Galatasaray, cf. de Salve, *op cit.*, pp. 244–252, for a discussion of the establishment of the school (de Salve was its first director). For the impact of attendance at this school on the lives of its students, see the long series of reminiscences of Suat Aray, "Bir Galatasaraylının Hatıraları" ("Memories of a Galatasaray Student"), which appeared in the magazine *Hayat* in the winter of 1958–1959. For a fictional indication of the social status of the school, note the thoughts of the aristocratic Sabiha Hanım in the novel of Halide Edib (Adıvar), *Sinekli Bakkal* (*The Fly-Filled Grocery*), when, observing her son, she thinks, "Although he graduated first in his class at Galatasaray, he is still only a minor clerk in the Finance Department." (Istanbul: Ahmet Halit Yaşaroğlu, 23rd printing, 1957), p. 28. More references to Galatasaray are found in this and other Turkish novels. *Sinekli Bakkal* exists in English as *The Clown and His Daughter* (London: George Allen & Unwin, 1935). Cf. also Eleanor Bisbee, *The New Turks* (Philadelphia: University of Pennsylvania

secondary school of this type in the land, it is by no means the only important one. Schools like *Vefa* and *Mercan Idadileri,* the *Istanbul Erkek Lisesi* (Istanbul Boys' Lycée), and the military schools at Monastir, Kuleli, and Erzurum seem to have had a similar impact on their students. In fact, one of these schools, the *Istanbul Erkek Lisesi,* has produced so many cabinet ministers in recent times that it has been called the "Ministers' School." [19] Actually, one suspects that it is in just such activities as selecting ministerial colleagues that school connections of this sort become most important in Turkish politics.

It would be extremely interesting to probe the secondary educational background of the deputies as well as their higher training. However, the data simply do not permit it. Enough information exists about the better-known figures to suggest that a highly disproportionate number of them came from one of the relatively select secondary institutions. In a very limited way, I shall refer to this information on occasion. But, unfortunately, I have not been able to obtain sufficient data for a general analysis of the significance of the secondary-level educational experience for the bulk of the 2,210 deputies. This inquiry, along with a number of other fascinating and highly promising lines of investigation — such as kinship connections among these politicians, average age at first marriage, rural versus urban upbringing, sibling position, wealth, Kurdish origin, and Shiite (*Alevi*) religious orientation — must be relegated to the long list of studies presently precluded by inadequate data.

The Political Significance of Educational Developments

The formation of the Westernized, secular military schools in the early nineteenth century constituted a wedge implanted in the Turkish social structure that ultimately split the educated ruling minority into two parts. On one side were the "modernists," influenced by a Western-oriented, secular education and desiring to remold Turkey into an effective state respected by the West. Frequently bearing the onerous official responsibility of *representing* the moribund empire, either on the field of battle or in the foyers of bureaucracy, these "modernists" almost perforce tended to view the empire's performance more personally and with standards at least partially absorbed from

---

Press, 1951), p. 90, where she speaks of Galatasaray, "... the first and most famous lycée in Turkey."

[19] See the article "Vekiller Okulu" ("Ministers' School"), by Orhan Tahsin, in *Hayat,* June 19, 1959, pp. 6–7, commemorating the 75th Anniversary of the *Istanbul Erkek Lisesi.* In this brief piece, over two dozen outstanding political figures of recent Grand National Assemblies who came from this school are named, and many intimate and durable friendships dating from those school days are cited.

those outsiders with whom they came into contact and conflict. Hence, it is important that all Turkish revolts to date, including the Young Turks, the Atatürk Revolution, and the "Gentle Coup" of May 27, 1960, have been engineered by *intellectual* and *official* cadres! They were revolutions primarily to maintain or enhance the prestige of the state, not essentially to admit a rising new class to power or adjust a society to major economic or social changes.[20] These uprisings did have strong social and economic consequences, but contrary to many other upheavals, such was not their main focus. Although the argument must not be pressed too far, in the Turkish case much of the character of these revolts can be understood in light of this intellectual and official background of the participants.[21]

Grimly opposed to these modernizing tendencies, in mentality and in action, was the other part of the educated elite — the *medrese*-trained intellectuals, oriented more to Islam than to the Ottoman state. Just as the ". . . Moslem youth who after 1860 attended the state schools where science was being taught, conceived the idea that Islamic teaching was an obstacle to progress and truth, . . ." so the *medrese* gradute clearly perceived the basic threat posed by the growing system of nonreligious, Westernized education to his Islamic conception of the proper path for the Ottoman Empire.[22] An educa-

---

[20] Cf. Max W. Thornburg, Graham Spry, and George Soule, *Turkey, an Economic Appraisal* (New York: The Twentieth Century Fund, 1949), p. 14. I use the term "intellectual" throughout to refer to a person possessing, for his society, a high level of formal education. The term is clearly ambiguous in ordinary language, often referring to attitudes or abilities. However, consultation of any standard dictionary also reveals the use of the term "intellectual" to refer to a member of "the educated class." That is how I have chosen to employ it.

[21] An interesting minor indication of the impact of an intellectual and official background lies in the program of *Türk Ocağı*, a very important politico-cultural organization formed in 1911–1912 by students at the military medical faculty. The intellectual characteristics of the founding personnel are well reflected in their goals and the proposed means for reaching these goals as stated in their *Program,* even allowing for the fact that this was a semipublic document in unsettled times. Ahmet Emin Yalman says that "According to its offical program, it [*Türk Ocağı*] set itself the tasks of 'working for the national education of the Turkish people, who constitute the most important element in Islam; of raising the intellectual, social, and economic level of the Turkish people; of improving the Turkish language; and of contributing to the uplift of the Turkish race. These tasks were to be accomplished by opening clubs, by giving evening courses, by public lectures, by establishing schools, and by publishing periodicals and books.'" *Turkey in the World War* (New Haven: Yale University Press, 1930), p. 193. Cf. Tunaya, *Türkiyede Siyasî Partiler, op. cit.,* pp. 378–386. Unfortunately, Tunaya gives the *Regulations* of the organization but not the *Official Program.*

[22] See Halide Edib (Adıvar), *Conflict of East and West in Turkey* (Lahore: Ashraf, 1935), p. 52.

tional dualism had been constructed in Turkey that resulted in the production of two conflicting mentalities. These were displayed most keenly in the struggle of the two institutions that dominated the higher educational system, namely the army and the religious organization.

The crucial significance of this dualism in Turkish history has been noted by many commentators, as well as by the official history of the Turkish Republic.[23] It is Ziya Gökalp, the intellectual father of Turkish nationalism, who puts this idea most cogently, referring to the two bifurcations previously discussed:

> In this country there are three layers of people differing from each other in civilization and education: the common people, the men educated in *medreses*, the men educated in (modern) secular schools. The first still are not freed from the effects of Far Eastern civilization; the second are still living in Eastern civilization; it is only the third group which has had some benefits from Western civilization. That means that one portion of our nation is living in an ancient, another in a medieval, and a third in a modern age. How can the life of a nation be normal with such a threefold life? How can we be a real nation without unifying this threefold education?[24]

The interrelations between these three educationally distinct elements provide us with the simplest theme in terms of which modern Turkish political development can be organized and understood. From the beginning of the nineteenth century nearly up to the present time, the tale has been one of gradual success for the Western-educated against the bitter resistance of the religiously trained. The role of the educational system in this development was central. In one sense, it was not until the new, faster-growing, secular state schools had produced sufficient graduates to tip the balance that the most profound changes in the nature of the regime occurred. Geoffrey Lewis is referring to this when he indicates the fundamental reason for the abortion of the *Tanzimat* reforms. He says that they failed because "... as yet the only educated class of any size among Muslim Turks was that of the [*medrese*-trained] *Ulema*...." Barbara Ward includes the First Constitutional Period and the Young Turk disappointment as well, suggesting that "... Midhat Pasha and Enver Pasha failed largely because their efforts were limited by the limited number of

---

[23] Among others, see *Histoire de la République Turque, op. cit.*, pp. 238–244; Niyazi Berkes, "The Historical Background of Turkish Secularism," in Richard N. Frye (ed.), *Islam and the West* ('s-Gravenhage: Mouton, 1957), p. 63; Karpat, *Turkey's Politics, op. cit.*, p. viii; "Atatürk," *Islam Ansiklopedisi, op. cit.*, pp. 777–778.

[24] Ziya Gökalp, *Turkish Nationalism and Western Civilization*, trans. and ed. by Niyazi Berkes (New York: Columbia University Press, 1959), p. 278. Also cf. Berkes's article, "Ziya Gökalp: His Contribution to Turkish Nationalism," *Middle East Journal*, VIII (Autumn 1954), p. 379.

educated sympathizers and executives upon whom they could call. . . ."[25]

Even by the time of the Atatürk Revolution, the best that could be said of the position of the Westernized intellectuals in Turkey was that they had established a precarious beachhead that gave them nominal control. The essence of the Atatürk Revolution is that it concentrated on the extension and consolidation of this beachhead to make it secure beyond all possible challenge. This effort involved the final expulsion of religion and the *medrese*-trained individual from the temple of politics and the attempt to make the uncongenial cities and larger towns of Anatolia habitable for the new class of Westernized Turkish intellectuals. It was not, as has occasionally been alleged, a revolution "from the bottom up" — an attempt to remold the society by starting with the peasant masses. Such an attempt was not in keeping with the movement's history nor with the attitudes of its leaders.[26] Moreover, the task was simply too immense for such an approach. As in most emergent nations, a smaller handle was necessary, a lever more easily grasped.

The grand strategy was that of making Turkey safe for the Westernized intellectuals who would lead her to modernity. A glance at the nature and chronology of the specific reform measures is revealing. First, the old regime was abolished and the sultanate terminated in November 1922. Shortly thereafter, the People's Party was created. Then, the final assault on the religious institution began with the abolition of the caliphate in March 1924. Religious tribunals were done away with, the fez was outlawed, and the religious dervish orders were proscribed. The wearing of religious garb outside religious buildings was forbidden. The Western calendar and time standards were adopted. The last vestiges of religious law were replaced by completely Western civil, commercial, and criminal codes. Deliberately using an art form offensive to traditional religion, statues of the Gazi (Atatürk) were erected in most of the important towns of Anatolia. The statement that Islam was the religion of the state was deleted from the constitution. Western numbers were adopted, and then, in 1928, a major step that had been talked about for some time was

[25] G. Lewis, *Turkey, op. cit.*, p. 36. Barbara Ward, *Turkey* (London: Oxford University Press, 1942), p. 31. Cf. also M. Philips Price, *A History of Turkey* (London: George Allen & Unwin, 1956), p. 131, where he says of Mustafa Kemal's early support: "The strength of this Radical group, out of which the Populist Party sprang, came from the young people who had benefitted by the increased education in Turkey after the 1908 Revolution."

[26] This is the main reason, for example, why there was no attempt at land reform under Atatürk, not "fear" of political repercussions. Cf. A. J. Meyer, *Middle Eastern Capitalism* (Cambridge, Mass.: Harvard University Press, 1959), p. 73.

taken when the Roman alphabet replaced the Arabic script. Arabic and Persian were removed from the curriculum of the lycées. Even earlier, a national (but primarily urban) system of education was established, a national railway network was being built, and the expansion of secular higher education begun.

This list could be extended. But the essential point is that most of these reforms were characteristically devoted to securing the grip of the state over the society, to putting the national house in order so as to command respect in the West, to removing the last possible challenge from the now defeated *medrese*-intellectual faction, and to enlarging the size of the dominant body of Westernized intellectuals. The immediate goal was *not* the fundamental improvement of the peasant's lot or the grant to him of increased political power. Lewis Thomas emphasizes this point most effectively:

> Thus the attempt to evoke and raise up enough truly new style Turks, enough thoroughly westernized Turks, to make a truly New Turkey viable had to begin with the ruling group itself rather than with the peasants. It was not only that large-scale and deep-seated changes in the peasants were practically impossible. Quite beyond that there was the consideration that only an upper class itself united in effective westernization and determined eventually to bridge the gap with the peasantry could hope for success in what would be a nationwide Operation Bootstraps.
>
> So, to begin with, Mustafa Kemal aimed his Operation Bootstraps principally at the partially westernized ruling group inherited from the Empire, for it was the only ready material with which he had to work.[27]

In other words, the basic bifurcation in Turkish society between the educated elite and uneducated masses actually provided Mustafa Kemal with a rather convenient "halfway house" in the reshaping of the country. He could, to a large extent, afford to forget about the submerged masses and concentrate on solidifying his hold over the dominant intellectual group. Then, once that initial battle was won, he could move on to the greater task of changing the masses.[28] Put another way, it can be said that he *exploited* the educational bifurcation in the society instead of deploring it, as other leaders have often done.

His tactics in his combat with the conservative-religionists are instructive in this connection. With great shrewdness he would mobilize all his forces on a specific, limited goal, without ever tipping his hand as to his next objective and thus permitting opposition to organize. Once the instant goal was achieved, he would then focus upon

[27] Thomas and Frye, *The United States and Turkey and Iran, op. cit.*, p. 72.
[28] Of course, Atatürk died in 1938, before even the initial phase of the "Angora Reform" was complete.

another target that, when known, usually bore a clear, strategic relation to the preceding effort. He has described this procedure, and the exigencies that led to it, in his own words:

> It would undoubtedly have been of little advantage if we would have put forward our demands at the very beginning in a resolution of such far-reaching importance. On the contrary, it was necessary to proceed by stages, to prepare the feeling and the spirit of the nation and to try to reach our aim by degrees, profiting meanwhile by our experience. This is actually what happened. If our attitude and our action during nine years are examined in their logical sequence, it is evident from the very first day that our general behaviour has never deviated from the lines laid down in our original resolution, nor from the purpose we had set out to achieve.... But we never disclosed the views we held. If we had done so we would have been looked upon as dreamers and illusionists.... The only practical and safe road to success lay in making each step perfectly understood at the right time.... This was how I acted.[29]

Thus, consciously or unconsciously, the grand *strategy* followed a pattern similar to the *tactical* approach, perhaps with equal success. The prime objective of the Atatürk Revolution was the completion of the Westernization of the Turkish intelligentsia. To quote Lewis Thomas again, it was "to get the necessary minimum of New Turks to enable his New Turkey to survive." [30] Bringing the uneducated masses into active political participation or improving their economic condition was initially quite secondary. Moreover, such an approach to Turkey's problems accords very well with the typical backgrounds of the political leaders of the period, who were predominantly intellectuals, and more than that, *official intellectuals*.

Awareness of this character of the Atatürk Revolution enables us to gain perspective on more recent political developments in Turkey. In a sense, what is occurring now is the *second stage* of the total Turkish revolution. The Atatürk Revolution accomplished the basic modernization of the educated elite and brought it into active political participation. Now the possibly more difficult task of modernizing the ill-educated masses of the society and of involving them in the political process is being undertaken. This is an incredibly complex

[29] Mustafa Kemal Atatürk, *Speech*..., *op. cit.*, p. 19. Cf. also pp. 16, 18, 598. It must be remembered that this was written in 1927, in the midst of some of the most far-reaching changes, with more to come.

[30] Thomas, in Thomas and Frye, *op. cit.*, p. 87, and see Lewis Thomas, "The National and International Relations of Turkey," in T. Cuyler Young (ed.), *Near Eastern Culture and Society* (Princeton, N.J.: Princeton University Press, 1951), pp. 179–180. For an interesting Soviet interpretation of modern Turkish history, see A. Miller, "Turkey's Path of Development," *PROD Translations,* III (June 1960), pp. 21–28.

and delicate, even dangerous, assignment. But the fact that the process has been able to be divided into two stages, rather than compounded by being telescoped into one, may partially account for the relative Turkish success compared with most other "emergent" nations. And, once again, we shall also see reflections of the existence of this "second stage" in some interesting changes in the social backgrounds of the top political leadership in Turkey through the years.

Educational Level of the Turkish Population and of the Deputies

The overwhelmingly intellectual character of the political leaders of modern Turkey is sharply reflected in even the most elementary aggregate profile of their formal education. As Figure 3.1 indicates, over 60 per cent of the 2,210 Turkish deputies serving between 1920 and 1957 had obtained some training at the *university* level. If the group for which I lack information is excluded, this proportion rises to almost three of every four deputies with some university training.[31]

Against a backdrop of information about levels of education in Turkish society as a whole, this material becomes significant. Unfortunately, I have not been able to secure statistics portraying the highest levels of education reached by the entire Turkish citizenry. A possibly even more stringent measure, however, can be employed. There are figures on the incidence of literacy in Turkey over a span of years. These are given in Figure 3.2.

Comparing Figures 3.1 and 3.2, we see that in a society in which about three fifths of the male population, on the average, *could not read and write,* at least three fifths of the top political leadership, on the other hand, was *university*-educated.[32]

---

[31] Most of the 327 "Unknowns" come from the First and Second Assemblies. The known educational level of these Assemblies was relatively low — compared to later Assemblies — and there is probably a disproportionate tendency for those with little or no education to fail to report that information. Therefore, the over-all figure of 60 per cent may be the more accurate aggregate measure. Even so, it is most impressive.

It must be kept in mind that I am, first of all, presenting a profile of the aggregate of all 2,210 deputies who served in any or all of the first ten Grand National Assemblies. There are, of course, numerous important trends and internal variations through time in the characteristics examined that are masked in the aggregate. These are described in the next section, after this gross panorama is complete.

[32] If I had been able to present figures for the male population over thirty years of age, to correspond exactly with the deputies, the contrast would have been even more striking, since the younger generation was always disproportionately literate.

Another set of background statistics highlights the same motif from a slightly different angle. Let us take the last year of the era under examination — 1957. In this year, the Turkish educational system was at the zenith of its development during the period. And let us look at the school distribution of youths at the appropriate age levels to try to ascertain what proportion went on to a university.

Figure 3.3 shows that less than 2 per cent of the youths of the proper age proceeded to higher education in 1957–1958. By con-

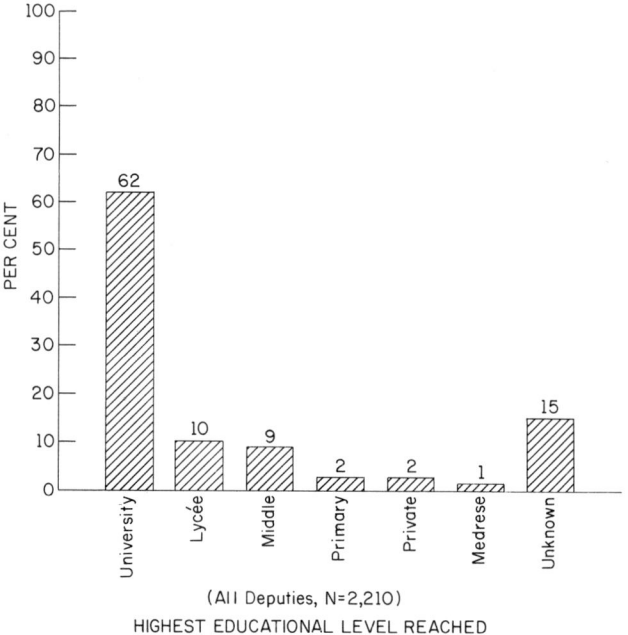

Figure 3.1. Educational attainments of all deputies, 1920–1957

NOTE: Though there were some variations, for most of the period under examination the basic route of passage through the Turkish educational system was as follows: The child entered primary school (*ilk okul*) at the age of six and remained there for five years; at the age of about eleven he proceeded to middle school (*orta okul*), which offered more or less of an added phase of primary-level education, lasting three years; thereafter, he passed on to a lycée (*lise*) for three more years, where he received his secondary education. From there he could continue to the university level at a professional school or faculty, usually requiring three or four more years of study.

Naturally, there are many different types of schools at all of these levels, especially in the secondary and university realms. I have coded a variety of specific schools according to basic educational level in order to obtain the classification here presented. This ranking of schools was done with the aid of advice from officials in the Turkish Ministry of Education, to whom I am indebted and grateful.

EDUCATION: THE HALLMARK OF THE ELITE 45

Figure 3.2. Literacy of Turkish population over six years of age, by sex and for selected years

SOURCE: *1955 Genel Nüfus Sayımı* (*1955 General Population Census*), (Ankara: Istatistik Umumi Müdürlüğü, Yayın No. 372, 1957), p. 25. Information for 1960 was supplied directly by the Turkish General Directorate of Statistics.

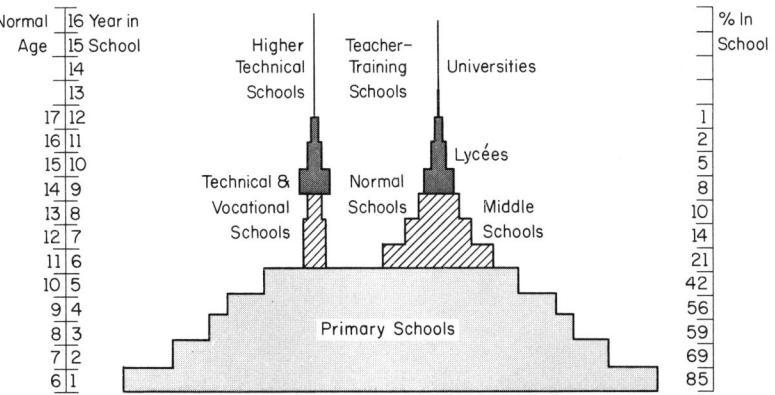

Figure 3.3. Distribution of Turkish youth enrolled in public schools in the school year 1957–1958

SOURCE: Data were supplied by the Test and Research Bureau of the Turkish Ministry of Education. The percentages used in school figures should be regarded as rough estimates, since they are projections from grade-level and age categories contained in indirect census-type materials rather than explicit information on how many children of each age group were actually in school. The percentages appear to err on the high side.

trast, when we inspect the individual Assemblies in the next section, we shall discover that in the contemporaneous Tenth Assembly (1954–1957) 77 per cent of the total membership had a university education, despite the fact that most of these deputies received that training when the percentage of all students going on to the university level was even slimmer.[33] In its broadest outline, then, the characterization of these top politicians as intellectuals in the context of their society seems to be strongly supported by their formal educational attainments as related to those of the bulk of their compatriots. Educationally, these deputies were about as atypical as they could be.

The Political Significance of Educational Differences

At this point it may be appropriate to ask whether the different educational backgrounds of deputies are reflected in specific behavioral differences between them. Are there any concrete instances in which distinctive educational backgrounds have had obvious political consequences? More generally, do certain types of political behavior of these Turkish politicians vary in accordance with differences in their educational training? The answer to both questions appears to be "yes." I shall first cite a few illustrative incidents and then apply a more general quantitative indicator.

---

[33] Though less significant, because of the absence of information about relevant larger populations (such as the *total* number of children at the appropriate age for each school level), the percentage distributions according to educational level of all Turkish youth *in school* for selected years are:

Percentages of All Turkish Students at Various Educational Levels[a]

Educational Level	Year						
	1912-1913[b]	1923-1924	1927-1928	1936-1937	1940-1941	1945-1946	1949-1950
University	1%	1%	1%	1%	1%	1%	1%
Technical and Professional	–	2	1	1	2	4	3
Lycée	4	–	1	2	2	2	1
Middle	–	2	4	7	9	4	4
Primary	94	95	93	89	86	89	91
Total	100%	100%	100%	100%	100%	100%	100%
(*N*) (in thousands)	(632)	(359)	(497)	(799)	(1,109)	(1,522)	(1,758)

a Figures are rounded and may not add to 100 per cent.
Sources: Ahmet Emin Yalman, *Turkey in the World War, op. cit.,* p. 82; *L'Instruction Publique en Turquie Républicaine, op. cit.,* page and table unnumbered; T. C. Başvekâlet Istatistik Umum Müdürlüğü, *Istatistik Yıllığı 1951 (Statistical Annual 1951),* Yayın No. 332 (Ankara: n.p., 1952), pp. 186-187, 189-190, 192, 198. For slightly different figures cf. *Histoire . . ., op. cit.,* p. 243, n. 2. As with all Turkish statistics presented, these are used to indicate general outlines, not to portray precise conditions.
b Of course, these data for 1912–1913 refer to the Ottoman Empire.

EDUCATION: THE HALLMARK OF THE ELITE

Insight is obtained from a glance at the educational background of the charismatic leader himself — Mustafa Kemal Atatürk. The Gazi related that the earliest thing he remembered about his childhood was a vigorous dispute between his mother and father concerning his education. His mother, of near-peasant stock, wanted young Mustafa to attend the religiously dominated local school. His father, on the other hand, who was a minor official, wished to send the boy to the school of one Şemsi Efendi, which was "... the first in Salonika where the teaching was done according to modern methods." [34] Going through with the customary matriculation ceremonies for the local religious school to placate his mother, he then quietly dropped out of that school after a few days and transferred to Şemsi Efendi's academy, where he could receive the more modern, secular education his father desired for him.

After a short while his father died, and Mustafa Kemal, his sister, and his mother went to live with his mother's brother, who was a peasant farmer. Mustafa was rather vividly exposed at this stage of his life to the vicissitudes of peasant existence. In fact, it can be argued that he would himself have been submerged into that mass had not educational opportunity rescued him. His mother became anxious about the boy's remaining without education; so she sent him to the house of an aunt in Salonika and enrolled him in the *Mülkiye Idadisi* (Civil Service Secondary School) there. After he was badly beaten by one of the teachers in this school, his family removed him.[35] Noticing the resplendent uniform of the son of a neighbor who was attending military school, Mustafa formed a determination to enter that type of training. His aunt was against this, but he took the entrance examination without her permission, and once he had gained admission, she relented.

After he finished the *Selânik Askeri Rüştiyesi* (Salonika Military Middle School), he went on to the *Manastir Askeri Idadisi* (Manastir Military Secondary School), at the same time taking special French lessons at the Brothers' School in Salonika. Completing this stage of his education, he entered the *Harb Okulu*, or *Harbiye* (War School, or War College), in March 1899. Although he wasted most of his

---

[34] The quotation is from the *Histoire...*, *op. cit.*, p. 18, n. 1. For the most accurate account of Mustafa Kemal's educational career, see the article "Atatürk" in *Islam Ansiklopedisi, op. cit.*, p. 719–720.

[35] Mustafa Kemal's family seems to have been more sensitive than most in this matter. Beatings were quite common and well justified in the popular mind. When the young boy was first taken to school, his parents signified their acceptance of such exercise of authority by saying to the *hoca* (religious teacher), "His flesh is yours, but his bones are ours." And among the numerous Turkish proverbs one very frequently quoted to children suggested that "Roses grow where the *hoca* strikes."

first year and neglected his studies, he became absorbed in his work during the second year.

> About this time, political thoughts slowly began to find a place in Mustafa Kemal's mind. They were the most severe days of the period of Abdülhamit II. The students of the War College, despite the tight precautions of the school administration, secretly read the works of the patriot Namık Kemal in their dormitory at night. The prosecution brought against the readers of these works awakened all the doubts of young minds and gave birth to the feeling that there was something rotten in governmental affairs.

Mustafa Kemal directly indicates the influence on his mind of these student experiences and says that it was in the War College that he, like many others, first became "politically aware." [36] This feeling was intensified in the *Harb Akademisi* (War Academy), where he completed his formal education, and in his early professional experiences.

It is often remarked that pupils in Turkish schools develop "extreme class solidarity," a solidarity that has been at times officially encouraged.[37] In Mustafa Kemal's case, aside from the special concern with politics developed during his years of higher education, his selection of comrades and cronies was greatly influenced by his educational experiences. A large proportion of the two entourages that he fashioned for himself — one official and one about as crude and unofficial as possible — consisted of classmates from the military schools. These ranged from his early drinking companion, Colonel Arif, whom Mustafa Kemal insisted on attaching to the military cabinet despite opposition, to the austere Ali Fuat (Cebesoy) Pasha, who was induced to stay with the Gazi at Çankaya in 1920 on the grounds that they were "classmates." [38]

The political significance of education can also be seen in the early organization of the Defense of Rights Committees in Anatolia, the core of which was frequently formed by a group of schoolmates.[39] Or, surveying official governmental actions, one spies a frequent tendency to emphasize formal education in drafting legislation, even where such emphasis is not customary, as in the press laws.[40] Further

---

[36] "Atatürk," *Islam Ansiklopedisi, op. cit.*, pp. 719–720.

[37] Bisbee, *op. cit.*, p. 86. See also Turkish Information Service, *Education in Turkey, op. cit.*, p. 5.

[38] See, Halide Edib (Adıvar), *The Turkish Ordeal* (New York: Century, 1928), p. 293, and Ali Fuat Cebesoy, *Siyasi Hatıralari (Political Memoirs)*, (Istanbul: Vatan Neşriyatı, 1957), p. 8, where Mustafa Kemal invites Ali Fuat, saying "You are my schoolmate."

[39] Cevat Dursunoğlu, *Milli Mücadelede Erzurum, op. cit., passim.*

[40] The last example in the period being examined is the Press Law of June 1956, which required reporters and similar employees to have at least a school-

examples will be given later to illustrate points about specific faculties and about the impact of foreign education on the deputies.

QUANTITATIVE DATA ON THE SIGNIFICANCE OF FORMAL EDUCATION

It is time now to turn to a more general indicator of the effect of different degrees of formal education on Turkey's national legislators. Since the internal climate and Regulations of the Assembly changed from time to time during the thirty-seven-year period, it is difficult to find a suitable behavioral measure in terms of which to check the import of the different social backgrounds being examined.

The one feasible and interesting behavioral measure that seems most appropriate for revealing the significance of different social backgrounds in this aggregate profile of the Turkish deputies is the *election rate*. Information will be presented about how many times different types of deputies were elected to the Grand National Assembly. We shall see what sorts of persons had brief careers and what sorts were repeatedly reelected.

Of course, it is difficult to state with precision exactly whose behavior is involved. One feels that he gains insight into the operation of the system as a whole from examining election rates; but it is difficult in the abstract to distinguish voluntary withdrawal from party purgation.[41] Nevertheless, I feel that the special characteristics of the Turkish case — the high prestige and perquisites of being a national legislator — reduce the cases of voluntary withdrawal to a minimum. For most of the period studied, this legislature acted more or less as a co-optative body, and so whatever variations in election rates are found to be associated with social background differences probably basically reflect the behavior of the top leaders who were making the fundamental recruiting decisions. Some interesting inferences into the sorts of considerations that seem to have been uppermost in these leaders' minds can be drawn from the data, though of course without certainty.

Incidentally, since half of the ten Assemblies being inspected lasted roughly three years and half lasted four years, one can use these reelection data as a rough measure of tenure or parliamentary longevity for the types of deputies described. However, unless otherwise stated, mean figures will refer to the average number of times a given

---

leaving certificate and owners and editors to be university graduates. Outside this period but most revealing of all are the requirements of the new Constitution of the Second Turkish Republic that members of the Senate and the President of the Republic must have had higher education! *Türkiye Cumhuriyeti Anayasası*, May 27, 1961, Article 72 and Article 95.

[41] The incidence of death seems to be slight and approximately randomly distributed in terms of most of these variables. Though I have no information, dropout because of illness is probably similar in character.

group of deputies was elected. In this case, there is an obvious floor of one (1.0) beyond which no mean can fall, and an equally obvious ceiling of ten (10.0) beyond which no mean can rise.[42] From another viewpoint, a classification of "one" indicates that the deputy was elected only once and was never reelected. A score of "two" indicates that he was reelected once, "three" means reelected twice, and so on, with the number of *re*elections being obviously equal to the score minus one. Median figures are also presented where they seem informative.

Now let us turn to the general question: In terms of these election rates, did the level of formal education of a deputy make much difference? In gross, Table 3.1 indicates a direct relationship between the level of formal education and the reelection rate for deputies. Particularly if we momentarily exclude the rather special categories of "Private" and "*Medrese*" education and concentrate on the products of the normal educational channels, it seems that university-trained people were preferred. With the exception of the lycée-middle inversion, there is a downward progression from university level to the lowest primary grade (*ilk*). The lycée-middle deviation is explicable essentially as a reflection of the change in the educational system itself in this period. As the lycée system grew, much larger numbers of lycée graduates entered into the last two or three Assemblies. But these Assemblies, for other reasons, displayed a very low reelection percentage, and the lycée category reflects this special circumstance. Looked at slightly differently, the table shows that 66 per cent of primary-school products, 53 per cent of middle-school products, and 61 per cent of lycée products were never reelected, whereas only 45 per cent of university products were never reelected.

Despite the relatively small numbers of deputies within the "Private" and "*Medrese*" categories, the found longevities are quite revealing. The categorization of "Private" education is really insufficiently descriptive. It can indicate a very high level of education or a very low one, being, in the latter case, a virtual euphemism for "no formal education." Detailed inspection of individual cases reveals that this fact accounts for the distribution of the figures. Half of the privately educated deputies lasted only for one Assembly. This half,

---

[42] This "ceiling" produces some bias in the results. The Ninth and Tenth Assemblies, most affected by the ceiling (as will become apparent), were different in certain respects from their predecessors. The categories most reflecting this difference will show somewhat lower election rates than might otherwise have been the case. However, the reelection percentage from the Tenth to the Eleventh Assemblies was relatively low, and once defeated for reelection, most deputies never returned to parliament. If all these factors are taken into consideration, only about one tenth of all 2,210 deputies seem to have been appreciably affected by the ceiling, and the resulting distortion would be even less.

Table 3.1

PARLIAMENTARY EXPERIENCE BY EDUCATIONAL LEVEL (ALL DEPUTIES)[a]

ASSEMBLIES ELECTED	HIGHEST EDUCATIONAL LEVEL REACHED															Total	
	University		Lycée		Middle		Primary		Private		Medrese		Unknown			
	No.	%	No.	%	No.	%	No.	%	No.	%	No.	%	No.	%	No.	%
One	615	45	132	61	105	53	23	66	22	50	6	26	299	91	1,202	54
Two	377	28	60	28	44	22	8	23	6	14	5	22	28	9	528	24
Three	156	11	8	4	21	11	2	6	3	7	2	9	1	—	193	9
Four	88	6	5	2	6	3	1	3	3	7	1	4	—	—	104	5
Five	44	3	8	4	7	4	—	—	2	5	1	4	—	—	63	3
Six	37	3	—	—	9	5	—	—	3	7	4	17	—	—	53	2
Seven	34	2	2	1	4	2	—	—	3	7	2	9	—	—	45	2
Eight	10	1	2	1	1	1	—	—	1	2	2	9	—	—	16	1
Nine	4	—	—	—	—	—	—	—	—	—	—	—	—	—	4	—
Ten	1	—	—	—	—	—	—	—	1	2	—	—	—	—	2	—
Total	1,366	100	217	100	197	100	35	100	44	100	23	100	328	100	2,210	100
Mean	2.19		1.69		2.06		1.54		2.77		3.70		1.08		1.98	
Median	1.18		0.82		0.84		0.76		1.00		2.56		0.55		0.92	

[a] Percentages may not add to 100 because of rounding.

judging from occupation, knowledge of languages, publications, etc., is mainly the "no formal education" subgroup. Most of the remainder of the privately educated, such as former President Celal Bayar (to take the most famous example), were extremely well-educated people; thus the high mean does not violate the general relationship.

The longevity of the "*Medrese*" group in an environment that was overwhelmingly hostile is also quite simply explained. Mustafa Kemal and his cohorts found it convenient to have a small group of tame *hocas* about to take the edge off religiously inspired opposition. These tractable clerics were used to introduce controversial religious legislation and perform similar tasks. Valuable and hard to find as they were, such men understandably had the highest reelection rate of all in this gross educational breakdown.[43]

Two other important points in Table 3.1 are, first, that the average deputy was reelected just about once (mean number of times elected, 1.98) and, second, that several of the distributions seem to be somewhat curvilinear, suggesting that if a man managed to survive one reelection, his chances for a prolonged career in parliament were considerably increased.

If each time elected is assumed to represent three and one-half years of Assembly service, the average deputy served for nearly seven years. Most intriguingly, this seems to be a rather conventional degree of stability for Western legislatures, but perhaps this is to be expected in a developing nation under conditions of virtual co-optation.

Significance of Knowledge of Foreign Languages

Let us now look at some additional characteristics of the deputies while continuing to preserve the basic breakdown into levels of formal education. The purpose of this aggregate view, which masks some important temporal variations, is to permit exactly such successive cross tabulations. Most of all, it will be important to inspect characteristics that might be a function of education. Foremost among these might well be knowledge (claimed!) of a foreign language. If education is held constant, does such knowledge seem to have any correlation with reelection and parliamentary longevity? Table 3.2 provides the answer.

First of all, as expected, the incidence of asserted knowledge of a foreign language varies directly with educational level. Three quarters of the university-trained deputies, but less than half of those with lycée training, one quarter of those at middle-school level, and a mere

---

[43] Dankwart Rustow's article, "Politics and Islam in Turkey, 1920–1955," in Frye (ed.), *Islam and the West, op. cit.*, pp. 69–107, provides an excellent examination of these practices and the general political role of the clerics in the G.N.A.

Table 3.2

PARLIAMENTARY EXPERIENCE BY EDUCATIONAL LEVEL AND KNOWLEDGE OF FOREIGN LANGUAGE[a] (PERCENTAGES)[b]

ASSEMBLIES ELECTED	University			Lycée			Middle			Primary			Private		
	Yes	No	?	Yes	No	?	Yes	No	?	Yes	No	?	Yes	No	?
One	41%	51%	77%	51%	67%	85%	46%	58%	36%	50%	68%	—%	45%	59%	43%
Two	28	30	16	31	27	8	14	24	36	25	23	—	5	12	43
Three	13	8	7	3	4	8	18	6	29	25	3	—	10	—	14
Four	7	5	—	4	1	1	2	4	—	—	3	—	5	12	—
Five	4	1	—	6	2	—	8	2	—	—	3	—	10	6	—
Six	3	2	—	—	—	—	10	3	—	—	—	—	10	6	—
Seven	3	3	—	2	—	—	—	—	—	—	—	—	10	6	—
Eight	1	—	—	2	—	—	2	—	—	—	—	—	—	—	—
Nine	—	—	—	—	—	—	—	—	—	—	—	—	5	—	—
Ten	—	—	—	—	—	—	—	—	—	—	—	—	—	—	—
Total	100%	100%	100%	100%	100%	100%	100%	100%	100%	100%	100%	100%	100%	100%	100%
(N)	(1011)	(269)	(86)	(96)	(108)	(13)	(50)	(133)	(14)	(4)	(31)	(—)	(20)	(17)	(7)
N (per cent)	74%	20%	6%	44%	50%	6%	25%	68%	7%	11%	89%	—	45%	39%	16%
Mean	2.34	1.93		2.04	1.44		2.52	1.89		1.75	1.52		3.35	2.53	
Diff. between Means	.41			.60			.63			.23			.82		

[a] The *medrese* group has been excluded because of lack of information and an initial N that was too small for this type of analysis (23). The "education-unknown" group has also been excluded. "Yes" means those knowing at least one foreign language, "No" covers those knowing no foreign language, and "?" indicates the number for which no information about foreign language proficiency was available. In the author's opinion, further information concerning the last group would act to increase the observed difference between means. In case of change in foreign language competence during a deputy's career, his maximal competence has been used.

[b] Percentages may not add to 100 because of rounding.

11 per cent of the deputies with only primary-level education claimed they knew a foreign language. Though hardly surprising, this information is interesting in another connection because it gives us a consistency check on the trustworthiness of the reporting of respondents. If there had been no association between level of education and knowledge of a foreign language, one would have been suspicious about the accuracy and sincerity of the information provided by the deputies about themselves. The present finding by no means *establishes* the validity of the answers provided; but viewing this result in conjunction with a similar face plausibility in numerous other instances, one has increased confidence in the accuracy of the data.

The main interest of Table 3.2 is that it reveals a markedly greater parliamentary longevity for those deputies with *some* foreign language competence as opposed to those with *none*, even when level of education is held constant. At each educational level the percentage of those *without* a foreign language who were *never* reelected is always at least 10 per cent more than the percentage of those *with* a foreign language and *never* reelected. The same fact is illustrated by the mean election rates for these two groups. At each educational level the mean election rate for those with foreign language competence is greater than for those without. Moreover, with the exception of the primary-school group, the difference between the two means increases as the level of education drops. In other words, as the amount of formal education declines, the seeming relative significance of foreign language competence for parliamentary tenure increases.

There seem to have been a few dominant social background considerations in recruiting formal political leaders in Turkey through most of these thirty-seven years. Outstanding among these criteria were: (1) that the individual have some claim to *intellectual* status, (2) that the individual have some *official* occupational status, and (3) that the individual have some fairly powerful *local* community position. Persons having all three characteristics were most favored and lasted longest in the Grand National Assembly. However, it was frequently difficult to find individuals combining the local position with the intellectual and official statuses. The inferred criteria are here presented in descending order of importance, which means that if one attribute had to be forsaken, it tended to be the local tie. Nevertheless, in most Assemblies there was a group of persons not having intellectual status or official status, and having only the local linkage. But there were few deputies without at least one of these three attributes, and those with more of them lasted longer than those with fewer.[44]

[44] Of course, it can be argued that the nature of these attributes is such that very few persons in Turkey would fail to possess one or another of the three.

In this matter of education and foreign language, as in others to come, we see a manifestation of the recruitment considerations just mentioned. The basic sign of intellectual status is formal education. However, such things as publication or familiarity with a major Western foreign language (as most of these languages were), even to the extent of only being able to claim knowledge of it in the *Parliamentary Annual*, also constituted lesser grounds for intellectual status. If an individual had the appropriate level of formal education, the other indicators of intellectual status assumed diminished importance. But in the absence of such formal educational credentials the importance of the lesser grounds for intellectual position increased relatively. In terms of the inferred criteria, the more "marginal" a deputy was, the greater became the importance of those few "desirable" social background characteristics he did possess.

The primary-level group seems to constitute the one exception to the interpretation just given. One might rightly attribute this to the comparatively small N involved — only four "Yes" cases. However, specific information about the deputies concerned is even more instructive. The primary-level group will be seen to be anomalous in certain later instances, and it contains people recruited mainly at two special times: as "showpieces" in the Fourth Assembly and after the "democratization" of 1950 (the Ninth Assembly). Moreover, the overwhelming majority of those knowing a foreign language knew a major Western language, namely French, German, or English. The point to be added here is that the four deputies with basic primary-level education who also claimed knowledge of a foreign language violate this general description. Each of the four knew one foreign language: two knew Arabic, and two knew Kurdish. Hence, in actuality none of the basic group knew a Western language, and the mean difference calculation does not really apply in the sense used here. On the other hand, inspection reveals that a similar refinement in terms of distinguishing Western and non-Western languages does not alter the character of the findings for the other groups with larger N's.

Number of Foreign Languages

So far linguistic competence has been examined merely in terms of the contrast between those who knew one or more foreign languages

---

This argument really depends on the interpretation of the third item, that of the "local position." What I mean by this is actually being in a position of relative power in an important local community. Even then, terms like "relative power" and "important community" need to be given more specific meaning. I shall return to this later on, though not with great success, for the only clear measures available relate to birthplace and voluntary association membership. Thus, my third item will be seen to be based essentially on impressionistic evidence. Nevertheless, I shall stick by it quite firmly.

and those who knew none. In this general vein, an interesting further question is whether the *number* of foreign languages a person knew had any appreciable relationship to his election rate. If the basic hypothesis about the favorable influence of intellectual status is accurate, we might anticipate that the more languages a deputy knew, other things being equal, the greater would his parliamentary longevity tend to be. Figure 3.4 furnishes this information. Because of the rather small number of deputies with less than university-level education who knew a foreign language the analysis will be confined to the university group.[45]

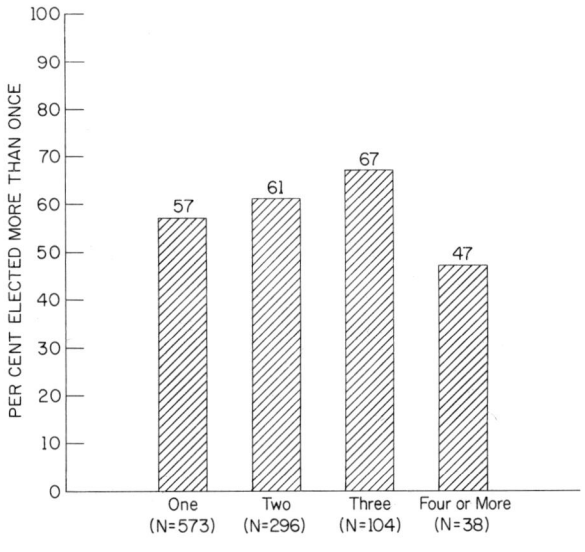

Figure 3.4. Percentage of those deputies with higher education and knowledge of a foreign language who were elected more than once, by number of foreign languages known

[45] For those interested, despite the low N's, the following table summarizes the lycée- and middle-level results. The figures are the mean number of times elected.

Number of Foreign Languages Known	Educational Level of Those Knowing at Least One Foreign Language			
	Lycée		*Middle School*	
One	($N = 65$)	1.91	($N = 37$)	2.14
Two	($N = 18$)	1.78	($N = 8$)	2.38
Three	($N = 10$)	2.90	($N = 5$)	4.20
Four or More	($N = 3$)	3.00	($N = 0$)	—

With the exception of the lycée-level group knowing two foreign languages, these data also fit the hypothesis, evincing the same sort of "step progression."

As is readily seen from Figure 3.4, the deputies knowing more languages were more frequently reelected. But then, in the final category — those knowing four or more languages — a reverse trend seems to be encountered. The reelection percentage drops sharply, even below the level holding for those knowing only one language. What happens here?

A detailed check of the other characteristics of these thirty-eight individuals claiming knowledge of four or more foreign languages, and also of the particular languages known, suggests no special factors that might be uniquely affecting this group. The nature of the relationship prompts the idea that this is a case of an optimum-value curve. Knowledge of foreign languages is possibly not the sort of achievement held to be increasingly good, without limit, such as amassing money or living additional years in good health is for many people. A marginal increase in one's knowledge of foreign languages could, for these politicians, apparently be undesirable from the viewpoint of their reelection possibilities.[46]

One plausible explanation is that knowing more than three foreign languages transformed a man in the eyes of the co-opting agents from a desirable intellectual into an undesirable "egghead," just as it is said sometimes that the armed forces in the United States really do not wish to recruit individuals of too great intelligence. One is tempted to label this the "Cassius complex," and I have the strong impression that such a factor was actually operative in these cases.

The Significance of Publication

Before rounding out this analysis by investigating the effect of publication on the deputies' election rates, I must warn the reader that my information about the incidence of publication by the Turkish deputies is much less complete than most of the other material. The deputies are apparently less careful in responding to this question than to others. Therefore, I may have disproportionately acquired information about publications for the better-known deputies for whom there were more sources. In addition, these better-known deputies tended to have longer careers than those less known. Thus a positive correlation of longevity with publication may be spurious. With this caveat in mind, let us examine Table 3.3, which controls for education by dealing only with those deputies having university-level training and which also controls for knowledge of foreign languages. In this

---

[46] An interesting sociological discussion of different types of values or goals, including the present optimum-value type, is presented in James March, "Group Norms and the Active Minority," *American Sociological Review*, XIX (1954), pp. 733–741.

Table 3.3

PARLIAMENTARY EXPERIENCE OF THOSE WITH UNIVERSITY EDUCATION, BY KNOWLEDGE OF FOREIGN LANGUAGES AND PUBLICATIONS[a]

ASSEMBLIES ELECTED	WITH FOREIGN LANGUAGE				WITHOUT FOREIGN LANGUAGE			
	Published		*Not Published*		*Published*		*Not Published*	
	No.	%	No.	%	No.	%	No.	%
Two	94	39	189	52	6	55	74	61
Three	61	26	67	19	2	18	20	17
Four	27	11	48	13	—	—	13	11
Five	19	8	21	6	1	9	3	2
Six	19	8	12	3	1	9	5	4
Seven	14	6	13	4	1	9	6	5
Eight	3	1	7	2	—	—	—	—
Nine	2	1	2	1	—	—	—	—
Ten	—	—	1	—	—	—	—	—
Totals	239	100	360	100	11	100	121	100
Mean	3.46		3.12		3.27		2.70	

[a] Percentages may not add to 100 because of rounding. "Unknowns" have been excluded.

context, the table illustrates the significance for parliamentary reelection of having published. Unfortunately, I have had to exclude those deputies who otherwise meet my criteria but were only elected once, since the incidence in this group of those for whom information about publications was lacking was quite high.

For whatever trust can be placed in them, these data also indicate the anticipated relationship between publication and parliamentary longevity. Since I have tried to restrict this comparison to persons for whom I had comparable sources of information, I feel that the essential direction of the association is probably accurate even though its strength is perhaps uncertain. Once again, the difference between the means, if accurate, is markedly greater in the group without a foreign language than in the group with foreign language knowledge (.57 against .34) — another case of a less important basis of intellectual status becoming increasingly significant in the absence of more prominent intellectual characteristics.

Age at First Election

Some inspection of the conditions under which the deputies were first elected may provide us with additional information for checking the hypotheses about the favored position of intellectuals. The age at

EDUCATION: THE HALLMARK OF THE ELITE 59

Table 3.4

AGES OF ALL DEPUTIES AT FIRST ELECTION, BY EDUCATIONAL LEVEL[a]

AGE	EDUCATIONAL LEVEL													
	University		Lycée		Middle		Primary		Private		Medrese		Unknown		Total	
	No.	%	No.	%	No.	%	No.	%	No.	%	No.	%	No.	%	No.	%
25–29	6	—	1	—	—	—	—	—	—	—	—	—	1	—	8	—
30–34	143	11	21	10	10	5	6	17	4	9	1	4	29	9	214	10
35–39	290	21	38	18	32	16	11	31	2	5	2	9	39	12	414	19
40–44	284	21	32	15	35	18	8	23	11	25	2	9	38	12	410	19
45–49	215	16	50	23	47	24	5	14	14	32	3	13	43	13	377	17
50–54	173	13	37	17	46	23	3	9	5	11	8	35	23	7	295	13
55–59	106	8	18	8	17	9	1	3	4	9	5	22	16	5	167	8
60–64	90	7	11	5	7	4	1	3	2	5	—	—	12	4	123	6
65–69	43	3	6	3	1	1	—	—	1	2	—	—	2	1	53	2
70 and Over	10	1	3	1	1	1	—	—	1	2	1	4	2	1	18	1
Unknown	6	—	—	—	1	1	—	—	—	—	1	4	123	38	131	6
Totals	1,366	100	217	100	197	100	35	100	44	100	23	100	328	100	2,210	100
Mean	45.4		46.3		46.5		41.3		47.2		50.2		44.6		45.5	

[a] Percentages may not add to 100 because of rounding.

which deputies having different educational backgrounds were *first elected* is one possibly interesting measure. Table 3.4 furnishes these figures.

With the exception of the anomalous primary-level group, there is evidence of a definite relationship between education and age at first election. Those deputies with higher levels of education tend to be initially elected at younger ages than those with less education. The university-trained deputies are the youngest of all groups when first elected, excluding the special primary group. As the level of formal education of a group drops, the average age at which its members were first elected increases. Intuitively, this sort of inverse relation between education and age at first election seems to accord well with the basic hypothesis about the importance of educational criteria for the recruitment of deputies. Other things being equal, one might expect that favored groups would tend to be selected at a younger age than less-favored groups.

First Election at a By-Election

Let us look at the device of bringing in new members through by-elections. Presumably, favored groups would be more likely to be introduced to parliamentary careers in this way than other groups; by-elections would be used to recruit deputies who were specially desired for one reason or another. Otherwise, in the Turkish case of virtually one-party rule, why bother to hold the by-election at all? There were many occasions when such elections were not held even though numerous vacancies through death and resignation existed.

In this regard, there are two interesting ways of examining those deputies initially elected at by-elections. First of all, if such entry was used to recruit legislators who were somewhat disproportionately desired by the leadership, then I should expect that the reelection rates of those so elected would be higher than the rates of those entering at normal elections. The data show this to be the case. As a group, and *within each educational level*, the 248 deputies who entered first at by-elections have a higher mean election rate than other deputies.

Second, according to my hypothesis, I should expect to find more of a tendency for those persons with higher educational levels to be initially elected at by-elections than those with less education, if this entrance route is indeed a means of introducing favored groups into political leadership and if intellectuals are favored. The data also reveal this to be the case, since 13.5 per cent of the university-educated deputies were first elected at a by-election, 8.3 per cent of the lycée-educated were so elected, 8.1 per cent of those educated at middle schools, and 2.9 per cent of those with primary-level education.

In summary, then, if we take two measures of supposedly preferred forms of entrance into the Grand National Assembly (namely at a relatively younger age and through by-election), we find in both cases a direct, steplike relationship between the indicator of preferential treatment and level of education. If we use inferred indicators of preferment other than the reelection rate indicator employed up to now, we still emerge with similar results. Thus confidence in the hypothesis regarding the preference for persons with some claim to intellectual status is increased.

School and Faculties

So far I have been referring to basic *levels* of education. Certain very prestigious *schools* on the lycée level have been mentioned, but unfortunately I do not have sufficient data regarding attendance at specific secondary schools to permit quantitative pursuit of that inquiry. On the other hand, there is information about attendance at specific schools and faculties on the university level. Moreover, there is ample evidence, both historical and contemporary, to indicate that there are wide differences of political behavior within the university group that seem likely to be correlated with attendance at one faculty or school rather than another. For instance, it has already been stressed that students at the military and military medical schools played a major part in the Young Turk revolution. Some of the most important quasi-political organizations of that era, like *Türk Ocağı* (Turkish Hearth), were founded in these schools by these students.[47]

At other end of the time spectrum, a comparable situation existed during the "Gentle Coup" of May 1960. Riots at the University of Istanbul, spearheaded by the law faculty students, and at the University of Ankara's political science and law faculties were a major stimulus to the coup. The severity with which the Menderes government suppressed these demonstrations increased the hostility to the regime, which was widespread among the educated segments of the society. Appropriately enough, both the final storm signal and the actual take-over itself involved the students at the War College, where Kemal Atatürk had achieved his first political awareness sixty years before. The silent protest march of the military cadets through central Ankara a few days before the seizure was almost a sure portent of the coup. Then, in the early hours of May 27, when power was actually seized by the military, the troops that moved into key government buildings

[47] Detailed information in English concerning some of this background is to be found in Ernest Edmondson Ramsaur, Jr., *The Young Turks* (Princeton: Princeton University Press, 1957), esp. pp. 18–19.

and installations in the capital were largely composed of these same cadets.[48]

Though this military school may be the best example of the special impact of particular institutions of higher education, it is by no means the only one. Throughout its history the Political Science (née Civil Service) School or Faculty has also impressed its particular spirit and outlook on its graduates. In this case, there is specific recent evidence that its students differ in important values from students of other higher-level schools.[49]

Further examples could be cited, but the general plausibility of the notion that differences in political behavior among the deputies are related to which faculties and schools of higher education they attended seems obvious. The very limitations of the educational system in Turkey heighten such an effect. In the United States, attending law school, medical school, an economics faculty, etc., generally means that individuals commonly trained have had a set of more-or-less similar educational experiences. However, since there are many schools of each type, the experiences of youths attending the same type of professional school may have little similarity aside from that contained in the general professional ethos and curriculum. In Turkey, on the contrary, there has usually been only one or, at most, two schools operating to provide each type of education. Thus, all those receiving political science training as a major discipline went to the *same school*. Those obtaining a legal education at the higher level all went either to the Istanbul or Ankara law faculty. The same can be said of medicine, engineering, and many other fields. Not only were there similarities in educational training, but there were many, many other common experiences for youths obtaining similar professional instruction. Persons of the same age and profession are much more likely to have known each other at school in Turkey than is the case in the United States. Moreover, since much more use is made of such

---

[48] On this vital school, see "Kahraman Yuvası" ("Hero's Nest"), *Akis*, June 9, 1960, pp. 22–23. Some details of the school's role in the coup are in "26 Mayıs gecesi Harp Okulunun içi" ("The Night of May 26 inside the War College"), *Akis*, October 3, 1960, pp. 22–23. Military cadets also participated in the two abortive coups of Colonel Talat Aydemir in 1962 and 1963. After the second such episode nearly the entire student body was expelled, and hundreds were tried in court for their actions. For an early warning regarding the headiness of the cadets' participation in the "Gentle Coup" of May 27, 1960, see Frederick W. Frey, "Arms and the Man in Turkish Politics," *Land Reborn*, XI, No. 2 (August 1960), p. 14.

[49] Cf. Herbert H. Hyman, Arif Payaslıoğlu, and Frederick W. Frey, "The Values of Turkish College Youth," *Public Opinion Quarterly*, XXII (Fall 1958), pp. 275–291, for a comparison of this faculty and Robert College in Istanbul with regard to certain values of their students. For valuable historical background, see B. Lewis, *Emergence . . ., op. cit.*, pp. 190–193.

contacts in Turkey, expectations are increased that differences in the type of higher education received may be behaviorally significant in politics.[50]

One of the first questions to be answered is whether some institutions of higher learning were disproportionately represented in the Grand National Assembly. Given the high incidence of deputies with university education, one may ask if all faculties and schools at this level were represented according to the numbers of their alumni, or if some were overrepresented and others underrepresented. It is difficult to obtain relevant general statistics covering the entire period from 1920 to 1957. However, I have secured figures indicating the number of graduates from all university-level institutions, save military schools, during the twelve-year period 1938–1950. It should be emphasized that the difference in years introduces a slight bias. New faculties and schools were being founded during the thirty-seven-year period. A faculty producing its first graduates in, say, 1943 would, with the same number of alumni, show a higher percentage in the twelve-year period than in the thirty-seven-year period. Nevertheless, the incidence of such cases is slight, and my general conclusions do not seem to be affected by it. Figure 3.5 compares the percentages contributed to the total body of university-educated *deputies* by the various types of higher educational institutions and the percentages of *all* male university-level graduates coming from the same types of institutions during the years 1938–1950.

The cases of overselection come entirely from two types of institutions: the political science and the law faculties. This is a rather interesting finding, for we see in this non-Western "developing" society with its relatively newly formed parliamentary institutions the same overrepresentation of the legally and administratively trained that we so frequently observe in the more established parliaments of the West.

The most underrepresented types of higher training are education, agriculture, medicine, and commerce. There seem to be two different underlying reasons for these cases. The first, and probably more significant, reason is that these were careers which, in the Turkish con-

---

[50] The greater use of social contacts of all sorts in Turkey is quite obvious even to the casual observer. It is important to recall that though Turkey is more modern than most of her neighbors, Turkish mores have not changed sufficiently to do away with the strongly felt need for the traditional "go-between" in many relationships. Furthermore, in addition to the deeper social and psychological causes for heavy emphasis on social contacts, one must also recognize that physical backwardness plays its part. For example, hotel accommodations are dismal in many areas of the country. Consequently, one tries to stay with friends, or friends of friends, if such arrangements are at all possible. Practical considerations of this type are important in extending the significance of concrete group memberships.

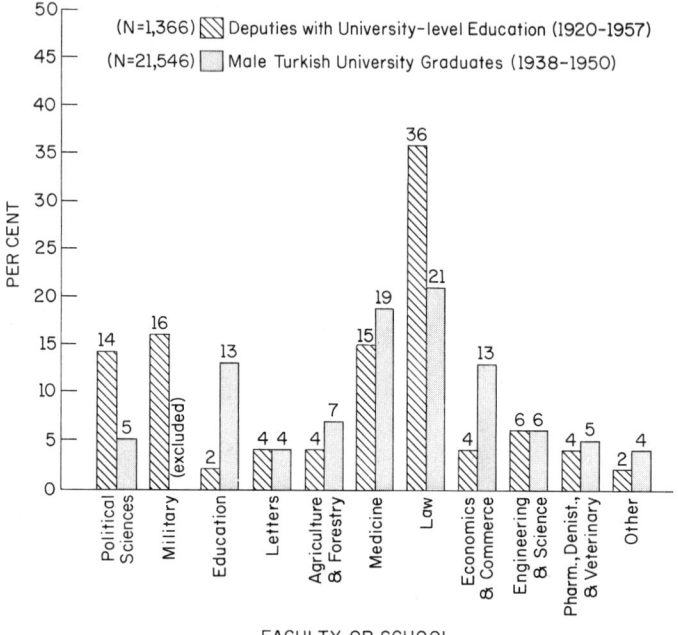

Figure 3.5. Types of higher education: university-educated deputies (1920–1957) and all male Turkish university graduates (1938–1950)

SOURCE: Adapted from 1951 *Istatistik Yıllığı*, pp. 199–201.

NOTE: Percentages do not add to 100 for the group of deputies because some individuals had more than one type of training. They do not add to 100 for the group of all male Turkish university graduates because of rounding. The subgroup with higher-level military education has been excluded from all calculations for the group of all male Turkish university graduates because of lack of information.

text at least, made demands on the time and efforts of the individual that were ill-suited to extensive political activity. In Max Weber's terms, these educators, agricultural experts, doctors, and businessmen were less "dispensable," less able to slip in and out of a hazardous political career without serious professional damage, than other groups. Second, in the case of those trained in economics and commerce, there does seem to have been a bias against recruiting such men on the part of the People's Party co-optors. But the general point is that legal and administrative training were overrepresented and other types underrepresented.

Table 3.5 provides information about the election rates of all deputies having higher education. The categories represent the basic

Table 3.5

POLITICAL EXPERIENCE BY TYPES OF HIGHER EDUCATION[a]

ASSEMBLIES SERVED	Pol. Science		Military		Education		Literature		Agriculture		Medicine		Law		Economics		Engin. & Sci.		Pharm., Dent., & Vet.		Other	
	No.	%	No.	%	No.	%	No.	%	No.	%	No.	%	No.	%	No.	%	No.	%	No.	%	No.	%
One	69	36	71	33	15	45	19	32	25	47	89	45	240	49	25	49	41	51	29	58	16	53
Two	46	24	44	21	4	12	23	38	17	32	54	27	147	30	20	39	28	35	13	26	7	23
Three	20	11	44	21	6	18	9	15	2	4	31	16	37	8	3	6	6	8	5	10	2	7
Four	19	10	20	9	4	12	3	5	—		9	5	31	6	1	2	2	3	3	6	1	3
Five	10	5	9	4	—		2	3	5	9	8	4	12	2	—		1	1	—		2	7
Six	11	6	13	6	—		3	5	1	2	1	1	9	2	1	2	1	1	—		—	
Seven	10	5	8	4	2	6	1	2	2	4	3	2	12	2	1	2	1	1	—		1	3
Eight	3	2	—		2	6	—		1	2	3	2	—		—		—		—		—	
Nine	1	1	2	1	—		—		—		—		1		—		—		—		—	
Ten	—		—		—		—		—		—		—		—		—		—		—	
Total	189	100	212	100	33	100	60	100	53	100	198	100	489	100	51	100	80	100	50	100	30	100
(% of Grand Total)	(14%)		(16%)		(2%)		(4%)		(4%)		(15%)		(36%)		(4%)		(6%)		(4%)		(2%)	
Mean	2.73		2.72		2.64		2.32		2.23		2.10		2.00		1.79		1.76		1.64		2.13	

[a] Percentages may not add to 100 because of rounding.

types of education received. It should be recalled from Table 3.1 that the mean election rate for all deputies with higher education was 2.19. In Table 3.5, the types of training are arranged from left to right in descending order of mean election rates. It is evident that political science and military training lead in producing parliamentary longevity.[51] They are followed fairly closely by education. Then there is a rather larger gap between these three and literature and agriculture, which are the only other two educational contingents above the general mean election rate of 2.19 for the entire university group.

If we take the general mean (2.19) as the dividing point, we discover an apparent basic distinction between the university groups above the mean and those below. Those below are mainly deputies trained in one of the "free professions" (*serbest meslekler*), while those above, with less homogeneity, have a bureaucratic or official type of higher education. This is certainly true of the top three groups — political science (civil service), military, and education. Virtually the only career outlet for persons possessing these types of training was government service. This finding seems to support the previously suggested second major criterion for the recruitment of leading politicians in Turkey, namely that preference was given not merely to intellectuals but to *official* intellectuals.

There are areas in which the findings of Figure 3.5 and Table 3.5 seem to conflict. One might expect that favored groups with a high election rate should also be numerically overrepresented in the legislature, and vice versa. Such is not uniformly the case. While the co-optors had considerable latitude in making their selections, they nevertheless had to operate in terms of a definite pool of *willing and available* talent. This pool contained a relatively large number of lawyers, even if the proportion of lawyers among the university-educated is considered. Thus lawyers are relatively overrepresented. On the other hand, this was not in the aggregate a favored group — not "official" — and so we find that the reelection rate for the legally educated is low.

The group consisting of those trained in the field of education, by contrast, is one of the favored groups, as its election rate reveals. But since the nature of the career was such that its followers were not very likely to be found in the pool of available talent, the group as a whole is underrepresented among the university-educated deputies. Similar considerations relate to the military. The over-all finding to be emphasized here again is that within the large group of the university-educated among the deputies those persons having an "official" type

---

[51] The 102 War Academy (*Harb Akademisi*) products had a mean election rate of 2.80, compared to 2.66 for the 110 War School (*Harb Okulu*) products.

of education seem disproportionately preferred, judging by election rates.[52]

Higher Education at Western Institutions

One final topic relating to the education of the deputies concerns their formal exposure to higher education in Western nations. What sorts of Turkish legislators received university-level training in Western countries, and where did they receive it? Table 3.6 provides information on this subject.

First of all, Table 3.6 shows that 260 deputies out of the 1,366 with higher education, or about 19 per cent, claimed to have studied at a university-level faculty in a Western country.[53] Once again I must caution the reader that the information concerning the foreign educational experiences of the deputies may be incomplete. There are a number of instances in which a deputy neglected to list any such training, yet I have discovered from other reliable sources that he possessed it. Consequently, though I feel that the general picture presented here of the sorts of foreign training received by the deputies is accurate, the specific dimensions may be awry in some cases. The data probably tend to underestimate the foreign educational contact. Hence, I can state that a sizable segment of the intellectual majority in the Assembly — at least about one fifth — had received high-level training at Western faculties.

---

[52] Of course, it can be argued that many of these educational findings are but a reflection of occupational differences. Thus, it was not those with higher education who were preferred but those persons engaging in certain occupations that demanded higher education. In this connection, what is necessary is to hold occupation constant and then ascertain the significance of educational differences. There is no doubt that occupation is another important social background distinction, and this procedure will be followed in the next chapter.

[53] This figure can be compared with some data from Henry E. Allen, *The Turkish Transformation* (Chicago: University of Chicago Press, 1935), p. 124: "In the year 1932-33, ... there were 267 Turkish students, 44 of whom were girls, pursuing courses of study in European countries under government guidance. This compares with 31 in the year 1923-24." Country distributions in 1932-1933 were roughly the same as for the deputies as a group, save that Belgium placed third and Switzerland fourth. Even with the addition of those studying abroad under *private* auspices, the proportion of deputies emanating from this relatively small group of students being educated in the West would seem to be very large.

By the end of the period being studied (1956), there were some 2,000 Turkish students in foreign countries. Furthermore, the distribution had changed markedly, with American educational institutions tending to replace French and German. Of the 2,000 Turkish students abroad in 1956, 816 were studying in the United States. (Turkish Information Office, *Education in Turkey, op. cit.,* p. 13)

68 THE AGGREGATE VIEW

Table 3.6 Deputies Obtaining Higher Education in Various Western Countries, by Type of Faculty Attended[a]

Country	Pol. Science		Military		Education		Literature		Agriculture		Medicine		Law		Econ. & Com.		Engin. & Sci.		Pharm., Dent. & Vet. Med.		Other		Country Totals (Students)	
	No.	%	No.	%	No.	%	No.	%	No.	%	No.	%	No.	%	No.	%	No.	%	No.	%	No.	%	No.	%
Austria	—	—	—	—	—	—	2	13	—	—	4	12	2	3	—	—	2	7	—	—	—	—	10	4
Belgium	4	11	—	—	—	—	—	—	1	5	—	—	3	5	1	4	3	10	—	—	—	—	12	5
France	23	66	7	54	3	43	8	50	5	24	16	47	33	52	4	17	6	21	1	25	7	47	113	43
Germany	3	9	4	31	1	14	5	31	14	67	16	47	10	16	9	39	12	41	2	50	3	20	79	30
Great Britain	3	9	2	15	—	—	—	—	—	—	—	—	1	2	3	13	—	—	—	—	1	7	10	4
Greece	—	—	—	—	—	—	—	—	—	—	1	3	—	—	—	—	—	—	1	25	—	—	2	1
Hungary	—	—	—	—	—	—	—	—	—	—	—	—	—	—	—	—	1	3	—	—	1	7	2	1
Italy	—	—	—	—	—	—	—	—	—	—	—	—	4	6	—	—	—	—	—	—	1	7	5	2
Rumania	—	—	—	—	—	—	—	—	—	—	—	—	—	—	—	—	—	—	—	—	—	—	1	—
Russia	—	—	—	—	2	29	1	6	—	—	1	3	1	2	—	—	1	3	—	—	—	—	4	2
Switzerland	5	14	—	—	—	—	1	6	—	—	4	12	12	19	8	35	4	14	—	—	2	13	38	15
U.S.A.	3	9	—	—	—	—	—	—	1	5	3	9	4	6	1	4	3	10	—	—	—	—	16	6
Yugoslavia	—	—	—	—	1	14	—	—	—	—	—	—	—	—	—	—	—	—	—	—	—	—	1	—
Total Persons	35[b]		13		7		16		21		34		63		23		29		4		15		293 (260)	
As % of all deputies with same type of education[c]	19%		6%		21%		27%		40%		17%		13%		45%		36%		8%		50%		(19%)	

[a] "Country Totals" column indicates the total number of deputies claiming to have studied in each country. Percentages are figured on the base 260, the sum of all deputies obtaining higher education in the West.

The percentages given under each type of education do not add to 100 because some individuals studied the same subject in more than one country. Hence, they are counted several times, while the percentages are computed on the base of the total number of different persons receiving the specific type of foreign education in Western countries. In other words, the percentages for the political science column indicate that of the 35 persons studying political science in a Western country, 66 per cent studied in France, 14 per cent in Switzerland, and so on. A man who had studied the subject in both countries would figure in both percentages, though he only enters once, of course, in the figure of 35 persons studying political science abroad.

[b] The percentages in this row indicate the proportion of all deputies having that same type of education who studied the subject abroad in the West. Thus, we see that 19 per cent of all deputies having university-level political science training studied political science in a Western nation. Naturally, this says nothing about whether they also studied that subject in Turkey or not. In most cases, the foreign study was in addition to study at a Turkish faculty.

France, Germany, and Switzerland, in that order, seem to have been especially favored among Western nations for providing this instruction. More than two out of five of those educated in the West went to school in France, and nearly one third studied in Germany. After observing the 15 per cent who studied in Switzerland, we see that no other Western nation trained more than 5 per cent of the total. In other words, two — possibly three — nations dominated this type of training of the deputies. All were continental European countries, and the basic cultural impact appears to have been either French or German.

Reflections of this continental European background are quite apparent in the formal structure of Turkish government, in the judicial system, in administrative practices, in the vocabulary of politics, in the educational system, and in many other areas of Turkish life and politics. Possibly the most illustrative single incident relates to the adoption by the Turks, in 1926, of new Western codes of law. A number of different codes were available. From these possibilities, the Swiss civil code, the German commercial code, and the Italian penal code were selected. A fundamental cause of the selection of the Swiss civil code — the most important of the three — is frequently represented to be the fact that the Minister of Justice of the time, Mahmut Esat (Bozkurt), received his legal training in Switzerland.[54]

Although a high proportion of those students receiving university-level education in the West seems to have been able to reach the Grand National Assembly, this foreign experience does not seem to have affected the length of a deputy's stay in that body. Direct comparisons of the foreign-educated and domestically educated university graduates failed to reveal significant differences in election rates.[55]

---

[54] See the articles by L. F. Fındıkoğlu and K. Lipstein in the special issue of the *International Social Science Bulletin* entitled "The Reception of Foreign Law in Turkey," Vol. IX, No. 1 (1957), pp. 13–20 and 70–81, respectively, esp. pp. 13–24, 74. Lipstein, for example, refers to the "... view ... that the preference of the Turkish legislature in 1926 for Swiss legislation must be attributed to the predilection of certain leading personalities who have received their legal education in Switzerland..." (p. 74). Fındıkoğlu states that Mahmut Esat's "... educational background disposed him favorably towards Swiss legislation" (p. 14). For yet another similar view, cf. H. E. Allen, *op. cit.,* pp. 13–14. On the earlier impact of Germany on Enver Pasha, see Alan Moorehead's fascinating *Gallipoli* (New York: Harper & Brothers, 1956), p. 23.

[55] It is interesting, however, to find that the official People's Party history (1923–1948) gives foreign education as one of three main reasons for the strong opposition to Mustafa Kemal that developed in the First Assembly. It contends that deputies who had studied or lived for a long time in a foreign country tended not to like the new Turkish government. Each such deputy wanted the government to be patterned after that of the particular Western nation in which he had lived or studied. Cf. *C.H.P. 25 Yil, op. cit.,* p. 8.

One additional aspect of Table 3.6 strikes the eye of an observer familiar with Turkish education. The subject areas in which Turkish faculties are best established are the areas where the smallest amounts of foreign experience are displayed. The political science, military, legal, and medical groups show relatively low incidences of study abroad. Thus, in a sense, the comparative lack of foreign contact in these fields may really be a measure of the strength of the Turkish faculties.[56]

SUMMARY

This chapter has been devoted to the educational aspects of the social backgrounds of Turkey's national legislators. First of all, the crucial role of educational distinctions in Turkish society has been stressed, with particular emphasis on two basic bifurcations: that between the educated ruling elite and the uneducated masses, and that within the ruling elite between those trained in secular, Western-type schools and those reared in the religious, *medrese* tradition. I have described the Atatürk Revolution as the resolution of the split *within* the educated elite by the final victory of the Westernized forces. That revolution solved the subordinate bifurcation within the dominant elite. Now, in the "second stage" of the over-all Turkish revolution, the society is coming to grips with the more crucial elite-mass bifurcation — it is struggling with the vital problem of bringing the peasant majority into active political and economic participation.

The aggregate educational data portray mainly the Kemalist modernizing cadre. The overwhelmingly intellectual character of its leaders relevant to their society is sharply silhouetted. Over 60 per cent of all deputies were *university*-educated in a nation where about 60 per cent of the male population, on the average in the same period, were *illiterate*.

After giving a few examples of the political significance of differences in formal education in Turkish politics, I investigated the number of times deputies with various amounts of formal education were elected to the Assembly. These rates generally varied positively

[56] Wilfred Cantwell Smith makes an analogous observation about Turkish society as a whole. While discussing foreign influences in Middle Eastern countries, he remarks that "... probably only in Turkey is it possible to be an intellectual entirely in one's own tongue. The Turkish intellectual probably knows French and regularly reads it; he may speak it fluently and may hold a Sorbonne degree. Yet he thinks and writes in Turkish, even intellectualist books. And another Turk who knows no French can follow what he has to say." "The Intellectuals in the Modern Development of the Islamic World," in S. N. Fisher (ed.), *Social Forces in the Middle East* (Ithaca: Cornell University Press, 1955), p. 202.

EDUCATION: THE HALLMARK OF THE ELITE 71

with the level of formal education; university people clearly displayed the greatest parliamentary longevity. A curvilinear pattern in the election rates was perceived; thus if a man managed to survive a few elections, his changes for further reelection seemed to be disproportionately high. The average deputy was elected twice (that is, reelected once) and served for a total period of about seven years.

It was suggested that three main social background criteria operated in the co-optative selection of most of the Turkish deputies. Some claim to intellectual status, to official status, and to a position of local power seems to have been essential, in approximately that order of importance. This chapter has been primarily concerned with the first of these criteria — the claim to intellectual status. Formal education constitutes the prime support of such a claim, and those persons with relatively more education were reelected more often than those with less education. Secondary bases for claiming intellectual status seem to be knowledge of a foreign language (especially a Western language) and publication. Over half the aggregate group of deputies claimed knowledge of a foreign language. If the formal educational level is held constant, those claiming knowledge of a foreign language had significantly higher reelection rates than those without such competence.

As the level of formal education declined, the apparent significance of each of the secondary bases for a claim of intellectual status increased in importance, as measured by its relationship to reelection chances. In other words, the fewer of the inferred recruitment criteria a deputy satisfied, the greater the differentiation in terms of the remaining criteria that he did satisfy.

The more foreign languages a deputy knew, with education held constant, the greater his parliamentary longevity, except that those who knew four or more foreign languages seemingly passed from the desired intellectual status into an "egghead" status and disproportionately failed to be reelected. Controlling both for education and for foreign language competence, I found that publication was associated with increased parliamentary longevity.

Deputies with higher levels of formal education tended to be first elected to the Assembly at younger ages than those with less education. Within each educational level, those first elected at a by-election had higher reelection rates than those regularly elected. Moreover, the higher the level of formal education, the greater the incidence of deputies first entering the parliament at a by-election. If younger age at first entry and first entry at a by-election can be assumed to reflect preferential selection, then these data further reinforce the contention that persons with some claim to intellectual status were preferred.

Illustrations were presented of the special political significance of particular institutions of higher learning, such as the military, medical, and political science faculties. The law and political science faculties were the only two appreciably overrepresented among the deputies, while persons with higher training in political science, military skills, and education had the highest reelection rates within the university-trained group. It was noted that these are all "official" types of training from which one proceeds to a governmental career.

At least one fifth of the deputies with higher education had studied abroad in the West, mainly on the continent of Europe in France, Germany, or Switzerland. The political influence of such training on the Turkish legal system was cited as an example of the significance of this social background variation. But there indirectly appeared to be no difference in reelection rates associated with the sundry types of foreign study.

In connection with the found differences in parliamentary longevity as related to the amount and type of formal education, foreign language competence, and publication, one might object that the truly important social background characteristic is occupation. The found educational differences may be merely a reflection of the fact that the preferred occupations were those requiring university education. To analyze this contention it would be necessary to hold occupation constant and ascertain whether educational differences within an occupational category still followed the general pattern I have discovered.

Simple as it may seem, this is actually rather hard to do in many cases. For example, all the medical men who became deputies had university-level training; thus it is impossible in that case to vary educational attainment. Much the same situation is found with the engineers, the military, the dentists, veterinarians, and pharmacists, and other groups. Nevertheless, some opportunity for this type of control is available, and I shall present the evidence in the next chapter, along with much other information on the occupational backgrounds of the Turkish deputies.

CHAPTER FOUR

Occupation: The Portal to Politics

A MAN'S OCCUPATION is second in importance only to his education in determining his social position in Turkish society. In one sense, the two are closely intertwined, since certain occupations demand specific types of high-level formal training. But the significance of occupational distinctions in Turkey is greater than this. Within the broad social strata established on educational grounds, the most crucial further determination of a man's status is that based upon his occupation. Other Turks tend to react to him largely in terms of judgments about his education *and* his vocation. The former permits a basic social placement, and the latter gives that placement its initial refinement. Together they go far toward deciding the political opportunities open to a man.

One way of illustrating this idea is to consider the imaginary Turkish town of Meçhul, a community of, say, ten thousand in Central Anatolia. If we are interested in comprehending the lives of two men in this town — call them Ahmet Aslan and Mehmet Kaplan — we learn a great deal about the probable position of each in local circles if we are informed that Ahmet is a lycée or university graduate while Mehmet has primary or no education. On this basis alone we can make some rather accurate predictions about the influence and behavior of the two men. We may be wrong in any individual case, but we shall be correct in such predictions far more often than not.

In a similar vein, let us suppose we learned that Ahmet was a doctor and Mehmet a merchant. Once again, on the basis of this information alone, a person with some experience in Anatolia could form a broad picture of the lives and behavior of the two men that would usually be fundamentally true. For example, to hark back to the *Şehir Kulübü* (City Club) mentioned by Mary Gough, one would be far more likely to find the doctor a member of that club than the merchant. In the Atatürk era, one would have found the doctor to be the head of the local People's House (*Halkevi*) much more often than the merchant. One could also make some rather shrewd estimates of the probable psychological attributes of the two men, their interests, the sorts of candidates they would be likely to support, and how one should relate himself to them. If an experienced observer wanted to get something done in Meçhul, he could probably tell you in advance with considerable accuracy whether it would be more profitable to work through the doctor or the merchant, "the grocer" or "the chief."

THE IMPORTANCE OF OCCUPATION IN TURKISH SOCIETY

General Evidence

There is much general evidence that supports this contention of the importance of occupation. Nearly all the informed writers cited previously as noting the fundamental significance of education in Turkey also mark the importance of occupational distinctions. Even the more specific previous examples have their precise parallels. The two levels of the coffeehouse in Mut, according to Mary Gough, were separated primarily on the basis of education. But what happens if we take a situation permitting more refined status distinctions? Mrs. Gough gives us a good example in her discussion of the gradation of seating in a cross-country bus, an increasingly important institution in transitional Turkey.[1]

> Seats in a Turkish bus are graded, tacitly, from front to back, the best ones being next to the driver. It is here that government officials, Army officers, ladies, or obviously wealthy people are put . . . . The first two, or even three, rows behind the driver are tolerably genteel, and to my mind more comfortable; the overflow from the front seat is to be found here, business men, schoolmasters, we ourselves. Then, gradually, going towards the back, the trilby and panama hats are replaced by cloth caps, neatly creased suits and western sports shirts by *şalvar* [baggy peasant pants] and collarless striped village shirts, smart frocks and high heeled sandals by flounced peasant dresses and *yemeni* [peasant shoes]. This grading of the seats seems to be due to custom rather than to any class prejudice, of which there is very little; also it

---

[1] Mary Gough, *The Plain and the Rough Places, op. cit.*, pp. 120–121 (italics mine).

is a very general rule to which there are frequent exceptions. One is quite likely to hear a villager say "Excuse me, my brother," as he climbs into the front seat beside a smart *memur* (official), or to see a village girl and her baby put there for greater comfort and decorum, if she is travelling alone. *One is very unlikely, however, to see a* memur *sitting at the back.*

Once again, Daniel Lerner, using survey data, also comes to a similar conclusion.[2]

> The differentia that count most in the disengagement of Transitionals are occupation, education, and of course literacy [an aspect of education]. The job is a major source of enlightenment, a channel through which experience of the larger world is acquired. Preconditions are schooling and literacy. Access to these channels differentiates modern men from their ancestors; and the distribution of such access is a fair index of modernization in any society.

Political Evidence

Instances of the *political* significance of occupational differences abound in modern Turkish history. "The Ottoman Empire was in its conception and essence an Islamic *military* institution...," as Sir Harry Luke observes.[3] The bifurcation within the educated elite between the "secular modernists" and the "religious traditionalists" was most vividly manifested in the conflict between the officers' corps and the *ulema*.[4] Later on, in numerous villages spread over the country, the same dispute involved as antagonists the schoolmaster and the *hoca*. Both occupational juxtapositions are now classic in Turkey.[5]

---

[2] Daniel Lerner, *The Passing of Traditional Society, op. cit.*, pp. 136–137.

[3] Sir Harry Luke, *The Old Turkey and the New* (London: Geoffrey Bles, rev. ed., 1955), p. 20 (my emphasis).

[4] Most symbolic of this was the famous "Menemen Incident," which was used officially to justify the induced termination of the Liberal Party in 1930 (November 17, according to the *Histoire, op. cit.,* p. 195, and December 18, according to Tunaya, *Türkiyede Siyasî Partiler, op. cit.,* p. 631). A number of Nakşibendi dervishes, led by one Dervish Mehmet, demonstrated on December 23, 1929, in Menemen near Izmir. A young army officer by the name of Kubilay (note the differences in name — Islamic and heroic Central Asian) attempted to intervene in the "reactionary" demonstration, whereupon the dervishes removed his head. The official *Histoire* describes this incident as "... the last open assault of the final agony of reaction, proving that the decision to dissolve the [Liberal] Party was justified, opportune and timely" (p. 195). Be that as it may, the characters — military and clerical — were appropriately cast.

[5] For a deservedly famous description of the tribulations of one young schoolmaster in Turkey, see Mahmut Makal, *A Village in Anatolia* (London: Valentine, Mitchell & Co., 1954). Note also that the village law makes both the village schoolmaster and the village *hoca* ex officio members of the village Council of Elders.

Notable also has been the regular ascription of importance to occupational differences by the state itself. For example, the Ottoman Senate ". . . was meant to include distinguished and experienced representatives of various professions. . . ."[6] Later, in 1922, Kâzım Karabekir Pasha proposed such a vocationally based second chamber for the Turkish Republic to Mustafa Kemal; and we have seen its recent partial institutionalization in the constituent Representative Assembly (*Temsilciler Meclisi*) set up after the coup of May 27, 1960.[7] Recall also that committee assignments in the Grand National Assembly were expressly made largely on the basis of occupational qualifications.

The political parties, as well as the state, have paid great heed to the vocational backgrounds of Turkish citizens. Ziya Gökalp, the intellect of the Unionist organization and the source of the idea for many an Atatürk reform, included in his program the conception that Turkey was to avoid internecine class struggle by emphasizing occupational groupings rather than class groupings. Historical antecedents for this, of course, lay in the guild organization of Turkish crafts throughout many centuries.[8]

Like many of Gökalp's suggestions, this one found its way into the official program of the People's Party. It was included in the "Populist" shaft of the party's "Six Arrows," or six leading principles (nationalism, republicanism, populism, reformism, secularism, and étaism). The 1935 People's Party *Program* put it this way:

> It is one of our main principles to consider the people of the Turkish Republic, not as composed of different classes, but as a community divided into various professions according to the requirements of the division of labor for the individual and social life of the Turkish people. The farmers, handicraftsmen, laborers and workmen, people exercising free professions, industrialists, merchants, and public servants are the main groups of [workers] constituting the Turkish community.[9]

---

[6] Ahmet Emin Yalman, *Turkey in the World War*, op. cit., p. 96.

[7] Cf. Mustafa Kemal, *Speech* . . ., op. cit., pp. 539–541. To Kâzım Pasha, Mustafa Kemal significantly replied: "In my humble opinion, the only way to obviate the dissensions foreshadowed by you is to *take care that the members of the Assembly shall be elected as far as possible from among distinguished men and experts* and to watch that very special importance is put on the internal organization of the Assembly for the election of members of committees on questions regarding their knowledge and experience." (My emphasis.) For some nineteenth-century illustrations of official recognition of occupational differences, see B. Lewis, *Emergence* . . ., op. cit., pp. 389, 392, and *passim*.

[8] Uriel Heyd, *The Foundations of Turkish Nationalism* (London: Luzac & Harvill Press, 1950), pp. 140–146, esp. p. 144.

[9] Webster, *The Turkey of Atatürk*, op. cit., p. 308, quoting the official party translation of Part II, Section 5c, of the *C.H.P. Programı*. Cf. Evrenol, *Revo-*

To extend the illustrations in time, we can look back to periods before the formation of the People's Party and then forward to the fifties and find further examples of the attention paid to occupational dictinctions by party organizations. Cevat Dursunoğlu's account of the creation of the pivotal Erzurum Defense of Rights Association repeatedly portrays the concern of the founders with occupational representation, special attention being paid to military, governmental, and religious personnel, as well as to intellectuals in general.[10] Concerning the fifties, a most revealing insight is obtained from a glance at the party ballots for the election of national deputies. Aside from the names of the party and its candidates, only one other item of information about the proposed slate was usually given — the occupations of the candidates.

---

lutionary Turkey, op. cit., p. 24, or Oğuzkan, *Adult Education in Turkey, op. cit.*, p. 11, where he explains that "... populism assumes that the republic is a society composed not of different classes in conflict but of various occupations, according to the requirements of the division of labour, whose harmonious functioning is essential."

[10] Dursunoğlu, *Millî Mücadele'de Erzurum, op. cit.*, pp. 26, 29, 38, 39, 41, 49–50, and *passim*. Cf. also Tunaya, *Türkiyede ..., op. cit.*, pp. 475–476. The occupational profile of the delegates to the Erzurum Congress, according to information presented by Dursunoğlu (pp. 109–112) was as follows:

VOCATION	No.	%
Law	4	7
Medicine	1	2
Dent., Pharm., & Vet. Med.	—	—
Engineering	—	—
(Professional)	**(5)**	**(9)**
Government	8	15
Military	6	11
Education	4	7
(Official)	**(18)**	**(33)**
Trade	5	9
Agriculture	10	19
Banking	—	—
(Economic)	**(15)**	**(28)**
Religion	7	13
Journalism	4	7
Other	—	—
Unknown	5	9
Total	54	100

There were at least nine other delegates who were prevented from attending by provincial governors loyal to the Istanbul regime. Even prior to Mustafa Kemal's hegemony, note the large "official" element — despite our classification, which tends to understate it.

Other indications of the political impact of vocational differences are the use made by both sides (Istanbul and Ankara) of religious leaders during the War for Independence, the deliberate addition of a dash of workers and peasants to flavor the Fourth Assembly and eliminate the bad taste of the events of 1930, and the fissure that overtly developed within the People's Party in 1945 as landowners and those allied with them opposed the Land Reform Bill.[11]

To complete the initial survey, let us now inspect the aggregate data to learn what occupations these deputies pursued, what other social background characteristics attended choice of occupation, and whether the election rate indicator turns up any important differences between occupational groups.

OCCUPATIONAL PROFILE OF THE POPULATION AND THE DEPUTIES

Classificatory Procedures

First, I must explain the system of occupational classification. Most of the individual vocational labels are straightforward and occasion little difficulty. "Agriculture," however, has been construed very strictly. If a man was both a farmer and a merchant, he was classified as a merchant and included under "Trade." The reason was that such a man would probably have rather different perspectives from one who was strictly a farmer and without mercantile experience. However, the "Agriculture" category does, unavoidably, contain some wealthy landowners and some agricultural experts, as will become apparent when the vocations are examined individually.

The "Trade" category includes merchants, workers, artisans, and a minute number of self-styled "industrialists." It should be thought of as being labeled "Trade, Industry, and Commerce." Familiarity with the Turkish economy of this period will indicate that "Trade" is perhaps the most apt single label.

"Religion" has also been construed quite strictly to keep the category as pure as possible. For example, the *dava vekili* (counselor before religious tribunals) of the early Assemblies has been classed as a lawyer. Despite some strong suspicions in individual cases, I have not

---

[11] On the land reform issue see, e.g., Karpat, *Turkey's Politics, op. cit.*, p. 119, where he says: "The deputies in the Assembly divided into two groups as soon as the debate on the law started; one in favor of the law, the other opposed to certain parts, namely to the drastic expropriation aspects of the law (Article 17). The first group was composed mainly of intellectuals and government officials who adopted a social-intellectual approach to land reform. The second group, composed mostly of deputies with some personal land interests involved, adopted a technical viewpoint. They insisted on preserving the existing agricultural structure and on strengthening it by improving the cultivation methods instead of partitioning the land."

placed men in the religious category unless I had definite evidence that they belonged there. Inference was not employed, and so the figures should be looked upon as minimal.[12]

Most of the individual vocations have been grouped into three general categories: "Professional," "Official," and "Economic." The first includes the so-called "free professions" (law, medicine, engineering, dentistry, pharmacy, veterinary medicine) and needs little elaboration. The second, "Official," includes those vocations whose primary orientation was the performance of a state function and nearly all of whose members were state employees. If a man was a lawyer working for the government, he was normally included under "Law." The same applies to similar situations in other vocations. As a result, the figures give a minimal representation of the degree of official background of the deputies. This was done deliberately so that if, as I suspected, the official element in the Assemblies would prove to be outstanding, I should not have increased its position by any of the classificatory decisions. Hence, the argument could proceed a fortiori.

The third general vocational category is called "Economic." It includes mainly deputies who made their living before election through private agricultural and commercial efforts, though some deviant cases have inevitably slipped through so broad a net as this must be. Most awkward in this respect is the category "Banking," for until quite late in the period studied many of these individuals worked for the government. Yet since concern with things economic and commercial seemed to be their *raison d'être,* I have somewhat reluctantly included them in the "Economic" group instead of leaving "Banking" as an isolated quasi-official category.

"Religion" and "Journalism" could have been combined under any of several rubrics relating to "symbol manipulation." However, the two professions are so distinct, almost antipodal, in so many ways in Turkey that I was convinced they must be kept separate. The other categories are either minuscule, residual, or "unknowns" and seem to require no discussion.

Occupational Profiles of All Deputies and Selected Comparison Groups

Table 4.1 will be our initial guide concerning the occupational characteristics of the Turkish political elite. It gives the percentage of all deputies during the 1920–1957 period who came from various

[12] Differences in classificatory procedures of this sort account for the discrepancy between the figures for religious representation given in this work and figures given by D. A. Rustow in his article on "Politics and Islam in Turkey, 1920–1955," in Frye (ed.), *Islam and the West, op. cit.,* p. 73, n. 5. Such differences are not destructive of Rustow's basic comment that the First Assembly (1920–1923) had a large congregation of clerics.

Table 4.1
OCCUPATIONAL DISTRIBUTION OF ALL DEPUTIES, 1920–1957

OCCUPATIONS	NUMBER	PERCENTAGE
Government	315	14
Military	223	10
Education	182	8
(Official)	**(720)**	**(33)**
Law	393	18
Medicine	193	9
Pharmacy	24	1
Dentistry	9	—
Veterinary Medicine	11	—
Engineering	57	3
(Professional)	**(687)**	**(31)**
Trade	294	13
Agriculture	191	9
Banking	38	2
(Economic)	**(523)**	**(24)**
Religion	83	4
Journalism	75	3
Art and Architecture	7	—
Tribal Chief	6	—
Housewife	2	—
Unknown	107	5
Total	2,210	100[a]

[a] Percentages may not add to exact total because of rounding.

vocations. It also makes use of the classification of most deputies into the three broad occupational groupings previously discussed: professional, official, and economic. Throughout, reference is to the deputy's main occupation prior to first election to the Assembly.

We see, first of all, that roughly one third of the deputies had official occupations, one third had professional occupations, and about a quarter had economic occupations. The remaining twelfth was divided largely into "unknowns" and those deputies with religious or journalistic occupational backgrounds. The largest single vocational group was that of the law, followed in order of size by government, trade, the military, medicine, agriculture, and education — to cite only the groups with one hundred or more members. Compared with other parliaments, the remarkable aspect of this distribution is the high incidence of persons with an official occupational background. The officials constitute the largest of the three basic groupings despite the conservative classificatory procedure.

Next we must once more ascertain how the Assembly compared with the society as a whole, or with its most relevant parts, along the dimension we are exploring. Was it merely a faithful reflection of the national occupational distribution of Turkish citizens? If it differed, which vocations were overrepresented, and which were underrepresented? Table 4.2 presents the gross occupational distribution of adult males in Turkey for selected years from 1927 through 1955.

Table 4.2

OCCUPATIONS OF THE TURKISH MALE POPULATION, FIFTEEN YEARS OF AGE AND OVER, IN SELECTED YEARS (PERCENTAGES)[a]

OCCUPATIONS	1927	1935	1940	1945	1950	1955
Professional and Technical	1.3%	1.1%	1.6%	1.5%	1.5%	1.9%
Government and Administration	1.6	7.0[c]	11.3[c]	10.1[c]	5.8	3.1
Agriculture	64.2	64.0	68.4	59.8	69.3	63.5
Entertainment, Sport, etc.[b]	2.5	0.8	0.9	0.6	2.3	3.7
Trade, Industry, and Commerce	12.7	18.5	13.1	17.4	16.9	19.7
Unknown	17.7[c]	8.6	4.7	10.7	6.0[c]	8.1[c]
Total	100%	100%	100%	100%	100%	100%
(N — in Thousands)	(3,976)	(4,445)	(4,906)	(5,526)	(6,333)	(7,209)

[a] SOURCE: Turkiye Cumhuriyeti Başvekâlet Istatistik Umum Müdürlüğü, *1955 Genel Nüfus Sayımı (1955 General Population Census)*, (Ankara: Republic of Turkey, Central Statistical Office, 1957), p. 27.
[b] Includes such occupations as hotel and restaurant workers.
[c] Armed forces included.

The data provided in Table 4.2 should be taken as only a crude guide to the relative proportions of persons in the listed vocations in Turkish society. Trend comparisons of this sort are complicated by the fact that at least three different occupational classification schemes were employed in the different censuses of these years, and the articulation of one scheme into the categories of another is beset with difficulties.[13]

[13] For a more detailed discussion (in Turkish) of these particular censuses, cf. Frederick W. Frey and Arif T. Payaslıoğlu, "Babalarının Mensup Olduğu

Approaching Table 4.2 with proper circumspection, we still observe gross differences between the distribution of occupations in Turkish society as a whole and the distribution in the Grand National Assembly. Turkish society is preponderantly agricultural in occupation. Just about two out of every three male Turks over fourteen years old were engaged primarily in agriculture. Among the deputies, however, agriculture occupied less than 10 per cent of the total group. Even allowing for understatement of the size of the agricultural element, agriculture was markedly underrepresented.

The "Trade, Industry, and Commerce" category included an average of about 16 per cent of the Turkish male population throughout the period and also had roughly equal representation in the national legislature (13 per cent).

The two general groupings that were greatly overrepresented were the professionals and the officials. Each had representation in the Assemblies of these thirty-seven years approximately ten to twenty times its weight in the male population.[14]

Further refinements in the vocational description of Turkish society, in order to produce more and more appropriate comparison groups and to ascertain where the true watershed of occupational divergence lay, would be most desirable. Unfortunately, available data do not permit extensive refinements, but we can probe a little more deeply. A more relevant comparison group than that of all males over fourteen years of age consists of all household heads. The occupational distribution of household heads is revealed by the 1955 census in greater detail than in previous years, so that comparison of specific occupations is possible. This information is found in Table 4.3.

Taking household heads as our comparison group rather than all males over fourteen seems to make scant difference. The same imbalances are present. Agriculture is greatly underrepresented, trade is about proportionately represented, and the free professions and official services are strongly overrepresented. In terms of specific single occupations, law is the most overrepresented, though we really

---

Meslekler Bakımından Siyasal Bilgiler Fakültesi Öğrencileri Üzerinde Bir İnceleme," *Ankara Üniversitesi Siyasal Bilgiler Fakültesi Dergisi,* XIII, No. 3 (September 1958), pp. 225–243, esp. pp. 237–239.

[14] The professional group seems to have been slightly more overrepresented than the official. One should note, however, that the "Government and Administration" category of Table 4.2 includes the armed forces during the years 1935, 1940, and 1945 — the years of World War II. Moreover, *all* the armed forces are included, officers *and men*. But the military deputies were *all* officers. The officers' corps of the armed forces is the better comparison group, rather than the armed forces as a whole, and of course the former is much smaller than the latter.

Table 4.3

Occupations of Household Heads, 1955[a]

Occupation	Number	Percentage
Law	6,520	0.15
Medicine	10,920	0.26
Engineering	5,590	0.13
Education	23,620	0.56
Art, etc.	6,420	0.15
Other Professional and Technical	16,520	0.30
(Professional and Technical)	**(69,590)**	**(1.6)**
Government	162,790	3.8
Religion	17,810	0.4
Agriculture	2,778,750	65.4
Trade, Industry, and Commerce	763,060	18.0
Service	136,210	3.2
Other, Unknown, and Unemployed	321,770	7.6
Total	4,249,980	100.0

[a] Percentages may not add to 100 because of rounding. This table was adapted from *1955 Genel Nüfus Sayımı, op. cit.*, pp. 52–53.

cannot analyze the military and governmental contingents since we cannot separate them.

A rather different comparison group that does diverge sharply with regard to occupation is that of *urban* Turks. Employed male Turks of known occupation in twenty large Turkish cities in 1945 were distributed as follows: professional and official, 31 per cent; agriculture, 9 per cent; trade, commerce, and industry, 60 per cent; and services, 1 per cent.

This is obviously closer to the parliamentary figures in some respects, but further apart in others. The agricultural representation is now 9 per cent in both groups, but trade is no longer equal in both. Using urban male Turks as our comparison group, we find trade acutely underrepresented. At the same time, professional and official elements are still represented in the Assembly at twice their relative numerical strength in the comparison group, even though they are not as extravagantly overweighted as in other comparisons.

It would be interesting to employ the body of all political party members, or all persons with university education, and other broad groups in Turkish society to make similar comparisons; but the data do not permit it. Hence we must be content with pointing out that the occupational character of the deputies to the Grand National Assembly was highly unrepresentative of Turkish society during the period examined. Above all, the deputies were disproportionately professional and official to a high degree.[15]

GENERAL ANALYSIS: BROAD INTEROCCUPATIONAL DIFFERENCES

Now let us seek some of the significance of these occupational differences. Close scrutiny will reveal an important and generally consistent pattern in the data presented. In brief, this pattern tends

Table 4.4

MEAN NUMBER OF TIMES ELECTED, ACCORDING TO OCCUPATION: ALL DEPUTIES, 1920–1957

OCCUPATIONS	MEAN TIMES ELECTED DEPUTY
Government	2.34
Military	2.52
Education	2.28
(Official)	**(2.38)**
Law	1.88
Medicine	2.07
Pharmacy	1.67
Dentistry	1.67
Veterinary Medicine	1.73
Engineering	1.56
(Professional)	**(1.89)**
Trade	1.65
Agriculture	1.86
Banking	1.97
(Economic)	**(1.75)**
Religion	1.83
Journalism	2.41
Art and Architecture	1.57
Tribal Chief	1.00
Housewife	2.00
Unknown	1.03
Over-All Mean	1.98

[15] For general comment by knowledgeable Turkish political scientists, cf. Yavuz Abadan, "Türkiye'de Siyasi Partiler ve Tazyik Grupları," *S.B.F. Yüzüncü Yıl Armağanı* (Ankara: Ankara Üniversitesi Siyasal Bilgiler Fakültesi, 1959), p. 95, and Bahri Savcı, "Partilerimizde Tabakalaşmanın Gerçek Mahiyeti ve Sosyal Muhtevalı Politika Meyli," *Siyasal Bilgiler Fakültesi Dergisi*, XIII (1958), p. 38.

to place the three basic occupational groups in a hierarchical array, with the official element most favored, the professional element less favored, and the economic element least favored.

To investigate this pattern, let us look first (in Table 4.4) at the main political indicator, the election rate. The mean election rate of the official element was 2.38, that of the professional element 1.89, and that of the economic element only 1.75, compared with an average election rate for all deputies of 1.98. Hence, in this crucial respect, persons having official occupations were clearly favored.

Actually, if we look at specific occupations inside these broad vocational groupings, the pattern seems to be generally reinforced. The three official occupations had higher election rates than all other occupations, with the single exception of journalism. This exception is, itself, rather interesting. Perusal of the individual dossiers of the seventy-five individuals comprising the journalistic group suggests strongly that these individuals were the quasi-official propagandists and publicists of the regime — a coterie of prestigious and favorable journalists (for example, Falih Rıfkı Atay and Yunus Nadi Abalıoğlu) who could usually be counted on to spread the doctrines of the regime. Also among the journalists and writers was a smaller group of famous literati (such as Halide Edib Adıvar) who were present as impressive, tolerable "independents."

Other nonofficial occupations with high election rates usually were close to official circles. It should be noted that the "Banking" group, the most official section within the "economic" element, also had the highest election rate of that category. It will be seen to be anomalous in other respects as well. Among the free professions, the doctors had the highest election rate. I have previously referred to the tradition of political activity among medical students and practicing doctors in Turkey. I might add that the majority of doctors active in Turkey during the period were most likely in official service, either with the military or working for domestic governmental agencies. It is only in recent years that the proportion of doctors engaged in private practice has loomed large.

First Election at a By-Election

If one assumes that first election at a by-election is a form of preferential treatment, one encounters a clear and predictable hierarchical ordering among the occupational categories. As shown in Table 4.5, the official group ranks first, with 14.7 per cent of all its members being initially elected at a by-election; the professional group ranks second, with 10.5 per cent; and the economic group ranks last, with 9.2 per cent. Military men were particularly likely to have been brought in at a by-election. Furthermore, in this case, too, the

Table 4.5

FIRST ELECTION AT A BY-ELECTION, ACCORDING TO OCCUPATION:
ALL DEPUTIES, 1920–1957

OCCUPATIONS	PERCENTAGE FIRST ELECTED AT A BY-ELECTION
Government	12.4
Military	19.0
Education	13.7
(Official)	**(14.7)**
Law	9.4
Medicine	13.5
Pharmacy	—
Dentistry	11.0
Veterinary Medicine	9.0
Engineering	12.0
(Professional)	**(10.5)**
Trade	8.5
Agriculture	7.9
Banking	21.0
(Economic)	**(9.2)**
Religion	6.0
Journalism	13.3
Other and Unknown	—
Total	11.2

journalistic group has a high rating (13.3 per cent), the bankers have by far the highest figure within the economic segment (in fact, the highest of all), and the doctors rank highest once more among the professionals.[16]

Foreign Language Competence and Publication

The same ordered pattern is displayed in Table 4.6, which summarizes the foreign language capacities and publication claims of the deputies. The official element professes knowledge of an average of 1.41 foreign languages per member; the professional element claims 1.05 such languages; and the economic contingent claims merely 0.65 languages per deputy. As before, the journalistic group has a very high rating (1.48), bankers differ markedly from the rest of the eco-

---

[16] The rank order correlation coefficient (r) between occupational groups arranged according to election rate and according to percentage first elected at a by-election is $+.648$, significant at the .01 level with $N = 14$.

Table 4.6

FOREIGN LANGUAGE COMPETENCE, PUBLICATION RECORD, AND UNIVERSITY EDUCATION OF DEPUTIES ACCORDING TO OCCUPATION: ALL DEPUTIES, 1920–1957

OCCUPATIONS	MEAN NUMBER OF FOREIGN LANGUAGES KNOWN	PERCENTAGE HAVING PUBLISHED	PERCENTAGE WITH UNIVERSITY EDUCATION
Government	1.26	21	76
Military	1.52	30	97
Education	1.50	50	77
(Official)	**(1.41)**	**(32)**	**(83)**
Law	0.74	19	95
Medicine	1.45	31	100
Pharmacy, Dentistry, and Veterinary Medicine	1.01	14	100
Engineering	1.72	13	100
(Professional)	**(1.05)**	**(23)**	**(97)**
Trade	0.52	2	20
Agriculture	0.68	12	34
Banking	1.36	10	54
(Economic)	**(0.65)**	**(7)**	**(28)**
Religion	1.64	27	19?
Journalism	1.48	66	70
Other	?	?	?
Unknown	?	?	?
All Deputies	1.09	18	73

nomic element, having a rating of 1.36 foreign languages per deputy; and the doctors once again have high proficiency among the professionals. The two exceptions in this instance are the strong ratings shown by engineers and by those in the religious category. Both these ratings seem to be directly related to particular professional requirements. The engineers had disproportionately to receive their education in a foreign country, and the clerics received instruction in Arabic and sometimes Persian as part of their vocational education.[17]

The same sort of relationships between the occupational groups

[17] Distinguishing between knowledge of Western and non-Western languages would eliminate the religious group's exalted position in this respect. However, since this was the only group that featured a high proportion of persons knowing non-Western languages, it was felt that this note would suffice.

hold with regard to publication. About one third of the official group listed publications, about one quarter of the professional group did the same, while only 7 per cent of the economic group claimed to have prepared published work.

Age on First Election

The only general tabulation of the data that does not essentially support the notion of a definite preferential ordering of occupational groups for Assembly recruitment is that giving the age on first election of all deputies. Relative youth at first election was used as an indicator of preferred status in the previous chapter. Here, however, the plain result is that the supposedly preferred groups are slightly *older* at first election than other occupational groups, though nearly all groups hover rather closely about the mean of 45.5 years. The military deputies are the only obvious exception. Turks ordinarily entered the Assembly for the first time as men in early middle age, regardless of occupation.

Table 4.7

AGE AT FIRST ELECTION ACCORDING TO OCCUPATION: ALL DEPUTIES, 1920–1957

OCCUPATIONS	MEAN AGE ON FIRST ELECTION
Government	46.1 years
Military	50.5
Education	44.2
(Official)	**(46.9)**
Law	43.6
Medicine	46.5
Pharmacy, Dentistry, and Veterinary Medicine	47.0
Engineering	44.3
(Professional)	**(44.7)**
Trade	44.6
Agriculture	45.1
Banking	42.5
(Economic)	**(44.6)**
Religion	46.1
Journalism	45.2
Other	?
Unknown	?
All Deputies	45.5

Localism

General Significance

We come now to some crude indicators of "localism" among the deputies — that is, relatively strong ties with the constituency represented by the deputy in the legislature, carrying with them important possibilities of local influence upon the deputy. Local pressures have been present throughout the history of the Grand National Assembly, even in the period sometimes called "the one-party dictatorship." In more recent years, with the introduction of a multi-party system, the impact of local considerations on deputies has seemingly grown rapidly.

One famous incident showing the pressures of localism occurred early in the history of the Assembly (December 1922). Superficially, it was nothing less than an attempt to deprive Gazi Mustafa Kemal himself of his deputyship by proposing a law that no person born outside Turkey, or, if so born, who had not resided in his constituency for five years or more, could be a deputy.[18] The Gazi satisfied neither requirement. Though the indignant Mustafa Kemal, perhaps correctly, viewed this as a personal assault, and though it had been traditional in Ottoman Assemblies to adopt a Burkean approach to representation, there existed a sincere current of thought that emphasized the responsibility of the deputy to his constituency as well as to the nation and that sought to augment such responsibility by insisting that the deputy reside in his district. Such ideas were specifically reiterated a few years later by an editorialist on the newspaper *Ikdam (Effort)*:[19]

> The mandate of our deputies expires this year [1927] and new elections will take place. As for me, the interests of the country inspire in me these reflections:
>
> 1) The deputy of an electoral constituency ought to originate from there or to have resided there for five years. For a deputy must know perfectly the condition and the people of his area . . . .
>
> 2) At the Grand National Assembly, it is not only necessary to take into account the question of party. All the deputies can be from the same party, but it is important that they belong to different specialties from the point of view of careers and knowledge. The interests of the country demand it, for the interests to be defended in parliament are numerous and varied.
>
> 3) The deputies must spend at least one month of each year in their respective electoral constituencies, to meet with their inhabitants, inquire about their ideas, and see things through their eyes . . . .

---

[18] "Atatürk," *Islam Ansiklopedisi, op. cit.*, p. 769. Mustafa Kemal, *Speech . . ., op. cit.*, p. 603.

[19] *Ikdam*, April 20, 1927. See also *Bulletin de Presse Hebdomadaire*, VII, No. 90. (Constantinople: Ambassade de France, 1927), p. 11.

Today, traveling through Anatolia, one frequently hears these sentiments voiced by lower-echelon local party politicians. And both the changes in political party regulations during the last fifteen years and the increased attention paid by the party central organizations to the local units scattered throughout the country are indications of the pervasive and increasing pressure of local forces on various national political figures.

Actually, the absence, not the presence, of such strong local ties would seem surprising to a person having general but not political knowledge about Turkish society. The attention accorded by many Turks to another Turk's birthplace can hardly fail to be noticed. On being introduced, an almost automatic question is *"Nerelisiniz?"* ("Where are you from?"). Usually the other party announces with obvious pride that he is *Trabzonlu,* or *Istanbullu,* or *Izmirli.* A highly disproportionate number of Turkish names are of the Payas*lı*oğlu, Ayaş*lı,* or Mersin*li* type, emphasizing place of family origin. These suffixes indicating geographical origin — roughly equivalent to our New York*er,* Californi*an,* Jersey*ite* — are used with much more apparent frequency than their English counterparts in the United States or Great Britain.

At Istanbul University the students tend to bunch together in groups according to the provinces from which they came. Large numbers of them live in the dormitory bearing the name of their province, if one is available. These boarding students, with the social solidarity produced by a sense of common origin and by common residence, were reportedly the leaders of the student demonstrations that portended the fall of the Menderes-Bayar regime in 1960.

Just as an obvious special camaraderie exists in later life between persons who have received lycée or university training in the same school, there also tends to be a special bond between persons from the same *memleket,* or place of origin, even though they have nothing else in common. The political significance of such ties is frequently observable, particularly in regard to appointments.[20] Moreover, in Turkey's largest cities there usually are formal associations of persons from various other provinces — associations designed to maintain ties with the original *memleket* and to aid it where possible. Karpat indicates that a similar, though less formal, institution is to be found in

---

[20] As one example among many, see R. D. Robinson, *Letters,* No. 67–73 (mimeo), where he indicates that Refik Koraltan, deputy from Konya and President of the Grand National Assembly, was probably most influential in securing the appointment of his fellow Konya resident, Eyüp Sabri Hayirlioğlu as President of Religious Affairs in 1953. On the provincial dormitories at the universities, see, e.g., Evan Fotos, "An Appreciation of Turkish University Life," *Middle Eastern Affairs,* VI, Nos. 8–9 (August-September 1955), p. 254.

Turkish towns, mediating the impersonality of town life for persons who have mates from their village already living in town.[21] These local ties also are very often reinforced by kinship connections that strengthen the relationship.

One can also cite a number of examples of the periodic political importance of a politician's being born within the present frontiers of Turkey. It has frequently been charged, by Turks and outside observers, that foreign birth produces a distinctive political mentality. Thus the Macedonians who took an active part in Ottoman and Turkish political life were sometimes viewed as being especially realistic and ruthless and subject to Western influences.[22] Turkish *émigrés* from Russia like Ahmet Ağaoğlu and Yusuf Akçura seem to have made a distinctive contribution to the growth of sentiments of "Turkism" and to organizations like *Türk Ocağı* and publications like *Türk Yurdu*.[23]

The immediate effect of such extra-Turkish origins on the behavior of a specific political personality can be seen in the activities of the early Foreign Minister of the Ankara government, Bekir Sami Bey. As Halide Edib has described him:

> Bekir Sami Bey belongs to a princely family in the northern Caucasus. He is first of all devoted to the Turkish cause. But next to that he wants the Caucasus in general and the northern Caucasus in particular to be free. What he has seen in the new Russia has convinced him that not only those border people but the entire world is in danger if the new Russian ideals are allowed to pass to the West and to take hold of Turkey. What he proposes is the unity of those border people with the Turks to form a federal buffer state between Russia and the West; and if necessary, to mobilize all those people under Turkey to fight the Bolshevist regime, and he wants England's support.[24]

[21] Kemal Karpat, "Social Themes in Contemporary Turkish Literature II," *Middle East Journal*, XIV, No. 2 (Spring 1960), p. 159. See also Karpat, *Turkey's Politics, op. cit.*, p. 93.

[22] Arnold J. Toynbee, *Turkey: A Past and a Future* (New York: George H. Doran, 1917), p. 33 n.; Halide Edib Adıvar, *Conflict of East and West in Turkey, op. cit.*, pp. 87–88; Bernard Lewis, "History-Writing and National Revival in Turkey," *Middle Eastern Affairs*, IV, Nos. 6–7 (June-July 1953), pp. 222–223. Several persons have commented on the fact that a number of the early nationalist leaders of Turkey seem to have been born on the periphery of the Ottoman Empire, with a possibly uniform psychological consequence. Cf. Heyd, *op. cit.*, p. 21, for comments on such a factor in the life of Ziya Gökalp, and see D. Rustow, "The Army and the Founding of the Turkish Republic," *World Politics*, XI (1959), p. 527, for interesting evidence on the prevalence of Macedonians in the Ankara government and Caucasians in the Istanbul government. Various Pan-Turkic or dynastic loyalties were associated with these geographical divisions.

[23] Ahmet Emin Yalman, *Turkey in the World War, op. cit.*, pp. 192–193.

[24] Halide Edib Adıvar, *The Turkish Ordeal, op. cit.*, p. 255. Cf.

Lloyd George, however, ridiculed this idea. Italy and France insisted on economic privileges in return for peace. Russia got wind of it, and Bekir Sami was forced to resign as Turkish Foreign Minister, since he had attempted the entire maneuver on his own initiative, thinking he could persuade Ankara to back him if he was successful with England, Italy, and France. The important point is the apparently great effect of Bekir Sami's social background — his personal ties with the Caucasus and his professional experience as a diplomat, which included a "mission to Moscow" to see the new Russia — on his political activities and on the early foreign policy of the Ankara regime.

These examples of the political significance of foreign birth can be brought up to date and ended with the experience of Samet Ağaoğlu, cabinet minister under the Menderes regime and son of Ahmet Ağaoğlu. Samet was born in the Caucasus in 1909 and came to Turkey with his father. Hardly a popular figure, one barb that has nettled him repeatedly is an allusion to his foreign origin in order to impugn his Turkish patriotism.[25] Other foreign-born Turks have had similar thrusts directed at them from time to time. In Turkey, as in most other countries, it is a definite political advantage to have been born within the national frontiers and to have strong ties with some important locality.

Localism: Aggregate Data

Table 4.8 furnishes information about the percentages of deputies born within the present boundaries of Turkey and the percentages of deputies born within at least one of the provinces they represented. Of course, if a deputy represented only one province, as most did, to qualify as being locally born he had to have been born in that specific province. If he represented more than one province, he had to have been born in one of the provinces he represented. Lacking better indicators, such as length of residence in each community, I shall employ these figures as rough measures of the relative degrees of localism among different groups of deputies and in different periods. In light of the previous general discussion of localism and the concept of *memleket* (birth district) in Turkey, such a procedure, though crude, seems reasonably promising.

Inspection of the table reveals that the ordering of the occupa-

---

Yakup Kadri Karaosmanoğlu, *Vatan Yolunda: Milli Mücadele Hatıraları* (Istanbul: Selek Yayınları, n.d.), p. 84; Rustow, "The Army...", *op. cit.*, p. 526; and Mustafa Kemal, *Speech...*, *op. cit.*, pp. 497–502.

[25] Cf. Karpat, *Turkey's Politics*, *op. cit.*, p. 96, n. 38, and p. 247, n. 4. For a very early instance of the importance of "pure Turkish" descent, see B. Lewis, *Emergence...*, *op. cit.*, p. 175, n. 8.

Table 4.8

PERCENTAGES OF DEPUTIES BORN IN TURKEY AND BORN IN A
CONSTITUENCY REPRESENTED, ACCORDING TO OCCUPATION:
ALL DEPUTIES, 1920–1957

OCCUPATIONS	PERCENTAGE BORN IN CONSTITUENCY	PERCENTAGE BORN IN TURKEY
Government	53	85
Military	36	78
Education	52	87
(Official)	**(48)**	**(84)**
Law	61	92
Medicine	49	87
Pharmacy, Dentistry, and Veterinary Medicine	45	89
Engineering	50	80
(Professional)	**(57)**	**(90)**
Trade	74	92
Agriculture	76	95
Banking	53	95
(Economic)	**(73)**	**(93)**
Religion	75	96
Journalism	39	84
Other	?	93
Unknown	?	?
All Deputies	58	89

tional groups is still preserved. The official element in each case is at one end of the spectrum, the professional group is in the middle, and the economic element is at the other end of the spectrum. The official element had the lowest percentage of its members (84 per cent) born within modern Turkish borders and also had the lowest percentage of its members (48 per cent) who could claim local birth — birth within a province represented. The corresponding figures for the professional group were 90 per cent and 57 per cent, and for the economic group were 93 per cent and 73 per cent. The dispersion of the individual percentages within the broad occupational groupings is greater than before (in the case of local birth), and the military and legal contingents produce the difference between the officials and the professionals. Yet once again the banking, journalistic, and, to a lesser degree, medical groups veer in the direction of the preferred official pattern.

In general, the over-all degree of "localism" seems quite high. Eighty-nine per cent of all deputies were born within the confines of present-day Turkey, even though the majority of them were born subjects of the much larger Ottoman Empire rather than citizens of the territorially reduced Turkish Republic. Using the measure of local birth, which by Western standards might be a strict measure of local connections, 58 per cent of all deputies were born in a province represented by them.

Once again, though, to interpret such information we need comparable material for Turkish society as a whole and, ideally, for a number of its larger parts. The latter is lacking; but the 1935 and 1945 censuses did elicit general information about the birthplaces of Turkish people. According to these sources, 94.0 per cent of all Turkish residents in 1935, and 95.6 per cent of all Turkish residents in 1945, were born within modern Turkey's frontiers. Hence, the deputies were slightly less likely to have been born within the country than the populace as a whole. However, if an adjustment could be made for age, the difference would undoubtedly become even smaller. Parliament and people seem relatively well matched in this respect. Another qualification makes the situation even clearer. Examining similar figures for Turkey's twenty largest cities over 30,000, we find that the percentage born in Turkey is exactly the same as the percentage of deputies born in Turkey, namely 89 per cent.

These sources also provide some interesting statistics on local birth. For the Turkish population as a whole, 86.9 per cent in 1935 were residing in the same province where they had been born (84.3 per cent in the same county — *kaza*), while in 1945 the corresponding figure was 90.7 per cent in the same province (88.3 per cent in the same *kaza*).[26] On the other hand, in Istanbul, Ankara, and Izmir provinces the percentages of residents born within the province were relatively low — only 30 per cent in Istanbul in 1960, for example.[27] In any event, though high compared with many other national legislatures, the percentage (58 per cent) of deputies born in a province represented seems to indicate a degree of localism, which, while strong, is definitely less than would be the case if the Assembly perfectly mirrored the populace in this respect.

[26] T.C. Başbakanlık İstatistik Genel Müdürlüğü, *21 Ekim 1945 Genel Nüfus Sayımı* (*General Population Census of October 21, 1945*), Yayın No. 286 (Ankara: n.p., 1950), pp. 150–151; General Directorate of Statistics, *Small Statistical Abstract of Turkey 1949*, No. 314 (Ankara: n.p., n.d.), p. 59. The *kaza* is roughly comparable to a county.

[27] Cf. the article in *Tanin*, July 22, 1961, reporting on the Sixth Geographical Association Congress in Ankara. In Izmir and Ankara the respective figures for 1960 were given as 68.1 per cent and 72.0 per cent. See also *Tanin*, July 15, 1961, for more general results.

Localism: Methodological Note

One final point of interpretation requires clarification. The ordering of the occupational groups, though preserved in Table 4.8, is in a sense inverted. It was previously argued that having strong local connections constituted one of the three main criteria for recruitment to the Grand National Assembly, ranking third after the possession of intellectual and official statuses. Now, however, the supposedly preferred occupational groups are found to rank lowest in degree of localism, and it is implicitly suggested that this, too, may be considered a mark of their preferred status.

This superficial paradox is resolved by pointing out that I am persisting in the assertion (shortly to be buttressed by more definite evidence) that relative lack of local connections was a drawback for the deputies. For this very reason, the percentage of persons without local ties in an occupational group is here taken as a measure of the preference accorded to the group in recruitment to the national legislature, provided that the reelection rate continues to show that the given occupational group *actually was preferred*. The easy solution to recruitment problems for the selectors was to cater to local popularity and to select local figures. The degree to which selectors were willing to choose counter to local preferences is probably a fairly good indication of the priority given by recruiters to securing members from specific occupational groups for the parliament.

What I am suggesting is that the localism criterion *was* operative, that groups *without* local connections and also without official occupational status would not have the high election rate of the group *with* local connections but without official status. And the fact that the lack of local connections did not lower even further election rates of those with preferred occupational positions is an indirect measure of the importance of such occupational status.

With adjustments, a similar argument could be used for those groups possessing any two of our three criteria (or even any one). This does not mean that the absence of one of the criteria increases the preference given a deputy. Such *would* be paradoxical. It *is* to say that with independent evidence of preferment in such a form as the election rate, and with independent evidence of the existence of the three recruitment criteria, continued relative preferment in the absence of one of the criteria illustrates the strength of the remaining two. Officials were preferred to professionals *despite* having fewer local connections. Professionals were preferred to those in the economic group *despite* having fewer local connections.

Of course, a vital question is: Why assume that deputies with local connections were preferred — why assume that this was a recruitment

96 THE AGGREGATE VIEW

criterion? At least superficially, Table 4.8 might be interpreted as indicating the opposite. Or one might plausibly object that the presence or absence of local connections, as shown in Table 4.8, was merely a reflection of professional situations, and thus quite naturally varied with occupation in the manner found, rather than being an independent criterion for parliamentary recruitment. It is to answer such objections that Table 4.9 has been prepared. It indicates the mean election rates for all locally born deputies as opposed to those not locally born — in total, in terms of the three broad occupational groupings, and in terms of each specific vocation. In other words,

Table 4.9

MEAN ELECTION RATES OF OCCUPATIONAL GROUPS OF DEPUTIES BY BIRTH IN A CONSTITUENCY REPRESENTED[a]

		MEAN ELECTION RATE	
OCCUPATIONS	NUMBER OF DEPUTIES	Constituency Born	Not Constituency Born
Government	296	2.54	2.11
Military	206	2.61	2.60
Education	180	2.42	2.16
(Official)	**(682)**	**(2.52)**	**(2.38)**
Law	381	1.89	1.84
Medicine	187	2.16	2.02
Pharmacy	24	1.70	1.64
Dentistry	9	2.00	1.40
Veterinary Medicine	11	1.33	2.20*
Engineering	56	1.79	1.36
(Professional)	**(668)**	**(1.94)**	**(1.85)**
Trade	289	1.73	1.45
Agriculture	185	1.88	1.95*
Banking	38	1.75	2.22*
(Economic)	**(512)**	**(1.79)**	**(1.72)**
Religion	52	2.49	1.85
Journalism	74	2.28	2.53*
Totals	1,988	2.081	2.089

[a] Because of lack of information 222 deputies were excluded. An asterisk indicates that the mean for those not locally born exceeds that for those who were locally born. Excluding the dentistry and veterinary groups because of their extremely small size and applying the sign test, we obtain $r=3$, which is significant at the .25 level with an N of 12. The Wilcoxon signed rank test yields a T of 21, which does not reach significance at the .10 level.

Table 4.9 ascertains what difference local birth made for the election rates of deputies possessed of the same vocation.

From the bottom of Table 4.9 we learn, first of all, that a gross division of all deputies into two classes, those who had a local birth connection with a province represented and those who did not, produces groups of almost exactly equal election rates.

However, when we control for broad occupational groupings, we discover that the locally born in all three instances have greater election rates than those without the local birth connection. Although the most favored group — the official — had the lowest percentage of its members with a local birth tie to a province represented, locally born deputies within this official group tended to last longer than those not locally born. For various reasons a lower percentage of this group had the local birth connection; but those who did have it were preferred. The same applies to the other two main occupational groups: the professional and the economic.

Moreover, ten of the fourteen specific occupations show the locally born deputies as having a higher election rate than those not locally born. Examination of individual dossiers reveals the exceptions, which are all outside the official group, to be produced mainly by persons within the specific nonofficial occupation but having a post or job that was official in character, such as bankers working in one of the state banks, agricultural experts working for the state, military veterinarians, and quasi-official journalists. They also tend to be persons of higher education. Hence, my general conclusion, after controlling for as many factors as the data permit, is that *deputies having local birth connections with a province represented tended to be preferred in recruitment to the Grand National Assembly.*[28]

This local preference manifested itself not so much in an across-the-board tendency toward longer terms for local deputies as in a tendency for there to be some deeply entrenched local politicians who served in parliament after parliament. The proportion of locally born deputies who served in only one parliament is not appreciably different from the proportion of those not locally born who had similarly

---

[28] Controlling for occupation, education, and local birth produced too few cases to be significant. For most of the free professions, as revealed in Table 4.6, just about 100 per cent of the group were university-educated, permitting no educational breakdown. Among the official group, though the percentages were not quite so extreme, the same difficulty prevailed. The nonuniversity group not locally born tended to be too small. However, since the university-educated deputies tended to be less local than others and still had a relatively higher election rate (like the official group), the observed differences of Table 4.9 could not be accounted for by the educational factor. On the contrary, if further analysis, controlling for education, were possible, it would in all probability strengthen the observed localism effect.

limited service. The differences in length of term come at the other end of the scale where the proportion of locally born deputies serving in four or five or more Assemblies is quite large. For this reason, and because of the moderate to slight differences between the election rate means of Table 4.9, this localism criterion appears to be the weakest of the three recruitment criteria proposed. On the other hand, my impression is that some of this weakness must be ascribed to the localism indicator's being less appropriate than the indicators of intellectual and official status. With a more suitable measure of localism, my hunch is that greater differences would appear.

Miscellaneous Characteristics of Vocational Groups

Having injected a forbidden "hunch" into the discussion, perhaps I have opened Pandora's box sufficiently to permit me to present miscellaneous information peripheral, but presumably related, to localism. This information consists of the percentages of deputies in various occupations who claimed elective experience in local government, membership in nonpolitical voluntary associations, and birth in Istanbul. Moreover, I shall list, according to occupational groups, the percentage of deputies from each group who were elected more than once to the parliament but who always represented the same constituency.

Elective Local Government Experience

The elective local government experience of the economic group is markedly greater than the experience of the official or professional groups, as shown in Table 4.10. This accords well with the picture

Table 4.10

Listed Elective Local Government Experience According to Broad Occupational Groupings: All Deputies, 1920–1957

Occupational Groups	Percentage Listing Local Governmental Experience
Official	11.4
Professional	11.5
Economic	25.8

I have been trying to sketch of this group as being elected to parliament essentially because of its local power, while the professional group and the official group were elected because of their intellectual and official statuses. The official group emerges as most preferred of all because it possesses *both* statuses, while the professional element tends to possess only intellectual credentials. In general, it is also noteworthy that most deputies lack the previous experience in elective office that typifies the American Congressman, if not his European counterpart.

Voluntary Associations

Though it is a mistake to assume that voluntary associations are of no importance in Turkish politics, Table 4.11 does suggest that

Table 4.11

LISTED MEMBERSHIP IN AT LEAST ONE VOLUNTARY ASSOCIATION ACCORDING TO BROAD OCCUPATIONAL GROUPINGS: ALL DEPUTIES, 1920–1957

OCCUPATIONAL GROUPS	PERCENTAGE LISTING VOLUNTARY ASSOCIATION MEMBERSHIP
Official	7.6
Professional	9.2
Economic	5.9

they, too, figure very much less in the life of a Turkish deputy than they do, for example, in the life of the typical American Congressman. Less than 10 per cent, on the average, of Turkish national legislators claim membership in such organizations, while in America the normal situation is for less than 10 per cent to *fail* to claim such membership.[29] Furthermore, most Turkish claims list only one such association, while American lawmakers and politicians are wont to list many. Even though my figures definitely understate the number of such memberships held by Turkish national politicians, the discrepancy is very apparent. Turkey was and is, very simply, a society far less organized into voluntary associations than American society, and this fact is well reflected in these data. Consequently, though many Turkish deputies are active in the Anatolian Club (*Anadolu Kulübü*) and like to gather at its bezique tables in Ankara in the winter, or at its resort on the Princes Islands in the summer, though they are beginning to seek out the presidencies of sports clubs in an apparent attempt to capitalize on that powerful brand of loyalty, and though they have long felt obliged to take an abnormally active role in

---

[29] See Donald Matthews, *United States Senators: A Study of the Recruitment of Political Leaders* (Unpublished Ph.D. dissertation, Department of Politics, Princeton University, 1952), pp. 141–143.

prestigious charitable organizations like the Red Crescent (*Kızılay*) or the Society for the Protection of Children (*Çocuk Esirgeme Kurumu*), these deputies are on the whole much less affected by such involvements than Western legislators.[30] In all probability, this situation will change as the nation proceeds with Westernization and its concomitant increase in organization.

The professional group seems to participate most in voluntary associations, followed by the officials and then by those of the economic group. Because their career interests more often demand participation in professional societies like bar and medicial associations, and Rotary Clubs, and because they tend to be more urban than the other groups, one might have expected such a result. The figures also reflect the charitable and professional nature of the existing associations and suggest the lack of the great fraternal organizations that influence much of American political and social life.[31] Perhaps their absence is one factor that makes politics such a prime interest for many Turkish citizens, with attendant benefits and severe problems. It can be argued that the lack of alternative outlets for partisanship, organizational activity, and similar urges helps to produce the exacerbation of political life that has done such periodic harm in Turkey, from the Young Turks to the Fatherland Front of Adnan Menderes. So much of an active person's attention is focused on politics that it can no longer be treated as the greatest of all *games* — as is typically the case in Anglo-American countries, according to Gabriel Almond's perceptive observation. Instead, it tends to become *war*. Without other interests and outlets, the clash of personalities becomes insufferably bitter and, sooner or later, produces excess and repression.

Constituency Stability

Approximately two out of every three Turkish deputies who were elected more than once represented only one constituency. In analyzing this situation and the figures of Table 4.12 on this topic, perhaps the

---

[30] The increase in size as well as number of voluntary associations in Turkey is whetting the interest of politicians in them. By way of example, in 1940 the Red Crescent had 80,316 members; in 1945 it had 211,535, and in 1950 it had 268,780. The Children's Protection Society had, in the same respective years: 61,000, 102,000, and 140,000. Other voluntary associations have grown similarly. T. C. Basvekâlet..., *Istatistik Yıllığı 1951*, pp. 166–169. Tunaya presents a list of voluntary associations in Turkey in 1946, in *Türkiye'de Siyasi Partiler op. cit.*, p. 548.

[31] An important possible exception is the Masonic organization, which is still rather different in function from its American counterpart. Cf. B. Lewis, *Emergence...*, *op. cit.*, pp. 73–74, and esp. 207–208, n. 4.

Table 4.12

PERCENTAGE OF DEPUTIES ELECTED MORE THAN ONCE BUT REPRESENTING ONLY ONE CONSTITUENCY IN THEIR CAREERS, ACCORDING TO BROAD OCCUPATIONAL GROUPINGS: ALL DEPUTIES, 1920–1957

Occupational Groups	Percentage from Only One Constituency
Official	63
Professional	76
Economic	82

following assumption is plausible: The more a deputy's selection depended on his local position, the greater the tendency for him to represent only one constituency — the harder for him to shift. As local factors entered less into his recruitment and continuation, the tendency for him to represent only one constituency should have decreased.

Table 4.12, in general, reflects a rather natural and strong tendency for a deputy, if reelected, to remain the representative of the constituency that first elected him. However, closer inspection reveals a number of violations of this trend and a familiar pattern in these violations. According to the hypothesized characteristics of the three main occupational groups, the group with the least tendency to represent only one constituency — because presumably least dependent on local connections — would be the official element. Similarly, next should come the professionals, and after them the group with the greatest consistency of representation, because it is most dependent on local ties — the economic group.

Table 4.12 shows that less than two thirds of the officials who participated in more than one Assembly always represented the same constituency, while more than three fourths of the professionals and four fifths of the economic group did so. Once more the same internal trends regarding the banking, journalistic, and medical subgroups are found, and the military subgroup is again the leader of the official element. Fifty-eight per cent of the reelected military members represented but one constituency as opposed to 72 per cent for the governmental and educational groups.

We can look at this same phenomenon from an antipodal point of view by separating from the aggregate group those deputies who displayed great *instability* in constituency represented. This group was quite small. Only thirty-two persons from the total of 2,210 were elected from three or more different constituencies. That is, only thirty-two out of the total of 482 deputies who were elected at least three times (and thus had the chance to represent three or more different constituencies) actually did so — some 7 per cent.

Of these thirty-two persons, twenty-eight were of the Republican People's Party, and four were members of the Democratic Party.[32] Twenty-five of the twenty-eight People's Party members represented their three or more constituencies between the First and the Eighth Assemblies, inclusive. Actually, twenty-seven deputies from the group represented three constituencies, four represented four constituencies, and one man represented five different provinces in the Grand National Assembly.[33] Since the twenty-eight People's Party deputies seem to constitute the solid core of this transient group while the four Democrats are rather anomalous, I have restricted my group analysis to the twenty-eight.

The outstanding points of difference between the entire aggregate group of deputies, the appropriate comparison group of 482 previously described, and this shifting group are again quite predictable in terms of the preceding hypotheses. The group that frequently switched constituencies was more highly educated, having 82 per cent with higher education as opposed to 78 per cent in the comparison group and 73 per cent in the aggregate group. Even more salient was the occupational difference. Thirty-two per cent of the aggregate group were in official occupations, 49 per cent of the appropriate comparison group were in such occupations, and 79 per cent of the shifting group had official occupations. The proportions of military men in all three groups, maintaining the same respective order and excluding unknowns, were 11 per cent, 19 per cent, and 36 per cent. Similarly, the proportions of government officials were 15 per cent, 19 per cent and 25 per cent, respectively. The constituency-changing group also had a higher average figure for foreign language knowledge, a higher publication percentage, and a younger average age at first election than the other two larger groups.

In essence, then, inspection from either end of the scale — that is, of those who were stable or those who were unstable in their specific constituencies represented — resulted in the same general finding. This finding supported the original hypothesis that the switching,

---

[32] The names of these thirty-two deputies, by party, are as follows: People's Republican Party — Inönü, Yurdakul, Dinç, M. M. Kansu, N. A. Kansu, Aykurt, Apaydın, Arıkan, Orbay, Kesebir, Rasım (from Kütahya), Gerede, Muş, Gövsa, Okyar, Atlı, Altay, Öktem, Örgeevren, Akgöl, Tanrıöver, Beyatlı, Uzer, Onaran, Yalçın, Tankut, and Cebesoy; Democratic Party — Menderes, Tunca, Yalman, Kırdar.

[33] Those serving four different constituencies were: Cebesoy, Tanrıöver, Beyatlı, Uzer. The man serving five was Onaran.

transient group would display intellectual and official status more frequently than the stable, localized group.³⁴

Metropolitanism

If several of the indicators relate to "localism," perhaps Table 4.13, giving the percentages of deputies who were born in Istanbul, relates to "metropolitanism," or the dominance of a country by its main city. Many developing nations currently confront this type of problem. In the West, writers on France have occasionally seen in the tremendous focusing of French life on Paris a cause of alleged French political debility. Canadian historians have often espoused a "metropolitan" theory of Canadian politics that sees the country as being exploited by the great eastern centers of Montreal and Toronto. Analogous ideas have had currency in the United States both academically and in the practical politics of Populism, "agrarian socialism," Progressivism, and similar movements.³⁵ Thus in Turkey, particularly during the Kemalist movement, the doctrine that the false sophistication of Istanbul was infecting the nation and producing weakness gained considerable support. The true strength of the Turks was thought to lie in Anatolia, not in European Turkey and the fatal city. Hence, it was not only for tactical reasons — Ankara's position on rail and telegraph lines — that Mustafa Kemal insisted on the drastic step of moving the capital to a bleak provincial town in Central Anatolia, hitherto known largely for its goats and cats.³⁶ It can also be interpreted as a measure to avoid the devious, effete atmosphere that was supposed to pervade Istanbul politics and to return, like Antaeus, to the earth of Anatolia from which sprang the strength and vigor of the essential Turk.

Table 4.13 suggests that the Kemalist revolution had considerable success in minimizing undue Istanbul influences, even though it was

---

³⁴ In the French Assembly under the Third Republic, clearly a much more locally based and oriented body than the G.N.A., only 5 per cent (instead of 33 per cent) of those who were elected more than once represented more than one constituency. See Mattei Dogan, "Political Ascent in a Class Society: French Deputies 1870–1958," in Dwaine Marvick (ed.), *Political Decision-Makers: Recruitment and Performance* (New York: The Free Press of Glencoe, 1961), p. 60. Dogan specifically states that in France, remaining in the same district was virtually a price of staying in office.

³⁵ See, for example, Herbert Leuthy, *France Against Herself* (New York: Praeger, 1955), pp. 13, 20–24, and *passim*; J. M. S. Careless, "Frontierism, Metropolitanism and Canadian History," *The Canadian Historical Review*, XXXV, No. 1 (March 1954), pp. 17, 18; Seymour Martin Lipset, *Agrarian Socialism* (Berkeley: University of California Press, 1950), *passim*.

³⁶ The complaints of the diplomatic community over the move were poignantly recorded in London in *The Times* of December 28, 1923: "Even the most chauvinistic Turks admit the drawbacks of living in a capital where half

Table 4.13

PERCENTAGES OF DEPUTIES BORN IN ISTANBUL, ACCORDING TO
OCCUPATIONAL GROUPINGS: ALL DEPUTIES, 1920–1957

OCCUPATIONAL GROUPS	PERCENTAGE BORN IN ISTANBUL
Official	21
Professional	16
Economic	9

not able to eradicate them completely. Of the entire group of 2,210 deputies only 16 per cent were born in Istanbul. This represents roughly four to six times what might have been expected on the basis of straight census projections, but it hardly seems worthy of description as "dominance." Furthermore, though I do not have comparable figures for the preceding Ottoman Assemblies, it seems most likely that the 16 per cent amounted to a considerable reduction, perhaps even to a minimal level. Istanbul had long been the center of what higher-level education and professional opportunities existed in Turkey, the arena for its political contests, and the hub of its cultural activities. Able families gravitated there; children raised there had special intellectual and social advantages not available elsewhere. The Ankara government could not afford to do without these relatively well-trained, capable, modern Turks, and this need is reflected in the figures. But these figures also cast suspicion on any allegation of continued political "dominance" in Kemalist Turkey by the Istanbul

---

a dozen flickering electric lights represent the public lighting of the town; where running water is almost unknown in the houses; where a donkey or a horse is as often as not tethered to the railings of the little house which serves as the Foreign Office; where open drains run down the middle of the streets; where the modern fine arts are confined to the manufacture and consumption of bad *rakı* and the playing outside the Assembly each day for half an hour by a very moderate band of such masterpieces as 'Tarara-Boomdehay' and 'After the Ball is Over'; where galoshes are more needed and used than razors; where the House of Parliament is no larger than many a public school cricket pavilion; where, in short, there is an almost perverse absence of every amenity and the presence of almost every conceivable disadvantage which could possibly hamper the rulers of a backward country which has to make up not only for the ravages of war but also for the neglect and stagnation of centuries." Quoted in Mears, *Modern Turkey, op. cit.*, pp. 24–25, n. 1. It was, in fact, questionable for a while whether the major foreign powers would give up their Istanbul embassies and come to Ankara. Dr. Adıvar was sent to Istanbul as the representative of the Ankara government to deal with these reluctant diplomats. *Ibid.*, p. 424. Of course, such a move and such complaints have been repeated many times since in the developing world.

elite, even though the subsequent trend and leadership analyses will show moderate retention of disproportionate formal influence.

Table 4.13 again reveals the anticipated pattern — official, professional, and economic. Twenty-one per cent of the officials, 16 per cent of the professionals, and only 9 per cent of the economic group were born in Istanbul. Moreover, the internal deviations within their groups, toward the official standard, of the medical, banking, and journalistic subgroups were again found. In general, one senses another indication of the "intellectual-official versus local-leader" split. This split underlies most of these aggregate data inspected from many different perspectives, and awareness of it makes the data more understandable.

By-Election

With the aggregate group of deputies classified according to occupation, there is an opportunity to check briefly into the significance of first being elected at a by-election and of the various foreign languages typically claimed as known by groups of deputies.

In the previous chapter, I mentioned that a greater percentage of the deputies with university-level education were elected first at a by-election and that this percentage fell with each reduction in educa-

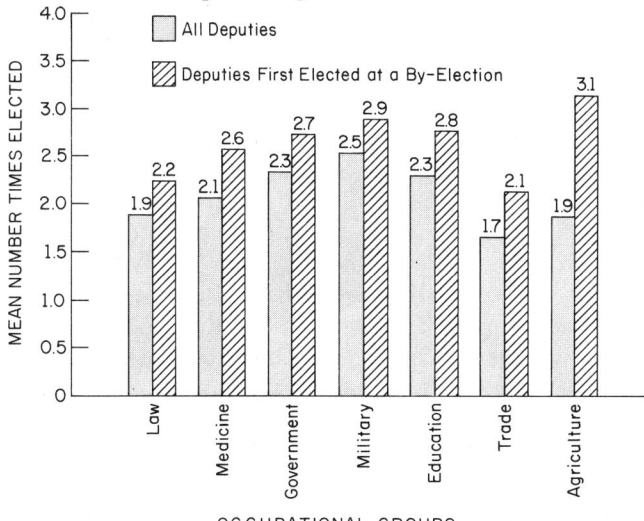

Figure 4.1. Mean number of times elected of all deputies and those deputies first elected at a by-election, according to major occupations: covering all deputies, 1920–1957

NOTE: The respective sizes of the groups of deputies first elected at a by-election were as follows: law, 37; medicine, 26; government, 39; military, 42; education, 25; trade, 25; and agriculture, 15.

tional level. Moreover, Table 4.5 has shown that the official sector had the highest percentage of its members first elected at a by-election, followed by the professionals, and then by the economic group.

In Figure 4.1 the mean election rates of each vocational group *as a whole* are compared with the mean election rates of those who were first elected at a by-election. This is, deliberately, a conservative procedure, since the observed differences would be increased by comparing the rates of those first elected at a by-election with those of the same occupation first elected normally. Nevertheless, in every single case, with occupation held constant, those first elected at a by-election had a higher mean election rate than their vocational group. Thus there is additional evidence that initial election at a by-election was a definite sigh of preferment.

Foreign Languages

Ziya Gökalp is reported to have said, late in his career, that he had never visited Europe, but he had "read it."[37] For many other Turkish political leaders, knowledge of a foreign language similarly opened a window to the West, permitting them to see and learn things that decidedly affected their political actions. Picking examples from only the highest levels, one thinks immediately of Enver's familiarity with German and the great influence of that culture on his mind, of Mustafa Kemal's reading forbidden French political literature while in the War College, of İnönü's efforts while in his sixties to add English to the French and German that he already knew because of his professed desire to understand better the British and American political systems that were replacing Continental systems as the models for postwar Turkey.[38]

Most recently, one recalls the oft-heard argument of the Menderes era that the Democratic Party leader understood Americans better than other Turkish politicians because he had been to the American College in Izmir and spoke English well. On the opposing side, analogous claims were heard concerning Kasım Gülek, then Secretary-General of the People's Party. One has the strong impression that in many cases deputies familiar with a Western language had an enlarged number of contacts with that culture and were relatively more responsive to its ideas and standards.

The preceding chapter examined the relation between education and knowledge of a foreign language and demonstrated that foreign language ability was clearly related to a deputy's chances for remaining a long time in the Assembly. The same effect is observed when oc-

[37] Webster, *The Turkey of Ataturk, op. cit.*, p. 139.
[38] For this aspect of Enver Pasha, see, e.g., Alan Moorehead, *Gallipoli* (New York: Harper & Bros., 1956), p. 23.

Table: Foreign Languages of Deputies by Occupational Groups[a]

Occupation[b]	Knew at Least One Foreign Language[c]		Foreign Languages Known (Percentage of Those Knowing a Foreign Language)								
	No.	%	French	German	English	Greek	Other Western	Arabic	Persian	Kurdish	Armenian
Government	188	77	93	13	19	6	8	11	6	2	3
Military	139	81	91	47	19	5	14[d]	6	2	—	—
Education	146	86	77	20	24	4	8	13	11	1	1
(Official)	**(473)**	**(81)**	**(91)**	**(26)**	**(22)**	**(5)**	**(10)**	**(11)**	**(7)**	**(1)**	**(1)**
Law	188	54	84	17	19	2	4	11	5	—	1
Medicine	171	95	89	26	17	7	3	3	1	—	1
Pharmacy	16	73	81	25	6	—	—	6	—	—	—
Veterinary Medicine	10	91	90	40	—	—	—	10	10	—	—
Engineering	49	74	82	51	43	—	8	2	—	—	—
(Professional)	**(434)**	**(71)**	**(88)**	**(26)**	**(20)**	**(4)**	**(4)**	**(6)**	**(3)**	**(—)**	**(1)**
Trade	91	37	66	27	16	5	7	14	—	1	1
Agriculture	82	49	61	32	17	9	2	13	1	2	—
Banking	29	81	90	24	38	3	6	7	7	—	3
(Economic)	**(202)**	**(45)**	**(67)**	**(29)**	**(20)**	**(6)**	**(5)**	**(13)**	**(1)**	**(1)**	**(1)**
Religion[e]	22	100	5	5	5	5	—	95	50	—	—
Journalism	60	84	90	13	25	5	7	8	10	—	—
Totals	1,191	68%	84%	25%	21%	5%	6%	11%	5%	1%	1%

[a] The specific language percentages indicate what percentage of the deputies who claimed knowledge of at least one foreign language knew the language named. Since many deputies knew more than one foreign language, these percentage totals do not add to 100.
[b] The dentistry group, which consisted of only five persons, has been excluded.
[c] This column gives the percentage of all deputies in the stated occupational group for whom information is available who claimed knowledge of at least one foreign language.
[d] Ten per cent of the military group who claimed a foreign language claimed Russian, which thus makes up the bulk of this total of 14 per cent claiming "Other, Western Languages."
[e] Most of the religious figures were in the First Assembly (1920–1923), for which this information about foreign language competence is lacking.

cupation is held constant. Here I shall merely indicate the types of foreign languages claimed by deputies from different occupations. This information is given in Table 4.14.

Over two thirds of all deputies for whom there is information knew one or more foreign languages. As the figures indicate, most of this knowledge was of Western languages. Moreover, the dominance of French cultural influences is clearly displayed. Eighty-four per cent of the deputies who knew a foreign language knew French. The official group, especially the bureaucrats and military, seems especially to have concentrated on that language, followed, in familiar order, by the professionals and then by the economic group.

This finding strongly supports the observations of many of the best historical writers on Turkey. For example, Allen remarked in the thirties that "French has long been the accepted second language in Turkey," and Karpat has more recently stated that "in all fields of [Turkish] literature the French influence was overwhelming." Bernard Lewis and others have noted the impact of French sociologists like Comte, Demolins, and Durkheim on Turkish political and social thought, while Tahsin Bekir Balta depicts the pervasive French influences on the whole structure and tone of Turkish administration.[39]

The general climate of Turkish political life cannot be understood without awareness of this French background. At present, American influences are replacing the French. Nevertheless, the residual impact of French culture is still an important force and is reflected in the approaches of Turkish politicians (especially some of the militant intellectuals) to many issues, ranging from foreign policy and state economic activities to education and the formation of a Turkish academy patterned after the French.

Though French influences were generally dominant, other Western peoples, particularly the Germans and the British and Americans, also had a significant impact on specific groups at particular times.[40] A more detailed inspection of Table 4.14 reveals some of these pat-

---

[39] Allen, *The Turkish Transformation, op. cit.*, p. 148, n. 7; Karpat, "Social Themes . . ." *op. cit.*, p. 33; B. Lewis, *Emergence . . ., op. cit.*, pp. 226–227 and *passim*; Tahsin Bekir Balta, "Turkish Administrative Law and Institutions," *International Social Science Bulletin*, IX (entitled "The Reception of Foreign Law in Turkey"), No. 1 (1957), *passim*. Cf. also Bernard Lewis, "The Impact of the French Revolution on Turkey," *Journal of World History*, I, No. 1 (1953), pp. 105–125. Allen, on p. 14, sums it up well when he says, "It is a simple matter for the traveller in Turkey to observe that French civilization has been of paramount importance in the Western impact upon the Turks."

[40] "The West has been generally regarded in Turkey as a bloc including all the countries West of the Baltic-Adriatic line. The influence exercised by some particular countries in this bloc has varied depending on Turkey's economic and political reliance upon these countries and upon her evaluation of what was 'best' in them. German influences have been felt strongly in the army, and,

terns. One quarter of all deputies speaking a foreign language spoke German. In the military group, however, nearly one half of all such deputies spoke German. Historical German contacts with the Turkish army are, of course, well known.[41] On the other hand, included in this group were a few (fourteen) Turkish naval officers, most of whom spoke English rather than German. In naval matters, Turkey traditionally looked to England rather than to Germany. Naval terms in the Turkish language have been borrowed mainly from English, army terms have been taken mainly from French, while in the modern Turkish air force the terminology is predominantly American.

The deputies with engineering and agricultural backgrounds also tended disproportionately to speak German, though English ranks a close second in engineering, reflecting the current predilection to go to the United States as well as Germany for higher education in that field and to consult American texts on technical engineering topics.

In the entire group of deputies, about one out of five who spoke a foreign language spoke English. Banking is the other occupational group that displayed a disproportionate number speaking English. As a whole, commercially inclined Turks are now concentrating on English, though this particular banking group is so small that the difference is not significant.

It is interesting to note the juxtaposition of Arabic and Persian. It seems plausible that where the two languages are found in comparable strength — are known by the same individual — the learning of both languages has usually been the result of academic training. This holds, in general, for many deputies who were lawyers, veterinarians, government officials, educators, religious leaders, and journalists. In the trade and agricultural groups, however, Arabic is relatively strong, while Persian is almost nonexistent. Thus such knowledge of Arabic might have been acquired largely as a result of living in an area of Turkey where Arabic is frequently spoken and might once more reflect the existence of strong local influences on these occupational groups. The numbers, however, are again quite small and preclude an estimate of the significance of the differences.

It is instructive to mark the tiny percentage of deputies who *professed* (or acknowledged) an ability to speak Kurdish, despite the

---

somewhat less so, in industry; English influence appeared in the philosophy of government; while the French continuously influenced politics, literature, arts, philosophy and, to a large extent, social habits. Since the Second World War, American ideas have made a general impact on the country and have replaced some of the previous influences." Karpat, *Turkey's Politics, op. cit.*, p. 324.

[41] Cf. Allen, *op. cit.*, p. 25, where he observes: "Germany's influence with Turkey's military class both before and during the [First] World War naturally caused many officers who were important in the government to look at the West through German eyes...."

fact that over one and one-half million people in Turkey in 1955 were listed as having Kurdish as their mother tongue and another 225,000 Turkish speakers claimed it as a second language.[42] Informal conversations with Turkish political leaders suggest that certain politicians were really of Kurdish background. Checking these reports against the non-Turkish language claimed by the involved deputy almost invariably indicated that he had failed to mention Kurdish. On the contrary, similar checks on the claimed knowledge of Armenian and Greek indicated that proficiency in those languages was usually reliably recorded.

---

[42] T. C. Başvekâlet..., *1955 Genel Nüfus Sayımı*, p. 40.

CHAPTER FIVE

Characteristics of Specific Occupations

SOME DATA pertain only to one occupation rather than to the entire group of deputies. Since these data frequently provide useful insight into important characteristics of the members of an occupational group, I shall now survey the various occupations and offer what seem to be the most interesting conclusions.

THE FREE PROFESSIONS

Law

The deputies to the Grand National Assembly with a professional background in the law were able to follow rather divergent career paths within that profession. These paths can be classified as follows: private practice as an attorney, judge, public prosecutor, lawyer in a governmental agency, legal education, and a residual category of lawyers who watched over their own financial interests, did nothing, etc. Naturally, in the course of the years many lawyers followed several of these paths. I have nevertheless tried to classify all legal deputies according to what can be regarded as their basic legal interest. The results of this classification show that about half the group were essentially lawyers in private practice, one quarter were judges, 10 per cent were public prosecutors, and 10 per cent were government lawyers.[1] Most simply it can be said that about half the legal contin-

---

[1] There were usually about three times as many judges as public prosecutors in Turkey. Cf. T. C. Başvekâlet..., *Istatistik Yıllığı 1951, op. cit.*, p. 134.

gent were "official" lawyers and half were "private" lawyers. Checking the election rates of legal deputies of different types indicates that the lawyers from private practice and the judges had rates that were relatively low (1.77 and 1.73, respectively) while the other types all had disproportionately high rates (all 2.00 and over).

It must again be stressed that these aggregate statistics mask very important internal changes in the character of the legal group. For the present purpose, the major change has been that the number of "private" lawyers has increased sharply in recent years while the relative number of "official" lawyers or judges has dwindled rapidly. To some extent this is merely a reflection of the growth of the free professions in Turkish society — a growth that has produced proportionately more lawyers and doctors in private practice.[2] But it is also a reflection of certain rather fundamental political currents that I shall describe in Part Three of this book.

The legal deputies were more likely to engage in secondary occupations than other professionals. More than one fifth of the total legal group listed such additional vocational experience. The most frequently named secondary pursuits were government, education, trade, agriculture, and journalism. Lawyers in private practice were more likely to have held some elective office in local government than other legal types, while judges most frequently listed membership in voluntary associations. Ninety-five per cent of the legal group had received higher education, leaving too small a remainder to permit internal analysis of the influence of education on parliamentary longevity.

Professional Health Specialists: Doctors, Pharmacists, and Dentists

The next three professional groups (doctors, pharmacists, and dentists) can be examined simultaneously to reveal an important difference between them. Of these professional health specialists, the doctors had by far the greatest parliamentary representation and the highest election rate (2.07 compared to 1.67 for each of the other two groups). In many respects the three groups otherwise seem to be similar. However, there is one very outstanding difference in professional background that distinguishes doctors in Turkey, as a group, from the other two health specialties. As late as 1950, only a little over one fourth of all Turkish doctors were engaged in private practice (26.9 per cent). Three fourths were found in official service — 24 per cent in the military, 40 per cent as regular government doctors,

---

[2] Cf. Yavuz Abadan, *Inkilâp Tarihine Giriş* (*Introduction to the History of the Revolution*), (Ankara: Ajans Türk Matbaası, 1960), p. 95. For a judgment on the situation in the 1930's, see Evrenol, *Revolutionary Turkey, op. cit.*, p. 65.

and 9 per cent as doctors in state economic enterprises and foundations.³

The employment situations of Turkish pharmacists and dentists were quite the opposite. Sixty-five per cent of all pharmacists and 85 per cent of all dentists in Turkey were engaged in private practice in 1950. It is difficult to escape interpreting some of the manifest differences in political behavior between the doctors on the one hand and the pharmacists and dentists on the other in terms of the greater official background and connections of Turkish doctors.

In classifying those doctors who became deputies to the Grand National Assembly I have tried to resolve all cases of doubt in favor of private practice so as not to err in favor of a previously observed trend. Nevertheless, 111 out of the group of 173 doctors for whom I have information (or 64 per cent) had to be classed as mainly *official* doctors. However, in this case, too, the gross figures obscure a clear trend in the more recent Assemblies toward inclusion of relatively more doctors from private practice.

Similar analysis of the deputies with occupations in pharmacy or dentistry indicated that 79 per cent of the pharmacists and 75 per cent of the dentists had previously been primarily engaged in *private* practice — percentages almost the reverse of those prevailing among doctors.

The members of these three health professions selected as deputies seem, in regard to type of employment, to have been reasonably representative of their professions, but the political role of the profession with the most official character (the medical profession) seems to contrast markedly with the other two. Furthermore, analysis of the election rates of those sixty-two doctors who specialized in private practice as opposed to the 111 doctors who were official in status shows that the medical *officials* had the higher rates. Comparable analysis of the pharmacists and dentists is precluded by the small size of those groups.

Many of the individual doctors were persons of considerable sophistication and great breadth of interest. Their high rate of publication (31 per cent) has already been noted. Most of these publications were professional in character. However, one quarter of the medical deputies who had published at all had published nonprofessional writings,

---

³ These data, and those following for pharmacists and dentists, are from the T. C. Başvekâlet . . ., *Istatistik Yıllığı 1951, op. cit.*, pp. 151–152. Interestingly enough, despite their marked difference in employment, doctors seem to cluster just as strongly in Istanbul, Ankara, and Izmir as the other health specialists. In 1950, 56.6 per cent of all Turkey's doctors, 51.6 per cent of all her pharmacists, and 64.3 per cent of all her dentists were found in those three cities that contained slightly over 10 per cent of the total population. *Ibid.*, p. 150.

many of them historical and literary. Every one of the fifty-five doctors who had published something — medical or otherwise — knew at least one foreign language, while none of the nine doctors who knew no foreign language had ever published. Doctors, as a group, ranked high in local government elective experience, being particularly active in the People's Houses.[4] As members of one of the few professional groups that became really *thoroughly* Westernized, they frequently were called upon or volunteered to apply this experience to political affairs. Over the years the medical profession "... furnished Turkey with many of its outstanding liberal leaders ...," though it supplied fewer of the organizational type of politician.[5]

Veterinarians and Engineers

There is little to add to the information already presented regarding the veterinary and engineering groups. The veterinary group is quite small. Actually, it contains two or three well-known figures who seem to have used their veterinary training to start them on the road to Westernization when other avenues were closed — men like the poet Mehmet Akif Ersoy, who had to be classed a veterinarian even though his fame came from his literary avocation, or the political writer Naki Akkerman. Ziya Gökalp himself received his higher-level instruction at the military veterinary school, though he has vocationally been classed as an educator. In one respect, such personages seem to bring out the potency of any systematic, objective, and disciplined Western-type training, no matter how pedestrian it may be by the West's own standards, in a society where the prevailing mentality was that of dogma and superficiality.

THE OFFICIALS

Government Officials (Bureaucrats)

In this analysis it would be useful to provide background material on all Turks engaged in the specific profession under discussion in addition to information about those who became deputies and about Turkish society as a whole. Thus an idea could be formed concerning what sorts of lawyers or merchants or military men became deputies

---

[4] E. W. F. Tomlin, *Life in Modern Turkey* (London: Thos. Nelson & Sons, 1947), p. 10.

[5] Allen, *The Turkish Transformation, op cit.*, p. 130. Cf. the interesting conversation between Dr. Adnan Adıvar and Ismet Inönü reported in Halide Edib (Adıvar), *The Turkish Ordeal, op. cit.*, p. 346, where Dr. Adnan says: "The fact that the medical and military departments in Turkey are most efficient is due to their having been Westernized fundamentally and without compromise."

— whether they were basically an accurate sample of their professional colleagues or whether within the profession certain selection criteria also seemed to be at work. If such criteria existed, it would be interesting to learn whether they were the same as those found to be generally operative, whether special considerations applied, or whether both general criteria and special criteria were simultaneously used in selecting the deputies coming from that profession.

Valuable as such analysis would be, Turkish statistics do not as a rule permit it — except for the governmental group. Because of the existence of a detailed history of the Political Science Faculty (*Mülkiye*) and the existence of more than the normal census material as well as additional monographic studies, it is possible to probe a bit more deeply into the characteristics of this group and its members who became deputies.

First, let us look at education. Three quarters of the bureaucrats in the Assembly had received higher education. Of this group, 68 per cent had attended the Political Science Faculty, 30 per cent had attended the law faculty, 5 per cent an economics faculty or university-level commercial school, and 7 per cent some other faculty or school. (The percentages add to more than one hundred because some individuals attended more than one type of institution.) In any event, the Political Science Faculty trained roughly two thirds of the bureaucratic deputies with higher education (52 per cent of the total bureaucratic contingent for whom education is known), and the law faculty trained something less than one third of those with higher education (23 per cent of the total contingent). Approximately one quarter of the total group had less than university-level education.

Let us compare this educational distribution of bureaucratic deputies with material on Turkish bureaucrats as a whole. Table 5.1 gives this information for the year 1938 — fairly near the middle of the entire thirty-seven-year period, and, appropriately enough, the year of Atatürk's death.

The educational differences between all Turkish bureaucrats and those who became deputies to the Grand National Assembly are striking. Strongly preferred were apparently those bureaucrats who had obtained higher education. The Turkish bureaucracy differed from Turkish society in that it was more highly educated; high-status Turkish bureaucrats differed from lower-status bureaucrats in that they were more highly educated; and those Turkish bureaucrats selected to be deputies to the Grand National Assembly differed from their high-status professional colleagues in that they were much more highly educated.

If those bureaucrats who received higher education are separated from the rest, a similar sort of comparison can be made regarding the

Table 5.1

HIGHEST EDUCATIONAL LEVELS REACHED BY TURKISH BUREAUCRATS (1938) AND TURKISH DEPUTIES WITH BUREAUCRATIC BACKGROUNDS (1920–1957) (PERCENTAGES)[a]

EDUCATION	TURKISH BUREAUCRATS			BUREAUCRATIC DEPUTIES
	Salaried	*Wages*	*Total*	
University and Prof. Schools (*Yüksek*)	35%	18%	28%	76%
Lycée (*Lise*)	10	8	9	11
Middle (*Orta*)	35	30	32	10
Primary (*Ilk*)	20	44	31	—
Private	—	—	—	3
Totals	100%	100%	100%	100%
(*N*)	(43,334)	(32,186)	(75,520)	(271)

SOURCE: T. C. Başvekâlet..., *Memurlar Istatistiği 1938* (Ankara: Istatistik Umum Müdürlüğü, 1939), pages and tables unnumbered.

[a] Unknowns excluded. "Salaried" (*maaşlı*) officials were of higher status and eligible for pension. Officials working for wages (*ücretli*) were of lower status and not eligible for pension.

specific faculties and schools attended by all Turkish bureaucrats and by those who became deputies. Only 6.5 per cent of all university-educated Turkish bureaucrats attended the Political Science Faculty, while 68 per cent of all university-educated bureaucratic deputies attended this faculty. On the other hand, the percentage of the university-educated in the two groups who attended the law faculty was almost exactly the same — 30 per cent in each case. The preference accorded to Political Science Faculty products is approximately as sharp in its own way as the general preference given to those with higher education.[6] With this in mind, let us peer more closely at the significance of variations in education for these governmental deputies.

The first inquiry was whether educational level was associated with differences in election rates within the group. Consequently, I

---

[6] One caution regarding these comparisons is that I have used a stricter procedure in classifying deputies as having a governmental vocational background than was used by the compilers of the data on the characteristics of Turkish government officials in 1938. This variation in classificatory procedures strongly heightens the differences observed between the two groups. These differences are so acute, however, that they would seem certain to persist in the face of any correction for classificatory bias. T. C. Başvekâlet..., *Memurlar Istatistiği 1938* (Ankara: Istatistik Umum Müdürlüğü, 1939), table unnumbered.

divided the governmental group into two categories — those with higher education and those without. To my surprise, those with university training showed an election rate that was appreciably lower than those who only had lycée or middle-school (*orta*) education. I realized from working over the individual dossiers that there was, within the governmental group, a body of local officials of less education who had established positions of considerable local power and who remained for a long time in the Assembly. However, I also felt sure that many of the graduates of the Political Science Faculty who had carved out important careers for themselves in national administration also had long tenures in parliament.

In other words, there seemed impressionistically to be two important subtypes within the governmental group of deputies. One type seemed to be that of the *local official*, possessing only a lycée or middle-school education, who nevertheless had established a position of local authority and maintained himself in the Assembly on this basis — satisfying the second and third basic recruitment criteria, official status and local influence. The other type seemed to be that of the member of the *national administrative elite*, a graduate of the proper school (the Political Science Faculty) and an official of the central government — satisfying the first and second recruitment criteria, intellectual and official status.

As a result of these considerations I refined the initial gross educational classification, dividing bureaucratic deputies with higher education into two subgroups — those from the elite Political Science Faculty and those from other faculties. The resulting changes in election rates were vivid. Previously, the election rate of the bureaucratic deputies with higher education had been 2.38, while the rate for those with lycée and middle-school education was 2.92.[7] Distinguishing the two types of higher education, Political Science Faculty and "other," gave the Political Science Faculty graduates a rate of 2.76, while those educated at other faculties dropped to 1.59!

This conception of additional preference criteria within the governmental group had proved sufficiently fruitful to warrant exploring it a little more fully. Another plausible hypothesis was that the preferred career line within the governmental service lay in the Ministry of the Interior, which ran Turkey's centralized internal affairs.[8] When I controlled for education as before and examined whether individual

---

[7] Those for whom education was unknown (43 persons) had an election rate of merely 1.17. Most of these would probably fall in the nonuniversity group and would act to reduce its over-all rate considerably.

[8] On this career line and the characteristics of its followers, see Albert Gorvine and Arif Payaslıoğlu, "The Administrative Career Service in Turkish Provincial Government," *International Review of Administrative Sciences*, XXIII (1957), pp. 467–474, esp. p. 468.

deputies with this Ministry of the Interior career line had higher election rates than those in other ministries or agencies, the results were as follows: For Political Science Faculty graduates, those from the Ministry of the Interior had an average election rate of 2.95, the others 2.36; for those who were not university-educated, those from the Ministry of the Interior had the astounding average election rate of 5.50, the others 2.32.

Again observe that the possession of the appropriate characteristic made more difference to those *without* the main claim to the desired status — i.e., in this case, membership in the national bureaucratic elite basically determined by attendance at the elite school, the Political Science Faculty — than it did to those *with* the essential qualification. In terms of years in the Assembly, a mean election rate of 5.50 would indicate that such deputies served roughly *twenty years* in the parliament on the average. However, the percentage of nonuniversity governmental deputies who served in the Ministry of the Interior in some capacity was only 22 per cent — fourteen persons out of sixty-five. On the other hand, 68 per cent of the Political Science Faculty governmental deputies served in that ministry — 96 out of 141. Interestingly, for those governmental deputies educated at other faculties, serving in the Ministry of the Interior made no difference at all; their election rate was already so low that much variation was impossible.

In slightly different terms, these findings relate once more to the "intellectual elite versus local influential" split. The governmental deputies in the Grand National Assembly who lasted for a reasonable length of time seem in general either to have been members of a national administrative elite formed from graduates of the Political Science Faculty who became members of the Ministry of the Interior or to have been local officials with strong positions in their communities. If the latter could also establish some claim to a position among the administrative elite — as a few did on the basis of participation in the Ministry of the Interior — they were able to remain longer than almost any other vocational group.

This phenomenon can be illustrated by another set of figures. If my general argument is correct, then those local officials who were able to establish some claim to *intellectual* status despite their lack of formal university-level education should have a higher mean election rate than similar officials without such claim. Foreign language ability is one basis for an assertion of some intellectual status. And in fact those governmental deputies with only lycée or middle-school education who claimed knowledge of a foreign language (twenty-seven persons) were found to have an average election rate of 4.41 as opposed to 2.00 for those not able to make such a claim (twenty-nine persons). For the Political Science Faculty group, those with a foreign language (111) had an election rate of 3.04 against 2.34 for those without (only twelve persons). Once again, the added factor made the most difference to the group that "needed" it most from the point of view of meeting the inferred criteria for recruitment. Finally, language, like service in the Ministry of the Interior, made no difference in the "out" group from other faculties (rates of 1.61 as opposed to 1.64).

A few more assorted items descriptive of these two main subgroups within the general category of bureaucratic deputies may help to complete the panorama. Twenty-nine per cent of the nonuniversity group had elective experience in local government, while only 8 per cent of the Political Science Faculty group had such experience. Twenty-six per cent of the nonuniversity group who spoke a foreign language spoke Arabic, while 8 per cent of the Political Science Faculty group spoke that language. On the other hand, for French the respective percentages were 81 per cent and 98 per cent. Approximately equal proportions of the deputies in the two groups had a secondary occupation (roughly 40 per cent). But this occupation was twice as likely to be education in the Political Science Faculty group as it was in the nonuniversity group. On the other hand, agriculture as a secondary occupation was claimed by more than four times as large a percentage of the nonuniversity group who had a secondary occupation as the Political Science Faculty group. Seventy-two per cent of the nonuniversity group had a local birth connection with one of the constituencies represented, whereas only 46 per cent of the Political Science Faculty group had such local ties.

Along almost any dimension selected, similarly sharp differences between the two groups are to be found. All together, they create a vivid impression of two distinct types of governmental deputies in the Assembly — both of whom, for diverse reasons, were able to establish themselves and endure. Within a crucial occupational group in the parliament we have once more come upon the elite-local division, which constitutes a main strand running through the weave of modern Turkish politics.

Military

The second specific vocation within the over-all "official" category is the military. In many respects, this group is much more homogeneous than the governmental group. For example, every professional military man who became a deputy and whose precise rank I could discover (over two thirds of the total) was an officer. Ninety-four per cent of all military deputies were from the army, and merely 6 per cent, fourteen persons, were from the navy. Ninety-seven per cent of all military deputies whose educations are known had university-level education. This group had fewer local connections than any occupational group, and there appears to be no sizable local element within the group comparable to that within the governmental contingent. At the same time, the military had the highest average election rate of any vocational group (2.52).

At its uppermost level, Turkish military education had two stages: The would-be officer went first to the War College (*Harbiye* or *Harb Okulu*) for two years and then, if he had done well and qualified, proceeded to the War Academy (*Harb Akademisi*) for two more years. In general, the War Academy graduates became General Staff officers and had greater prestige.

Of the military deputies who had higher education (some 193 persons), 49 per cent had attended the War Academy, 45 per cent just the War College, 2 per cent the Naval War Academy, and 5 per cent the Naval War College. The War Academy graduates tended to have greater foreign language competence, more publications, slightly greater activity in voluntary associations, fewer secondary occupations, a somewhat increased incidence of Istanbul births, and less elective local government experience. Even more significantly, they had a mean election rate of 2.82 as opposed to a rate of 2.50 for the War College graduates and to 1.88 for a combined residual group of twenty-four "education unknowns," three lycée and two middle-school graduates. Again, within the vocational group, those deputies with greater education are seen to be preferred!

Seventy per cent of the War Academy graduates whose ranks are known had achieved the level of general or admiral. Only 40 per cent from the War College had obtained similar rank. Over one half of the military group as a whole had attained general officer status. Ninety-five per cent of the entire group were field-grade officers or higher, that is, major or above in rank.

This bloc of military deputies seems definitely to have been a very sizable chunk of the upper levels of the Turkish military establishment. In this connection, however, despite the presence of Atatürk (who was elected five times), İnönü (who was elected ten times), Ali Fuat Cebesoy and Kâzım Özalp (each elected nine times), and similar pashas in their midst, the general officers as a group had a lower average election rate than the group of all military deputies at other ranks — 2.30 as opposed to 2.75.

In sum, then, within a relatively homogeneous military contingent in the Assembly, the type of higher military education obtained seems to have been the main social background factor affecting parliamentary longevity. One detects some minor hints of the division between the national elite and the local leader that was found to be so prominent in the governmental group, but they are very subdued. Besides being most preferred, the military were also the least local of all the vocational groups.

Educators

It seems fruitful to distinguish two types of internal divisions within the educational category, the last group of the official element. First of all, there is the distinction between higher or university-level educational activity and work on lower levels. There is little doubt that the former carried appreciably more national prestige than the latter, though the nonuniversity administrator may have wielded more effective local power.[9] Secondly, there is the distinction between teaching and educational administration, which I have altered to a distinction between those educators who had some administrative experience and those who apparently had none.

Quite plainly, simultaneous application of these two classificatory principles to the group of educator deputies would produce four categories: university administrators, university teachers, nonuniversity administrators, nonuniversity teachers. Internal analysis of this group proceeded essentially in these terms, though I must issue a caution that the group of university administrators consisted of merely fourteen persons compared to forty-two, sixty-seven, and forty-six in the other groups, respectively.

The mean election rates for the four groups were 2.07 for the university administrators, 2.57 for the university teachers, 2.59 for the nonuniversity administrators, and 1.92 for the nonuniversity

---

[9] On the prestige of university professors, see, for example, Bernard Lewis, "Democracy in Turkey," *Middle Eastern Affairs*, X, No. 2 (February 1959), p. 67, or Evan Fotos, "An Appreciation of Turkish University Life," *op. cit.*, p. 256. By comparison, note that Neşet Halil (Atay), in his useful study, *Büyük Meclis ve Inkilap* (Ankara: T.B.M.M. Matbaası, 1933), p. 40, says of the position of the nonuniversity teacher in the twenties that "In neither primary, middle, nor advanced schools is 'teaching' a profession. Teachers' salaries differ according to the income of the locality and instruction programs differ according to the particular opinions of the [individual] school's Training and Instruction Committee." For more discussion on the role of the teacher in this period, see Osman Ergin, *Türkiye Maarif Tarihi, op. cit.*, pp. 1471–1483.

At the same time, there is also much truth in George Lenczowski's observation that "The secret of Kemal's success may largely be attributed to the strict enforcement of educational reform. The new generation of village and high-school teachers constituted — with the People's Party members — a zealous cadre which spread Kemalist ideals and trained the minds of Turkish youth. Teachers became Kemal's most devoted propagandists...." *The Middle East in World Affairs, op. cit.*, p. 123. Numerous other statements stressing this same point are also available. The teacher has been, and is today in Turkey, one of the main protagonists of the Kemalist Revolution — along with the army officer and the government official.

teachers. Utilizing the even more simple division of administrators versus teachers, regardless of the level of educational employment, furnishes respective election rates of 2.52 and 1.95.[10] Performing the same dichotomous analysis according to the level of educational employment rather than administrative experience gives the university group a mean election rate of 2.44 and the nonuniversity group a rating of 2.24. In short, such manipulations seem to indicate that both factors, the level of education at which the person worked and whether he had administrative experience, were associated with preferred recruitment to the Assembly. No clear-cut pattern emerges.

Inspection of the other social background characteristics associated with each of these groups, and especially with the two most durable groups — the university teachers and the nonuniversity administrators — suggests that we are confronting another version of the division between the intellectual elite and the local leader previously encountered among the bureaucratic group. Contrasting the university teachers with the nonuniversity administrators, both of whom had virtually the same high election rate, we discover that the former were more likely to have been born in Istanbul (43 per cent versus 12 per cent), were better educated (90 per cent university-trained versus 78 per cent university-trained), more frequently were educated abroad (48 per cent versus 12 per cent), were more likely to know a foreign language (100 per cent versus 82 per cent), had published more often (79 per cent versus 42 per cent), and were more likely to claim membership in a voluntary association (31 per cent versus 16 per cent). On the other side, the nonuniversity administrators had a higher incidence of local government experience (13 per cent versus none for the university teachers) and a greater percentage of persons born in Turkey but outside Istanbul (69 per cent versus 45 per cent). Other general differences were that the nonuniversity administrators were more likely to have had purely pedagogical training, while university teachers of course attended quite a range of schools and faculties. More important, the nonuniversity administrators were much more likely to have had a local birth connection with one of the constituencies they represented than were the university teachers.

If all educator deputies are taken as a whole, one other item worthy of attention is that the election rate of those persons who, themselves, had university-level education, regardless of where they were working, was 2.36, whereas the election rate of those with lower-level education was 2.26. In other words, again, if vocation is held constant, those deputies with higher education were preferred.

---

[10] Nine of the university teachers also had nonuniversity-level experience in educational administration.

Economic Occupations

Trade

The last of the three broad occupational groupings is the economic. Let us consider the "Trade, Industry, and Labor" category first. In general, this group had a low election rate, a low level of formal education, and a relatively high level of localism. Actually, a detailed internal analysis has failed to produce much to add to the general description. In most respects the trade group is rather homogeneous. For instance, 80 per cent of the group had less than university-level education. Such education seems to have been occupationally superfluous in what has been repeatedly described as a small trader's economy.[11] There is virtually no difference between the election rates of the traders with higher education and those without such training (1.67 and 1.69). However, this group as a whole has an extremely low election rate — only the late-arriving engineers being lower. After consideration of their individual dossiers, it is hard to avoid the conception that the traders were included in the Assembly most reluctantly and certainly minimally during the People's Party era. Sixty-two per cent lasted only for one Assembly, and another 25 per cent were dropped after just one reelection, making 87 per cent who failed of more than one reelection.

There was a display batch of *laborers* added in the Fourth Assembly who were kept on for slightly longer than the rest of the trade group, but even these dwindled away rapidly compared to the normal run of officials. The mean election rate for the nineteen laborers who have appeared in the parliament is 1.74 — just three of them managing to have more than one reelection.

Discerning various career lines besides laborer within the trade group also failed to produce appreciable differences between deputies. I separated the trade contingent into merchants, workers, and owners or executives of larger enterprises, plus an unfortunately large group who had made no further specification of their vocation than saying that they were concerned with trade — some 42 per cent of

---

[11] In 1927, only 3.1 per cent of Turkey's industrial establishments were listed as having more than ten workers on their payrolls. In 1935, Webster indicates that there were only 300,000 to 400,000 persons in Turkey engaged in industrial occupations. Webster, *Turkey of Ataturk, op. cit.,* pp. 255, 247. Cf. *Histoire...*, *op. cit.,* p. 163; Karpat, *Turkey's Politics, op cit.,* pp. 109–110; Osman Okyar, "Economic Framework for Industrialization: Turkish Experiences in Retrospect," *Middle Eastern Affairs,* IX, Nos. 8–9 (August–September 1958), pp. 262–264; the International Bank for Reconstruction and Development, *The Economy of Turkey* (Baltimore: Johns Hopkins University Press, 1951), p. 160. On the origins of what entrepreneurship exists, consult Alec P. Alexander, "Industrial Entrepreneurship in Turkey: Origins and Growth," *Economic Development and Cultural Change,* VIII (July 1960), pp. 349–365.

the total. The resulting election rate variations were negligible. One third of the owner-executives, one quarter of the merchants, 14 per cent of the unspecified group, and none of the workers had higher education. No differences were found between the groups regarding birthplace, voluntary association membership, publication, etc., mainly because the percentages were so low for all members of the group. There was an observable tendency for the merchants to have had markedly more experience in local government and for those who had a secondary occupation, usually agriculture, to last a little longer in the legislature. But the dominant picture is one of uniformity among a group that was very much present on sufferance.

Agriculture

It is sometimes said that there have been only four vocations historically open to the Turk who wanted to be socially accepted: the military, government, religion, and agriculture. Trade was supposedly despised and relegated to the minorities. The free professions had not yet had their present vogue and tended also to be left to suspect *gâvurs* (infidels) or more suspect irreligious Turks, like the doctors who ". . . put the accursed wine into their medicine," as the *hoca* of *Sinekli Bakkal* expressed it. Journalism was not yet recognized as an existing profession. Thus, according to these oversimplified but not wholly inaccurate ideas, agriculture was the only *economic* pursuit that the Turk traditionally could follow with honor, even though it was by far the least prestigious of the four honorable occupations.[12] Something of its marginal status is reflected in the analysis of the group of deputies with agricultural occupational backgrounds.

First of all, the agricultural group of deputies appears to have had a somewhat higher over-all election rate than the traders (1.86 as opposed to 1.65). Secondly, and more important, 30 per cent of the agricultural group for whom education is known had received higher education, and this education had a very perceptible effect on the election rates of those involved. For the university-educated agriculturists the average rate was 2.36; for the nonuniversity agriculturists the average rate was 1.65. In other words, the agricultural group had

---

[12] See, e.g., IBRD, *The Economy of Turkey, op cit.*, pp. 3–4; M. Philips Price, *A History of Turkey* (London: George Allen & Unwin, 1956), p. 166; Selma Ekrem, *Turkey, Old and New* (New York: Scribners, 1947), pp. 46–47. The results of a national sample survey of the values of all public lycée-level students in Turkey as they relate to occupational prestige and selection will shortly be available in material prepared by F. W. Frey, G. W. Angell, Jr., and A. Ş. Sanay. Similar information was also obtained in the national attitudinal survey of the Turkish peasantry conducted in 1962. See Frederick W. Frey, "Surveying Peasant Attitudes in Turkey," *Public Opinion Quarterly*, XXVII (Fall 1963), pp. 335–355.

a larger share of well-educated members than the trade group, and this education seems to have mattered more than in the very low level trade group. Again, approximately one fifth of the agricultural group consisted of agricultural engineers and experts working for the government. The agricultural officials had an election rate of 2.28, while all other agriculturists had a rate of merely 1.76. In short, one finds within this agricultural element a subgroup of the favorite sons of the regime, and this group is markedly distinct from the rest of the contingent.

The official faction within the agricultural group was not responsible for the entire difference between the agriculturists and the traders in the Grand National Assembly. Instead, it appears that education makes far more difference to these agricultural deputies than does governmental employment. Holding education constant by considering only those members of the entire group who had higher-level training alters the election rate means for the deputies employed as official agricultural experts and engineers, on the one hand, and those engaged in private agriculture, on the other, to 2.38 and 2.34, respectively. Hence, in further internal analysis of the agricultural deputies I have preserved the educational distinction rather than the employment distinction.

The university-educated agriculturists rather naturally knew more foreign languages than the rest; they were somewhat more often members of voluntary associations, though the rate was low for both groups; they were much more likely to represent more than one constituency (33 per cent against 7 per cent); and of those who represented but one constituency, the university group was less likely to have been born in that constituency (60 per cent versus 82 per cent). Understandably, the university group published more frequently than those with less education. Still, within the university group the twenty-one deputies who published had a mean election rate of 3.38, and the thirty-seven who failed to publish had a rate of 1.74.

Banking

The small size of the banking group precludes detailed analysis of the sort presented for most other occupations. Twenty-three out of the total of thirty-eight persons, or 61 per cent, did claim some experience in state banks. The division between those with such experience and those without might have provided an interesting avenue for investigation, as might the educational division between university and nonuniversity groups. However, in each case one of the subgroups produced by such division was so small that internal analysis became highly unreliable. This problem was compounded by the fact that one of the banking deputies, Celal Bayar, was so different from the rest in his political longevity and career that his influence in successive cross tabulations produced marked distortions. Bayar was elected to parliament ten times — the only man to match İnönü in longevity. In the rest of the banking group, no man was elected more than five times.

Religion

Sixty-four of the eighty-three members of the group of deputies professionally occupied with religion belonged to the First Assembly (1920–1923). I have very little information about these deputies because the parliamentary *Albüm* covering that Assembly is less ample than those of later Assemblies. Consequently, for this group, too, detailed internal analysis is impossible. Probably the most outstanding fact concerning the religious group is that most of these clerics participated only in the First Assembly, after which they were rather severely weeded out as secularism became a principal point of the Atatürk reform. Between the Fourth and Seventh Assemblies, inclusive — some fifteen years and four elections — not one new deputy with religion as his occupation was elected to the Grand National Assembly!

The clerics who remained after 1923 can best be described as a group of tame *hocas* who were used to make more palatable this bitter but salutary dose of laicism and to take the sting out of the predictable charges of a "godless regime." These acceptable clerics lasted quite a long time in politics, ten of them being elected five times or more.[13] Most of them had strong ties with some locality. All but two of those religious deputies serving in more than two Assemblies had a secondary occupation — education, agriculture, law, or trade. One senses that after a while their local connections became almost as important for their retention in the national legislature as their religious association.[14]

---

[13] Their names: elected five times — Dinç, Izbudak, and Gedik; elected six times — Demiralay, Ulusan, and Aydın; elected seven times — Onat and Özdamar; elected eight times — Kaplan and Gerçeker.

[14] On religion and politics in Turkey, see such writings as Dankwart Rustow, "Politics and Islam in Turkey, 1920–1955," in Frye, *op. cit.*; Howard A. Reed, "The Religious Life of Modern Turkish Muslims," in Frye, *op. cit.*, pp. 108–148; Niyazi Berkes, "Historical Background of Turkish Secularism," in Frye, *op. cit.*; Howard A. Reed, "Revival of Islam in Secular Turkey," *Middle East Journal*, VIII (1954), pp. 267–282; Reed, "Secularism and Islam in Turkish Politics," *Current History*, XXXII (1957), pp. 333–338; Bernard Lewis, "Islamic Revival in Turkey," *International Affairs*, XXVIII (1952), pp. 38–48; Robert N. Bellah, "Religious Aspects of Modernization in Turkey and Japan," *American Journal of Sociology*, LXIV (1958), pp. 1–5; Lewis V. Thomas, "Recent Developments in Turkish Islam," *Middle East Journal*, VI (1952), pp. 22–40; Paul Stirling, "Religious Change in Republican Turkey," *Middle East Journal*,

JOURNALISM

The printing press was introduced into Turkey in 1727, but the first major newspapers were not established until the second quarter of the nineteenth century, and journalism as a distinct and respectable profession dates only from just before the First World War.[15] Even today, Turkish academics, for example, are quick to deny, as a blow to their prestige, any suggested association with the press — though academics in the West often do much the same thing. In fact, perhaps the overall status of journalism as a profession in Turkey is not too different from its position in America; the top editors, publishers, and columnists are fairly well respected, while the workaday reporters are viewed with some disdain as lacking in normal human sensitivity and restraint.

By 1920, however, the Turkish press was an institution of such importance that it could not be ignored by any regime, no matter what other institutions the regime controlled. Certainly the Atatürk, İnönü, and Menderes regimes, in their different fashions, dramatically illustrate the accuracy of this contention. One apparent device for ensuring the cooperation of at least a major segment of the press was that of including a number of prominent editors, publishers, and writers among the deputies to the Grand National Assembly. We have already seen that in many respects the journalistic group in the Assembly was one of the most favored. Now some of the internal characteristics of this vocational group will be examined more minutely.

The first refinement was to divide the entire group of seventy-five journalists and writers into three parts according to their main activity within their occupation. The first group consisted of owners, publishers, and editors constituting 53 per cent of the total; the second, of regular reporters constituting 39 per cent of the total; and the third,

---

XII (1958), pp. 395–408; Karpat, *Turkey's Politics, op. cit.*, pp. 271–292; B. Lewis, *Emergence . . ., op. cit.*, pp. 395–436.

[15] On the press in Turkey, consult, among others: Ahmet Emin (Yalman), *The Development of Modern Turkey as Measured by Its Press* (New York: Columbia University Press, 1914), *Turkey in the World War, op. cit.*, "The Turkish Press" in Mears, *op. cit.*, pp. 450–474; B. Lewis, *Emergence . . ., op. cit., passim*, esp. citations, p. 93, n. 37; "The Press in Turkey" (supplement to *The European Press Today*) (Washington: Library of Congress, European Affairs Division, November 1949); *Türkiyede Çıkan Gazete ve Mecmualar* (Ankara: Basım-Yayın ve Turizm Bakanlığı, 1961); Frederick W. Frey, "Turkey's 'War,' " *The Nation*, CXC (May 14, 1960), pp. 419–420; and the periodic coverage provided by the monthly bulletin of the International Press Institute in Zurich, Switzerland, *IPI Report*. No really definitive work on the contemporary political role of the Turkish press has yet been produced. The most comprehensive recent study is provided by Kemal Karpat in a contribution to Ward and Rustow (eds.), *Political Modernization in Japan and Turkey, op. cit.*, pp. 255–282.

of six writers (Halide Edib Adıvar, Reşat Nuri Güntekin, and others) who made up 8 per cent of the total. In further discussion I shall call the first group the "editors" and the second group the "reporters." Since it is so small, the group of writers will not be analyzed in more detail.

The high status of the journalistic deputies is reflected in the fact that over half of them were owners, editors, or publishers. The editor-reporter distinction can be looked upon as another partial reflection of the division between the national elite and the local leader groups already emphasized in other professions. Seventy-two per cent of the editors and only 61 per cent of the reporters had higher education.[16] For that higher education, 64 per cent of the editors went to the law faculty, while the reporters were more scattered over several faculties, only 29 per cent attending the law faculty. Foreign language knowledge in the two groups was about equal. In regard to birthplace, 36 per cent of the editors were born in Istanbul, while only 24 per cent of the reporters were born there. There is a moderate difference in the election rates of those editors who had Istanbul or foreign birth as opposed to those born outside Istanbul in Turkey (2.56 and 2.76, respectively). Exactly the same sort of relationship, but more pronounced, existed for the reporters, where those born in Istanbul or abroad had an average election rate of only 1.60 and those born outside Istanbul in Turkey had a rate of 2.57. In the broad comparison of the election rates of editors versus reporters the editors were markedly favored, possessing a mean rate of 2.62 contrasted to 2.07 for the reporters.

There are definite signs that the reporters had more local connections than the editors. Sixty-two per cent of the reporters elected more than once represented only one constituency in parliament as opposed to only 50 per cent of the editors. Of those persons who represented only one constituency, half the reporters and only one seventh of the editors were born in that constituency. Thirty-one per cent of the reporters had held an elective post in local government, while merely 10 per cent of the editors had had such experience.

In the journalistic group as a whole, those with secondary occupations had a mean election rate of 2.59 as opposed to 2.08 for those without an additional occupation. Within the editor-reporter sub-

---

[16] Incidentally, the prominent secondary schools of Istanbul seem to have been especially well represented among these journalists. I have information on the secondary education of over half the group. Twelve of twenty-two editors went to Galatasaray, Vefa, Mercan, or *Istanbul Erkek Lisesi* — eight of these twelve to Galatasaray alone. Five of the twelve reporters went to one of those four secondary schools — three to Galatasaray. Three out of five "writers" attended these select schools, making a grand total of twenty out of thirty-nine — twelve of the twenty attending Galatasaray.

groups, this difference is still preserved. The editors with a secondary occupation had an average election rate of 2.92; those without had a rate of 2.19. The reporters with another occupation had a rate of 2.16; those without had a rate of 1.90.[17] Once again, occupational diversity seems to have brought a deputy into greater favor with those responsible for parliamentary recruitment.

Summary

I have sought, in Chapters 4 and 5, to describe the occupational characteristics of the aggregate group of all deputies to the Grand National Assembly from 1920 to 1957. This information has been presented in general terms, in terms permitting comparisons between broad occupational groups, and in some detail for each individual vocation. The use of three main occupational categories — official, professional, and economic — seemed to provide a regular and meaningful arrangement of the data. Throughout, an attempt was made to furnish specific examples of the significance of occupational and related experiences for the political behavior of important people and for the governmental system.

About one third of all deputies serving during the period under examination had occupations classified as "official" in character, another third had occupations that were labeled "professional," and about one quarter followed "economic" occupations. Law had the largest contingent, some 18 per cent of the total; next in order was

[17] Possibly the differences in election rates associated with the possession of a secondary occupation are merely the result of the fact that I have more information on this score from the famous deputies who lasted longer in the Assembly. Deputies were not asked to list secondary occupations in the official questionnaire returned by them at the beginning of each Assembly and reported in the *Parliamentary Annual*. Thus, my finding may simply reveal the fact that there are more outside sources of information about the famous deputies who lasted a long time in parliament; one is more likely to know about the secondary occupations of this group that already has a disproportionately high election rate.

In the present instance, and in others where the characteristic involved was not explicitly investigated in the official questionnaire, I have examined this problem. I report the results here to illustrate the method in all these investigations. It is true that I had sources other than the *Parliamentary Annual* for 72 per cent of those journalists with secondary occupations and only for 31 per cent of those said to be without such occupations. This might seem to suggest that the finding of an election rate difference is simply an artifact of greater coverage of well-known politicians. However, the election rate of those *without* secondary occupation for whom I had an outside source was 2.00, which was slightly lower than that of those for whom my only source was the *Annual*. A similar result is found for those *with* secondary occupation and leads me to the conclusion that the original finding is not simply the result of informational differences concerning the subgroups of journalistic deputies.

government (bureaucrats), with 14 per cent; trade had 13 per cent; the military had 10 per cent; medicine and agriculture had 9 per cent each; and religion, journalism, and engineering (or science) had 3 per cent each. The military group ranked first in mean number of times elected, journalism second, government third, education fourth, medicine fifth, and so on. The official group clearly had the highest average election rate, trailed by the professionals, with the economic group being lowest.

Compared to all adult male Turks and to all household heads, agricultural occupations were drastically underrepresented in the Assembly, while professional and official occupations were greatly overrepresented. Compared to all male adult urban Turks, trade was underrepresented, and the professionals and officials were overrepresented, though not so extremely.

Various analyses repeatedly produced the same ordered pattern among the three broad occupational groups being considered: The officials came out first, the professionals second, and the economic group third. This was true for the percentage of deputies first elected at a by-election, for knowledge of foreign languages, and for the incidence of publication among members. The one exception to the pattern was that of age at first election. The typical deputy was first elected when he was forty-five years of age, and there was very little difference between occupational groups. What difference there was indicated that the officials were slightly older than the other two groups. The military men were especially likely to have been brought in at a by-election and to have been about five years older than most entering deputies.

Numerous examples of the importance of "localism" in Turkish politics were given, and it was pointed out that there was always in the Assembly a sizable group of deputies with strong local ties. In fact, the data reveal a basic division among the deputies between a relatively cosmopolitan national elite and a body of local influentials. It is important that the same type of political division found at this high level of Turkish society has been found again and again in studies at all levels of government in Western societies. The cosmopolitan-parochial, national-local, urban-rural, official-private, intellectual-practical sort of social background clustering among these Turkish politicians seems to be repeated with variations all over the world in many different polities and cultures. Surely here is an attitudinal and structural regularity eminently worthy of increased attention on the part of political scientists.

Birth in various special regions (Macedonia, the Caucasus, the Levant) has frequently been regarded in Turkey as leading to distinctive forms of political activity. Moreover, in Turkey as in many other lands, birth on the periphery of the country has been viewed as leading to a heightened nationalism. This hypernationalism may be a reaction to an increased political vulnerability whose source is a popular tendency to be suspicious of those not clearly members of the dominant group. In any event, in Turkey as elsewhere, birth within the national frontiers and strong ties with a particular locality seem to have been distinct political advantages.

Eighty-nine per cent of all deputies were born within present-day Turkish boundaries, while 58 per cent were born within a constituency represented in the Assembly. Along both these dimensions, the officials were the least local, the professionals were again intermediate, and the economic group was the most local. Though the degree of localism seems to have been relatively high compared to other national legislatures, there was appreciably less localism than would have been the case if the parliament were fully representative. Nearly 90 per cent of all Turks, on the average over the period being examined, were resident in the same *county* in which they were born.

If occupation is held constant, birth within a constituency seemed to be associated with a higher mean election rate. This was not so much an across-the-board tendency for all locally based deputies to have longer terms as a tendency for there to be some deeply entrenched local politicians who served in Assembly after Assembly.

The deputies had very limited experience in elective local governmental office, though the economic group, as expected, had significantly more such experience than the officials or the professionals. There was also very meager membership in voluntary associations, partly reflecting, of course, the low degree of organization of Turkish society in this respect.

The hypothesis was advanced that the more a deputy's selection depended on his local position, the greater would be the tendency for him to represent only one constituency — that is, not to switch constituencies. The locally based deputy would have greater need for constituency stability than the elite-based deputy. Verily, it was found that the officials displayed the greatest constituency mobility (or instability), the professionals next, and the economic contingent the least. From another viewpoint, the deputies who shifted constituency three or more times were predictably found to be better educated, more likely to have an official occupation, and less likely to have an economic occupation than those elected as often but representing only one constituency.

"Metropolitanism," or the tendency for one or a few large cities to dominate the politics of a nation, was also considered through examination of the number of deputies born in Istanbul — the "fatal city." Only 16 per cent of all deputies were born in the metropolis, which was more than one would expect if the Assembly were perfectly representative, but hardly a figure suggesting dominance. The officials were most likely to have been born in Istanbul, the professionals next, and the economic group was least likely to have been born there.

In every single case, with occupation held constant, those deputies first elected at a by-election had a higher mean election rate than those normally elected.

About two thirds of all deputies for whom information was available claimed knowledge of a foreign language. French was clearly the favored foreign tongue, especially among the officials. Some 84 per cent of all deputies who spoke a foreign language spoke French. German was the second-best-known language, claimed by one fourth of all deputies knowing a foreign language. However, nearly one half of the military men and a disproportionate number of engineers and agriculturists knew German. Engineers and bankers were most likely to know English, which was claimed by over one fifth of those knowing a foreign language. Knowledge of Kurdish was very little professed (or acknowledged).

Certain salient characteristics of specific occupational groups were also examined. Lawyers in the Assembly were found to have come about equally from the private practice of law and from an official capacity. Lawyers from private practice and those who were judges had relatively low election rates, while the other types of lawyers had relatively high rates. On the other hand, nearly two thirds of the doctors had an official position. In general, doctors had an appreciably higher over-all election rate than any of the other "free professions." Official doctors had a higher mean election rate than doctors engaged in private practice before becoming a deputy. Doctors were compared with deputies from the other two health professions: dentistry and pharmacy. The latter two occupational contingents were only about one quarter official and were much lower in parliamentary longevity.

Internal analysis of the governmental (bureaucratic) group sharply revealed the national elite/local influential distinction. Education at the Political Science Faculty and service in the Ministry of the Interior seemed to be the decisive recruitment factors for this group, in addition to local influence. Both the deputies from the elite faculty and those with strong local ties tended to remain a long time in the Assembly. Deputies from either of these two subgroups who had worked in the powerful Ministry of the Interior lasted longer than their colleagues without such experience.

The military contingent in the parliament consisted entirely of former officers and came overwhelmingly from the army. More than one half of all deputies from a professional military background and whose ranks were known were general officers. Rank, however, was not associated with parliamentary longevity. Education, on the other hand, was significantly related to repeated selection as a deputy. Those military men from the higher-level War Academy had a larger mean election rate than those from the lower-level War College. The 223 military deputies comprised a sizable portion of the topmost level of the Turkish military establishment during this period.

Among educators, university teachers and nonuniversity administrators appear to have been preferred.

Very few significant internal divisions were found among the group engaged in trade, industry, and commerce.

In the agricultural group, those with university education clearly lasted longer than those without. Official status also seemed originally to have been a strongly favorable factor, but when education was held constant, it dwindled to a very weakly favorable factor.[18]

Over one half of the group of journalists were editors or publishers, and these individuals displayed a higher mean election rate than did the reporters.

In conclusion, I should emphasize again that the most durable deputies seemed to be of two basic types: the deputy who was from the official elite and the deputy whom I have described as the local leader. Besides his official occupation, the former type usually possessed the highest level of education obtainable, was more urban in background and habits, more cosmopolitan in training, experience, and outlook, and was recognized by those at the same level as belonging with them to a dominant national elite within the occupation and the society. The local potentate was usually of moderate education, less urban, and less broad in his cultural values, but a power in his own community and probably viewed as a man of great capacity at that lower level.

The pressures on the two types of men were quite different. The national elite member depended for his political rise on the opinions of him held by other members of the same elite. If he met exceptionally well the standards of his fellow officers, bureaucrats, or educators, his chances of political ascent were great. Psychologically, he seems to have been primarily attuned to this group, which was essentially distinguished by education and occupation from the rest of the Turks.

The local leader, on the contrary, seems to have been dependent for his political rise on the support of his local community (at least on its prime movers), and to have been much more sensitive to its stirrings

---

[18] "Favorableness" simply refers to association with a relatively higher mean number of times elected.

and probably less sensitive to many broad national issues than the elite member.

In power terms, the elite controlled the major formal institutions of the society, namely the army, the bureaucracy, the educational system — those vertical networks of authority and communications in which Western training was so useful. The local leaders controlled the individual villages, towns, and small regions in most aspects of their behavior not determined by formally authoritative institutions or by ingrained tradition.

Realistic politicians had always recognized that compromise and cooperation between these two elements was essential to effective government, and so we find the two strands interwoven in the personnel of the parliament. The national elite was dominant at the level of the national legislature, and much of the tone and tempo of Turkish political life must be understood on that basis — especially its "tutelary" character. But even in the heyday of the "one-party dictatorship" the elite had to incorporate and consider some of the local politicians and leaders who commanded the allegiance of important communities.

CHAPTER SIX

Fathers, Faiths, and Females

LIKE HIS SINS, the occupation and social status of the father are often visited upon the son. Family status almost indubitably will have affected the educational and vocational vistas presented to the child, the doors of contact opened for him, his confidence and style in personal relations with others, his satisfaction with his present lot, his optimism or pessimism toward the future, and even his distinctive set of political values. Knowledge of his family of origin's social status compared with his own equips us better to comprehend many aspects of his general and political behavior.

The relationship of a given person's social status to that of his family of origin is usually labeled social mobility. The political importance attached to matters of social mobility naturally varies from polity to polity and ideology to ideology. More often than not, however, such questions lie at the heart of political dispute. And while perceived social mobility is probably more determinative of political perspectives and behavior than actual social mobility, there exists an obvious connection between the two for most groups with some pretensions to rationality. Thus, for a deeper understanding of individual participants, of specific political institutions, and of the functioning of the polity as a whole, information about the social mobility of members of that polity seems highly desirable.

A variety of indicators should ideally be employed in an investigation of the relative social statuses of a man and his parental family — items such as the amount and sources of income, the educational levels of the parents and all their children, the area of residence and the nature of the dwelling, the religious, racial, and ethnic backgrounds. However, when the use of merely a single indicator is possible, the indicator most commonly employed is the father's occupation. It is the one measure with which all others seem to correlate most highly. By this time it should be no secret that this is the indicator I shall apply to the aggregate group of deputies to the Turkish Grand National Assembly.

THE FATHERS OF THE DEPUTIES: OCCUPATIONAL MOBILITY

Impressionistic Evidence

No broad, quantitative studies of social mobility in Turkey exist.[1] A frequent verdict of the impressionistic literature is that there was, and is, relatively high social mobility in Turkish society. Comments like the following are typical:

"Social mobility in the Ottoman Empire enabled humble peasants and rank-and-file soldiers to raise themselves to the highest governmental positions." (Karpat, *Turkey's Politics, op. cit.*, p. 5.)

"Turkish society is essentially an open class society. On every level of class structure, upward and downward mobility are common features...." (Oğuzkan, *Adult Education in Turkey, op. cit.*, p. 10.)

"Turkish society has always been fluid." (Bisbee, *The New Turks, op. cit.*, p. 214.)

"The mud-hut-to-palace life was a common occurrence with the Ottomans — too common to be news. Vertical mobility is even more marked a characteristic of Kemâlist society." (Webster, *The Turkey of Atatürk, op. cit.*, p. 166.)

On the other hand, one can also find numerous references to the importance of family background — to a pride of privileged, semi-aristocratic households, which traditionally have had an abundance of the most valued things that Turkey has to offer. Such a conception pervades Halide Edib's personal reminiscences and her novels of early twentieth-century Istanbul life, in which she consistently refers to ideas of "class," "station," "strata," and the like. A. T. J. Matthews strives to make the social reality behind this conception more explicit

---

[1] A partial remedy for this deficiency will be available in some of the forthcoming articles emanating from the study of the basic value systems of a national sample of lycée-level students in Turkey conducted by G. W. Angell, A. Ş. Sanay, and the author, with the cooperation of the Turkish Ministry of Education and its Test and Research Bureau. The previously cited survey of peasant attitudes also provides much relevant material. Another gap, also partially filled by the aforementioned research, is the lack of reliable information on the social status of various occupations.

in the following passage from his study of *Emergent Turkish Administrators*:[2]

> One of the main criteria that has traditionally been used to evaluate the fitness of an individual for employment in Turkish society has been the type of family he comes from. This has been a reasonably reliable criterion until recently. The worth and character of a person was likely to be a reflection of the social standing of his family. In other words, the family being the single most significant social unit (and not the individual) tended to result in the members of a family being trained and educated in accordance with the social and vocational expectations of that family.

Webster found evidence of the same stratification in the educational system, remarking: "In general, in the pre-Republic days, the children of economically and intellectually favored families composed the bulk of the schools' enrollments. This situation has continued to a certain extent." [3] And Kemal Karpat comments on current political life in Turkey: "The present party leaders of Turkey, with only minor exceptions, belong to rich or politically and socially prominent sections of the population. Many times individuals with little experience in public life and questionable educational background are catapulted into leading positions in the parties merely because of family background." [4]

Specific names can be cited to bolster claims either of great mobility or of the durable advantages of family prestige. Atatürk's father was a petty official, Enver Pasha's a bridge keeper. The other members of the Young Turk triumvirate — Talât and Cemal Pashas — were also of humble origin. Şükrü Saracoğlu, the People's Party Premier of the late forties, had a saddle maker as a father. But on the other side of the ledger, for example, former People's Party General-Secretary Kasım Gülek and former Democratic Party Foreign Minister Fuad Köprülü are scions of most illustrious families and were unquestionably aided in their careers by this fact. The fathers of Rauf Orbay, Ali Fuat Cebesoy, and many more prominent political leaders were pashas. Other deputies, like Adnan Menderes, were sons of large landowners of great local sway and thus were given an unmistakable head start in their political lives.

In their more moderate forms, there is nothing really incompatible in all these statements and ideas. Viewed as a whole and compared to most other non-Western societies, Turkish society seems to have displayed a high degree of social mobility. It stemmed partly from

---

[2] A. T. J. Matthews, *Emergent Turkish Administrators* (Ankara: Faculty of Political Sciences, Ankara University Press, 1955), p. 25.

[3] Webster, *The Turkey of Atatürk, op. cit.*, p. 215.

[4] Karpat, *Turkey's Politics, op. cit.*, p. 392.

the nomadic Turkic heritage, partly from a strong Islamic tradition of the equality of all believers, and partly from the prevailing recruitment patterns of the Turkish army and bureaucracy. Low social origins placed less of a barrier before the rise of a Turkish youth who was able to provide himself with the requisite educational training and vocational skills than would exist in most other non-Western countries.[5] Essentially, this remains true today.

Nevertheless, it also seems to be that a rather widespread "log-cabin-to-White-House," "rags-to-riches" type of myth has led to some exaggeration of this Turkish social mobility, both within Turkey and without. It appears to be undeniable that self-conscious social classes — whatever the minor vagaries of the specific definition of "social class" may be — do exist in Turkey; that most Turks do tend to remain in the same social class as their parents; and that such class memberships are one important influence on the political and social behavior of Turkish citizens. Perhaps Turhan Oğuzkan puts the situation most simply when he says that "A poor family background does not constitute a serious handicap; although a good family background is an advantage, it is no sure guarantee of success." [6]

Occupational Mobility among a Select Group of Deputies

Before inspecting the data to ascertain as far as possible the degree of occupational mobility in the aggregate group of deputies, I must again introduce a caveat. Unfortunately, the *Parliamentary Annual* and *Album,* the obituaries, most of the school annuals, the *Who's Who,* and the other publications that furnish social background information about prominent Turks usually fail to provide any information about fathers' occupations. As a result, I have been able to assemble such information quite laboriously for only 344 persons out of 2,210, or some 16 per cent. Nor do these persons approximate a random sample of the entire group. They are sharply atypical in some respects, as will become evident. However, since we know the population characteristics along many dimensions and we know the same characteristics of the group for which there are data on fathers' oc-

---

[5] Of course, there are significant differences in social mobility between different subgroups of the Turkish people. As Bernard Lewis has observed, "The army had always drawn its recruits from a wider circle than the religious hierarchy, with its entrenched dynasties of rank and wealth, or the bureaucracy, with its inevitable bias in favor of the capital and its insistence on traditional, formal education." *Emergence...*, op. cit., p. 457. Under the republics of Turkey, another career that has aided social mobility has been teaching. Today the teaching profession probably reaches more deeply into Turkish society for its recruits than any other major career line — with the possible exception of the military.

[6] Oğuzkan, *Adult Education in Turkey,* op. cit., p. 10.

cupations, this information can be used to make certain plausible inferences from the known group to the total group of deputies. In other words, we know much about the nature and degree of the biases in this "sampling procedure."

In general, the group of 344 contains a disproportionate number of famous and durable politicians and of deputies trained at the Political Science Faculty. In most respects it is a more "select" group than the whole body of deputies. For instance, three fourths of the aggregate group of deputies had university-level education, but nine tenths of the special group had reached that level of formal training. On the average, the deputies of the aggregate group knew 1.09 foreign languages, while the deputies in the special group for whom fathers' vocations are known knew 1.51 foreign languages. One third of all deputies had official occupations, while over half of the special group had such positions.

What use can be made of the information obtained for this special group of deputies for whom the fathers' vocations are known? How can one overcome the bias in the coverage and obtain some useful information on this important topic? It seems fairly plausible to assume that the occupational mobility of the special group members would have been no more — and probably less — than that of the remainder of the deputies for whom there is no information. The special group contains a disproportionate number of famous, durable, and well-educated deputies. Presumably, its members were aided in reaching this privileged position by family advantages. One can assume that the occupational statuses of their fathers, according to contemporary criteria, were higher than those of the rest of the deputies because they seem to have been able to provide their sons with more advantages.

One partial check on this assumption is furnished by comparing the occupations of the fathers of the special group deputies who failed to get higher education with the fathers' occupations of those who secured such education. If one also regards trade, agriculture, and religion as the least lofty of the occupations being considered, one finds that 64 per cent of the thirty special group members *without* higher educations had fathers from those less prestigious occupations while merely 42 per cent of the 292 special group members *with* higher education had fathers engaged in those occupations. In other words, the better-educated special group members were more likely to have had fathers in occupations with higher social status.[7]

The same sort of difference should hold when the entire special group, better educated as it was, is contrasted with the rest of the

---

[7] Chi square is 4.965, significant at the .05 level with one degree of freedom.

deputies. In short, the chances for upward occupational mobility would be less for the special group members than for the rest of the deputies. Their starting points were higher, and the present measures have a low ceiling. If one finds scant mobility among the special group, this finding is not very informative. There was probably more mobility among the rest of the deputies, but one has no idea *how much more*. On the other hand, if considerable occupational mobility existed even among the special group, then we infer that there must be at least that degree of mobility, and probably more, among the rest of the deputies.

Table 6.1 presents the vocational relationships between the special group of deputies and their fathers. Analysis of the table indicates that 27 per cent of the special group of deputies were in the same occupation as their fathers. Nearly three quarters were in different occupations. The religious subgroup displays the highest percentage of occupational stability, the fathers of twelve out of thirteen clerics also being clerics. Next in order of occupational stability come the agriculturists (with 80 per cent in the same occupation), the military group (with just under half being sons of military men), trade (with 43 per cent), and government (with 38 per cent).

In one sense, these figures reinforce previous comments about the traditional vocations of Turkish society. The four outstanding vocations mentioned previously — government, the military, religion, and agriculture — along with trade (which was low in status but nevertheless a common occupation in traditional Turkish society) dominate the distribution of fathers' occupations. Four out of every five fathers listed were in one of these vocations. Only these five vocations display any marked degree of occupational stability. From another point of view, this suggests that it is rather inappropriate to rate the free professions, which have achieved their important growth only in recent decades, by the same standards one applies to the other groups. Actually, analyses of occupational mobility are to some extent confounded by sharp changes in the occupational structure of Turkish society.

Looking at larger occupational groupings instead of at specific vocations may simplify the picture. Fifty-six per cent of the economic group also had fathers with economic occupations; 51 per cent of the officials also had fathers who were officials; and only 12 per cent of the professionals had fathers who were professionals. Over half (57 per cent) of the deputies for whom we have information had moved into different *gross* occupational categories from those of their fathers. While this result appears to reflect somewhat less mobility than that prevalent among American Senators, for example, it indicates that a sizable proportion of top-level Turkish politicians did

FATHERS, FAITHS, AND FEMALES

Table 6.1
DEPUTIES' OCCUPATIONS COMPARED WITH THEIR FATHERS' OCCUPATIONS

Deputies' Occupations	Government	Military	Education	(Official)	Law	Medicine	Other Prof.	(Professional)	Trade and Agric.	Banking	(Economic)	Religion	Journalism	Other	Total (Deputies) %	No.[a]
Government	38%	7%	5%	(50%)	17%	2%	1%	(20%)	16%	—%	(16%)	15%	—%	—%	31	105
Military	13	47	—	(60)	3	2	—	(3)	28	—	(28)	3	—	6[b]	9	32
Education	31	7	9	(47)	13	2	—	(15)	29	—	(29)	9	—	—	13	45
(Official)	(32)	(14)	(5)	(51)	(14)	(2)	(1)	(17)	(21)	(—)	(21)	(12)	(—)	(1)	(53)	(182)
Law	20	9	7	(36)	2	2	2	(6)	36	—	(36)	18	2	—	13	44
Medicine	19	22	5	(46)	11	8	11	(19)	27	—	(27)	8	—	—	11	37
Other Prof.	11	11	—	(22)	—	—	—	(11)	33	—	(33)	33	—	—	3	9
(Professional)	(19)	(14)	(6)	(39)	(6)	(4)	(2)	(12)	(32)	(—)	(32)	(16)	(—)	(—)	(26)	(90)
Trade and Agric.	—	6	—	(6)	—	—	—	(—)	71	—	(71)	18	—	6	5	17
Banking	50	—	—	(50)	—	—	—	(—)	17	—	(17)	33	—	—	2	6
(Economic)	(13)	(4)	(—)	(17)	(—)	(—)	(—)	(—)	(56)	(—)	(56)	(22)	(—)	(4)	(7)	(23)
Religion	—	—	—	(—)	—	7	—	(7)	8	—	(8)	92	—	—	4	13
Journalism	38	24	—	(62)	—	—	—	(—)	17	—	(17)	3	10	—	8	29
Other	—	20	—	(20)	—	—	—	(—)	—	—	(—)	—	—	80[c]	1	5
Total (Fathers): %	26	14	4	(44)	9	3	1	(12)	25	—	(25)	16	1	2	100	
No.	89	47	14	(150)	30	9	3	(42)	86	—	(86)	53	4	7		344[d]

[a] Some of these N's are extremely small and the internal percentages, therefore, highly unreliable.
[b] Two tribal chiefs.
[c] Four tribal chiefs.
[d] The total of fathers whose occupations are indicated is 344. The total of sons, however, is only 342, since I knew the father's occupations for two deputies whose own occupations I did not know.

move out of their fathers' occupational footsteps into different careers of their own.[8] It also reflects the novelty and the popularity of the free professions in Turkish society.

One final note may further illuminate these suggestive but inconclusive findings. Lacking basic studies of the prestige of various occupations in Turkey, and impressionistically aware of some acute changes in the respect accorded to certain occupations, one finds it rather difficult to determine the most vital factor of all — which deputies have risen and which have fallen in occupational status vis à vis their fathers. For much of the period being examined, the official vocations seemingly stood at the apex of the prestige scale. At the end of the period, the free professions appear to have taken over first place. Hence, the only recourse seemed to be the crude one of combining the official and professional groups and contrasting them with the economic group. Moving from the latter to the former is considered a rise in occupational status, the reverse movement a decline. All else is viewed as stability in occupational status. Obviously, this procedure understates the degree of occupational mobility that might be revealed by less bludgeonlike tools.

Of those eighty-six deputies whose fathers were engaged in trade or agriculture, only twelve were themselves occupied with those economic pursuits. One man professed religion as his occupation, and all the rest can be deemed to have risen in occupational status — twenty-nine into the professions, thirty-eight into official careers, five into journalism, and one into banking. In other words, 14 per cent remained constant, while 84 per cent of those for whom rising was possible, according to this very limited analysis, rose in occupational status.

There were, on the contrary, 192 deputies in the group who had fathers in professional or official occupations and who could have fallen in vocational status. Of these deputies, only four were in trade or agriculture — some 2 per cent. Thus, downward occupational mobility seems, as anticipated for these outstanding politicians, to have been almost nil.

All in all, if observed social mobility is even higher among the rest of the deputies for whom I have no information, my tentative conclusion is that although Turkey's political leaders during the First Republic included an important contingent of men springing from prestigious fathers, there was also a wide representation of men who

---

[8] Cf. D. Matthews, *United States Senators...*, *op. cit.*, pp. 118–119. Lamentably, existing social background studies of political leaders have accumulated very little useful material on the fathers' vocations of those leaders; much comparative analysis is impossible. Insight into the British situation is provided by Guttsman's previously cited articles.

FATHERS, FAITHS, AND FEMALES   143

had risen from lower social origins. The top political leadership in Turkey was not the preserve of a small coterie of social aristocrats, and the lowest levels of the society were not without representation, in the sense of having no men of direct experience with their style of life in the national legislature.

Religious Orientation

An eyebrow or two may involuntarily have twitched and crept upward when I claimed earlier that education and occupation are the basic social distinctions in Turkish society. The skeptic may have queried, "What of religion and sex?" Surely being non-Muslim or female exerts tremendous force on the life of a person living in Turkey. The necessarily awkward formulation of the last sentence ("a person living in Turkey"), in fact, reflects this force, since one rarely calls a non-Muslim Turkish citizen a "Turk."

Bernard Lewis has emphasized the point that religion was historically ". . . the fundamental division of mankind among the Muslim peoples. . . ." Traditional Ottoman society classified men essentially into Muslim, *Zimmî*, and *Harbî* — the believer, the subjugated unbeliever, and the hostile unbeliever — with appropriate codes of conduct toward each.[9] The very structure of the Ottoman state, in the *millet* system, institutionalized religious differences between subjects into a distinctive form of governmental administration.[10]

It has been argued at times that the influence of this Islamic heritage, and of the *millet* system in particular, has been to make "second-class citizens" of today's non-Muslim Turkish populace, despite the secularism and formal legal protections of the Turkish Republic.[11] Though problems of religious discrimination are less acute in Turkey than in many Western nations, and though many Turks would find the best expression of their ideas in the tolerant character of the old Turkish sergeant in Reşat Nuri's fine novel *Afternoon Sun* (*Akşam Güneşi*) or in the wise dervish of Franz Werfel's pro-Armenian epic *The Forty Days of Musa Dagh*, one cannot in general deny the existence of significant degrees of religious prejudice.[12] This bias

---

[9] See B. Lewis, *Emergence . . .*, *op. cit.*, pp. 8, 323, and *passim*, for a basic discussion of the role of religion in the Ottoman Empire.

[10] There is much literature on the *millet* system. Cf., e.g., Luke, *The Old Turkey and the New*, *op cit.*; B. Lewis, *Emergence . . .*, *op. cit.*, Ch. X.

[11] For example, see Harry J. Psomiades, "Turkey: Progress and Problems," *Middle Eastern Affairs*, VIII, No. 3 (March 1957), pp. 94–95.

[12] "The old sergeant raised his bushy eyebrows and looked into my face with a smile of mild contempt. 'What's religion got to do with you or me, Doctor? That's a matter between him and God . . . . If I were to shove my

has been reflected in such things as the tacit refusals to accept non-Muslim but otherwise qualified girls as Red Crescent nurses or to accept non-Muslim boys as military officers.[13] More tragically, it helped to produce the confiscatory capital levy (*Varlık Vergisi*), which was directed at the non-Muslim commercial community in the war years of 1942–1943, and the severe Istanbul riots of September 1955.[14] Even today, the moral stigma attached by many to the word *gâvur* (infidel, non-Muslim, unbeliever) is almost palpable.

Non-Muslim Deputies

What has been the impact of such religious attitudes on the character of political representation in Turkey? How have they affected the group of deputies with whom we are immediately concerned? To answer this question it is, first of all, important to note that the non-Muslim religious communities were apparently effectively represented in late Ottoman political life. According to Turhan Feyzioğlu, the 1908 Chamber of Deputies included 142 Turks, sixty Arabs, twenty-five Albanians, twenty-three Greeks, twelve Armenians, five Jews, four Bulgars, and three Serbs.[15] Naturally, Muslims dominated, as they did in the empire as a whole. But there was a sizable group of Christian deputies, and Christians and Jews were also represented in the cabinet. Furthermore, these Christian deputies tended to band together in reaction to a number of political issues.

---

horse into the stream here, and make him go through his religious ablutions, if I were to give him a good drubbing and make him say his prayers, if I were to cut off his food and drink and subject him to a religious fast — seeing that he's not a human being, what good would all that be? Some five or six years ago, there was a doctor here called Ilya Efendi. I don't know now that he is dead whether he was a Christian or an old Jew; all I know is that he was better than a whole host of Moslems. He helped those in trouble. God forbid, but if I were in the Almighty's place, I'd send down a light every night on the tomb of that Ilya Efendi.'" Reşat Nuri Güntekin, *Afternoon Sun* (London: Heinemann, 1951), pp. 3–4. Franz Werfel, *The Forty Days of Musa Dagh* (New York: The Modern Library, 1934).

[13] On these matters, see, for example, Allen, *The Turkish Transformation*, *op. cit.*, pp. 81–83; Webster, *The Turkey of Atatürk*, *op cit.*, pp. 280–281; B. Lewis, *Emergence...*, *op. cit.*, pp. 350–351.

[14] The *Varlık Vergisi* is described in detail in Faik Ökte, *Varlık Vergisi Faciası* (*The Capital Levy Tragedy*) (Istanbul: Nebioğlu Yayınevi, 1951), and in English in B. Lewis, *Emergence...*, *op. cit.*, pp. 291–296. No thorough account of the Istanbul riots has yet been published, partly for political reasons. After the records of the Yassıada Trials are available, a detailed study may be possible.

[15] Turhan Feyzioğlu, "Les Partis Politiques en Turquie: Du Parti Unique à la Democratie," *Revue Française de Science Politique*, IV, No. 1 (January–March 1954), pp. 131–155.

Their religious backgrounds clearly affected their political behavior.[16]

If all this is true, then why was religion not ranked with education and occupation? The simple answer is that the Turkish Republic is not the Ottoman Empire, even the late Ottoman Empire. Though minority religious status is a vitally important matter for those to whom it applies, nearly 99 per cent of the country is now Muslim. Consequently, while of reduced but still compelling force where applicable, the non-Muslim religious distinction does not have its former impact because there are now too few non-Muslims for it to have retained its over-all social significance.

With the Atatürk Revolution and the fight to oust the Greek invader from Anatolia, the representation of non-Muslim communities in the Turkish national legislature declined precipitously. In the mid-twenties the Greek newspapers in Athens occasionally irritated the Turks by complaining about the lack of Christian Greeks in the Grand National Assembly and harping on the fact that there were four Turks in the Greek Assembly.[17] The Turkish reply given in the daily press was that the idea of "Greeks" in the "Turkish Assembly" was ridiculous. Moreover, the Turkish editorialists cited previous Greek perfidy and the resultant bitterness in Turkey, while adding that such persons were perfectly free to be elected by the people but were apparently not wanted.[18]

In the thirties there were informal places made on the list of Independent members elected to parliament, with the approval of the People's Party, for two representatives of the Greek community and one each for the Jewish and Armenian communities, according to Ritter von Kral.[19] Since that time such minimal representation — which is, however, not disproportionate — has continued. Subsequent *Parliamentary Annuals* sometimes explicitly note the few *gayri Müslümanlar* (non-Muslims) of each session. In particular, three non-Muslim deputies from Istanbul were found in each of the

---

[16] Price, *A History of Turkey, op cit.,* p. 882; Lewis, *Emergence...*, *op. cit.*, p. 374; Mears, *Modern Turkey, op. cit.,* p. 54.

[17] Incidentally, meager available evidence seems to indicate that the Turks themselves, when minority citizens in another nation, have generally behaved quite admirably. Cf, e.g., H. L. Kostanick, "Turkish Resettlement of Refugees from Bulgaria, 1950–1953," *Middle East Journal,* IX, No. 1 (Winter 1955), p. 42: "The Turkish Muslims had been a model minority group because of their consistent support of the Bulgarian government and their lack of anti-Bulgarian feeling."

[18] *Bulletin de Presse Hebdomadaire,* No. 106, August 14, 1927, pp. 2–4.

[19] H. C. Armstrong, in *Grey Wolf* (London: Arthur Barker, 1932), p. 285, alleges that Saffet Arıkan, former People's Party General-Secretary, was a Jew, but I have been unable to substantiate this. August, Ritter von Kral, *Kamâl Atatürk's Land* (Wein: Wilhelm Braumüller, 1938), p. 27.

last three Assemblies (the Eighth through the Tenth), perhaps inaugurating a minor tradition.

Thirteen deputies (0.6 per cent), excluding Christian-Muslim converts (like Ahmet Bilinski-Rüstem of the First Assembly), definitely were non-Muslim, and there were probably a few more.[20] Of these, six were Greek Orthodox, one was Turk Orthodox, two were Armenian, two were Jewish, and two (Marmaralı and Soriano) were definitely non-Muslim but of unknown religion.[21] Nine of the thirteen (69 per cent) were professional men, with doctors being especially popular — there were six of them, almost half of the group. Eleven out of the thirteen (85 per cent) had university-level education, while the other two had lycée-level training. In general, in regard to vocation and education, the non-Muslim group seems to have been professional rather than official and to have had higher formal education than the dominant Muslim delegation.

Not surprisingly, these thirteen deputies spoke an average of 3.3 foreign languages each. None spoke less than two such languages, one spoke seven, and one spoke eight, perhaps reflecting the incredible linguistic competence of some members of the non-Muslim community in Istanbul. Ten out of thirteen were born in Turkey, the other three in Greece. Half of the ten born in Turkey were born in Istanbul. Several others gravitated there, for eight of the thirteen represented Istanbul in the Assembly and apparently lived there. The other five represented Ankara, Afyon, Eskişehir, and Niğde (two). Five of the thirteen had published. Only one, Fakaçelli, the sole regular People's Party man, was elected first at a by-election; and the same man was the youngest of all at first election (forty-one), while the oldest was seventy-two. The group as a whole tended to be much older than the average Muslim deputy on first election, having a mean age of 59.1 years and with eight of thirteen being over sixty on first entering parliament. The election rate for the group was a mere 1.54 (compared to 2.00 for the Muslims), and eight out of the thirteen were elected only once. No man served in more than three Assemblies.

These thirteen non-Muslims seem to have served as a token or symbol, elected because of their minority religious background, rather than as fully participating members of the Assembly. Moreover, this situation will most likely continue in the near future until it is resolved by an attitudinal improvement leading to the loss of force of the religious distinction itself.

---

[20] I considered only those deputies whose non-Muslim status had been definitely established.

[21] The thirteen names are: Fakaçelli, Konus, Hacopulos, Moshos, Taptas, Tarver, Özdamar, Türker, A. V. Bayar, Adato, Bodrumlu, Marmaralı, and Soriano.

Intra-Muslim Distinction

Before leaving the subject of religion I must mention another regrettable omission in the data. Any perceptive resident in Turkey soon comes to realize that the intra-Muslim distinction between *Sunni* and *Shi'i* (*Alevi*), orthodox and schismatic, is of considerable social significance. Turkey has traditionally been the arch-Sunnite nation — a stronghold of orthodoxy, at least on official levels. However, sincere estimates of the number of *Alevi,* or Shiites, in the country range from 5 per cent to 20 or even 40 per cent.[22]

No census figures on this matter have ever been presented, largely because this is still a sensitive subject in Turkey. Since the Shiite profession generally bears an incontestable taint, such beliefs are commonly concealed before outsiders, though the days of Sultan Selim the First's attempt to exterminate 40,000 Shiites have long since fortunately passed. It would be interesting to learn if the Shiite-Sunnite religious division is associated with any important variations in political behavior and how adequately the Turkish *Alevi* persuasion is represented in the Assembly. There is occasional conjecture about Shiite support for the People's Party, but reliable data are at present impossible to acquire.[23]

WOMEN DEPUTIES

In most areas of the world — "developed" or "underdeveloped" — there seems to be marked incompatibility between the female role in society and certain occupational roles, especially that of politician. In the United States, women won national suffrage in 1920 through the Nineteenth Amendment. With only minor exceptions, they appear to exercise that suffrage today with frequency and care comparable to men. Yet the proportion of women in elective office is minuscule — and seems stabilized at that level. In Britain, Ross has estimated that female candidates are more than twice as unlikely to be successful in being elected to parliament as men, and that women are still more unlikely even to be nominated.[24] Similar observations have been made

---

[22] E.g., Geoffrey Lewis, *Turkey, op. cit.,* p. 88; R. D. Robinson, *The First Turkish Republic, op cit.,* pp. 37, 328, n. 11.

[23] Equally frustrating is the impossibility of investigating Kurdish representation. Some moderately well-informed inferences regarding Kurdish background can be made for a few deputies, but substantial and reliable information is so lacking that I have not been able to pursue the investigation with profit.

[24] J. F. S. Ross, "Women and Parliamentary Elections," *British Journal of Sociology,* IV, No. 1 (March 1953), pp. 14–16. Looking at a different, but allied, profession, only as late as 1949 did the first woman become a King's Counsel in Britain. Langston Day, "Women King's Counsel in Britain," *American Bar Association Journal,* XXXV, No. 11 (November 1949), p. 915.

in France, Germany, Canada, New Zealand, and other countries, and even in Scandinavia, which pioneered in granting political rights to women.[25] Nor is the phenomenon restricted to Western democracies of one type or another. Despite Soviet twitting of the United States about the lack of females in Congress compared with the number of females in the Supreme Soviet, detailed studies indicate a similar dearth of feminine voices in the top policy-making councils of the Soviet Union, both on the national level and on the level of the individual republics and oblasts.[26] Moreover, in all these countries, direct female political participation still smacks of "... an 'example' to be followed ... an effort to change the old conceptions, rather than a change already accomplished." [27] It seems that in most societies, although divergent in their political practices, "The man is expected to be dominant in action directed toward the world outside the family; the woman is to accept his leadership passively. She is not expected, therefore, to see herself as an effective agent in politics." [28]

The Progress of Female Emancipation in Turkey

Few countries have more fully emphasized these separate social and political roles for male and female than traditional Turkey. As Howard Reed has remarked, Islam itself was "... essentially a male preserve...." [29] Women were granted some legal control over their own property, which provided a foothold for future reforms; but in marriage and divorce practices, in the sanctioning of limited polygamy, even in the customary place of prayer in the mosque, the superior status of male over female was expressed. Around this religious affirmation of masculine superiority, a strong web of additional social practices grew up, resulting in a situation in which the well-bred Turkish lady was virtually confined to her home, family, and a few close female friends for her entire life.

The fascinating autobiographical writings of Irfan Orga and Selma Ekrem portray this condition unforgettably. Orga describes his mother as "... content to be solely an ornament in her husband's home." He depicts his surprise, even as a youth, when she "interfered

[25] On this general topic, see Maurice Duverger, *The Political Role of Women* (Paris: UNESCO, 1955).

[26] Cf. George Schueller, *The Politburo* (Hoover Institute Studies, Series B, Elite Studies No. 2; Stanford: Stanford University Press, 1951), p. 43, and John A. Armstrong, *The Soviet Bureaucratic Elite: A Case Study of the Ukraninian Apparatus* (New York: Frederick Praeger, 1959), p. 45.

[27] Duverger, *op. cit.*, p. 10.

[28] Angus Campbell *et al.*, *The American Voter* (New York: John Wiley, 1960), p. 490.

[29] Howard Reed, "The Religious Life of Modern Turkish Muslims" in Frye (ed.), *Islam and the West, op cit.*, p. 119.

in a masculine conversation" concerning politics. The unquestioned assumption in the early Orga household was that the men of that household mediated almost all contacts between its females and the outside world. This conception had its physical implementation in the *kafes* (cage), or shutters, which covered all windows and kept passing males from catching even a stray glimpse of a female inside. After the great agonies and changes of World War I, when Orga's mother went through her own personal emancipation and removed the *kafes* work to let in light and air, she was regarded by the entire neighborhood as a fast woman, formerly good but now on the highroad to sin. When she also began to consider removing her veil, the grandmother told her:

> And now you talk of leaving aside your veil. Why, I lived for thirty years with my husband, and I never went out without his permission and I had to keep my face covered all the time. If I went out in the carriage with Murat [the coachman], immediately all the windows were closed and sometimes the blinds were drawn, too. I say it is a scandal that women today are revealing their faces. God will punish them!

Apparently, the reliability and alacrity of the deity were not equally trusted by others, for when the mother did go without her veil for the first time in Istanbul she was stoned and spat upon.[30]

Selma Ekrem describes the separate areas for women on trolley cars and ferryboats as well as the rigid division of the house into the closed *harem* portion for females and the open *selamlık* for males, though she also points out that these severe restrictions were much more thoroughly enforced among fashionable ladies in the cities than among peasant women. The latter mingled with men more naturally, largely because of economic necessity: both worked together in the fields.[31]

Almost all occupations were denied these urban cloistered women. Even more distressingly, education was also restricted. De Salve, describing Turkish education in 1875, writes:

> There is in Turkey no school for young Mohammedan ladies; it has, no doubt, been thought that the life in the harem which awaits them renders all education useless.... Turkish family-life is so walled up

---

[30] See Irfan Orga, *Portrait of a Turkish Family* (New York: Macmillan, 1950), pp. 4, 66, 79–80, 116, 201–202, and *passim*.

[31] Selma Ekrem, *Turkey, Old and New, op. cit.*, and *Unveiled: The Autobiography of a Turkish Girl* (New York: Ives Washburn, 1942). Halide Edib, too, regularly stresses the difference between the roles of upper-class and peasant women. See also Mary Mills Patrick, "Women," in Mears (ed.), *Modern Turkey, op. cit.*, pp. 141–149, and her autobiography, *Under Five Sultans* (New York: Century, 1929).

that very little of it is known, and most of the descriptions which have been given of it are purely imaginary. The Turkish lady, unacquainted with serious work, lives in her harem occupied with trifles, unless she gives her attention to her offspring; she only goes out accompanied by her slaves and eunuchs, and clad in her ancient costume, which is certainly not deficient in originality, the Paris fashionplates being but little consulted. Sultan Mahmoud, who desired to change the male costume, never attempted anything of the kind with regard to female dress.[32]

Considering this somewhat overstated picture, and contrasting it with conditions in contemporary Turkey, one is inclined to agree with the official brochure of the Turkish Information Office, *Women in Modern Turkey*, which states: "It would be almost impossible for anyone acquainted only with present-day Turkey to imagine the condition of subjection in which women were forced to live only twenty-five years ago. . . ." That condition is further described as being ". . . the status of a household object in a masculine abode, assigned duties, but accorded not the slightest rights or responsibilities." [33]

The event that dealt the initial shattering blow to female "subjugation" was the First World War. Mobilization forced many women out of the home for the first time and into work as clerks, teachers, factory workers, nurses, and minor officials. We find in 1916 the first introduction of civil marriage and the establishment of restrictions on completely arbitrary divorce-by-repudiation. Shortly thereafter, written permission of the first wife was legally required before an additional marriage could be officially approved, and the first provision for coeducation at the University of Istanbul was made.[34] Women began to take an active role in the *Türk Ocağı* organization, even to the extent of speaking at public meetings. Brave souls, like Orga's mother, appeared without the veil, and discussion of political rights for women began to be heard even before there were widespread political rights for men.

In a very few years, this small flame of feminist agitation was spread by the second violent storm that struck Turkey — the War for Independence against the Greeks and the Allies of World War I. Once again, adversity forced women into hitherto forbidden or de-

---

[32] De Salve, "Education in Turkey," *op. cit.*, p. 239. The author adds, however, that within the family the influence of such ladies over their husbands and children seemed to be great.

[33] Turkish Information Office, *Women in Modern Turkey*, Turkey Today, No. 6 (New York: Turkish Information Office, n.d.), p. 3.

[34] Howard Reed, "Revival of Islam is Secular Turkey," *op. cit.*, pp. 268–269; Ahmed Emin (Yalman), *Turkey in the World War*, *op cit.*, Ch. 20, esp. pp. 231–238; Halide Edib (Adıvar), *Conflict of East and West in Turkey*, *op. cit.*, p. 236 and *passim*; Barbara Ward, *Turkey*, *op. cit.*, pp. 32–33; Eleanor Bisbee, *The New Turks*, *op. cit.*, Ch. 4.

spised activities. They became ammunition carriers, nurses, even fighters on rare occasions. More important, they were indispensable in keeping the agricultural economy going while their weary husbands were once more under arms. Refet (Bele) Pasha, one of the Turkish commanders, is quoted as having said, "We owe our success to the Anatolian peasant women — for hundreds and hundreds of miles they transported the ammunition on carts or on their backs along roadless wastes, protecting the ammunition with the scanty covers with which they covered their babies, who accompanied them tied to their backs.[35] If one detects the enthusiasm and hyperbole of Halide Edib intermingled with the idea of Refet Pasha, still the accuracy of the basic observation is not belied. The contribution of Turkey's women, both upper-class and peasant, to the victory in the War for Independence was there for all to see.

The emancipation of women became one of the cardinal tenets of the Atatürk Reform, which followed the military and diplomatic victories of the early 1920's. Indeed, since Islam had supported male hegemony so dramatically, a blow for women's rights — for their own sake and as part of the move toward "civilization" — was also a blow against archaic religion. The campaign against the veil was as much a campaign *against* the *hoca* as it was one *for* the modern female![36]

The Social Position of Women in Turkish Society

The legal achievements of the Atatürk Reform created a new juridical position of virtual equality for Turkish women. The educational reforms deliberately attempted to continue earlier efforts to provide girls with contemporary academic training. Exemplary females were encouraged to enter professions such as the law, medicine, dentistry, journalism, and of course teaching. By 1946, there were 11,250 female teachers in Turkey's schools, nearly 30 per cent of the total teaching force, and these teachers were instructing a body of students that now included over half a million girls, roughly one third of the total. In the legal profession, by 1948 there were 101 women judges and public prosecutors who had received law faculty training, nineteen women who were assistant judges, and twenty-six who were law clerks

---

[35] Halide Edib (Adıvar), *The Turkish Ordeal, op. cit.*, p. 293.

[36] Obversely, the cries of "atheism," "godlessness," "infidel," that were used as undercover weapons against the Atatürk reforms were frequently followed by shouts for the "protection of our women" and protests against unveiled faces and bodies not enshrouded in voluminous *çarşafs.* Cf. Halide Edib (Adıvar), *Memoirs of Halide Edib* (New York: Century, 1926), p. 269: "The common and the most explosive weapons they [the early opposition] used were reactionary, women and religion being the supreme ones."

in various courts and tribunals.[37] There were even women pilots and, that still rarer *avis*, women deputies to the Grand National Assembly. Moreover, this development was not confined to a few show occupations, as Geoffrey Lewis has noted:

> The propagandists who boast of the fact that all professions are open to Turkish women, are missing the point; other Muslim countries have their few but well-publicized women doctors, teachers and lawyers. But Turkey has women shop-assistants, clerks and telephone operators too; the test of female emancipation is not whether a small number of highly-gifted or highly-placed women can gate-crash one particular masculine preserve, but whether any girl at all who wants a job can get one, of right, and at the same rate of pay as a man. In this respect Turkey is a model to Asia, and perhaps not to Asia alone.[38]

To point out this amazing broadening of the accepted role of the female in Turkey — even to repeat the statement that Turkey might furnish a model for other nations in this respect — is not to contend that no problems remain or even that they are not serious problems. The development described here has only slowly and painfully been extended from cities to towns and villages. "Professional work, such as school teaching and nursing," according to Kemal Karpat, "becomes difficult for women in towns, where a woman's morality is measured according to the degree of her attachment to home and family. So any woman who ventures to take an outside job is considered of dubious morality...."[39] Such towns are growing fewer in number all the time, but many still exist. Among the peasants, male authority remains supreme and is still reflected — though less often — in the man's riding the family donkey while the woman plods on foot, or in the man's walking ahead with his sons, unencumbered, while his wife and daughters labor in the rear with bundles and babies. To take another example, within the confines of the village, Stirling reports that "no one is ever forbidden entry to an *oda* [communal social room] or to a house, except on grounds of sex differentiation."[40]

---

[37] Turkish Information Office, *Women in Turkey, op. cit.*, pp. 7-8. Cf. also Abul H. K. Sassani, *Education in Turkey* (Washington: Office of Education, 1952), p. 5.

[38] G. Lewis, *Turkey, op. cit.*, p. 186.

[39] Karpat, "Social Themes...," *op. cit.*, pp. 160–161.

[40] On the position of village women, one can find these ideas stated in: Makal, *A Village in Anatolia, op. cit.*, pp. 68–70, 140, and *passim*; Ibrahim Yasa, *Hasanoğlan* (Ankara: Yeni Matbaa, 1957), p. 119; Paul Stirling, "Social Ranking in a Turkish Village," *British Journal of Sociology*, IV (March 1953), p. 36 ("...with rare exceptions, all women rank automatically lower than all men"); Kemal Karpat, "Social Effects of Farm Mechanization in Turkish Villages," *Social Research*, XXVII (Spring 1960), p. 98.

In most respects, the life and outlook of the intellectual professional female is far more similar to that of her male counterpart in education and vocation than it is to her uneducated sister.[41] It is for this reason that I have considered the educational and occupational distinctions to be politically the most vital, even though sex differences, too, are of extreme social significance.

Even within an urban environment, women have not uniformly obtained social status equal to that of men in Turkey. "There are many men, even in self-consciously modern Ankara, who buy their wives European clothes but leave them at home most of the time in the time-honored Eastern way." [42] One is often struck by the preponderance of males at cinemas, night clubs, cocktail parties, and the like, where roughly equal representation of the sexes is the rule in the West. One knows sophisticated modern Turks for a long time, in many cases, before one meets their wives.

Part of the reason for women's more restricted social position is simply adherence to the more reticent social norms of Europe rather than those of America. But much of the explanation seems to lie in the vestiges of older Turkish attitudes toward women, which have not been completely eradicated. A further reflection of the same phenomenon is that in 1959 only about one quarter of all students at the lycée level of education in Turkey — the basic step toward indisputable intellectual status — were girls. Sending one's daughter to a lycée or beyond is regarded by perceptive Turks as being one of the truest signs of modernity or Westernization. In the same vein, less than half of a national sample of these lycée-level students in 1959 felt that they approved of *full-time* careers for unmarried women, and only 8.7 per cent approved of such careers for married women.

Perhaps a just description of the present situation is that in the cities of Turkey the social position of women is beginning to approximate that of women in the West — which is still hardly one of equality, especially in politics. In the towns and villages, male superiority, while weakened, remains the rule.[43] However, pictured against the scene of merely a few decades ago, the progress in "female emancipation" must be regarded as truly remarkable.

---

[41] For a rather amusing illustration of this, see Halide Edib Adıvar's description of the Women of Ankara versus the Women of Istanbul in the Ankara chapter of the Red Crescent, *Turkish Ordeal, op. cit.*, pp. 246–247.

[42] Webster, *The Turkey of Atatürk, op. cit.*, p. 277.

[43] Extensive quantitative information on this topic and many other matters discussed in this book will be forthcoming from the national attitudinal survey of a large sample of Turkish villagers directed by the author and sponsored by the Turkish government and U.S. A.I.D. in 1962. Cf. Frederick W. Frey, "Surveying Peasant Attitudes in Turkey," *op. cit.*, pp. 335–355.

The Characteristics of Female Deputies

Turkish women first received voting rights in the municipal elections of 1930. They obtained national voting rights, along with the right to become a deputy to the Grand National Assembly, in time for them to participate in the 1935 elections and the Fifth Assembly (1935-1939). All together, from that time until 1957, that is, from the Fifth through the Tenth Assemblies, thirty-eight women served as deputies. As a group, they had an average election rate of 1.74 compared to 2.00 for all men. Let us remember that a ceiling of six sessions prevailed and may have acted artificially to reduce this comparative election rate for women. Nevertheless, the basic finding is that women are grossly underrepresented in the national legislature of Turkey as in other nations, and that when they did wend their way to the parliament, they tended to have relatively abbreviated careers.[44]

Another sign of the rather grudging acceptance of women is that only one of the thirty-eight female deputies was first elected at a by-election. Not one served in all six possible Assemblies, nor even in five of six. Only eight of thirty-eight were reelected more than once.

Two thirds of the women deputies had received university-level education. Though slightly lower than the male proportion, this shows the women to be even more outstanding than their masculine colleagues, since the proportion of university-educated women in Turkey was so much smaller. Educationally, this was definitely an elite group of women. Rather interestingly, they differed sharply from the men in type of faculty attended, being much more likely to have come from the faculties of letters and of science or from schools of education. Twenty out of twenty-six with higher education (77 per cent) were trained in these disciplines.

Not surprisingly, teaching was the dominant vocation, occupying nearly two thirds of the entire group. No other occupation enlisted more than the 8 per cent (three persons) found in the second largest category, medicine. The women knew 1.26 foreign languages each, on the average, with French and English prevailing. Over one third of those who knew a foreign language knew English, mirroring the popularity of that language both for the most recent generations and for girls in particular. Female deputies tended to be noticeably younger on first election than males — being forty-one and a half years instead of forty-five and a half, on the average.

One quite revealing finding is that the women deputies were much more likely than men to have been born in Istanbul and not to have had any local birth connection with a constituency represented. Forty-

---

[44] For a revealing vignette on the selection of Turkey's "first" female deputy by Mustafa Kemal personally, see Afetinan, *Kemâl Atatürk'ü Anarken* (*Recalling Kemal Atatürk*), (Ankara: Güzel Sanatlar Matbaası, 1956), pp. 66-67.

two per cent of the female group were born in Istanbul, compared with 16 per cent of the males. Only 26 per cent of the women had a local birth connection with a constituency represented, while 58 per cent of the males had such connection. In other words, the women in the Assembly appear highly urban and cosmopolitan, rather than local, when contrasted with male deputies. Such a finding supports the previous observations about the concentration of feminine advancement in the cities. These women legislators emerge as extremely well educated, professional (only two could be classed as "housewives"), urban, and cosmopolitan when placed alongside Turkish women as a whole.

The general impression acquired from these data is that the ladies were present in the parliament as an obeisance to principle more than anything else. It was deemed "the thing to do," and they lingered on the fringes of the legislature without ever becoming a large enough or a sufficiently well placed group to have an important part in parliamentary affairs. Not one female became chairman of a permanent committee, and only two of thirty-eight barely managed to become what I shall style a "top formal leader," essentially through party position. The women did hold office in the permanent parliamentary committees quite frequently, but always in the same appropriate slot — secretary or clerk (*kâtip*). This accords with the repeated findings in other countries that women, if they do get into the national legislature, tend to be less active than men, tend to be found in activities relating to health, education, and welfare (the legislative matters most proximate to the traditional female role), and tend to be rarely if ever in important positions of political leadership.[45] Turkey is no exception to this tendency.

Summary

An aggregate view of all deputies to the Grand National Assembly between 1920 and 1957 necessarily overlooks changes through time. Thus Part Three will be a direct analysis of such temporal changes. First, however, the briefest possible recapitulation of the findings of this chapter plus reemphasis of a few interpretations from earlier chapters of Part Two seems warranted.

The occupations of the fathers of some 16 per cent of the total group of deputies were analyzed, particularly in comparison with their sons' occupations. This special group of 16 per cent for whom information about fathers' occupations was available contained a dispro-

---

[45] Duverger, *The Political Role of Women*, op. cit., pp. 122–124.

portionate number of famous and durable deputies and of graduates from the Political Science Faculty. It was, on the whole, better educated and more official in occupation than the rest of the deputies.

Three fourths of the deputies in this special group were in occupations different from those of their fathers. The occupations with the greatest continuity from father to son were religion, agriculture, military, trade, and government, in that order. In broader terms, the deputies with occupations classed as economic were most likely to have had fathers in the same occupational classification, the officials were next, and the professionals by far the least likely. Still, over half the deputies had moved into a *broad* occupational classification different from that of their fathers.

It was assumed that occupational mobility among the special group under direct analysis would be less than occupational mobility among the remainder of the deputies. If the official and professional occupations are regarded as carrying the most prestige during the period under investigation and the economic occupations as least prestigious, then 84 per cent of those deputies for whom *upward* occupational mobility was possible displayed such mobility. On the contrary, only 2 per cent of those for whom *downward* mobility was possible displayed such mobility. All in all, a considerable sprinkling of men with lower occupational and social status (according to their families of orientation), and of men who had displayed marked upward occupational mobility, apparently seasoned the national legislature.

Token representations of non-Muslims and women were discovered among the aggregate group of deputies. There were a baker's dozen non-Muslims and some thirty-eight females. The non-Muslims were better educated than the rest of the deputies, while the females, though slightly less well educated than the males, also manifested exceptional educational attainments when compared with their female compatriots. Both groups were more urban and less locally oriented than others. The non-Muslims (all males) were primarily professional in occupation, and the females were engaged mainly in teaching. The members of both groups had appreciably lower reelection rates than the rest of their colleagues. They appear to have been present primarily for symbolic purposes and to have had negligible group impact on high-level decision making.

Three fundamental criteria seem to have been operative in the semi-co-optative recruitment and retention of these top-level Turkish politicians. These criteria were that the deputy have some claim — the stronger the better — to intellectual status, to official status, and to a position of power in his particular locality. The relative incidence of intellectuals and officials in the Assembly has been shown to have been extremely great. Moreover, various indicators of preferential treatment, especially the average election rates for different groups of deputies, have repeatedly reflected the favor shown to politicians with these attributes.

Though deputies satisfying all three criteria were most preferred of all, I have also found a sharp tendency in many cases for the criteria to divide these national legislators into two subgroups: those with intellectual and official status on the one hand, and those with local connections and influence on the other. There are signs of latent tension between a national elite, determined by education and vocation, and the local politicos. And I have hinted that this national versus local rift would show up again in later analyses and would be vital to the understanding of the most recent developments in Turkish politics. At least in the aggregate view, the national element appeared to be paramount.

To leap from some knowledge of the social backgrounds of national politicians to inferences about the power structure of the society is quite dangerous. Even to proceed from such knowledge to judgments about the political behavior of these same politicians can be treacherous, especially without the aid of detailed studies about the general political significance of the social background experiences involved — that is, without studies of political socialization in its broadest sense. Minimally required are studies of how lawyers commonly differ in their political attitudes and behavior from military men, studies of the political implications of various levels of education, studies of how age affects political outlook, etc.

While unacceptable as direct evidence, speculations about the distribution of power based on inferences from social background analysis may nevertheless be useful if viewed as hypotheses or suggestions demanding more explicit confirmation. In this connection, it is hard to resist mentioning the obvious possible relationship between the social backgrounds of Turkey's deputies and the typical mode of action of government in the Turkish revolution. Until quite recently this revolution has been essentially a revolution "from the top down." The fuel of reform has been the philosophy of Turkish *intellectuals,* the vehicle has been the official and semiofficial *state apparatus,* and the road has been that of *edict and regulation.* It is difficult to avoid ascribing much of this distinctive style to the particular social backgrounds of Turkish political leaders — to their strongly intellectual and official character.

Indeed, perceptive writers on contemporary Turkey have already done so. Thus, for instance, the International Bank team, in its study *The Economy of Turkey,* has written:

> Most of the Turkish leaders were former soldiers or government officials. Accustomed to authoritative plans of action, they were naturally

impatient with the individually organized and uncontrolled activities of private enterprise.[46]

As another example, Bernard Lewis has used such factors in interpreting the "authoritarian centralism" of the Young Turk movement, and the étatism of the Kemalists.[47] The intellectualism, the imperiousness, and the "tutelary" bureaucratic approach to national problems that typified Turkish government during most of the First Republic, all would seem to accord with the modal social background of its members.[48]

It is more rarely noted, however, that some of the great *virtues* as well as the faults of this revolutionary elite also seem to be linked to the social backgrounds from which its members sprang. Their intellectual ability placed at the disposal of the main modernizing agency — the state — much of the outstanding talent of the society. Their official background enabled their leaders many times to call upon the magnificent Turkish traditions of sober-minded devotion to duty and sacrifice of self for suprapersonal ends. Their shared backlog of experiences helped to produce a homogeneity of values and an ease of communication without which their great achievements in chaotic and critical times might well have been impossible. Finally, the fact that the modernizing cadre was so strategically placed in the existing power and communications structures of Turkish society, and did not have to fight its way to the center of power from a peripheral position, greatly speeded the march toward modernity. It will be important to keep these broad considerations in mind as we examine detailed changes through time.

---

[46] *Op. cit.*, p. 7.

[47] B. Lewis, *Emergence*..., *op. cit.*, pp. 200, 277.

[48] For one illustration of what this approach meant on the local level, see Joseph S. Szyliowicz, *Erdemli: A Case Study in the Political Integration of the Turkish Villager* (unpublished Ph.D. dissertation, Department of Public Law and Government, Columbia University, 1961), pp. 201–202. Szyliowicz says: "The concept of tutelage is the guiding principle of government–local government relations in Turkey and local government units are closely controlled by the central government." He also quotes A. H. Hanson, a British authority on Turkish local government, to the effect that "The basic fact about tutelage is that there are literally no decisions made by a local government authority which either (*a*) do not require approval by a higher authority or (*b*) cannot be reversed or amended by a higher authority..., i.e., the administrative and judicial organs of the central government." See also A. H. Hanson, "On Local Self-Government in Turkey," in A. H. Hanson, Tahir Aktan, Fatma Mansur, and Ibrahim Yasa (eds.), *Studies in Turkish Local Government* (Public Administration Institute for Turkey and the Middle East; Ankara: Yeni Matbaa, 1955), p. 177.

PART THREE

Analyses of Change

CHAPTER SEVEN

The Ten Assemblies

THE THIRTY-SEVEN YEARS from 1920 to 1957 witnessed a now famous, deep transformation of Turkish society and Turkish politics. In 1920, the Turkish trunk of the once mighty Ottoman Empire was fighting what seemed to be a forlorn "National Struggle" to preserve a viable semblance of sovereign identity. Its antagonists were not only the invading Greeks and their Allied supporters but fellow Turks who remained loyal to the "captive" Sultan-Caliph, Mehmet VI (Vahdeddin), and his government in Istanbul. Under the leadership of Mustafa Kemal and his associates, the rebel assembly became a national legislature, its executive committee a national government, and the divided and beleaguered Anatolian and Thracian remnants of the Ottoman mélange the Turkish nation.

Having preserved Turkish autonomy, the Kemalists proceeded to construct a single-party, tutelary government that tried to drive, prod, lecture, lead, and even occasionally cajole selected portions of Turkish society into that modernity which would redeem its self-respect. At the same time, the twin themes of democracy and economic improvement were increasingly worked into the Kemalist propaganda harmony that influenced new generations of Turkish youths who were shrewdly assigned the responsibility of being "guardians of the regime."

The death of Atatürk in 1938, the victory of the "democracies" over fascism in World War II, and particularly the absorption by Turkey's young intellectuals of much of the democratic and materialistic content of the basic message of Kemalism were among the factors that undermined the single-party, tutelary approach to national development. These swelling currents were recognized by Ismet Inönü,

Atatürk's successor as chief of state and party, who used his great personal authority to help introduce the first truly multi-party political system in Turkey in the years following the Second World War. In 1950, the initial "acid test" of the sincerity of Turkey's movement toward democracy was passed. After the first scrupulously fair and open national election in the history of the Republic, the People's Party was clearly defeated, and it honorably relinquished power to the Democratic Party of Bayar, Menderes, Köprülü, and Koraltan.

Our investigation period ends with the first seven years of the Menderes-Bayar regime — a time in which, following three or four early years of good feeling, political life grew increasingly bitter and taut. The Democratic leaders began to pursue a path that could lead only to a return to authoritarianism and a reversal of the democratic progress which had so strenuously been achieved. However, the great semi-autonomous institutions (the political parties, the press, the universities, the judiciary, the bureaucracy, the public school system), which had been erected in the preceding thirty years to link citizen and government and to integrate large elements of Turkish society and connect them with the highest levels of political decision making, stubbornly resisted the recrudescence of authoritarianism. Their rearguard action essentially prevented Menderes and Bayar from dominating Turkish political institutions and compelled the Democratic Party leaders to invoke force in the agency of the Turkish armed forces to obtain a commanding grip on the society. But such forceful action put to the military a very momentous choice: whether to permit itself to be used to repress those institutions which it had long supported or to violate the Turkish soldier's by now well-established and obviously essential tradition of political neutrality.[1] We know, of course, that the military chose the latter as the lesser evil.

These major political developments were apparently reflected in, and strongly affected by, changes in the sorts of men reaching the formal acme of political power in Turkey, the Grand National Assembly. Marked variations in the social backgrounds of Turkish deputies

---

[1] For more details, see Frederick W. Frey, "Arms and the Man in Turkish Politics," *op. cit.* See also Daniel Lerner and Richard D. Robinson, "Swords and Ploughshares: The Turkish Army as a Modernizing Force," *World Politics*, XIII, No. 1 (October 1960), pp. 19–44, and Dankwart A. Rustow, "The Army and the Founding of the Turkish Republic," *op. cit.*, pp. 513–552. A Turkish reaction to these articles is offered by Nermin Abadan, "Türkiye'de Ordu ve Siyaset" ("The Army and Politics in Turkey"), *op. cit.* A fascinating, blow-by-blow account of the coup was published in the Istanbul daily, *Milliyet (Nation)*, in a long series of articles commencing on May 27, 1962. See, also, Dankwart Rustow, "The Military," in Ward and Rustow (eds.), *Political Modernization in Japan and Turkey, op. cit.*, pp. 352–388, and two forthcoming articles by George Harris in the *Middle East Journal*, 1965.

occurred during these thirty-seven eventful years. Moreover, these variations seem to fall into a rather consistent pattern that suggests a crude hypothesis about alterations in the distribution of political power in modern Turkey. Therefore let us examine the gross changes in the social profiles of our ten Assemblies and then investigate relative alterations through time in important subgroups within the Assemblies.

Parliamentary Service

Table 7.1 lists the ten Assemblies with which we shall be dealing and the duration of each Assembly. It also provides fundamental information about the deputies' completeness of service, previous experience, and the percentage of each Assembly reelected to the subsequent Assembly.

Resignation

The sharp decline in the percentage of resignations from the Grand National Assembly reflects the growth in status of that body and the consolidation of the Kemalist hold on the national government. Participation in the First Assembly, formed during the bleakest days of the "National Struggle," was apparently viewed by many Turks who had been elected deputies as rather like *boarding* a sinking ship. More than two dozen never came to the Assembly to which they had been elected, and nearly a dozen more put in a brief appearance and then failed to show up again.[2]

A glance at the reasons for the more normal resignations occurring during the First Assembly gives one some insight into the relative status of the deputyship as opposed to other posts. Members of the Assembly resigned to become religious leaders (*müftü*), judges, public prosecutors, provincial governors (*vali* and *mutasarrıf*), county prefects (*kaymakam*), ambassadors, and even local directors of the state monopolies. As the prestige of the Grand National Assembly mounted, resignations to accept such posts became increasingly rare.[3]

---

[2] It must also be observed that travel in Anatolia in such unsettled times was frequently quite hazardous. For example, Ziya Bey, deputy-elect from Gümüşhane, was killed by bandits on May 13, 1920, near Çarşamba, on the Black Sea coast, while on his way to join the Assembly. For an illustrative Turkish comment, cf. Süleyman Külçe, *Mareşal Fevzi Çakmak* (Istanbul: Cumhuriyet Matbaası, 1953), I, p. 139.

[3] A. T. J. Matthews, in his study *Emergent Turkish Administrators*, found that the prestige of the national legislator *for actual and prospective bureaucrats* was surpassed only by that of the provincial governor from a list which included "general, judge, diplomat, professor, chief dept. administrator, big businessman, engineer, doctor, and lawyer." The status of the deputy among the general populace would, impressionistically, seem to be even higher than that of the *Vali* (provincial governor). Cf. A. T. J. Matthews, *op. cit.*, p. 21.

Table 7.1
PARLIAMENTARY SERVICE, EXPERIENCE, AND REELECTION, BY ASSEMBLY (PERCENTAGES)[a]

Assembly			Service					RELECTED[b]	PREVIOUS EXPERIENCE	DEPUTY TOTAL[c]
No.	Years	Resigned	Died	Elected Late	Removed	Completed				
I	1920–1923	16%	5%	7%	1%	70%		30%	23%[d]	437
II	1923–1927	6	8	14	1	72		67	37	333
III	1927–1931	3	5	6	1	86		74	63	333
IV	1931–1935	3	7	10	1	80		85	71	348
V	1935–1939	2	8	10	—	80		73	66	444
VI	1939–1943	1	10	10	—	80		75	68	470
VII	1943–1946	1	6	8	—	85		61	67	492
VIII	1946–1950	1	8	7	1	83		12	59	499
IX	1950–1954	1	5	4	—	90		54	19	494
X	1954–1957	1	3	—	—	96		48[e]	49	537

[a] Percentages may not add to 100 because of rounding.
[b] Excludes those who died.
[c] Absolute number of persons elected to a deputyship during Assembly.
[d] Experience in previous Ottoman Assemblies.
[e] To the Eleventh Assembly (1957-1960).

In the critical early years Mustafa Kemal and his colleagues may have felt it necessary to utilize in other areas some of the talent found in the Assembly, and thus may have requested that various persons resign to accept administrative and legal posts. Once again, with the consolidation of the regime in later years, this was no longer necessary.

In all, roughly one out of every six deputies elected to the First Grand National Assembly resigned his seat, and though certain special factors may have reinforced this tendency, it would seem generally to reflect the early lack of status and security of the Ankara legislature. The percentage of resignations declined quickly in the subsequent four parliaments, so that by the end of the Atatürk era at the termination of the Fifth Assembly, resignations had dropped to an apparently normal level of 1 per cent. The stabilization of the role of the Grand National Assembly in Turkish politics is well illustrated by these figures.

Complete Tenure

A corresponding indication of the same trend can be found in the column of Table 7.1 giving the percentage of the members of each Assembly who served a complete term in office — who neither arrived late nor left early. There is a steady trend toward a higher percentage of deputies serving a complete term. This trend is weakened if we adjust for the percentage of deaths in each parliament, as we should. Nevertheless it is a statistical counterpart of the decline in resignations. In most recent times, nearly every man elected to a deputyship has remained in that post during the entire session for which he was chosen.

Death

The proportion of deputies who died in the course of an Assembly has remained fairly constant over the years, varying around a mean of some 5 per cent. The greatest relative incidence of deaths occurred in the Sixth Assembly, when about one man in ten died in office, double the average figure. Basically, the explanation is that the solid troop of loyal supporters that Mustafa Kemal gathered about him in the Assembly and retained for several parliaments was reaching old age and dying off. This is an important consideration in viewing the major recent political changes in Turkey, which commenced in earnest about the time of the beginnings of World War II and which reached first fruition in 1946 and 1950.

Late Election

The figures in Table 7.1 displaying the percentage of each Assembly that was elected late (at a by-election) are a somewhat different barometer of political change in Turkey. The greatest percentages are found in the Second through the Sixth Assemblies, with the one exception of the Third Assembly. These Assemblies constitute the true heyday of Kemalism. They begin in 1923, when Mustafa Kemal formed the People's Republican Party and proclaimed the Republic. He weeded out the recalcitrant and the reactionary from the First Assembly (as is reflected in the very low reelection rate of 30 per cent for that parliament) and formed a disciplined legislative phalanx of supporters. The core of this body of deputies remained relatively stable for the following fifteen years of Mustafa Kemal's life and carried over into the first parliament after his death, the Sixth Assembly. One common method of introducing into the legislature individuals whom the People's Party leadership decided were helpful to its plans was to secure their election at a by-election if, for one reason or another, their candidacy had not been placed in the general election. The single-party control was such that these by-elections were to a large extent devices for adjusting the composition of the Assembly to the demands of the existing leadership.

With the advent of the multi-party system the percentage of deputies elected at a by-election abruptly decreases. It is difficult to know whether this decrease is due to the characteristics of the multiparty system in general as it operated in Turkey, or whether it emanates from the particular nature of the Menderes-Bayar regime. Certainly it is true that the Democratic Party leaders in the Tenth Assembly (and in the Eleventh Assembly as well) refused to hold by-elections even though nearly a score of vacancies existed and the other parties repeatedly pressed for such contests. Moreover, the percentage of deputies who were elected late would naturally decline with the reduction in resignations and the increase in deputies serving a complete term.

Removal and Rejection of Credentials

After the first few parliaments, when the political dust in Turkey had settled, there was a cessation of outright removals of deputies from parliament. In the initial four Assemblies, fifteen men were removed for one reason or another, ranging from conviction of treason, murder, or felony to nonattendance. Then, excluding the Eighth Assembly, the next five Assemblies saw only four persons removed, and three of the four simply had their election credentials rejected. In the Eighth Assembly four persons were removed, all through the rejection of their election credentials. In more recent multi-party times, partisan use of the verification of credentials by the Assembly seems to have developed. Five of the six rejections after 1946 were of deputies from minority parties, though a hopeful sign is the absence of any rejections at all in the Tenth and Eleventh Assemblies.[4]

Reelection

Three important observations are suggested by examination of the column of Table 7.1 that furnishes the percentage of each Assembly reelected to the following parliament, excluding those who died. First of all, the average reelection rate was high, especially from 1923 to 1946 — the single-party years. Considerable governmental continuity was thus provided, with usually about three fourths of the deputies being retained.

In the second place, we find two glaring exceptions to this general situation of governmental continuity. Less than one third of the First Assembly survived in the Second, and only about one eighth of the Eighth Assembly carried over into the Ninth. The high casualty rate for the First Assembly has already been explained; Mustafa Kemal personally removed its more unreliable, obstreperous, and dissident elements in order to form the cohesive legislative group that was to see the great Kemalist reforms through to completion. The extremely low reelection rate of the Eighth Assembly, on the other hand, reflects the broad defeat of the People's Party's incumbent candidates in the crucial 1950 election, when that party took its historic tumble from power.

The third point to note is that even after the Democratic Party was firmly in control, the reelection rate seems to have become stabilized at a definitely lower level — about 50 per cent, if the use of only two points can mark a trend. The Democrats renominated and reelected fewer of their incumbent deputies than the People's Party had done when it was in control. Naturally, conditions were significantly different, especially in regard to the party system. However, this shifting and change of personnel also typifies the Democratic

---

[4] The deputies removed after the Fourth Assembly were: Muhittin Birgen (Mardin — VI), removed; Nasuhi Erzurumlu (Samsun — VII), cred. rej.; Yavuz Abadan (Eskişehir — VIII), cred. rej.; Zeki Rıza Sporel (Istanbul — VIII), cred. rej.; Burhan Cahit Morkaya (Istanbul — VIII), cred. rej.; Abdürrahman Munip Berkan (Istanbul — VIII), cred. rej.; Sebati Ataman (Zonguldak — IX), cred. rej.; Tahsin Coşkun (Kastamonu — IX), cred. rej. In the last three Assemblies of the First Republic there was also a marked tendency toward partisan use of the threat to remove a deputy's legislative immunity, so as to render him vulnerable to civil and criminal litigation. After 1950, prominent opposition leaders like Kasım Gülek and Osman Bölükbaşı were harassed in this fashion. Unfortunately, it would lead us too far afield to discuss this tactic in the present work. For a list of the fourteen cases up to 1958 in which immunity was actually lifted, see *T.B.M.M. Teşkilatı Esasiye Kanunu ve Dahilî Nizamname, op. cit.* (*Dahili Niz. Notları*, No. 97), pp. 129–130.

Party's top-level operations in other respects, as we shall see. So we must make a mental note of this drop in the reelection rate of deputies in its era of control, and recall it later on.

Prior Parliamentary Experience

The final column of percentages from Table 7.1 gives the proportion of each Assembly that had seen previous parliamentary service. It is only a partial function of the reelection figures, since it includes deputies with previous experience who had interruptions in their legislative careers (were not reelected from the *preceding* Assembly), and it also is affected by the rise in the total size of the Assemblies. One interesting result is that nearly one quarter of the total membership of the First Assembly is known to have had previous experience in one of the Ottoman Assemblies; thus there was a carry-over of valuable experience in the Turkish polity despite the manifest hostility of Kemalism to its Ottoman heritage. Another fact to note is the relative lack of experience found among the Ninth Assembly's deputies, the first Assembly of the Democratic Party era. The question is immediately raised as to how much this inexperience had to do with the sway of the more experienced Democratic Party leadership over the Assembly — a question I am, unfortunately, not able to answer at the present time.

Age

The attention paid to differences in absolute and relative age in Turkish society is noticeably greater than that accorded age differences in America. Within the family, the oldest son and daughter are often addressed by special titles of respect (*ağa bey* and *abla*), rather than by their given names. They frequently wield great power over the rest of the children, with the oldest boy being particularly likely to serve as a parental surrogate. Moreover, even within the most modern social sets of Ankara, Istanbul, and Izmir, young adults, no matter how famous, commonly defer to the aged with the traditional gesture of kissing the elderly individual's hand and then pressing it to their foreheads.

Political examples of the significance of age distinctions in Turkey are easily found. Paul Stirling reports on the village in Kayseri Province where he worked that "... although seniority is not a sufficient condition, it is a necessary condition for the exercise of public authority." [5] Ibrahim Yasa's study of the village of Hasanoğlan, near Ankara, depicts quite clearly the generational cast that village political

---

[5] Stirling, "Social Ranking...," *op. cit.*, p. 37.

disputes were wont to take.⁶ Dankwart Rustow has shown that in the early national struggle, "The age difference between the [cabinet] supporters of the Sultan and of Mustafa Kemal [was] by far the most remarkable contrast between the two groups." The median age of Ottoman ministers was more than seventeen years greater than that of the ministers surrounding Mustafa Kemal. Rustow concludes that "The relative youth of the Anatolian military commanders," in the early days of the revolution, "goes a long way toward explaining their readiness to support new political ideas." ⁷ I have already mentioned the special pitch of Kemalist propaganda and programs toward youth. More recently, high-level political antagonists distinguished in background from their opponents mainly by age differences are to be found in the "Thirty-five" (*otuzbeşler*), who constituted a vital progressive wing within the People's Party in the crucial late 1940's, or in the "Fourteen" (the defeated authoritarian segment of the Committee of National Union, after the coup of May 1960), who differed sharply in age from the older, milder majority group in the military junta.⁸

In short, age still seems frequently to confer a special, traditional prestige in contemporary Turkey — a prestige that is declining but remains residually strong in the villages and even in the cities. For example, Ismet Inönü's crest of snow-white hair contributes significantly to the more respectful treatment he is publicly accorded in the bitter political strife of Turkish campaigns.⁹ On the other hand, along with age there frequently seems to go a conservatism, a religiosity, and a rigidity inimical to the total transformation of society that nationalist leaders want to effect. Consequently, the Kemalists tended to make their appeal to youth and to sacrifice the political leverage that a greater inclusion of older men in their ranks might have given them. Such a dilemma and such a reaction appear to be quite common in the "emerging nations."

Table 7.2 presents information about the average ages and ages

---

⁶ Yasa, *Hasanoğlan, op. cit.*, pp. 156–157. The Village Council, it should be noted, is called the Council of *Elders* (*Ihtiyar Meclisi*).

⁷ Dankwart Rustow, "The Army and the Founding of the Turkish Republic," *op. cit.*, 529–536 and Table I, p. 527. Khadduri finds the same age phenomenon to be rather typical for Middle Eastern military in general: "The elements which showed intense interest in political activities were the younger rather than the older army officers." Majid Khadduri, "The Army Officer: His Role in Middle Eastern Politics," in Fisher (ed.), *Social Forces in the Middle East, op. cit.*, p. 174.

⁸ Also note, for example, the numerous references to age and generational differences by Cevat Dursunoğlu, *op. cit.*, pp. 52, 99, and especially 119, when describing the early revolutionary organizational efforts in Erzurum in 1919–1920.

⁹ For instance, cf. Richard D. Robinson, *Letters, op. cit.*, No. 70-3.

Table 7.2
Average Age and Average Age at First Election of Deputies, by Assembly

| | \multicolumn{10}{c}{Assembly} | | | | | | | | | |
	I	II	III	IV	V	VI	VII	VIII	IX	X
Average Age[a]	43.0	43.2	46.2	48.3	51.8	53.3	54.0	52.8	47.8	46.7
Difference in Average Age from Subsequent Assembly	0.2	3.0	2.1	3.5	1.5	0.7	−1.2	−5.0	−1.1	−0.8
Average Age on First Election	43.0	42.3	43.3	43.4	45.0	46.1	45.9	46.2	45.9	43.9

[a] Age at time of first Assembly meeting.

at first election of the deputies to each of the ten Assemblies studied. The average age of the Turkish deputies has been somewhat younger than that of most national legislators in the West. The average of the mean ages in the ten individual Assemblies is 48.7 years, and in six of the ten Asemblies the average age of the deputies was under 48.8 years. By comparison, the average of the mean ages in the British House of Commons from 1918 through 1935 was 50.1 years. French deputies under the Third Republic averaged about fifty years of age. The median ages in the Canadian Commons from 1921 through 1945 ranged from 50.2 to 52.9. United States Senators in 1945 averaged 58 years of age and in 1949 averaged 56.5. United States Representatives to the Seventy-seventh Congress had an average age of 52 years. The German Bundestag of 1949 averaged 50 years, and the New Zealand parliament of 1938 averaged 55 years. As these scattered figures indicate, most Western national legislators average fifty years of age or over; they are primarily of men of solid middle age.[10]

Comparable data for many emerging nations are lacking. However, existing data suggest that there is a tendency for other non-Western legislators, like the Turkish, to be somewhat younger than their Western counterparts. (Indeed, so are the general populations of these countries.) The Indian Lok Sabha of 1952, for instance, had an average age level of 46.3 years. Members of the same house seem to have been even younger between 1957 and 1961, while the Pakistani legislators serving between 1956 and 1958 appear to have had an age distribution roughly comparable to the Turkish.[11] Repeated observations of this type attest to the tendency of those who would drastically alter the basic structure of a society to rely on relatively young adherents.

[10] J. F. S. Ross, *Parliamentary Representation* (London: Eyre & Spottiswoods, 2nd ed., 1948), p. 32; Mattei Dogan, "Political Ascent in a Class Society: French Deputies 1870–1958," in Dwaine Marvick (ed.), *op. cit.*, p. 61; Norman Ward, *The Canadian House of Commons: Representation* (Toronto: University of Toronto Press, 1950), p. 129; D. Matthews, *U.S. Senators...*, *op. cit.*, p. 56; Madge M. McKinney, "Personnel of the 77th Congress," *American Political Science Review*, XXXVI (February 1942), p. 67; Otto Kircheimer, "The Composition of the German Bundestag, 1950," *Western Political Quarterly*, III, No. 4 (1950), p. 591; L. C. Webb, *Government in New Zealand* (Wellington, 1940), pp. 47–48. It is useful to note that the average ages of the 1928 and 1949 German Bundestags were each 50 years, while that of the 1932 legislature was only 44 years. Gerth cites evidence indicating that the Nazi Party was distinguished by its relative youth. In its transforming (revolutionary) social aims it can be likened to many nationalist movements in emerging nations; Hans H. Gerth, "The Nazi Party: Its Leadership and Composition," *American Journal of Sociology*, XLV, No. 4 (1940), pp. 530–531.

[11] W. H. Morris-Jones, *The Parliament of India* (Philadelphia: University of Pennsylvania Press, 1957), p. 115; Karl von Vorys, "The Legislator in Underdeveloped Countries, " *PROD*, III (November 1959), p. 25, Table III.

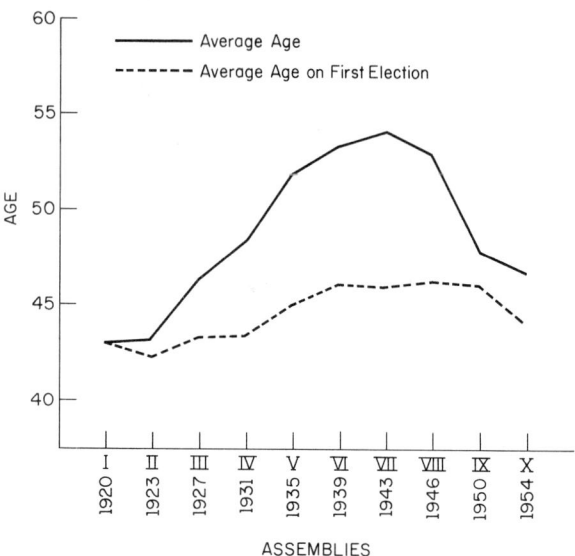

Figure 7.1. Average age and average age on first election, by Assembly

More revealing of the patterns of Turkish politics is the change in average age from Assembly to Assembly (graphically depicted in Figure 7.1). We see a steady and rather smooth rise in average age from the First Assembly right up through the Seventh Assembly — in other words, throughout the single-party period. Then a decline sets in with the Eighth Assembly, the commencement of the multi-party era in Turkey, and accelerates with the accession to power of the Democrats. Though there was some tendency to elect older replacements to the Assembly in the single-party period, the constant rise in average age is very much the product of the aging of the stable Atatürk cohort, which constituted the core of the legislature throughout most of this era. In general, the slope of the average age curve very neatly distinguishes the single-party and multi-party periods.

An interesting way of inspecting these data is to look at the differences in average age between adjacent Assemblies. Within the single-party period, we find the greatest differences between the Second and Third, Third and Fourth, and Fourth and Fifth Assemblies. This, again, reflects the continuity that prevailed in these "Atatürk years." Between the First and Second Assemblies there is a difference of merely 0.2 years in average age, and there was very little carry-over of personnel. Between the Fifth and Sixth Assemblies, the Sixth and Seventh, and the Seventh and Eighth, we also find reduced average age differences. In the Sixth and Seventh Assemblies the single-party regime still operated, but the Atatürk leadership had passed to the hands of Inönü, while new forces in Turkish society were beginning to command recognition. The Eighth Assembly marked the beginning of the multi-party system, in attenuated but nonetheless significant form, even though the People's Party remained in power. With the Ninth Assembly came the biggest age change of all, a *drop* of five years in the average age of the Assembly, reflecting the victory of the Democratic Party and its dominance in the parliament. Then, strangely enough, instead of another *rise* in the average age level of deputies, as the Democratic Party acts to consolidate and stabilize its power, we find a continuing *decline* — though naturally at a reduced rate — in the average age of Turkish deputies. I must add here that the average age of the Eleventh Assembly (not given in the table) was 45.9 years, still *lower* than that of the Tenth.

In these figures, and in others, is reflected the shifting, rather amorphous quality of the Democratic Party leadership as portrayed in the social composition of its parliamentary echelon. The social background evidence suggests the possibility that the device of deliberate fluctuations in personnel and their placement within the highest level of the party was used by the few stable individuals at the top, namely Menderes and Bayar and one or two others, to aid their control over the party and to forestall the rise of opposition within the organization. For one reason or another, most Democratic deputies did not linger long enough in the Assembly, or in positions of leadership, to be able to offer a threat to those at the pinnacle of formal power.

The average age of deputies *on first election* to parliament has fluctuated much less than their actual ages in each session. There was a trend toward choosing older deputies on first election throughout the single-party period, but it was less than the change in actual age.

Marital and Parental Status

When the Democratic Party came to power in the Ninth Assembly, there was an increase in the percentage of married deputies. The figure moved up over 90 per cent for the first time, as revealed in Table 7.3. By itself, the change is quite slight and might easily be overlooked. However, it falls into a pattern deserving attention. Part of the appeal of the Democrats was that they catered to the growing restlessness of local forces in Turkish society. They gave local party units more influence in selecting parliamentary candidates. In policy formation they seemed to put more emphasis on the satisfaction of local demands, and they included in their Assembly delegation more persons typifying local norms and possessing local contacts. Local elements were given the feeling that, for the first time, *they really mattered*. In fact, this rise in local power, capitalized on by the

Table 7.3

MARITAL AND PARENTAL STATUS OF DEPUTIES, BY ASSEMBLY

	I	II	III	IV	V	VI	VII	VIII	IX	X
						ASSEMBLY[c]				
Per Cent Married	?	89%	85%	86%	84%	89%	87%	89%	93%	91%
Per Cent with Children[a]	?	?	91%	90%	87%	90%	90%	92%	92%	90%
Average Number of Children	?	?	2.8	2.8	2.6	2.6	2.5	2.6	2.5	2.4
N (marriage)[b]	—	222	311	338	438	464	486	494	494	536
N (children)[b]	—	—	245	311	393	430	448	464	475	505

[a] The percentage base consists of all married, divorced, or widowed deputies. One intriguing entry in an *Annual* was "Not married [not divorced or widowed], two children."
[b] The total number of deputies for whom information was available.
[c] The information offered for Assemblies prior to the Fifth has been obtained by backward projections from later data. It is felt that such projections are unlikely to be more than two or three percentage points in error. No data are presented for the First and Second Assemblies in some cases because of insufficient coverage. The marital data for Second Assembly members are based upon only 67 per cent returns.

Democrats but internally affecting all parties, is a major issue in contemporary Turkish political life. In the present case, the slight but significant increase in the proportion of married men among the deputies, men evincing the sober-mindedness that local opinion ascribes to those who have assumed marital responsibilities, is part of this general pattern.

The average number of children for all married, divorced, or widowed deputies is also presented in Table 7.3. A mild decline in the size of the families is seen. In light of the rise in age of the deputies from 1920 to 1946, giving them time in which to have had more offspring, and the inclusion of more provincial types under the Democrats (small-town merchants, large-scale farmers, etc.), this decline gains in significance. For example, in the Ninth Assembly one Democratic deputy had fourteen children, one had twelve, and one had eleven — all three deputies being farmers. Up to that time, no deputy had ever had more than nine children. But despite this infusion of a few more prolific rural representatives, the mean number of children per deputy declined.[12] If the deputies can be said to typify the procreative habits of Turkish intellectuals, then perhaps there is hope that a voluntary reduction in the size of families may begin to spread to other portions of the society and reduce the alarmingly high 3 per cent annual rate of population increase, which is giving "empty" Anatolia population pressure pangs for the first time.

Education

Levels of Formal Training

The great importance of educational distinctions in Turkish society and politics was discussed at some length in Chapter 3. Internal inspection of changes in formal education through time in the ten Grand National Assemblies under examination reinforces this estimation. The predominance of university-trained people in the national legislature has remained relatively constant over the years from 1920 to 1957. Approximately three fourths of each Assembly, except the First and possibly the Second, was drawn from the 1 per cent of

[12] This trend is probably better illustrated in the following figures, giving the deputies who had *more than three children* as a percentage of all deputies with children, for the Third through the Tenth Assemblies.

	Assembly							
	III	IV	V	VI	VII	VIII	IX	X
More than Three Children	31%	31%	29%	26%	24%	26%	21%	17%

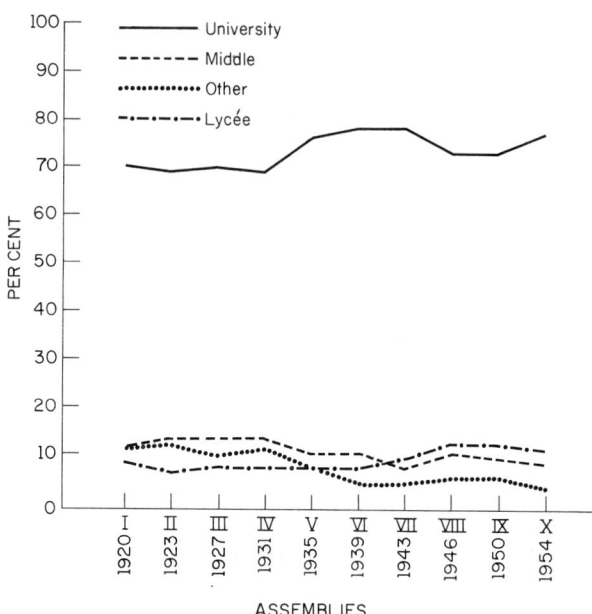

Figure 7.2. Educational levels of deputies, by Assembly

NOTE: The data on the First Assembly are of uncertain reliability because of insufficient coverage. Information regarding education was available for merely one third of that Assembly. Coverage of the Second Assembly was 80 per cent and was more than 99 per cent for all other Assemblies.

In the Eleventh Assembly, elected in 1957, 72 per cent of all deputies had university-level education, 13 per cent had lycée-level training, 8 per cent middle-level, 5 per cent primary-level, and the remainder either private education or *medrese* education (0.5 per cent).

the population that had received some higher education. This is the outstanding finding shown in Figure 7.2.

Certain changes in the Turkish educational system are somewhat wanly reflected in Figure 7.2. The percentage of deputies with a middle-school-level education declined slightly, while the percentage with a lycée-level education increased slightly. As the educational system developed, the basic line of demarcation for being "well educated" was raised from the middle-school level, as described by Webster for the mid-thirties, to the lycée level.[13] The "other" category employed on the graph represents mainly persons who had a private or *medrese* education. Its decline also reflects the growth of the public school system and the abolition of the *medrese* system of religious education.

[13] Cf. Chapter 3, footnote 3.

Foreign Languages

Several of the main currents revealed by the preceding examinations of changes in the age, familial status, and education of Turkish deputies are further illustrated by statistics on the foreign language proficiencies claimed by these men. Table 7.4 shows the percentage of the deputies to each Assembly who claimed to know one, two, three, or four or more foreign languages. It also gives the average number of foreign languages claimed per deputy for each Assembly, the percentage of those knowing a foreign language who knew French, and the same percentage for those who knew a non-Western foreign language.

Once more, the single-party and multi-party periods are clearly distinguished by variations in the social backgrounds of the deputies. In general, the foreign language competence of the deputies declined with the introduction of the multi-party system in the Eighth Assembly. The proportion of deputies who claimed knowledge of *no* foreign language jumps from a fairly stable one in five in the single-party era to roughly one in three after 1946. Similarly, the average number of foreign languages claimed per deputy diminishes from around 1.3 to less than one.

A hint of the approaching change in the social characteristics of Turkish political leadership is to be found in the Seventh Assembly, the last of the single-party Assemblies. As has been remarked in other cases, "the dam leaked before it burst" — small but apparent alterations in the social composition of the Grand National Assembly can be seen, *in retrospect,* to have presaged larger, fundamental changes. The last single-party Assembly, the Seventh, swung in the direction of future changes along nearly every dimension of social background we are considering. This indicates that changes within the People's Party in the directions that later proved to be dominant occurred prior to the opening-up of political life. It is as if the party attempted to incorporate and recognize the newer forces in the Turkish political system by co-opting some individuals representative of these forces — some younger, less experienced, less educated, less linguistically proficient, more local, and more professional and commercial elements — but did so too little and too late.

Although the Eighth Assembly was the first truly multi-party Assembly, and though it differed conspicuously in social background from its predecessors, the People's Party was still in unquestionable command. Its deputies made up the great majority of the Assembly and gave it its essential social-background character. Hence, the changes in that character were, in most instances, changes in the People's Party itself as well as changes produced by the injection into the Assembly of some threescore persons from opposition parties.

178 ANALYSES OF CHANGE

Table 7.4
FOREIGN LANGUAGE CLAIMS OF DEPUTIES, BY ASSEMBLY (PERCENTAGES)

ASSEMBLY	FOREIGN LANGUAGES CLAIMED						AVERAGE NO. OF FOREIGN LANGUAGES	FRENCH[a]	NON-WESTERN[a]	DEPUTY TOTAL
	None	One	Two	Three	Four or More	Unknown				
I	24%	45%	17%	12%	2%	(75%)	1.23	81%	20%	437
II	17	47	22	12	3	(40)	1.36	82	24	333
III	17	48	22	12	2	(23)	1.32	85	22	333
IV	26	41	20	11	2	(3)	1.22	82	21	348
V	22	40	24	10	4	—	1.32	88	17	444
VI	21	43	23	10	3	—	1.30	91	16	470
VII	22	42	24	9	3	—	1.26	92	13	492
VIII	31	38	22	6	2	—	1.09	87	11	499
IX	35	38	18	7	2	—	1.01	84	12	494
X	35	41	16	7	1	—	0.96	78	7	537

[a] Percentage base is all deputies claiming at least one foreign language.

The slight dip in foreign language proficiency of deputies to the Fourth Assembly is largely due to the deliberate inclusion of a few more farmers and merchants in that parliament. This interesting action was seemingly taken in order to absorb, in well-advertised fashion, a symbolic portion of the underlying opposition in the country, which had been aroused by the abortion of the Liberal Party in the preceding year.[14] The important aspect of these anomalous characteristics of the Fourth Assembly, when the social representation of the Assembly was briefly broadened, is that they almost invariably are in the same direction as later major changes in the backgrounds of Turkish deputies. As an examination of party characteristics will suggest even more strongly, there seems to have been early and basic opposition to the dominant Kemalist officers and officials — opposition that is revealed through occasional cracks in the Kemalist front, as in the Fourth Assembly, and that bursts through to power in 1950. It appears to have been an opposition that was latent and growing from the very start of the Grand National Assembly.

The paramount position of French in the foreign linguistic skills of Turkish deputies, especially in the single-party era, is again well portrayed by Table 7.4. Normally, more than four of every five deputies knowing a foreign language knew French. In one sense, the cultural time lag that typifies political leadership in a rapidly changing society is partially evident here. In the last decade or so, English has surpassed French as the most popular Western — and second — language for Turkish youth. However, most of today's deputies were educated in the Atatürk and İnönü periods, when the position of French was only beginning to be challenged. The fact that politicians usually receive their formal education (sometimes their only real chance to obtain certain types of information or skills, such as foreign language proficiency) about twenty years before they become political leaders, and often before they have any conscious thought of entering a political career, can result in a perhaps unavoidable but still lamentable waste of opportunities. In the Tenth Assembly, when Turkey's relations with the United States and the Soviet Union were much more critical than her relations with France, only 30 per cent of her national legislators who knew another language knew English, compared to 78 per cent who knew French. Only three persons, less than 1 per cent, knew Russian. In this Tenth Assembly, however, we do see an incipient change in foreign language knowledge wherein French begins to show a noticeable decline and English an even more acute rise.

Throughout the entire thirty-seven-year period, excluding the First Assembly, for which the figures are unreliable, there was a steady

[14] See Chapter 11.

drop in the percentage of deputies knowing non-Western second languages. This trend continued regardless of the type of party system that prevailed and regardless of which party was in power. It is in a special sense significant, for I shall argue that the Democratic Party, though willing to support a mild religious "revival" (actually, a partial easing of previous restraints rather than a revival), was basically quite modern in its top personnel and quite committed in its own way to a continuation of modernization, even while trying to make political capital out of the religious issue. One small reflection of this general situation is the continuation under Democratic rule of the decline in deputies knowing non-Western languages, even though changes in the school system and curricula explain most of the decline.

Occupation

Scrutiny of the changes in the occupational characteristics of Turkish deputies provides a basic key to the understanding of some other variations in social background that have already been noted. Table 7.5 furnishes the necessary data.

Many highly revealing trends in Turkish politics are reflected in this table. Let us first of all look at each occupation, reading across the table, to ascertain its changes in representation through time. I have put "Law" first this time because of a very pronounced steady rise in the percentage of lawyers in the Grand National Assembly. Between 1920 (or 1923) and 1957, the proportion of deputies from the legal profession doubled, changing from one in eight to one in every four. By the end of the period, the lawyers, who had been the third or fourth largest occupational group in the Assembly, became the largest single group, ten percentage points ahead of the second largest group, trade.

A closer look at the figures reveals that the legal contingent remained quite stable, at around 12 or 13 per cent of the Assembly, for the first six parliaments of the ten being examined, that is, from 1920 to 1943. Then this legal group rose sharply in size in the last single-party Assembly, when the People's Party introduced an enlarged legal element into its ranks. It rose moderately again with the introduction of a multi-party system in the Eighth Assembly, and jumped ahead with a bound when the Democrats came to power in 1950. Here is a rather vivid demonstration of several points previously mentioned. Changes in the character of the People's Party itself in the last years of the single-party era heralded further changes under the multi-party system, which were accelerated when the Democratic Party took over in the Ninth Assembly of 1950. One gains the impression from these data of mounting pressures gradually eroding a structure, which first

Table 7.5
OCCUPATIONS OF DEPUTIES, BY ASSEMBLY (PERCENTAGES)

OCCUPATION	I	II	III	IV	V	VI	VII	VIII	IX	X
Law	13%	12%	12%	13%	12%	13%	17%	19%	26%	27%
Medicine	4	7	8	7	9	11	10	11	13	11
Dent., Pharmacy, & Vet. Med.	1	—	1	1	2	2	2	3	2	2
Engineering	—	1	1	1	1	1	2	2	4	4
Government	23	25	25	20	19	18	19	14	10	9
Military	15	20	19	16	18	16	14	11	6	4
Education	5	9	10	9	11	13	14	11	6	8
Trade	12	7	9	11	10	10	7	13	17	17
Agriculture	6	6	6	10	8	6	7	9	10	10
Banking	1	1	1	1	1	3	2	2	2	2
Religion	17	7	4	3	3	2	1	1	1	1
Journalism	2	4	5	7	5	5	3	3	4	4
Other	2	—	—	—	—	—	1	—	—	1
Total[a]	100%	100%	100%	100%	100%	100%	100%	100%	100%	100%
Unknown	(15%)	(12%)	—	(1%)	—	—	—	—	—	—
Total Number of Deputies	437	333	333	348	444	470	492	499	494	537

[a] Percentages may add to 99 or 101 because of rounding.

shows relatively slight strains and cracks, is shored up, and then succumbs entirely with a startling and resounding crash.

It is most intriguing that as the Turkish parliament became better established, and as it developed a multi-party system more like the well-known national legislatures of the West, it also came to resemble those bodies in the sense that the legal profession became the largest occupational group. Here is a "developing" society whose political elite is in the process of taking on the same occupational hue as that of its models in the West — apparently entirely from natural and internal causes.

Whether we style this the rise of a dominant group of "specialists on persuasion" as the elite becomes more "pluralistic" (a generalization rendered dubious by the data on the journalists and other occupational groups), or whether we restrict ourselves merely to remarking the rise in the percentage of lawyers, we seem to be observing in Turkey, as the polity formally moves toward "democracy," the development of that legal predominance which is so widespread and distinctive a characteristic of modern Western parliaments. And the fact that the development coincides so clearly with the striving toward a viable multi-party system perhaps beckons us to further consideration of a Lasswellian-type hypothesis that stages of political development, if not actual distributions of power, may be marked by regularities in the differential participation in formal politics of distinctive social groups. Certainly the Turkish case lends at least initial support to such a view. Furthermore, it may well show the phenomenon *in process,* so that if the trend and the development continue, there will be an excellent opportunity to look back and try to associate specific social forces with specific degrees of change in representation.

Turning to the second occupational group in the Assembly, we discover that the percentage of medical doctors also rose in the course of the thirty-seven-year period. The rise was less acute than that of the lawyers and more uniform. Similarly, there was an increase in the percentage of dentists, pharmacists, and veterinarians, and in the percentage of engineers, over the ten Assemblies. In recent times, engineering has become the most prestigious vocation in Turkish society, and there appears to be a corresponding upturn in the proportion of engineers in the parliament.

In the official sector of the occupational groupings is the nearly "equal and opposite reaction" to the expansion of the professional delegation just examined. The number of government officials declined from approximately a quarter of the Asembly — the largest single group — to less than 10 per cent. The military contingent dwindled from about 15 or 20 per cent down to a mere 4 per cent, that is, from being second in size only to the governmental group to a three-way tie for seventh place in a twelve-place list! A marked but less acute reduction confronted the educators in the Assembly. All in all, the ranks of officialdom in the Grand National Assembly have been hard hit by the trends of the times in Turkish politics.

Inspection of internal changes — a search for watersheds within the over-all picture — leads us once more to the same dividing points: that between the First and Second Assemblies, that between the Seventh and Eighth, and that between the Eighth and Ninth. Alterations that commence in the Eighth Assembly (1946) are amplified in the Ninth (1950) with the advent of Menderes and Bayar. The result is the incontestable loss of its leading position in the parliament by the "official" group.

Trade and agriculture, especially the former, resemble the professions in their increased strength in the Grand National Assembly in modern, multi-party times in Turkey. Along with the provincial lawyer, the small-town merchant or tradesman seems to typify the changed Assemblies of the Democratic Party's decade of control, just as the official and the officer typified the Kemalist epoch. The First Assembly had a sizable delegation of merchants — some 12 per cent. However, this delegation was reduced more than any other, save that of the clerics, in Atatürk's Second Assembly. A little later, in the Fourth Assembly, when the representational base of parliament was extended, the merchant group reached its largest size in the single-party (People's Party) period. Finally, of course, in the Eighth Assembly and with the accession of the Democrats, the trading contingent became the second largest group in the legislature. It is as if this deliberately slighted group builds up strength — and umbrage — as a result of the modernizing and democratizing successes of the Kemalists and ultimately moves into a commanding position, with its professional allies, as the Democratic Party.

The journalistic group in the ten Assemblies remained quite constant in size, varying around a mean of some 4 per cent regardless of the nature of the party system or which party was in power. This situation may reflect the care taken by all parties to develop a small but essential band of reliable press supporters, part of which they included in their parliamentary delegations.

In the religious group, on the other hand, we find the greatest fluctuation of all. The clerics plummeted from a position as the second largest element in the First Assembly, with at least 17 per cent of all deputies, to being the smallest of all occupational groups in the Tenth Assembly, with a scant 1 per cent of all deputies. Most of this loss was suffered between the First and Second Assemblies. At that time, Mustafa Kemal pruned essentially two main occupational groups — the *hocas* and the merchants. He pruned the clerical group apparently to kill it, except for the few "tame *hocas*" discussed previously. The political strength and character of the merchants, however, was seemingly such that he could not and did not need to cut them down as severely, though his attitude is portrayed in their nearly 50 per cent reduction in relative size.

The over-all situation in regard to the basic occupational groupings is dramatically sketched in Figure 7.3. The trends are so clear that no additional comments seem necessary.

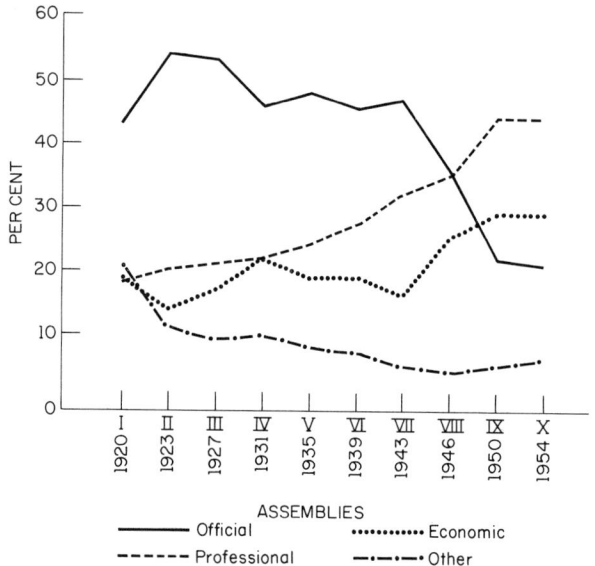

Figure 7.3. Broad occupational classification of deputies, by Assembly

REGIONALISM AND LOCALISM

Though we know that the aggregate group of deputies came in significant proportions from all regions of Turkey, we must now inspect the birthplaces of the deputies to each Assembly lest we overlook important but countervailing internal variations not shown in the aggregate picture. Ideally, along with other information about the deputies, I should offer at least the statistics giving the birthplace distribution of the total Turkish population at the time of each Assembly, which would permit an estimation of how "representative" each Assembly was.

Unhappily, the necessary birthplace figures are not available for the years prior to 1950. But there is information from a number of censuses on the size of the total population of each of the main agricultural regions of the country. We also know that the degree of

BIRTHPLACES OF DEPUTIES, BY REGION (PERCENTAGES)[a]

ASSEMBLY	Region[b]									FOREIGN-BORN	UNKNOWN	TOTAL[a]
	North Central 1	Aegean 2	Marmara 3	Mediterranean 4	North-east 5	South-east 6	Black Sea 7	East Central 8	South Central 9			
I	10	11	13	7	7	12	12	11	7	11	(33)	100
II	10	14	20	6	4	8	10	7	6	13	(17)	100
III	8 (15)	17 (17)	24 (14)	5 (8)	3 (6)	4 (7)	11 (15)	6 (9)	6 (9)	16	—	100
IV	11	16	22	5	3	3	11	5	7	15	(2)	100
V	9 (14)	13 (17)	28 (14)	5 (8)	3 (6)	3 (7)	8 (15)	5 (10)	5 (9)	21	—	100
VI	8 (14)	16 (17)	29 (14)	8 (9)	4 (7)	2 (7)	8 (15)	4 (9)	6 (9)	14	—	100
VII	8	14	33	7	5	2	8	6	5	13	—	100
VIII	10 (14)	13 (17)	24 (14)	9 (10)	6 (7)	6 (7)	9 (15)	8 (9)	6 (9)	9	—	100
IX	10 (15)	12 (16)	21 (14)	9 (10)	5 (7)	7 (7)	13 (14)	8 (9)	7 (8)	9	—	100
X	10 (15)	12 (16)	16 (14)	9 (10)	7 (7)	8 (7)	14 (14)	9 (9)	8 (8)	8	—	100

[a] May not add to 100 because of rounding. Unknowns excluded in computing percentages.
[b] For an enumeration of the provinces in the regions, see Appendix B. For their geographical location, see the map in the frontispiece.

geographical mobility in Turkey, particularly before the end of the Second World War, was quite small. In other words, the great bulk of the people resident in a region had been born there (over 90 per cent); consequently, the regional residential percentages are not very different from the regional birthplace percentages.[15] For background, then, I shall furnish the percentage of the Turkish population residing in each of the nine regions. These are given for selected years in parentheses below the deputies' birthplace percentages in the rows of Table 7.6.

Table 7.6 adds another dimension to the consistent pattern that has emerged from the preceding investigations. No glaring discrepancies existed between the distribution of the population in the country as a whole and the distribution of the deputies according to their birthplaces. Thus the Assembly can be generally said to have been reasonably representative of the nation in a geographical sense. However, in the entire thirty-seven years there was only one region that was consistently overrepresented. And that region, the Marmara (including Istanbul), was appreciably overrepresented in every Assembly between the First and the Tenth. Its overrepresentation came at the expense of nearly all other regions, though the Aegean Region and, to a lesser extent, the Mediterranean fared less poorly than Eastern and Central Anatolia.

The disproportionate inclusion of deputies born in the Marmara area — overwhelmingly from the city of Istanbul — seems to have been strongest in the single-party period.[16] In the First Assembly,

---

[15] For example, the comparison between the residential and birthplace percentages for the nine regions in the year 1950 was as follows:

	REGION										
	1	2	3	4	5	6	7	8	9	Foreign	(Istanbul)
Percentage of Turkish Population Born in the Region	14	15	10	9	7	7	15	9	10	4	(3.4)
Percentage of Turkish Population Resident in the Region	15	16	14	10	7	7	14	9	8	—	(5.6)

SOURCES: Compiled from *1955 Genel Nüfus Sayımı*; *Nüfus Sayımları 1927–1950*; *İstatistik Yıllığı 1951*.

[16] The percentages of deputies born in the *province* of Istanbul itself were as follows:

	ASSEMBLY									
	I	II	III	IV	V	VI	VII	VIII	IX	X
Deputies	8%	13%	17%	16%	24%	22%	26%	15%	15%	11%
(Turkish population)			(6%)		(6%)	(6%)		(6%)	(6%)	

before the assumption of firm control by Mustafa Kemal, the number of deputies born in the Marmara-Istanbul Region corresponded quite closely to the population of that region. Then, in the Second Assembly, the beginning of the one-party period, the proportion of *Istanbullular* (those born in Istanbul) rose sharply. This proportion continued to rise essentially throughout the remainder of the People's Party era. The peak was reached in the Seventh Assembly, when one deputy out of every three had been born in the Marmara-Istanbul Region — one in every four in Istanbul itself.

As before, the situation begins to change with the introduction of the multi-party system in the Eighth Assembly. The percentage of *Istanbullular* drops almost ten percentage points, and this trend is visibly continued under the Democratic Party regime. By the Ninth and Tenth Assemblies the distribution of the deputies according to birthplace matched rather closely the distribution of the entire Turkish population, and slightly more closely the distribution of that population at the time of birth of the average deputy. The more cosmopolitan Istanbul elite had lost its exaggerated representation, while the more locally oriented areas of Anatolia had obtained representation commensurate with their numbers.

The same phenomenon is reflected in the column of Table 7.6 that gives the percentage of deputies born outside the present borders of the Turkish Republic. However, in this instance the decline begins with the end of the Atatürk years in the Fifth Assembly. All in all, we discover once again, from another vantage point, evidence of the same tendencies toward what has been called "localism" — the decline of the national elite and the growth in power of provincial Anatolia.

It is now time to look directly at the incidence of localism, defined technically as the percentage of deputies born in the area they represented in the Assembly, hence ostensibly with their roots in their specific constituencies. This information is presented initially in Figure 7.4, which gives for each Assembly the percentage of deputies who were born in the same province they represented in the parliament. Throughout the years from 1920 to 1957 there were from fifty-seven to seventy-two provinces that comprised the set of constituencies of all deputies in the Assembly.

The U-shaped pattern in the figure clearly shows the basic trend in modern Turkish politics toward increased representation of local forces and the rising power of provincial Anatolia as contrasted to the more urban, cosmopolitan, nationalistic Kemalist elite. A high degree of localism is apparent in the First Assembly, with some 62 per cent of all deputies for whom I have information being born in the province represented in parliament. This percentage declined slightly in the Second Assembly, and then more rapidly in each of the following

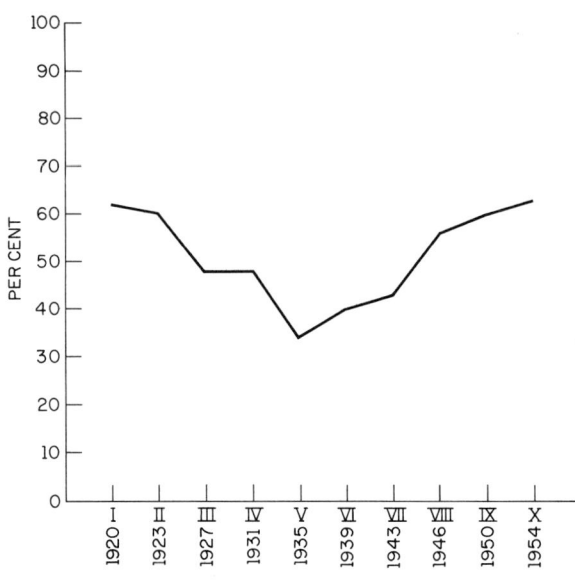

Figure 7.4. Percentage of deputies born in constituency represented, by Assembly

Assemblies of the Atatürk era until it reached a low of 34 per cent in the Fifth and final Atatürk Assembly (Atatürk died in 1938). From the First through the Fifth Assemblies the percentage of locally born deputies was cut almost in half. Note again that the trend was temporarily halted in the anomalous Fourth Assembly.

With the death of Atatürk and the accession of Inönü there began a rise in localism, slight at first in the Sixth and Seventh Assemblies, but mounting markedly with the first election of a multi-party Assembly in 1946. This trend continued under the Democrats so that a high point of localism was reached in the Tenth and last Assembly of the period. Actually, in the Eleventh Assembly the percentage of localism climbed still further to 66 per cent.

The slope of this localism curve rather neatly depicts another aspect of the fundamental movement of recent Turkish politics. Its negative sign from the First Assembly through the Fifth portrays the development and rise of the Kemalist movement, a modernizing elite resting heavily on officers and bureaucrats who were primarily national, nationalistic, and political in their social outlook. After the death of Atatürk the always latent opposition gathers enough strength to compel its reluctant recognition, and then finally breaks openly into power with the introduction of the multi-party system in 1946 and the victory of the Democrats in 1950. The change is reflected in the rising localism curve following the Fifth Assembly. The dominant composition of the top political leadership now has become legal and commercial in occupation, local in origin, and localistic and economic in social outlook.

One more set of figures will serve to complete this picture. In Table 7.7 the local birth statistics are broken down by region to show the percentage of the deputies, representing provinces within the nine agricultural regions, who were born in the *region* represented.

Two outstanding facts emerge from this table, both indicated by the rectangles enclosing certain figures. First of all, we see that from the Second Assembly through the Seventh — that is, throughout the entire single-party period — both the Aegean and the Marmara Regions were above the national average figure in the percentage of deputies representing the region who were born within the region. Secondly, and correspondingly, we observe that the eastern regions regularly fell below the national figure from the Third through the Seventh Asemblies. The same eastern regions were significantly above the national figure in the First and Tenth Assemblies, while the Aegean and Marmara Regions were below that figure in the same Assemblies. The resemblance between the First (pre-Kemalist) Assembly and the Ninth and Tenth (Democratic Party) Assemblies is once again very striking.

We are dealing here, of course, with the percentage of each regional delegation to parliament that was born within the region represented. The absolute size of the regional delegation is irrelevant. Consequently, the Kemalist overrepresentation of the Marmara Region and the relatively strong representation of the Aegean Region do not affect the figures, which seem to display a relative tendency during the single-party era to include more locally born deputies in the Aegean and Marmara Regions and less in the eastern regions. Exactly the opposite tendency was a feature of the First Assembly as well as the Ninth and Tenth Assemblies.

These data immediately bring to mind the broad regional differences in relative modernization that are so pronounced in Turkey. In general, these differences are that the western portions of the nation, especially the littoral areas, are the most developed, and that development progressively declines as one moves eastward and inland. The standards used in making this evaluation are: urbanization, literacy, a low birth rate, the production of cash crops, the degree of occupational specialization, the incidence of female education, and the incidence of manufacturing establishments employing more than ten persons.[17]

---

[17] For a graphic portrayal of this general situation consult the series of statistical maps presented in George and Barbara Helling, *Rural Turkey: A New Socio-Statistical Appraisal* (Istanbul: Fakülteler Matbaası, 1958).

Table 7.7
Deputies Born in Region of Constituency Represented (Percentages)[a]

Assembly	North Central 1	Aegean 2	Marmara 3	Mediterranean 4	North-east 5	South-east 6	Black Sea 7	East Central 8	South Central 9	Unknown	Total for All Deputies[b]
I	62	65	60	52	**83**	**81**	**82**	**84**	**81**	(34)	72
II	55	**71**	**67**	59	54	**75**	58	**68**	**73**	(17)	64
III	49	**68**	**72**	45	29	50	51	50	**58**	—	55
IV	**62**	**62**	**70**	**58**	30	43	51	45	56	(1)	56
V	**42**	**53**	**67**	41	24	23	33	32	36	—	41
VI	44	**62**	**68**	**56**	32	24	39	34	47	—	47
VII	43	**58**	**72**	**51**	41	26	35	**49**	45	—	49
VIII	62	64	**77**	**80**	**67**	**65**	**49**	**69**	**73**	—	66
IX	66	53	63	**84**	58	**81**	67	**75**	**71**	—	68
X	64	51	57	**82**	**81**	**88**	**81**	**79**	**74**	—	71

[a] The foreign-born have been excluded.
[b] The total column gives the percentage of all deputies born in Turkey who were born in the region including the province represented. All regional percentages exceeding this total percentage are in boldface type.

The People's Party in the single-party period, and especially in the Atatürk years, apparently allocated local representation disproportionately to the more modern areas of the country, the Aegean and Marmara Regions, while damping with special care the local representation of the more backward East. The central regions, intermediate in development, are also intermediate in local representation. We see also, in other intermediate cases, that the Black Sea Region, which was the most modern in the East, usually had the highest degree of local representation in that area during the single-party period, and that the Mediterranean Region, ranking third in modernity, especially in more recent times, also ranks third in terms of the incidence of local representation in the single-party period. However, it must be recalled that we are examining the *relative* distribution of the *existing degree* of localism in each Assembly, having ignored variations in the over-all level of localism and in the sizes of the regional contingents in parliament.

In general, combining the findings of Tables 7.6 and 7.7 with my conception of the ebb and flow of recent Turkish politics produces the impression that *the parties have tended to grant a higher degree of local representation to the delegations from those areas of which they were unsure.* This may seem paradoxical in the case of the People's Party, for it both overrepresented the western portions of the country and accorded those areas the highest degree of local representation. However, the East was so impossible from the Kemalist viewpoint that it was rigidly controlled; it was so unsure that it was *made* sure. Political life was closed. The West, on the other hand, was more modern and more powerful; thus political life could be and needed to be relatively more open. At the same time, the West was the bailiwick of the lawyers, merchants, and commercial elements who opposed Kemalist methods while desiring modernization according to their own lights. Hence, the Kemalists grudgingly accepted some influence from local forces in this area led by these lawyers and merchants. They were sufficiently modern so as not to appear to jeopardize the entire Kemalist program, while at the same time they were sufficiently powerful and dissatisfied so as to compel at least limited recognition.

Over several decades, the People's Party's control of the East seems gradually to have become a position of real party strength in that region. Politics in the area is even today frequently a matter of negotiation between great *ağas* and tribal chiefs on one side and party representatives on the other.[18] Perhaps the recollection of the People's

[18] Revealing illustrations of this situation are to be found in the articles of *Cumhuriyet* of September 25, 1961, describing the electoral campaign in the eastern regions.

Party's power remains strong, perhaps the erection of an opposition organization to contest entrenched strength is doubly difficult in this fairly backward section, or perhaps the principles of the party were effectively inculcated in some crucial segments of the population. Whatever the reason, recent election statistics indicate that the East has become an area of relative strength for the People's Party and relative weakness for the Democratic Party and its successor, the Justice Party. Conversely, the West and the littoral areas have generally become areas of strength for the Democrats and the Justice Party.

In accordance with my hypothesis, the Democratic Ninth and Tenth Assemblies feature a comparatively high degree of local representation in the eastern delegations, where the Democratic Party was relatively weak, and a lower degree in the Aegean and Marmara Regions, the Democratic bastions. The greater the uncertainty concerning the political support of the area, the higher the incidence of parliamentary localism. In fact, this relationship seems capable of extension to the party system as a whole. As the parties have moved into a situation of true interparty competition — a situation of increased need for popular support and simultaneous uncertainty regarding that support — there has been an acute rise in localism within all the political parties of Turkey, including the People's Party, to whose philosophy and leadership this localism was originally rather repugnant.

WOMEN DEPUTIES

The compression of political time in the emerging nations is well illustrated by the role of women in these polities. In the West the struggle for political rights for all adult males usually far antedated, in any significant sense, the struggle for female political rights. In Turkey, on the other hand, female suffrage and officeholding quite early entered into the composite ideal of political modernization held by Turkish progressives. From the pre–World War I activities and meetings of the *Türk Ocağı* organization, the nationalist movement in Turkey implicitly undertook a commitment to accord Turkish women formal political rights. Though there had been some discussion of the topic throughout the twenties and frequent rumors of imminent legislative action, it was in the early thirties (the time of the anomalous Fourth Asembly!) that the official bequest of voting and candidacy rights was made. Women first brightened the dark corridors of the Grand National Assembly building in Ankara in the Fifth Assembly of 1935. There were eighteen of them, some 4.1 per cent of the total number of deputies.

Although the experience of Turkey *differs* from that of the West in that female political emancipation came much earlier, relatively, in the political development of the country, the Turkish experience with female national legislators strongly *resembles* that of the West in another respect. After the initial flurry, the incidence of female deputies declined appreciably, so that in recent times their representation in the parliament can only be called token. In the Sixth Assembly women comprised 3.4 per cent of the total number of deputies, 3.3 per cent in the Seventh Assembly, 2.0 per cent in the Eighth Assembly, 0.6 per cent in the Ninth Assembly, and 0.7 per cent in the Tenth Assembly.[19]

Though the general trend is plainly downward, it seems likely that it may show a partial upswing in the near future. While the political parties have "Women's Arms" of widely varying degrees of activity, Turkish politicians have not yet paid any profound attention to whatever "women's vote" exists in the country. It is probably very small at present. But as the interparty competition for votes increases, as male dominance decreases, and as the communications system of the country develops and the politicians become more adept in using modern campaign methods, it seems likely that they will try to gain the advantage by augmented appeals to female voters. One such appeal is obviously the inclusion of more women candidates among the party's Assembly lists. In this fashion, the proportion of female deputies might well rise somewhat in the near future, particularly under the system of proportional representation of the "Second Republic." However, on the basis of Western experience, which may be becoming increasingly applicable to Turkey if the social background changes being discussed are any criterion, any rise in female representation in the Grand National Assembly would probably be slight.

Summary

The findings regarding the completeness of the deputies' terms of service clearly depicted the Grand National Assembly's consolidation of its position after an uncertain start. Resignations dropped from 16 per cent in the First Assembly to a stable 1 per cent by the end of the Fifth Assembly. There was a concomitant rise in the percentage of each Assembly serving a complete term. Recruitment of new members through by-elections was fairly common in the single-party years. An average of just under 10 per cent of each Assembly from the Second (1923) through the Seventh (1943) was elected in this fashion. In the three Assemblies from 1950 to 1960 (the Ninth, Tenth, and Eleventh), however, under the Democrats, by-elections virtually lapsed.

[19] Eight women, 1.3 per cent of the Eleventh Assembly, were elected in 1957.

The co-optative procedures of the single-party era resulted in considerable continuity in personnel from parliament to parliament. More than two thirds of all incumbents were reelected in each of the six Assemblies from 1927 to 1946. The two great turnovers in Assembly membership occurred in 1923 and in 1950. Less than one third of the members of the obstreperous First Assembly were reelected to the Kemalist-dominated Second Assembly, and only about one eighth of the People's Party–led Eighth Assembly survived the Democratic victory in 1950. After 1950, while the Democrats had overwhelming control over the Assembly, the average carry-over of personnel settled to a lower level. Just about half the incumbents of each of these parliaments (the Ninth and Tenth) moved on to the next.

The Turkish national legislature during the First Republic was slightly younger on the average than comparable Western legislatures. The mean of the average ages for all ten Assemblies was 48.7 years. Changes in these average age figures also revealed the formation and survival of a solid Kemalist legislative phalanx. With the advent of the multi-party system and the Democratic Party, the average age of the deputies dropped in each Assembly from 1946 to 1960. Seemingly, no Democratic phalanx comparable in relative size to the Kemalist was developed. Compared with the average age figures, there was greater stability in the average ages of the deputies *on first election* to the Assembly. These figures ranged about a mean of some forty-four years.

Most of the deputies in each parliament were married, though there was a very slight increase to above 90 per cent under the Democrats. On the other hand, the average number of children of the married deputies declined perceptibly during more recent years.

The one great rock of consistency over the entire span of four decades was that of the continued high educational level of the deputies. Over all ten Assemblies between 70 and 80 per cent of the deputies had always obtained university-level training. The occupational, age, linguistic, cosmopolitan, and other characteristics of these politicians all varied significantly during these momentous years, but the elite educational status of the deputies never wavered. The highly educated still dominate the top formal echelon of Turkish politics, and have done so since the foundation of the Republic.

After World War II and the opening-up of the Turkish political system there was, however, a decline in the foreign language competence of the deputies, even though, at the end of our period, nearly two thirds of them still claimed knowledge of a foreign tongue. There was a particularly precipitous drop in the percentage of deputies claiming knowledge of a non-Western language (largely Arabic and Persian).

In clear contrast to the consistency in educational background over the ten Assemblies, the altered *occupational* composition of the parliaments is probably the most notable discovery of this part of the analysis. Much of the political history of the era is wrapped up in the decline of the officials and the rise of the professional and economic contingents in the Grand National Assembly. The "new man in Turkish politics" is the lawyer and the merchant, replacing the soldier and the bureaucrat at the pinnacle of formal power. Of keenest interest is the association of this change with the advent of the multi-party system, even though the gross change was presaged by milder alterations within the single party itself. As the Turkish political system took on more of the formal *institutional* aspects of Western-type parliamentary democracy, it also came increasingly to resemble the Western polities in the strongly legalistic background of its formally authoritative decision-makers.

By and large, the Assemblies were reasonably representative of the nation in terms of the geographical distribution of the birthplaces of the deputies. The Marmara Region, containing Istanbul, was the only area consistently overrepresented. Next most prominent in this respect was the Aegean Region, containing Izmir. The overrepresentation of the Marmara and Aegean Regions was most acute in the single-party period.

A highly revealing U-shaped curve was found to express the incidence of "localism" among the deputies during the Assemblies of the First Republic. Birth in the constituency represented in parliament started out at a relatively high 62 per cent in the First Assembly, sank progressively to a low of 34 per cent by the time of Atatürk's death in the Fifth Assembly, and then began to rise again. With the beginning of the multi-party system after World War II, the proportion leaped to over half the Assembly locally born, and by 1960 it had climbed to two thirds of the Assembly. Next to the change in occupational background, and certainly allied with it, these two sharp trends in the incidence of "localism" among the deputies stand out as the most significant of the descriptive findings of this portion of the analysis.

I hypothesized a general tendency (1) for rising interparty competition to increase localism and (2) for the political parties to present a higher degree of localism in those areas where the party was most dubious of its strength. The greatest relative incidence of localism during the single-party years was found in the western and littoral regions, while under the Democrats the eastern and interior regions displayed the greatest localism. This finding seems to support the second hypothesis.

A token representation of female deputies entered the Assembly in

1935, making up some 4 per cent of its membership. This small group of females declined relatively in size over the following years until it was apparently stabilized at the minuscule level of about 1 per cent of the total body of deputies.

Two more general findings of this investigation of changes across the ten Assemblies should be noted. The first is that *variations in social background seem to mark off several distinctive subperiods* within the over-all period of thirty-seven years and ten Assemblies. Moreover, these subperiods distinguished by social background variations coincide with alterations in the characteristic political party system of Turkey. Regardless of the causal relationship, the changes and trends in the social backgrounds of the deputies are associated with apparent changes and trends in the style of political life and the nature of the political party system — indeed, with the apparent allocation and distribution of power in the society. The particular subperiods noted were: (1) that of the First Assembly (1920–1923), prior to the establishment of the single-party dominance; (2) the Atatürk era of the Second through Fifth Assemblies (1923–1939), the period of Kemalist control; (3) the İnönü era of the Sixth and Seventh Assemblies (1939–1946), when the stirrings of new forces were first heeded within the continuing single-party framework; (4) the Eighth Assembly (1946–1950), a transitional period in which the multi-party system was introduced even though the People's Party remained in power and in which the accumulated drives produced by the impact of Kemalist success and the Second World War on Turkey were first articulated; and (5) the Democratic Party era of the Ninth and Tenth (and Eleventh) Assemblies (1950–1957, 1960), when, for the first time in the history of the Republic, power was democratically transferred and a new and fundamentally different regime was established. With the overthrow of the Menderes-Bayar regime by the military in 1960, the First Turkish Republic, a definite epoch in the political history of modern Turkey, came to an end.

The second and even more important finding of this survey has been that along a number of related dimensions *the deputies have changed from being primarily a national elite group, oriented toward the tutelary development of the country, to being primarily an assemblage of local politicians, oriented toward more immediate local and political advantages.* The more recent deputies are younger, have less previous legislative experience, and are more likely to be married. Fewer deputies know a foreign language, and those who do are less likely to know French and more likely to know English. Most important of all, the deputies are much more likely to have been born in the constituency they represent; they are more likely to have been born in provincial Anatolia rather than in Istanbul; and they are much more likely to be lawyers, other professional men, or merchants than to be military men or bureaucrats. These trends fall into a relatively consistent pattern that I have termed the increase of "localism" in Turkish political life because I believe that the "new man in Turkish politics" is one who accords main emphasis to local considerations rather than one who accords dominant emphasis to national problems and pressures.

If this evalution is correct, it should help one gain perspective on the key conflict of contemporary Turkish politics. This is the conflict between the residual "national elite," basically found within or in support of the People's Party (perhaps until recently), and the new breed of local politicians, basically found in the Democratic Party and its successor. The local politicos, however, now have obtained strong representation, even dominance, in all political parties. The nationalistic politicians, with strong external support from some of the military, the bureaucracy, and generally from intellectuals, want to continue intensive Turkish development under as strong central surveillance as seems politically feasible. They favor major sacrifices of present consumption and satisfaction so as to invest in creating a stronger industrialized nation in the future. They tend to be, like their Kemalist forebears, intellectual and official in their approach to politics even if they are no longer so overwhelmingly official in vocation. The localists, on the contrary, are much more closely attuned to the immediate satisfaction of local expectations, both as a device for obtaining political power and from conviction. They tend to emphasize local initiative, free enterprise, a relaxation of religious restrictions, and an interpretation of "democracy" that caters to local interests.

The conjunction of the growing power of this "localism" in Turkish politics, the tragic experience of the Menderes-Bayar perversion of the original spirit of the Democratic Party, and the "revolution of rising expectations," which has currently hit vital parts of the society with real force, has produced the beginnings of a severe political crisis.

Many sectors of the populace are now starting to demand a sharp improvement in their standards of living and in the nation's general economic position. At the same time, the reaction to the Menderes-Bayar attempt at political control has resulted in altered political institutions that make very probable the emergence of weak government. There is now a two-house legislature and a President of the Republic elected for a seven-year term, in contrast to the legislative term of four years for the lower house and staggered six-year terms for the members of the upper house. There is a Supreme Court with powers of judicial review of national legislation, and there is a system of proportional representation that, under the present multi-party system, seems likely to produce a series of improbable coalitions.

These institutional arrangements, the recrudescence of bitter intraelite hostility, and the heightened impact of local pressures seem to reduce the chances for strong and effective government at the very time when rising popular expectations are placing even greater demands on that government. With the frustration of popular expectations, unrest and discontent ensue. Among the puissant Turkish military, less constrained by the now fractured tradition of political neutrality, this leads to coups. Among civilians it leads to extremism. However, the Turks have repeatedly demonstrated that they possess the political talent to get themselves out of their apparent difficulties. They have great capacities for self-sacrifice and a broad and deep commitment to their nation and to democracy as they perceive it, which must not be underestimated. One can hope, therefore, that this discouraging prognosis will prove false.

CHAPTER EIGHT

New Deputies and Cohort Groups

IN THE PRECEDING CHAPTER I investigated changes through time in the social backgrounds of *all* deputies to each of the first ten Grand National Assemblies. In this chapter I shall sketch the social characteristics of *newly elected* deputies in each parliament.

THE RECRUITS

Every Assembly had a group of members who carried over from previous Assemblies and a group of recruits. The relative size of the carry-over group as opposed to the newly elected group should be considered in evaluating all the data of this chapter. However, *trends* in recruitment patterns may possibly be more sharply delineated by concentrating on the *new* members introduced into each parliament. If the over-all composition of the Assembly (which was a partially co-optative body) reflects the politics and tactics of the top party leadership, then variations in the social backgrounds of the periodic new recruits to the Assembly may provide magnified insight into the adjustments in policy and tactics made through time by that leadership. The social characteristics of the new members may fluctuate more extremely and more revealingly than those of the Assembly as a whole.

In this chapter I shall also exploit the technique of cohort analysis to illuminate the differential adjustments in Assembly recruitment patterns. Very simply, this consists of taking a group of people (the cohort) distinguished by some common characteristic at a given time (such as age or being initially elected to the same parliament) and tracing subsequent alterations in the character of this cohort by examining it at periodic intervals (say, every five years, or at each successive parliament regardless of elapsed time between parliaments).[1]

Obviously, the gross variations in the social backgrounds of deputies to the ten Assemblies could have been produced by injecting into an Assembly a divergent group of new members, by selectively weeding out the old members, or by doing both. The cohort analysis dealing with progressive alterations in the characteristics of new members as they became old members will complement the analysis of the newly elected deputies and complete this portion of the picture.[2]

Age

Let us first glance at the ages of the appropriate classes of deputies and then proceed to the more important topics of birthplace, localism, education, and occupation. Figure 8.1 contrasts the average ages of all newly elected deputies and all carry-over deputies during the ten Assemblies. The average age of both groups combined into the Assembly as a whole is also given.

Throughout the first four Assemblies the average age of newly elected deputies remained rather constant at around forty-three years, though there was a mild rise in age among the entrants to the Fourth parliament. Then in the Fifth Assembly an older group of deputies was recruited, and there was a sharp increase of about five years in average age up to a level of roughly forty-nine. This plateau continued through the Eighth Assembly, the last of the People's Party's reign, with no appreciable break at the end of the single-party era in the Seventh Assembly similar to that almost unfailingly found before. With the coming of the Democrats, the average age of newly elected deputies began to decline, and by the Tenth Assembly it once more approximated the age level of the First Assembly.

No ready hypothesis comes to mind to explain the sharp rise in the age level of newly elected deputies in the Fifth Assembly and the

[1] For a discussion of cohort analysis as applied to social surveys other than those of demography, see William M. Evan, "Cohort Analysis of Survey Data: A Procedure for Studying Long-term Opinion Change," *Public Opinion Quarterly*, XXIII, No. 1 (Spring 1959), pp. 63–72.

[2] The cohort analysis will be quite brief because it naturally recapitulates most of the findings given in our aggregate profile of all deputies, which was a sort of inverse cohort analysis, using the "election rate" as a main dependent variable. What was necessarily neglected in the aggregate profile was a comparison of the election rate *with the timing of a deputy's initial election*, rather than with his educational level, occupation, etc. Consequently, the cohort analysis of this chapter will focus primarily on the longevity of the various cohorts — in other words, on what their varying reelection performances were.

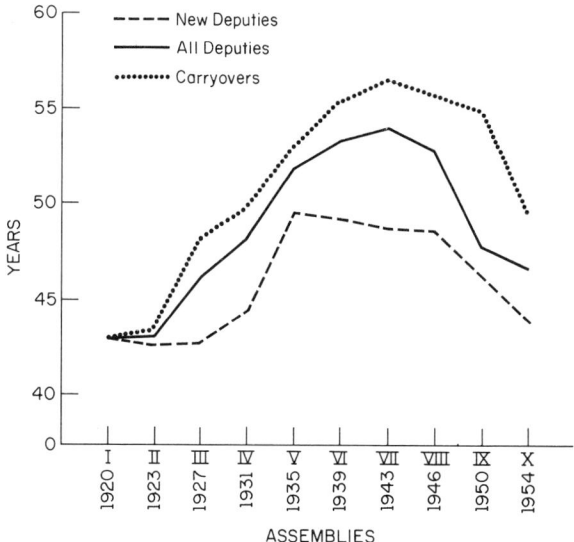

Figure 8.1. Average ages of new deputies, carryover deputies, and all deputies, by Assembly

stability of that level for three subsequent parliaments. With the Kemalists' consolidation of their position and the establishment of the primacy of the Grand National Assembly in Turkish political life, one might expect the parliament to display a rise in the ages of its recruits. As the legislature gained in prestige and power, competition for seats would increase, and a more obvious demonstration of competence would be required to win candidacy — a demonstration that took longer to make. Such a trend among the newly elected deputies would appear to be an expected concomitant of the political stabilization of the regime. But the sharp rise in the Fifth Assembly, which was not a turning point in other instances, and the lack of a break between the Seventh and Eighth Assemblies, which constituted a clear turning point in other instances, seem at variance with the general pattern of change previously discussed.

On the other hand, the average age of the *carry-over* group rises regularly up to the turning point between the Seventh and Eighth Assemblies, after which it declines slightly at first and then more sharply. The rise generally reflects the continuation of many members of this group from one parliament to another in the single-party era. However, the increase in average age of this previously experienced group between the Second and Third Assemblies — some five and one half years — is greater than the life of the Second Assembly, indicating that some of the younger members of the Second Assembly were disproportionately eliminated in the Third.

The age discrepancy between the newly elected and the carry-overs was greatest from the Sixth through the Ninth Assemblies. It would be interesting to learn if this increased age differential was associated with any increase in problems of communication and accommodation between the recruits and the carry-over deputies, but again the relevant data are not available. Surely it is plausible to suspect that the absorption of new members into a legislative body will be more difficult if the new members and the old are markedly different in social background. But it would be enlightening to learn what *types* of social background differences seem to engender the greatest strain in this respect.

Birthplace and Localism

A major motive behind this inspection of the newly elected deputies has been the feeling that changes in the composition of the Assembly would be magnified and highlighted in the changes in social composition of the body of new recruits. The figures on the birthplaces of the newly elected deputies seem to illustrate this idea. Alterations in birthplace patterns previously found for the entire group of deputies (see Table 7.6) are accentuated in the statistics for the newly elected deputies. Table 8.1 gives the percentage of *all* deputies born in a region as well as the percentage of *newly elected* deputies born there. In each column the figure for all deputies is to the left of the dash, and the figure for the newly elected is to the right.

The statistics for the Marmara Region, which includes Istanbul, illustrate the accentuation of differences and trends in the newly elected group. In the Second Assembly, the percentage of newly elected deputies who were born in the Marmara Region was exactly equal to the percentage of the entire Assembly born in that region. However, under the People's Party in the single-party era there was a clear tendency to draw a disproportionate segment of the political leadership from this more modern and developed area. This tendency is shown even more sharply in the data on the newly elected deputies than in the over-all figures for the Assemblies as a whole.

Thus, in the Third Assembly the over-all percentage of deputies born in the Marmara Region was 24 per cent, while 34 per cent of the newly elected had been born in that region. In the anomalous Fourth Assembly the over-all figure drops to 22 per cent, but the figure for the newly elected plummets even further down to some 15 per cent. Returning to the more characteristic pattern, we see that in the Fifth Assembly the over-all level is back up to 28 per cent and the level for the newly elected has risen to an all-time high of 39 per

Table 8.1

REGIONAL BIRTHPLACES OF ALL DEPUTIES AND NEWLY ELECTED DEPUTIES, BY ASSEMBLY (PERCENTAGES)

BIRTHPLACE (Region)	ASSEMBLY									
	I	II	III	IV	V	VI	VII	VIII	IX	X
North Central	10%	10– 7%	8– 6%	11– 17%	9– 7%	8– 9%	8–10%	10–12%	10–10%	10–11%
Aegean	11	14–15	17–16	16– 12	13– 7	16–16	14–13	13–13	12–12	12– 7
Marmara	13	20–20	24–34	22– 15	28–39	29–30	33–31	24–19	21–20	16–13
Mediterranean	7	6– 7	5– 4	5– 9	5– 5	8–11	7– 6	9–10	9– 8	9–10
Northeast	7	4– 7	3– 2	3– 3	3– 1	4– 3	5– 4	6– 5	5– 4	7– 9
Southeast	12	8– 8	4– 0	3– 1	3– 0	2– 2	2– 4	6– 9	7– 6	8– 8
Black Sea	12	10–10	11–12	11– 12	8– 6	8– 8	8– 6	9–10	13–14	14–15
East Central	11	7– 6	6– 5	5– 2	5– 5	4– 3	6– 8	8– 9	8– 8	9–11
South Central	7	6– 7	6– 4	7– 12	5– 3	6– 6	5– 6	6– 7	7– 7	8– 9
Foreign	11	13–13	16–16	15– 18	21–26	14–12	13–12	9– 5	9– 9	8– 7
(Istanbul)	(8)	(13–13)	(17–28)	(16–14)	(24–31)	(22–23)	(26–26)	(15–13)	(15–15)	(11– 9)
(Unknown)	(33)	(17–22)	—	(2– 6)	(0– 1)	—	—	—	—	—
Total per cent[a]	100%	100%	100%	100%	100%	100%	100%	100%	100%	100%
N[b]	360	280–161	333–122	346–101	443–149	470–152	492–163	499–204	494–402	537–271

[a] Percentages may not add to 100 because of rounding. Istanbul and the unknowns are not included in the percentage computations.
[b] Those for whom age was unknown have been excluded (77 in the First Assembly; 53–48 in the Second; 2–2 in the Fourth and 1–1 in the Fifth).

cent, or nearly two of every five new deputies from the Marmara Region. The percentage for all deputies continues to climb in the following Sixth Assembly and even into the Seventh. But the downward trend that affects the over-all figures only in the Eighth Assembly is presaged two parliaments earlier by the Sixth Assembly's drop in the percentage of new deputies born in the Marmara Region. The Seventh Assembly figure remains at the same level, but the decline continues in earnest in the subsequent three Assemblies. (See the graphic representation in Figure 8.2.) It is in this fashion that the group of newly elected deputies seems to be a bellwether for the parliament as a whole.

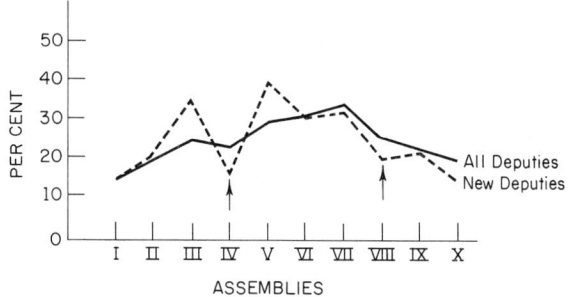

Figure 8.2. Percentages of new deputies and of all deputies born in the Marmara Region, by Assembly

Though the Marmara-Istanbul change is the clearest of all, several other trends in the birthplace patterns of newly elected deputies seem worthy of mention. For instance, under the Kemalists the eastern regions decline even more abruptly in representation among the newly elected than in the parliament as a whole. Part of this phenomenon derives from the fact that the deputies from those regions tended to be installed by the People's Party and to remain in the parliament for some time. Nevertheless, the fact that from 1927 through 1939, over four Assembly elections, only one newly elected deputy was born in the Southeastern Region seems to indicate a slighting of that area in the Kemalist recruitment scheme. A similar observation applies to the North Central Region, though in this case and others the Fourth Assembly situation is anomalous and in the direction of later multiparty and Democratic Party trends. The East Central Region is another case in point as is the Northeastern Region, though in attenuated and belated form.

The differences between the birthplace patterns of the newly elected deputies under the Kemalists and those prevailing under the Democrats are illustrated in Table 8.2, which compares the Fifth Assembly

Table 8.2

COMPARATIVE REGIONAL RECRUITMENT OF NEW MEMBERS
IN THE FIFTH AND TENTH ASSEMBLIES

REGION	PERCENTAGE OF NEWLY ELECTED DEPUTIES FROM REGION COMPARED TO THE PERCENTAGE OF ALL DEPUTIES FROM THE REGION	
	Fifth Assembly	Tenth Assembly
North Central	−	+
Aegean	−	−
Marmara	+	−
Mediterranean	0	+
Northeastern	−	+
Southeastern	−	0
Black Sea	−	+
East Central	0	+
South Central	−	+
Foreign	+	−
(Istanbul)	+	−

+ The percentage of newly elected deputies born in region was higher than percentage of all deputies born in region.
0 The two percentages were equal.
− The percentage of newly elected deputies born in region was lower than percentage of all deputies born in region.

(the last Kemalist legislature) with the Tenth Assembly (the last Democratic Assembly of the period). The table shows the relationship between the percentage of all deputies born in a region and the percentage of the newly elected deputies born in that region. If the newly elected deputies' regional birth percentage is higher, a plus sign is given in the table. If the two percentages are equal, a zero is used, and if the newly elected deputies' percentage is less than that of all deputies, a minus sign is shown. If the relationship of the newly elected deputies to the over-all group reflects the emphases in regional recruitment placed by the parliamentary leaders of the time (in this case the Kemalists versus the Democrats), then the table should permit us crudely to contrast these emphases — to see whether they resembled each other or differed appreciably.[3]

[3] It is true, of course, that the Fifth Assembly was essentially a "nominated" or "co-opted" Assembly, while the Tenth was freely elected. Hence, the electoral system and the choices of the voters intervened in one situation much more than in another. Can we, therefore, take the newly elected of the Tenth Assembly as reflective of the Democratic Party's regional recruitment emphases?

The relative domination of the election and the Assembly by the Democratic Party suggests that the comparison is permissible. At the time of the election,

So construed, Table 8.2 reveals the important social background differences between the Kemalist leadership under Atatürk and İnönü and the Democratic Party leadership under Menderes and Bayar. The Kemalists in the Fifth Assembly tended disproportionately to introduce new members born in the Marmara-Istanbul Region or of foreign birth into the parliament, while the Democrats of the Tenth Assembly tended to introduce deputies born in the Eastern and Central Regions. Note the clear regional tendency toward opposition in the special signs displayed in Table 8.2. In only one instance out of eleven are the signs the same. In seven instances they are diametrically opposite.

Localism

The data on "localism," that is, the percentage of deputies born in the *province* they represented in parliament, also display the newly elected group as a body in which the basic trends in the deputies' social backgrounds are etched in sharper contrast. Peaks and troughs in the over-all figures are markedly exaggerated in the figures for newly elected deputies, as can be understood from Figure 8.3.

The outstanding points for comparison are the Third, Fourth, Eighth, and Tenth Assemblies. In the Third Assembly the newly elected deputies lead the downward trend in localism, which was a general feature of the Kemalist period. The consistently aberrant Fourth Assembly, on the other hand, in which the Kemalists tried to accommodate some of the opposition currents that had become manifest in the Liberal Party of 1930, moved in the opposite direction in almost all respects, and thus the newly elected to that Assembly were more local than the continuing members. This adjustment was counter to the basic thrust of Kemalism, however, and was abandoned with abandon in the Fifth Assembly, after the apparent crisis had passed.

With Atatürk's death a seeming retrenchment set in. Changes in the types of the deputies recruited were not encouraged in the remaining two single-party parliaments. New deputies did not differ from the carry-overs in degree of localism, and the over-all proportion remained steady at about 42 per cent born in their constituencies.

In the Eighth Assembly, the commencement of the multi-party

---

of the 272 newly elected deputies 242 were Democrats. In the Assembly as a whole, 490 out of 535 were Democrats. Thus, the Democratic nominees were overwhelmingly elected with scant change in their lists by the electorate. It can be argued that the D.P.'s slates were prepared with an eye to electoral success, whereas the Kemalist lists were not. This does not conflict at all with our point, however, which is that the regional recruitment emphases of the two regimes were quite different. Part of the difference seems to have been due to political tactics and the character of the party system, and part was due to differences in basic policy.

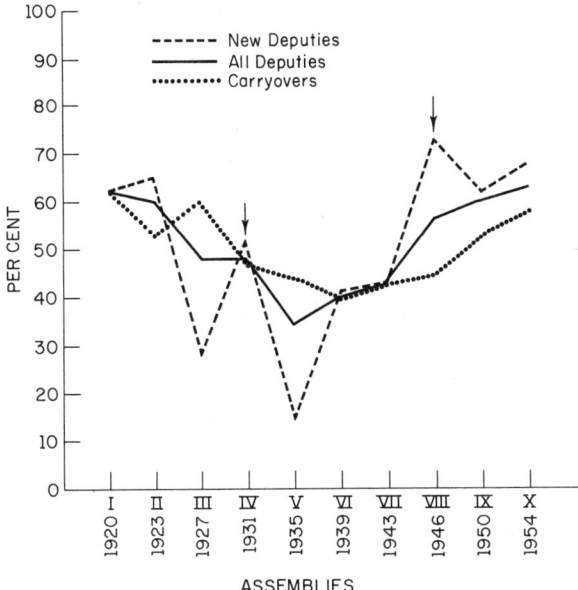

Figure 8.3. Percentages of new deputies, carryover deputies, and all deputies born in the province represented, by Assembly

period, the legislature as a whole experienced an acute rise in localism, particularly in the new recruits. Another brief leveling-off occurred in the Ninth Assembly, but the upward trend continued in the Tenth (and Eleventh) Assembly and was still paced by the newly elected deputies.[4]

[4] The greater localism of the newly elected in recent years may be due to a tendency for deputies to get elected *for the first time* from their home (birth) provinces and then, once established in party politics, to switch to another constituency. But the data on the percentage of deputies first elected to a given parliament and then reelected to the subsequent parliament and who represented the same constituency on both occasions do not support such a view. As the following figures show, very little constituency switching has been done, though fully in keeping with the general thesis I have presented, the incidence of switching was very slightly greater in the single-party era. If the influence of local forces in Turkish politics is growing as I have suggested, constituency switching will probably decrease to an even lower level in the future.

	ASSEMBLY IN WHICH FIRST ELECTED									
	I	II	III	IV	V	VI	VII	VIII	IX	X
Percentage of Deputies Reelected Representing Same Constituency in the Next Assembly	69	91	76	88	88	90	75	89	88	91

Education

Inspection of the changes in social background of all deputies from parliament to parliament shows that with a few minor exceptions the educational profile remained rather constant through time. It was the one consistent characteristic in a general pattern of change. Like the comparable statistics for the over-all group, the stability of the educational figures for newly elected deputies, in contrast to the variability of the other data, is quite pronounced. In other words, when the over-all profile varies, the profile for the newly elected varies more extremely in the same direction; but when the over-all profile does not vary, the newly elected deputies' profile also remains stable, giving further evidence of the regular relationship between the characteristics of the two groups.

As shown in Table 8.3, the resemblance between the Fourth Assembly and the initial Assembly of the multi-party period, the Eighth, is again striking. As a whole, however, these data on education are not appreciably different from those of Figure 7.2, and the comments made in Chapter 7 are also applicable here.

Table 8.3

EDUCATIONAL LEVELS OF NEWLY ELECTED DEPUTIES, BY ASSEMBLY (PERCENTAGES)[a]

EDUCATIONAL LEVEL	ASSEMBLY									
	I	II	III	IV	V	VI	VII	VIII	IX	X
University	70	72	76	**64**	82	74	73	**62**	74	74
Lycée	8	5	9	10	8	13	15	17	12	14
Middle	11	12	12	12	7	12	9	16	9	8
Primary	—	—	—	13	—	—	—	3	2	3
Private	6	5	4	1	2	1	3	1	2	1
Medrese	1	6	1	—	1	—	—	—	1	—
Unknown	(63)	(19)	—	(2)	(1)	—	—	—	—	—

[a] The data for the First Assembly are highly unreliable since the education of two thirds of the deputies is unknown. In particular, the incidence of *medrese* education and of those without any education at all would undoubtedly be significantly larger. Percentages may not add to 100 because of rounding. The figures for the Fourth and Eighth Assemblies are emphasized again to stress their similarity.

Occupation

When we turn to an analysis of the occupational backgrounds of the newly elected deputies, the highlighting of general trends through changes in the composition of the new recruits is once more apparent. The importance of official elements in the Kemalist era and the decline of these officials together with the rise of the professionals and merchants under the multi-party system are accentuated. The details are given in Table 8.4 and should be compared with Table 7.5 and Figure 7.3.

For most of the occupational categories, variations in representation in the over-all group of deputies were amplified in the variations among the newly elected. The differences between the two groups were not as pronounced among the professionals as they were among the other occupational groups. The rise in the proportion of professionals among the newly elected led the rise in professionals in the Assembly as a whole, but the difference between the two percentages never exceeded ten percentage points (the maximum in the Seventh Assembly) and normally was in the neighborhood of five percentage points. The increased incidence of members of the "free professions" was perhaps the most prominent occupational trend over the entire period, but the change seems to have resulted as much from selective deletion of old members as from selective recruitment of the new.

More acute differences can be found by examining the official occupations. For example, in the deviant Fourth Assembly the percentage of officials in the parliament as a whole dropped from 53 per cent to 46 per cent. But the percentage of deputies with an official occupational background among the newly elected deputies to the Fourth Assembly, compared to the Third, dropped from 57 per cent to 23 per cent. The percentage of officials among the newly elected to the Fourth Assembly was exactly half that of the Assembly as a whole — 23 per cent compared to 46 per cent. In the Eighth Assembly, while 36 per cent of the entire Assembly had official occupational backgrounds, only 23 per cent of the newly elected to that Assembly had such backgrounds.

Scrutiny of specific occupations within the official group strengthens the perception of this trend. From the Third to the Fourth Assembly the proportion of bureaucrats dropped from 25 to 20 per cent for all deputies, but dropped from 23 to a mere 7 per cent for the newly elected. The representation of the military provides an even clearer case. From the Third to the Fourth Assembly the over-all military representation declined from 19 to 16 per cent, while military personnel among the newly elected dropped from 16 to 8 per cent. By the Eighth Assembly the military men among the newly elected numbered a scant 3 per cent. In every Assembly from the Sixth through the Tenth, inclusive, the percentage of military men among the newly elected was less than the percentage in the parliament as a whole.

The figures for the economic contingent show a rise in representation among the newly elected as sharp as the decline of the officials. In particular, the rise of the merchant group is as steep as the decline

Table 8.4

OCCUPATIONS OF NEWLY ELECTED DEPUTIES, BY ASSEMBLY (PERCENTAGES)[a]

OCCUPATION	I	II	III	IV	V	VI	VII	VIII	IX	X
Government	23	23	23	7	15	12	14	12	10	10
Military	15	19	23	8	18	12	9	3	5	5
Education	5	9	11	8	15	14	15	7	6	8
(Official)	**(43)**	**(52)**	**(57)**	**(23)**	**(47)**	**(38)**	**(38)**	**(23)**	**(21)**	**(23)**
Law	13	16	9	17	9	13	24	21	26	26
Medicine	4	6	7	5	14	13	12	10	13	8
Dent., Pharm., & Vet. Med.	1	—	2	2	5	3	2	4	2	2
Engineering	—	2	2	4	1	2	4	3	4	5
(Professional)	**(18)**	**(25)**	**(20)**	**(28)**	**(29)**	**(30)**	**(42)**	**(42)**	**(46)**	**(41)**
Trade	12	6	9	20	10	15	5	22	17	19
Agriculture	6	5	7	21	8	7	8	12	9	11
Banking	1	1	2	—	3	3	3	2	2	2
(Economic)	**(19)**	**(12)**	**(17)**	**(41)**	**(21)**	**(25)**	**(16)**	**(40)**	**(28)**	**(32)**
Religion	17	7	2	—	—	—	—	—	1	—
Journalism	2	5	5	7	1	6	3	3	4	3
Other	2	—	—	—	1	1	1	—	—	1
Unknown	(15)	(18)	—	(2)	(1)	—	—	—	—	—

[a] Totals may not add to 100 because of rounding. Unknowns were excluded in computing percentages.

of the military. Picking the same Assemblies for comparison, we see that from the Third to the Fourth Assembly the over-all rise in the mercantile group was from 9 to 11 per cent while the rise in merchants among the newly elected to each parliament was from 9 to 20 per cent. In the Fourth Assembly, the relative size of the merchant group among the newly elected was about double the size of that group in the parliament as a whole — 20 per cent compared to 11 per cent. And once more in the Eighth Assembly the representation of the merchants in the parliament as a whole was 13 per cent, while their representation among the newly elected was 22 per cent.

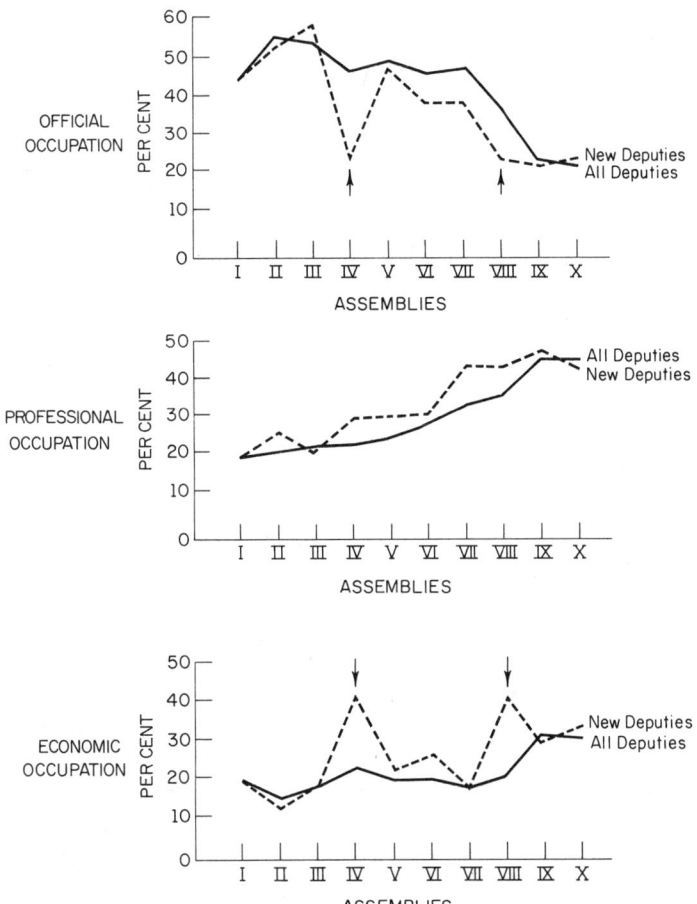

Figure 8.4. Occupational distributions of new deputies and all deputies, by Assembly

A graphic depiction of the broad occupational changes is presented in Figure 8.4. Note there again the similar "peaking" in the Fourth and Eighth Assemblies, particularly for the official and economic groups. This repeated finding is interesting on at least two counts.

First of all, it suggests, along with many other data from this study, that *the opposition to the Kemalists which erupted in the post–World War II period had been smoldering for a long time.* It flared up in 1930 under the abortive Liberal Party. To ease the pain of that induced abortion, the Fourth Assembly, which was elected in 1931, was to a certain extent "opened up," and social elements that were being increasingly deleted from the parliament were momentarily replenished, especially the more locally oriented mercantile and laboring groups.

With the coming of the multi-party system the same elements that were accorded an ephemeral recognition in the Fourth Assembly emerge as the distinctively different components of the new political alignment. As a matter of fact, this latent opposition to the Kemalists can be traced back to the First Assembly, which was *pre*-Kemalist in many respects.

The second observation prompted by these data on the relative similarity between the Fourth and Eighth Assemblies is that *the Kemalists were at least partially aware of the social nature of their opposition* — if one can judge this from the character of the redressive action they took in the Fourth Assembly. They apparently perceived temporary tactical utility in the incorporation of more local merchants and laborers in the Assembly, though the situation regarding the professionals is far less clear. The earlier and later excision of these types from the Assembly thus appears even more to have been a deliberate and self-conscious strategy. The social nature of the political battle lines seems to have been at least partly appreciated quite early in the struggle.

Cohort Analysis

Each group of newly elected deputies who entered the parliament in the same Assembly can be considered a cohort. At periodic intervals the differential changes in its composition can be examined as it proceeds through its parliamentary life. Rather than using arbitrary periods of *chronological time* for an interval, such as every five years, I shall use *parliamentary time* and reexamine the group's composition at each successive new parliament, regardless of elapsed time. In general, the findings will of course parallel those presented through the use of the "election rate" in the aggregate profile of all 2,210 men ever elected deputy to any of the first ten Grand National Assemblies. Rather than repeat those findings, I shall state here that the cohort analysis essentially (and necessarily) produced the same broad results, and I shall thus concentrate on items of information produced by the cohort analysis that amplify and deepen the aggregate profile previously sketched.[5]

Which groups of newly elected deputies, if any, lasted a relatively long time in the legislature and which had relatively short tenures? We know what sorts of people, in social background terms, lasted longest. But what was the situation with regard to time of entrance into parliament rather than with regard to social background? Has there been any trend among the cohorts in this respect? Do any cohorts seem to have been especially favored?[6]

The relevant data are presented from two different points of view in Tables 8.5 and 8.6. Table 8.5 gives the percentage of the original

Table 8.5

COHORT ANALYSIS: PERCENTAGE OF COHORT REMAINING AT SUCCESSIVE ASSEMBLIES

ASSEMBLY OF FIRST ELECTION	ASSEMBLY INTERVALS (Percentage remaining after N Assemblies)									COHORT'S ORIGINAL NUMBER
	1	2	3	4	5	6	7	8	9	
I	28	19	16	16	14	9	8	2	1	437
II	62	47	42	35	29	19	2	—		209
III	61	58	42	34	19	2	—			122
IV	65	38	27	15	6	3				101
V	64	46	26	3	3					149
VI	60	32	7	4						152
VII	59	7	—							163
VIII	22	11								204
IX	55									402
X	a									271

a As stated above, 51 per cent were actually reelected to the Eleventh Assembly; but my investigation stops with the Tenth Assembly, and therefore this entry is blank.

[5] The main difference between the aggregate profile results and those of the cohort analysis was that the official occupational recruitment preference largely disappeared in the multi-party era. The aggregate profile was dominated by the single-party situation since 60 per cent of the total group of deputies were from that period. The intellectual and local criteria continued in force, however, as the present findings suggest.

[6] Ideally, other factors than time of entry into the Assembly should be controlled in this analysis. I have not done so because the numbers quickly get so small as to preclude reliability. Conclusions must therefore be more tentative.

cohort remaining at each successive Assembly. In other words, the Assembly at which a cohort was first elected is indicated on the vertical stub of the table. The horizontal stub indicates the percentage of the original group left after one parliament, after two parliaments, and so on, up to nine. Note that there is an appreciable "ceiling effect" here — a varying upper limit for the length of each cohort's service. Since there were only ten Assemblies in the period of investigation, no cohort could exceed nine reelections. Moreover, this limit was reduced by one Assembly for each successive cohort until the entering cohort of the Tenth Assembly had, for us, no possibility of a longer term. (Actually, 51 per cent of those who first entered in the Tenth Assembly were reelected to the Eleventh and last Assembly of the "First Republic.") Table 8.5, however, is arranged so as to facilitate comparison between cohorts regardless of the ceiling effect. It indicates what percentage of each cohort remained after one parliament, after two, etc. The ceiling simply acts to reduce by one the number of possible figures for each successive cohort and to limit the number of possible comparisons at longer and longer intervals. Nevertheless, comparisons between all cohorts for whom information is given in the same columns of Table 8.5 are eminently suitable, and such comparisons will be made.

Even casual inspection of the column of Table 8.5 indicating the percentage of each cohort returning after one Assembly again reveals the characteristic unity of the single-party era. From the Second through the Seventh Assemblies the percentage of each cohort returning remains close to 60 per cent. Cohort II, the first completely

Table 8.6

RANK ORDERINGS OF THE PERCENTAGES OF EACH COHORT
REMAINING AT SUCCESSIVE ASSEMBLIES

ASSEMBLY OF FIRST ELECTION	ASSEMBLY INTERVALS								
	1	2	3	4	5	6	7	8	9
I	8	6	5	3	3	2	1	1	1
II	3	2	1.5	1	1	1	2	2	
III	4	1	1.5	2	2	4	3		
IV	1	4	3	4	4	3			
V	2	3	4	6	5				
VI	5	5	6	5					
VII	6	8	7						
VIII	9	7							
IX	7								
X									

Kemalist group, has in general the longest service of all the cohorts.

One way of making these relationships clear is to assign a rank order to all the cohorts within each interval, the highest percentage ranking first, and so on. This produces the results depicted in Table 8.6.

For a total comparison between cohorts, with adjustment for differences in the varying upper limits of possible service and the varying sizes of the rank orders, we can express each cohort's rank in each interval as a decimal (e.g., in the fourth interval Cohort I ranked third of six, thus scoring .5).[7] If we average all the decimal scores so obtained for each cohort, we get the length-of-service, or longevity, ordering of the cohorts shown in Table 8.7. The lower the score, the higher the average ranking of the cohort.

Table 8.7

AVERAGE LONGEVITY RANKINGS OF ALL COHORTS

COHORT	SCORE
II	.39
III	.50
IV	.55
V	.63
I	.64
VI	.72
IX	.78
VII	.89
VIII	.94

[7] While this procedure has the advantage of straightforwardness and simplicity, it is not without built-in bias. It assumes, for instance, that ranking second on a four-place list is equivalent somehow to ranking fourth on an eight-place list. More questionably, it assumes that ranking second on a three-place list is equivalent to ranking fourth on a six-place list. Similarly, the top rank would decline in significance (increase in score) as the size of the list decreased, dwindling in significance (rising in score) from .11 in a nine-place list to .50 in a two-place list and being equivalent to being last on a one-place list (1.00). From some points of view these results seem desirable; from other viewpoints they seem undesirable. In the present case, however, the results obtained from using other procedures, such as averaging the absolute rank scores, hardly vary at all from the above procedure (adjacent Cohorts I and V switch positions, and Cohorts IX and VII tie instead of being seventh and eighth, respectively). Since the main bias is to increase the scores of those cohorts with the highest upper limits on longevity (i.e., Cohorts I, II, III, IV, as opposed to later cohorts), and since the finding is that these cohorts nevertheless have the lowest scores — the highest longevity ranking — I feel justified in utilizing the procedure. Its bias runs counter to my finding and argument.

Ordered in this fashion, the outstanding but hardly surprising finding of our analysis is that *the cohorts entering parliament in the Kemalist era had by far the greatest durability.* Most long-lived of all was the group that entered in the Second Assembly when Mustafa Kemal created the basic legislative phalanx that was to carry through the great Atatürk reforms. After the Kemalist cohorts, the group in the First Assembly, including a sizable Kemalist nucleus that survived, is the next most durable. Below it in average longevity rank come the İnönü cohorts of the Sixth and Seventh Assemblies, and then the Democratic and multi-party cohorts (except for the intervening Cohort VII).

Another way of looking at the longevity of these cohort groups is to utilize a concept analogous to that which is used in physics of the "half life" of radioactive materials. I shall speak of the "quarter life" and "tenth life" of a cohort and mean by these expressions, respectively, the number of "Assembly intervals" (say, 2.4 Assemblies or 4.7 Assemblies) that had passed when exactly one fourth or one tenth of the original cohort was left in the parliament.[8] Figure 8.5 presents

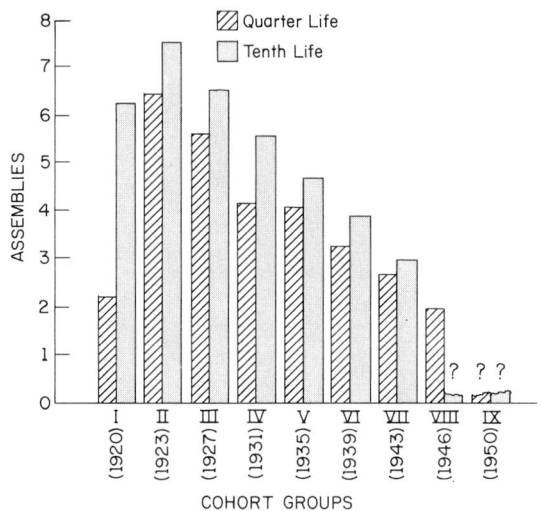

Figure 8.5. "Quarter life" and "tenth life" of cohort groups, by Assembly intervals and date of entry into the deputyship

[8] Since a cohort could decline past either of these points and then increase beyond them again, it is theoretically possible, but unlikely, to have more than one "quarter life" or "tenth life" figure. However, such a situation did not in fact occur. The "Assembly interval" statistics given were computed by interpolation.

this information. Note again that these "quarter life" and "tenth life" calculations are independent of any ceiling effect. Figure 8.5 suggests a regular decline in cohort longevity after the First Assembly. But these indices by nature and by design strongly reflect such factors as the wholesale elimination of People's Party deputies that occurred in 1950.

The obvious general import of these findings is essentially the same as that already obtained using other methods. The Kemalist cohorts display markedly greater longevity than all others. Cohort I has an intermediate rank in terms of its "quarter life" but contained a small core group that lasted extremely long in the Grand National Assembly — a fact partially reflected in its relatively long "tenth life." As of the end of the Tenth Assembly in 1957, Cohort VIII had not yet reached its "tenth life," and Cohort IX had reached neither its "quarter" nor its "tenth life" — hence the question marks above their entries in the figure.

Localism

One matter of particular interest, in view of the importance of the growth of localism in the more recent Assemblies, was whether the cohorts tended to become more or less "local" from parliament to parliament — that is, whether a greater or smaller percentage of their members were born in the constituencies they represented.

Plausible initial hypotheses could be formed to suggest either development. It could be argued that once elected the deputy became less dependent on local support for reelection. He became a better-connected member of his political party and might be expected to switch his constituency to some place more convenient, if he so desired. Similarly, those deputies without the local connection, once they had fought and won an election and had become known as the deputy from province X, might have been more likely to secure reelection. They usually already possessed the characteristics of education and occupation that counted most heavily in national political circles, and they had now achieved a new local base as well. But one could, on the contrary, contend that those *with* the local birth tie would be more likely to endure in parliament because their base of support in the local community would be less fickle than other forms of support and because the political party, under a single- or a multi-party system, still depended heavily on local support for its strength. It could more easily find men with other characteristics than men who could command this local allegiance and consequent local power.

The cohort data on "localism" are furnished in Table 8.8. I have indicated for each successive Assembly interval the percentage of the cohort that was born in the constituency represented in parliament.

Table 8.8

COHORT ANALYSIS: PERCENTAGE BORN IN CONSTITUENCY REPRESENTED, BY ASSEMBLY INTERVALS

COHORT	ASSEMBLY INTERVALS									
	0	1	2	3	4	5	6	7	8	9
I	62	53	57	60	57	69	68	68	13	20
II	65	62	56	53	53	57	65	40	100	
III	28	24	24	29	38	30	0	4		
IV	52	39	39	56	67	17	—			
V	35	18	24	38	50	50				
VI	41	36	46	36	17					
VII	43	57	50	—						
VIII	73	73	83							
IX	62	57								
X	68									

In the column headed 0 is the percentage "locally" born of each cohort at the time of its first election — that is, when *no* Assemblies had passed since its entry into parliament.

These data should be compared with those of Table 8.5, which show the percentage of each cohort remaining at each Assembly interval. It is clear that by the time of the Ninth and Tenth Assemblies the absolute number of deputies left from almost all earlier cohorts was extremely small. This means that figures along the outer diagonals of the table — the diagonals running from lower left to upper right and pertaining to the Ninth and Tenth Assemblies — will be quite unreliable for at least the first seven cohorts.

Though striking trends are absent in Table 8.8, two observations seem warranted. First of all, *there appears to be tendency for "localism" to decline in the initial reelection of the cohort.* In seven out of nine cases, the incidence of "localism" after one Assembly is less than the incidence of "localism" at the inception of the cohort: column 1 is less than column 0 ($p = 0.18$, two-tailed binomial test). It may well be that once obtaining election, the nonlocal group is in the short run preferred. Once having achieved the status of an official deputy from a province, the nonlocal politician is able to develop the local contacts and influence requisite in many cases for reelection. Or it may be that once in parliament his other qualities are sufficiently displayed so that room is made for him despite his lack of local support.

The second observation prompted by Table 8.8 seems to support the latter suggestion. There is a tendency toward an increase in the "localism" of the cohort after about two to four Assemblies have passed — an increase that usually more than offsets the first interval decline. In other words, *those members of the cohort who become really entrenched in parliament are disproportionately likely to have been born in the constituency represented.*

This is hardly a novel report concerning a Western-type, freely elected legislature. But it is revealing of the underlying, yet very real, partial and controlled responsiveness of the single-party Assemblies of the Kemalist "dictatorship." While the hegemony of the national elite in the Kemalist movement was unmistakable, the Kemalist leaders apparently recognized the dormant but great power of local forces in Turkish politics and co-opted a sufficient portion of local leadership to ensure relative local quiescence. After Mustafa Kemal's death, however, these local pressures grew more rapidly than the desire or ability of the People's Party to absorb them, with the result that they erupted so violently in the open election of 1950 that the party was blown from power. Even today, the People's Party is internally adjusting to the belatedly recognized alterations in Turkish society that it largely wrought.

Continuity in Constituency Represented

Another intriguing question to be answered by the cohort analysis was whether there was a tendency for those deputies who were reelected each time increasingly to represent the same constituency they represented in the preceding parliament. I suspected that the answer would be "yes," but the answer has turned out to be "no." No visible trend emerges in any direction.

Table 8.9 provides the precise information. The percentages given are those of the deputies from each cohort who were reelected *and* who represented the same constituency they represented in the immediately preceding Assembly as compared to the total reelected group. Thus, column 1 gives the percentage of each returned cohort, after the passage of one Assembly from the Assembly of initial election, that represented the same constituency as in the previous parliament. The diagonals running from the lower left to the upper right of the table separate the nine Assemblies (Second through Tenth) from one another. The diagonal farthest to the right is that of the Tenth Assembly; the diagonal farthest to the left including only the 69 per cent is that of the Second Assembly. It says that 69 per cent of the cohort elected in the First Assembly *and reelected to the Second* represented the same constituency in the Second Assembly.

Examined either for trends in the cohorts as they "age" or for characteristics that distinguish the nine Assemblies along the drawn diagonals, these data seem not to present any clear pattern. All per-

220   ANALYSES OF CHANGE

Table 8.9

COHORT ANALYSIS: PERCENTAGE REPRESENTING SAME CONSTITUENCY AS IN IMMEDIATELY PRECEDING ASSEMBLY, BY ASSEMBLY INTERVALS[a]

COHORT	ASSEMBLY INTERVALS								
	1	2	3	4	5	6	7	8	9
I	69	85	92	80	86	95	82	50	60
II	91	85	74	82	84	77	60	100	
III	76	93	96	93	70	50	—		
IV	88	95	93	93	17	67			
V	88	90	82	50	50				
VI	90	81	55	50					
VII	75	83	—						
VIII	89	87							
IX	88								
X	(91)								

[a] The previous caveat about the unreliability of the last two (Ninth and Tenth Assembly) figures for Cohorts I through VII, inclusive, again applies.

centages increase in the Sixth Assembly, and all but one, which remains constant, decrease in the Eighth Assembly, reflecting a degree of relative constancy in the former and relative fluidity in the latter. But, other than that, the table appears to show no significant pattern among the cohorts in regard to presence or absence of relative stability in constituency represented. However, the percentages as a whole are quite high — most of them over eighty, portraying a great deal of constituency stability among the deputies over the years. Constituency switching, though done, was not the rule.

Education

The cohort analysis of the deputies' educations will again show the importance of education brought out in the study of "election rates." Table 8.10 gives the percentage of each cohort with university-level education, utilizing the same presentational procedure as in the previous tables.

In seven out of nine cases the cohort had a greater percentage of members with university education in its first *re*election than it had in

Table 8.10

COHORT ANALYSIS: PERCENTAGE WITH UNIVERSITY-LEVEL
EDUCATION, BY ASSEMBLY INTERVALS[a]

COHORT	ASSEMBLY INTERVALS									
	0	1	2	3	4	5	6	7	8	9
I	70	64	57	60	60	66	65	74	75	60
II	69	72	74	78	74	74	83	80	100	
III	76	80	82	84	83	91	100	—		
IV	64	70	82	78	73	100	100			
V	82	89	91	85	75	100				
VI	74	86	86	91	83					
VII	73	80	75	—						
VIII	62	61	74							
IX	74	79								
X	(74)									

[a] The figures in the last two diagonals from lower left to upper right are unreliable for Cohorts I through VII.

its initial election. The exceptions are characteristically Cohorts I and VIII. With one slight exception, for all four of the main Kemalist cohorts (II through V) the lowest university-level educational percentage was at the first election of the cohort. Subsequent educational levels were always higher than the initial level. In fact, the same holds true of the Inönü cohorts (VI and VII) and of Cohort IX as well, while Cohort VIII differs slightly from the others in this respect by only two percentage points. We thus encounter from yet another perspective evidence of the importance of education in parliamentary recruitment. More significantly, we have another indication that the importance of education was relatively stable despite the alterations in the party system that so affected other characteristics of the deputies.

Additional Information

The cohort analysis reveals several other anticipated trends, which will not be presented in detail here. For instance, the proportion of deputies first elected at a young age naturally increases in the cohort as time passes. In the Kemalist cohorts (II through V) the percentage of deputies born in the Marmara Region or foreign-born rises at successive Assembly intervals. Cohort II also shows a tendency for deputies born in the Northeastern Region to endure relatively well, and Cohort III shows a trend toward an increased proportion of deputies born in the Aegean Region after about three Assembly intervals. However, with one exception to be cited in the next chapter, the most significant of the findings from the cohort analysis are those already presented.

SUMMARY

In order to obtain deeper insight into changes over time in patterns of recruitment to the Grand National Assembly, we have looked at the deputies newly elected to each parliament and at the deputies organized into cohort groups. Variations in the social backgrounds of the entire group of deputies were usually strongly amplified among the newly elected members. On the whole, the analysis tended to reinforce conclusions about basic trends in Turkish politics that had been drawn from inspection of the over-all differences between Assemblies.

The average age of new deputies was fairly constant at forty-three to forty-four years during the first four Assemblies. In the Fifth Assembly of 1935, however, it jumped to an average of approximately forty-nine. It remained stable at that new level until the Ninth Assembly of 1954, when it began to fall. By the Tenth Assembly (1957) it was down to about forty-four years once more. No compelling reason was discovered for this pattern, which is quite different from the usual timing of social background changes that we have found.

Over-all trends in regional recruitment, as indicated by the distribution of the deputies' birthplaces, were accentuated among the newly elected deputies. In the single-party era, the Marmara-Istanbul area was even more overrepresented among new members than among the parliament as a whole. Later on, the geographical recruitment pattern of the Democratic Party was seen to be almost antipodal to that of the Kemalist People's Party, at least as revealed by a comparison of new deputies to the Fifth and Tenth Assemblies.

The data on "localism," that is, the percentage of deputies born in the province represented in the G.N.A., also display greater and more characteristic variation among the new deputies than among the carry-over deputies or the whole Assembly. On the other hand, the high level of formal education of the deputies remained about as consistent among the newly elected as among the rest of the legislators. It was the one strikingly stable social background characteristic for the subgroup of freshman deputies to each Assembly just as it was for each Assembly as a whole.

Occupationally, the greatest fluctuations among the new deputies occurred in the official and economic ranks. The over-all decline of the officials was anticipated and led by a decline in newly elected deputies from the previously dominant official occupations. An analogous increase in the newly elected group from economic occupations was also found. The professionals, however, increased steadily but gradually throughout the entire period among newly elected deputies.

Across many social background dimensions, the new recruits brought into the Fourth Assembly, to mitigate the death of the Liberal Party and suppression of the currents it unleashed, resembled the new recruits of the Eighth Assembly — the first multi-party Assembly (in which there was also a revamped People's Party).

All in all, the analysis of the newly elected deputies suggests: (1) that this group was indeed a bellwether for future trends; (2) that the sociopolitical upheaval that occurred in Turkey after World War II had been smoldering throughout the preceding two decades; and (3) that the Kemalists were at least partially aware of its social nature and tried on one occasion to damp it through special, anomalous recruitment emphases.

The cohort analysis revealed, to no one's great surprise, that the single-party, Kemalist cohorts of the Second through the Fifth Assemblies were by far the most durable. They were followed in longevity by the survivors of the First Assembly and then by the Inönü and Menderes cohorts. The four Kemalist cohorts each had a "quarter life" of four to six Assemblies (that is, four to six Assemblies elapsed before exactly one fourth of the group originally elected together was left in parliament). The First Assembly cohort had a "quarter life" of about two Assemblies, as did the Eighth Assembly cohort. Cohorts VI and VII of the post-Atatürk, single-party period had "quarter lives" of approximately three Assemblies.

There appeared to be a tendency for the "localism" of the cohort to decline in the initial reelection of its members, but then to increase again, even past the original level, after the passage of from two to four Assemblies.

No visible trend in constituency continuity was found (that is, in a cohort's having a higher or lower percentage through time of members representing the same constituency they previously represented). The elite educational status of the deputies, however, was once again revealed. Better-educated deputies were disproportionately retained in all cohorts for all Assemblies.

CHAPTER NINE

Elites within an Elite: Levels of Formal Leadership

AS A LEGISLATIVE BODY, the Grand National Assembly was divided into a number of specialized permanent committees, each of which normally had officers such as a chairman, vice-chairman, rapporteur, secretary, and, if needed, treasurer. The Assembly as a whole also had a group of officers, including a President, Vice-Presidents, administrative members, and secretaries or clerks. After 1923, the Assembly elected from its own members the President of the Republic, who in turn appointed the Prime Minister and, in consultation with the Prime Minister, the rest of the cabinet — subject, of course, to the approval of the parliament. There were usually about fifteen ministerial posts to be filled. Finally, the political parties had two top-level organs that were wholly or largely composed of deputies: the Central Executive Committee of the party and the Executive Committee of the party's Assembly Group.[1]

The pivotal question of this chapter is whether the various formal levels of political leadership in and about the Assembly differed appreciably from one another in terms of social background and, if so, precisely how they differed. In addition, changes through time in the social composition of Assembly leadership will be compared with the previously described changes in over-all Assembly composition. On the basis of the inferred recruitment criteria, on the basis of the suggested leadership styles of different political regimes in modern Turkey, and on the basis of the standard sociological hypothesis that as the group differs from its larger social environment so the leader-

[1] These posts were discussed in Chapter 1.

ship of the group will differ from the group, one would hypothesize that the leaders within the Assembly would differ from the entire membership in known directions. For instance, top leaders would be disproportionately intellectual and official under Atatürk and disproportionately professional (especially legal) under Menderes and Bayar. The data to be presented will permit us to check this type of historical and sociological hypothesis.

Establishment of Leadership Levels

A panel of nine judges who seemed to be at least as well informed about the history and workings of the Grand National Assembly as any numerically comparable and accessible group was selected. Three main standards governed the selection of the panel: (1) that the members be intimately familiar with the operations of the Assembly and with Turkish politics in general — preferably *professionally* familiar; (2) that the members' familiarity with the Assembly extend far back into the history of that body — ideally, back to 1920; (3) that the members be as diversified in background and outlook as possible within the considerable limitations imposed by conformity to the first two standards. The first two criteria were established to ensure that the panel members had the opportunity, skill, and inclination to make the observations necessary for accurate judgments about the relative power of these offices and committees. The third criterion was designed to minimize the possibility of a uniform bias among the judges that would not be detected in the reliability checks.

The resulting panel of nine judges was composed of three long-time officials of the Secretariat of the Grand National Assembly; three professors of political science at Ankara University (two of whom had also been deputies and members of top-ranking party organs and one of whom had been a cabinet minister); one important and long-term party politician still very active in politics; one American professor distinguished for his detailed knowledge of Turkish political history and contemporary politics; and one younger Turkish political scientist of American training and wide familiarity with contemporary Turkish political and administrative life.

Three major uniform biases were possible among the panel. The first was that its members necessarily were predominantly older men. Only such men would normally have the familiarity with the earlier Assemblies that the rating task demanded. However, two of the panel were middle-aged, and two were relatively young men (in their thirties). A comparison of the ratings of this younger group with those of the five older members revealed no significant differences. The second possible bias was the limited occupational spread. The judges were officials, academics, or professional politicians. Again, internal checks revealed no significant rating differences between these three occupational groups of judges, but no comparison with an outside control group was made, largely because it proved difficult to find such a control group with adequate knowledge of the Assembly. The third possible bias was that the bulk of the panelists were known to be supporters of the Republican People's Party. I feel that no appreciable warping of judgments resulted from this fact, but I cannot offer positive evidence to support that feeling.

The judges were presented with a list of nearly all the major posts of the Assembly and of the political parties and were asked to rate these posts according to their importance. "Importance" was defined in the following fashion: the respondents were instructed to imagine that the *same* individual occupied each of the posts and then to rate the posts according to the relative *influence* of each over the regular activities of the Assembly, including the cabinet.[2] A rating scale ranging from zero to one hundred, similar to that used by teachers in the Turkish school system, was employed because of its familiarity and relative simplicity. The judges gave a rank of one hundred to the office or offices considered most important and graded all other offices accordingly. If offices were felt to be equal in importance, it was possible to give them equal numerical "grades." The judges were also given a separate list of all the permanent committees of the Assembly and were asked to rank these, relative to each other, in a similar fashion. Since the ranges of the ratings were comparable, the scores were not standardized.

---

[2] Readers familiar with the literature on power analysis will realize that the procedure utilized is the "panel" variant of the "attribution" method of locating power wielders. As such, it has all the particular demerits (and, of course, merits) of that technique. Cf., e.g., Robert A. Dahl, "The Concept of Power," *Behavioral Science*, II (1957), pp. 201–215; James G. March, "An Introduction to the Theory and Measurement of Influence," *American Political Science Review*, XLIX (1955), pp. 431–451; Robert E. Agger, "Power Attributions in the Local Community: Theoretical and Research Considerations," *Social Forces*, XXXIV (1956), pp. 322–331; Peter H. Rossi, "Community Decision Making," *Administrative Science Quarterly*, I (1957), pp. 415–443; Raymond Wolfinger, "Reputation and Reality in the Study of 'Community Power,'" *American Sociological Review*, XXV (1960), pp. 636–644.

The present procedure has a further drawback: the question asked is essentially the "general" influence question, which does not clearly specify the *scope* of the relationship. Different posts and committees are probably differentially influential according to the particular issues (actually, types of behavior) involved.

My reason for not specifying various scopes was simply that of practicality. With the "general" question, the instrument was four long pages in length and demanded 160 post ratings and 81 committee ratings. I felt that this degree of complexity was maximal and thus chose to ask the "general" question rather than fail to make other office and time distinctions that seemed more crucial.

Both general knowledge of recent Turkish political history and the analysis of changes through time in the deputies' social backgrounds indicated that there were several distinct "eras" or subperiods within the total thirty-seven-year period under investigation. It seemed highly probable that the relative importance of the various posts and committees would at least have varied between these basic subperiods. In some cases, such as between the First and Second Assemblies, the very framework of formal government had been changed. Accordingly, the judges were asked to make separate ratings for each of four subperiods: (1) the period of the *First Assembly* (1920–1923); (2) the period of the *Atatürk Era* (the Second through the Fifth Assemblies, 1923–1939); (3) the late single-party period, or the *İnönü Era* (the Sixth through the Eighth Assemblies, 1939–1950); and (4) the *Democratic Party Era* (the Ninth and Tenth Assemblies, 1950–1957).[3] Separation of the Eighth Assembly (1946–1950) into a period of its own would have been highly desirable. However, four periods seemed maximal in order to avoid respondent fatigue and instrument formidability.

The agreement between the judges' ratings of these posts and committees was very high. Comparing *each* judge's rank order of all posts for each period with the rank order produced by averaging *all* the judges' scores for each post and ranking the posts accordingly for each period, we get a mean rank order correlation coefficient of .847 with a standard deviation from that mean of .051. The analogous figures for all committees are .783 as the mean rank order correlation coefficient and .045 as the standard deviation from that mean.[4] A detailed description of the agreement between the judges' ratings is given in Appendix C. It suffices to say here that the agreement in judgment seems sufficiently high to produce confidence in the reliability of the ratings.

---

[3] Of course, the Democratic Party Era actually was terminated by the military *coup d'état* of May 27, 1960, and thus includes the Eleventh Assembly, which is outside present coverage in this respect.

[4] Both figures are statistically significant at the .01 level using the minimal N of 20. Of course, there is a degree of contamination in the procedure employed in that the two rank orders were not totally independent of each other. Each judge's rating comprised one ninth of the average rating for all judges with which the individual's ratings were compared. The ideal procedure would have been to compare each judge's ratings separately with every other judge's ratings and to summarize the results of such comparisons. This, however, would have involved computing 288 correlations, and my resources of time, funds, and energy were unequal to that task. Though the compromise procedure employed unfortunately overstates the degree of agreement between the judges, I feel that the agreement is sufficiently great and the bias of the procedure sufficiently slight to justify the compromise.

Ratings of Posts and Committees

The average scores given to the various posts and committees by the group of judges provide interesting insight into some aspects of Turkish political life. I shall briefly discuss those ratings here, taking up the posts for the four periods first and then examining the ratings of the committees.

The First Assembly Period

I have separated the thirty-one posts ranked by the judges into eight echelons, or groups of posts, attempting as much as possible to preserve the "natural" clusterings evident in the array of average scores by making the cutting points generally conform to the greatest numerical differences between adjacent ranks. To facilitate later calculations that use the average scores, I have assigned to each group an index number between zero and ten that roughly corresponds to the tens digit of the average of the group's scores.[5]

Table 9.1

JUDGES' RANKINGS OF TOP POLITICAL POSTS FOR THE PERIOD 1920–1923 [a]

Echelon	Posts	Average Score	Index
1.	President of the G.N.A. (*Divanı Riyaset Reisi*) . . .	100	10
2.	President of Executive Committee of the Defense of Rights of Anatolia and Rumelia Group (*Anadolu ve Rumeli Mudafaai Hukuk Grubu Idare Heyeti Reisi*)	94	
	Chief of the General Staff (*Erkâni Harbiyei Umumiye Reisi*)	93	9
	Chairman of the Council of Ministers (*Icra Vekilleri Heyeti Reisi*)	92	
3.	Minister of National Defense (*Mudafaai Milliye Vekili*)	77	
	Deputy President of the G.N.A. (*Divanı Riyaset Reisisani*)	77	7
	Foreign Minister (*Hariciye Vekili*)	74	
4.	Finance Minister (*Maliye Vekili*)	68	
	First Vice-President of the G.N.A. (*Divanı Riyaset, Birinci Reis Vekili*)	66	
	Minister of the Interior (*Dahiliye Vekili*)	65	6
	Second Vice-President of the G.N.A. (*Divanı Riyaset, Ikinci Reis Vekili*)	64	
	Minister of Justice (*Adliye Vekili*)	63	
5.	Minister of Education (*Maarif Vekili*)	56	5

[5] I have strayed from this procedure only where necessary to avoid fractions.

Echelon	Posts	Average Score	Index
6.	Minister of Religious Law and Pious Foundations (*Seriye ve Evkaf Vekili*)	49	
	Minister of Health and Social Welfare (*Sıhhiye ve Muaveneti İçtimaiye Vekili*)	48	
	Chairman of a Permanent G.N.A. Committee (*Daimi Encümen Reisi*)	47	4
	Minister of Economics (*Iktisat Vekili*)	46	
	Minister of Public Works (*Nafia Vekili*)	45	
7.	Vice-President of the Defense of Rights of Anatolia and Rumelia Group, Executive Committee (*Reis Vekili*)	42	
	Administrative Officer of D.R.A.R.G.E.C. (*Idare Memuru*)	41	
	Treasurer of the D.R.A.R.G.E.C. (*Sandık Emini*)	40	
	Administrative Officer of the G.N.A. (*Riyaset Divanı Idare Memuru*)	40	
	Clerk of the G.N.A. (*Divanı Riyaset Divan Kâtibi*)	38	3
	Vice-Chairman of a Permanent G.N.A. Committee (*Daimi Encümen Reis Vekili*)	38	
	Secretary of the D.R.A.R.G.E.C. (*Kâtip*)	38	
	G.N.A. Section President (*Şübe Reisi*)	38	
	Member of the D.R.A.R.G.E.C. (*Üye*)	37	
	Rapporteur of a Permanent G.N.A. Committee (*Mazbata Muharriri*)	37	
8.	Treasurer of a Permanent G.N.A. Committee (*Murakıp*)	32	
	G.N.A. Section Secretary (*Şübe Kâtibi*)	32	2
	Secretary of a Permanent G.N.A. Committee (*Kâtip*)	27	

a Thirty-one posts are rated. The mean score is 55; the median score is 47, and the range is 73. Average correlation between judges' rank orders and the rank order of the average scores of all judges is .824 with a standard deviation from that mean of .109.

Examining the ratings of the posts of the First Assembly, we see initially that all the judges agreed in placing the President of the Grand National Assembly (formally, the President of the Council of the Presidency of the Grand National Assembly) at the top of the list. Below this "pinnacle post," but also of outstanding importance, are three offices: the President of the Executive Committee of the Defense of Rights of Anatolia and Rumelia Group; the Chief of the General Staff; and the Chairman of the Council of Ministers. These three offices can be taken to represent control over party, military, and government, respectively. This pattern will be repeated in each of the remaining three periods, with the essential modification that the military Chief of Staff retires from direct political participation. One crucial feature is that the same man, Mustafa Kemal, held the two top posts — that of formal head of the state (insofar as there was a state at this time) and head of the only political party. The diminished position of the Prime Minister relative to that of the head of state, here shown in its early form, should also be noted as an important and characteristic deviation from the most common Western pattern.

The third group of posts, containing the Deputy President of the G.N.A. plus the Ministers of National Defense and Foreign Affairs, corresponds to later groupings of the presiding Assembly post with the most important ministries into a third echelon of command. That these most important ministries are, in the First Assembly, those of Defense and Foreign Affairs reflects the position in which the deputies found themselves: they were fighting for their lives while attempting to obtain international recognition for what was in many respects a new nation. Considerations of defense and foreign policy thus loomed uppermost in their minds.

Below these top ministerial and Assembly posts we find, in the fourth echelon, other ministerial and Assembly positions, estimated to be relatively important but a notch below those already named. The fifth echelon is that of the single post of the Ministry of Education, and the sixth consists of the less powerful ministries plus the office of chairman of a permanent committee of the Assembly. At the lowest levels of importance are the secondary positions in the Defense of Rights Group, in the Assembly as a whole, in its branches, and in its permanent committees. Note that secondary party positions generally rank ahead of secondary Assembly positions, which in turn rank ahead of secondary permanent committee positions. This pattern, too, will repeatedly reoccur. Also note the rather wide gulf between the top position in the Defense of Rights Group and the next highest party post, that of Vice-President of the group.

In analyzing these office-power ratings, I shall regularly note the "distance" between offices as shown by their respective scores in different periods. Does this "distance" between the top party post, for example, and the second- and third-level party posts increase or decrease in subsequent periods? In terms of their scores, do the various party offices seem to be rather evenly distributed over the entire range of scores, or is there more concentration at the ends of the scale in some periods than in others? Questions of this type warrant attention, along with questions regarding the relative location in the positional spectrum of a particular office through time.

The Atatürk Era

Table 9.2 shows how the judges rated the top political positions for the Atatürk Era, the apogee of Kemalism. First of all, we see

Table 9.2

Judges' Rankings of Top Political Posts for the Period 1923–1939 [a]

Echelon	Posts	Average Score	Index
1.	President of the Republic (*Cumhurbaşkanı*)	100	10
	General-President of the Republican People's Party (*Cumhuriyet Halk Partisi Genel Başkanı*)	99	
2.	Prime Minister (*Başbakan*)	94	9
3.	General-Secretary of the R.P.P. (*C.H.P. Genel Sekreteri*)	87	8
4.	Minister of the Interior (*Dahiliye Bakanı*)	79	
	Foreign Minister (*Hariciye Bakanı*)	78	
	President of the G.N.A. (*Başkanlık Divanı Başkanı*)	78	
	Finance Minister (*Maliye Bakanı*)	77	
	Leader of the Liberal Republican Party (*Serbest Cumhuriyet Fırkası Lideri*)	77	7
	Minister of National Defense (*Milli Mudafaa Bakanı*)	74	
	R.P.P. Assembly Group Vice-President (*C.H.P. Meclis Grubu Başkan Vekili*)	71	
	Minister of Education (*Maarif Bakanı*)	69	
	Minister of Justice (*Adliye Bakanı*)	68	
5.	General-Secretary of the Liberal Republican Party (*S.C.F. Kâtibi Umumisi*)	64	
	President of the Central Committee of the Progressive Party (*Terakkiperver Fırkası Reisi*)	64	
	Minister of Public Works (*Nafia Bakanı*)	63	6
	Minister of Economics (*Iktisat Bakanı*)	62	
	Minister of Health and Social Welfare (*Sıhhat ve İçtimai Muavenet Bakanı*)	62	
6.	Minister of Agriculture (*Ziraat Bakanı*)	58	
	G.N.A. Permanent Committee Chairman (*Daimi Encümen Reisi*)	58	
	R.P.P. General Executive Committee Member (*C.H.P. Genel Idare Heyeti Üyesi*)	58	
	Progressive Party Central Committee Deputy President (*T.P.F. Reisisani*)	57	5
	Minister of Customs and Monopolies (*Gümruk ve Inhisarlar Bakanı*)	56	
	G.N.A. Vice-President (*Başkanlık Divanı Başkan Vekili*)	55	
	R.P.P. Regional Inspector (*C.H.P. Bölge Mufettişi*)	53	
	Progressive Party Central Committee General Secretary (*T.P.F. Umumi Kâtibi*)	53	

Echelon	Posts	Average Score	Index
7.	R.P.P. Assembly Group Treasurer (*C.H.P. Meclis Grubu Veznedarı*)	51	
	R.P.P. Assembly Group Secretary (*C.H.P. Meclis Grubu Kâtibi*)	50	
	R.P.P. Assembly Group Executive Committee Member (*C.H.P. Meclis Grubu Idare Heyeti Üyesi*)	48	
	G.N.A. Permanent Committee Rapporteur (*Daimi Encümen Sözcüsü*)	46	4
	Liberal Republican Party Central Unit Member (*S.C.F. Merkez Ocak Üyesi*)	45	
	G.N.A. Permanent Committee Vice-Chairman (*Daimi Encümen Başkan Vekili*)	45	
	Progressive Party Central Committee Member (*T.P.F. Heyeti Merkezi Azası*)	42	
	G.N.A. Administrative Officer (*Başkanlık Divanı Idare Üyesi*)	41	
8.	G.N.A. Permanent Committee Treasurer (*Daimi Encümen Veznedarı*)	33	
	G.N.A. Permanent Committee Secretary (*Daimi Encümen Kâtibi*)	33	3
	G.N.A. Clerk (*Başkanlık Divanı Kâtibi*)	32	

[a] Thirty-seven posts are rated. The mean score is 62; the median score is 58, and the range is 68. Average correlation between judges' rank orders and the rank order of the average scores of all judges is .858 with a standard deviation from that mean of .041. The special "Political Undersecretaries" (*Siyasî Müsteşarlar*) of the Fifth Assembly have been ignored.

now two definite aspects to the pinnacle position in Turkish politics: head of state and head of party. After the formation of the People's Party in the fall of 1923, that party's leadership became extremely important. Party and government constituted the twin reins of power — a fact that is reflected in the exalted rating of the chief office of each institution. The formal political impact of Kemal Atatürk can be sensed from the fact that he occupied both of these positions throughout this entire subperiod.

Just below the "pinnacle post," which was the combined formal leadership of state and party, we now find a position that might be labeled "chief lieutenant" or "second-in-command." In the table this station is shown as that of Prime Minister — the formal head of *government* below the head of state. In the Kemalist scheme this position, too, had its direct party counterpart, which, unfortunately, was omitted from the questionnaire and is not shown on the table. This was the Vice-Presidency of the People's Party. And once again both offices were occupied by the same individual — Ismet Inönü — throughout most of the Atatürk Era.

At the third echelon of the formal hierarchy we find the post of General-Secretary of the People's Party. It was at this level that the separation of personnel between government and party began. In fact, the relationship between the General-Secretary of the party and the Minister of the Interior (the highest ministerial office of the fourth echelon and, roughly, the governmental counterpart of the General-Secretary) illustrates the branching characteristic of this structural level. For a short while in the Fifth Assembly the intimate connection between party and governmental administration was legally recognized by making the Minister of the Interior ex-officio the General-Secretary of the party, and the provincial governor (*Vali*) ex-officio the provincial party chairman of his assigned province. However, below this level analogous party and governmental posts were almost always occupied by different persons, just as they were always occupied by the same person above it.[6]

The fourth level of formal power consisted mainly of the most important ministries (Interior, Foreign Affairs, Finance, Defense, Education, and Justice), the President of the Grand National Assembly, and the Vice-Presidents (two) of the Assembly Group of the People's Party. Here also was located the leader of the Liberal Republican Party (Ali Fethi Okyar).

In the fifth echelon we find the ministries of average importance, along with the General-Secretary of the Liberal Party and the President of the Progressive Party. The sixth level features the least important ministries, permanent committee chairmen in the Assembly, the Vice-Presidents of the Assembly, and several mid-range party officers. Finally, the bottom two rungs of the ladder of formal power were occupied, respectively, by low-level party leaders and by the minor officers of the Assembly and its permanent committees.

Several general aspects of this array of offices deserve particular comment. First of all, the relative parliamentary significance of the two short-lived opposition parties, the Progressive Party of 1924 and the Liberal Party of 1930, can perhaps be inferred from the rankings of their comparable offices. In every case the Liberal Party office has been awarded the higher rating. It is also revealing that the influence of the Liberal Party's leader was rated as inferior to the President, Vice-President (our inference), and the General-Secretary of

---

[6] Technically, we should say that the personnel isomorphism of the structures of formal power across the broad scopes of party and governmental affairs was greatest at the highest levels — there was more individual overlap at the top.

the People's Party. Actually, it was placed at the approximate level of that of the Vice-Presidents of the People's Party's Assembly Group. The importance credited to the head of the Progressive Party places him still lower in the firmament, down to the level of the weakest ministerial stars and below an ordinary member of the Central Executive Committee of the People's Party. Moreover, these rankings in their present form take no account of the relative duration of the offices involved. Some flashed very briefly across the political horizon. Later I shall introduce this added time factor, which will reduce further the significance of the opposition party leaders.

The generally ample articulation of the People's Party can be sensed from the data of Table 9.2. There is a full complement of top party offices from the level of the General-President on down. A prominent party post is found at six of the eight hierarchical levels distinguished in the table. The General-President, in the person of Atatürk, was unmistakably the most powerful formal party leader. But there were no large gaps in the ranks below him. The "distance" between adjacent party leaders cannot be called great.

Within the party, as within the Kemalist state, a rather effective "political infrastructure" had been created. While Mustafa Kemal Atatürk lived, and in the earlier years of Ismet Inönü's ascendancy, the predominant flow of influence may have been from the pinnacle post down to the rest of the organization. However, within the party as within the whole society, in recent years the infrastructure has served rather well as a mechanism for the "upward" transmission of certain influences — for what is sometimes called "the articulation of interests." To make a virtue of ambiguity, we might say that the fine articulation found in the party's structure has been one factor in fostering its use as an instrument for the "articulation of interests." A highly developed channel was present, so that the force necessary at least partially to reverse the flow of influence was alone required, rather than the creation of the very channel itself.

Comparison of the highest-ranking ministerial posts with those of the previous subperiod is also interesting. In the 1920–1923 period of the First Assembly, the Defense and Foreign Affairs positions led the ministerial parade. This seemed only natural in light of the major goals of that Assembly. In the Atatürk Era, however, the outstanding ministries in order of rank were: Interior, again Foreign Affairs, but then Finance before Defense. This altered arrangement, too, seems fully in keeping with the concentration on the profound domestic reforms of Kemalism rather than such overriding concern with Turkey's survival and its international relations.

The preceding detailed comments should not obfuscate the impressive general similarity in structure between the posts as arrayed in Table 9.1 for the First Assembly Period and as arrayed in Table 9.2 for the Atatürk Era. In each case we found a "pinnacle post," a "chief lieutenant's post" (actually three of them in the First Assembly), stations for high-level party and ministerial leaders, a brace of middle-level party and ministerial figures, and then low-level ministerial and party leaders mixed in with and followed by minor Assembly and committee officials. Both in the nature and number of echelons and in the allocation of specific offices to particular levels in the overall array of posts, an obvious general similarity of pattern seems to stretch across subperiods.

The Inönü Era

This consistency is etched even more sharply into the figures of Table 9.3, which provides the post rankings for the third period — the late single-party, or Inönü, era. The greater similarity between the Atatürk and Inönü Eras as opposed to their similarity to either the First Assembly Era or the Democratic Party Era seems to be fully in keeping with the previous data and with the broad picture of the fundamental characteristics of these political epochs.

Since the general pattern previously discovered in the First Assembly and Atatürk Eras manifestly prevails in the Inönü Era, there seems little point in recapitulating the detailed examination made for those periods. Instead, I shall point out the few most significant changes in positional arrangement. For instance, if the differences between scores are taken as a guide, the distance between the pinnacle post and both the Prime Ministry and the General-Secretaryship of the People's Party increased. Put epigrammatically, Inönü had no Inönü!

The Foreign Minister moved to the apex of the ministerial pyramid, probably because this was the period including the Second World War and the commencement of the "cold war." The increased salience of economic problems is reflected in the rise of the Finance Minister from third place among ministers to second — a rise that continues in the next period until the Finance Ministry becomes the top cabinet portfolio.

The relative positions of the People's Party and the Democratic Party in the Eighth Assembly are portrayed in the respective scores of their leaders. The Democratic Party leader ranks in influence below the level of the General-Secretary of the People's Party. A further item of interest is the seemingly weaker articulation of the Democratic Party at the highest levels of leadership. There is an appreciable gap between the Democratic Party President and the second-highest Democratic Party office — that of the President of the party's Assembly Group. No Democratic Party offices corresponding to those of Vice-President and General-Secretary of the People's Party are to be found.

The power of the lieutenants relative to that of the leader seems clearly reduced. This fact in conjunction with the accelerated turnover among Democratic deputies as a whole and the relatively great shifting of Democratic ministers seems to reveal a general lack of positional stability within the party that may have contributed to the observed ascendancy of the party leader.

Table 9.3

JUDGES' RANKINGS OF TOP POLITICAL POSTS FOR THE PERIOD 1939–1950 [a]

Echelon	Posts	Average Score	Index
1.	President of the Republic (*Cumhurbaşkanı*)	100	
	R.P.P. General-President (*C.H.P. Genel Başkanı*)	97	10
2.	Prime Minister (*Başbakan*)	91	9
3.	R.P.P. General-Secretary (*C.H.P. Genel Sekreteri*)	82	
	G.N.A. President (*Başkanlık Divanı Başkanı*)	81	
	Foreign Minister (*Dışişleri Bakanı*)	80	
	Finance Minister (*Maliye Bakanı*)	79	8
	Minister of the Interior (*İçişleri Bakanı*)	78	
	Democratic Party President (*D.P. Başkanı*)	78	
4.	Minister of National Defense (*Millî Savunma Bakanı*)	75	
	Minister of Justice (*Adalet Bakanı*)	74	
	Minister of Education (*Millî Eğitim Bakanı*)	73	7
	R.P.P. Assembly Group Vice-President (*C.H.P. Meclis Grubu Başkan Vekili*)	71	
	Ministry of State and Assistant Prime Minister (*Devlet Bakanı ve Başbakan Yardımcısı*)	69	
5.	Minister of Economics (*Ekonomi Bakanı*)	64	
	Minister of Works (*Bayındırlık Bakanı*)	64	
	Minister of Health and Social Welfare (*Sağlık ve Sosyal Yardım Bakanı*)	62	
	Minister of Agriculture (*Tarım Bakanı*)	61	
	Minister of State Enterprises (*İşletmeler Bakanı*)	59	
	Minister of Trade (*Ticaret Bakanı*)	59	
	Minister of Communications (*Ulaştırma Bakanı*)	59	6
	D.P. Assembly Group President (*D.P. Meclis Grubu İdare Kurulu Başkanı*)	59	
	Minister of Labor (*Çalışma Bakanı*)	58	
	Minister of Customs and Monopolies (*Gümrük ve Tekel Bakanı*)	57	
	G.N.A. Vice-President (*Başkanlık Divanı Başkan Vekili*)	57	
	D.P. General Executive Committee Member (*D.P. Genel İdare Kurulu Üyesi*)	57	

Echelon	Posts	Average Score	Index
6.	G.N.A. Permanent Committee Chairman (*Daimî Encümen Başkanı*)	55	
	Minister of State (*Devlet Bakanı*)	54	
	R.P.P. General Executive Committee Member (*C.H.P. Genel Idare Heyeti Üyesi*)	52	
	R.P.P. Assembly Group Treasurer (*C.H.P. Meclis Grubu Veznedarı*)	51	5
	R.P.P. Regional Inspector (*C.H.P. Bölge Müfettişi*)	51	
	D.P. Assembly Group Vice-President (*D.P. Meclis Grubu Başkan Vekili*)	51	
	R.P.P. Assembly Group Secretary (*C.H.P. Meclis Grubu Kâtibi*)	50	
	R.P.P. Assembly Group Executive Committee Member (*C.H.P. Meclis Grubu Idare Heyeti Üyesi*)	48	
	D.P. Assembly Group Treasurer (*D.P. Meclis Grubu Muhasibi*)	48	
7.	G.N.A. Permanent Committee Rapporteur (*Daimî Encümen Sözcüsü*)	44	
	G.N.A. Administrative Officer (*Başkanlık Divanı Idare Üyesi*)	44	
	D.P. Assembly Group Secretary (*D.P. Meclis Grubu Kâtibi*)	43	4
	G.N.A. Permanent Committee Vice-Chairman (*Daimî Encümen Başkan Vekili*)	42	
8.	D.P. Assembly Group Executive Committee Member (*D.P. Meclis Grubu Idare Kurulu Üyesi*)	39	
	G.N.A. Clerk (*Başkanlık Divanı Kâtibi*)	38	
	G.N.A. Permanent Committee Treasurer (*Daimî Encümen Murakıbı*)	34	3
	G.N.A. Permanent Committee Secretary (*Daimî Encümen Kâtibi*)	32	

a Forty-three posts are rated. The mean score is 61; the median score is 58.6, and the range is 68. Average correlation between judges' rank orders and the rank order of the average scores of all judges is .871 with a standard deviation from that mean of .061.

The Democratic Party Era

During the Democratic Party Era from 1950 to 1957, several major changes in leadership positions occurred. These are apparent in the listings of Table 9.4.

Paramount among the changes from the preceding period are two. First of all, the dual-faceted pinnacle post remains, but its formal

Table 9.4
JUDGES' RANKINGS OF TOP POLITICAL POSTS FOR THE PERIOD 1950–1957 [a]

Echelon	Posts	Average Score	Index
1.	Prime Minister (*Başvekil*)	100	10
	D.P. President (*D.P. Reisi*)	100	
2.	President of the Republic (*Cumhurreisi*)	93	9
	R.P.P. General-President (*C.H.P. Genel Başkanı*)	92	
3.	R.P.P. General-Secretary (*C.H.P. Genel Sekreteri*)	79	7
	G.N.A. President (*Riyaset Divanı Reisi*)	78	
4.	Finance Minister (*Maliye Vekili*)	73	
	Minister of the Interior (*Dahiliye Vekili*)	69	
	Foreign Minister (*Hariciye Vekili*)	66	6
	D.P. Assembly Group President (*D.P. Meclis Grubu Reisi*)	65	
	Minister of Justice (*Adliye Vekili*)	63	
	R.P.P. Assembly Group Vice-President (*C.H.P. Meclis Grubu Başkan Vekili*)	62	
	Minister of National Defense (*Milli Müdafaa Vekili*)	61	
	R.P.P. General Executive Committee Member (*C.H.P. Genel Idare Heyeti Üyesi*)	61	
5.	Minister of Education (*Maarif Vekili*)	59	
	D.P. Assembly Group Vice-President (*D.P. Meclis Grubu Reis Vekili*)	59	
	Minister of State and Assistant Prime Minister (*Devlet Vekili ve Başvekil Yardımcısı*)	58	
	Minister of Economics and Trade (*Iktisat ve Ticaret Vekili*)	58	
	G.N.A. Vice-President (*Riyaset Divanı Reisvekili*)	58	5
	Minister of Agriculture (*Ziraat Vekili*)	56	
	G.N.A. Permanent Committee Chairman (*Daimi Encümen Reisi*)	56	
	Minister of Labor (*Çalışma Vekili*)	54	
	Minister of Public Works (*Nafia Vekili*)	53	
6.	Minister of Communications (*Münakalat Vekili*)	50	
	Minister of State Enterprises (*Işletmeler Vekili*)	50	
	Minister of State (*Devlet Vekili*)	49	
	Minister of Customs and Monopolies (*Gümrük ve Inhisarlar Vekili*)	49	4
	Minister of Health and Social Welfare (*Sıhhat ve Içtimai Muavenet Vekili*)	49	
	D.P. General Executive Committee Treasurer (*D.P. Genel Idare Kurulu Muhasibi*)	49	
	D.P. Assembly Group Treasurer (*D.P. Meclis Grubu Muhasibi*)	48	

Echelon	Posts	Average Score	Index
	R.P.P. Party Assembly Member (*C.H.P. Parti Meclisi Üyesi*)	48	4
7.	R.P.P. Assembly Group Treasurer (*C.H.P. Meclis Grubu Veznedarı*)	45	
	D.P. General Executive Committee Secretary (*D.P. Genel İdare Kurulu Kâtibi*)	45	
	R.P.P. Assembly Group Secretary (*C.H.P. Meclis Grubu Kâtibi*)	44	
	D.P. General Executive Committee Member (*D.P. Genel İdare Kurulu Üyesi*)	44	3
	D.P. Assembly Group Secretary (*D.P. Meclis Grubu Kâtibi*)	44	
	G.N.A. Permanent Committee Rapporteur (*Daimi Encümen Sözcüsü*)	44	
	G.N.A. Administrative Officer (*Riyaset Divanı İdare Amiri*)	44	
	G.N.A. Permanent Committee Vice-Chairman (*Daimi Encümen Reisvekili*)	43	
	D.P. Assembly Group Executive Committee Member (*D.P. Meclis Grubu İdare Kurulu Üyesi*)	41	
	G.N.A. Permanent Committee Treasurer (*Daimi Encümen Murakıbı*)	40	
	R.P.P. Assembly Group Executive Committee Member (*C.H.P. Meclis Grubu İdare Heyeti Üyesi*)	38	
8.	G.N.A. Permanent Committee Secretary (*Daimi Encümen Kâtibi*)	34	
	G.N.A. Clerk (*Riyaset Divanı Kâtibi*)	32	
	Nation Party Assembly Group President (*Millet Partisi Meclis Grubu Başkanı*)	31	
	Nation Party Assembly Group Secretary (*Millet Partisi Meclis Grubu Kâtibi*)	25	
	Peasant Party Assembly Group President (*T.K.P. Meclis Grubu İdare Heyeti Reisi*)	22	2
	Peasant Party Assembly Group Vice-President (*T.K.P. Meclis Grubu İdare Heyeti Reisvekili*)	22	
	Peasant Party Assembly Group Secretary (*T.K.P. Grubu İdare Heyeti Kâtibi*)	20	

[a] Forty-nine posts are rated. The mean score is 54; the median score is 50.3, and the range is 80. Average correlation between judges' rank orders and the rank order of the average scores of all judges is .833 with a standard deviation from that mean of .086.

character has been altered. Its governmental aspect is no longer that of the Presidency of the Republic; it has, instead, become that of the Prime Ministry. As in other respects, the formal structure of Turkish government has come more to resemble the prevailing Western pattern, with the chief of *state* becoming more of a figurehead (though still far from being completely so in Turkey), while the responsible head of *government* gains in power.

Actually, this change in the governmental side of the pinnacle post seems to be directly related to a development in its party facet. A sharp Democratic Party propaganda point in the pre-1950 attacks on the incumbent People's Party was the allegedly partisan character of the Turkish head of state, the President of the Republic — in this case İnönü. The head of state was also the active head of the People's Party. Prior to the 1950 election, the Democrats amended their *Party Regulations* so as to stipulate that if they came to power and the Democratic Party President became President of the Republic, he would be deemed to have withdrawn from the Presidency of the party.[7] Thus, under most normal circumstances, the Prime Minister would either be, or become (à la Menderes), President of the party. The People's Party quickly adopted a similar provision (which it later dropped).[8] In short, the *governmental* post which was now normally associated with the top *political party* post was that of Prime Minister rather than President of the Republic. Hence, we find the Prime Ministry moving past the Presidency of the Republic in the judges' rankings — a rather neat indication of how thoroughly Turkish government had become party government since the era of the First Assembly. The highest levels of both formal and actual political power in contemporary Turkey are obtained through strategic location in the dominant political party of the country.[9]

The second outstanding change in the patterning of offices for the fourth subperiod is obviously that Democratic Party positions now surpass comparable People's Party posts, at least at the top levels. However, that the People's Party was still a force to be reckoned with is reflected in the relatively high ratings of its leading offices compared to those of the Democrats in the preceding period, when the Democrats were in the minority. The rankings also clearly indicate that though other political parties existed in the country and even had puny parliamentary contingents, essentially a two-party system pre-

[7] *Demokrat Parti Tüzük ve Programı* (*Democratic Party Regulations and Program*), (Ankara: Güneş Matbaacılık, 1949), Article 18.

[8] Cf. *C.H.P. Program Ve Tüzüğü* (*Republican People's Party Program and Regulations*), (Ankara: publisher not indicated, 1947), Article 73. Inspection of later *R.P.P. Regulations* reveals no such provision regarding the General-President.

[9] Other factors were also at work to produce this result, prominent among them being perhaps the felt awkwardness of a governmental arrangement under which the Prime Minister had primary legal responsibility for the conduct of an administration in which the President of the Republic could and did regularly interfere. For a presentation of this thesis cf. George Harris, *A Political History of Turkey, 1945–1950* (unpublished Ph.D. dissertation, Department of History, Harvard University, 1956).

vailed. The lowest rankings of the forty-nine posts were awarded to the top positions of the Nation Party and the Peasant Party.

The articulation of the Democratic Party had improved since the preceding period in that the spacing of offices over the various levels of leadership was more even. Both the Democratic and People's parties had posts in five of the eight levels distinguished. Nevertheless, Table 9.4 indicates that the *top-level* articulation of the Democratic Party was still less elaborate than that of the People's Party. Specifically, Menderes's lieutenants had relatively less formal power than did those of İnönü, the most conspicuous gap being the continued absence of a Democratic counterpart to the General-Secretary of the People's Party. Also, membership on the General Executive Committee of the People's Party seems to have counted for more than membership on the same committee for the Democrats. With these two exceptions, the respective party posts are rather well matched.

Previously observed patterns are generally repeated for ministerial posts. Finance became the number-one cabinet slot, while Interior moved up again to number two. The basically domestic orientation of the regime is evidenced in the relative decline of the Foreign Ministry and National Defense Ministry portfolios.

Committees

The four comparable tables presenting the rankings of the permanent committees of the Grand National Assembly for each of the four periods are given in Appendix D. Here I shall merely adumbrate the general shape of the results.

In each period, five "natural" groupings of the committees appeared. Differences between committees were less pronounced than differences between posts. The ranges of the committee-power ratings were usually in the neighborhood of fifty points, running from about ninety to forty. The five committee groupings found in each of the four subperiods bear an extremely strong relationship to one another, especially those of the last three subperiods.

The paramount committee for the last three periods — actually in a group by itself — was always the Budget Committee, the permanent committee reviewing the governmental budget. During the First Assembly this committee was accompanied at the top, quite understandably, by the National Defense and Constitutional Committees.

After the Budget Committee in ascribed importance are the committees corresponding to the leading ministries as depicted in the ratings of the posts. The Ministry of Justice always heads this group and is followed by Interior, Foreign Affairs, National Defense, Education, Constitution (not a ministerial committee), and Finance. Next comes a third clustering consisting of intermediate ministerial committees such as Public Works, Health and Social Welfare, Labor, Trade, and Agriculture, plus the Petitions Committee. The fourth level contains the Customs and Monopolies Committee and the Communications Committee — weak ministries — while at the bottom are the "housekeeping" committees of the Assembly (the Governmental and Assembly Accounts Committees as well as the Assembly Library Committee). In most recent years, there seems to be a slight tendency for the other two major nonministerial committees besides the Budget Committee — the Constitutional Committee and the Petitions Committee — to rise in importance. This tendency, however, may simply have been due to a greater insulation of the ministries from parliamentary control under the heavy Democratic Party majorities of the fifties.[10]

Questioning of several judges as well as my own impressions of Turkish political life led me arbitrarily to assign to membership on the Budget Committee a formal power index weight of one (1.0). The other four levels of committee membership were correspondingly assigned weights of .8, .6, .4, and .2. Assigning weights in this fashion enabled me to make allowance for the relatively abstract way in which I had inquired about the formal importance of being a permanent committee chairman, rapporteur, or other officer. Clearly, the rating to be given to such an office should vary with the importance ascribed to the *committee* as well as that accorded to the committee *office*. Multiplying in each case the committee office scores by these committee importance weights would produce an adjusted committee score taking account both of ascribed committee *office* importance and committee *subject* importance in a plausible though partially arbitrary fashion.

Formal Power Scores

My major purpose in devising this procedure was to permit the assignment to each deputy of a summary score crudely reflective of that deputy's formal power position in each Assembly in which he served. Consequently, before I can discuss social background differences between the leadership levels of the Assembly, I must apply the post and committee ratings to each deputy of each parliament.

Since what is desired is a summary rating of the formal power of each deputy over the course of each Assembly, it is necessary to take

---

[10] Neşet Halil (Atay), *Büyük Meclis ve Inkilap, op. cit.*, p. 133, discerns three types of permanent committees in the G.N.A.: (1) committees concerned with Assembly services (Constitution, Petitions, Accounts, Library); (2) committees supervising ministries; (3) the Budget Committee. My data suggest the utility of separating the relatively important Constitutional and Petitions Committees from the three remaining, unimportant service committees.

account of the length of time a deputy served in any given post or committee. It was practically impossible, however, to compute for each of the 4,387 incumbents the exact number of days spent in each post, convert this to a fraction of the total life in days of the Assembly, and then multiply this figure by the ascribed importance of the post involved.

As a result, I followed a simplified procedure, using the fact that each Assembly was divided, officially, into from three to five "sessions" (*içtima* or *toplantı*), corresponding to the annual sessions of the U.S. Congress. With the exception of the "extraordinary" (*fevkalâde* or *olağanüstü*) session — the introductory session of each Assembly — the sessions were almost always about one year in length. Each deputy was given the full index score for each post held or committee membership occupied for each full session in which he held that position or membership. Each deputy who held a post or committee membership for less than the full session was given half credit — half the index score accorded to that position. Thus a deputy who held the post of Minister of Education for the first three sessions of the Eighth Assembly, but who then resigned in the middle of the fourth session to become an ordinary member of the Permanent Committee on Education for the remainder of that session plus the fifth session, would receive 24.5 points for his ministerial post (7 for each complete session, 3.5 for the partial session) and an additional .9 point for his committee membership (.6 for the full fifth session and .3 for the partial fourth session). A deputy of the same Assembly who served as an ordinary member of the Budget Committee for five sessions and held no other post or membership received five points, one for each full session served.

The general result of the application of these procedures was an array of deputies for each of the ten Assemblies according to the deputies' formal power scores. Since working directly with such arrays was still not convenient, I was confronted with the task of reducing each array, by some logical and uniform procedure, to a few specified categories.

The basic distinction I desired to make was that between "leaders" and "backbenchers," those who held some formal position of leadership and those who held none. Since I was possibly interested in the relative sizes of these groups in different periods and parliaments, I did not choose cutting points arbitrarily in terms of size.

Considering that the essential characteristic of the backbencher was that he held no leadership position (other than the committee membership assigned to each nonleader deputy), I decided to let the cutoff point be the maximal score a deputy could obtain by serving throughout the Assembly on its most important committee. In all cases this was the score obtained by a regular member of the Budget Committee — usually four or five points, depending on the number of sessions. Anyone having a higher score must have held some leadership post.[11]

Within the group of leaders, I wanted to make at least one further distinction between elements labeled "top leaders" and "middle leaders." Again, instead of defining them in terms of their relative sizes, I computed the lowest possible score for a man who served as a minister in all but one of the sessions of a given Assembly and made that the cutoff point between top and middle leaders. The greater turnover among ministers as compared to committee members induced me to make a slight reduction in my previous demand for service in the post throughout all sessions of the Assembly. In essence, however, the top leaders were those who had at least the equivalent of durable ministerial importance, while the middle leaders were those who occupied Assembly offices and minor party offices or held ministerial posts only briefly.[12]

Within the group of backbenchers was an element that I labeled the "inconsequentials." These were backbench deputies who had scores lower than that obtained by a deputy who served a full term on any committee except on a lowly "housekeeping" committee (Accounts or Library). I hoped to isolate in this fashion a group of especially powerless deputies. This effort was disappointing since a sizable portion of the "inconsequentials" frequently turned out to be deputies who did not serve a full term in the Assembly, either dying or resigning in mid-passage. The group of "inconsequentials" was therefore divided into two parts, those who had served the life of the Assembly and those who had not. After this division, unhappily, an initially rather small group sometimes became too tiny for reliable comparisons, and so I have contented myself with analysis in terms of the three major strata: top leaders, middle leaders, and backbenchers.

Table 9.5 gives the percentage of the deputies to each Assembly found in the four leadership groups described earlier. Application of the formal power weights to the ten Assemblies yields a rather constant structuring of about 10 per cent of the deputies as top leaders, some 15 to 25 per cent as middle leaders, well over half as backbenchers, and a varying residue as inconsequentials. In the most recent Assemblies, under the multi-party system, the relative size of the top leadership group has dwindled, and the relative size of the middle leadership group

[11] In the first two Assemblies a deputy could normally have more than one committee membership. An adjustment was made to allow for this fact, yielding a leader-backbencher cutoff point of 7 instead of 4 or 5.

[12] The lowest ministerial score per session being 5, the top versus middle leader demarcation was set as follows: scores greater than 14 were classed as top leaders for all four-session Assemblies and scores greater than 19 were classed as top leaders for all five-session Assemblies.

Table 9.5

LEADERSHIP GROUPS BY ASSEMBLY (PERCENTAGES)

LEADERSHIP GROUP	ASSEMBLY									
	I	II	III	IV	V	VI	VII	VIII	IX	X
Top Leaders	8%	11%	8%	10%	10%	10%	12%	9%	7%	7%
Middle Leaders	13	13	21	17	14	15	12	24	26	21
Backbenchers	44	53	55	53	62	54	60	55	62	68
Inconsequentials	35	23	15	21	14	20	16	12	5	4
Total[a]	100%	100%	100%	100%	100%	100%	100%	100%	100%	100%
N	437	333	333	348	444	470	492	499	494	537

[a] May not add to 100 because of rounding.

246   ANALYSES OF CHANGE

has increased, probably because of an increase in the number of party posts to be filled. As resignations and late elections virtually ceased, the contingent of inconsequentials also diminished. In any event, the general results seem intuitively plausible. Let us now inspect these leadership groups for differences in social background.[13]

CHARACTERISTICS OF LEADERSHIP GROUPS

In examining the social characteristics of the top leaders, middle leaders, and backbenchers, I shall use some of the data as a partial check on the validity and significance of the leadership distinctions. For instance, it would generally be assumed that top leaders would be

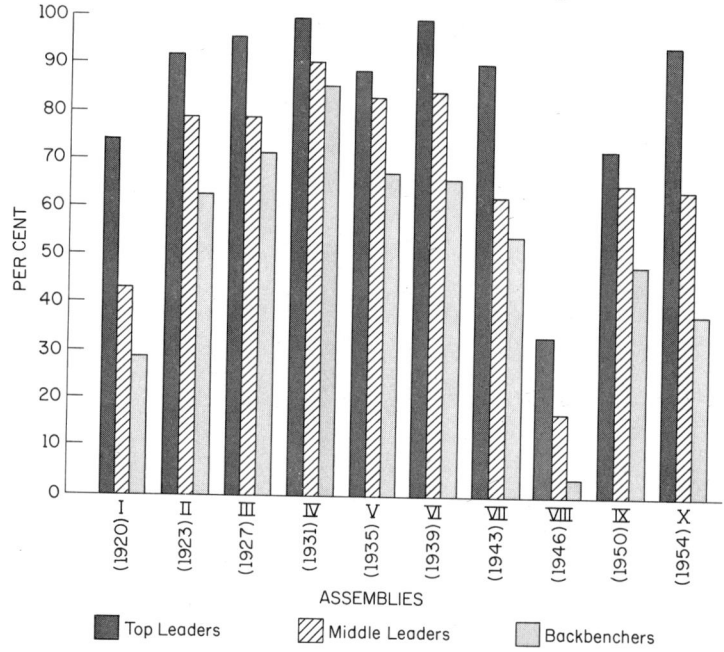

Figure 9.1. Deputies reelected to the subsequent Assembly, by leadership level

[13] The constancy of the ratings, in terms of the relative size of the leadership levels through time, is not emphasized for the simple reason that much of it might be a mere artifact of the rating scheme. That scheme, applied rigidly to each Assembly with the assumption of complete stability in original position for all deputies, would produce results different — *but not grossly different* — from those of Table 9.5. For example, the number of top leadership posts *available* was generally in the neighborhood of (though less than) 10 per cent of the size of the Assembly and remained comparatively stable despite some growth. The same consideration applies to the middle leadership and back-bench levels.

reelected more often than middle leaders, who in turn would be reelected more often than backbenchers. If this proves to be the case, only a slight increase in the confidence accorded the procedure and results can be claimed. However, if the assumption is *not* supported by the data, considerable doubt about the validity of the procedures may well arise.

As Figure 9.1 indicates, there is a strong tendency in the expected direction. In each of the ten Assemblies under investigation there is a perfect downward step progression in the percentages of top leaders, middle leaders, and backbenchers reelected to the subsequent Assembly. Those deputies with a higher leadership rating in any given Assembly were quite disproportionately retained in the subsequent Assembly.

Previous Parliamentary Experience

A complementary assumption about differences between leadership groups comes to mind, though it is somewhat less important than that regarding reelection rates. In most national parliaments the legislators in positions of formal leadership usually tend to have greater parlia-

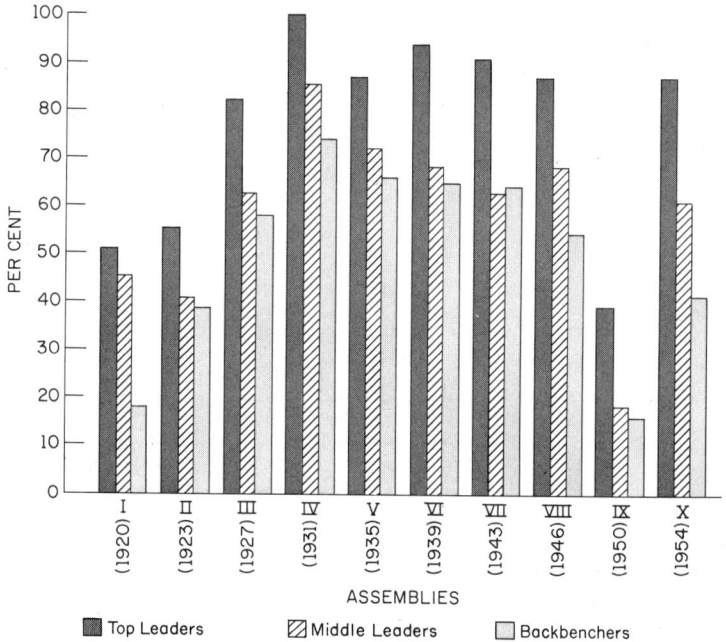

Figure 9.2. Deputies with previous Assembly experience, by leadership level

NOTE: The percentages in the First Assembly refer to experience in an Ottoman Assembly. The figures given are minimal and are to be taken as more suggestive than precise.

mentary experience than the backbenchers. If I have truly distinguished meaningful levels of leadership in the Grand National Assembly, the same increase in experience might be expected to be associated with elevation to leadership level. Again, the data confirm the hypothesis. Figure 9.2 shows the percentage of each leadership group with experience in at least one prior Assembly. In nine out of ten Assemblies there is the same downward step progression, though the differences between the middle leaders and backbenchers are occasionally rather slight. In general, the higher the formal leadership position of the deputy, the more likely he was to have had prior parliamentary experience.

Cohort Progression to Leadership

It is rewarding here to apply to the cohort groups (analyzed in Chapter 8) the leadership information we now have gained. In this way we can discover whether there is any pattern in the experiences of the various cohorts with regard to changes in their formal power positions. Did the cohorts rise or fall in power in successive parliaments? Is there any regularity in the timing of when the cohorts attained their maximal power? Did some cohorts become more powerful than others? Relevant data are found in Table 9.6. Quite naturally, the cohort starts off at a low level of formal power, its percentage of top leaders usually being less than one fourth that of the nonentering deputies. The few entering cohort members who did reach the uppermost echelon did so largely through *party* positions rather than ministerial or Assembly posts.

Table 9.6

FORMAL POWER RATINGS OF COHORT GROUPS — PERCENTAGE OF TOP LEADERS

	COHORT ASSEMBLY OF ENTRANCE									
	I	II	III	IV	V	VI	VII	VIII	IX	X
Cohort at Entry	8	8	4	—	4	2	3	3	5	2
Nonentering Deputies		17	11	14	14	14	16	14	14	12
Maximal Cohort Power	21	20	18	26	18	13	8	22	11	
Elapsed Assemblies for Maximal Power	7	6	3	3	2	2	1	2	1	

In general, the cohorts attained their peak power two to three parliaments after initial election, though the figures are significantly affected by alterations in party fortunes and by the previously discussed "ceiling effect," which impinges on the cohort analysis. Nevertheless, the basic impression is that an entering group of deputies took two to three successive parliaments to reach its maximal power position, after which it dropped two or three points below that maximum.

For most of the Atatürk cohorts, the maximum was such that about one of every five *remaining* members of the cohort had secured top leadership status. The debacle of 1950 resulted in a drastic worsening of the fortunes of the İnönü cohorts of the Sixth and Seventh Assemblies, while the "ceiling effect" makes any generalization about the multiple-party cohorts quite unreliable.

Age on First Election

Another plausible assumption that can be applied to the leadership level distinctions is that the preferred and the powerful would tend to have been first elected to the Assembly at a younger age than other deputies. Obviously, this characteristic is not independent of previous parliamentary experience. However, since the parliamentary experience involved in the data of Figure 9.2 was at the minimal level of service in any single prior Assembly, age at first election seems sufficiently distinct to warrant its presentation in Figure 9.3. This depicts the average ages at first election of the three leadership groups of each Assembly.

Using this third quasi-control, we also find that in nine cases out of ten there is a perfect step progression between the three leadership

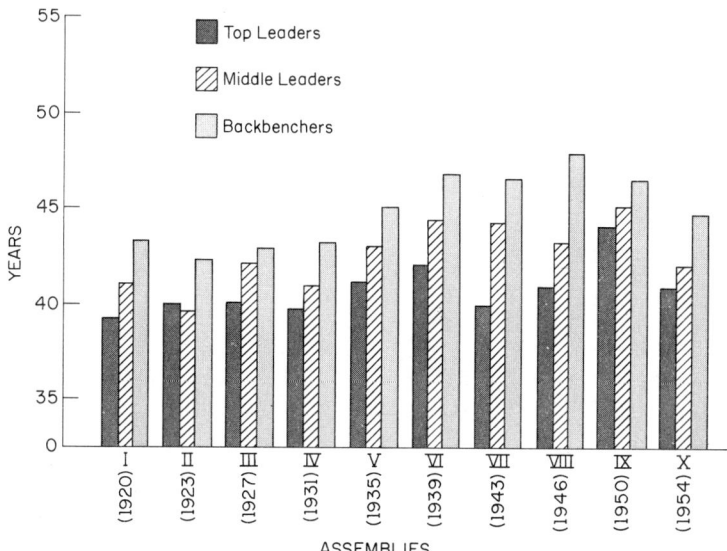

Figure 9.3. Average age on first election, by leadership level

levels — a progression in the direction that, it was assumed, would hold between meaningfully different levels of leadership in the Assembly.

The relatively young age at which top leaders, on the average, first entered parliament expresses a rather important fact about Turkish political life. Though the outstanding political figures of the country generally started adult life in a vocation other than politics, they became professional politicians quite early in their careers. By about the age of forty they had already secured their initial election to the national legislature. The commanding political positions in Turkey are consequently not ordinarily held by prestigious outsiders who move into the political arena after the culmination of a successful career in another pursuit. On the contrary, the leading offices are held by men who are truly professional politicians, having focused their energies on politics in early maturity and usually having risen to prominence by dint of hard and able effort on behalf of a political party.

Turkish politics, in short, are *professional party* politics, which in many ways have come to resemble those of Continental Europe more than those of Turkey's Muslim neighbors.

Age

Figure 9.4, comparing the average actual ages of deputies in the three leadership levels, instead of their average ages on first election, reveals

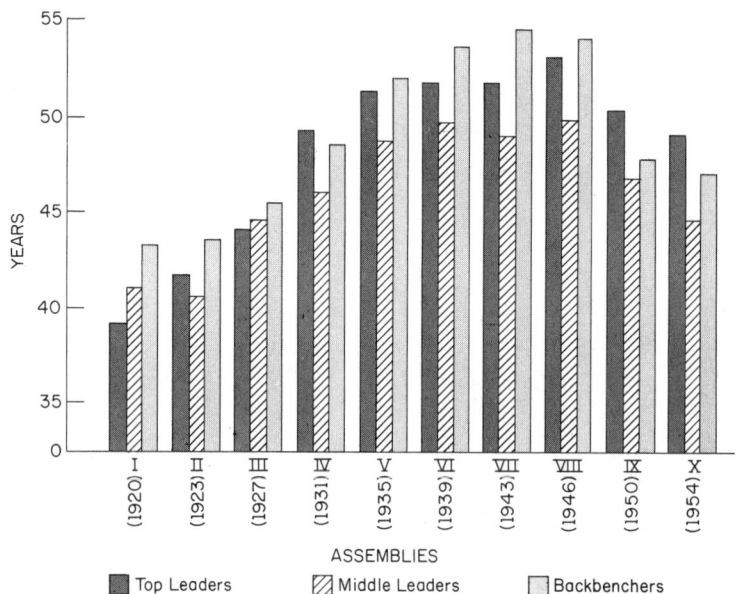

Figure 9.4. Average age of deputies, by leadership level

that a U-shaped curve generally replaces the regular step progression. By the Fourth Assembly, the top leaders and the backbenchers are normally seen to be of roughly comparable age, while the middle leaders are quite consistently younger than the other two groups.

The middle leadership echelon seems in general to have been much more of a way station than a stable unit in the leadership hierarchy. Inspection of the individual dossiers of deputies suggests that tenure in the middle leadership level was much more ephemeral than in either the top leadership or backbench level. The greatest fluidity in personnel is found in this intermediate echelon. Many backbenchers flowed into the middle leadership sector rather early in their careers. They would linger at this level for one or two Assemblies, after which they would either continue their rise to the top leadership level and establish themselves there or, more frequently, would tumble back to the backbench level or out of parliament completely. Those who regressed to the backbench level but were able to consolidate their positions at that level and remain in parliament seem disproportionately to have been the deputies with strong local ties.

Marital Status and Birthplace

Calculation of the marital statuses of deputies at the three leadership levels reveals no significant differences between the groups. I had suspected that the top and middle leaders might show a slightly higher incidence of bachelors, but no such pattern was found. On the other hand, when I checked the average number of children of the married and widowed deputies at each leadership level, I did find in six out of eight cases (insufficient data were available for the first two Assemblies) that the backbenchers had larger families than either of the two groups of leaders, perhaps betokening differences in "modernization."

Similar evidence pointing toward the greater modernity of top and middle leaders lies in the data on the birthplaces of the deputies of the three leadership groups, displayed in Figure 9.5. In general, the top and middle leader groups tended to have a higher incidence of deputies born in the Aegean and Marmara Regions of Turkey — the most modern and highly developed areas of the land.

Women

Very few women found their way to positions of great importance in the Assembly. Women participated in six of the ten parliaments under inspection. In five of these six parliaments there were *no* women who were top leaders! Only in the Seventh Assembly, when two female deputies, Dr. Fatma Memik and Tezer Taşkıran, achieved enough importance from membership on the General Executive Committees of the People's Party and its Independent Group, did women gain brief

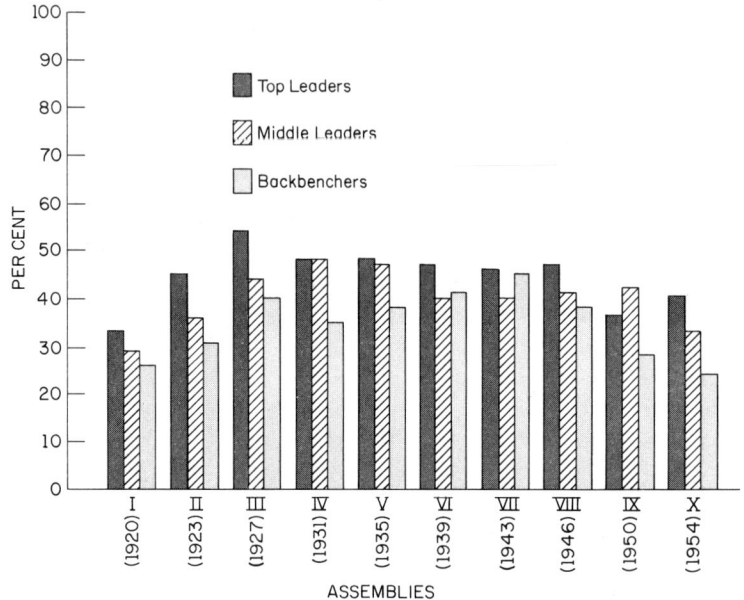

Figure 9.5. Deputies born in the Marmara and Aegean Regions, by leadership level

entry into the upper precincts of power. On the other hand, women did display a tendency to gain middle leader ranking largely because they frequently became the secretaries of several of the less important permanent parliamentary committees. In all, over the six Assemblies in which women participated, thirty-eight different women held sixty-six incumbencies. Of those sixty-six female deputyships, in terms of formal power, 3 per cent must be accorded the status of top leaders (compared to roughly 10 per cent for all deputies), 24 per cent are assigned to the middle leader category (compared to approximately 19 per cent of all deputies), 64 per cent were backbenchers (compared to about 60 per cent of all deputies), and some 9 per cent of the female incumbencies were at the inconsequential level (compared to nearly 12 per cent of all deputies). In short, the women in the Assembly clearly failed to breach the highest walls of formal power even though they did obtain mid-range leadership of a special sort with slightly increased frequency.

Education

The most interesting question, in terms of the preceding analysis of recruitment and retention in the Assembly, is whether the three criteria then found to be most important are equally vital in the allocation of formal leadership positions. Are the three leadership groups markedly distinguished from one another in terms of those characteristics which constituted a claim to intellectual status, to official status, or to a role of local influence? As before, we shall look first at intellectual status, judged to be the most important of the three recruitment and retention criteria.

When formal education is taken as an indicator of intellectual status, the data show that the three leadership groups are indeed sharply distinguished from one another. The distinction, as portrayed in Figure 9.6, was especially clear between the two leader groups, on the one hand, and the backbench group, on the other. In every case, both of the leader groups have a markedly higher percentage of deputies who obtained university-level education. In fact, for the last eight Assemblies — that is, since 1927 — the lower of the two leader groups in the proportion of its deputies with university training has always been at least sixteen percentage points higher in that respect than the backbench group. In seven out of ten cases we have again a downward step progression between the three leadership levels, the three minor exceptions being inversions between the top and middle leader groups.

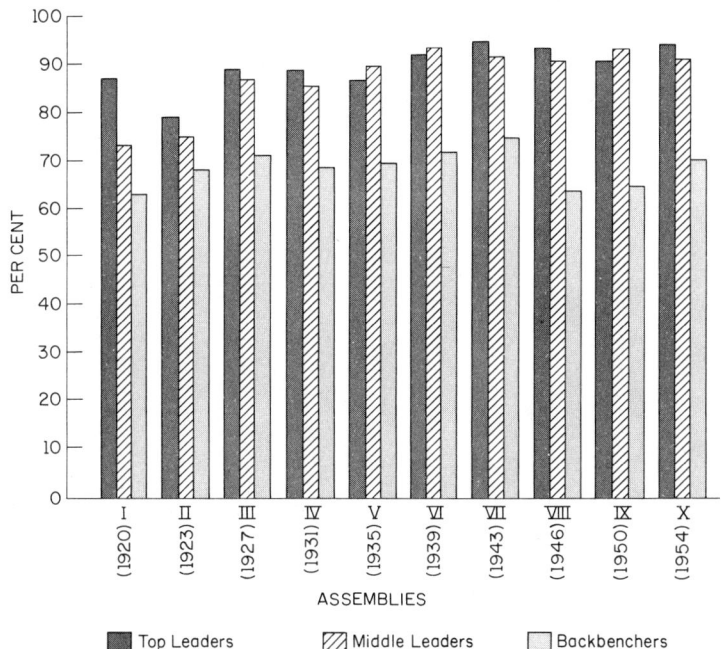

Figure 9.6. Deputies with university-level education, by leadership level

NOTE: The data for the First Assembly are rather unreliable because of insufficient coverage — merely 161 deputies from a total of 437.

Of all the social background characteristics examined, education most clearly and consistently distinguished between the designated leadership levels in the Assembly. The educational difference remained crucial and stable throughout all ten Assemblies, all four eras, all changes in the internal party system and in external environment. Just as the Grand National Assembly differed from the adult Turkish populace in being distinctly superior in formal education, so the higher leaders of that Assembly clearly differed from the less formally powerful members in being better educated. Though political power in Turkey has changed hands in the past two decades, both the hands that relinquished power and those that grasped it were attached to relative intellectuals who had high levels of formal education in common, differ as they did in other respects. This fact must not be forgotten even as we engage in the essential task of trying to fathom the psychology and political role of the Turkish peasant. At its highest levels, Turkish political life is still dominated by relative intellectuals in Turkish society.

Foreign Language Competence

Further insight into the leadership significance of a claim to intellectual status can be garnered from data on a more marginal characteristic — foreign language competence. Figure 9.7 gives the average number of foreign languages spoken by the members of each of the three leadership groups.

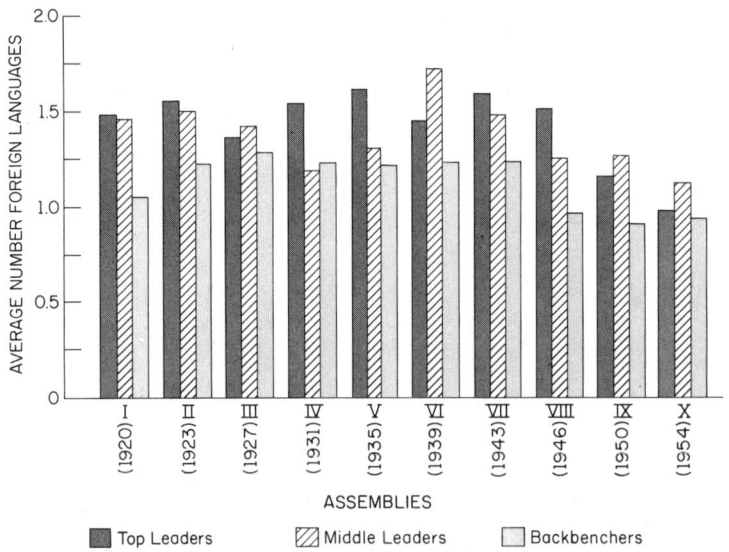

Figure 9.7. Average number of foreign languages claimed per deputy, by leadership level

Though knowledge of a foreign tongue was definitely a secondary characteristic, still in nine out of ten cases both leader groups have appreciably higher averages than the backbench group. Not surprisingly, within the leader groups the foreign language distinction becomes much less reliable, there being four inversions. The general pattern seems, nevertheless, to be once more in accordance with the suggested hypotheses.[14]

Occupation

The *educational* backgrounds of the deputies, grouped into the three main leadership levels of the Assembly, reveal the stable, dominantly intellectual cast of the uppermost echelons of Turkish politics. The *occupational* backgrounds furnish us with a profound insight into the major *changes* that took place within the leadership groups – changes occurring inside the framework of the continued intellectual character of the political hierarchy. The gross figures are furnished in Table 9.7, which gives for each Assembly the percentage of each leadership level in "professional," "official," and "economic" occupations.

These data graphically illustrate the major movements of Turkish politics: the hegemony of the officials in the single-party heyday, their decline, and their replacement as the dominant occupational group by the professionals after the free elections of 1950. After the anomalous First Assembly, which again is seen to resemble the Ninth and Tenth Assemblies in many respects, we view a steady rise in the percentage of top leaders who were professionals. Similarly, we note a sharp decline in the percentage of top leaders who had official occupational backgrounds. However, there was an appreciable lag in the reduction of the official element at the top leadership level contrasted to its reduction at the middle leadership and backbench levels. The officials remained the largest contingent in the uppermost Assembly level right up until

---

[14] I have not presented data on the publication records of each leadership level because the proportion publishing in some of the levels is regularly so small as to preclude reliable comparisons. The information about the types of foreign languages spoken by those deputies who asserted foreign language competence is, however, rather interesting, inasmuch as the two leader groups appear to be distinguished from the backbenchers by a greater tendency to claim French as a foreign language. At each leadership level, the percentage of *those with foreign language competence* who spoke French is given in the table.

Leadership Level	I	II	III	IV	V	VI	VII	VIII	IX	X
Top Leaders	100%	94%	96%	94%	93%	91%	95%	95%	96%	85%
Middle Leaders	78	92	98	93	94	95	90	93	83	80
Backbenchers	69	77	84	84	85	89	91	87	80	78

Table 9.7

OCCUPATIONAL CATEGORIES OF DEPUTIES, BY LEADERSHIP LEVELS AND ASSEMBLIES (PERCENTAGES)[a]

LEADERSHIP LEVEL AND OCCUPATION	ASSEMBLY									
	I	II	III	IV	V	VI	VII	VIII	IX	X
Top Leaders:										
Official	49%	66%	61%	60%	65%	61%	50%	49%	30%	29%
Professional	37	18	21	23	24	31	38	38	49	58
Economic	3	11	11	11	7	6	9	11	18	13
Middle Leaders:										
Official	57	50	65	53	51	46	43	38	32	29
Professional	17	26	18	26	30	32	43	49	54	51
Economic	13	7	8	9	15	14	8	17	12	15
Backbenchers:										
Official	43	55	53	47	44	43	47	35	17	19
Professional	17	19	25	23	25	26	30	30	41	42
Economic	18	13	14	21	22	24	18	29	35	34
N	373	297	332	346	443	470	492	499	494	536

[a] "Inconsequentials," unknowns, and those classed occupationally as "other," are excluded. See Chapter 4 for a description of the occupational categories. Because of the exclusions, percentages within leadership levels do not add to 100. As before, the N refers to all deputies for whom information was available and includes the "Inconsequentials" and "Others."

LEVELS OF FORMAL LEADERSHIP   257

1950, and this fact may have contributed to any existing misperception of the basic groundswell of change — a change acclaimed to be so surprising in 1950, though clear portents were present.

Figure 9.8 gives us perhaps a clearer view of the parliamentary position of each of the three occupational groups, showing the percentage that each group contributed to the three leadership levels. If random distribution in terms of occupation is assumed, a vocational group should have contributed about the same percentage to each of the three leadership levels — say, 20 per cent of each, or 50 per cent of each — depending on the total size of the occupational group in the Assembly as a whole. The three columns for each group should be

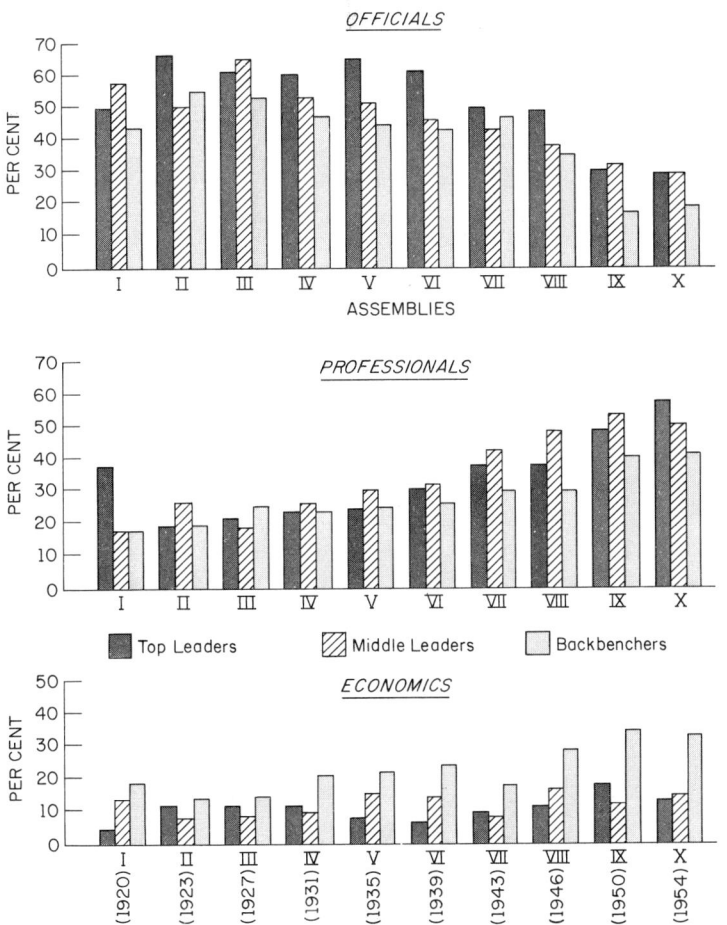

Figure 9.8. Broad occupational categories of deputies, by leadership level

roughly the same size. But we see that between the First and Tenth Assemblies, with one exception, the professionals contributed most heavily to the middle leadership level of the parliament. In that Tenth Assembly, however, the group had the downward step progression that reflects truly disproportionate access to power. Moreover, the individual columns are the longest of any such entries for the Tenth Assembly, indicating numerical superiority as well as disproportionate access to power. The professionals clearly stand out as the formally and numerically dominant occupational element in the most recent Democratic Party Assemblies.

If the professionals have assumed dominance in recent times, the officials displayed even greater superiority in the parliaments of the single-party era. From 1923 to 1950, with one exception, they had their highest percentage in the top leadership group. Even after 1950, their relative distribution maintained much of its basic form. The most egregious change, from the officials' viewpoint, was their over-all reduction in numbers linked to a comparative drop in top leadership representation.

The same retention of basic pattern in the face of gross numerical changes is to be seen in the economic group. Here, however, the situation was, in a sense, reversed. Instead of retaining a disproportionate access to power even though suffering an over-all loss of numbers, the economic group experienced a marked rise in numerical representation that they were unable to parlay into a more favorable power position. They remained the broad occupational group with the least access to the formal seats of influence in Turkish government. Thus I must introduce an important qualification to the description of the basic occupational trends of recent political life in Turkey. With the introduction of the multi-party system and the accession of the Democrats, the Assembly as a whole occupationally assumed more of a professional and economic (or commercial) character. Nevertheless, these two occupational groups must not be indiscriminately lumped together as equally typical of the newer developments. A fundamental difference exists between them. The professionals reached the formal founts of power, while the economic members were unable to break free of their backbench location. Both the professional group and the economic group greatly increased their representation, but only the professional group greatly increased its relative share of formal power.

What of specific vocations within the gross occupational categories? What variations, if any, existed within the larger groupings? To answer such questions I shall review briefly the data for the major specific vocational contingents in the Assembly. The information on the two largest professional groupings, law and medicine, is supplied in Figure 9.9.

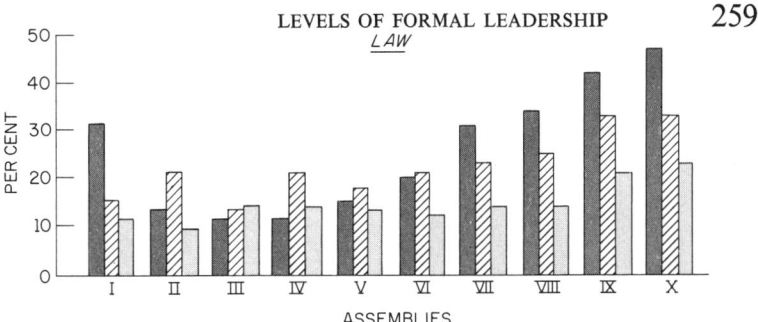

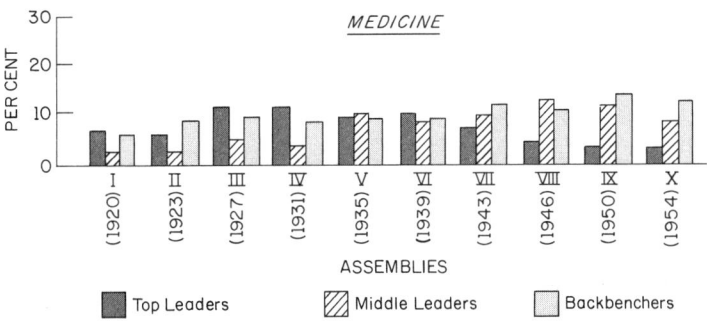

Figure 9.9. Deputies with legal and medical vocations, by leadership level

The position of the lawyers in the Assembly proves to have been quite different from that of the doctors. The doctors were not usually favored with any acutely disproportionate amount of formal power, with the possible exception of the Third and Fourth Assemblies. For the most part, and especially in the more recent parliaments (in particular contrast to the lawyers), the doctors played a predominantly backbench role so far as formal importance was concerned.

The core of the professional delegation, and that element which contributed most heavily to its rise, was the lawyers. In the First Assembly the legal deputies were patently well placed in positions of leadership. Thereafter, with the Kemalist consolidation, they lost that favored aspect and were relegated to a middle leadership role until the Seventh Assembly, when they burst through to disproportionate representation among the top leaders once again. It is particularly noteworthy that this breakthrough occurred prior to 1950 or even 1946. In other words, the lawyers led the rise of the professionals to formal power. By the Tenth Assembly nearly one half of the top political leaders of Turkish government were lawyers.

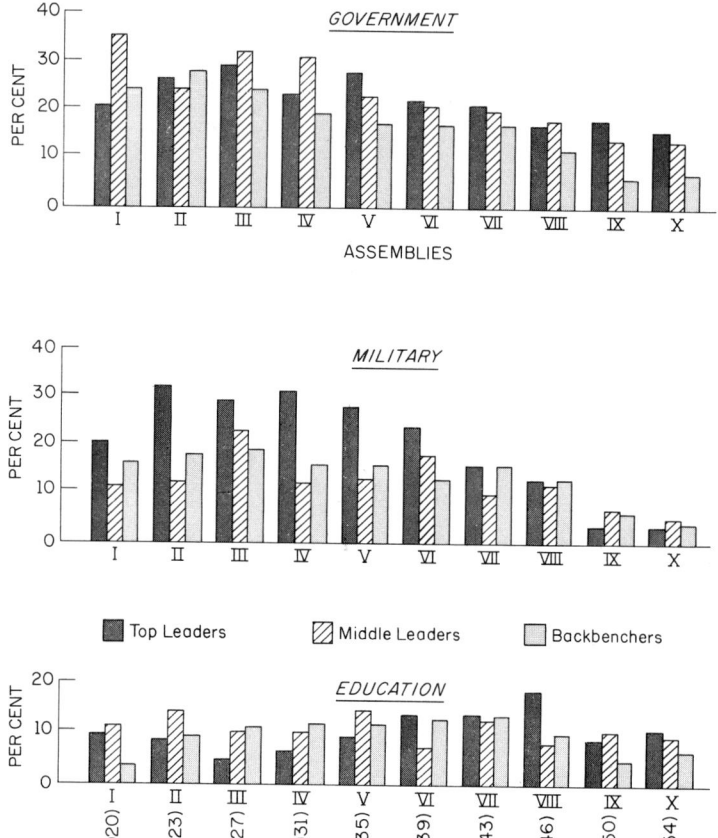

Figure 9.10. Deputies with governmental, military, and educational vocations, by leadership level

Figure 9.10 presents the equally interesting results for the three official vocations — government, military, and education. In the single-party era, the governmental deputies appear to have been cast as middle leaders nearly as much as top leaders. It is clear, nevertheless, that they were disproportionately likely to be found in a leadership position as opposed to being a mere backbencher, though the differences between the percentages are not as sharp as for the lawyers or as for the military men. One mildly surprising revelation is that under the Democratic Party's reign the *relative* access of former bureaucrats to high positions increased, even though their *absolute* numbers and, consequently, their representation at high levels decreased.

The most dramatic decline of all was that suffered by the military.

From the Second up to the Seventh Assembly the military group was the most favored. In most instances it was the largest vocational contingent at the top leadership level, and it was more overrepresented at that level than any comparable group. The total size of the contingent of deputies from military backgrounds began to dwindle sometime prior to any severe decline in military representation in the most powerful echelon of politics. The upper-level decline began about the Sixth Assembly and continued strongly in the Seventh and Eighth Assemblies. But the shocking casualties occurred with the advent of the Democrats in 1950, when military personnel fell to a scant and unaccustomed 3 per cent of the top leadership group. However, this drop was not solely due to a general reduction of military deputies. It also reflected a reversal of the former preferred entry of military deputies to top leadership positions. The small troop of deputies with military backgrounds in the Ninth and Tenth Assemblies began to have a backbench or middle leader character rather than its erstwhile top leadership cast.

This loss by the military first of its over-all strength in the Assembly and then of its lingering strength at top leadership levels seems to be one important background factor in understanding the military *coup d'état* of May 27, 1960. Three outstanding factors aiding the separation of the military from politics (unusual in Turkish history) were: (1) that retired officers were disproportionately represented in the Assembly and even more strongly and durably in its most influential councils; (2) that when such representation dwindled, the People's Party government was still ostensibly carrying out the programs that most of the officers' corps favored; and (3) that there had developed a "neutral army" tradition of significant potency.

The essential background to the coup, from the point of view of the military's involvement, was the gradual obliteration of all three of these restraining factors. As I have just shown, the military ultimately lost both its large general representation and, more slowly, its top-level contingent. Furthermore, after the first few "honeymoon" years, the Democratic Party began to tamper with the cherished programs supported and even, to a large extent, inaugurated by the army. The government ceased to carry out the programs endorsed by the military and, in the eyes of many officers, began to undermine and sabotage some of those programs. By 1957, the army was restrained mainly by the "neutral army" tradition coupled with sheer inertia. When the Democrats, with the aim of suppressing the People's Party, began to take action that willy-nilly involved the army in politics, the "neutral army" tradition was finally sundered, and the military group decided to take matters into its own hands. It is in this sense that knowledge of the alterations in the deputies' vocational backgrounds at the various levels of formal leadership contributes to an understanding of these critical developments in modern Turkish political life — developments which brought an end to the "First Republic," with whose politics we are here concerned.[15]

The educators in the Assembly appear to have been primarily middle leaders and backbenchers in the Atatürk Era. Under Inönü they increased in importance until, in the Eighth Assembly, they surpassed both the governmental and military deputies in their contribution to the top leadership echelon. With the coming of the Democrats, their over-all importance also declined, though, like the bureaucrats and unlike the military, they nevertheless remained disproportionately likely to be leaders rather than backbenchers.

The last two vocations for which I shall provide leadership data are those of trade and agriculture, which along with the small group of bankers make up the "economic" occupational category. Figure 9.11 displays these data.

The general tendency for merchant deputies to be backbenchers is apparent from the figure. Just as these commercial elements were underrepresented in the parliament as a whole, so they were still further underrepresented in the leadership groups of the parliament.

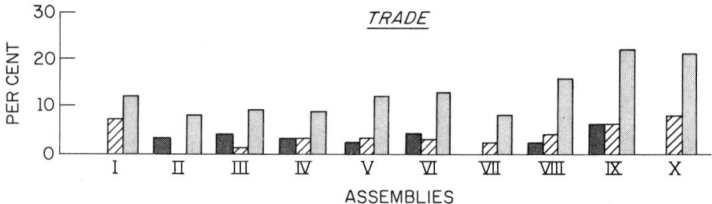

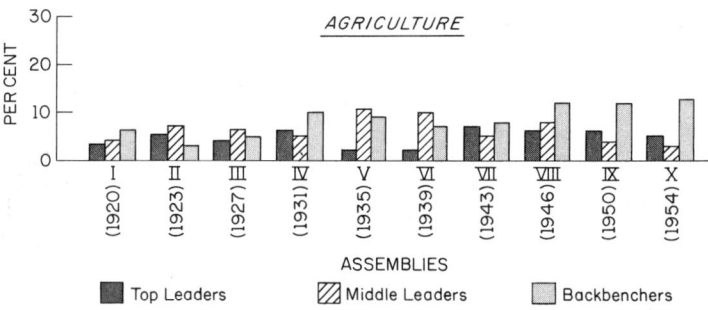

Figure 9.11. Deputies with "trade" and agricultural vocations, by leadership level

[15] For fuller discussion of these events from this viewpoint, see Frederick W. Frey, "Arms and the Man in Turkish Politics," *op. cit.*

Up to the Eighth Assembly, the deputies with backgrounds in agriculture fared better. Those agriculturists who found their way to positions of importance, however, tended not to be from peasant ranks. Instead, they were mainly agricultural engineers and technicians. After the introduction of the multi-party system, the size of the agricultural group increased moderately, but its relative access to formal power decreased. In the Tenth Assembly, at the end of the thirty-seven-year period, both economic groups have the poorest leadership ratings of any of the major vocational groupings in the Assembly.

Localism

So far, the findings concerning the social backgrounds of deputies at the various levels of formal leadership in the Assembly have closely paralleled the previous findings with regard to recruitment and retention. That is, the intellectual and occupational qualities associated with preferred recruitment and retention also were associated with greater access to positions of power in the Assembly.

What of the third recruitment criterion — some plausible claim to local connection and influence? Does this characteristic also distinguish the three levels of formal leadership? The answer to this question, interpreted from Figure 9.12, must be that there seems to be no

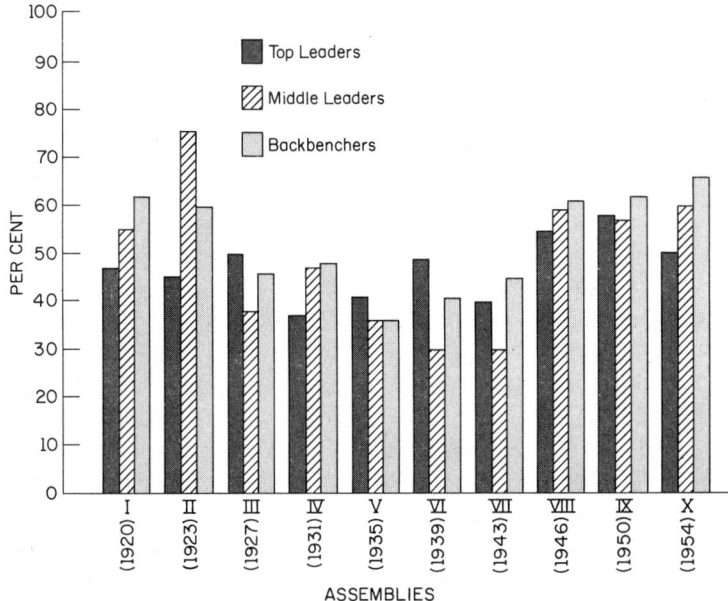

Figure 9.12. Deputies born in the province they represented in the Assembly, by leadership level

association between "localism" (defined as birth in the constituency represented) and level of leadership attained.

No outstanding pattern appears in Figure 9.12, except perhaps for the mild tendency of backbenchers in the last four Assemblies to be somewhat more local than the two leader groups. Actually, such a general finding should come as no surprise. Of the three recruitment criteria previously discussed, I tried to suggest that localism was rather different from the other two. In many respects it ran counter to traits subsumed under the educational and occupational characteristics, which were deemed more important. Insofar as this was true, localism seems to have been much more of a *recruitment* criterion than a factor conducive to achieving a position of formal importance. Even under the Democrats, the inclusion of more deputies with stronger ties to local communities might have been viewed as tactically valuable in political campaigning; but such local types were, if anything, slightly hampered rather than favored in achieving formal positions of influence in the Assembly. On the other hand, if the influence of local politicians keeps rising in the future as it has in the recent past, the character of the Assembly may become so broadly affected as to permit the localists to penetrate the highest levels of formal power and may make localism even there a positive rather than a weakly negative or inconsequential factor, as it seems to be today.

Summary

This chapter has been concerned with the analysis of levels of formal leadership in the Grand National Assembly, and of differences between groups of top leaders, middle leaders, and backbenchers. The alterations through time in the social composition of these leadership groups were also examined.

A panel of nine judges rated the "importance" (power) of all the posts and committees of the Assembly and the political parties for each of the four periods into which the epoch of the First Turkish Republic had been divided. These periods were: (1) the pre-Kemalist First Assembly (1920–1923); (2) the single-party, arch-Kemalist "Atatürk Era" (1923–1939), including the Second through the Fifth Assemblies; (3) the late single-party and early multi-party "İnönü Era" (1939–1950), covering the Sixth through the Eighth Assemblies; and (4) the multi-party "Democratic Party Era" (1950–1957, 1950–1960), covering the Ninth through the Tenth or Eleventh Assemblies.

The judges' ratings, which displayed a high degree of agreement, divided the offices of each period into eight echelons of relative influence. The basic structure represented by these divisions was as follows:

Level 1. The "pinnacle post" of Turkish politics, formed by a single individual's bestraddling the two posts of head of the dominant political party and head of the state (or government). The party chieftainship seems to have been the more dynamic office.

Level 2. A less-stable "chief lieutenant's post," occupied by the man who held simultaneously the second-highest positions in both party and government (though under the multi-party system the leader of the main opposition party would also be placed at this level).

Level 3. A "sublieutenant's level" consisting of the People's Party General-Secretary and the President of the G.N.A. At this level the party and governmental officeholding usually began to diverge.

Level 4. The "top ministerial echelon," composed essentially of the Ministers of Finance, Foreign Affairs, Interior, and Defense.

Level 5. The "ordinary ministerial level," consisting of most of the remaining ministers plus some of the leading party officials in the parliamentary group.

Level 6. The "weak ministerial level," comprising holders of the least prestigious ministerial portfolios, such as Customs and Monopolies or Transportation, as well as a few party and Assembly officials.

Level 7. The intermediate party and Assembly officials.

Level 8. Minor party and Assembly officials.

Very revealing changes in the relative power positions of some of these offices occurred over the four periods under investigation. For example, the official side of the "pinnacle post" changed from that of President of the Republic to that of Prime Minister, reflecting an alteration in the governmental position occupied by the leader of the dominant political party. The relative importance of various leading ministries also switched in an interesting fashion. The ministries of Foreign Affairs and of Defense were uppermost in the First Assembly period. During the Atatürk Era the leading ministries were, in descending order, Interior, Foreign Affairs, and Finance. In the İnönü Era the ministerial parade was led by Foreign Affairs, followed by Finance and then by Interior. And under the Democrats, the Finance Ministry, which had been rising steadily, finally reached the head of the list, followed by Interior and then by Foreign Affairs.

Almost from its inception, the articulation of leadership positions under the People's Party seems to have been rather full. Ordinarily, party offices were found at six of the eight leadership levels adumbrated earlier. Though less fully articulated at the start of its parliamentary career, the Democratic Party quickly came to present a similar array of offices, with one glaring exception. It never established any lieutenant's position comparable to that of the General-Secretary of the People's Party.

The rankings of the permanent committees of the Assembly produced a structure with five levels of influence. In every period the Budget Committee emerged as the most influential of these bodies. In the second rank came the committees corresponding to the leading ministries (Justice, Interior, Foreign Affairs, National Defense, Education, and Finance), plus the Constitutional Committee. In the middle rank appeared the committees corresponding to ministries intermediate in importance, such as Public Works, Health and Social Welfare, Labor, Agriculture, and Trade, plus the Petitions Committee. The fourth level consisted of committee counterparts of the weak ministries, such as Customs and Monopolies or Communications and Transportation. And, finally, at the bottom of the structure were the "housekeeping" committees, like Government Accounts, Assembly Accounts, and the committee directing the Assembly Library.

The ratings of the posts and the committees were applied to each deputy of each Assembly, also taking into consideration the length of time the deputy held a given post or committee assignment. By utilizing the resultant formal power scores obtained for each legislator, all deputies were classified as top leaders, middle leaders, backbenchers, or inconsequentials. Looking at the Assemblies as the units of analysis, we found that the percentages of deputies at each level of formal power remained rather constant over the four decades of the First Republic. On the whole, about a tenth of each Assembly emerged as top leaders, between a sixth and a fourth qualified as middle leaders, one half to two thirds filled the backbenches, and, with somewhat more fluctuation, a fifth or less were classed as inconsequentials. Probably the most intriguing change in this pattern through time was that under the multi-party system the percentage of top leaders dropped by about a third — from 10 or 11 per cent down to 7 per cent — and the percentage of middle leaders sharply increased, probably because of the increase in available party posts.

Confidence in the validity of the judges' power ratings was increased by the findings that in every one of the ten Assemblies, deputies with higher leadership classifications also had higher reelection percentages and more prior parliamentary experience, as was to be expected if such deputies really were as influential as the ratings indicated.

The cohort analysis of the preceding chapter was briefly reinvoked to indicate that a cohort group usually obtained its maximal power approximately two or three Assemblies after its formation. After that peak, the formal power of the cohort declined slightly to a level just below the peak. This fact, combined with more impressionistic observations, suggests that it took the typical top leader about two Assemblies after his initial election — or some seven to eight years —

to work his way up to the formal apex of the political pyramid. If he did not reach it in that length of time, he was unlikely ever to make it.

Top leaders were younger *on first election* than middle leaders, who were in turn younger than backbenchers. The representative top leader entered professional politics and the Assembly at a relatively early age. By about forty he had usually obtained a deputyship, though many persons first entered politics at the elevated level of a national legislator.

When we looked at average age, rather than age on first election, we discerned a U-shaped distribution, rather than the step progression previously encountered. Middle leaders tended to be younger than either top leaders or backbenchers. In fact, the middle leadership echelon seems basically to have been transitional group. Members moving into it either rose to top leadership positions or regressed to backbench status — perhaps even falling completely out of the Assembly. Few deputies consistently remained middle leaders as they did top leaders or backbenchers.

The two leader echelons tended to have a higher incidence of deputies born in the Aegean and Marmara Regions than did the rank and file. They also tended to have fewer children than the backbenchers. These items may be regarded, along with education and occupation, as indicators of "modernity." Altogether, they suggest that the formal leaders were appreciably more "modern" than the bulk of the deputies.

In five of the six Assemblies in which they participated, no female deputy became a top leader. Only in the Seventh Assembly (1943–1946) did two women achieve this level of formal influence — both through party position. Women did become middle leaders quite frequently through occupancy of the secretaryships of permanent parliamentary committees.

The three leadership levels were generally and strikingly distinguished from one another by formal education. In particular, top and middle leaders were markedly better educated than backbenchers. A similar pattern held with regard to foreign language competence. Considering only those deputies who spoke a foreign language, leaders were also more likely to have French as that foreign language than were backbenchers.

As in the preceding analyses, the educational data displayed the greatest consistency over time, and the occupational distributions revealed the greatest changes in the character of the deputies. The proportion of officials loomed especially large in the top leadership echelon up until the Democratic victory in the election of 1950, which produced the Ninth Assembly. Thereafter, professionals replaced officials as the formally most powerful group. Lawyers spearheaded the rise of the professionals, while military men suffered the severest losses in the rout of the officials. On the other hand, the economic contingent, led by the merchants, sharply increased in over-all size and in percentage of the total Assembly membership, but failed to achieve anything like a commensurate gain in the top leadership or even middle leadership ranks. Thus two occupational elements sharply increased in size during the post–World War II Assemblies: the lawyers and the traders. But only the lawyers were able to parlay that over-all increase in size into greatly augmented representation at the top leadership level.

There was an appreciable lag between the gross decline in the proportion of deputies with official occupational backgrounds and the decline in the relative size of their top leadership delegation. However, by the Tenth Assembly (1954–1957), nearly one half of the top leaders of Turkish government came from the legal profession. This was the most favored position any occupational group had ever been able to achieve. The military, in their heyday, only mustered one third of the top leaders. But by the Tenth Assembly their ranks had been sliced to a paltry 3 per cent of the top leader group.

Though it was found that the educational and occupational characteristics associated with preferred recruitment to and retention in the Assembly were also associated with greater access to formal power, no such association with access to formal power was found for the third recruitment criterion — "localism," or birth in the constituency represented. While rising ever since Kemal's death, localism, like mercantile occupation, remained more of a key to *entry* into the Assembly than to the uppermost portals of power within that body.

CHAPTER TEN

Elites within an Elite: Cabinets and Ministries

THE TOP LEADERS among the deputies normally included political party stalwarts and a few outstanding officials of the Assembly as well as the durable cabinet ministers. Since the cabinet was the most authoritative executive organ of the land and since there exists a good deal of information about the social characteristics of cabinets in other countries, I shall briefly and separately examine the social backgrounds of Turkish cabinets and individual ministries.

THE CABINET

Our first concern is the size and stability of the ten cabinets of our period. Figure 10.1 portrays the official size and the total number of persons participating in each cabinet ("total personnel"). It also gives the number of cabinet ministers for each Assembly who served throughout the *full* Assembly term in the *same* ministry. Thus, the figure crudely reflects the degree of turnover in the cabinet and ministries of each parliament. Actually, it may understate that turnover in a few cases, since only regularly appointed ministers are considered in the analysis. Acting and deputy ministers have been excluded. Menderes, for instance, in the Ninth and Tenth Assemblies, made considerable use of such temporary appointments. He employed the practice so extensively at times that the legal limit placed upon the number of such appointments was approached and the practice became a political issue. However, aside from this well-known case and some heightened

269

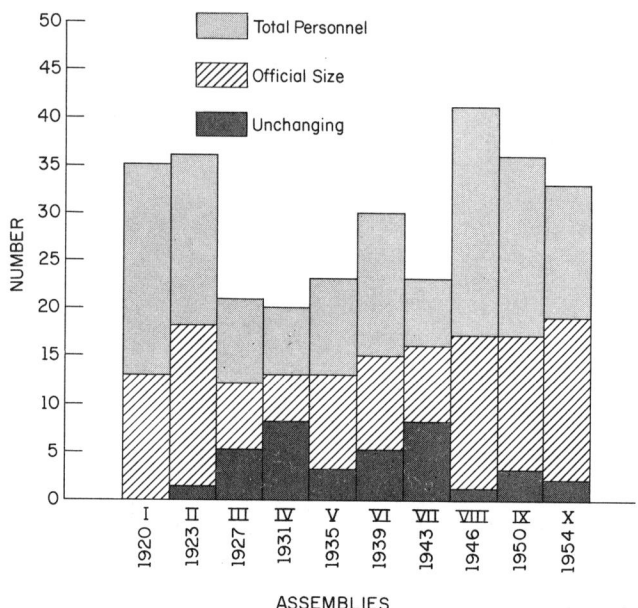

Figure 10.1. Official and total sizes of cabinets: ministers serving a complete term in the same ministry, by Assembly

NOTE: When the official size of the cabinet changed during the course of an Assembly, the most typical (usually largest) size was selected. The total personnel — i.e., total size — figure is the base for all subsequent cabinet percentages unless otherwise stated.

use of acting and deputy ministers in the First Assembly, the regularly appointed ministers generally held almost all portfolios.

Though Figure 10.1 traces a mild rise in the *official* sizes of the cabinets over the years, the broad picture in this respect is one of relative constancy. For example, the most conspicuous differences in official composition between the cabinets of the Fourth and the Tenth Assemblies were the added presence in the latter of several Ministers of State, a Minister of Labor, and a Minister of State Enterprises. Otherwise, the basic ministerial positions remained the same. That distention of the cabinet which has recently caused severe problems of coordination and control in some other parliamentary systems did not occur.

The total number of persons holding cabinet rank in any given Assembly varied from a minimum of twenty in the Fourth Assembly to a maximum of forty-one in the Eighth. About two or three dozen people were normally enough to staff all available posts for the term of the parliament. Comparison of the total size of the cabinet with its official size affords some insight into the degree of turnover in cabinet membership. Such a gross calculation, however, must be treated with care because, in one instance, a single ministry might have changed hands many times while the rest remained constant and in another case the turnover might have been spread among many ministries. For this reason I have added to Figure 10.1 the number of cabinet personnel who served a complete Assembly term in the same ministerial post.

It is apparent that the most stable period in terms of cabinet personnel was again the single-party era from the Third through the Seventh Assemblies. Particularly firm were the cabinets of the Third, Fourth, Fifth, and Seventh Assemblies. The Sixth Assembly cabinet was less stable than the other single-party cabinets primarily because of Atatürk's death and the changes in personnel that attended Ismet Inönü's assumption of the "pinnacle post." Excluding the President of the Republic but including the Premier, only four of the twelve cabinet ministers in office on November 10, 1938 — the date of Atatürk's death — were still in their same ministerial slots two months later at the turn of the year.[1] In the Sixth Assembly it took Inönü still more time and maneuvering to assemble the core of his "team."

The rest of the cabinets display relatively low stability in personnel. In the contumacious First Assembly, cabinet officials were often directly and individually elected by the Committee of the Whole House (*T.B.M.M. Umumî Heyeti*). Fluidity (sometimes better termed "near chaos") was the result. In the Second Assembly, Mustafa Kemal was still experimenting and gathering his working cadre of ministers, as well as fighting off the high-level challenge of the Progressive Party.

The great inconstancy in membership of the People's Party's cabinets of the Eighth Assembly lays bare the internal writhing that was going on within that organization during the eventful years from 1946 to 1950. In the course of this one Assembly, as the People's Party thrashed out an answer to the momentous question of whether it was going to remain a semiauthoritarian *parti unique* or take the tremendous step of truly permitting a multi-party system, three different Premiers held office — Recep Peker, Hasan Saka, and Şemsettin

---

[1] Cf. Dankwart Rustow, "Politics and Islam in Turkey, 1920–1955," in Frye (ed.), *op. cit.*, p. 89, n. 36, and *T.B.M.M. Yıllığı* (*G.N.A. Annual*), Devre V, *İçtima* 1 (Ankara: T.B.M.M. Matbaası, 1928–1958), pp. 243, 249. Rustow speaks of "five of eleven" who "retained their posts." There is no real discrepancy. He apparently includes Şükrü Saracoğlu, who remained in the cabinet though he switched from Minister of Justice to Foreign Minister, and excludes the Premier (though mentioning former Premier Bayar who was replaced by Saydam) to get eleven instead of twelve. But for Kemal's death the Fifth Assembly cabinet would probably have been the most stable of all.

Table 10.1
Reelection, Parliamentary and Ministerial Experience of Ministers, by Assembly (Percentages)[a]

Description	I	II	III	IV	V	VI	VII	VIII	IX	X
Reelection of Cabinet Ministers:										
Reelected to Subsequent Assembly	71%	76%	81%	95%	78%	87%	91%	20%	89%	79%
Never Reelected	20	11	5	—	17	3	—	63	8	18
Reelected after Interval	6	5	10	—	—	—	9	12	—	—
Died	3	8	5	5	4	10	—	5	3	3
(All Deputies Reelected to Subsequent Assembly)	30%	67%	74%	85%	73%	75%	61%	11%	52%	47%
Experience of Cabinet Ministers:										
Average Previous Parliamentary Experience, in Number of Assemblies Served	(—)	(0.61)	(1.33)	(2.00)	(2.48)	(2.34)	(2.78)	(2.51)	(0.86)	(1.33)
No Previous Parliamentary Experience	29%[b]	38%	10%	10%	22%	13%	4%	7%	75%	30%
(All Deputies — No Previous Parliamentary Experience)	77[b]	63	37	29	34	32	33	41	81	51
Previous Ministerial Experience	9[b]	43	76	65	65	53	65	29	6	48

[a] May not add to 100 because of rounding. The base N's for the cabinet are throughout the same as the "total personnel" statistics of Figure 10.1.
[b] Figure refers to the Ottoman Assembly.

Günaltay. This was one third of the total number of Premiers from 1923 to 1957.

The rather low stability of the cabinets of the Ninth and Tenth Assemblies also depicts a degree of internal party dispute and the trials of forming a "team." But more than that, it would seem to expose a rather definite policy of induced cabinet turnover, especially if scrutinized in conjunction with the very pronounced increase in the use of acting and deputy ministers already emphasized. It is difficult for a cabinet minister engaged in a high-level game of musical chairs to build enough of a following in any of his brief stops to become a possible rival to the entrenched. Such a consideration seems not to have escaped Adnan Menderes. In the cabinets of the Ninth Assembly, only Menderes, Bayar, and Foreign Minister Köprülü, remained constant throughout. In the Tenth Assembly, only Menderes and Bayar kept their grips on their posts for the full Assembly, though Kalafat, Yardımcı, Ethem Menderes, and Zorlu changed posts while surviving as cabinet ministers for the entire parliament.

Reelection and Prior Experience

The reelection chances and the relative amounts of previous parliamentary experience of cabinet ministers are shown in Table 10.1 to be superior, as expected. Data for all deputies are again furnished to ease comparison. The relative stability of the single-party cabinets is illustrated once more in the statistics on the previous ministerial experience of cabinet members.

Regional Origin

There is no need to present a table showing the percentage of women in the last six cabinets — those for which they were eligible. The percentage was always zero. Not one female ever held a ministerial post in the entire First Republic! I shall, instead, examine the places of birth and the regions represented by the members of the various cabinets. Table 10.2 indicates that cabinet ministers tended to have been born in the Marmara and Aegean Regions, or else outside Turkey, even more than did the entire body of deputies. Furthermore, unlike the situation in the Assembly as a whole, there seems to be scant indication of a decline in this tendency in recent times.

One rather surprising and interesting finding from Table 10.2 is that the relative cabinet preferment of deputies born in the Marmara Region is very mild and plainly less than that of deputies born in the Aegean Region, regardless of party system and who was in power. In nine out of the ten Assemblies the Aegean Region contributed more heavily to ministerial ranks than to the parliament as a whole. The

Table 10.2
Regions of Birth of Cabinet Members, by Assemblies (Percentages)

REGION	I	II	III	IV	V	VI	VII	VIII	IX	X	Total[a]
North Central	3%	—%	—%	—%	—%	3%	4%	2%	14%	9%	4%
Aegean	11	30	43	25	17	20	26	17	31	30	23
Marmara	29	30	19	25	26	33	22	22	22	21	26
Mediterranean	3	5	—	—	—	—	4	12	3	3	5
Northeastern	3	—	5	—	9	7	—	5	8	3	4
Southeastern	3	3	5	5	—	—	—	5	—	—	2
Black Sea	11	8	—	—	—	7	9	12	6	9	7
East Central	6	—	—	—	—	—	4	7	3	3	4
South Central	6	3	—	10	22	10	9	5	—	6	6
Foreign	14	16	29	35	26	20	22	12	24	25	16
Unknown	11	5	—	—	—	—	—	—	—	—	3
Totals[b]	100%	100%	100%	100%	100%	100%	100%	100%	100%	100%	100%
(Istanbul)	(20)	(22)	(19)	(15)	(13)	(27)	(22)	(17)	(17)	(15)	(20)
All Deputies:											
Aegean	11%	14%	17%	16%	13%	16%	14%	13%	12%	12%	
Marmara	13	20	24	22	28	29	33	24	21	16	

[a] Percentage given is that of all incumbencies born in region. In the entire thirty-seven years, there were 176 separate ministerial incumbencies, counting a given man as many times as he appeared as a minister in different Assemblies.
[b] May not add to 100 because of rounding.

same was true for the Marmara Region in only five of the ten Assemblies.

Table 10.3 sets forth the ministerial personnel of each Assembly according to the agricultural regions in which their constituencies lay. Alterations in the patterns of regional representation by cabinet ministers seem to coincide with the four subperiods previously distinguished. In the First Assembly, the most even regional distribution of ministers prevailed, and the greatest number of different provinces was represented. Then, in the Atatürk years, we witness a steep increase in the incidence of cabinet members representing the Aegean Region. By the Fifth Assembly, 43 per cent of all ministers had their constituencies in that area.

Under Ismet Inönü a pronounced reversal of this trend occurred. The percentage of ministers representing the Aegean Region was halved, and there appeared a widening of representation and a rather striking rise in the proportion of cabinet members who were elected from the Black Sea Region. In general, the Eighth Assembly has the second-best spread in cabinet representation — and the second-largest number of different provinces represented — of all ten Assemblies, though it had the largest total cabinet size as well.

Finally, under the Democratic Party of Menderes and Bayar, the Aegean Region resumes its disproportionate strength and even surpasses its maximum percentage of the Fifth Assembly. Another symbolic straw in the wind was that Bayar chose Istanbul rather than Ankara as his constituency, in contrast to what Atatürk and Inönü had normally done while President of the Republic. Moreover, Prime Minister Menderes also represented Istanbul instead of Ankara.

Localism

In the preceding chapter we found no salient patterned differences in "localism" (the percentage of deputies born in the province represented) between the leadership levels of the ten Assemblies. Some of the value of this separate inspection of cabinet personnel is displayed when we examine the "localism" of the ministers of the ten Assemblies contrasted with that of all deputies, as in Figure 10.2.

With minor discrepancies, the general similarity between the "localism" trends of both groups is apparent. Both sets of figures assume a basically U-shaped curve reflecting a decline in "localism" under Atatürk, a rise under Inönü, and then, under the multi-party system and Democratic rule, a continued ascent to the original level or beyond.

Even more significant, however, is the relative magnitude of the two percentages in each Assembly. In almost every case the percentage of "localism" among cabinet personnel is *less* than that for all

Table 10.3

REGIONAL REPRESENTATION OF CABINET MEMBERS, BY ASSEMBLIES (PERCENTAGES)

REGION	I	II	III	IV	V	VI	VII	VIII	IX	X
North Central	9%	14%	14%	15%	9%	17%	17%	7%	22%	3%
Aegean	23	38	38	40	43	20	22	12	39	45
Marmara	17	22	19	15	22	17	9	15	22	18
Mediterranean	9	8	10	5	4	3	9	15	3	3
Northeastern	6	3	—	—	4	7	—	5	6	3
Southeastern	3	—	5	5	—	3	—	10	—	—
Black Sea	11	11	10	5	9	17	22	24	8	9
East Central	11	3	5	10	9	3	4	10	—	3
South Central	11	3	—	5	9	13	17	2	—	6
Totals[a]	100%	100%	100%	100%	100%	100%	100%	100%	100%	100%
Number of Different Provinces	28	19	15	16	16	20	16	26	21	18

[a] May not add to 100 because of rounding.

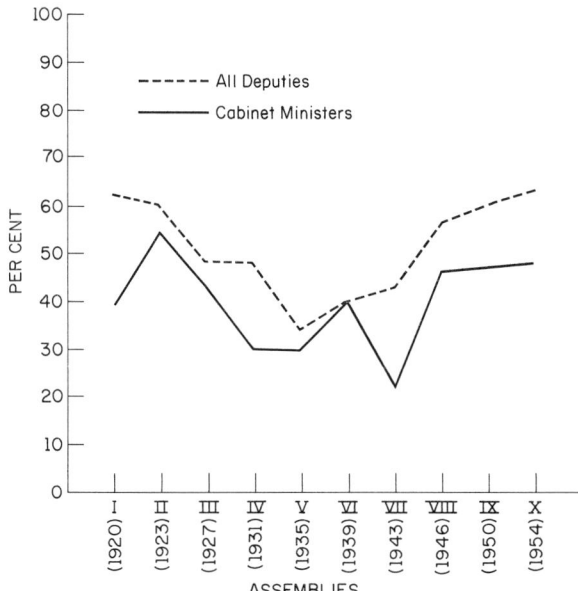

Figure 10.2. Birth in province represented, cabinet ministers and all deputies, by Assembly

NOTE: All unknowns have been excluded in these computations. Unknowns occurred only in the first two Assemblies: four persons in the First and one in the Second.

deputies — the one anomaly occurring in the Sixth Assembly, when the percentages were equal. Barring further evidence to the contrary, it would seem that deputies with strong local connections, as inferred from local birth, were regularly slighted in recruitment to posts of cabinet rank.

This fact reemphasizes the difference of the local influence recruitment criterion from the other two. Besides being weaker than the other criteria in its gross association with the election rate and being otherwise incompatible with them in some respects, "localism" seems different in its significance for the attainment of a position in the highest official unit of government. This difference is essentially that top leaders and cabinet ministers do *not* show a relatively increased incidence of "localism" when contrasted with backbenchers or all deputies. On the contrary, however, they *do* show a higher incidence of education, foreign language competence, publication, and membership in official and then legal occupational groups — the indicators for the other two recruitment criteria. In fact, with regard to "localism" among *cabinet ministers,* exactly the opposite is true. The ministerial group is regularly lower than the rank-and-file group in terms of the preferred recruitment characteristic ("localism").

Evidence of this type is what has produced the conviction that the weaker but still discernible recruitment preference accorded in many cases to those with strong local connections was very much a grudging accommodation on the part of Turkey's dominant political leaders to some of the perceived "hard facts" of political life. Even in the Kemalist prime, attention was paid to local forces and figures. In recent years, the surge of such forces and figures has become one of the most striking aspects of Turkish politics. But the inmost keep of the fortress of political power — the cabinet — still has not succumbed to the point of yielding a representation to the localists proportionate to their numbers in the Assembly as a whole, even though by the Tenth Assembly just under half of all cabinet members had been born in the province they represented. Note also that since the localism differences between leadership levels have been seen to be slight, the present finding suggests that the "top leader" localists have been primarily political party figures rather than cabinet ministers.

Education and Foreign Language Competence

The educational level of the cabinet was always extremely high, as the pattern unearthed by this analysis so far would lead us to expect. What is particularly noteworthy, however, is the fact that the percentage of *cabinet* personnel having obtained university-level education is even higher than the comparable percentage for each group of *top leaders*. Figure 10.3 exhibits this relationship in nine of the ten Assemblies, excepting only the First Assembly, where the percentages of university-educated among the two groups were equal. In fact, after 1927 only *three* men without university training attained ministerial rank: Celâl Bayar, Ali Rana Tarhan, and Atıf Inan! [2]

The cabinet can probably be considered to be an even more select group than the larger band of top leaders, which also included high party and Assembly officials, though some less durable cabinet ministers were middle leaders. We thus note another instance of the repeatedly observed fact that as the level of formal power rises, the incidence of incumbents of high social status, as least as measured by education and occupation, also rises. As the parliament differed from

[2] Bayar studied at a French school in Bursa prior to his embarking on a career in banking; but his education was mostly at the hands of his cleric-teacher father, and he has therefore been classed as privately educated. Ali Rana Tarhan attended Galatasaray Lycée and studied postal administration in Germany and Belgium. Atıf Inan went to the lycée in Izmir and also studied in Germany. Tarhan spoke German, French, and English; Bayar, French; and Inan, German. All three men were marginal cases in regard to formal educational classification and certainly qualified as intellectuals in Turkish society.

the general population in social background, so the upper leadership groups of the parliament differed from the parliament as a whole. Now we also find that the most puissant organ of all, the cabinet, differs from the top leadership group in precisely the same fashion.

On the average, more than one third of the members of each cabinet had received some formal education at the lycée or university level outside Turkey. Thus, the government at its uppermost reaches of authority could draw upon a considerable fund of first-hand experience with foreign practices and progress.

Even those ministers who had not actually studied abroad normally had a degree of access to Western culture through their knowledge of its dominant languages. Rare was the cabinet minister who could claim no foreign language competence. Moreover, we see from Figure 10.4 that the same ordered relationship between cabinet ministers, the broader group of top leaders, and the group of all deputies holds for foreign language competence as well as for formal education. The cabinet ministers were even more proficient than the top leaders, who, in turn, surpassed the group of all deputies.

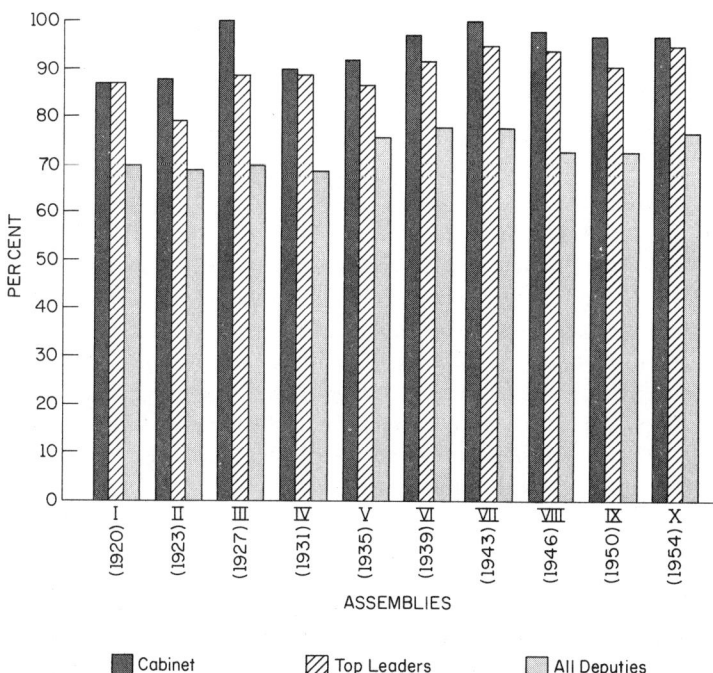

Figure 10.3. University-level education of cabinet ministers, top leaders, and all deputies, by Assembly

280 ANALYSES OF CHANGE

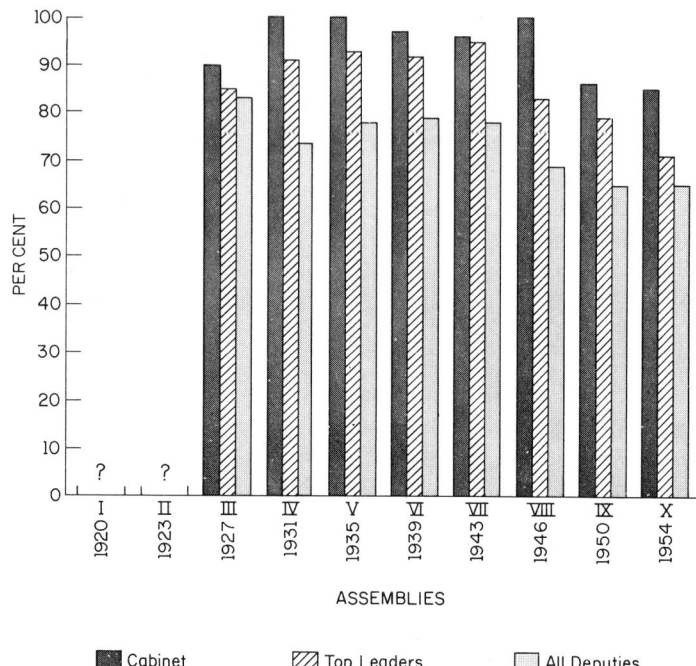

Figure 10.4. Persons claiming knowledge of at least one foreign language: cabinet ministers, top leaders, and all deputies, by Assembly

NOTE: Data for the First and Second Assemblies are not presented because of the high incidence of unknowns.

Though insufficient coverage precludes statistical presentation, inspection of the dossiers of the cabinet personnel suggests the significance of secondary-school education for many of these men, as indicated in Chapter 3. At least eighteen individuals attended the Istanbul Boys Lycée (*Istanbul Erkek Lisesi*), a minimum of eleven attended Galatasaray Lycée, four or more went to Mercan and Vefa Lycées, more than that number to the old Izmir Lycée (*Izmir Idadisi*), and so on. Similarly, the number of classmates from these institutions who were found in the same cabinet seems, impressionistically, far to exceed chance expectations. It is unfortunate that lack of information prevents further pursuit of this topic.

One allied matter, however, is that of the specific faculties attended by those ministers with university-level education. This material is summarized in Table 10.4, which illustrates the predominance of four faculties: law, political science, military, and medicine. About four out of every five cabinet appointments were of men trained in

Table 10.4

FACULTIES ATTENDED BY CABINET MINISTERS WITH HIGHER EDUCATION, BY ASSEMBLIES (PERCENTAGES)[a]

FACULTY	ASSEMBLY									
	I	II	III	IV	V	VI	VII	VIII	IX	X
Law	26%	31%	33%	20%	19%	28%	43%	35%	51%	53%
Medicine	15	14	14	15	14	14	13	13	6	13
Engineering	—	—	—	—	—	—	—	—	6	13
Political Science	30	24	24	30	38	24	26	38	23	22
Military[b]	37	34	29	20	29	34	17	15	9	—
Agriculture	—	—	5	5	5	7	9	8	6	—
Economics	—	—	—	—	10	6	4	—	11	16
Other[c]	—	—	—	5	—	—	4	11	—	—

[a] Percentages may not add to 100 because of rounding or because individuals may have attended more than one faculty and therefore have been counted more than once.
[b] The War College or the War Academy.
[c] The faculties of letters and of education, plus the pedagogical schools.

these four faculties.[3] Moreover, the table shows us again the precipitous decline of the military man in politics in recent times and the concomitant rise of the lawyer. Under the Democratic Party, more than half of all cabinet appointments were awarded to legally trained individuals.

Occupation

The occupational data naturally form a similar picture, though slightly less sharp because some persons with legal training went into occupations other than law. Adnan Menderes himself, for example, has been classed under the vocation of agriculture rather than law. His legal training came rather late in life, and both his general background and his livelihood revolved more about his position as a large landowner than about his legal work. Studying law while a deputy, he never really entered the practice of law. Other deputies with law faculty training directly entered the bureaucracy as government officials on graduation, and these have frequently been classed under government if they seemed to have been regular bureaucrats. In any event, the distribution of ministers according to faculties of higher education and their distribution according to occupation, as shown in Table 10.5, generally elicit similar interpretive comments.

Capillary Recruitment

Waves of change in the social characteristics of deputies to the Grand National Assembly in Turkey seem definitely not to hit that body broadside, affecting all internal levels equally and simultaneously. Rather — to adjust the metaphor — a sort of *capillary action* appears to occur. The lowest levels of formal power are affected first. If the pressure continues, the middle leaders are then altered, and only after a noticeable time lag is there a seepage into the highest levels of leadership and the cabinet. This observation has been suggested by the slower rise in the incidence of lawyers at high levels of formal leadership compared to their rise at lower levels, as well as by the current tardiness of the economic group in penetrating both the top leader echelon and the cabinet despite the over-all growth of the economic group in the Assembly as a whole. Obversely, the manifest stickiness in the decline of the military from the highest levels of formal power, compared with their more rapid disappearance from backbench levels, also illustrates this phenomenon.

Capillary action generally works slowly relative to other processes of change. Both physiologically and in our special metaphorical usage of the term to describe a form of change in political personnel,

[3] That is, at no more than six schools, since there were medical and law faculties in both Istanbul and Ankara that were attended.

CABINETS AND MINISTRIES 283

Table 10.5
OCCUPATIONS OF CABINET MINISTERS, BY ASSEMBLIES (PERCENTAGES)[a]

OCCUPATION	ASSEMBLY									
	I	II	III	IV	V	VI	VII	VIII	IX	X
Government	20%	16%	19%	30%	35%	23%	26%	24%	17%	18%
Military	29	27	29	20	26	33	17	15	8	9
Education	6	16	14	10	9	7	9	15	17	9
(Official)	(54)	(59)	(62)	(60)	(70)	(63)	(52)	(54)	(42)	(27)
Law	17	14	24	15	9	13	22	20	31	33
Medicine	9	11	10	15	13	13	13	12	6	12
Engineering	—	3	—	—	—	—	—	—	6	12
(Professional)	(26)	(27)	(33)	(30)	(22)	(27)	(35)	(32)	(42)	(58)
Trade	—	—	5	—	—	3	—	—	3	3
Agriculture	6	8	—	5	4	7	9	10	6	3
Banking	3	3	—	5	4	—	4	5	6	9
(Economic)	(9)	(11)	(5)	(10)	(9)	(10)	(13)	(15)	(14)	(15)
Religion	9	—	—	—	—	—	—	—	—	—
Journalism	3	—	—	—	—	—	—	—	3	—
Unknown	—	3	—	—	—	—	—	—	—	—
N's	35	36	21	20	23	30	23	41	36	33

[a] Percentages may not add to 100 because of rounding.

gradualness can be said to be its distinctive characteristic. When the demands of the environment are not severe, the slowness of the capillary process might be said to be conducive to the smoothest possible functioning of the organism — to alteration with a minimal amount of disruption and tension. In purely political terms, the gradual infusion of new personnel from lower levels of power to higher levels probably promotes maximal continuity in policy and reduces the strains resulting from change. Hence, the mechanism can be said to be "conservative" in the most favorable sense of the word.

Obviously, however, there is another side to the evaluation. If an alteration in the environment, or in other parts of the system itself, demands rapid change in recruitment, the type of process that we have broadly christened "capillary action" is unlikely to be adequate. Phased gradual absorption may simply be too slow a process under certain conditions, and the pressures demanding more rapid change may burst out elsewhere in the body politic, not infrequently rupturing vital organs at the same time. In a sense, the transfusion of new blood into the Grand National Assembly by the momentous elections of 1946 and 1950 may be looked upon as a traumatic adjustment correcting imbalances that the sluggish capillary-action recruitment process of the Assembly had permitted to develop. However, severe damage to the Turkish body politic may well have been produced.

In politics this absorptive process is subject to human regulation. One of the major tasks of an effective political system is to equate the pressure for recognition emanating from emerging forces in the society with the recruitment of representatives from those forces.[4] A cogent argument might be offered that the Atatürk-İnönü regimes, for all their many virtues, fell down seriously in this respect. The pent-up vexation of the repressed forces — the professional and economic sectors of the society — unnaturally agitates Turkish politics today.

THE INDIVIDUAL MINISTRIES

In this section we shall try to discover whether there was any uniformity in the social characteristics of the deputies who obtained each of the specific ministries. If so, how did the set of occupants of a given ministerial chair differ from the occupants of the other ministerial positions?

The investigation will be quite brief, noting merely the most outstanding points of homogeneity and diversity. Additional incentive

---

[4] An excellent case study of this process in American administration is to be found in Philip Selznick, *T.V.A. and the Grass Roots* (Berkeley: University of California Press, 1949).

for such a limited approach is produced by the fact that the groups of deputies having held the same portfolio are small, with the result that internal analysis loses statistical significance and becomes at best simply insightful and suggestive.

The analysis is restricted to the body of ministers holding office from the Second Assembly on — that is, from 1923 through 1957. The First Assembly ministers have been excluded because of their frequently unique method of appointment, and because of divergencies in the types of ministries involved. With the most minor exceptions, we are thus dealing with all the main ministries of the First Turkish Republic, excluding the final Eleventh Assembly.

Table 10.6 summarizes information about a number of characteristics of the grouped incumbents of the several ministries. The ministerial posts have been arrayed in descending order of ascribed power, as reflected in the averages of the power scores from the three relevant subperiods (Assemblies II–V, VI–VIII, and IX–X), which are given in the first column. Though the ministerial groups are extremely small in some instances, I have nevertheless computed rank order correlation coefficients for the power ranking as contrasted with the rank order of each of the other columns of the table. Two of these correlations proved to be significant at the .05 level. One of the two was that of the power score ranking versus the ranking of average ministerial tenure expressed in terms of Assembly sessions. The correlation indicates that the more powerful the post, the greater the incumbent's stability in office — that is, the higher the average tenure.[5] The most prominent exception to this relationship was that of the Ministry of Health and Social Welfare, which was the one post most consistently occupied by a specialist of established professional competence.

The second significant correlation was the negative one between formal power and the percentage of each ministerial group with *no* ministerial experience prior to first entering the given office.[6] The more powerful the office, the lower the percentage of occupants without prior ministerial experience — or, expressed positively, the greater the power of the office, the greater the percentage of occupants with previous experience in another ministry.[7]

This finding also increases one's confidence in the power ratings used. It indicates that ministers usually first entered the cabinet through ministries independently found to be less powerful. Only

[5] $N = 18$. Rho $= .592$.
[6] $N = 18$. Rho $= -.586$.
[7] The most notable anomaly in the ranking is that of the Ministry of State Enterprises, which was formed late in the Eighth Assembly and had only six occupants.

Table 10.6 VARIOUS CHARACTERISTICS OF MINISTERS, 1923–1957

Post[a]	Average Power Score	Average Tenure in Sessions	Average Age on First Election	Average Age on First Appointment	Average Years Elapsed, First Election to First Appointment	Average Foreign Languages	Average Prior Parliamentary Experience	Percentage with No Prior Ministerial Experience	N
President of the Republic	97.7	13.7	37.0	54.0	17.0	1.60	4.3	—%	3
Prime Minister	95.0	4.6	36.9	54.2	17.3	1.67	4.3	22	9
Finance Minister	76.3	3.4	40.1	44.1	4.0	1.50	0.9	58	10
Interior Minister	75.3	2.4	45.0	52.4	7.4	1.18	1.5	53	17
Foreign Minister	74.8	4.1	40.3	49.7	9.4	1.50	2.2	60	10
Defense Minister	70.0	2.4	45.7	51.8	6.1	1.65	1.1	35	17
Justice Minister	68.3	2.4	42.6	49.5	6.9	1.41	1.4	47	17
Education Minister	67.0	2.2	38.8	42.2	3.4	1.42	0.6	79	19
Minister of State (A.P.M.)[b]	63.5	1.7	40.7	47.6	6.9	1.43	1.6	57	7
Economics and Trade Minister[c]	60.8	1.7	41.2	46.2	5.0	1.37	0.9	67	30
Public Works Minister	60.0	2.2	42.8	49.6	6.8	1.59	1.3	63	19
Agriculture Minister	58.3	2.6	40.8	46.1	5.3	1.29	1.2	79	14
Health Minister	57.7	4.1	46.9	50.1	3.2	1.50	1.0	70	10
Labor Minister	56.0	1.8	41.6	44.8	3.2	1.44	0.4	56	9
Transportation Minister	54.5	1.9	43.3	50.1	6.8	2.00	1.5	75	12
State Enterprises Minister	54.5	1.8	43.8	48.0	4.2	1.33	0.7	33	6
Customs Minister	54.0	2.8	42.1	47.6	5.5	1.42	1.2	92	12
Minister of State[d]	51.5	1.3	40.8	48.7	7.9	1.69	1.1	69	16

[a] All ministries below Education in the table, with the exception of Public Works and Health, were not in existence for the full nine Assemblies.
[b] Minister of State and Assistant Prime Minister.
[c] Three separate ministries have been combined under this heading: the Ministry of Economics (*Iktisat*), the Ministry of Trade (*Ticaret*), and the Ministry of Economics and Trade (*Iktisat ve Ticaret*).
[d] Minister of State alone — not Assistant Prime Minister.

after their novitiate in such weaker positions were they generally able to move on to posts that were more influential. If one makes the plausible assumption that the normal passage to political leadership would be from less powerful to more powerful positions, the present finding exhibits the expected relationship between office power and the previous ministerial experience of the incumbents.

Two other correlations narrowly missed significance at the .05 level. These were, first, a correlation between office power and the average number of years that elapsed between the occupants' first elections to the Assembly and their first appointments to the particular ministry, and, second, that between office power and the average prior parliamentary experience (in sessions) of the ministerial office-holders.[8] Again, the relationship between power and both stability and experience is evident, though the nonpower indicators being employed are hardly independent of one another. The remaining data speak largely for themselves and will be referred to in the discussion of the most conspicuous characteristics of each group of ministers.

Presidents of the Republic

Only three individuals held the post of President of the Republic during these thirty-four years: Mustafa Kemal Atatürk, Ismet Inönü, and Mahmut Celâl Bayar. Atatürk had the longest tenure, some eighteen sessions. Inönü ranked second in this respect with fifteen sessions, and Bayar last with nine sessions (thirteen, if we add the Eleventh Assembly to complete the epoch). Both Atatürk and Inönü were military officers, while Bayar claimed private-sector banking as his vocation. This particular occupational difference can be said, in terms of the previous analysis, to have been highly symbolic of regime policy styles.

All three individuals were elected to the First Assembly in 1920 while still under age forty. Atatürk and Bayar remained in the Assembly until wrenched from it by death and force, respectively. The superficially frail but actually incredibly durable Inönü carried over to the first Assembly of the Second Republic, indeed becoming its initial Prime Minister at the age of seventy-eight just as he had been the initial Prime Minister of the First Republic half a lifetime before at the age of thirty-nine. Inönü and Bayar were the only deputies to serve throughout the entire First Republic, for forty years from 1920 to 1960.

Atatürk's family background has been sketched; Inönü's father

---

[8] With $N = 18$, a rho of .475 is necessary for significance at the .05 level. The two specified rank order correlation coefficients (rhos) were .469 and .460, respectively.

was a legal official; and Celâl Bayar's father was a religious teacher and *müftü* — a fact that again, some might argue, is not without symbolic import. Before assuming the Presidency of the Republic, Atatürk had experience as President of the First Grand National Assembly; İnönü had been Chief of the General Staff, Foreign Minister, and Prime Minister; and Bayar had held the early portfolio of (Population) Exchange, Reconstruction and Resettlement (*Mübadele, Imar ve Iskân*), plus the Ministry of Economics and the Prime Ministry. All three individuals had been at the helm of their political parties, Atatürk and Bayar as party President and İnönü primarily as Vice-President.

The Prime Ministers

Nine deputies reached the level of the Prime Ministry in the First Turkish Republic. Seven of the nine were born in the Aegean and Marmara Regions or outside present-day Turkey (Saka and Günaltay were the exceptions). Two thirds of the Premiers had official vocations, and five of the nine went either to the War Academy or to the Political Science School. Seven of the nine had prior ministerial experience (exceptions: Günaltay and Menderes), and all had at least one full Assembly as a deputy before becoming head of the administration. The average previous parliamentary experience was 4.3 Assemblies, as shown on Table 10.6. İnönü held the office for the longest time, some sixteen sessions, and Adnan Menderes was second in this respect with thirteen sessions in office, including the Eleventh Assembly.

All the Premiers, except Ali Fethi Okyar, were listed as having held important positions in their parties prior to attaining the Premiership. All but Refik Saydam were married and had children, and all spoke French, save Adnan Menderes, who spoke English. However, not all the Prime Ministers came from privileged and prestigious origins. For example, Şükrü Saracoğlu's father was a saddlemaker, and Refik Saydam's father was a merchant dealing in oils and fats.

The Finance Ministers

The Finance Ministers, as Table 10.6 divulges, deviate from expected ministerial characteristics in being younger at first appointment, in having had fewer years elapse between first election and first appointment, and in the average number of children produced by those married. Apparently, bright young specialists who had distinguished themselves in governmental financial affairs were co-opted to this post. Eleven of the twelve Finance Ministers had university-level education (exception: Ataç), and ten of these eleven had attended the Political Science Faculty! Of the dozen, eight have been classed as governmental officials by occupation, two as bankers, and one each as an educator and an agriculturist. Seven of the twelve had no previous ministerial experience. Eleven of the Finance Ministers spoke a foreign language, all eleven speaking French and four also speaking English. Seven of the total group of twelve were born in the Marmara and Aegean Regions or outside Turkey. Fuat Ağralı stayed longest in the post, a total of fourteen parliamentary sessions. Renda and Polatkan ranked second and third, respectively, with nine and eight sessions of service, though Polatkan added four more in the Eleventh Assembly, before meeting the hangman's noose.

The Ministers of the Interior

The seventeen Ministers of the Interior are shown on Table 10.6 to have been rather anomalous in that they were surprisingly older on first election to the Assembly and ranked last in foreign language proficiency. Sixteen of the seventeen (exception: Göle) were born outside present-day Turkey or in the Marmara or Aegean Region. Six of the seventeen were born in the province of Istanbul alone, and eight in the Marmara Region. The entire group had received higher education, ten of them at either the War Academy or Political Science School. Nine persons, just over half the group, were classified as official in occupation, six as professional (three legal and three medical), while two were journalists. Just over half the group also had no ministerial experience previous to their asumption of this post. On the other hand, all but two Ministers of the Interior (Ethem Menderes and Cemil Uybadın) had held prior Assembly offices, mainly as permanent committee officials. Nine of the seventeen had been chairmen of such committees, though, interestingly enough, only one had been chairman of the Interior Committee. Ten of the seventeen listed themselves as holding prominent political party posts before ministerial appointment. The Ministers of the Interior ranked second only to the Prime Ministers in the sizes of their families, having produced an average of 2.67 children each. Şükrü Kaya had the longest tenure in office of the seventeen ministers, remaining on duty for fourteen parliamentary sessions. A distant second in this respect was Ethem Menderes, who held the post for five sessions, or Namık Gedik, with seven, if we consider the Eleventh Assembly as well.

The Foreign Ministers

The Foreign Ministers also emanated largely from the Aegean, Marmara, and foreign regions. Only one of the ten deputies who occupied this office was born within Turkey but outside the Aegean and Marmara Regions. This was Hasan Saka from Trabzon. The Aegean Region alone provided half of the total group.

All the Foreign Ministers had received university-level education — half of them at the law faculties and two at the Political Science Faculty. Seven of the ten were listed as having received higher instruction abroad. All but Ethem Menderes claimed knowledge of a foreign language, every such individual speaking French, two speaking German, and two speaking English as well. All but two Foreign Ministers had previous parliamentary experience, the average being 2.2 Assemblies. On the other hand, six of the ten had no taste of ministerial activity before becoming Foreign Minister. Four ministers had previously held office on the Assembly's Foreign Affairs Committee. Tevfik Rüştü Aras held the portfolio longest — a period of seventeen sessions, from early in the Second Assembly until the death of Atatürk in the fourth session of the Fifth Assembly. Second in longevity was Fuat Köprülü, who served for eight sessions.

The Ministers of National Defense

For a powerful ministry, the seventeen Ministers of National Defense were also relatively old on first election to parliament. Once again, few of them were born within Turkey but outside the Aegean and Marmara Regions — just three of the seventeen, all born in the strategically important Northeastern Region. Seven of the seventeen were born outside the confines of present-day Turkey, most of these being the sons of military and official personnel stationed on the frontiers of the Ottoman Empire.

All the Defense Ministers had received university-level education. Not surprisingly, about half — eight persons — had attended the War Academy or War College. However, six had obtained legal education, and three had gone to the Political Science Faculty. Five of the six Defense Ministers who had legal training served under the Democratic Party regimes of the Ninth and Tenth Assemblies — another revealing comment on the decline of the military under Menderes and Bayar!

A glance at the occupations of the ministers is similarly suggestive. Eight have been classed as military, five as legal, and four as governmental. Until 1950, *seven military men,* three bureaucrats, and *one lawyer* (Birsel) held the post. After 1950, *one military man* (Kurtbek), one legally trained bureaucrat (Yılmaz), and *four lawyers* occupied the Defense Ministry!

Fifteen of the seventeen individuals knew a foreign language, all fifteen knowing French, four knowing German, four knowing English, and two knowing Russian. Seven of the total group had no prior parliamentary experience in the Grand National Assembly before that parliament in which they first became Defense Minister. Eleven of the group had other ministerial experience before assuming the

Defense post, and twelve of the seventeen had previously occupied Assembly offices. The Defense Ministers ranked third in the sizes of their families, behind the Prime Ministers and the Interior Ministers. They had an average of 2.53 children for each married man.

No one held the Defense Ministry for a very long stretch, perhaps by design. Kâzım Özalp survived longest — some seven sessions — with Apaydın and Artunkal ranking just behind him with six sessions each. The last man to serve a full Assembly term in office was Artunkal in the Seventh Assembly from 1943 to 1946. Subsequently, for the rest of the period, no man served more than two and one-half sessions in office. Both the change from men of military background to men of legal orientation and the heightened instability in office of the Defense Ministers may be viewed as having contributed to — and perhaps being symptomatic of — the widespread disaffection of the military from the Menderes regime.

The Ministers of Justice

Seventeen men occupied the post of Minister of Justice in our period. Twelve of these were born in the Aegean or Marmara Region or outside Turkey. All the Ministers of Justice obtained higher education, fourteen at the law faculties, two in political science, and one (Ali Fethi Okyar) at the War Academy. Twelve of the seventeen incumbents have been occupationally classed as lawyers, two each as bureaucrats and educators, and one as a soldier. Six Ministers of Justice had no experience as a deputy in the Grand National Assembly prior to that Assembly in which they received their first appointment to the Justice Ministry. Eight had no previous ministerial experience. On the other hand, publications were listed by ten of the seventeen ministers, most writings being in the legal field.

The average number of children was 1.64, placing the Justice Ministers second lowest of the eighteen ministerial groups in this regard. All but two of the group spoke a foreign language, fourteen speaking French, four English, two German. Moreover, there were persons who spoke various other Western languages such as Italian, Greek, and Russian. Ten men had held office in the Assembly or in one of its permanent committees before gaining ministerial rank, and five of these had been officers (chairman or rapporteur) of either the Justice or Constitutional Committees. One gains the impression that *the more specialized or technical the ministerial post, the more relevant was service on its counterpart parliamentary permanent committee for recruitment to that post.* The individual with the longest tenure as Minister of Justice was Şükrü Saracoğlu, who served for eight sessions; second was Mahmut Esat Bozkurt, who served for six sessions.

The Ministers of Education

Next we come to the nineteen Ministers of Education. These were geographically much better distributed. True, ten of them were from either the Acgean or Marmara Region or outside Turkey. But, despite this, every geographical region except the North Central was represented, in the sense that a Minister of Education had been born in one of the provinces of the region. All Ministers of Education except Hamdullah Suphi Tanrıöver had had university-level training, and Tanrıöver had attended Galatasaray Lycée. The distribution over the various university faculties was also greater than for many other ministerial groups. Seven different types of faculties were recorded, with the faculties of law, political science, and letters making the largest contributions to the group — four ministers apiece. Occupationally, however, eleven of the nineteen ministers have been classed as educators, since they were professionally engaged in teaching or educational administration. The remaining ministers were scattered among six other occupations, none having more than two representatives.

Education stands at about the bottom of the powerful ministries — or at the top of the ministries of lesser importance — and this fact is reflected in the relative lack of stability and experience of the Ministers of Education. As seen in Table 10.6, the average tenure was merely 2.2 sessions. Hasan Ali Yücel, the able but controversial Minister of Education of the late single-party, İnönü years, held the job for the longest span — ten sessions, from Atatürk's death to the end of the Seventh Assembly in 1946. After him, the next most durable ministers were Saffet Arıkan and Tevfik İleri, both of whom were in office less than five sessions — an appreciable drop. Fifteen of the nineteen persons had no ministerial experience prior to assuming command of the Turkish educational system, and ten of the nineteen had never had any prior parliamentary experience at all before that Assembly in which they became Minister of Education. The group of Education Ministers ranks seventeenth of eighteen in the average prior parliamentary experience of its members. Ten of the nineteen members of this group had held an Assembly office before becoming minister.

All but one of the Ministers of Education (exception: İleri) spoke a foreign language, each of these speaking French, four also speaking English and four German. Nine had publications which they claimed, and the average size of their families was 2.0 children for each of the sixteen married men. Ten of the total of nineteen did not appear to have held any prominent political party post previous to becoming minister.

Ministers of Economics and Trade

Three different but related economic ministeries have been combined into one joint description of the ministers of "Economics and Trade" in Table 10.6. From the Second Assembly to the third session of the Eighth Assembly there was a Ministry of Economics, headed by eleven different deputies over that period. In the Second Assembly there also existed a Ministry of Trade, which was dropped in the Third, Fourth, and Fifth Assemblies, and then revived in the Sixth. In the third session of the Eighth Assembly the two separate Ministries of Economics and of Trade were merged into a combined Ministry of Economics and Trade. The following description applies to the thirty individuals who held any of these three ministerial posts: Minister of Economics, Minister of Trade, and Minister of Economics and Trade. Two persons, Hasan Saka and Rahmi Köken, held the posts of Minister of Economics and Minister of Trade at different times. Each has been counted only once in my calculations.

As indicated by Table 10.6, the average tenure and the average parliamentary experience of these economics ministers were low. The Ministers of Economics actually rated higher in these respects than either the Ministers of Trade or the joint ministers. But, even so, the most durable incumbent of any of the three was Celâl Bayar, who served a modest seven sessions as Minister of Economics before becoming Prime Minister. No one else served more than four sessions in office. Of the entire group of thirty, only one man (Fuat Sirmen in the Seventh Assembly) held one of these three economic ministries throughout the course of a complete Assembly. Moreover, twenty-one of the thirty ministers had no ministerial experience prior to assuming these economic posts.

Twenty-two of the thirty men were either foreign-born or born in the Marmara or Aegean Region. Twenty-seven had seen university education, two asserted "private" training (Bayar and Ali Cenani), and one reached the lycée level (Inan). Law, political science, and economics were the dominant forms of higher training, fifteen attending law faculties, ten political science faculties, and four economics faculties (three persons attended two of these three types of school). Vocationally, lawyers and bureaucrats predominated, but there was a noticeable sprinkling of other occupations. Ten men were lawyers, ten were government officials, three were bankers, three were educators, two were classed under trade, and one each was a doctor and an agriculturist. All but three of the group professed knowledge of a foreign language. Once again, nearly all of those who knew a foreign language knew French, some twenty-five of twenty-seven. English ranked second, being known by six ministers, while German was known by five.

Half of the group claimed no important political party position before entering ministerial office, but just over two thirds (22) did have experience in Assembly and permanent committee offices previous to that entry. Nineteen had held committee posts, and these were generally in either the Economics or Budget Committee. Finally, the average married economics minister had two children.

The Ministers of Public Works

The Ministers of Public Works are intermediate in power and intermediate in most other respects as well. They appear in the middle of most of the rankings of Table 10.6. Eleventh in power, they are tied for eleventh in average tenure, rank thirteenth in relative youth at first election, eighth in relative age at first ministerial appointment, eighth in average prior parliamentary experience, eleventh in percentage with no prior ministerial experience, and sixth in the average number of foreign languages known.

This fairly consistent middle position is maintained along other dimensions. Eleven of the nineteen Public Works Ministers were born in the Aegean or Marmara Region or outside Turkey, but the over-all distribution of ministers was greater than for the more influential ministries. Only two regions (Northeastern and East Central) failed to place a locally born product atop the ministry. Educationally, all sixteen persons whose educational backgrounds were known had received university-level training. Six had attended one of the military colleges, six the Political Science Faculty, and five a law faculty. Three of these men had attended both law and political science faculties. Rather interestingly, only two individuals had engineering training (Zeytinoğlu and Çavuşoğlu), both of whom were selected by the Democratic Party's administration. With regard to occupation, three have been classed as engineers (adding Ahmet Muhtar Cilli, whose education is unknown, to the above two, who were trained engineers). Six Ministers of Public Works were military officers, five were bureaucrats, two each were lawyers and agriculturists, and one (Süleyman Sırrı) was of unknown occupation.

Six of the group had no prior parliamentary experience, and double that figure were without previous ministerial experience. Again, in partial compensation, the story with regard to experience in Assembly and permanent committee offices is better. Twelve of the total of nineteen deputies held such posts, ten of these having been the chairman of a permanent committee. Moreover, thirteen ministers listed previous political party posts of importance.

Perhaps appropriately, in family production the Public Works Ministers ranked rather high — fifth of the eighteen, as a matter of fact, each married man producing an average of 2.16 offspring.

The Ministers of Agriculture

The Ministers of Agriculture as a group rate rather low along the dimensions displayed in Table 10.6, but in this case there are the exceptions of anomalously high ratings in average tenure and youth at first election, and low ratings in the average number of foreign languages and prior ministerial experience. The group stood next to the bottom in the last two rank orders. The longest tenure was that of Muhlis Erkmen — twelve sessions. Hatipoğlu and Ökmen were second with six sessions each.

Nine of the fourteen agricultural ministers were born in the Aegean, Marmara, and foreign regions. Thirteen of them went to universities, four to law faculties, six to political science, and five to advanced agricultural schools (two attended two of these faculties). Six of the group had agricultural occupations, six were government officials, and the other two were a lawyer and an educator. All the agriculturists, however, were agricultural teachers and officials. Twelve of the fourteen spoke a foreign language, eleven of these French, four German, and two English.

Six of the ministers had no prior parliamentary experience, and eleven had no previous ministerial experience. Eleven did, on the other hand, have experience in Assembly and permanent committee offices, eight of these being committee chairmen. Just over half the group listed no important prior political party position. Finally, the average number of children was 1.83.

Other Ministries

Since the remaining ministries come at the tail end of the hierarchy, I shall mention merely a few of the most outstanding characteristics of each. For example, the ten *Ministers of Health* were all professional doctors, heavily from the Aegean-Marmara Region, nearly three fourths without prior ministerial experience, but nearly three fourths with experience as a permanent committee chairman. As Table 10.6 brings out, their average tenure in office was much higher than their power position would have led one to expect. The longest individual tenure was that of Refik Saydam, who was in office for sixteen sessions. Hulusi Alataş was second in this respect with eleven sessions in office.

The *Ministry of Labor* was inaugurated only in the second session of the Eighth Assembly, and just nine persons have held that post. Hayrettin Erkmen held it for the longest period — just five sessions. Regional birth distribution was relatively wide. Law dominated the higher educational training that all the ministers received, and law (four) and education (three) were the vocational leaders. Over half the ministers had no prior ministerial experience, but seven of the nine previously had experience of Assembly and permanent committee offices.

The *Ministry of Transportation and Communication (Ulaştırma or Münakalat)* was formed at the commencement of the Sixth Assembly in 1939. Seven of its dozen ministers had been military men, and two had been engineers. The geographical distribution of the birthplaces of these individuals was relatively wide, six different regions being represented. Three quarters of the group had no ministerial experience prior to becoming Minister of Transportation, half of them held no prior Assembly or permanent committee office, and just under half (five) had no previous parliamentary experience. All but one knew a foreign language, and, once again, all of these knew French. German ranked second with six persons knowing it, English third with five.

Just six individuals served as *Minister of State Enterprises,* a post created in the third session of the Eighth Assembly. With such a small group, internal analysis is not rewarding; the only prominent feature worth attention is that two thirds of the group were lawyers.

The *Ministry of Customs and Monopolies* was formed in December, 1930, in the first session of the Fourth Assembly. Since then, twelve deputies have occupied its highest office, Ali Rana Tarhan holding it for the longest time, a total of ten sessions. As with most of the less powerful ministries, there is relatively good distribution of regional birthplaces, five different regions being represented, though three quarters of all the ministers came from the Marmara, Aegean, and foreign regions. Law and political science constituted the basic training of the eleven who had higher education, nine attending those faculties. Two thirds of the group were lawyers or bureaucrats. The prior ministerial experience of these Customs Ministers was extremely slight. Only one man, Şevket Adalan, had held office before entering this ministry, and he had appeared just briefly as Minister of Agriculture in the same session as that of his appointment to Customs and Monopolies.

The last of these ministerial groups is that of the *Ministers of State.* Once more, this is a relatively recent post, formed in the Eighth Assembly. The added designation of one of the Ministers of State as Assistant Prime Minister made it a more important post, as shown in Table 10.6, a development that was greatly heightened under the Second Republic. The two most notable characteristics of these ministers were that three fourths were lawyers and that just under three fourths of them were listed as having held important political party posts before ministerial appointment. On the other hand, it is also necessary to note that over three quarters of these ministers had no ministerial experience prior to this appointment. The office seems in general to have been awarded to party politicians whose presence in the cabinet was felt essential but who could not easily be worked into the regular ministerial openings. The Prime Ministerial Assistants, in particular, included such well-known names as Faik Ahmet Barutçu, Nihat Erim, Samet Ağaoğlu, Celâl Yardımcı, Fatin Rüştü Zorlu, and Fuat Köprülü, most of whom held other ministries at one time or another.

Summary

This chapter has been devoted to an examination of the highest executive level of Turkish government — the cabinet. That body has been inspected both collectively, as a unit, and in terms of each of the ministerial offices which comprised it. The size and stability of the cabinet as an entity were first considered. In its *official size,* the cabinet displayed a relatively high degree of stability over the four decades under scrutiny. That elephantiasis of the cabinet which has plagued many other parliamentary systems was not found in Turkey. The official cabinet consisted of a dozen to a dozen and a half posts throughout the First Republic.

Greater fluctuation was found, however, in the *total size* of the cabinet — that is, in the total number of persons holding cabinet portfolios in each of the ten Assemblies. Comparing the total size of the cabinet with its official size in order to get a crude measure of stability in personnel, we learned that the single-party years witnessed the greatest degree of stability. The one internal exception to that trend was the Sixth Assembly, in which Ismet Inönü reconstructed the cabinet after the death of Kemal Atatürk. More generally, gross cabinet turnover usually seemed to reflect each new regime's efforts to form an effective and compatible ministerial "team." This ordinarily required one Assembly, after which cabinet instability decreased. All in all, about two or three dozen persons normally participated in the cabinet during the course of an Assembly — or just about two occupants for every ministerial chair.

Cabinet ministers were reelected with appreciably greater frequency than ordinary deputies and were more likely to have had prior *parliamentary* experience. Three fourths to four fifths of the cabinet were usually returned to the subsequent Assembly as opposed to about one half to two thirds of all deputies. Again, about twice as large a percentage of all deputies as opposed to all cabinet ministers was without previous parliamentary experience.

There was a good deal of fluctuation in the previous *ministerial* experience of cabinet members. In the single-party years, about two thirds of the cabinet had held earlier ministerial office, but at other times the proportion fell below one in ten with prior ministerial experience. Whenever anything like a multi-party system was operative, the amount of top-level executive experience on which the government could call depended very much on the fortunes of party warfare. What sorts of administrative problems, if any, were engendered by widespread lack of prior ministerial experience among cabinet members we do not know. The present data do suggest that an answer to this question could best be provided through comparison of the First, Eighth, and Ninth Assembly cabinets with their closest, more experienced counterparts.

Cabinet members were very disproportionately born in the Aegean and Marmara Regions or else outside present-day Turkey. The Turkish populations of these areas appear to have been relatively the most modern of their time. If we consider all persons who held a ministerial position over the thirty-seven-year period from 1920 to 1957, we discover that nearly half were born in the Aegean or Marmara area. If we add to this group those born outside Turkey, the group swells to two thirds of the total which came from these three limited areas. One fifth of all ministers were born in Istanbul Province alone, though the Aegean Region seems to have contributed even more disproportionately than the Marmara Region to the ministerial ranks.

The four basic subperiods or political eras that were unearthed by our previous analyses reappeared quite strikingly in the pattern of constituency representation of cabinet ministers. A rather even regional distribution in the cabinet was found during the First Assembly. Then, in the Atatürk years, the Aegean Region's contingent of ministers increased sharply. This trend was reversed under Inönü during the late single-party period, when representation was broadened and the Black Sea Region in particular made substantial gains. Finally, under the Democrats, the Aegean Region again mounted disproportionate strength in the cabinet, even surpassing its previous maximum and approaching a clear majority.

"Localism" (birth in the constituency represented) was consistently and markedly less among cabinet members than among all deputies. This stands in contrast to a lack of consistent differences between broad leadership levels in terms of localism. Hence, we infer that "top leaders" who were born in the constituency they represented in the Assembly were primarily political party officials in contradistinction to cabinet officers. However, these findings regarding localism must be interpreted with recognition of the sharp, continued, absolute rise in the incidence of localism in both the parliament as a whole and in the cabinet over the last few decades.

The cabinet consistently had a slightly higher incidence of the university-educated than did the group of "top leaders," who, of course, were in turn much more highly educated than the rest of the deputies. The same sort of pattern prevailed with regard to foreign language competence: the cabinet differed from the top leader group as the latter differed from the rank and file. About one third of the cabinet, on the average, had obtained higher education in a foreign country, and nearly all ministers knew at least one foreign language. Thus, there seems to have been a rather high degree of exposure to the West, either directly or through foreign language instruction and printed media.

About four of every five cabinet ministers came from one of but four types of faculty: law, political science, medicine, and military. Law was especially prominent under the Democrats. Not surprisingly, the occupational data generally reflect the same pattern.

The infusion of new blood into the Assembly appeared to follow what we have called a *capillary* process — that is, change generally seeped up slowly from below to the highest levels of authority. There was a definite "lead time" and "lag time" in the change of personnel at the top of the authoritative structure as compared to the bottom. Such a process would seem to promote continuity in policy, the reduction of tension within the legislature, and the maintenance of experienced leadership. However, the intrinsic slowness of the process would also seem to render it inadequate for the accomplishment of rapid change. Much of the current hostility and bitterness of Turkish political life can perhaps be understood in terms of the slow and meager way in which the People's Party during the single-party era absorbed the very social forces that its own reforms were encouraging, even though the analysis also shows that some efforts at absorption were made well before the advent of the multi-party system.

The second section of the chapter dealt with the characteristics of holders of each individual ministry. Though emphasis was here placed on the particular and distinctive qualities of the incumbents of each office, a few more general findings did emerge. For example, the more powerful the post, according to the formal power ratings, the greater the incumbents' stability in office and the greater the probability of their having had prior ministerial experience in another post. It would also seem that the more technical or specialized the ministry, the more important was previous service on its counterpart permanent committee of the Assembly. On the whole, and similar to the permanent parliamentary commitees, most of the ministers tended to have had educational or occupational specialization relevant to their ministerial activities. In this respect the Grand National Assembly seems to resemble the French model much more than the British: occupational and educational specialization appear to be quite significant background factors in determining the area of parliamentary concentration and officeholding of the deputy. Political specialization, for which social background provides the basic credentials, is a salient feature of this topmost stratum of Turkish political life.

Finally, probably the most dramatic of the particular findings pertaining to only one ministry concerned the role of military men in the National Defense Ministry. We learned that before 1950, seven of eleven Defense Ministers were military men, whereas after 1950, under the Democrats, only one of six Defense Ministers was a military man. Moreover, the instability of tenure of the Defense Minister increased during the latter era. Hence, I must add another important bit of social background evidence to the composite picture of the factors behind the military termination of the Menderes-Bayar regime in 1960. On almost every count, after 1950, military representation in the highest councils of the state suffered most grievously. Previous decline became virtual annihilation.

CHAPTER ELEVEN

Political Parties: 1920-1946

The Role of the Party in Turkish Politics

TURKISH POLITICS ARE PARTY POLITICS. This has been true, with few exceptions, since 1908 and the victory of the Union and Progress Association in the initial election of the Second Constitutional Period.[1] Within the power structure of Turkish society, the political party is the main unofficial link between the government and the larger, extragovernmental groups of people on whose support the government depends and whose activities it must mobilize — voters, interest groups, local communities, social strata, and the like. Furthermore, the formal structure of power adopted by the Turks from Western models, and which had sufficiently broad legitimacy to make it a conditioning force, invested power in a legislature (the Grand National Assembly) and also in an executive (the cabinet), supposedly controlled by that legislature. Regardless of which organ more influenced the other, the concerting of their activities was absolutely essential to the realization of most national aims. It was again the party which performed this second unifying function. Hence, the political party

---

[1] Unfortunately, though a great many studies of the Union and Progress exist, there is no thorough investigation of the process by which it established a national, highly articulated, deep-reaching party organization. In addition to the possibly great theoretical significance of such a study of this original party-political organization in one "traditional" society, it would be a valuable aid in understanding subsequent political developments in Turkey, since the Union and Progress served as an implicit model and partial foundation for the later creation of the Defense of Rights and People's Party organizations.

in Turkey during the period studied had at least two vital integrative effects: It was the primary agency for providing the requisite *intra*governmental coordination at the highest level, and it was the basic institution mediating between government and the *extra*governmental systems in the society.

In more personal terms, the direct significance of party for national political leaders of Turkey was: (1) that the party was the main channel for recruitment into politics and for promotion once recruited, (2) that the day-to-day behavior of the deputy as a deputy constantly occurred within an organized party context, and (3) that the symbols of party and the identification with party permeated the entire approach to politics of the deputy and the politically active populace.

To be even more specific, the personal impact of party on the lives of Turkish deputies can be seen in party control over nominations and in the fact that the would-be leader usually rose to eminence and power through party activity and with party support. He received his most practical training in political tactics from his party comrades or, more recently, from his enemies (the word is used advisedly) in opposition parties. As the social background data have repeatedly suggested, the best-trodden paths to top political office traversed the organized party hierarchies. Indeed, the "pinnacle post" itself — a distinctive feature of the Turkish polity in the First Republic — was characteristically the ultimate amalgamation of party and government, with the former being perhaps the more dynamic element of the pair.

The prime concern in the formation and maintenance of the cabinet was usually control over the dominant party. Illustrative insight into this situation can be obtained from a comparison of majority party caucuses with the subsequent Assembly debates on the same topic. Free voting and relatively open discussion were more common in the party caucus than on the rostrum or floor of the Assembly. Despite much co-optation, the cabinet still had to take pains on occasion to "bring the party along" — to secure its assent. If that was done, Assembly consent was often perfunctory.[2]

---

[2] For a similar comment, see B. Lewis, "Democracy in Turkey," *op. cit.*, p. 59. The most dramatic illustrations of the importance of the party caucuses are perhaps the following. First, there is the debate over the proclamation of the Republic on October 29, 1923. The People's Party caucus met at 10:00 A.M. After an impasse, Mustafa Kemal presented his draft proclamation to some party leaders at about 12:30 P.M. and then to the entire caucus at 1:30 P.M. It was debated, article by article, until 6:00 P.M., at which time the caucus closed and the Assembly immediately opened. The Assembly deliberated on other questions while its Constitutional Committee considered the draft proclamation, after which the Assembly as a whole debated the proclamation. Yet it still managed to enact the proclamation by 8:30 P.M. — that is, in just two and one-

A final example is the extreme party loyalty and commitment that prevail in Turkish political life, despite the superficially slight differences between the parties' avowed programs. Anyone who has attended even a small provincial congress of one of the major parties and who has become alarmed lest the zeal of the participants, in response to banal oratory, collapse the rickety cinema in which such affairs are normally held can give graphic testimony to the partisan cast of the Turk's approach to politics.[3] It is perhaps in this respect above all — the existence of extensive, powerful, highly organized, grass roots parties — that Turkey differs institutionally from the other Middle Eastern nations with whom we frequently compare her.[4]

Party and Governmental Control

In accordance with their official backgrounds, the typical style of the Kemalists in achieving the great national transformation they desired was that of command. The strategy was that of revolution from the top down, not from the bottom up. Falih Rıfkı Atay, editor of the main People's Party newspapers during the Atatürk Era and a close associate of Mustafa Kemal, fixes the Kemalist course quite well in the following passage from his recent memoirs of the Atatürk years: [5]

> We [the Turkish people prior to Mustafa Kemal and 1923] had been unable to see anything other than evolution as a principle. [However] in a society which is under the sway of institutions of the Middle Ages, the revolution of advanced ideas does not come from below, it comes from above. The great Russian revolutionary was Peter the Great.

---

half hours, compared to a minimum of four and one-half hours for the party. Cf. Atatürk, *Speech* . . ., *op. cit.*, pp. 652–657.

The other well-known example is that of the "revolt" within the Democratic Party's caucus (parliamentary group meeting) in the fall and winter of 1955. Here turbulent scenes in the caucus, close elections, and even the forced resignation of the cabinet contrast with the party's bloc voting in the Assembly on similar issues at the same time. For a brief discussion, cf. Karpat, *Turkey's Politics, op. cit.*, pp. 426–427.

[3] The contrast between the unimaginative, stereotyped, humorless oratory of political meetings in Turkey and the often devastatingly clever humor of the political cartoonists, or the shrewd wit of the politicans in private conversation, is very sharp and very intriguing. Most politicians appear to feel that the public does not relish humor at the hustings.

[4] For instance, one learns a great deal about political conditions in Turkey as opposed to those in Iran by contrasting, say, the People's Party, the Democratic Party, and the Justice Party of Turkey with the National Front (or the Iran Party), the Mardom Party, and the Melliun Party of Iran. The same holds for the contrast between the People's Party, the Wafd, and Nasser's latest venture in quasi-party formation.

[5] Falih Rıfkı Atay, *Çankaya: Atatürk Devri Hatıraları* (*Çankaya: Memories of the Atatürk Era*), (Istanbul: Dünya Yayınları, 1960), II, p. 335.

The first Ottoman revolutionaries were the Sultans and the Viziers. In such societies, only "counter revolutions," that is, reaction, come from below.

Not surprisingly, the standard Kemalist attitude toward the role of the political party was to view it primarily as *a mechanism for social control from above*. The party was an organization for securing the necessary governmental and societal integration — a disciplined set of power and communications relations functioning mainly to implement certain decisions of top leadership and to provide that leadership with information not normally forthcoming through regular bureaucratic and military channels. Such an orientation toward party is reflected, for example, in the great concentration of formal power in the hands of the party's leaders, as revealed in the *R.P.P. Regulations*. It is shown in the stern disciplinary pledges exacted of new party members, and it vividly emerges in the official union of the party and bureaucratic apparatuses in the mid-thirties. Most importantly of all, the conventional Kemalist view of the role of the party organization as being quasi-official and policy-implementing rather than policy-formulating was manifested in the establishment and preservation of the *single*-party system itself. The party was commonly considered to be, and to a considerable extent actually was, a vital instrument of social control, wielded by the party leader and his chief lieutenants.

At the same time, one of the fundamental later changes in the Turkish political system of the First Republic was an alteration in the internal power structure of the People's Party — a major deviation from the practice of the Kemalist years, though a deviation that was germinating even then. It was an alteration away from the concentrated and relatively unilateral distribution of power just described to one in which power was more dispersed and more reciprocal. Much more influence began to flow up and rather less began to flow down the formal hierarchy. Most relevant of all for our immediate purposes, these structural changes were associated with changes in the social characteristics of the personnel involved.

Party and Opposition

The political party, as an integrative power structure, can operate not only to concert *governmental* activities or the activities of government and supportive extragovernmental groups. Quite obviously, party organization can also concert the activities of *opposition* elements — can integrate and focus various forms of resistance to governmental power — and normally does so in the West. In Turkey, party organization was not *always* the monopoly of a single party during the years from 1920 to 1957 or even during the years from

1923 to 1945, though it is true that there was *often* such a monopoly. Opposition party organizations of assorted real and artificial types did exist in the Assembly during these years. Indeed, the growth and development of such organized opposition was a salient factor in producing the described change in the internal power structure of the People's Party. The social backgrounds of these opposition movements, as they differed from one another and from the dominant party group in the Assembly, are especially interesting.

In this treatment of interparty differences in the social backgrounds of Turkish deputies I shall proceed in chronological fashion, commencing with the First Assembly and examining in turn each important manifestation of organized opposition and the majority party it confronted. To complete the total portrayal of the social backgrounds of parties and movements in the Assembly, we simply need to add the characteristics of the People's Party during the parliaments in which there was no overt formal opposition — in actuality, only the Fourth and Fifth Assemblies. However, in these cases the material previously presented for the Assembly as a whole affords the desired description of the sole party in those Assemblies, the People's Party. So I shall omit those data.

The specific party groups, then, are as follows: the First and Second Groups of the First Assembly; the Progressive Republican Party; the Liberal Republican Party; the Independent Groups of the People's Party in the Sixth and Seventh Assemblies; and the Democratic Party, the Nation Party, and the Freedom Party in one or more of the last three Assemblies. With the exception previously noted regarding the Fourth and Fifth Assemblies, we shall be dealing with the People's Party in all Assemblies after the First. We shall also look briefly at one very important clique which emerged within the People's Party, that of the famous "thirty-five." The single-party years will be examined in this chapter and the multi-party years in the next.

Finally, we shall investigate the deputies' speaking and voting records in the Grand National Assembly. The data on speaking cover most of the sessions of the First Assembly and relate to the number of times each deputy spoke and the length of each of his utterances. The voting data cover all Assemblies but the Second, though information concerning the First and Third Assemblies is extensive but incomplete. I have not found it profitable to examine the entire voting record of each deputy and correlate the total voting pattern with social background characteristics. Doing so on a trial basis merely produced the social background configurations that distinguished the parties from one another. Instead, I have concentrated on the more interesting phenomenon of majority party voting *deviance*. I have tried to separate those mavericks within the governmental party who voted in parliament against a governmental proposal. In short, since the overriding party discipline obliterated the most common and visible effects of social background, I have focused on the outstanding cases in which that party discipline broke down, looking there for a possible relationship between social background characteristics and deviant voting.

THE FIRST AND SECOND GROUPS OF THE FIRST ASSEMBLY

In recollection of the bitter partisanship of the Second Constitutional Period, the Defense of Rights Association started out with an antiparty bias. In fact, it went so far as to affirm this antiparty outlook specifically in its *Program and Regulations,* stipulating that "This national association is free from every sort of party current," and deliberately donning the title "Association" (*cemiyet*) rather than "Party" (*fırka*).[6] Such an orientation proved feasible, perhaps even sagacious, up to the inauguration of the Grand National Assembly in 1920. After that, the need for the legislative-executive coordination that party normally provides became agonizingly apparent. The First Asembly was a remarkably heterogeneous, cantankerous, and insecure body. For example, Mustafa Kemal's strong-armed crony, Kılıç Ali, gives the following colorful description of this Assembly:[7]

> The First Grand National Assembly was an utterly different world.
> There you could find people who had pulled on jackets over their loose robes, people ranging from a number of bigoted individuals who wore the fez to Kurds and Circassians wrapped up in their national costumes, astrakhan-wearing nationalists, the doctor, pharmacist, commander, *ulema,* judge, dervish, sheikh, lawyer, telegraph official — pasha, bey, efendi, ağa, hacı, hoca, of every sort, from every occupation, all the types of a society.

These rather wild differences in social background were quickly embodied in a plethora of cliques, factions, and followings. Such divisions, when coupled with a formal structure of power that is best described as "convention government," produced a leadership crisis in which the entire nationalist cause nearly foundered.[8] To remedy

---

[6] Cf. Tunaya, *Türkiyede Siyasî Partiler, op. cit.,* pp. 478, 516, 529.

[7] Ali Kılıç, *Kılıç Ali Hatıralarını Anlatıyor* (*Kılıç Ali Presents His Reminiscences*), (Istanbul: Sel Yayınları, 1955), p. 67. Note that Ali describes most of these people in terms of their occupations. The same practice is widely followed in similar works of other Turkish writers.

[8] For a depiction of these various groups see, among others, *Histoire . . .,* pp. 86–87; Halide Edib (Adıvar), *The Turkish Ordeal, op. cit.,* pp. 183–184; Mears, "The Kemâlist Movement," in Mears, *Modern Turkey, op. cit.,* pp.

matters, Mustafa Kemal had "recourse" to the formation of a unifying parliamentary party of his own in May 1921. This organization took the name of the Defense of Rights *Group*. A little over a year later, some of the opposition to Mustafa Kemal and his associates also organized rather more clearly.[9] They remained nominally in the Defense of Rights Group, whose net had been broadly cast, but they were styled the "*Second Group*" of that parliamentary party — the Kemalists being labeled the "*First Group*." In any event, these two groups were the initial, important, organized antagonists in the Grand National Assembly.

Size

The First Group was somewhat less than twice as large as the Second Group, numbering 197 to the Second Group's 118.[10] There were also 122 deputies who were not listed as having had any affiliation with either group. The large majority of those without group allegiance were the inactive, "inconsequential" members of the First Assembly. For example, no one from the First Group resigned his deputyship or was removed. Only three persons from the Second Group (3 per cent) resigned, and no one from that group was removed. Just one man from each of the two groups died during the course of the As-

---

574-575; Atatürk, Speech..., *op. cit.,* pp. 502-504. The factions most commonly distinguished are: the Solidarity, or Union, Group (*Tesanüt Grubu*); the Independence Group (*Istiklal Grubu*); the Defense of Rights Faction (*Müdafaai Hukuk Zümresi*); the People's Faction (*Halk Zümresi*); the Reform Group (*Islahat Grubu*); the conservative Islamists (mostly clerics); the moderate conservatives; a small labor element; and an equally small band of those labeled "more or less Communist."

[9] There is a misprint of the date in Tunaya, where it is given as "*Temmuz* (July), 1338 (1923)," on p. 537. Of course, 1338 was 1922, which is the correct date. On the creation of the Second Group, see, e.g., Speech..., *op. cit.,* pp. 533 ff. Mustafa Kemal considered Rauf Bey (Orbay) to be in league with the Second Group, but he was never listed as a member. Cf. Tunaya, *Türkiyede Siyasî Partiler, op. cit.,* pp. 536-539, and the First Assembly *Albüm,* pp. 242-250, where the names of the First and Second Group members are given. Tunaya adds four names to the *Albüm* list, and I have also included these four in the Second Group.

[10] Several authors, both Western and Turkish, have represented the size of the Second Group as being "about forty." For instance, M. Sadık Yiğitbaş, in his work, *Kiğı* (Istanbul: Cemal Asmi Matbaası, 1950), p. 241, makes much of the fact that his local favorite, Hüseyin Avni (Ulaş), an important leader of the Second Group, was elected a Vice President of the Assembly despite the fact that the First Group numbered 200 and the Second Group 40. Perhaps this figure of two score refers to active members which these authors have distinguished in some unexplained fashion. But our speaking analysis shows that 78 of the 118 persons listed by Tunaya as being in the Second Group (or of the 114 in the official *Albüm*) actually appeared as Assembly speakers in our 10 per cent sample of the pages of the First Assembly *Debates.*

sembly. On the other hand, of those without group ties, sixty-seven deputies resigned their posts (55 per cent), six were removed (5 per cent), and twenty-two died (18 per cent).

Age

The Nationalist Movement as a whole was distinguished by its youth, and so was the First Assembly. Surprisingly, within the First Assembly the Second Group was moderately but noticeably younger than the First Group. Since the adherents of the Second Group were more conservative, I had expected them to be, if anything, older rather than younger than their antagonists. Just over half (52 per cent) of the Second Group members were under forty years of age, while the comparable figure for the First Group was something over one third (37 per cent). The average ages for the two groups were: First Group, 43.6 years; and Second Group, 41.5 years. Both groups were younger than the unaffiliated, who had about one quarter (27 per cent) of their members under forty and an average age of 46.5 years, though in this last case the incidence of those for whom information was lacking approaches half the group. If we look at prior experience in an Ottoman Assembly instead of age, we find that the First Group members emerge on top, with 30 per cent of the First Group having such legislative experience, 22 per cent of the Second Group, and but 13 per cent of the unaffiliated.

Geographical Representation and Birthplace

Where did the group members come from, both with regard to constituency represented and region of birth? Were the First and Second Groups different in these respects? If we separate the regions in which there was substantial Allied and Greek occupation from the remainder of the country and look at the group connections of the deputies representing these regions, we discover an interesting fact. Deputies from the occupied regions (the North Central, Aegean, Marmara, Mediterranean, and South Central Regions) contributed 59 per cent of the total numerical strength of the First Group and merely 44 per cent of the strength of the Second Group, a difference of some fifteen percentage points.[11] Succinctly, the First Group deputies tended disproportionately to represent the occupied regions of the country and the Second Group members the unoccupied regions. Of course, I am merely hypothesizing that the fact of Allied occupation was a decisive characteristic of the two differentiated regions. One could, with considerable cogency, argue that some other characteristic, such as greater Westernization or higher per capita income, was the

[11] Chi square is 6.96, significant at the .01 level with one degree of freedom. N's are: First Group, 197; Second Group, 118.

underlying regional similarity. I do not have time to enter into *all* the superficially attractive *ex post* explanations for this intriguing finding, and I shall merely say a word or two more about *my own* superficially attractive *ex post* explanation.

While not denying that other factors were probably also at work, my general impression is that Mustafa Kemal's supporters in the Assembly did tend to come from the regions enumerated at least partly *because* they were occupied regions. As such, the local resistance groups had to be more cautious and could not organize as effectively as those in the unoccupied eastern regions of Turkey. The occupied regions depended more upon Mustafa Kemal's support and were more readily influenced by him. It was easier for him to secure nominations for his supporters from the occupied provinces than to induce the actively functioning, self-conscious Defense of Rights organizations in the unoccupied provinces to adopt his candidates. These organizations frequently seemed to have felt that they had started the resistance movement before he arrived on the scene — as they had — and that they should have every bit as determinative a voice in the shaping of the movement as Kemal. Locally rooted, relatively well established, and aware of their independent earlier struggles in resistance to Allied demands, the organizations of the unoccupied areas of Turkey proved to be least tractable of all.

Partial evidence for this conclusion is the fact that the most stubborn regional hostility to Mustafa Kemal's leadership came from precisely those areas in the unoccupied zone where the Nationalist Movement began. The two regions in which the Second Group was most strongly represented were the Northeastern and Black Sea Regions — the original base of overt operations by Kemal and the Defense of Rights Association. A full 30 per cent of the Second Group represented these two regions in the Assembly, while just 15 per cent of the members of the First Group represented these regions. Carrying the analysis one step further, if we look at the delegation from the province of Erzurum, where the local Defense of Rights Association was of particularly great historic importance and where the first momentous congress of the Nationalist Movement was held, we learn that eight of the province's ten deputies were Second Group members, four of them leaders of that opposition. The two non–Second Group deputies can hardly be said to have been Kemalist stalwarts. One had no group affiliation and resigned in the first session of the Assembly. The other (Asım Vasfı Araslı) did belong to the First Group, but had one of the most negative voting records of anyone in that group, voting against government proposals at least nineteen times. In fact, the voting analysis for the First Assembly, though inconclusive, generally seems to support the emphasis here given to the factor of Allied occupation as influencing support for Mustafa Kemal and his First Group.

The intergroup patterns of regional birth are basically similar to those of constituency representation, a fact that is hardly astounding for a parliament in which over 60 per cent of the deputies were born in the province represented. Making the distinction between those born in the more developed Aegean, Marmara, and foreign areas, on one side, and those born in Turkey but not in the Aegean or Marmara Region, on the other, we discover that 39 per cent of the First Group fell into the Aegean-Marmara-foreign-birth category while just 18 per cent of the Second Group were so born. The social background differences between the First and Second Groups in very many ways anticipate the later differences between the People's Party and the Democratic Party; and, in fact, they also presage later developments in the characteristics of the Assembly as a whole, which moved, after the Kemalist heyday, in the directions in which the Second Group tended to deviate from the First Group.

Localism

From the entire canvas I have painted so far the reader might well be able himself to predict how the two groups would differ from one another along the dimension of "localism," or birth in the province represented. The incidence of localism among Second Group members was indeed appreciably higher than that among First Group members: 71 per cent contrasted with 59 per cent.[12] The anticipated pattern is again found. The Second Group would seem to have had stronger local ties than the First Group if we accept this indicator.

Occupation

I have not analyzed the differences in educational level between the two groups simply because the proportions of those for whom educational information is lacking are so great that the comparison becomes quite unreliable.

The information regarding occupation, however, is much more complete and is presented in Table 11.1. The most striking finding from Table 11.1 coincides with the expectation induced by the previous analyses. The paramount occupational difference between the First and Second Groups was the markedly higher proportion of lawyers in

[12] Chi square is 3.37, significant at the .10 level with one degree of freedom. N's are: First Group, 159; Second Group, 86. The null hypothesis is that the found differences would occur through random division of the deputies into two groups without regard to localism. The chi square test is, of course, not here used to make any inference to some larger population from which we have some sort of "sample." We are dealing with the entire population of our concern; thus, any found difference is in that sense "significant."

Table 11.1
PARTY GROUPINGS IN THE FIRST ASSEMBLY, BY OCCUPATION (PERCENTAGES)

OCCUPATION	PARTY			ASSEMBLY
	First Group	Second Group	No Group	
Government	25%	20%	22%	23%
Military	15	13	19	15
Education	6	5	1	5
(Official)	**(46)**	**(37)**	**(42)**	**(43)**
Law	9	24	8	13
Medicine	6	2	3	4
Dentistry, Pharmacy, and Veterinary Medicine	—	1	1	1
Engineering	—	1	—	—
(Professional)	**(16)**	**(27)**	**(11)**	**(18)**
Trade	10	14	11	12
Agriculture	9	2	5	6
Banking	1	—	—	1
(Economic)	**(21)**	**(16)**	**(16)**	**(19)**
Religion	13	15	29	17
Journalism	3	3	—	2
Other	2	2	1	2
(Unknown)[a]	(3)	(14)	(34)	(15)
Total	100%	100%	100%	100%
N	197	118	122	437

[a] The "unknowns" are in parentheses because they have been excluded from the computation of the occupational percentages. The "unknowns," however, are included in the N's, so that to get the base for the occupational percentages one must compute the absolute number of "unknowns" by applying the given percentage to the proper N and subtracting the resultant figure from that N. Over-all and subtotals may not add to designated figure because of rounding.

the Second Group — 24 per cent as opposed to 9 per cent. The legalistic resistance to the Kemalists began in the First Assembly and presaged later developments. Moreover, the other occupation whose representation in the Second Group exceeded its First Group representation was predictably that of trade. We find law and trade overcontributing to the opposition from the very start of the Grand National Assembly.

The occupational contingents that were overrepresented in the First Group were agriculture, government, medicine, and the military, in that order, though the differences are quite small and statistically insignificant. The lack of one specific difference between the First and Second Groups is most interesting. Though a slightly greater incidence of men of religion existed in the Second Group, the relationship was basically one of equality. It was not true, as is sometimes claimed, that the Second Group differed from the First by being populated by *hocas* and *ulema*, even though some of the men classed as lawyers might well have been designated clerics. As Tarık Tunaya and Dankwart Rustow have pointed out, there were clerics and nonclerics in both groups.[13] The proportions on the two contending sides were not dissimilar. It is also significant to note that the clerics seemed particularly reluctant to participate at all in the Assembly and in its internal partisan strife. I make this inference from the large proportion of the nonaffiliated (29 per cent) who wore the white turban (*sarık*) of the man of religion.

Reelection and Leadership Level

What effect, if any, did membership in the First or Second Group have on the reelection chances and formal power positions of the deputies? The first part of this question was answered in Chapter 2, where I pointed out the decimation of the Second Group in the election of 1923. Only three of the 118 were reelected to the next Assembly, and only eight more members of the group were reelected to any subsequent Assembly other than the Second after a hiatus in their political careers.[14] Of these eleven survivors of the Second Group, nine were well below average for that group in their spoken participation in the parliament, though the negative voting of the eleven was only slightly below the mean figure for the Second Group.

The First Group had 58 per cent of its members reelected to the Second Assembly and another 4 per cent reelected to a later Assembly after missing the Second. Even the unaffiliated did better with regard

---

[13] Tunaya, *Türkiyede Siyasî Partiler*, op. cit., p. 530. D. Rustow, "Politics and Islam...," in Frye (ed.), op. cit., p. 85, n. 26.

[14] The three men reelected to the Second Assembly were: Ali Rıza from Amasya, Mehmet from Biga, and Ali Rıza from Kırşehir. The first was a cleric and the last two were merchants. Mehmet was also elected to the Third Assembly, Ali Rıza from Amasya faded out with the Second Assembly, and Ali Rıza from Kırşehir was hanged in the purge of 1926 by the Ankara Independence Tribunal, as were several other former Second Group members.

The eight men not reelected to the Second Assembly but reelected to some later Assembly were: Arif (Özdemir) from Bitlis (reelected in Assembly VIII), Emin from Canık (IV), Neşet (Akkor) from Çankırı (VIII), Mustafa Durak (Sakarya) from Erzurum (V, VI), Süleyman Necati (Güneri) from Erzurum (V), Haydar Lûtfi (Aslan) from İçel (VIII), Cemal (Mersinli) from Isparta (VI), and Sırrı (Bellioğlu) from İzmit (IV). Four were government officials, two were lawyers, one was a military man, and one was a journalist.

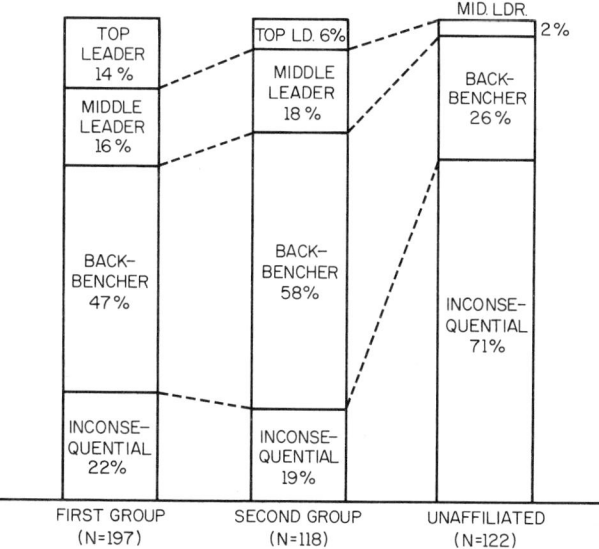

Figure 11.1. Party groupings in the First Assembly, by leadership levels

to reelection than the Second Group, since 8 per cent of the former entered the Second Assembly and another 5 per cent entered later Assemblies.[15]

The distribution of formal power between the groups is given in Figure 11.1. Though less pronounced than in later opposition parties, there was even in the chaotic First Assembly a tendency for the opposition to fall into the middle levels of power and to be found less frequently at the extremes of top leadership or unimportance. The other item of interest from the figure is the lowly status of the unaffiliated group. It was basically an inactive element. The 71 per cent of its members falling into the "inconsequential" stratum exposes this fact, as will the behavioral analyses.

Speaking in the First Assembly

An important aspect of the role of deputy in Turkey is that of speaking in the Grand National Assembly. The aspiring young legislator and the more experienced solon both create, alter, and maintain their reputations, in part, by ascending the rostrum of the Assembly and effectively addressing their colleagues. One may endure in the Assembly without speaking, but it is extremely unlikely that one could

[15] Those dying during the First Assembly, and thus, I trust, ineligible for reelection, have been excluded from all percentage calculations.

reach a position of leadership without actively and frequently participating in parliamentary debate. As early as the First Assembly, for example, Mustafa Kemal found it a useful tactic to condemn a deputy who incurred his wrath on the grounds of that deputy's failure to speak in the Assembly.[16] Today, in conversation with leading politicians in Turkey one quite regularly hears them praise a party comrade for being adept in Assembly debate, and sometimes even contend that this talent more than compensates for certain important and acknowledged faults of the individual under discussion. Similarly, one encounters the appraisal of a young deputy which says that he is intelligent and industrious, "but just doesn't speak up enough in the Assembly and won't get anywhere, really, until he does." Furthermore, insofar as speaking is more free of party control than voting, its correlation with social background characteristics may be particularly rewarding.

The rigorous, quantitative examination of speaking patterns in a large legislative body is a most time-consuming labor. Since the same can be said of the other research processes which have gone into the preparation of the data presented in this work, compromises have been necessary. The analysis of speaking has been restricted to the First Assembly. It deals only with the number of times a deputy spoke and the length of his remarks. Originally, I attempted to include a classification of the topic on which the deputy spoke, but I found that such a classification could not be adequately performed without much additional research for which I had not the resources.

The basic procedure followed in this analysis of speaking behavior in the First Assembly was simply to take a 10 per cent systematic sample — with a randomly selected starting point — of the pages of the verbatim *Parliamentary Debates* of the Assembly (*T.B.M.M. Zabıt Ceridesi*). I covered the first two of the three years of life of that body, from April 23, 1920, to April 4, 1922 — some eighteen volumes of debates.[17] Each time a deputy spoke, excluding Assembly

---

[16] "It is true," said Mustafa Kemal, "that a deputy of Brusa (Bursa), who, during his whole time of being a deputy, had not once appeared on the speaker's rostrum, nor ever spoken a word in the Chamber in defence of the interests of the nation and the Republic, the deputy of Brusa, I say, Nureddin Pasha, introduced a lengthy motion against wearing hats and mounted the rostrum to defend it." *Speech...*, *op. cit.*, p. 722. For three examples among many of a deputy's being praised for his Assembly oratory, see Ziya Göğem, *Daday'lı Halit Beğ Akmansü*, 2 vols. (Istanbul, Halk Basımevi, 1954), p. 179; Ahmet Şevket Elman, *Dr. Reşit Galip* (Ankara: Yeni Matbaa, 1955), p. 385 and *passim*; and Samet Ağaoğlu, *Babamın Arkadaşları* (Istanbul: Nebioğlu Yayınları, 1958), p. 101. The last also concerns Dr. Reşit Galip, though the author chooses to use no names.

[17] At the time of data collection only these eighteen volumes had been translated into the Roman script.

officials speaking as officials, that fact was recorded, and the length of his speech in column inches was also recorded. For each deputy I was able thereby to count the number of times he spoke in the 10 per cent sample of the Assembly debates, as well as the total number of column inches per speech. All remarks less than an inch were classed as one inch. In general, the bias that exists in this procedure tends to magnify somewhat the speaking activity of deputies, especially those who spoke very briefly but often. In view of the nature of the results, however, the bias does not seem to be very grave. The overall rate of participation is rather low.

Table 11.2

PARTY GROUPINGS IN THE FIRST ASSEMBLY,
BY INCIDENCE OF SPEAKING (PERCENTAGES)

TIMES SPEAKING	PARTY			ASSEMBLY
	First Group	Second Group	No Group	
None	38%	34%	74%	47%
1–10	37	32	16	30
11–60	19	19	10	16
61–299	7	15	1	7
Totals[a]	100%	100%	100%	100%
Average Number of Times	16.2	21.7	3.3	14.1
N	197	118	122	437

[a] May not add to 100 because of rounding.

Incidence of Speaking

Table 11.2 groups the deputies according to party and shows the number of times they spoke. Always recalling that we are dealing with a 10 per cent sample of the debates, we see first that just under half the deputies did not speak at all. Once more we observe the relationship between group membership and parliamentary activity. Somewhat over a third of the First and Second Group members failed to speak, while three fourths of the unaffiliated group never spoke. The other major revelation of Table 11.2 is that the Second Group members tended to be somewhat more active orally in the Assembly than the First Group members, particularly at the uppermost level of speaking. The average number of times the deputies of each group spoke also reflects this fact, standing at 16.2 for the First Group and 21.7 for the Second Group. Generalizing roughly from our sample, we find that the typical affiliated deputy spoke about six to twelve times a month.

The basic analysis of speaking patterns will be in terms of the total number of column inches spoken per deputy rather than in terms of the number of times that a deputy spoke, since I consider the former slightly more significant as a single indicator. Nevertheless, it is interesting to ascertain whether the number of times a deputy spoke had any clear relationship to his reelection fate. For this information we must consult Table 11.3.

Table 11.3

PARTY GROUPINGS IN THE FIRST ASSEMBLY, BY REELECTION AND INCIDENCE OF SPEAKING (PERCENTAGES)

REELECTION	PARTY AND TIMES SPEAKING							
	First Group				*Second Group*			
	None	1–10	11–60	61–299	None	1–10	11–60	61–299
Reelected	38%	59%	84%	85%	3%	5%	—%	—%
Later Reelection	3	4	5	8	8	8	5	6
Never Reelected	59	37	11	8	90	87	95	94
Totals[a]	100%	100%	100%	100%	100%	100%	100%	100%
N	73	73	37	13	40	38	22	18

[a] May not add to 100 because of rounding.

Reading across the table, we note one quite distinct fact. In the First Group the higher the level of speaking activity, the greater the reelection percentage. The more a First Group member spoke in parliament, the better his reelection chances. Perfect step relationships between these two variables are found for the First Group members. The Second Group pattern, on the other hand, is much less clear, partly at least because so few individuals were ever reelected that the figures become quite small and unreliable. Nevertheless, if anything, increased speaking activity apparently reduced a Second Group member's electoral chances. If we use total column inches instead of number of times speaking as our indicator, exactly the same type of pattern emerges, save that the Second Group results suggest slightly more unequivocally that increased verbal activity in the Assembly decreased the reelection percentages for those individuals.

Amount of Speaking

A deputy may have spoken many times in parliament and still not have made much of an impact. He may have spoken very, very briefly each time. Supposedly, a better single measure of the speaking role of the legislator would be the total number of column inches his speaking occupied in the debate transcript — what I shall call his "amount" of speaking. At any rate, this is the indicator I have chosen to employ. Table 11.4 gives the general breakdown for each party grouping.

Table 11.4

PARTY GROUPINGS IN THE FIRST ASSEMBLY,
BY AMOUNT OF SPEAKING (PERCENTAGES)

VOLUME (Column Inches)	PARTY			ASSEMBLY
	First Group	Second Group	No Group	
None (Silent Deputies)	38%	34%	74%	47%
1–19 (Moderate Speakers)	35	34	17	30
20 or More (Orators)	27	32	9	24
Totals[a]	100%	100%	100%	100%
Average Column Inches per Deputy	37.5	42.7	6.4	30.2
N	197	118	122	437

[a] May not add to 100 because of rounding.

The results of Table 11.4 are essentially identical with those of Table 11.2. Table 11.4 has been presented simply for reference, since I shall be using column inches, or "amount," as a basic analytic tool. Note, however, that the general distribution for amount of speaking is heavily skewed. Regardless of category, most deputies spoke far less than the average figure for the category in which they are found. A few individuals spoke a great amount and have appreciably hiked the average.

A list of the prominent persons from each group who appeared in each of the speaking classifications is given in Appendix E. One significant finding is that, even after discounting all utterances made as an Assembly officer, Mustafa Kemal still ranked fourth in the total amount of speaking with 417 column inches, surpassed only by Ahmet Ferit Tek with 637, Tunalı Hilmi with 459, and Mehmet Vehbi with 426. Though Kemal spoke only seventy-one times in this sample and ranked twenty-third in that respect, a little further research is illuminating. If we consider only those deputies who spoke at length (more than 100 column inches), we discover that Mustafa Kemal had far and away the greatest *average length per speech* — some 5.9 column inches compared to Ahmet Muhtar, who was second with 4.2. Only six persons from the First and Second Groups spoke more than 100 times and averaged more than three column inches per time. And this computation excludes all Mustafa Kemal's remarks as President of the Assembly. To no negligible degree, Mustafa Kemal *talked* his way to authority over the First Assembly, and that itself is one of the most revealing facts of all about the man and this period in Turkish political history!

Age

Scrutinizing the relationship between age, party, and speaking yields one broad observation. The First Assembly was dominated on both sides of the major political fence by relative youth. Regardless of party, the younger the deputy, the more he spoke in the First Assembly, as Figure 11.2 shows.

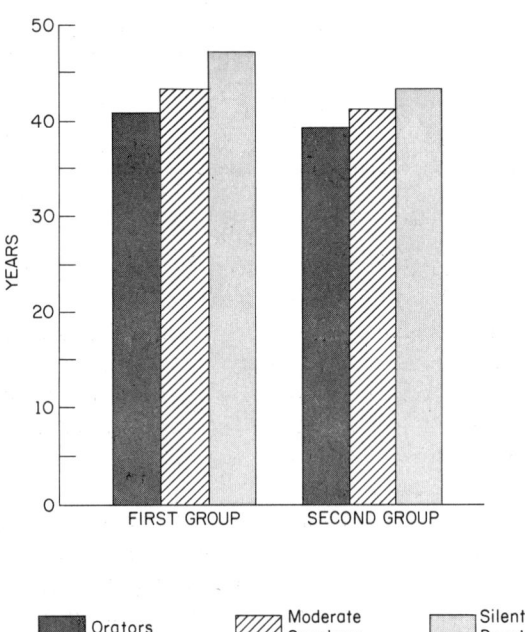

Figure 11.2. Average age of deputies, by party group and amount of speaking in the First Assembly

Prior Legislative Experience

When we check the situation concerning prior legislative experience, a rather different result catches our attention. (See Figure 11.3.) For the Second Group, there is no distinct relationship between previous experience in an Ottoman Assembly and the amount of speaking. True, the percentages display a regular rise as one moves to a

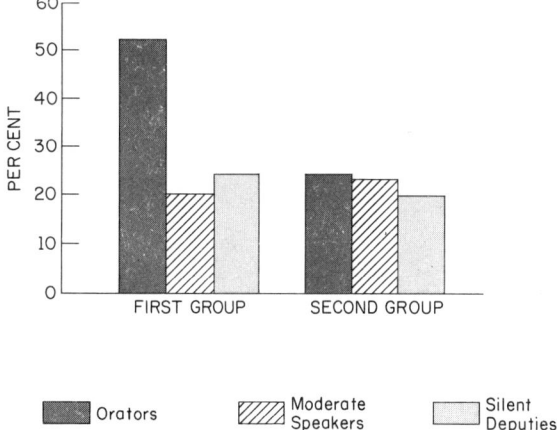

Figure 11.3. *Previous parliamentary experience of deputies, by party group and amount of speaking in the First Assembly*

NOTE: This figure gives the percentage of deputies of each type having prior experience in the Ottoman National Assembly.

greater amount of speaking, but the terminal difference is only four percentage points. On the contrary, for the First Group, despite what one might have predicted on the basis of the preceding finding regarding age and speaking, there is a very pronounced tendency for the "orators" to have had prior legislative experience. Over half were deputies to an Ottoman Assembly — commonly the last one — whereas less than one quarter of the "moderate speakers" and the "silent deputies" of the First Group had such experience. A majority of those who bore the brunt of the First Group's oratorical efforts were experienced parliamentarians.

Leadership Levels

In both groups there was plainly an association between formal power and speaking. Those holding positions of influence spoke more than the rest of the deputies, providing another plausible reason for confidence in the validity of the power ratings. Table 11.5 furnishes these data.

Table 11.5

PARTY GROUPINGS IN THE FIRST ASSEMBLY, BY LEADERSHIP LEVEL
AND AMOUNT OF SPEAKING (PERCENTAGES)

LEADERSHIP LEVEL	PARTY AND AMOUNT OF SPEAKING					
	First Group			Second Group		
	Silent	Moderate	Orator	Silent	Moderate	Orator
Top Leaders	3%	9%	37%	—%	5%	13%
Middle Leaders	12	14	26	5	18	32
Backbenchers	42	61	35	63	58	53
Inconsequentials	43	16	2	33	20	3
Totals[a]	100%	100%	100%	100%	100%	100%
N	74	69	54	40	40	38

[a] May not add to 100 because of rounding.

Region Represented and Localism

When we look at speaking, with party held constant, we do not unearth any conspicuous association between the region represented and the volume of speaking. A fairly clear trend that was the same for both the First and Second Groups emerged in just three regions. The Mediterranean and Southeastern Regions contributed to each party a disproportionate number of deputies who spoke sparingly, while the Black Sea Region contributed an immoderate proportion of "orators" to each party. Within the First Group, the "orators" tended to come in abnormal degree from the Aegean, Marmara, Black Sea, and South Central Regions, and the "silent deputies" from the Mediterranean and Southeastern Regions, as I have said, plus the East Central Region. In the Second Group the "orators" tended to represent the North Central, Northeastern, and Black Sea Regions, and the "silent deputies" represented the Mediterranean and Southeastern areas.

The data on "localism" are more telling. They show that for the First Group the speaking burden was carried disproportionately by those deputies who were *not* born in the province represented. The pattern in the Second Group is less unmistakable, but it seems to be in the opposite direction. Certainly it is true that the "orators" among the Second Group members were the most often of all locally born, with some 73 per cent being born in the province they represented at Ankara. (See Figure 11.4.)

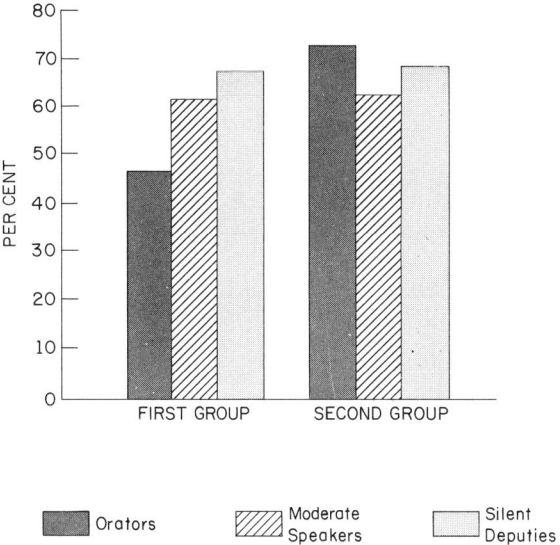

Figure 11.4. Percentage of deputies born in province represented, by party group and amount of speaking in the First Assembly

Occupation

The final dimension of this analysis is that of occupation. Within the parties, was there any association between the type of occupation a deputy pursued prior to his election and the amount of his speaking in parliament? Table 11.6 must be consulted for the specific figures.

Several rather fascinating patterns are brought out. First of all, scanning the gross occupational classifications, we uncover major relationships which tend to hold regardless of party. The professionals spoke a disproportionate amount whether they were in the First or Second Group, though they contributed comparatively less to the "orators" of the Second Group than to those of the First Group. For the officials, the pattern is one of no pattern. Compared to the two other broad vocational groups, no one speaking pattern seems to be typical of the officials. The economic group, on the other hand, has as marked a tendency toward silence as the professionals do toward speaking. Regardless of party, the downward progression of the economic group's representation as speaking level rises is most striking.

With regard to particular vocations, equally interesting configurations appear. All the professionals display the broad pattern characteristic of that classification as a whole. The lawyers of the First Group, however, evince a more acute tendency to be among the

Table 11.6

Party Groupings in the First Assembly, by Occupation and Amount of Speaking (Percentages)

OCCUPATION	PARTY AND AMOUNT OF SPEAKING					
	First Group			Second Group		
	Silent	Moderate	Orator	Silent	Moderate	Orator
Government	29%	21%	26%	28%	18%	14%
Military	13	16	15	6	18	14
Education	4	7	7	—	6	8
(Official)	(46)	(44)	(48)	(34)	(41)	(36)
Law	4	7	19	19	29	22
Medicine	1	6	13	—	—	6
Dentistry, etc.	—	—	—	—	3	—
Engineering	—	—	—	—	—	3
(Professions)	(6)	(13)	(31)	(19)	(32)	(31)
Trade	13	12	6	22	15	6
Agriculture	16	9	2	3	3	—
Banking	—	1	2	—	—	—
(Economic)	(29)	(22)	(9)	(25)	(18)	(6)
Religion	16	15	7	16	6	22
Journalism	1	3	4	—	3	6
Other	1	3	—	6	—	—
Totals[a]	100%	100%	100%	100%	100%	100%
N	69	68	54	32	34	36

[a] Percentages may not add to designated grand and subtotals because of rounding.

voluble than do those of the Second Group. The other main groups that display a definitely similar pattern toward active speaking in the Assembly are the journalists and the educators. In fact, the table as a whole seems almost to argue for the sort of conception that Harold Lasswell had in mind when he developed the phrase "specialists in persuasion" — those who are adept at, and prone to use, one particular set of influential behaviors out of many, the behaviors we inadequately style "persuasion." The practitioners of several specific occupations in Turkey, irrespective of party, seem to find one legislative behavior which is frequently deemed influential — addressing the Assembly — more congenial than do deputies from other occupations, if we can infer congeniality from disproportionate practice.

By the same measure, who found speaking least congenial? Obviously, the merchants and the agriculturists. Perhaps this is a clue to the tardy rise in power of these two occupational groups in the more recent Assemblies, despite their over-all rise in numbers. If, as the Assembly becomes more and more Westernized and democratized, the position of the "specialist in persuasion" is enhanced (that is, the polity is restructured so as to make certain forms of influential behavior more effective and other forms less effective), and if the merchants and agriculturists find these influential behaviors — among which is speaking in the Assembly — as uncongenial as the data suggest, then their lowly power position can be readily understood. Psychologically, their previous social background renders one vital form of influence relatively unavailable to them, at least in the sense that they do not employ it as frequently and as capably as others, probably because they do not feel as adept in its use as those from different social backgrounds. Here, definitely, would seem to be an interesting and fruitful area for further exploration.

Let us conclude this investigation of the parties and speaking patterns of the First Assembly with an examination of the religious group. We previously found that the clerics were distributed between the First and Second Groups in roughly equal proportions. Quantity of religious representation did not seem to distinguish the parties. We now learn, however, that the types of *behavior* of the clerics in the two groups were, at least as far as speaking was concerned, sharply different. The religious deputies of the First Group displayed a clear bias in the direction of low speaking activity. Such is not true of the *hocas* of the Second Group. The latter tended either not to speak at all or, in contradistinction to the First Group, to speak very, very much. Their greatest contribution was to the ranks of the "orators" of the Second Group, comprising almost a quarter of that category. In short, the speaking patterns of the religious deputies of the two parties were quite divergent.

The Progressive Republican and Republican People's Parties of the Second Assembly

Just from the names of these parties as contrasted with that of the Defense of Rights Group we see that Turkey's world position and governmental structure have changed. The War for Independence has been won, and the Ottoman sultanate has been replaced by a republic. Moreover, the relations between the cabinet and the Assembly are no longer what they were. The phoenix is rising and is in many features a startlingly different bird. Nevertheless, probing beneath the plumage we uncover several important traces of old ailments. Not the least of these is the Progressive Republican Party, which, to purloin a phrase, was in many ways neither progressive nor republican.

Genesis of the Progressive Party

Though formed in the Second Assembly, the Progressive Party was a rather special extension of the anti-Kemalist opposition of the First Assembly. This statement may seem strange since Mustafa Kemal had eliminated all but three of the Second Group's partisans from the Assembly elected in 1923. However, even within the more reliable First Group of the First Assembly (1920) — and up to its highest echelons — there had lurked a stubborn resistance to Kemal and Ismet (Inönü). Discord, frequently personal and petty but at times high-principled and profound, ran like a fault below the surface agreement.

The Progressive Party, in its parliamentary mien, featured a number of able, disgruntled, and still very influential former associates of Mustafa Kemal in the leadership of the First Group. It included notables like ex-Premier Hüseyin Rauf (Orbay), military pashas with the stature of Kâzım Karabekir, Ali Fuat (Cebesoy), Refet (Bele), and Cafer Tayyar (Eğilmez). It attracted civil leaders like Dr. Adnan (Adıvar) and Bekir Sami. Men of this stamp were intellectually adroit, possessed important reputations that often spanned the country, and had become accustomed to the exercise of power and the satisfaction of being heeded. From the Kemalist standpoint this made them all the more dangerous.

Whether through an honest unawareness of how seriously their views differed from those of Kemal, or through duplicity and "thousands of tricks," as Kemal later interpreted it, these individuals passed the candidacy test imposed by the Gazi in the 1923 election. Along with the other deputies to the Second Assembly, they formally subscribed to the Kemalist program and pledged to support it. Nevertheless, they ultimately found themselves engaged in organized opposition to that program, at least in its more developed form, which they may or may not have foreseen. The tale that lies therein is a fascinating one that I shall sketch only in barest outline here.[18]

---

[18] Useful sources of information about the Progressive Republican Party (*Terakkiperver Cumhuriyet Fırkası*) are: Tunaya, *Türkiyede Siyasî Partiler, op. cit.*, pp. 606–622; Atatürk, *Speech...*, *op. cit.*, pp. 572–722, and *passim*; *Histoire...*, *op. cit.*, pp. 185–194; Rustow, "Politics and Islam...," in Frye (ed.), *op. cit.*, pp. 87–88, and "The Army and the Founding of the Turkish Republic," *op. cit.*, pp. 547–549; Atay, *Çankaya...*, *op. cit.*, Vol. II, pp. 345–361; Cemal Kutay, *Halit Paşa, Ali Çetinkaya Vuruşması* (Istanbul: Nürgök Matbaası, 1955), pp. 38–39. A wild and melodramatic account is given in Armstrong's *Grey Wolf*, *op. cit.*, pp. 260–280, and a much better biographical treatment in Dagobert von Mikusch, *Mustapha Kemal* (Garden City: Doubleday, Doran, 1931), pp. 310–313, 337–343, 345–366. Interesting details also emerge from the biography of Halit Beğ (Akmansü), who was an important parliamentary member of the Progressive Party, in Göğem, *op. cit.*, I, pp. 163–277.

On the more picayune level of personalities, several antecedent clashes contributed to the formation of the Progressive Party. Most flagrant of all was the hostility that had been bared between Rauf (Orbay) and Ismet (Inönü). In fact, this reached such a state of open enmity, at least on Rauf's part, that it led to his resignation as Premier in August 1923, when he utterly refused to comply with the requirements of normal protocol and officially greet Ismet on the latter's triumphal return from conducting the Lausanne Treaty negotiations.[19] The hostility grew worse during the following year and a half. In several crucial debates within the Assembly Group of the People's Party, these two individuals acted as standard-bearers for contending points of view and grappled with a relish that clearly exceeded even the momentous issues at stake.

Another example of personal rivalry that figured in the generation of the Progressive Party, though in a much more latent fashion, was the edginess of several illustrious generals toward Mustafa Kemal's ascendancy. While matters of principle were probably more salient, close reading of Kâzım Karabekir's book *The Principles of Our War for Independence* or Ali Fuat Pasha's various *Memoirs* reveals the feeling of these renowned soldiers that Kemal had usurped some of the credit rightfully belonging to them and had turned it to political account.[20] Their professional attainments and vital role in the National Struggle had become submerged in the general adulation of the Gazi. Nor was the Gazi averse to this development. His reciprocal sensitivity was reflected, for instance, in the banning of Karabekir's book, though probably more basic tactical considerations also urged that action. In any event, a history of personal animosities of varying intensity helped provoke and pattern the organized opposition to the Kemalists that was the Progressive Party.

Fundamental and growing policy differences were an even more significant cause of the development of opposition than was personal antagonism. The swelling disaffection of First Group members such as Rauf, Kâzım Karabekir, Dr. Adnan, and others was directly related to specific programmatic differences between what they wanted and what the Kemalists wanted. The opposition favored a constitutional monarchy with a strong legislature. They envisioned a state in which religion maintained a position not much different from

[19] Cf. Atatürk, *Speech* ..., *op. cit.*, pp. 620–642.
[20] Kâzım Karabekir, *İstiklâl Harbimizin Esasları* (Istanbul: Sinan Matbaası Neşriyat Evi, 1933); Cebesoy, Gl. *Ali Fuat Cebesoy'un Siyasî Hatıraları, op. cit.*, and *Millî Mücadele Hatıraları* (*Recollections of the National Struggle*), (Istanbul: Vatan Matbaası, 1953–1957). In the cases of Ali Fuat and Refet Pashas it was well known at the highest levels that their performances as commanders in the field were not wholly successful, and sensitivity on this score may have contributed to their estrangement from Kemal and Ismet.

that which it possessed before the war. They foresaw a society in which government granted a relatively important role to the localities. And they claim to have desired internal arrangements within the political parties in which power would be more dispersed. Behind all these ideas there lay the conservative aim of making the new Turkey — if there was ever to be a *new* Turkey in any basic sense — conform as far as possible to the customs and traditions of the old. Change was to be gradual and evolutionary, not swift and revolutionary in the Kemalist mode.

Favoring ideas of this sort, the future Progressives found the transforming trend of the Kemalist program increasingly repugnant. The termination of the sultanate was opposed by Rauf, for instance, as strongly as was possible for him without completely exposing his position and being forced over into ineffectiveness in the Second Group camp. At that time he went so far as to express in rather transparent language his mistrust of Mustafa Kemal's intentions.[21] The proclamation of the Republic, which followed the demise of the sultanate was still more irksome, since the formal institutionalization of the break with the past made its reversal less feasible. The Republic symbolized much that the future Progressives opposed, despite their eventual inclusion of "Republican" in their party's name.[22] Finally,

---

[21] The arguments supposedly given by Rauf in personal explanation of his attitudes are quite expressive of the significance of social background — in this case the status and occupation of his father. Asked by Mustafa Kemal for his own convictions regarding the sultanate and caliphate, Rauf replied: "I am devoted heart and soul to the Throne and Caliphate, because my father [a famous admiral and member of the Ottoman Senate] has received benefits from the Padishah and was one of the dignitaries of the Ottoman Empire.... Regarding my attachment to the Caliphate, it is imposed on me by my education [upbringing — *terbiye*]." Atatürk, *Speech*..., *op. cit.*, pp. 572–573; *Nutuk*, *op. cit.*, p. 490. Later on, in one Assembly debate, it was stated that Rauf should return to the Caucasus, whence his father originally came! *Ibid.*, p. 704.

[22] This matter of the name of the Progressive Republican Party is rather interesting and revealing, though superficially confusing. According to Tunaya and Kutay, the dissentient group originally favored two other names: the *Rescue*, or *Redemption*, *Party* (*Istihlâs Fırkası*) and the Radical Republican Party (*Cezri Cumhuriyet Fırkası*). The first of these two labels reflects the party's true conception of its goal — that of saving the Ottoman heritage from Kemalist spoliation, even though limited reform in the late Ottoman institutions was essential. The second name is superficially as ambiguous as the one finally chosen, for the "Radical" relates to the Radical Socialist Party of France, which, along with the British Conservative Party, served as a partial model for the Progressives. Tunaya, *Türkiyede Siyasî Partiler*, *op. cit.*, p. 609; Kutay, *Halit Paşa, Ali Çetinkaya Vuruşması*, *op. cit.*, pp. 38–39.

The official (Kemalist) history of the Turkish Republic asserts that there were three different versions of the Progressive Party's *Program* and that the first version contained no reference to republican principles — in fact, did

the abolition of the caliphate, resulting in the removal of the last representatives of the House of Osman from the soil of Turkey, acted to seal the determination of the opposition openly to resist before it was too late. They had, however, miscalculated; it was already too late!

The Postindependence Crisis: A Stage of Political Development

Examined from the most general perspective, the opposition that culminated in the Progressive Republican Party can perhaps be characterized as that of the "Postindependence Conservatives." Most nationalist movements have as their paramount initial goal the acquisition or maintenance of independence for their country. It has become quite commonplace to observe that this aim is essentially negative and self-terminating, yielding only a temporary unity. Once independence is achieved, dissension sets in. Divergent views of the most desirable future program for the nationalist movement come to the fore and are contested. The conflicting opinions are either reconciled to some degree, dominated by a single vision, or else linger on the scene, unreconciled, to produce a debility that leads eventually to another upheaval. This stage of the immediate, postindependence resolution of differences has proved to be crucial for the nationalist movements of many emerging nations. In Turkey, the short and unhappy career of the Progressive Republican Party was the final phase of this stage of political development. It was the last truly dangerous traditional threat to Kemalist hegemony.

Ardent Nationalists and the Problem of Power

Underlying the specific programmatic differences of opinions in the "postindependence crisis" is usually a basic conflict of views regarding the preferred power structure of the society, for the short run and possibly for the long run as well. A dichotomous classification of the various positions in this conflict is generally an oversimplification, but I shall resort to it anyway for heuristic purposes. On the one side there tend to be the more *ardent nationalists*. These individuals have been deeply affected, psychologically, by their awareness of the disrespect in which their nation is held by the more technically developed world. They desire above all things, consciously or un-

---

not even mention the word. *Histoire*..., *op. cit.*, p. 186. The Kemalist view was that the final name of the party was pure camouflage. It was apparently successful camouflage, however, since it was largely in irritated reaction to rumors of the Progressive Party's choice of a name that the People's Party added the word "Republican" to its own designation, scandalized that the party which introduced the Republic should nearly be outmaneuvered in formally claiming association with it. Cf. *C.H.P. 25 Yıl, 1923–1948, op cit.*, p. 17; Atay, *Çankaya, op. cit.*, Vol. II, pp. 345–346.

consciously, to alter this situation and compel respect.[23] Associated with this profound status reaction there is frequently a very genuine concern with raising the level of life of the peasant masses of the society, coming as a result of altruism, empathy, or the awareness of mutual involvement in foreign eyes.

Singly or together, both values induce the placing of a high priority on the achievement of specific improvements and reforms. To effect these policies, an increase in the society's ability to concert the activities of large numbers of its citizens is required. For example, a national system of education is usually desired. Investment must be stimulated and channeled, not merely into the most productive ventures, but also into those projects which will convince the more developed nations and the emerging nation itself that it is beginning to compete effectively with those who have held it in disrepute — compete at the developed nation's own game. Antimalaria campaigns must be waged, an increasingly potent military establishment must be sustained, and improvements in communications must be introduced. For all these valued programs, taxes must be collected, resources allocated, and the present consumption of various groups restricted, thereby incurring resentment.

In short, in the absence of broad consensus favoring all these activities (and the postindependence crisis is a stage in which conflict rather than consensus prevails) the only means of securing the necessary concerting of activities for reform is through the orderly exercise of power — through creating known interpersonal relationships such that some individuals can and do regularly determine certain specific behaviors of other individuals. The less the consensus, the fewer the determinative individuals must be — the greater the concentration of power — if one demands that these activities *be* concerted and that these programs *be* carried out.[24]

---

[23] Reflections of this status reaction are replete throughout Mustafa Kemal's career and writings, but Halide Edib gives us perhaps the most graphic example when she quotes him as follows: "They shall know that we are as good as they are! They shall treat us as their equal! Never will we bow our heads to them! To the last man we will stand against them till we break their civilization on their heads." Adıvar, *The Turkish Ordeal, op. cit.*, p. 149.

[24] We are using the term "consensus" in a rather special way not to mean *uniformity* of opinion but, instead, to mean that compatibility of opinions, uniform or not, which produces a *voluntary* concerting of activities. Amplification of some of the ideas of this section is to be found in Frederick W. Frey, "Political Development, Power and Communications in Turkey," in Lucian W. Pye (ed.), *Communications and Political Development* (Princeton: Princeton University Press, 1963), pp. 298–326, and in Frederick W. Frey, "Education and Politics in Turkey," in Ward and Rustow (eds.), *Political Modernization in Japan and Turkey, op. cit.*, pp. 205–235.

In most developing societies, the power structure adequate to the implementation of the reforms and improvements advocated by the more ardent nationalists is lacking. Therefore, one problem they confront is that of creating such a structure. Practically, it appears that the easiest procedure is to establish the requisite linkages by augmenting decisively the position of one or a few of the institutions of the society rather than to attempt a more balanced development. The government, the party, or the army (or all three controlled by the same individuals) becomes dominant. The *over-all level* of power in the society is increased, but largely in a way that also increases the *concentration* of power. Moreover, in the stated absence of consensus, a more balanced development involving less concentration of power renders the achievement of the desired programs much more perilous. Powerful elements that are uncooperative can frustrate "progress."

Of course, the sort of development just described is contrary to most conceptions of democracy. Not surprisingly, it is rare that we find much democracy in most of the actively emerging nations. At best, in most cases, including the Turkey of 1924, there is a sincere commitment by the ardent nationalists to *eventual* democracy *after* they feel sufficient progress has been made toward the realization of the most vital of their specific programs. A preparatory, tutelary regime is established. Turkey is, in this respect, of special interest because of the very clarity of this pattern and the fact that she was fortunate enough to have leaders who tried to live up to the long-run democratic pledge after engaging in short-run authoritarianism. Knowledge of the social backgrounds of these leaders and their opponents, I believe, contributes toward an understanding of the conditions under which such a development is likely to occur.[25]

The Postindependence Conservatives

While the ardent nationalists so keenly desire specific programs that they feel obliged to establish a short-run concentration in the society's power structure, other nationalist leaders often react quite differently. They wanted independence for various reasons, but they

---

[25] The model of political development in the emerging nations, which is here very generally and partially outlined would seem to suggest that Western policy-makers and political analysts might be well advised to spend less time wondering how to avoid the short-run tendencies toward authoritarianism in the developing world and spend more time investigating when and how to channel that development toward democracy (greater distribution and reciprocity of power) after the nationalist leaders appear to have achieved the most important of their specific, programmatic aims. From this vantage, technical aid, even to authoritarian governments, may have pay-offs if it hastens a future concern with the distribution of power, though of course many other factors are involved.

do not endorse the postindependence programs of the ardent nationalists with anything like the same enthusiasm. They are opposed to the short-run elaboration and concentration of power, which they feel will only too surely result in an attempt at a long-run dictatorship. These individuals I have styled the "postindependence conservatives" because their opposition occurs during the postindependence resolution of the divergent strands within the nationalist movement and because they argue against the drastic program and the concentration of power envisioned by their opponents. To this category I assign the Progressive Republicans.

The Chronology and Character of the Progressive Party

Late in October 1924, Kâzım Karabekir and Ali Fuat Pashas resigned their posts as army inspectors general to concentrate on their Assembly activities. At the same time Refet Pasha withdrew his previous resignation from his deputyship. These and other dissidents met with Rauf. About a week thereafter a major interpellation of the government was brought in the Assembly and provoked a bitter debate lasting several days. In the debate, the deep hostility of Rauf Bey and his associates to the developments I have discussed was revealed more clearly than ever before. In addition, a large portion of the Istanbul press vigorously supported the stand that Rauf and the opposition were taking. Though Ismet Pasha's government won the vote of confidence by 148 votes to 19, after the debate there occurred several resignations from the People's Party. Finally, on November 17, 1924, the Progressive Republican Party was officially founded, or, as Mustafa Kemal preferred to say, "unmasked itself." [26]

The party, which was definitely one of parliamentary origin, mustered only twenty-nine deputies under its banner. Nevertheless, for many reasons, some of which have been given, one must endorse Falih Rıfkı Atay's judgment that it was "... a sincere and important movement," not just the venting of personal pique and local grievances.[27] The extraparliamentary organization of the party was never very extensive. Its first branch was set up in Urfa, and the party's greatest strength remained in the East. It held only one congress, that in Istanbul in mid-May of 1925. The social support of the party

[26] *Speech...*, p. 717.
[27] *Çankaya, op. cit.*, p. 347: "*Terakkiperver Cumhuriyet Partisi, ciddî ve büyük bir hareket idi.*" Tunaya lists twenty-eight deputies as Progressive Party members as does Kutay, but Tunaya (on p. 606) in listing the leaders of the party also includes Faik of Ordu, whom he did not include on the general list. We have thus taken twenty-nine as the true size. Akmansü, incidentally, claims only twenty-seven deputies as members. Tunaya, *Türkiyede Siyasî Partiler, op. cit.*, pp. 606, 621; Kutay, *op. cit.*, p. 39; *Göğem, op. cit.*, p. 177, n. 1.

has been variously described as including unregenerate Unionists, the still ambitious First Assembly discards who had been in the Second Group, religious reactionaries, sincere democrats and conservatives, sensational and sober elements of the press, "cosmopolitans," and certain units of the armed forces. Actually, no definitive analysis of the support of the Progressive Party has yet been made.

The *Manifesto* and the *Program* of the party contain many provisions indicative of its areas of divergence from the People's Party, despite the fact that the documents were undoubtedly watered down to facilitate legal approval of the party. (That legal approval, it must not be forgotten, was given.) [28] The party documents emphasize that the Progressive Republican Party is opposed to despotism. They also stress greater control over the administration. Individual rights are insisted upon, and it is stated that no amendment to the constitution should be made without a clear mandate from the nation. Suggestive of a future dispute is the provision that a deputy elected to the Presidency of the Republic should lose his capacity as a deputy. Local initiative in many matters was stressed, including primary education, social welfare functions, and the like.[29] Moreover, the party was generally considered to affirm the importance of greater conformity to Turkish traditions, greater decentralization within political parties, and reforms such as the direct election of deputies.[30] The decentralizing impact upon the existing structure of formal power in Turkey of many of these proposals should not be overlooked.

The Progressive Republican Party lasted less than seven months. It was abolished by cabinet decree on June 5, 1925. With grim literality we can say that it met a violent end, for six of its twenty-nine deputies were executed a little over one year later, and several others were compelled to flee Turkey. The opposition movement that was focused in the Progressive Party precipitated the one severe purge of the Kemalist era.

The violence and harshness of Kemal's reaction to the Progressive Party prompts the question, "Why? What was there about this party that it should have been dealt with so differently from those who had opposed Kemal under the aegis of the Second Group?" Once again, social background information provides a key to the answer and is buttressed by other types of evidence.

---

[28] Also note Mustafa Kemal's guarded interview with a correspondent from the London *Times* on December 11, 1924, in which Kemal presented his democratic side, though dodging pointed comments on the Progressive Party. *Atatürk'ün Söylev ve Demeçleri* (Ankara: Türk Tarih Kurumu Basımevı, 1954), III, p. 76.

[29] Tunaya, *Türkiyede Siyasî Partiler, op. cit.*, pp. 615–620.

[30] Göğem, *op. cit.*, p. 177, n. 1.

Background Characteristics of the Progressive Party and the People's Party

Let us now contrast the social backgrounds of deputies from the Progressive Republican Party and the Republican People's Party, bearing in mind the nature of the contending factions in the preceding Assembly. Whereas more of the First Group than the Second Group had previous parliamentary experience, there was no difference in prior Assembly experience between the Progressive and People's Party delegations. Since 62 per cent of the Progressives and 63 per cent of the People's Party suporters had held a deputyship in the First Assembly, both parties could draw on an ample fund of experience. Again, there was no appreciable difference between the percentages of the two parties born in the Marmara, Aegean, and foreign regions. Some 45 per cent of the Progressives and 48 per cent of the *Halkçılar* (People's Party members) were born in these regions. However, within Istanbul alone a sharp difference does emerge: 30 per cent of the Progressives and only 11 per cent of the *Halkçılar* were born in Istanbul Province. In these respects we see that the Progressive Republican Party does not at all resemble the Second Group. On the contrary, it is an exaggeration of the very qualities in which the First Group differed from the Second Group. It has the same general make-up as the People's Party, only more so. Inspection of additional dimensions will demonstrate this fact.

Whereas 61 per cent of the People's Party's deputies were born in the province they represented, just 50 per cent of the Progressives had such local connection. Only 12 per cent of the *Halkçılar* represented a constituency in the Marmara Region, while 31 per cent of the Progressives represented a province in that region. Moreover, six of the twelve leaders of the Progressive Party had their constituencies in the Marmara Region.

The educational data for the First Assembly were too skimpy to contrast the First and Second Groups in this respect. Though coverage is still not really satisfactory, the data for the Second Assembly are more complete.[31] While 85 per cent of the Progressives had university-level education, only 68 per cent of the *Halkçılar* reached the university level. In other words, the Progressive Party presented an even more intellectual front than the People's Party.

The Progressive Party endured so briefly that holding a party office did not contribute sufficiently to the incumbent's formal power score to place him among the top leaders, and the Progressives were excluded from important Assembly and cabinet posts. As a result, no Progressive Party member fell into the top leader category, and

[31] Information is available for 20 of 29 Progressives and 245 of 309 People's Party deputies.

just three (10 per cent) reached the middle leader echelon. The corresponding figures for the People's Party were: top leaders, thirty-eight (12 per cent); middle leaders, forty-one (13 per cent). Not one of the Progressives was reelected to the Third Assembly, while just under three of every four People's Party deputies (72 per cent) were reelected. There was a tendency, however, toward a later utilization of some of the outstanding talent of the Progressive Party after the dark clouds of 1924-1925 had blown over. Nine of the twenty-nine members reentered the Assembly after a considerable hiatus. Nearly half of these, some four persons, reappeared in the Sixth Assembly, the first after the death of Atatürk.

The one characteristic in terms of which the Progressives did not resemble and even exceed the People's Party, as contrasted to the

Table 11.7

PROGRESSIVE REPUBLICAN AND PEOPLE'S PARTIES, BY OCCUPATION (PERCENTAGES)

OCCUPATION	PARTIES		
	Progressive Republican	*Republican People's*	*Total*
Government	28%	25%	25%
Military	44	18	20
Education	4	9	9
(Official)	**(76)**	**(52)**	**(54)**
Law	8	12	12
Medicine	4	7	7
Dentistry, Pharmacy, and Veterinary Medicine	—	—	—
Engineering	4	1	1
(Professional)	**(16)**	**(21)**	**(20)**
Trade	—	8	7
Agriculture	—	6	6
Banking	4	1	1
(Economic)	**(4)**	**(15)**	**(14)**
Religion	4	7	7
Journalism	—	5	4
(Unknown)[a]	(14)	(12)	(12)
Total[a]	100%	100%	100%
N	29	304	333

[a] Percentages may not add to designated figure because of rounding. Unknowns excluded in computing percentages.

Second Group, was that of age. Both the Second Group and the Progressive Party had average ages slightly under that of the People's Party. For the Progressives the figure was 41.7 years, and for the *Halkçılar* it was 43.9. Both groups, however, were relatively young.

It is when we turn to occupation that the most revealing differences appear. These data are furnished in Table 11.7. Not only was the Progressive Republican Party more intellectual and less local than the People's Republican Party, but the Progressives were also much more official in character. Three quarters of the Progressives had official occupations, compared to half the *Halkçılar*. Instead of having fewer lawyers and fewer traders than the opposition, the People's Party is now in the position of having a larger proportion of men from these vocations. Most significant of all, 44 per cent of the Progressives were military men, while just 18 per cent of the People's Party's deputies were from the military. The Progressive Party had a greater proportionate representation than did the People's Party from the very vocational group that was most favored in the Kemalist period. In its parliamentary shape, then, this was not the same sort of opposition as that of the Second Group and that which will again be encountered with the Democratic Party — primarily legalistic and commercial in composition. This was an opposition that drew from the very same sources as the Kemalists — intellectuals, bureaucrats, and especially military men. As such, it was possibly the most pernicious development of all in Kemalist eyes, for if successful it threatened to undermine the very foundations of Kemalist strength! For this reason above all the Progressive Republican Party was crushed.

Final scrutiny of Mustafa Kemal's personal reactions to the Progressive Party's challenge will support and illustrate this general interpretation resulting from the social background data. Kemal realized very well that his power ultimately depended on his control over the military, and he was always extremely sensitive to any stirrings among the armed forces.[32] Consequently, when he first learned of the resignations of Kâzım Karabekir and Ali Fuat Pashas from their posts as inspectors general, he relates that he "... did not hesitate for a moment to tell [himself] that [he] was face to face with a plot." Furthermore, he also surmised that the plotters, the future Progressives, had previously drafted a plan of campaign, and that "They found that, in order to succeed, they must have the army on their side." As a result, they had worked on the army for a year to win it over, trying to get various commanders to make common cause with them.[33]

---

[32] For a more detailed examinations, see Frederick W. Frey, "Arms and the Man in Turkish Politics," *op. cit.*

[33] *Speech...*, *op. cit.*, p. 688.

The Gazi's "countermeasures" were typically decisive. He requested Marshal Fevzi (Çakmak), the prestigious Chief of the Turkish General Staff, to resign his seat in the Assembly, and Fevzi Pasha readily agreed. Then Kemal dispatched telegrams to all commanders who were also deputies informing them of Fevzi's resignation and asking them to do the same. All complied except for Cafer Tayyar and Cevat Pashas, whereupon their military functions were terminated. Thus, the direct connection between military commanders and the Assembly was severed. Most of the resigned and retired commanders were thereby channeled into overt political activity in the Progressive Republican Party. In such a position they were less dangerous than if they had maintained formal authority in both the party and the army. Even so, their reputations and previous contacts with the armed forces were still a threat so long as they were prominent in the political life of the nation. Hence, the final step, which was rationalized in terms of the Kurdish Rebellion in the East and the attempt on Mustafa Kemal's life in Izmir, was the suppression of the Progressive Republican Party. There was no room at the top for opposition that tried to mobilize support from the main sources of Kemalist strength. Hostile pressure so close to the jugular could not be tolerated.

The Liberal Republican Party of the Third Assembly

Mustafa Kemal was many things: an "ardent nationalist," a brilliant and imperious commander, a lonely man with an incredible perception of human relations in general and of power in particular, a sensitive egocentric who was able to maintain his intellectual honesty in nearly all fundamental matters, a lover of individual animals and masses of men who could be utterly ruthless to individual human beings, a demander but not a giver of loyalty, and above all a man of diverse facets who cannot be well understood in terms of any one of them. One thing he was not, however, and that was a despot. His personal inclinations may have driven him in that direction on occasion, but his mind would never permit it. He had imbibed too thoroughly and understood too well the fundamental values of the West.

An essential difference between Mustafa Kemal and his erstwhile associates who later became Progressives was that Kemal believed in a policy of placing certain basic reforms (especially the curtailment of the power of the religious institution) first and foremost, while making "democracy" a secondary and contingent goal. Nevertheless, there *was* a sincere and growing Kemalist commitment to democratic development as one of the principal aims for Turkish society. Tarık Tunaya perceptively remarks that in most Turkish eyes, "Turkey's becoming a Western state means that she is obliged to meet all the requirements of a democratic system." [34] Mustafa Kemal, with the aforementioned reservation, would have subscribed to this proposition. In fact, he articulated it increasingly as the years — and the direst of the crises — passed.[35] Though he was shrewdly cognizant of the dangers of a premature rush toward democratic institutions, which would only fragment power before the cultural foundations for democratic development had even been laid, and though there were exasperated periods in which an emotional authoritarianism dominated an intellectually derived democratic urge, he unfailingly returned to the democratic theme.

There are many illustrations of the originally implicit and sub-

---

[34] Tarık Z. Tunaya, *Türkiyenin Siyasî Hayatında Batılılaşma Hareketleri* (*Westernizing Movements in Turkey's Political Life*), (Istanbul: Yedigün Matbaası, 1960), p. 119.

[35] Though Kemal might say in 1921 in the Assembly that "We resemble neither the democrats nor the socialists. The form of our administration is equivalent neither to that of the democratic governments nor the socialists. We resemble ourselves, and glory in it," he was speaking for tactical advantage, defending the structure of the government of the First Assembly from those who likened it to the Bolsheviks or who demanded to know why it did not resemble the more typical arrangements of Western democracies. Cf. Yakup Kadri Karaosmanoğlu, *Atatürk* (Istanbul: Remzi Kitabevi, 1946?), pp. 80–84.

The early ambivalence of Kemal regarding the weight to be attached to democratic progress is reflected in the fact that at about the same time as the above statement he justified the Constitutional Act of 1921 to Kâzım Karabekir mainly on the grounds that it introduced the "principle of democracy (populism)" into the administration. *Speech*..., *op. cit.*, pp. 506–507; *Nutuk*..., *op. cit.*, p. 428. (The actual word is *halkçılık*, better translated as "populism," though the relationship to "democracy" is definitely present.)

In his speeches in the early and mid-twenties, Kemal rarely if ever used the word "democracy" (*demokrasi*), though the idea was frequently referred to through the concepts of popular sovereignty, representative government, freedom, and so on. Interestingly, if one can judge from scanning his collected saying and speeches (*Atatürk'ün Söylev ve Demeçleri, op. cit.*), he began to utilize the word "democracy" more frequently in 1930, around the time of the formation of the Liberal Party. Then he abandoned it once more after the demise of that party, as the world situation became stormy and he became concerned about keeping Turkey neutral in a well-foreseen conflict between the Western democracies and the dictatorships. Thus, the term "democracy" appears in the three volumes of collected speeches probably only about half a dozen times in all, and at least three of these occur late in 1930 and early in 1931 (Vol. II, pp. 261, 287; Vol. I, p. 352).

Whether the specific term was enunciated or not, the idea of democracy was definitely expressed with mounting force and frequency, We even find Kemal arguing in 1933 that a republican regime was, *ipso facto*, committed to democracy. See Afetinan, *Atatürk Hakkında Hatıralar ve Belgeler* (*Reminiscences and Documents Concerning Atatürk*), (Ankara: Türk Tarih Kurumu Basımevi, 1959), pp. 250–251. See footnote 36.

sequently explicit Kemalist adherence to democratic values. I shall give only a few highlights. The initial illustration might well be the First Grand National Assembly itself, "the first government in the East created by the people and acting for the people," as Halide Edib contends. It was a broadly based body, as I have shown. It acted according to very democratic procedures, almost to the point of futility, and pursuant to a self-enacted constitution stating that sovereignty belonged to the nation. The constitution further specified that the Assembly was the national representative of a "people actually and individually guiding their own destiny" (Article 1). Kemal did not merely concur in these democratic emphases, he often suggested and encouraged them. Moreover, though Mustafa Kemal was granted extraordinary powers for brief periods by the Assembly; he took exceptional pains to work with it and through it. Whether he could have dominated it by force is an intriguing but moot and irrelevant issue; the point is that though possessed of a good chance for success at coercion, he made no real attempt to use it — as a matter of principle.[36]

The political party founded and headed by Mustafa Kemal provides further insight into his approach to politics. Its very name, the *People's* Republican Party, helped at least in part to create expectations, of which Kemal was well aware, regarding Kemalist values. These expectations were reinforced by the "populist" (*halkçılık*) plank of the party's *Program*, which was later written into the Constitution of the Republic. This plank originally hailed the unity of the Turkish population and its freedom from class strife, and emphasized the equality of Turkish citizens in the eyes of the party and state. It also mentioned the party's concern with serving the people and comprehending their needs. Though the word "democracy" was not expressly used in the first formulation of "populism," by the thirties it had come to be associated with this section of the People's Party *Program*.

---

[36] The Halide Edib (Adıvar) quotation is from her *Conflict of East and West in Turkey, op. cit.*, p. 132.

Tevfik Bıyıklıoğlu affords us some good observations on Mustafa Kemal's principles in the anthology *Yakınlarından Hatıralar* (*Remembrances by Those Close to Him*), (Istanbul: Sel Yayınları, 1955), pp. 86-88. Bıyıklıoğlu, after commenting on the sincerity of Kemal's desire for a loyal opposition party, stresses the point that "Atatürk possessed a democratic outlook. Although he held in his hands all the opportunities, the force and the endless confidence and love of the nation which were necessary and sufficient for establishing a dictatorship, he never fell into that course." (p. 88.)

For a glimpse of the relationship in Kemal's mind between the fundamental Kemalist programs and democratic procedures, see the slightly ambiguous conversation related by Hasan Rıza Soyak on p. 12 of the same work.

Today, of course, it is explicitly mentioned as an inherent part of the fundamental notion of "populism." [37]

Other principles may have been given greater prominence at various times, and the party's actions may frequently have contradicted its profession of democracy, but the fact remains that the democratic principle did exist as an acknowledged goal and was increasingly heeded by growing numbers of Turkish citizens and politicians as time passed. In a negative way, we could point out that though authoritarian practices were widely used to restrict the expression of dissent, no totalitarian "terror" ever stalked Kemalist Turkey. Still more important, *no ideology justifying authoritarianism or dictatorship was ever developed!* Democracy was greatly aided in its growth by the rejection of most alternative ideologies. Repressive measures were almost always regarded as temporary and unfortunate, even though of practical necessity, and they were productive of what Duverger has aptly called a "bad conscience." [38] This bad conscience was eased,

---

[37] The official *Histoire...*, *op. cit.*, printed in 1935, refers to "la démocratie turque," p. 164. Recent *R.P.P. Programs* give a prominent place not only to "democracy" (in the introduction and under "populism") but also to the "multi-party system" (under "republicanism"). See C. H. P. Beyoğlu Ilçesi Eviyaçelebi Ocağı, *C.H.P. 'nin el Kitabı (R.P.P. Handbook)*, (Istanbul: Şevket Unal Matbaası, 1958), pp. 17–18. Though typically not employing the word *demokrasi*, the 1927 *R.P.P. Regulations* proclaim that the party is dedicated to government "by the people and for the people" — a phrase often taken to be an effective brief definition of "democracy." *Cumhuriyet Halk Fırkası Nizamnamesi 1927*, Article 4 (Ankara: Zelliç Biraderler Matbaası, 1929).

[38] Maurice Duverger, *Les Partis Politiques* (Paris: Librairie Armand Colin, 1951), pp. 307–312.

With regard to the use of force and repression in Turkey, Mustafa Kemal made the following comments to a foreign reporter in 1930: "Even the guard standing at the door is not afraid of me. If you want, ask him. Government cannot be built on fear. The government that relies on bullets does not endure. Such a government, even dictatorship, is necessary only on the appearance of rebellion *for a temporary period*." (My italics) (*Atatürk'ün Söylev ve Demeçleri, op. cit.*, Vol. III, p. 87.)

Bernard Lewis has described the dictatorial aspect of the Kemalist regime in the following terms: "Force and repression were used to establish and maintain the Republic during the period of revolutionary struggle, but there was little danger to life and to personal liberty. Turkey under Kemal was a dictatorship, but without the monstrous apparatus of surveillance and repression, the terror of the doorbell and the concentration camp, the furtive over-the-shoulder glance. Political activity against the regime was banned and newspapers were under strict control, but apart from that, talk and even books were comparatively free.... Real violence was rare, and was usually in response to violent opposition." "Democracy in Turkey," *op. cit.*, p. 59. The essential reason for this state of affairs was that democracy was a positive value for Kemal, and authoritarianism was simply a device for ensuring the success of specific revolutionary programs that were still more highly valued.

Hence, it is not surprising to find Mustafa Kemal repeating in 1935 to an-

periodically, through attempts to live up to democratic norms by permitting the organization of opposition. The outstanding example of this process is the party I shall examine next — the Liberal Republican Party.

Chronology and Character of the Liberal Party

In 1930, five years after the termination of the Progressive Party, four years after the trials of July 1926, and after Assembly passage of many basic reforms, Gazi Mustafa Kemal determined to permit an experiment with a loyal opposition party. Following an exchange of correspondence with his friend and former Premier, "gentle" Ali Fethi (Okyar), Fethi was summoned from his quasi-exile as Ambassador to France and was vouchsafed the right to construct the Liberal Republican Party. Kemal envisioned a gentlemanly parliamentary dialogue between trusted leaders of both parties. He could view this mild contest with Olympian detachment; it would have the welcome side effect of further elevating his own position vis à vis all other politicians and statesmen, and it would "prove to the world that a well-mannered political life exists among the Turks also." [39] He

---

other foreigner who had asked him why he disliked to be called a dictator: "I am not a dictator. They say that I am powerful; yes, this is true. There is nothing that I want that I shall not be able to achieve; because I do not know how to act reluctantly and weakly. In my view a dictator is one who subjugates others to his will. I do not want to govern by breaking hearts, I want to win them." (*Atatürk'ün Söylev ve Demeçleri, op. cit.*, p. 98.)

These comments again reflect the long-range, antidictatorial bent of Kemalist doctrine even amid its short-run dictatorial practices. However, an authoritarian ideology was *not* developed but a definite and positive democratic commitment *was* slowly developed, as much through the implicit logic of certain actions as in words. This democratic impulse was generally a minor strand among bolder patterns. But it was always heeded to some extent and became increasingly influential with time.

[39] Süreyya Ilmen, *Dört Ay Yaşamış Olan Zavallı Serbest Fırka* (*The Unfortunate Liberal Party Which Lasted Four Months*), (Istanbul: Muallim Fuad Gücüyener Yayınevi, 1951), p. 8. Numerous other reasons for the formation of the Liberal Party have been adduced, most of them relating to varying degrees of alleged disagreement between Mustafa Kemal and Ismet Pashas. They are cited in Tunaya, *Türkiyede Siyasî Partiler, op. cit.*, pp. 623–624. Kemal's ideal picture of relations between the two parties is to be found in several places, for example, Ilmen, *op. cit.*, or *Atatürk'ün Söylev ve Demeçleri, op. cit.*, II, p. 258. Basic sources on the Liberal Party include, in addition to the above: Ahmet Ağaoğlu, *Serbest Fırka Hatıraları* (*Memories of the Liberal Party*), (Istanbul: Nebioğlu Yayınları, 1950); Samet Ağaoğlu, *op. cit.*; *Histoire . . ., op. cit.*, pp. 194–195; Karpat, *Turkey's Politics, op. cit.*, pp. 64–68; Rustow, "Politics and Islam . . .," in Frye (ed.), *op. cit.*, p. 88; and Walter F. Weiker, "The Free Party of 1930 in Turkey," *op. cit.*

Kemal had written to Fethi; "Since my youth I have been in favor of a system in which honest individuals and political parties would express and

assured Fethi that he was not active as President of the People's Party and that he would remain neutral in the salutary parliamentary contest between two *republican* and *secular* parties. As proof of his sincerity his sister, Makbule, was registered in the Liberal Party with much publicity.

On August 12, 1930, the Liberal Republican Party was formally launched. In its program it stressed nearly all the points stressed by the People's Party. Two main differences should be noted. The first is the Liberal Party's more negative attitude toward etatism and its accent on private enterprise (Article 5). Actually, economic affairs in general occupy a more prominent place in the Liberal outlook. Second, there is a more explicit insistence on political individualism. Individual rights, freedom of conscience, freedom of ideas and freedom of assembly, popular control over administration, women's rights, and direct elections are clearly advocated. Thus there is much in the program of the Liberal Party that heralds the Democratic Party's propaganda appeal between 1946 and 1950.[40]

When we examine the organization of the Liberal Party, its kinship with the Democratic Party and with that party's successor, the Justice Party, emerges even more distinctly. The parliamentary activities of the Liberal Party were, in Tunaya's expression, "unproductive." The party enlisted only fourteen members and made a profound impact in only one debate, while participating in just thirteen sittings altogether.[41] In the country, however, the reception and performance were more impressive. After some initial apprehensiveness, strong local support for the party was displayed in many areas. Yasa tells us of the thrust of the party in the small village of Hasanoğlan in Ankara Province.[42] We learn from Samet Ağaoğlu of the rapid growth of the Kars branch of the party.[43] Ilmen describes a similarly speedy growth in Istanbul.[44] But most significantly, the greatest activity and enthusiasm were manifested in the Izmir and Aegean Regions, later the central bastions of both the Democratic Party and the Justice Party.[45] Outstanding among the young politicians who gained early

---

freely debate ideas in the Assembly or before the nation for the benefit of the country...." See Tunaya, *Türkiyede Siyasî Partiler, op. cit.*, p. 633. (Translation by Karpat, *Turkey's Politics, op cit.*, p. 65, n. 96.)

[40] The Liberal *Program* is given in Tunaya, *Türkiyede Siyasi Partiler, op. cit.*, pp. 633–635.

[41] *Ibid.*, p. 625, n. 9. Tunaya lists twelve members (p. 622), but the *Yıllık* lists fourteen, and I have accepted the latter listing. *T.B.M.M. Yıllığı, op. cit., Devre* III, *İçtima* 3, p. 492.

[42] *Op. cit.*, p. 156, n. 1.

[43] *Op. cit.*, p. 115.

[44] *Op. cit.*, pp. 72–73.

[45] Tunaya, *Türkiyede Siyasî Partiler, op cit.*, p. 630.

eminence in the party was the Aydın organization's chairman, a youthful landowner, Adnan Bey — to be better known a decade and a half later, after service in the People's Party, as Adnan Menderes.[46] In several important respects, then, the Liberal Party was a presentiment of things to come.

Relations between the two political organizations deteriorated as rapidly as the Liberal Party grew, to a considerable extent because of that growth. The personal bitterness that has marked all party politics in Turkey infected many of the leaders on both sides. Matters were made worse by the conviction within the People's Party that religious and social reactionaries were appearing above ground once more and infiltrating the Liberal organization. The basic Kemalist reforms might once again be placed in jeopardy. Despite the unpleasant repercussions of halting for the second time what was widely intereperted to be democratic growth, the reforms could not yet be risked. The Liberal Republican Party was induced to abolish itself on December 18, 1930, just ninety-nine days after its auspicious start.

Background Characteristics of the Liberal Party and the People's Party

What sorts of backgrounds did the Liberal Party's deputies to the Grand National Assembly have? Where do they fit into the broad and detailed picture? Were there any differences between them and the People's Party's delegation? I shall now attempt to answer these queries. Since the Liberal contingent numbered but fourteen men, the breakdowns become highly unreliable, and I shall offer only the grossest comparisons.

First of all, unlike the Second Group and Progressive oppositions, the Liberal deputies were four years older, on the average, than those in the People's Party — 50.7 years to 46.4. One quarter of the *Halkçılar* were under forty, but none of the Liberals were under that age. The fourteen Liberals were spread over thirteen different provincial constituencies, suggesting the artificial character of the parliamentary group of the party. Most political parties in Turkey and elsewhere display greater geographical concentration of strength.

Coming to birthplace, we learn that exactly one half of the Liberals were born outside Turkey, compared to 14 per cent of the People's Party's deputies. And we see that thirteen of the fourteen Liberals (93 per cent) were born outside their constituencies compared to half of those from the People's Party. The local roots in Turkey of the parliamentary Liberal Party were almost nonexistent, in sharp contrast

---

[46] For a brief period Menderes first adopted the last name of Ertekin, switching to Menderes while a deputy in the Fifth Assembly.

to the strong local support given the extraparliamentary Liberal organization in many parts of the country.

A similar trend is evident with regard to several other characteristics. All of the Liberal deputies had received university-level education, while two thirds of the People's Party's deputies had reached that level. The Liberals were also somewhat more experienced in the Assembly, 79 per cent of them having served before, as against 63 per cent of the *Halkçılar* with previous experience. The same sort of differences appear when we look at occupation, one of the most critical background dimensions. Eleven of the fourteen Liberals (79 per cent) were officials in contrast to an official representation of just over one half (52 per cent) in the People's Party group. Examining the military men in particular, we discover that every other Liberal deputy was a military man, as against approximately one in six (17 per cent) of the People's Party deputies. Finally, checking on their reelection fates, we observe that six of the fourteen Liberal deputies were elected to the subsequent Assembly, some 43 per cent, a very high relative return for an opposition group, though 76 per cent of the People's Party returned.

All in all, as with the Progressive Party, we see that the Liberals in the Assembly outdid the People's Party's deputies in those very characteristics which typified the People's Party. The Liberals were less local, more likely to have been born outside Turkey or in the Marmara-Aegean Region, and more experienced in the parliament. They had a higher over-all level of formal education, and were more official and military in their occupational make-up. Was this another opposition movement similar to the Progressives? If so, why the mild treatment and relatively high rate of reelection for an opposition group?

The answer, of course, is that there was one striking difference between the two parties that has not been reflected in the social background data. The Progressives were a real threat to the Kemalists because they were so much like them in social characteristics that they imperiled the basic sources of Kemalist strength. The parliamentary Liberals were even more like the Kemalists, so that they were no danger. "In the first movement," as Tunaya explains, "the founders were the Gazi's rivals; in the second, however, they were his own personnel." [47] The Liberals resembled — again, even outdid — the Kemalists in official and intellectual background *because Kemal inserted into the small party his own trusted comrades and adherents.*

Thus, *in the Assembly* and its relations therein with the bloc of People's Party deputies, the Liberal Party was a kitten compared to

---

[47] Tunaya, *Türkiyede Siyasî Partiler, op. cit.*, p. 624.

the Progressive Party. But it is superficial to accept too readily the common comment that the Liberal Republican Party was, all things considered, a much less serious competitor to the People's Party. It was perhaps in one crucial respect more dangerous. The Progressive Party was like the Cheshire cat in its late stages of appearance — all head and no body. The fangs were readily perceived, and measures to eliminate the beast were hastily prepared, to add a note of grim realism to the whimsy of Lewis Carroll. The Liberal *movement* — for so we must truly label it — was a creature with an artificial and puny head onto which there grew an increasingly powerful body and tail. Being less of a direct threat, its strength was underestimated. That strength, lying in the expanding and increasingly restive professional and commercial classes in the country, in the modern, locally oriented, but anti–People's Party denizens of littoral Turkey, was diffuse and not easily assaulted. It continued to develop and spread until, in 1950, it unseated the People's Party after twenty-seven years of rule.

THE INDEPENDENT GROUP OF THE REPUBLICAN PEOPLE'S PARTY

The Origin of the Group

To mollify the popular reaction to the demise of the Liberal Party, to maintain some of the external appearances of democracy in the face of European cries of "mock parliamentarism," and to sustain the self-image of the People's Party as being democratically inclined if not currently democratic, the Gazi indicated to the party early in March 1931 that it was necessary to hold another general election "... to confirm, against doubtful and hesitant views, the trust and confidence of the nation which have been given to it [the People's Party]." [48] In this election, nominations for the candidates who would represent the People's Party were at least ostensibly opened up. Nominating proposals were solicited from various sources, and the party newspaper, *Hâkimiyeti Milliye (National Sovereignty)*, began publishing in early April a list of some 1,176 nominees for 287 party candidacies. However, analysis of the occupations of the over-all group of proposed nominees, as contrasted to the occupations of the deputies actually nominated by the party and elected (no party nominee failed of election), reveals few differences.[49] Nevertheless, it

---

[48] On the situation in Turkey and on the European reaction see, respectively, Webster, *The Turkey of Atatürk, op. cit.*, p. 111, and von Kral, *Kemal Atatürk's Land, op. cit.*, p. 26. For Mustafa Kemal's statement on the renewal of the mandate of the R.P.P., see *T.B.M.M. Yıllığı, op. cit., Devre* IV, *Fevkalâde İçtima*, p. 307.

[49] For an occupational breakdown of the proposed nominees (unfortunately into seventy categories) consult the *Yıllık* just cited, pp. 308 ff.

is true that a small band of farmers and laborers, hitherto largely unrepresented in the Assembly, was introduced into parliament at this time. Also, to complete the gesture, thirty deputyships — to be filled by means of write-in votes — were left open for "independent" candidates.[50] A related development that occurred about one year later was the establishment of the first of the People's Houses (*Halkevleri*) in fourteen provincial capitals.

The symbolic and retrospective significance of these measures is clearly greater than their impact on Turkish public opinion at the time, for they were followed in the mid-thirties by a general hardening of the domestic policies of the regime and by a concomitant rise in discontent among many segments of the burgeoning elite. Before long, the discontented began increasingly to exploit the democratic theme in the Kemalists' own corpus of propaganda and implicit in the Kemalists' earlier actions — to press for a liberalization of political life. A group of scattered "independents" in the Assembly could hardly pass, even *pro forma*, as a true and organized opposition. To remedy matters once again the People's Party decided at its Fifth National Congress in 1939 to create within the People's Party a twenty-one-man Independent Group (*Müstakil Grup*) to act as an obvious — though rather fictitious — opposition. This Independent Group commenced its activity in the Sixth Assembly and continued into the Seventh Assembly, until it was terminated by the extraordinary National Congress (*Kurultay*) of the People's Party at the start of the multi-party era in 1946, its members then reentering the People's Party fold.[51]

The President of the People's Party was also the formal President of the Independent Group, which was more immediately headed by its own Vice-President (Ali Rana Tarhan), who reported directly to

---

[50] These alterations in the composition of the Assembly were, of course, the result of a decision by Kemal and his associates in command of the People's Party. The rationale for the establishment of the independent seats is given in the official *Histoire...*: "As for the seats left for independent candidates, this was a gesture, to give proof of the fidelity of the Republican People's Party to democratic principles and of its explicit desire to see its acts submitted to control, which will always in the history of the Republic be appreciated and admired." Cf. *Histoire...*, *op. cit.*, pp. 195–196.

[51] On the Fifth National Congress and the Independent Group, see *T.B.M.M. Yıllığı*, *op. cit.*, *Devre* VI, *Fevkalâde İçtima*, pp. 492, 498–499, 502–510, 539, 541–544, 631–632. Some of the remarks on the operations of the R.P.P. in the Assembly, e.g., those of Hikmet Bayur, are quite interesting. Cf. also Tunaya, *Türkiyede Siyasî Partiler*, *op. cit.*, pp. 562–563; Karpat, *Turkey's Politics*, *op. cit.*, pp. 75, 117, n. 53, 396–397; Feyzioğlu, "Les Partis Politiques en Turquie," *op. cit.*; and, especially, Hilmi Uran, *Hatıralarım* (*Memoirs*), (Ankara: Ayyıldız Matbaası, 1959), pp. 344–345.

the People's Party President (İnönü) and "took orders from him." [52] The members of Independent Group could attend the meetings of the regular People's Party Group even though they could not participate in the discussions or vote. On the other hand, only the members of the Independent Group attended the meetings of that group. It was stipulated that the deputies of the Independent Group could not become People's Party cabinet members (tacitly recognizing that there was no chance of its becoming sufficiently powerful or independent to form a government on its own).

Even the staunchest *Halkçılar* have confessed that the Independent Group was independent only in name and indulged only in the mildest criticism and remonstrance — much milder than that which occurred within the Assembly Group caucus of the People's Party itself. At the same time, it should not be overlooked that the Fifth National Congress of the People's Party, which set up the Independent Group, was something of a watershed for the mounting democratic currents within that party, and that the Independent Group was conceived by many to be — and actually was — *a device for accustoming people to the operations of a multi-party regime.* Though an artificial opposition, it was not just a cynical piece of camouflage either in intention or in effect. For this reason it warrants our attention.

Background Characteristics of the Independent Group and the Regular People's Party

Again my findings must be merely suggestive and will be offered without detailed breakdowns because there were only twenty-two Independent Group members in the Sixth Assembly and thirty-five in the Seventh.

In both Assemblies the Independents were noticeably younger than the Regulars. For the Sixth Assembly the average age of the Independents was exactly 50.0 years and that of the Regulars was 53.4 years. In the Seventh Assembly the difference was even more pronounced, with the Independents having an average age of 45.5 years and the Regulars an average of 54.5 years. The men assigned to (or possibly volunteering for) the Independent Group tended to be younger deputies than those of the main group. Correspondingly, they also tended to have markedly less experience. In the Sixth Assembly 32 per cent of the Regulars and 41 per cent of the Independents had no previous experience, while in the next parliament 30 per cent of the Regulars had seen no previous service as opposed to 74 per cent of the Independents.

The usual birthplace comparison reveals that the Independents

---

[52] Uran, *ibid.,* p. 344.

were more likely to have been born in the Marmara, Aegean, and foreign regions. While 77 per cent of the Independents of the Sixth Assembly and 80 per cent of the Independents of the Seventh Assembly were born in these regions, only 58 per cent of the Regulars in each Assembly were born there. Similarly, the "localism" of the Independents was less than that of the regular People's Party deputies. For the two Assemblies, respectively, 42 and 45 per cent of the Regulars were born in the provinces they represented, and just 23 and 29 per cent of the Independents were so born.

In the same fashion, the Independents were better educated and more competent at foreign languages than the Regulars. For each group and for the two Assemblies, respectively, the percentages of members with university-level training were as follows: Independents, 86 and 89 per cent; Regulars, 77 and 78 per cent. The figures regarding those claiming knowledge of a foreign language were: Independents, 95 and 98 per cent; Regulars, 77 and 76 per cent. The Independents were also more likely to know French and more likely to list a publication.

The essential occupational difference between the two groups is also rather revealing. The proportions of officials in each were almost exactly equal, varying between 45 and 47 per cent, or just under half of each group. The important difference was that the Independents regularly had about 10 per cent more professionals and fewer "economics" than the Regular group. In the Sixth Assembly, there were also more journalists in the Independent Group, but in the Seventh Assembly there were less.

If we look, finally, at the reelection percentages for the two groups, we get a hint of the lack of severity of the opposition waged by the Independents. Nine tenths of the Independents of the Sixth Assembly were reelected to the subsequent parliament in contrast to just three fourths of the Regulars. In the Seventh Assembly the situation was reversed, but not sharply. Sixty-one per cent of the Regulars were reelected, while 46 per cent of the Independents survived. It cannot be claimed that the Independents, like the Second Group and the Progressives, were at all punished with regard to their tenure in parliament for their participation in the "opposition." The "opposition" was so feeble that partisan feelings were not aroused.

The general picture that emerges from these data is that of the Independent Group member as being younger, less experienced, more intellectual and cosmopolitan, less local, and more likely to be professional in his occupation than the regular People's Party deputies. If we can judge from the incidence of people like Ali Rana Tarhan and Fuat Sirmen (current President of the National Assembly of the Second Republic), the Independents would seem to have been intelligent but less personally committed and definitely second echelon members of the People's Party. With a few possible exceptions, such as Kemalî Bayazıt and Hıfzı Oğuz Bekata, one gets the impression that most of the Independent Group members were deliberately chosen as men or women who were respected for their probity and intellect, but who were less partisan and had less organizational influence than equally able people in the Regular group. Hence, their background and character as well as their power position helps to account for the innocuous nature of their opposition. The data also seem to suggest a relative decline during the Seventh Assembly of whatever impact the Independent Group did have, since the group became still younger, still more drawn from products of the Marmara Region, still less formally powerful, and appreciably less favored for reelection.

CHAPTER TWELVE

Political Parties: 1946-1957

THE SERIES OF REAL and artificial opposition movements that has been described culminated in the cessation of single-party rule and in the introduction of a multi-party system in the years 1945–1950. Throughout the single-party period there had been a groping toward some form of democracy that was consonant with the preservation of basic Kemalist reforms. The succession of ventures at organized opposition is perhaps the best evidence of this democratic predilection, although inspection of the themes of Kemalist propaganda and other observations also yield confirmatory evidence. In any event, by the end of the Second World War the internal Turkish pressures toward a major revamping of the political system were so great, both within and without the People's Party, that they could no longer easily be stifled or appeased.

The specific events that precipitated the liberalization of 1945–1950 are too involved and varied to permit adequate description here.[1] Included were such factors as pent-up resentment against the

---

[1] Fortunately, several valuable studies deal specifically with Turkish politics during these years, and we are able to refer to them for background information that is not so conveniently available for earlier party developments. Especially useful are Karpat, *Turkey's Politics, op. cit.*; Harris, *A Political History of Turkey, 1945–1950, op. cit.*; B. Lewis, *Emergence . . ., op. cit.*, pp. 297–306, and *passim*; Tunaya, *Türkiyede Siyasî Partiler, op. cit.*, pp. 646 ff.; and Robinson, *The First Turkish Republic, op. cit.*, pp. 124–161. Revealing views of participants are found in Ahmet Emin Yalman, *Turkey in My Time* (Norman: University of Oklahoma Press, 1956), Chs. 19–20, and "The Struggle for Multi-party Government in Turkey," *Middle East Journal,* I (January 1947),

government because of wartime austerities and restrictions; the government's apparent chagrin over its own failures, such as the capital levy (*Varlık Vergisi*); the prestige of the victorious democracies of the West; the death of the charismatic leader to whose will it was so easy to succumb and to demand that others succumb; the desire to join the United Nations as a fully accepted democratic member; internal disputes within the People's Party over land reform and other substantive issues; and a renewal of Russian encroachments that led to a search for external support from the United States, adding to the contacts between America and Turkey and further diminishing the already anemic appeal of authoritarian communism for the Turks. Also important was the impact on Turkey of the Kemalist programs that had greatly extended many forms of communication and had reared in the expanded school system a younger generation now reaching power for whom individual rights and direct political participation were values of heightened priority.

Basic changes in Turkish social structure had also occurred. Especially significant was the growth of the professional and commercial components of the elite. To this growth the dominant party had adjusted only minimally and reluctantly. *An alternative elite had developed.* This elite had been neither co-opted nor quashed, possibly because the tremendous problem of eliminating anachronistic religion as a political force had monopolized the attention of the Kemalist high command. An elite head for the body of latent opposition in the country had been formed.

Finally, among the factors leading to the establishment of the multi-party system in 1945-1950, we must include the most vital factor of all — the spread of intense, personally salient democratic conviction over important portions of the Turkish elite. External factors were indubitably involved, but the Turks achieved this democratic development primarily because large groups of them sincerely wanted it and were willing to struggle for it!

By the same token, we must not neglect the legitimate place accorded democratic strivings by the ideology of Kemalism, which not only encouraged the democrats but also sapped much of the defensive position of would-be authoritarians. The liberalization of

---

pp. 46–58; Kasım Gülek, "Democracy Takes Root in Turkey," *Foreign Affairs*, XXX, No. 1 (1951), pp. 135–144; Uran, *Hatıralarım (Memoirs), op. cit.*, 431–548. Additional details and an overview of the entire process are presented in Kerim Kami Key, "The Origins of Turkish Political Parties," *World Affairs Interpreter*, XXVI, No. 1 (1955), pp. 49–60, and in Feyzioğlu, "Les Partis Politiques en Turquie," *op. cit.* A careful chronology of events is found in Gotthard Jäschke, *Die Türkei in den Jahren 1942–1951* (Wiesbaden: Otto Harrassowitz, 1955).

1945-1950, then, was the product of a conjunction of prior democratic tendencies in Kemalism and in the antecedent Turkish heritage with the more immediate, specific influences that I have in part enumerated. This liberalization has resulted in a fundamental transformation of the entire Turkish political system, the consequences of which are still being worked out. Hence, it is with the Eighth Assembly that we first encounter contemporary Turkey.

The Eighth Assembly

The years of the Eighth Assembly (1946-1950) were sharply different in some respects from those following 1950, particularly since the People's Party was still in power and since the overt transition to an accepted multi-party system had only just begun. Not yet had power been democratically transferred, and there was a real uncertainty in most informed minds as to whether it would ever be so transferred.

Of prime significance for Eighth Assembly activities was the fact that the organization of the Democratic Party, founded in January of 1946, was not complete at the time of the 1946 general election.[2] Thus, the composition of the Democratic Party contingent in the Eighth Assembly was to a certain extent warped by special organizational limitations as well as by probable electoral skulduggery in Istanbul. It therefore seems wise to distinguish it from the Democratic Party's Assembly Group of the Ninth and Tenth Assemblies. Similarly, it appears fruitful to distinguish very clearly between the People's Party's parliamentary delegations before and after the fall from power in 1950 — to separate the minority People's Party from the party when it was in office. Consequently, I shall treat the political parties of the Eighth Assembly separately before concluding my scrutiny of social background differences among Turkey's parliamentary parties with an examination of the Ninth and Tenth Assemblies.

Social Backgrounds of the Democratic and Republican People's Parties

From all that has previously been said, one could probably predict how the social backgrounds of the Democratic Party (D.P.) deputies to the Eighth Assembly differed from those of the People's Party

---

[2] The first party formed after World War II was the National Recovery Party (*Millî Kalkınma Partisi*), founded on July 18, 1945. It did not prosper, and the Democratic Party, established six months later, gathered to itself most of the strands of opposition. Tunaya, *Türkiyede Siyasî Partiler...*, *op. cit.*, pp. 638-645. The Democrats had completed about half of their organization at election time.

(R.P.P.) deputies. The Democrats were younger (average age 48.9 years versus 53.2 years for the R.P.P.), had markedly less legislative experience (83 per cent without prior Assembly experience versus 35 per cent for the R.P.P.), were somewhat more likely to have been born in the Aegean-Marmara Region despite the tampering with the Istanbul vote (45 per cent from these regions versus 36 per cent for the R.P.P.), and were more likely to have been born within the province represented (67 per cent locally born versus 56 per cent for the R.P.P.). The Democrats had a lower percentage of deputies who had obtained university-level education (69 per cent compared to 74 per cent for the R.P.P.), but those Democratic deputies who did get to the university were much more likely to have received legal training there (48 per cent versus 32 per cent for the university-educated of the R.P.P.). The university-educated Democrats were correspondingly much less likely to have received bureaucratic or military training (political science faculty: D.P., 8 per cent, R.P.P., 18 per cent; military schools: D.P., none; R.P.P., 18 per cent). Thirty-two per cent of the People's Party deputies knew more than one foreign language, while only 23 per cent of the D.P. deputies knew more than one such language.[3]

As usual, some of the most revealing differences of all emerge when we come to occupation. The interparty differences expressed in terms of the broad occupational groupings are portrayed in Figure 12.1.

The Democrats were notably more professional and economic and less official in occupation. Looking inside the broad occupational

[3] In these and in subsequent interparty comparisons, the percentages are based on an allocation of deputies to party groups according to the alignments prevailing at the end of the given Assembly, or, for those deputies with incomplete service in an Assembly, according to the deputy's last affiliation. Thus, for the Eighth Assembly, I have separated from the Democratic Party group those deputies who left it to join the Nation Party (seventeen), to join the People's Party (three), or to become Independents (six), while adding to the D.P. ranks two converted R.P.P. members it picked up. The total, net Democratic contingent, on which the percentages are based, thus became thirty-six. Computed in the same way, the base for all R.P.P. percentages was 435, and there were also nineteen Nation Party deputies and nine Independents in the Assembly, making the grand total of 499 persons. A splinter group of the D.P., the so-called Independent Democratic Party (*Müstakil Demokrat Parti*) has been included with the main body. The very minor discrepancies between our figures and those of other sources (e.g., Tunaya or the official *Isim Defteri*) are due to slightly different allocation procedures. Naturally, the procedures I have adopted seem most reasonable for my purposes.

The nineteen-man Nation Party (*Millet Partisi*) group will not be examined because of its small size and especially because it did not differ outstandingly or regularly from the other two parties, though on the whole it tended to resemble the D.P. more than the R.P.P.

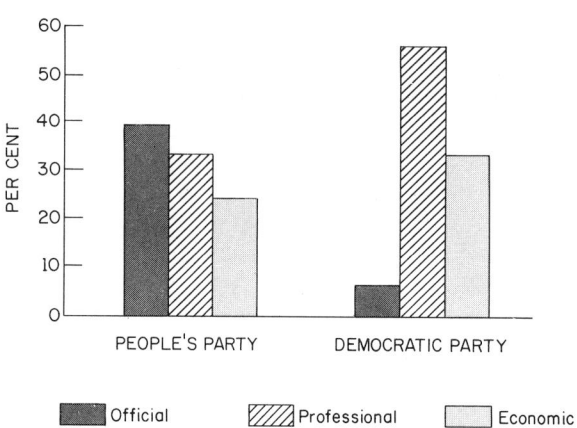

Figure 12.1. Broad occupational distribution of deputies in the Eighth Assembly, by party

classifications we learn that the most striking differences between the parties were that the Democratic group contained 33 per cent lawyers against just 18 per cent for the R.P.P. group, while the R.P.P. group had 15 per cent bureaucrats and 13 per cent military men compared with nary a representative from either of these two important vocations in the basic D.P. contingent! All four of the deputies originally elected under the D.P. banner and whom I have classed as bureaucrats, plus the sole military man originally elected as a D.P. candidate, left the Democratic Party and moved to the Nation Party in the course of the Assembly.[4]

We must not forget that these differences between the Democratic Party and the People's Party occurred in an Assembly in which the basic social background characteristics of the People's Party had already shown a strong general movement in the direction of the Democratic Party. In other words, the R.P.P. delegation to the Eighth Assembly can be compared to the R.P.P. delegation to the Seventh Assembly, data for which were presented in the preceding chapter. Such a comparison reveals that the Eighth Assembly's R.P.P. group differed from the Seventh Assembly's R.P.P. group exactly as the

[4] There were among the D.P. deputies a few other men (e.g., Refik Koraltan) with bureaucratic or military experience. But these men were placed in other vocations (law for Koraltan) which were regarded as more basic for them according to our regular criteria. Thus, by applying the same criteria to all deputies, the present striking difference was obtained. The names of the five renegade D. P. officials are: military — Sadık Aldoğan; bureaucratic — Ahmet Oğuz, Enis Akaygen, Ahmet Tahtakılıç, and Suphi Batur.

For a statement about the occupational backgrounds of the 250 D.P. candidates in the 1946 election, see Karpat, *Turkey's Politics, op. cit.*, p. 163.

Table 12.1

COMPARISON OF THE PEOPLE'S PARTY ASSEMBLY GROUP OF THE SEVENTH
AND EIGHTH ASSEMBLIES WITH THE DEMOCRATIC PARTY ASSEMBLY GROUP
OF THE EIGHTH ASSEMBLY ALONG SELECTED DIMENSIONS

SOCIAL BACKGROUND DIMENSION	R.P.P. SEVENTH ASSEMBLY	R.P.P. EIGHTH ASSEMBLY	D.P. EIGHTH ASSEMBLY
Average Age in Years	54.5	53.2	48.9
Previous Assembly Experience	70%	65%	17%
Born in Province Represented	45%	56%	67%
Official Occupation	47%	39%	6%
University-Level Education	78%	74%	69%
Foreign Language Proficiency	76%	71%	64%
N	(453)	(435)	(36)

D.P. contingent of the Eighth Assembly differed from the R.P.P. contingent of that same Assembly. Despite a major adjustment within the R.P.P. in the Eighth Assembly, the Democratic Party still clearly differs from it and is even further down the road along which the People's Party was traveling. Table 12.1, comparing the R.P.P. groups of the Seventh and Eighth Assemblies with the D.P. group of the Eighth Assembly along several dimensions, will illustrate this point. Note the regularity and direction of the progressions.

Factions within the People's Party: The "Thirty-Five"

In the course of the Eighth Assembly the People's Party went through a soul-searching crisis over the fundamental issue of whether to permit the liberalization of political life that was being urged or to attempt to sit on things, probably forcibly, for a longer spell. It is difficult to find moments when the internal lines of conflict were sufficiently clear and known so as to permit social background analysis. In late August of 1947, however, at a meeting of the R.P.P. Assembly Group, a bloc of thirty-five votes was cast in opposition to the policies of Premier Recep Peker, protagonist of the stern, antiliberalization viewpoint. The names of the members of this opposition bloc were given to the press, whereupon they were ingeniously christened the "thirty-five." As a result, we are able to check briefly into their social backgrounds compared to those of the R.P.P. deputies who did not register a protest at that time.[5]

[5] Cf. Tunaya, *Türkiyede Siyasî Partiler...*, *op. cit.*, pp. 563–564. Originally, the number of opposition votes was placed at thirty-four and was then raised to thirty-five the following day. Tunaya lists the members of this group, follow-

The most common description of the "thirty-five" has been that they were "younger" than the rest of the People's Party deputies.[6] My analysis shows this to have been true and to have been one of the more pronounced differences between the two groups, which do not differ greatly in most social background characteristics. Over half the "thirty-five" were under the age of forty-five, while less than a quarter of the other R.P.P. deputies were in the same age bracket. The mean age difference between the two groups was seven years, 46.8 for the "thirty-five" and 53.8 for the others.

This is the sort of fact that I have in mind when I refer to the importance of the appearance of a "new political generation" in the postwar years. These more liberal R.P.P. deputies, born after the turn of the century, had generally received at least their higher education in *Kemalist* Turkey, imbibing the Kemalist outlook and differentially experiencing its democratic content in particular. They were also in most cases too young to have participated in the National Struggle and were more oriented to the later attempts at domestic social and economic development than to the independence effort.

With regard to previous parliamentary experience, the "thirty-five" occupied an intermediate position. They had fewer members with no previous experience (27 per cent against 36 per cent), but they also had fewer members with long experience (15 per cent having served in more than two prior Assemblies versus 35 per cent) — rather naturally, when one considers their age. Less than one man in eight among the "thirty-five" had served in an Atatürk Assembly in contrast to one in three for the residual R.P.P. group.

The only other differences of note between the two groups lie in the areas of education and occupation. One of the very conspicuous characteristics of the "thirty-five" is a high level of education. Eighty-five per cent reached the university level as opposed to 73 per cent of the rest of the People's Party deputies. Considered against the high over-all level of education in the Assembly and against the intergroup educational differences obtained in other comparisons, this is a rather striking distinction.

---

ing *Vatan* (August 27, 1947). In the Tunaya-*Vatan* list there are only thirty-four names. One of these names is that of a Hilmi Hakkıoğlu, but there does not seem to have been a deputy with that name. Of the five Hilmis in the Assembly, the most likely candidate seems to be Hilmi Atlıoğlu, R.P.P. deputy from Ankara who died in 1948. But since I am not certain, we have limited our list to the remaining thirty-three names. The Eighth Assembly *Yıllık* gives thirty-four as the number (p. 911, *Toplantı: Olğ.*, 1) but no names.

[6] See, e.g., Tunaya, *Türkiyede Siyasî Partiler...*, *op. cit.*, p. 563; Karpat, *Turkey's Politics, op. cit.*, p. 197; B. Lewis, *Emergence...*, *op cit.*, p. 302; G. Lewis, *Turkey, op. cit.*, p. 126 (2nd rev. ed.).

Occupationally, I had expected that the "thirty-five" might turn out to be more professional and economic than the main body of the People's Party, mistakenly viewing the recalcitrants as like the extraparty opposition, the Democrats. Such a conception proved to be wrong. The "thirty-five" were slightly more official than the other R.P.P. deputies (52 per cent versus 42 per cent) and less professional (21 per cent versus 36 per cent). If we momentarily ignore the warning flag that the small size of the group raises and look within the broad occupational breakdowns, one very interesting refinement comes to the fore. Inside the official classification, the factional proportions of bureaucrats are almost equal, but the proportion of military men is less in the "thirty-five" and the proportion of educators sharply more (27 per cent against 12 per cent).

The last finding led me to check the individual dossiers of the "thirty-five" for their vocational connections with university-level education, since I was aware that several prominent university professors were included in the group and that other outstanding members, such as Ismail Rüştü Aksal and Kasım Gülek, had strongly intellectual backgrounds. This further check turned out to be most rewarding. More than half (five of nine) of those I had listed as educators were university professors, and five individuals whom I had classified as belonging to some other vocation also had experience as university professors. Thus, exactly 30 per cent of the entire group had *taught* in Turkish *universities.* If we add two other deputies who were not classed as educators but who had professional experience as teachers and educational administrators, plus the four nonuniversity educators, to the above group, we get the surprising total of just under half the entire group of the "thirty-five" — some 48 per cent — which had been professionally involved in the field of education. And these calculations still exclude intellectuals like Aksal and Gülek, whom we might style as university-oriented in much of their approach to politics.

Adding the insights produced by these data to other inmpressions of Turkish political developments, one forms the notion that while the "new man in Turkish politics," as a whole, may have been the lawyer, engineer, and merchant, the new man in the People's Party was, to an important degree, the young university professor. His commitment to individual freedom and democracy aroused him to fight first against authoritarian elements within the People's Party and then, with even more vigor, against the antidemocratic moves of Menderes and Bayar. At the same time, the young professor's intellectual qualities disposed him toward planning and state-supervised development, emphasized in the R.P.P. Certainly within the People's Party of today one perceives, especially in positions of leadership, many examples of this university-formed intellectual. Names like Turhan Feyzioğlu, Fethi

Çelikbaş, Turan Güneş, Nihat Erim, and others come immediately to mind. Always granting significant individual differences, we can still say that, in considerable measure, these people tend to speak a common language, share many social and political norms, and work especially well with one another. In fact, it is not too great an exaggeration to say that much of the fate of the People's Party and of Turkey itself may rest in their hands, and more particularly on their relations with the other new men both in and out of their party — the lawyers and the men of commerce.

Political Parties in the Ninth and Tenth Assemblies

With the direct support of Ismet Inönü, the liberal elements within the People's Party won their battle. During the last two years of the Eighth Assembly, the electoral law was made more democratic, the formal structure of the R.P.P. was also democratized, and governmental harassment of the Democratic Party largely ceased. Finally, on May 14, 1950, the democratic convictions of the People's Party were put to the ultimate test. A completely free national election was held — the first since 1920 — and the People's Party lost.

Its convictions were about all of the R.P.P. that survived the election. The party salvaged only 69 seats out of 487, though the popular vote was closer, 54 per cent for the Democratic Party and 40 per cent for the People's Party. Honorably resisting last-minute cries to deny the election results and stay in power by force, the R.P.P. remained true to its newly dominant liberalism, surrendered power, and went into opposition. The decade of Menderes and Bayar began, amid widespread enthusiasm and optimism for the future.

It was really only the bony rump of the People's Party that survived the electoral debacle. The provinces resisting the anti-R.P.P. trend were almost entirely in the east. Consequently, the social characteristics of the R.P.P. deputies, largely limited to this area, were rather divergent from those which had typified the party in previous Assemblies. Though in the following Tenth Assembly the R.P.P. made a partial adjustment to its wounded, minority condition, the People's Party's Assembly Group in that parliament, too, must be looked on as being primarily a rump. Only in the Eleventh Assembly did the party's parliamentary group return to a more normal, though still minority, condition.

Age

In the Ninth Assembly the R.P.P. deputies were older than the Democrats, averaging 51.7 years as opposed to 47.0 years. By the Tenth Assembly, the People's Party had made a major adjustment in this respect and had reduced the average age of its parliamentary delegation by eight years, down to a figure of 43.7 as contrasted to 46.7 for the D.P. deputies. In these times, as the party leader's (Inönü's) age became more and more a matter of concern and speculation, the R.P.P. rejuvenated the rest of its organization right up to the level of the Party Assembly (*Parti Meclisi*).[7]

Birthplace

The birthplaces of the Democratic deputies were relatively widely distributed over all of Turkey compared to the People's Party when it was in power. Furthermore, the distribution increased slightly in the Tenth Assembly as compared to the Ninth. In the Ninth, for instance, one third of the Democrats were born in the Aegean-Marmara Region, while in the Tenth this proportion dropped to just over one fourth. No single region spawned more than 15 per cent of the total Democratic delegation in the Tenth Assembly (the Marmara and Black Sea Regions each reaching that figure), while on the other hand no region contributed less than 6 per cent (the lowest being the Northeastern Region). The birthplaces of the deputies from the People's Party were, on the contrary, highly concentrated. In the Ninth Assembly, three eastern regions — the Northeastern, the Black Sea, and the East Central Regions — produced 55 per cent of the total R.P.P. group, and in the Tenth Assembly this percentage rose to the extreme level of 94 per cent.

Localism

The rump characteristics of the People's Party's Assembly Group are also plain to see in the data on "localism," or birth in the province represented. The D.P. percentages for the Ninth and Tenth Assemblies were 59 per cent locally born and 63 per cent locally born. Similar figures for the R.P.P. were 63 per cent and 91 per cent locally born. Only rather atypical, deeply entrenched, locally oriented politi-

---

[7] These and the subsequent statistics are based on the following totals. For the Ninth Assembly: D.P., 394; R.P.P., 71. For the Tenth Assembly: D.P., 451; R.P.P., 32; F.P. (Freedom Party), 36. These figures represent the basic party strengths at the end of each Assembly, with the main exception of the seventy-one R.P.P. total for the Ninth Assembly. The last figure includes twelve deputies who resigned from the People's Party during the sessions, nine entering the D.P., and three becoming independents. The Democratic Party's total for the Ninth Assembly excludes twenty-two deputies who resigned from that party and maintained a quasi-organized identity as independent Democrats. The grand totals for the two Assemblies — respectively, 494 and 537 — are finally obtained by adding seven "others" (Nation Party, Peasant Party, and independents) to the Ninth Assembly figures and fourteen "others" to the Tenth Assembly figures.

cians in the virtually impregnable eastern bastions of the People's Party managed to withstand the electoral onslaughts of 1950 and 1954 and gain election on the R.P.P. ticket. Not until 1957 do more familiar characteristics reappear, and even then it is plain that the traumatic experiences of the preceding two elections fundamentally altered the structure of the R.P.P. Local influences subside somewhat but remain at a newly established high level.

Assembly Experience and Reelection

A new situation with regard to previous parliamentary experience and the proportions of the parties being reelected also prevails. In earlier eras a high degree of inter-Assembly stability was displayed by the party in power. The percentages of deputies with prior experience and of deputies who secured reelection to the subsequent Assembly were large. But in the Ninth Assembly 88 per cent of the D.P. contingent had no previous parliamentary experience. More significantly, in the Tenth Assembly, after having been in power during the previous four years and winning the 1954 election by a margin even more lopsided than that of 1950, 51 per cent of the Democratic deputies still had no prior parliamentary experience. With regard to reelection, 63 per cent of the Democrats were reelected after the Ninth Assembly and only 51 per cent after the Tenth.

Naturally, for the suffering People's Party deputies, positions were even more insecure. Forty-four per cent in the Ninth Assembly and 72 per cent in the Tenth had no prior experience, while but 20 per cent of the Ninth Assembly People's Party deputies were reelected to the Tenth. In this last respect, however, the R.P.P. did better between the Tenth and Eleventh Assemblies, reelecting 72 per cent of its small band of thirty-two souls, a higher percentage than that which held for the D.P., though not surprisingly so. Any truly viable party can be cut down only so far; it has an irreducible core which cannot be shaken and on which it can always rebuild.

Education and Foreign Language

If we examine education and occupation, we see that, in adversity, the People's Party came even more to resemble the Democratic Party. With regard to education, in the Ninth Assembly the R.P.P. was still slightly better educated than the D.P. Seventy-nine per cent of the R.P.P. deputies had university-level education as opposed to 73 per cent of the D.P. deputies. Sixty-nine per cent of the former spoke a foreign language against 64 per cent of the latter. By the Tenth Assembly, though, the Democratic Party's percentage with university-level education had climbed just a bit to 76 per cent, while the People's Party's figures had fallen to the relatively low level of 62 per cent.

The same happened with regard to foreign language competence. Seventy-four per cent of the Democrats claimed proficiency at a foreign language, a rise of some 10 per cent over the Ninth Assembly figure, and merely 44 per cent of the R.P.P. deputies made such a claim, a drop of 25 per cent.

Occupation

The broad occupational changes are indicated in Table 12.2. Basically, we see that the People's Party became less official and more professional and economic in vocational background as we move from the Ninth to the Tenth Assembly, whereas the Democratic Party's composition remained quite steady.

Table 12.2

OCCUPATIONS OF DEMOCRATIC AND PEOPLE'S PARTY DEPUTIES, NINTH AND TENTH ASSEMBLIES (PERCENTAGES)

OCCUPATIONAL GROUP	NINTH ASSEMBLY		TENTH ASSEMBLY	
	D.P.	R.P.P.	D.P.	R.P.P.
Official	19%	35%	20%	25%
Professional	46	35	45	41
Economic	29	25	31	31
Other	6	5	4	3
N	(394)	(71)	(451)	(32)

The Freedom Party

Before inspecting certain voting patterns in the Assembly, a capsule description of the thirty-six members of the Freedom Party (*Hürriyet Partisi*) of the Tenth Assembly seems to be needed. It was a large enough group to permit the very limited breakdowns I have deliberately been employing throughout these party analyses. And in view of its separation from the Democratic Party and later merger with the People's Party it may give some insight into the nature of the growing movement late in the 1950's away from the Democrats and toward opposition, if not always toward the R.P.P.

In most respects the Freedom Party deputies were like the Democrats, from whom they had split. Thus I shall concentrate solely on the differences between the two groups. The first important difference lies in the greater incidence within the Freedom Party of persons born in the Aegean-Marmara Region. Fifty-eight per cent of the Freedom Party deputies (*Hürriyetçiler*) had their origins in those two regions as opposed to 27 per cent of the Democrats. Secondly, the *Hürriyet-*

çiler had a larger percentage of deputies with university-level education than the Democrats, 86 per cent versus 76 per cent. Eighty-one per cent of the *Hürriyetçiler* claimed knowledge of a foreign language in contrast to 64 per cent of the Democrats. And lastly, the Freedom Party had relatively more professionals and officials than the Democratic Party (three fourths against two thirds), and had fewer "economics" (14 per cent against 31 per cent).

In short, the social background data suggest that the Freedom Party deputies, when contrasted with their former Democratic comrades, were *more cosmopolitan, more intellectual, and less commercial.* That description is redolent of the new type of People's Party deputy portrayed earlier.

The Voting Behavior of Deputies

In Turkey, as in many other political systems where party discipline is very strong, analysis of the social backgrounds of national legislators grouped according to their voting behaviors is not particularly fruitful. One merely obtains the social background differences that distinguish the parties from one another, since the parties tend to vote as largely unbroken blocs. One group membership, that of belonging to a political party, completely overshadows all other memberships in directly affecting this very visible political behavior — voting. Consequently, if one is seeking to uncover the behavioral significance of different social backgrounds for national legislators, the most effective strategy would seem to be to concentrate on political actions other than voting — actions less dominated by party control, such as speechmaking, contacts with interest groups, frequency of visitations to the constituency, and attendance in the parliament.

Sometimes, however, as in the present case, the absence of information about other legislative behaviors nevertheless compels one to examine the relationship between social background and voting patterns under these very conditions of strict party discipline. Voting records are just about the only precise behavioral indicator available. Under such circumstances, one useful tactic, it would seem, is to try to deal with those instances in which party discipline broke down, either for all deputies during a brief period of time or among certain limited subgroups of deputies. Such is the approach I have used in investigating the relationship between social background and voting behavior in the Grand National Assembly. I shall not examine gross voting patterns. I shall instead focus upon instances of the collapse of party discipline, at least in individual cases. I shall consider the action of a member of the governmental party who voted *against* a governmental proposal in the Assembly — who acted contrary to the demands made upon him in the name of party discipline. Were the governmental party members who violated party discipline different in their social backgrounds from those who conformed to it? This is the interesting, but quite limited, question which this voting analysis purports to answer.

My initial concern was whether there *were* any such mavericks — whether party discipline ever broke down in more than one or two cases per Assembly. To answer this query I tabulated for each Assembly: (1) the number of governmental proposals on which negative votes (governmental or not) had been cast; (2) the number of governmental proposals with governmental party negative votes; (3) the total number of negative votes cast against governmental proposals; (4) the total number of governmental party negative votes cast against governmental proposals; and (5) the total number of governmental deputies who cast negative votes on governmental proposals. This information is presented in Table 12.3, to which I have also added for comparative purposes the total number of governmental deputies (party resignees excluded).

Table 12.3 provides another insight into the nature of Turkish politics in the component epochs of the over-all thirty-seven-year period. It is another piece of evidence confirming the reality of the subperiods that have been distinguished and their characterization. Note that, with regard to the frequency of dissident *voting behavior* within the governmental party, we once again observe the same basic, temporal patterns we discerned in terms of inter-Assembly changes in the *social background characteristics* of the deputies. The First Assembly resembles the Eighth, Ninth, and Tenth, and there is an internal peaking in the Fourth Assembly of the single-party years that also presages the later developments of the post–World War II years. In general, however, the relative lack of voting opposition in the Assembly during the single-party years stands out like the proverbial sore thumb. The finding is so evident from the table that it does not seem to require further comment. I shall simply emphasize again the tremendous congruence between the voting pattern displayed in Table 12.3 and the social background patterns that were brought out in Chapter 7.

Governmental party discipline was obviously weakest in the First Assembly. I have, therefore, analyzed in some detail the characteristics of negative voters in that Assembly, the results of which I shall outline here. On the other hand, the incidence of negative voting in the Third through the Seventh Assemblies was so slight as to preclude analysis of any single Assembly. Instead, I have combined all dissident governmental party voters from those five Assemblies into one aggregate group and have analyzed them as such. Then, finally, I have

Table 12.3

NEGATIVE VOTING ON GOVERNMENT PROPOSALS, BY ASSEMBLY

Assembly	Government Proposals with Negative Votes	Government Proposals with Gov't Party Negative Votes	Government Proposals, Total Negative Votes Cast	Government Proposals, Total Gov't Party Negative Votes	Government Proposals, Total Negative Voting Deputies (Gov't)	Total Government Deputies
I[a]	134	112	2,286	967	178	197
II[a]	n.d.	n.d.	n.d.	n.d.	n.d.	n.a.
III[a]	4	4	17	17	16	319
IV	24	24	43	43	23	348
V[b]	3	3	6	6	5	444
VI	4	4	12	12	9	444
VII	14	14	40	40	19	453
VIII	188	31	2,121	172	95	435
IX	177	84	1,670	303	155	394
X	128	39	1,593	107	63	451

[a] Linguistic difficulties have precluded complete coverage for these Assemblies, though Assemblies I and III are largely complete. For the former, *İçtima* (Sessions) 1–3 are covered and for the latter, *İçtima* 2–4.
[b] The few Independents are included with the R.P.P.

treated each of the last three multi-party Assemblies separately. In reporting the results, I shall simply note the most pronounced differences between those members of the governmental party who violated party discipline and those whose voting record was one of complete conformity. Needless to say, abstention, which can be an act of resistance to party discipline, has been ignored throughout, since I had no means of distinguishing rebellious abstention from that resulting from illness or conflicting obligation.

Deviant Voting in the First Assembly

Considering the anomalous and rather chaotic conditions of the First Assembly, one might wonder if party affiliation had any clear behavioral significance at all for the deputies to that body. Of course, I have already shown, through the analysis of speaking patterns, that there were notable differences in behavior between the First and Second Groups, even though important cross-party behavioral similarities between background groups also emerged. The incidence of speaking, however, is a rather neutral behavioral indicator, so it will be interesting to note whether the voting against governmental proposals was appreciably more intense in one party than in another.

The answer to this question is that the voting behavior of the pro-government, First Group members was plainly different from that of the members of the opposition Second Group. Party did make a difference, as Figure 12.2 illustrates. The average number of anti-

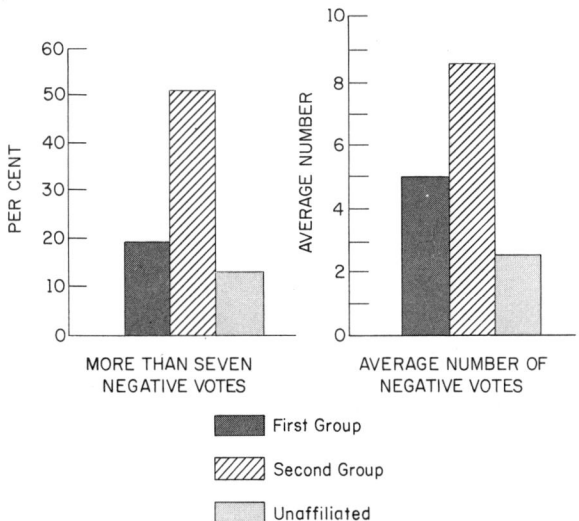

Figure 12.2. Negative voting on governmental proposals during the First Assembly, by faction

governmental votes cast by First Group members was only a little over half that of Second Group members, though the First Group figure itself is high enough to suggest the absence of the strong party discipline that was displayed in the subsequent Kemalist Assemblies. Over half the Second Group voted more than seven times against governmental proposals, while less than one fifth of the First Group cast more than seven negative votes. (The low figures for the "Unaffiliated" again reflect lack of participation in the Assembly more than support for the government.)

To examine the social background differences that might be related to voting behavior, I have held the dominant factor, party affiliation, constant. I have divided each party group into two subgroups: those who voted more than seven times against governmental proposals and those who voted seven or fewer times against such proposals. I shall call those casting more than seven antigovernmental votes the "Negatives" and those with seven or fewer the "Positives," remembering always that the so-called "Positives" of the opposition, the Second Group, could hardly be called government supporters.

Age, Birthplace, and "Localism"

Regardless of party, the Negatives were older, on the average, than the Positives, though the differences were very slim. *Regardless of party,* the Negatives were less likely to have been born in the Marmara Region or outside Turkey than were the Positives. Still more striking is the fact that the Negatives, *regardless of party,* were always at least 11 per cent more "local" — more likely to have been born in the province represented — than the Positives.[8] (Figure 12.3 presents the "localism" data.) Hence, voting opposition to governmental proposals in the First Assembly came disproportionately from older, more "Anatolian," more "local" deputies, regardless of party.

Occupation

The educational information is, unfortunately, too limited to permit analysis, but a few revealing insights are suggested by inspection of the relationship between occupation and voting behavior in the First Assembly. The most conspicuous findings are the following. While lawyers in the Second Group tended to have a slightly higher proportion of representatives among the Negatives than among the Positives, no definite pattern was found for the legal group as a whole. Speaking

---

[8] Unknowns are excluded. N's for the Positives and Negatives of each party group are: First Group, 132, 27; Second Group, 40, 46; unaffiliated, 37, 10. Once again, in view of the proportion of unknowns (total: 27 per cent) and the small cell in at least one case, these figures should be taken as suggestive and not conclusive.

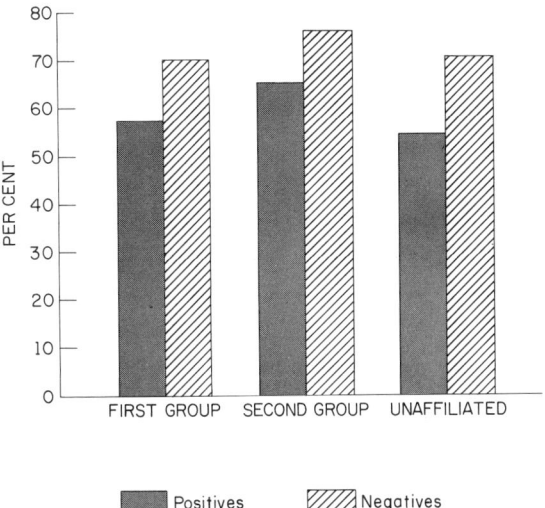

Figure 12.3. Percentage of deputies born in province represented, by voting support of governmental proposals and faction

NOTE: The category labeled "Positives" refers to deputies who voted seven or fewer times against governmental proposals, while the "Negatives" are those who voted more than seven times against such proposals.

more than voting distinguished the lawyers! The military, on the other hand, were always prominently Positive in voting behavior *regardless of which party they had joined.* Within each party group the percentage of military Positives was always about two to three times that of military Negatives (though this finding may be partly attributable to the absence of some service personnel for military duties). The same was not true of the bureaucrats, however, whose record was rather ambiguous. In fact, for all vocations, the only other pattern that was as clear and unmistakable, regardless of party, as the Positive voting of the military was that of the religious group. Appropriately, *the clerics' voting record was as Negative as the military's record was Positive.* The percentage contributions made by these two vocations to the Positives and Negatives of each party group are shown in Figure 12.4.[9] The fundamental antagonists of the early Kemalist Revolution again stand revealed.

Parliamentary Experience, Reelection, and Speaking

Holding party allegiance constant, we learn that the Positives were distinguished by a higher level of prior parliamentary experience in

[9] The N's for the Positives and Negatives of each party group are: First Group, 154, 35; Second Group, 51, 51; unaffiliated, 66, 14.

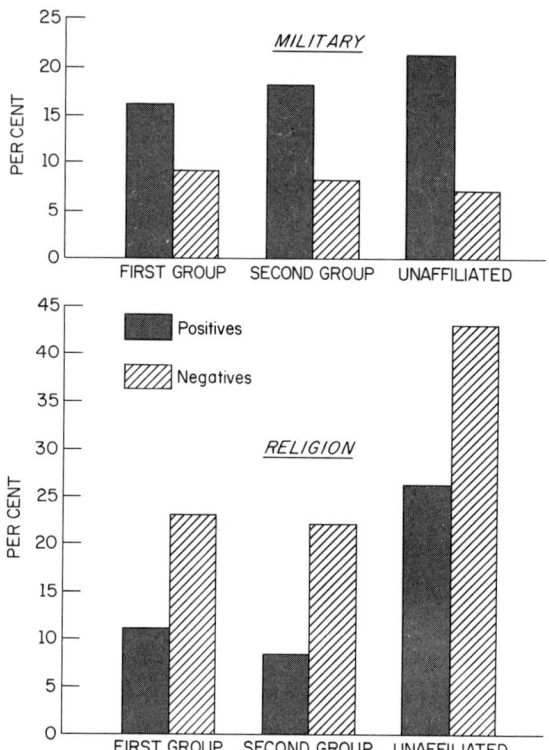

Figure 12.4. Governmental voting support of deputies with military and religious occupational backgrounds, by faction

Ottoman Assemblies. Thirty-five per cent of the Positives of the First Group had previous experience in an Istanbul parliament in contrast to a mere 11 per cent of the First Group Negatives with such experience. In the Second Group, 29 per cent of the Positives were experienced against just 15 per cent of the Negatives. *Regardless of party, the more experienced deputies were less likely to oppose the government by Assembly vote.*

Regarding reelection, the rate of return of the Second Group was so low that internal analysis of the returnees is impossible. For the First Group, however, three fifths of the Positives as opposed to two fifths of the Negatives were reelected to the Second Assembly (61 per cent versus 43 per cent). Within the governmental party as well as without, a price was paid for opposition! It is also interesting to compare voting behavior and speaking behavior within parties. In essence, I found that the Positives of the First Group spoke more than the Negatives, while the reverse is true for the Second Group and the unaffiliated. In the last two factions the Negatives tended to be more vocal.

Formal Power

The relationship between leadership position and voting behavior within each party is also interesting. It is portrayed most clearly by the proportions of the Positives and Negatives of the First and Second Groups who achieved top or middle leader status. In the First Group, 34 per cent of the Positives were classed as top or middle leaders as opposed to just 16 per cent of the Negatives. In the Second Group, however, the same difference does not show up — the proportions of Positives and Negatives reaching positions of leadership were equal (23 and 24 per cent). Actually, only 2 per cent of the Positives of the Second Group were top leaders against 10 per cent of the Negatives of that group who were top leaders. In short, and quite naturally, those deputies with voting records relatively favorable to the government contributed disproportionately heavily to the leadership echelon within the First Group, while those deputies with antigovernmental voting records seem to have been slightly better located in the leadership levels of the Second Group.

Constituency Location and Enemy Occupation

Earlier I suggested that Kemal's support tended to come more from the areas of the country that were under Allied occupation than from the unoccupied areas where the less clandestine resistance organizations were active and where the first nationalist congresses were held. The analysis of speaking supported that contention as did the analysis of the regional origins of the political parties. Now there is an opportunity for a further check in terms of the voting behaviors of the deputies and the party groups. Were there regional variations of the sort I have implied? Did the deputies from the occupied areas give Kemal more voting support than deputies from the unoccupied portions of the country?

One method of casting light on this subject is to inspect for each region the incidence of negative voting on governmental proposals, comparing the regions with each other. To do this I computed the average number of antigovernmental votes cast by the deputies from each of the nine regions and then ranked the regions according to these average figures. The results are given in Table 12.4.

The occupied western and littoral regions have the lowest incidence of antigovernmental votes, and the unoccupied or very slightly occupied eastern and interior regions have the highest rates of voting opposition. However, it is impossible to separate the factor of Allied and Greek occupation from the factors of relative regional development

Table 12.4

AVERAGE NUMBER OF NEGATIVE VOTES CAST ON GOVERNMENT PROPOSALS, PER DEPUTY, BY REGION[a]

REGION	AVERAGE NEGATIVE VOTES
Marmara (Extensively Occupied)	3.9
Aegean (Extensively Occupied)	5.3
Mediterranean (Extensively Occupied)	5.4
East Central (Essentially Unoccupied)	5.5
Northeastern (Essentially Unoccupied)	6.4
North Central (Slightly Occupied — Eskişehir, Kütahya)	6.7
Southeastern (Slightly Occupied — Urfa)	6.7
Black Sea (Slightly Occupied — Samsun and Zonguldak)	6.8
South Central (Slightly Occupied — Afyon, Akşehir, Konya)	10.2

[a] For the disposition of the occupying forces of the Entente and Greece in Turkey during the first phases of the War of Independence, see the map devoted to this topic and appended to Mustafa Kemal's *Speech, op. cit.*

and contact with the West, since the areas of enemy occupation and of greatest regional development are basically coterminous. Also, when we hold party constant, the only uniform trend is for the Marmara and Aegean deputies to be disproportionately Positive in each party group. The other regional patterns are weak or mixed, except that — in contradiction to my argument — the deputies from the Northeastern Region seem to have been more Positive than Negative in each party!

Deviant Voting Behavior in the Single-Party Years

Just as the incidence of antigovernmental voting in the single-party Assemblies was impressively low, so there seem to be very few clear differences in social background between those government deputies to these Assemblies who cast negative votes on government proposals and those who never once registered opposition. The control of the Kemalist hierarchy over the Assembly is amply illustrated in these facts. Combining all the R.P.P. negative voters from the Third through the Seventh Assemblies yields a total of seventy-three incumbencies, as opposed to 2,014 incumbencies from which no negative vote ever issued. ("Incumbency" indicates that a deputy was counted once for each Assembly in which he appeared.) The only noticeable social background differences — and these were very slight — between the two groups lay in the area of vocation. The Negatives (those who cast a vote against a government proposal) included a higher percentage of lawyers than the Unwavering (19 per cent versus 13 per cent) and had a lower proportion of military men (12 per cent versus 17 per cent). Though the remaining differences between specific vocations were too frail to warrant their being reported here, they did cumulate to produce the broad occupational differences one suspected: the Negatives were 34 per cent professional compared to 26 per cent for the Unwavering, were only 42 per cent official compared to 48 per cent official for the Unwavering, and were 18 per cent economic compared to 15 per cent for the Unwavering. The differences are obviously slim, and the general lack of social background variations tends to confirm the triviality of the voting deviations. Nevertheless, the slight occupational differences that do exist are in the anticipated direction. They point to the same social undercurrents which the previous analyses have repeatedly found — the growth of a legalistic and commercial counterelite within the top strata of Turkish society.[10]

Antigovernmental Voting within the People's Party of the Eighth Assembly

Some ninety-five R.P.P. deputies, or 22 per cent of the entire parliamentary group of the party, voted against a governmental proposal in the Eighth Assembly. This was a higher proportion of internal opposition than the party had ever experienced during the single-party years, but it still seems not to have been a unified, major revolt — at least with regard to voting behavior. The average number of antigovernmental votes cast by the ninety-five Negatives was less than two, and only five R.P.P. deputies registered more than three opposing votes.

In line with the blandness of this internal voting opposition, there are few sharp social background distinctions between the R.P.P. Negatives

[10] Examination of the names of members of certain small, more negative subgroups within the body of the seventy-three negative-voting R.P.P. deputies from the Third through the Seventh Assemblies is rewarding. Those deputies who cast negative votes in more than one Assembly were: Emin Sazak, R. Ş. Ince, S. Sırrı İçöz, Hüsnü Kitabcı, and Hakkı Tarık Us. At least two of these five later joined the Democratic Party. (Kitabcı was an "independent" in the Fourth Assembly.)

In the Seventh Assembly (1943–1946), the following R.P.P. deputies cast more than one antigovernmental vote: Fuat Köprülü (4), Refik Koraltan (3), Adnan Menderes (3), Ali Rıza Esen (3), Celâl Bayar (2), Hikmet Bayur (2), Hazım Atıf Kuyucak (2), Recep Peker (2), Emin Sazak (2). Of these nine, four were the founders of the D.P. in the next Assembly, one (Sazak) joined the D.P. as a backbench deputy in that Assembly, one (Bayur) became a prominent independent, one (Kuyucak) resigned to return to his professorship, one (Recep Peker) was to be the beleaguered and ousted R.P.P. Premier who fought liberalization, and the last (Esen) was an R.P.P. backbencher.

and the R.P.P. Unwavering of the Eighth Assembly. Those differences that did exist can be summarized quite succinctly. The Negatives tended to be slightly younger than the Unwavering (average age: 51.6 years versus 53.7), had less prior parliamentary experience, were slightly more likely to have been born in the province represented, and came more heavily from the ranks of the middle leaders than from either top leadership or backbench positions. (Note, however, how similar these differences are to those which distinguished the Second Group from the First Group.) Though the educational levels of the two groups were almost exactly equal, the Negatives had a somewhat higher precentage of individuals knowing two or more foreign languages than did the Unwavering. Finally, the Negatives were 47 per cent official in occupation compared to 36 per cent for the Unwavering. The groups were equal in the percentage of members with economic vocations, but the Unwavering contained a greater proportion of professionals, 35 per cent against 25 per cent.

Obviously, the patterns described do not depict any striking and intuitively suggestive differences between the two intra-R.P.P. groups, largely because the struggle that went on within the party was not well reflected in the voting of the R.P.P. deputies in the *Assembly*. Furthermore, the antigovernmental voting that did occur at varying times in the life of the Eighth Assembly would probably have emanated from several different sources and for divergent reasons. In the early sessions of that body, the R.P.P. minority protest would most likely have sprung from the liberal elements of the party, such as the "thirty-five." In the later sessions, after the liberals won their battle and had begun to push through democratizing legislation, the R.P.P. minority protest would have sprung from the defeated strong-armed faction of the party. As they stand, our social background data seem to reflect the latter elements more than the former. But the picture as a whole is mixed, and, in view of the very low rate of negative voting, more involved analysis does not seem to be very promising.

Antigovernmental Voting within the Democratic Party of the Ninth and Tenth Assemblies

In the Ninth and especially the Tenth Assemblies there was resistance within the Democratic Party to the coercive course being taken by Menderes and Bayar. This internal restiveness carried over into the Eleventh Assembly, outside our purview, and is of keen interest to anyone concerned about the political future of Turkey. The diversion of the Democratic Party from its original democratic commitment is one of the great tragedies of modern Turkish history. Its consequence has not only been the exacerbation of Turkish political life and the production of a military coup to remedy the patent failure of civil politics, but also the formal fragmentation of governmental power (in the new Constitution) and a frustrating, artificial politics which impedes development in other sectors.

Most supposedly objective observers of the Turkish scene admit that there is room for — indeed, a vital *need* for — a responsible major political party occupying the position in the political spectrum held by the Democratic Party of 1948-1953. Despite the earnestness with which the adherents of the minority parties in Turkey espouse their causes, there is an important segment of informed opinion in the country which believes that the preferred party system is one in which two major parties are arrayed against one another in democratic conflict. And the two most probable candidates for these party roles have seemed to be the People's Party on the left and some counterpart of the earlier Democratic Party on the responsible right. However, for many in Turkey one of the crucial problems confronting the nation today is that of obtaining just such a democratic, responsible, moderately conservative party of the right to fill the void opened by the Democratic Party's abandonment of its democratic commitment.

One method of examining the chances for the development of a responsible party of the right in Turkey might well be to look at the opposition within the Democratic Party to the repressive measures of Menderes and Bayar. This opposition may perhaps be the nucleus around which a democratic and secular right-wing party could be organized. Certainly, such an idea has been prominent in Turkey in the years since May 1960, plainly extending as far as the Committee of National Union itself. It is with this concern in mind that one approaches the inspection of the social backgrounds of those Democratic deputies who voted against the Democratic Party government in the Ninth and Tenth Assemblies.

Before expectations start climbing, however, let us say that despite a few interesting findings, the analysis has not proved to be as fruitful as had been hoped. The essential reason would seem to be our old acquaintance: the fact that the internal opposition to the antidemocratic measures of Menderes & Co. was expressed almost entirely in the party caucus, and not in voting on the Assembly floor. Moreover, the opposition that was manifested through Assembly votes included disagreement with policies of the government other than its antidemocratic proposals. Hence, the analysis of the social backgrounds of the negative voters within the D.P. is rather beclouded by the intrusion of extraneous issues and suffers from an inability to deal with the most appropriate behavioral indicator — activity within the party caucus. The social background findings would thus seem to be greatly diluted and contaminated.

In the Ninth Assembly, 155 Democratic deputies, or 39 per cent of the total D.P. delegation of 394 persons, voted against a proposal of their government. Of these 155 Negatives, 62 per cent voted only once in opposition, and the remaining 38 per cent voted twice or more against their party. To elaborate the independent variable and supply an additional point of reference in ascertaining significant differences, I have maintained in this analysis the division of all the D.P. Negatives into these two groups: those voting just once against their party and those voting more than once against their party. For the Ninth Assembly, I shall compare these two groups with the larger body of the Unwavering within the Democratic Party, looking for progressive differences between the More Negative, the Less Negative, and the Unwavering. Where feasible, such a procedure inspires more confidence than mere dichotomous examination.

Unfortunately, in the Tenth Assembly the total number of Negatives was just 63 deputies, 14 per cent of the over-all D.P. contingent of 451 persons. Hence, I have not been able to break down this Negative group still further into those who were More Negative and those who were Less Negative. Our comparison will simply be between the Negatives and the Unwavering of the Tenth Assembly.

One further cautionary observation seems necessary. Though the division of the Ninth Assembly Negatives into two groups of greater and lesser opposition permits more conclusive analysis, this gain must be balanced against the fact that the restrictive actions of the D.P. leadership did not really commence until the last stages of the Ninth Assembly — late 1953 and early 1954. Thus, antidemocratic activity was probably not an important cause of much of the negative D.P. voting found in the Ninth Assembly. In the Tenth Assembly, where repressive D.P. policies were more of an issue, the small number of Negatives compels dichotomous analysis. In general, the Tenth Assembly data would seem more relevant to the question posed.

The differences found between the various Negative groups and the Unwavering of the Democratic Party in the two Assemblies can be fairly quickly summarized. First of all, the Negatives were (again, as in the R.P.P.) always younger, on the average, than the Unwavering. Figure 12.5 illustrates this fact and indicates the nature of the type of comparison I shall be making.[11]

Insofar as this opposition was centered about resistance to antidemocratic tendencies within the Democratic Party (by no means a wholly plausible assumption), the findings with regard to age might be said to be encouraging. They indicate that the opposition within the D.P. was disproportionately composed of younger deputies, which

[11] The N's for the various groups are: Ninth Assembly: More Negative — 59, Less Negative — 96, Unwavering — 239; Tenth Assembly: Negative — 63, Unwavering — 388.

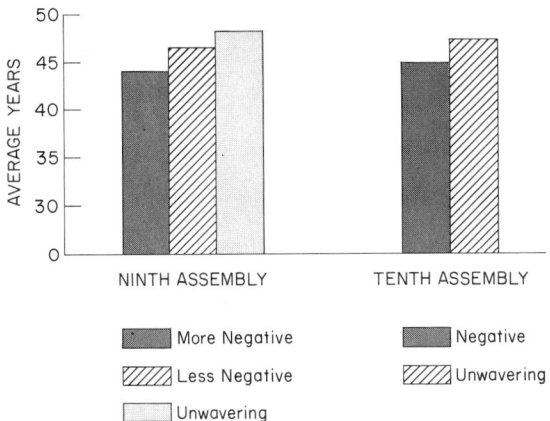

Figure 12.5. Average age of Democratic Party deputies in the Ninth and Tenth Assemblies, by governmental voting support

NOTE: "More Negative" with regard to Ninth Assembly Democratic deputies indicates more than one negative vote against a Democratic governmental proposal. "Less Negative" indicates exactly one such negative vote, while "Unwavering" refers to those Democratic deputies who never voted against a legislative proposal of the Democratic government. In the Tenth Assembly, the "Unwavering" category maintains the same meaning, but the "Negative" category refers to all Democratic deputies who voted at least once against a Democratic governmental proposal, thus combining the "More Negative" and "Less Negative" categories of the Ninth Assembly.

may mean that the chances for more democratic leadership on the right should improve in the future as the younger politicians of whom these Negative D.P. deputies may be a reflection come into a more dominant position. However, many alternative explanations are possible, not least persuasive of which is that relative youth is always more likely to be in opposition simply because it is youth, trying to work its way into the positions occupied by more senior persons, and not because of any particular ideological commitment. Certainly our consistent previous findings relating youth and opposition would support this latter interpretation. In any event, there remains the rather clear finding that the Negatives of the D.P. in the Ninth and Tenth Assemblies were younger than the resolute and unwavering supporters of the D.P. leadership in those Assemblies.

Another interesting finding, though one that is much less definite, is that the D.P. Negatives seem (again) to have been more "local," more likely to have been born in the province represented in parliament, than the Unwavering. In the Ninth Assembly, the Unwavering were 56 per cent "local" as opposed to 65 and 63 per cent, respectively, for the Less Negative and More Negative. In the Tenth Assembly, the Unwavering were 62 per cent "local" and the Negatives 65 per cent. These differences are quite slight, however, so that this finding must remain entirely tentative and suggestive.

Now that the nature of the analytical procedure has been illustrated, verbal description of the remaining differences between the various Negatives and the Unwavering of the Democratic Party in the Ninth and Tenth Assemblies should suffice. Glancing at the leadership positions of the Negatives in each Assembly, we discover no outstanding differences between the groups in the Ninth Assembly, but when we come to the Tenth, such a difference does emerge. The Negatives of the Tenth Assembly (again) came relatively much more from the ranks of the middle leaders than did the Unwavering. More than one in three of the Negatives was a middle leader (35 per cent), while less than half that proportion of the Unwavering (17 per cent) were middle leaders. Nor was this difference produced by a marked reduction of top leaders among the Negatives. Instead, it was related to a reduction of backbenchers and inconsequentials. The younger, rising middle echelon of leadership within the Democratic Party in the Tenth Assembly seems to have contributed disproportionately to the internal opposition in the Assembly to the party leaders' proposals.

No pronounced regional or educational differences between the Negatives and the Unwavering were discovered, but an interesting, though mild, occupational variation did appear. In short, the Negatives in both Assemblies were more professional in occupation than the Unwavering (49 per cent to 44 per cent), and were even less populated by traders and agriculturists, who remained most loyal of all to the regular D.P. leadership. The official elements in each of the groups were of almost exactly the same size.

It is tempting to use this last finding as a final vehicle to comment on the nature of the resistance to Menderes and Bayar that mounted during these critical years. That resistance was not uniform across the country. From all appearances, those mercantile and agricultural elements which supported the Democrats hardly wavered in that support through the long decade. Curtailment of newly won democratic rights does not seem to have struck these vocational groups as being a fundamental political issue. The political restrictions of the D.P. regime caused few if any apparently adverse reactions among the traders and farmers. On the other hand, the intellectual and professional support that had been given to the Democrats from 1946 on was significantly undermined by the repressions of the Menderes-Bayar government. Both these facts are wanly reflected in the above social background data from the formative years of the internal D.P. opposition.

Though only a small number of the professional people who had supported the early Democratic Party seem to have made the considerable leap over to the People's Party, many of them did quit the D.P. for less distant, minority parties, and even more of them simply suffered a visible decline in their enthusiasm for the D.P. though still remaining in the party. The key to many forthcoming political developments in Turkey may rest with this basically anti–People's Party, but responsible and democratic, professional segment of the once-again-bifurcated Turkish intellectual elite.

SUMMARY

Chapters 11 and 12 have shown how thoroughly Turkish politics are party politics. They have been partisan since before the establishment of the First Republic — under single-party and multi-party systems, through People's Party, Democratic Party, and coalition regimes, in times of war and of peace, and after a traumatic military take-over. The highly organized, competitive, grass-roots cast of post–World War II political life in Turkey is one of the striking features distinguishing her from most of her Near Eastern neighbors.[12]

Party organization performed at least two vital integrative functions in both the single- and multiple-party systems: (1) it furnished essential *intra*governmental coordination between the executive and legislative organs of government, and (2) it was the main agency linking the national government with the many *extra*governmental groups in the society on whose support that government depended. The daily lives and future plans of Turkey's leading politicians were deeply embedded in a party context.

Under the single-party system, the party started out primarily as an instrument of social control — a lever for the downward exertion of influence that was to be wielded almost exclusively by the party chiefs. Once the organizational network was erected, however, those lower down in the hierarchy began to discover how to manipulate the system, especially since it had a partially democratic formal structure. Influence began to flow reciprocally in two directions rather than unilaterally in one — up from lower levels as well as down from on high. A crucial element in a potentially democratic political infrastructure had been created.

Just as the political party served as an invaluable device in the government's attempt to mobilize the society for modernization, it

[12] A national survey of the peasant (village) population of Turkey in 1962 carried out by the author and his associates indicates that, prior to the abolition of village-level party cells (*ocaklar*) under the military junta of 1960–1961, about two thirds of the villagers of Turkey lived in communities which had local party organizations. Furthermore, over three fifths lived in villages where *more than one* party had such a local organization.

also served to integrate opposition to the government. Tacit recognition of this fact was the paramount reason behind the tutelary insistence on a *single*-party system. "Progressive" governmental forces were to be integrated through party; "reactionary" opposition forces were better left uncoordinated by denying them political party organization. Nevertheless, largely because of the concurrent commitment to democracy as well as to reform, the organization of attenuated forms of opposition was sporadically allowed. After the Second World War, this development culminated in the transition to a true multi-party system with all-too-earnest combat between extensive and fully articulated political parties. Examination of the social backgrounds of the deputies enrolled in these various parties and groups sharply increases our perception of the nature of the political struggles and problems confronted by the Turkish political system during this formative era.

The First and Second Groups

The First Grand National Assembly, elected in 1920 under relatively free conditions, was divided into two main factions: a Kemalist First Group and an opposition Second Group, both ostensibly within the fold of the Association for the Defense of Rights of Anatolia and Rumelia. These two factions were rather clearly distinguished from one another in social background. Though both bodies were youthful, the First Group was slightly older and had a greater proportion of members possessing prior legislative experience in an Ottoman Assembly. The First Group deputies were more likely to have been elected from an occupied region (or, taking another perspective, a western, littoral, and more modern region). The Second Group drew disproportionately from the Northeastern and Black Sea Regions, where the occupation was less extensive and the local resistance organizations had been operating more openly. The First Group also displayed a higher percentage of members born in the presumably more cosmopolitan Aegean-Marmara Region or outside present-day Turkey. The Second Group was more "local" than the First Group, that is, featured more deputies born in the province they represented in the Assembly. The Second Group also contained relatively more lawyers and merchants, while the clerics were about equally distributed between the two factions. In general, the differences in social background between the First and Second Groups of the very First Assembly presage later differences between the People's Party and the Democratic Party as well as subsequent trends in the social composition of the Assembly as a whole, regardless of party. Locally oriented legal and commercial opposition to the Kemalist program seems to have been evident from the very start of the Atatürk Revolution, even though it was generally upstaged by the duel between secular and religious forces.

Analysis of the amount of speaking by the deputies to the First Assembly, with faction held constant, brought out the significance of several social background factors. A 10 per cent sample of parliamentary debates revealed that half the deputies never spoke at all. The Second Group members were somewhat more vocal than the First Group members. However, the more voluble the First Group member, the more likely he was to be reelected to the following Assembly. A similar tabulation for the Second Group is futile because of the fact that only three of its 118 members were reelected. None of the three spoke frequently or at length. Most significantly, Mustafa Kemal was the deputy with the greatest average length per speech — even after exclusion of his utterances as President of the Assembly — and he also spoke quite often. He seems certainly to have made every effort to *talk* his way to leadership over this sometimes unruly body, rather than readily resorting to coercion.

Regardless of party, the deputies who spoke more often tended to be younger men. The "orators" of the First Group were particularly likely to have had prior parliamentary experience, and there was a positive association between formal power and amount of speaking within both groups. The deputies who were not locally based carried more of the speaking burden for the First Group, while "locals" debated most voluminously for the Second Group. Regardless of party, the professionals tended to speak a great deal, and those from economic occupations (mainly trade and agriculture) tended to keep silent. Such a finding calls to mind Harold Lasswell's phrase about "specialists in persuasion." In any event, we find that one particular type of influential behavior — speaking before parliament — was disproportionately used by deputies with a professional background and was disproportionately shunned by deputies with commercial and agricultural backgrounds. Moreover, democratization of the political system probably increased the importance of this particular influential behavior, a fact that helps to account for the striking rise of professional men in general and lawyers in particular as the system was opened up.

Finally, we found that though the clerics were present in about the same proportion in each faction, those in the First Group spoke very little, while those in the Second Group either remained silent or else spoke a great deal.

The Progressive Party of 1924

In Turkey, as in many emerging nations, elimination of direct foreign intervention and achievement of essentially uncontested independence precipitated what I have called a "postindependence crisis." Once the blinders imposed by the struggle to free the country from foreign domination were cast off, the team began to pull in opposite directions. One element, the "ardent nationalists," so desired to inaugurate "essential reforms" that it was willing to bear a curb bit and a tight rein. The other element, the "postindependence conservatives," placed much less emphasis on reform, desired to preserve most of the status quo (under which they had frequently been privileged), and balked strenuously at returning to severe harness. The clash between these elements was most sharply revealed in the short and unhappy career of the Progressive Party.

In the analysis of the Turkish postindependence crisis, one point must not be overlooked. The Turkish case is instructive — indeed, nearly classic — partly because of its relative simplicity. Compared with other situations, the lines of conflict were clearly drawn. Resolution of the conflict was thus easier in many respects. The dilemma of numerous other developing nations is that the "ardent nationalists" do not themselves display even minimal agreement on "what is to be done." Internal strife renders them ineffective and easy prey to infiltration by their opposition. On the other hand, they sporadically muster sufficient effectiveness to break the traditional network of social and political relations, with the result that a jerky, drifting, unsatisfying, and inconsistent pattern of social change ensues. The Turkish pattern is in many respects more model than typical: but a visible model is of great value to the analyst of political development.

In social background, the Progressive Party was almost an extreme version of the People's Party. It differed from the R.P.P. as the R.P.P. differed from the Second Group and the adult populace as a whole. Its members were less "local" and slightly more cosmopolitan in origin than their R.P.P. rivals. They were more likely to represent a constituency in the Marmara Region. Relatively more of them had a university-level education. And, most significantly of all, they were more official in occupation, over three fourths falling into that category as opposed to just over one half the People's Party group. Forty-four per cent of the Progressive deputies were military men against 18 per cent of the R.P.P. deputies. As I have said, this was an opposition which drew from the very same social sources as the Kemalists. As such, it threatened, if successful, to undermine the very foundations of Kemalist strength — particularly in the army. For this reason above all the Progressive Party was crushed.

The Liberal Republican Party of 1930

The Kemalist message included a commitment to democracy that was not abandoned even in the heady days of single-party power. No ideology of totalitarianism ever developed. Moreover, there was a continual, if often rather feeble, groping toward formal institutionalization of that democratic commitment. The Liberal Republican Party of 1930 was the most significant venture of this sort during the single-party years.

Superficially, in social background terms, the parliamentary head of the Liberal Republican Party greatly resembled that of the unfortunate Progressive Party. The Liberals had in exaggerated form all the social characteristics that distinguished the People's Party. They were relative cosmopolitans with virtually no "localism." All possessed university-level education. Nearly four fifths had previous Assembly experience. Furthermore, once again, over three fourths of the Liberals were officials as contrasted to just over half the People's Party deputies. Even the incidence of military men resembled the Progressive Party–People's Party relationship: half the Liberals were military as opposed to 17 per cent of the R.P.P. members. The parliamentary Liberals might seem to have been the reincarnation of the Progressives except for one thing — rather than being a spontaneous and deeply hostile opposition, they consisted largely of cronies and comrades of Mustafa Kemal. The party was formed at the Gazi's behest and was to provide loyal, gentlemanly, parliamentary opposition. However, dissident elements in many parts of the nation rallied to the Liberal standard — particularly, it would seem, locally oriented legal and commercial figures. The Kemalists, alarmed by this flare-up of opposition, induced the parliamentary Liberals to dissolve their party, but dealt very mildly with most of the members.

The Independent Group of the People's Party

Chastened by their experience with opposition by formally independent political parties, yet unwilling or unable to relinquish all appearances of democratic contention, the Kemalists finally resorted to the establishment of a pseudo-opposition within their own ranks — the Independent Group of the People's Party. Social background analysis helps to reveal the artificial character of the enterprise. The Independent Group members were younger, less experienced, more intellectual and cosmopolitan, and more professional in occupation than the regular R.P.P. deputies. Though intellectually able, they seem to have been personally less committed to politics and definitely in the second echelon of party power. They seem to have been led by respected figures, but men somewhat apart from the mainstream of party life.

Moreover, judging from the social background data, the Independent Group seems to have declined from the Sixth Assembly, when it commenced, to the Seventh Assembly, at the end of which it expired. In the latter Assembly it became still younger, still more drawn from the Marmara Region, still less formally powerful, and much less favored for reelection.

The Parties of the Eighth Assembly (1946-1950)

Though the People's Party was still in power and a completely free election had not yet occurred, the Eighth Assembly was the first true multi-party Assembly of the First Republic. In it we perceive the first momentous adjustment of the parliament to the many social changes that the Kemalists had wrought or encountered. And in it we find the initial confrontation of the People's Party and the Democratic Party in a struggle that persists in its basic outlines even today. Comparison of the social characteristics of these two major parties is deeply revealing of the social conflict and transformation through which the Turkish polity is still passing.

The Democrats of the Eighth Assembly differed markedly in social background from their People's Party antagonists, even though the People's Party in that Assembly had already made a considerable move in the direction of the Democrats. In general, the Democrats of the Eighth Assembly differed from the People's Party deputies of the Eighth Assembly as those R.P.P. deputies themselves differed from the R.P.P. of the preceding Seventh Assembly. The D.P. deputies were younger, less experienced, and drawn more from the Aegean-Marmara Region. They were less likely to be university-trained and less likely to know a foreign language. Most conspicuously, they were clearly more "local" and more professional and economic in their occupations. The contingent of officials in the D.P. ranks was sharply reduced.

In the course of the Eighth Assembly a great political transformation swept over Turkish society. The single-party closed system gave way to a relatively open, competitive multi-party structure. Some of the most critical early battles in this struggle were fought within the People's Party as a new and more democratic reform element grappled with a powerful faction of single-party diehards. Analysis of the most famous band of reformers within the R.P.P. — the "thirty-five" — produced some interesting social background data to add to the usual observation that the reformers were younger than their opponents. The liberalizers, perhaps the vanguard of a new generation of political leaders born and raised in a Kemalist Turkey, were also distinguished from the rest of the R.P.P. by their very high level of education and their occupational connections with education. Just under half the group had been professional educators. We must add the young university professor to the lawyer and the merchant as the decisive new men of Turkish politics.

Parties in the Ninth and Tenth Assemblies

In the Ninth and Tenth Assemblies, during the era of Democratic Party control, both the D.P. and the R.P.P. became younger, with an especially steep drop in average age among the People's Party deputies, shifting their figure from above that of the D.P. to below. The birthplaces of the Democratic Party deputies were more evenly distributed over the country than those of the R.P.P. had ever been. The latter party, in adversity, was reduced almost entirely to its representation from the eastern provinces. The R.P.P. actually became more "local" than the Democrats, even though over three fifths of each party was now made up of deputies who were born in the province they represented in parliament — a new peak.

The educational qualifications of the Democratic Party deputies rose, while those of the R.P.P. fell. The D.P. retained a rather steady occupational blend, while the R.P.P. became more professional, more economic, and less official. In many ways, the competition for votes tended to reduce the social background differences between the parties and to produce convergence about a new norm in which the locally based lawyer became the modal figure.

Considerable turnover in personnel, as compared with the People's Party, was a feature of the operation of the Democrats in power, though some of this was probably due to the fundamental change in the political system. The reelection rate of D.P. deputies was substantially lower than that of R.P.P. deputies when the latter were in power. Less than two thirds of the Ninth Assembly Democrats were reelected to the Tenth Assembly, and but half of the Tenth Assembly Democrats were reelected to the Eleventh Assembly, despite overwhelming D.P. control of each of these bodies in terms of the percentage of seats won. The turnover seems to be attributable more to lack of renomination than to losses at the polls.

In the Tenth Assembly a group of deputies broke off from the Democratic Party and founded the important but short-lived Freedom Party, later largely absorbed into the R.P.P. Not surprisingly, these Freedom Party deputies were like the Democrats, from whom they split, in most social background characteristics. The key differences between the two were that the Freedom Party supporters were more often drawn from the Aegean-Marmara Region, better educated, more professional and official in occupation, and less economic. They appear to have been a rather able group of intellectual, cosmopolitan, and less commercially oriented deputies who, rather surprisingly, drew their main electoral support in the campaign of 1957 from the eastern provinces.

Voting Behavior of the Deputies

Since party discipline was ordinarily very strong and members usually voted in party blocs, only deviant voting behavior was analyzed — cases in which a member of the party in power voted against a proposal of the government. The analysis again brought out the various subepochs in the political history of the First Republic that had been previously and independently distinguished on the basis of social background variations. In other words, variations in social background and in deviant voting behavior form similar temporal patterns. The open First Assembly resembles the multi-party Assemblies (Eighth through Tenth) in the increased incidence of deviant voting just as they resemble each other in the distribution of certain social background characteristics among the deputies. Once again, the Fourth Assembly was anomalous within the single-party period and indicated the direction of later trends. The strong Kemalist control during the single-party years is well reflected in the virtual absence of deviant voting throughout those years.

Party did make a difference in voting behavior in the First Assembly even though the organized groups of that Assembly might better be described by the term "faction" than the term "party." The First Group averaged only half as many antigovernmental votes as the Second Group, though it still displayed enough contumacy clearly to separate itself from the more disciplined Kemalist Assemblies that followed.

Regardless of party, several social background characteristics marked those First Assembly members who voted disproportionately against the government. The antigovernmental votes came most often from the older, more "Anatolian," and more locally based deputies. The military were inordinately low in voting opposition, regardless of party, while the clerics were inordinately high. Regardless of party, the experienced deputies supported the government more consistently than the inexperienced. Within the First Group, deviant voting was punished by disproportionate elimination from the Assembly at the next election. A clear price was paid for opposition. Those who voted most often with the government also spoke most among the First Group members, while those who most often voted against the government were the leading speakers of the Second Group. The incidence of antigovernmental voting by deputies from the extensively occupied regions was less than that from the unoccupied and only slightly occupied regions.

Virtually no strong social background differences were found to characterize the few deviant voters during the single-party years. The group of mavericks featured a slightly higher percentage of lawyers, a slightly lower percentage of military men, and were also somewhat more professional and economic in occupation. But the differences were quite slim.

Naturally, in the multi-party years things changed. Party discipline became less rigid, though it still remained strong. Just over a fifth of the People's Party deputies in the Eighth Assembly voted at least once against their government, appreciably more than ever before in the party's history. However, the average number of deviant votes cast by the ninety-five mavericks was less than two apiece — hardly betokening a major revolt or even faithfully reflecting the turmoil that did erupt within the party. The maverick voters tended to be slightly younger, less experienced, more "local," more official, and disproportionately from the middle leader echelon, though once again all differences are relatively slight.

Finally, in the Ninth Assembly, under the Democratic Party, two fifths of the government deputies voted against a governmental proposal. In the Tenth Assembly this fraction dropped to about one eighth. Once more, the Negatives were always younger than the party stalwarts. They were also very slightly more "local." In the Tenth Assembly, as in the Eighth, they were more likely to come from middle leader ranks; they were also more professional and were less economic in occupation. In the Assembly, as in the nation, the main internal opposition to the wayward Democratic leadership seemed to be centered in the party's professional and intellectual elements rather than in its strong mercantile and agricultural components.

Conclusion

CHAPTER THIRTEEN

Emphases and Evaluations

AFTER LISTENING TO THE acknowledged savants of his time, the writer of the *Rubáiyát* once ruefully remarked that he had "... heard great argument, but evermore came out by the same door wherein [he] went." Throughout this work, as the data have been presented, I have sought to open as many different doors as seemed justified by the evidence at hand. Factual summaries have been provided for all substantive chapters and can be readily referred to by the interested reader. Broader interpretations of the information offered have also been inserted in the text wherever they seemed appropriate. However, since these interpretive comments are less easily located than the end-of-chapter data summaries, and since I should like to collect, reassert, and elaborate some of the interpretive suggestions made, I shall devote this final chapter to a series of emphases and evaluations rather than to a tedious and unnecessary comprehensive factual summary.

COMMENTS ON THE TURKISH POLITICAL SYSTEM

Many divergent insights into the nature of the Turkish political system under the First Republic are suggested by the analysis of the social backgrounds of the country's leading politicians — the deputies to the Grand National Assembly. The aggregate profile, for example, revealed the importance of three main social background characteristics: intellectual status, official status, and a position of local influence. However, all three characteristics were rarely possessed by a single individual. On the contrary, two different types of well-entrenched deputies appeared to emerge from the analysis. One type belonged to the national elite, possessing intellectual and official status but ordinarily without strong local connections. The other was the local potentate, often without strong claim to intellectual status and without official position, at least on the national level. Under the Kemalists, the national elite figures with intellectual and official backgrounds dominated the political life of the nation and for some time ran the country in near-model tutelary fashion. Gradually, however, and partially as a result of the success of that tutelary development, an important alternative elite component gathered strength. Instead of being predominantly *intellectual* and *official* in background, this elite arm displayed a different combination of the salient background elements. It was primarily *intellectual* and *local* in character, being led to a large extent by lawyers and men of trade and commerce. No less "modern" in many ways than the official-intellectual national elite, it differed primarily and understandably in paying greater heed to local interests and in emphasizing short-run economic and commercial considerations over previously erected national goals.

The analysis has stressed the protracted latency of this opposition to the Kemalist elite, and the fact that it was sporadically visible and even dimly recognized by the dominant official-intellectuals, even though their eyes habitually scanned the ranks of the religious for their most formidable opposition. The sizable mercantile and clerical delegations of the First Assembly were largely eliminated in the Second Assembly. The religious contingent, regarded as Public Enemy No. 1, disappeared from the national legislature and never reappeared. The merchants, however, were briefly seen again in the conciliatory Fourth Assembly, and reappeared in mounting numbers, along with the swelling tide of lawyers, on the advent of the multi-party system.

Many of these changes in the social backgrounds of the deputies moved so consistently together and coincided so meaningfully with alterations in the political system and in the dominant regime that they can be figuratively represented (see Figure 13.1).

In this composite and suggestive figure, let us recognize that the curve might just as easily have been inverted without altering the nature of the relationship being discussed. What I am stressing is the association between the slope of the graph (the *change* in social background) and the character of the political system and dominant regime. In other words, the vertical axis of the graph can be taken to represent variation in any one of a number of different social background variables. Change in that variable will quite frequently be seen to flow in one direction, be it up or down, from the starting point in the First Assembly to a high or low point in the Fifth Assembly, the apogee of Kemalism. Or, on other occasions, if the movement is

EMPHASES AND EVALUATIONS 389

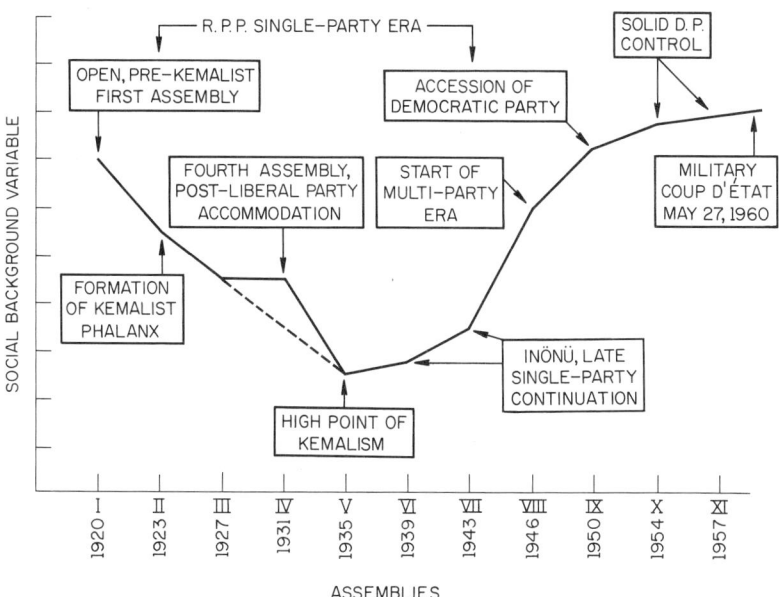

Figure 13.1. Composite representation of social background and broad political changes, 1920–1960

not quite so extreme, it will at least be seen that the Second Assembly differs sharply from the First and that there is a plateau across the Kemalist years from the Second through the Fifth Assemblies. Moreover, there almost always will have been a deviation from the established Kemalist trend in the accommodative Fourth Assembly.

Then, after the Fifth Assembly and Atatürk's death, the curve will reverse its direction (change the sign of its slope), but only slightly. During the late single-party period under İnönü it will form a slightly tilted plateau, signifying the "holding operation" aspect of that era. A sharp acceleration of that mild reversal of direction occurs in the Eighth Assembly with the transition to a multi-party system under the People's Party, and this reversal is continued, though in abated form, under the Democrats up to the *coup d'état* of May 1960. The pattern just described holds roughly for such factors as "localism" (birth in the constituency represented in parliament), average age, incidence of deputies from "economic" and official occupations, knowledge of foreign languages, knowledge of French in particular, and birth in the Marmara Region. The most outstanding exception to this over-all trend is that of education. The new legal and commercial elite that replaced the officials during the multi-party years was just as "intellectual" — just as highly educated — as its predecessors.

Though at least some local interests were clearly more amply represented in Ankara, it was not the case that the common man had come to parliament.

The entire assemblage of social background variations seemed to mark off five internal "eras" within the over-all period of the First Republic. These were: (1) the era of the First Assembly (1920–1923), prior to the formation of the Kemalist phalanx; (2) the Atatürk Era (1923–1939), the Second through the Fifth Assemblies, when the Kemalists were in full sway; (3) the late single-party or İnönü Era (1939–1946), the Sixth and Seventh Assemblies, during which the Kemalist drive became ossified; (4) the transitional Eighth Assembly (1946–1950), the advent of the multi-party system under the People's Party — a time of momentous internal adjustments in the Turkish political system; and finally (5) the Democratic Party Era (1950–1960), the Ninth through the Eleventh Assemblies. Not only do these variations in social background mark off periods that coincide with manifest changes in the structure of the political system and character of the dominant regime, but the independent analysis of deviant voting behavior revealed variations that reinforce the social background findings.

Awareness of these social background trends contributes decisively to an understanding of many political developments in Turkey, both recent and remote. For example, the character of the Progressive Party of 1924 and the relatively drastic action taken to terminate that party must be understood in light of the high proportion of military commanders and prominent civil officials making up that organization. At the end of the period under study, the very military action that extinguished the First Republic must in part be understood in terms of the sharp decline in representation and power of erstwhile military men in the Grand National Assembly and its cabinet. The importance of the military men's feeling that they had lost "their representatives" among the deputies, and the dismay of these highly nationalistic soldiers over what they regarded as obvious truckling to local interests by the Democrats, are graphically recorded in the reports of the planning of the coup.[1]

A comment on the current political malaise in Turkey under the Second Republic must be added here. As is usually the case, the military take-over of May 1960 and even the two abortive coups since then were prompted and permitted by a strongly perceived failure of civilian government. What caused this failure? How could such an auspicious start deteriorate in this fashion? Was it due to the sheer magnitude of the problem of opening up a tutelary system — of sharing

---

[1] See the *Milliyet* articles cited on p. 162.

power in a developing society? Or was there some basic flaw in the Kemalist course that undermined their efforts?

A social background study of this sort cannot hope to provide a complete answer to these vital questions, but it does suggest a few crucial observations. Put in the barest possible terms, what we have witnessed in Turkey in the past two decades is *the resurrection of severe intraelite conflict*. The Kemalist unity, which itself resolved a bitter and debilitating dogfight within the Turkish elite, has been fractured. No integrated elite offers discipline and direction to Turkish society today. Warring elite elements engage in the intense infighting that produces in Turkey, as in many other nations, simultaneous stagnation and instability. That elite unity which permitted mobilization of the society for rapid reform has degenerated into the war of each against all, which typifies so many stagnant nations today.

At first thought, one would be inclined to question the importance of this observation. There are many societies, among them our own, in which a good deal of intraelite conflict is to be found. Indeed, some would style this part of the essence of democracy. But the significance of the resurrection of intraelite conflict in Turkey is somewhat different. First of all, the breakdown of elite unity occurred just at the time when modernizing influences were being widely extended to the rural masses of the society for the first time — when the first major incursion into the "second stage" of the Turkish Revolution was taking place. Under almost any circumstances these would have been delicate and trying times. The problem of maintaining a balance between bringing the villagers into more active political and social participation and yet not permitting their demands, expectations, and interventions to run rampant would have been difficult under optimal conditions. However, under conditions of renewed and virulent intraelite conflict, the temptation presented opportunistic elite elements to engage in short-run pandering to nascent village expectations has proved almost impossible to resist.

Elite unity broke down in pathological form just as the vote was given to the peasant. The intraelite conflict thus became qualitatively different. It was no longer solely *intra*elite. It was transferred, sometimes in violent fashion, to the villages. More significantly, it was now true that a party well ensconced in the affections of a majority of the villagers, as was the Democratic Party, was under very few restraints in its dealings with its elite and party rivals. An *insulating* power base had been found. Newly enfranchised peasants cared little about the niceties of electoral and parliamentary freedom so long as the wheat subsidies and debt moratoria were forthcoming, especially since they had been impressed by one rather incontestable fact: only under the Democrats had any political party acted as if they, the peasants, really mattered. Though all parties were keenly aware of just how much they mattered by this time, the Democrats, under whom the change had actually come about, commandeered the credit.

Another point to be made in this connection concerns the absence of most of the established techniques for dealing with intraelite conflict that have been laboriously developed under durable democratic regimes. In this case we confront a negative legacy or concealed cost of Kemalism or any other tutelary regime. By the very nature of benevolent authoritarianism, it furnishes scant instruction and practice in the vital arts of political accommodation, compromise, and adjustment. Experience in tolerating public criticism by the "outs" without trampling on their rights in vexation and also experience on the part of the "outs" in keeping criticism within those bounds which prevent animosity from getting out of hand were both lacking. It is hard for a tutelary regime to provide instruction in manipulating a democratic polity.

Social background information of the type I have been inspecting furnishes valuable perspective on another aspect of the origins of this resurrection of virulent intraelite conflict. Like many political analysts, I have made much of various patterns of recruitment to top-level political positions in Turkey. I have concentrated on the *recruitment process*. However, recruitment is but one side of a dual phenomenon: the flow of personnel through an institution. That institution or system's *release processes* are also of critical importance, and these have generally been neglected by political scientists.

A little thought reveals numerous instances of political systems' becoming clogged because of inadequate mechanisms for the release of political personnel who are no longer abreast of their times or whose sheer presence blocks the admission of pressing new elements. One thinks immediately of Joseph Chamberlain waiting for years for "Elijah's mantle" to drop from Gladstone's shoulders to his.[2] One thinks of the U.S. Supreme Court, and one should also think of the U.S. Congress. A vital question to be asked about any political system concerns the mechanisms for releasing existing political leadership so as to adjust to changes in the society. A system in which the number of leaders is numerically fixed will be disadvantaged in this respect as opposed to a numerically flexible system. The same holds for a system which has set terms of office. A system in which power rather automatically accrues to a politician on the basis of seniority will tend

---

[2] Despite his magnificent achievements, not the least of which is the sacrificial dedication he has shown in assuming power under the Second Republic, when he and his party lose popularity by such a course but when there is really no alternative government, Ismet Inönü's extremely long career may have undermined a whole generation of potential R.P.P. leaders.

to have release inflexibility, as will, in more general terms, a system in which authority is allocated on an ascriptive basis. A competitive electoral system offers definite advantages in maintaining release flexibility just as it may have commensurate problems in ensuring sufficient stability of personnel to obtain reasonable decisional constancy and effectiveness.

Tutelary systems seem to be particularly susceptible to release difficulties. I have shown how the Kemalists, with their eyes averted to the dangers of reactionary religion, failed to perceive adequately and allow for the burgeoning power of professional, commercial, and local interests on their other flank. They maintained the monopolization of power by the officials too long and only began to absorb the rising professional, commercial, and local elements on their other flank too little and too late. By that time these groups had become convinced that the Kemalists and the People's Party were hopelessly opposed to anything except the tight, tutelary, official-dominated system that they had long before introduced. While I have argued that the slow, "capillary action" recruitment process of the standard legislative system makes adjustment to rapid social change quite difficult, some of this social background rigidity on the part of the Kemalists must be ascribed to the inadequacy of the mechanisms they developed for the release of incumbent personnel. With no second chamber or other honorific exit from a deputyship, with no strong electoral pressures to compel adjustment to social transformation, and with a system of quite limited (though increasing) feedback and reciprocal influence, they lost their adaptive flexibility.

Some Hypotheses and Generalizations

Social background research will become truly fruitful only when a series of strategically placed, carefully accomplished studies has been achieved. The present work purports merely to be one early element in such a series. Nevertheless, if these Turkish findings are compared with data from other nations, some intriguing generalities are already discernible. Consider, for example, the following summary of findings from a recent survey of social background literature in the United States:

1. Public leadership is a man's role today. Male dominance in public affairs is the rule.

2. Public leadership is a more common activity during the middle years of life than during either youth or advanced age. Advanced age, however, clearly outranks youth.

3. Formal public leadership on national issues is not often in the hands of members of ethnic and religious minority groups.

4. Formal public leadership is most likely to be held by people in the middle and upper social classes and by those with above-average formal education.[3]

Though summarizing social background research on American political leaders, every one of the four findings is strikingly true of Turkey — a non-Western nation with a sharply different political heritage and, for much of the period I have investigated, with a markedly divergent political structure. Moreover, the findings seem to hold for Great Britain, France, New Zealand, Canada, Germany, India, and points east and west. Furthermore, one can actually increase the specificity of the above generalizations or suggest additional propositions without greatly diminishing the wide, cross-national, and cross-cultural accuracy of the set of statements.

It is quite notable how consistently the average age of most national legislatures over the world hovers about a mean of some fifty years. Though subject to slightly more variation, the average age at first election generally turns out to be around forty-five years. Pursuing the investigation a little more deeply in the few cases where appropriate data have been collected continues to reveal regularities. For example, I have found in Turkey under the First Republic that the average tenure — the average length of a deputy's total career in parliament — was approximately seven years. The British and French political systems are, of course, significantly different from one another and even more different from the Turkish system during the single-party, co-optative period. Nonetheless, the average tenures of M.P.'s and French deputies were quite close to the Turkish figure and to each other. In the House of Commons between the two world wars the figure was nine years, while under the Third Republic of France it was nine and one-half years, and under the Fourth Republic the figure would seem to have been about eight years or less.[4] Despite the considerable differences in culture and system, the parliamentary longevity of national legislators in Britain, France, and Turkey seems to cover a comparable span of years.

Let us look briefly at the reelection rates of the aggregate group of deputies in France under the Third and Fourth Republics and in Turkey under the First Republic. Once again, some interesting regularities emerge. Table 13.1 gives the percentage of all deputies

---

[3] Cf. Wendell Bell, Richard Hill, and Charles Wright, *Public Leadership* (San Francisco: Chandler, 1961), pp. 180–181. I have closely paraphrased their language.

[4] Dogan, "Political Ascent in a Class Society: French Deputies, 1870–1958," in Marvick (ed.), *Political Decision-Makers, op cit.*, pp. 58–60. Dogan's British figure, however, may be contradicted by J. F. S. Ross. Cf. *Parliamentary Representation, op cit.*, pp. 40, 107.

Table 13.1

NUMBER OF TIMES ELECTED, ALL DEPUTIES IN FRANCE UNDER THE THIRD AND FOURTH REPUBLICS AND IN TURKEY UNDER THE FIRST REPUBLIC (PERCENTAGES)[a]

	NUMBER OF TIMES ELECTED DEPUTY				
	One	Two	Three	More than Three	
France, Third Republic	46%	21%	14%	19%	($N = 4,892$)
France, Fourth Republic	40%	17%	16%	27%	($N = 1,112$)
Turkey	54%	24%	9%	13%	($N = 2,210$)

[a] French data are from Dogan, *op. cit.*, p. 59. The Turkish data exclude the Eleventh Assembly.

who were elected only once, elected twice, and so on, for each nation.

Whether one finds these data compelling or not depends, of course, on his expectations. To me, the fact that two to three fifths of the deputies were only elected once, another fifth, approximately, elected twice, a tenth or more elected three times, and so on, despite the great differences in political system and culture, suggests the possible presence of common underlying influences. This impression is fortified by what seem to be similar findings from several other nations, such as Canada and Britain, contained, unfortunately, in reports that do not give precise figures for a direct comparison. More specifically, one slight surprise emerging from the present comparison is that the stability of tenure in Turkey seems to have been less than that in France, despite the fact that Turkey had for much of this time a co-optative single-party system and her deputies did not have to take the usual electoral risks.

One of the most graphic regularities has already been discussed — namely the recent dominance of the multi-party Turkish legislature by men from the legal profession. Though there are a few striking exceptions, such as Germany, and though most national legislatures are not so heavily populated by lawyers as those of the United States and some of the British Commonwealth nations, the fact that lawyers tend to be the largest single occupational group in parliament after parliament all over the world is certainly one of the outstanding facts to emerge from the existing body of social background studies. The Turkish case is particularly instructive in this connection. As I have stressed, we have been able to witness in Turkey a dramatic transition in the occupational composition of the Assembly. Neatly associated with the transition from a single-party, tutelary regime to a multiparty, Western-type democratic regime was a concomitant flushing of the previously dominant officials from their positions in the legislature and their replacement by a flood of lawyers and merchant-businessmen. What the causal connection will ultimately prove to be is difficult to say at present. But the change to the formal institutions of a Western, multi-party, parliamentary democracy clearly was associated with a gross change in political personnel that made the Turkish Assembly for the first time take on the full social background aspect of a Western legislature.

The inevitable question that snaps at the heels of such a factual observation is "Why should this be so?" Most assuredly, the answer will be complex, compounded of several different elements, not least of which will be the conscious following of a Western model. However, I wish to emphasize again the idea that different institutional arrangements place a premium on different sorts of skills. Under one type of political system one kind of influential behavior becomes disproportionately effective, while under a divergent type of system another kind of influential behavior produces more powerful results. The existing social background evidence suggests that a Western, multi-party, parliamentary democracy gives special sway to persons adept in verbal presentation, superior in their comprehension of the formal and legal intricacies of government, facile at interpersonal relations, particularly in the sense of not "putting other people off," and with the stamina and ability to attend to a plethora of organizational and administrative details and duties. As I have said, this seems to be what Harold Lasswell had in mind when he wrote of "specialists in persuasion," even though that label may understandably seem simplistic to many people. Certainly the social background data from Western legislatures highlight what J. F. S. Ross long ago called the "huge proportion of members belong[ing] to the *talking classes*, and in particular to the legal profession." [5] It has been difficult to know, however, whether this phenomenon was due primarily to Western culture in some general way or to specific Western institutions. The Turkish data suggest the latter, though ultimately, of course, one cannot separate the two.

One final generalization seems worthy of a brief spotlight. In perusing the literature on the social backgrounds of politicians in many parts of the world and at various levels of authority, one thing that has impressed me is the virtual ubiquity of the cosmopolitan versus

---

[5] Cf. Ross, *Parliamentary Representation, op. cit.*, p. 115, and, e.g., Harold D. Lasswell, Daniel Lerner, and C. Easton Rothwell, *The Comparative Study of Elites*, Hoover Institute Studies, Series B, Elites, No. 1 (Stanford: Stanford University Press, 1952), p. 16.

parochial, national elite versus local potentate polarization of politics. In nation after nation, modern or emergent, this dimension is a main axis for political alignment. The social and psychological causes of this phenomenon should be a major concern of political analysts. Moreover, at least in Turkey, as we have seen, the opening up of the tutelary developmental system and the inauguration of a Western, multi-party parliamentary structure emphatically increased the representation of local forces, that is, of *local elites*.[6] Does democratic interparty competition generally tend to lead to augmented influence of local elites? If so, how does the developing country keep this from "going too far," from degenerating into a selfish, narrow, logrolling politics that stymies national planning, obscures national goals, and wipes out the willingness to make national sacrifices? Such is the grave concern of many citizens in a number of developing countries at the present time.

More Limited Hypotheses and Leads

A variety of lesser leads and hypotheses emerges from a "case study" of this type — findings that nevertheless seem to warrant further investigation elsewhere and at other times. A few illustrations of such observations are as follows:

1. Localism, as exemplified by birth within the constituency represented, residence there, and having a position of local leadership, tends to be most emphasized in recruitment by the political parties in those areas where their voting support is weakest. This seems quite reasonable on the grounds that where the party platform is less popular the party turns to another, superficially neutral, type of appeal. However, some nations display a very powerful local bias in politics, whereas other nations are seemingly able to strike more of a balance. What is it about the institutional situation and political culture of a nation that determines the incidence of localism in the political system? What are the probable consequences of different elitist-localist mixes? These questions and many similar ones urgently require investigation in the developing nations.

2. The middle leader position in the national legislature is inherently a transitional stage. It consists of relatively young and able politicians who enter it after they leave neophyte status. But they

---

[6] One view of the current party situation in Turkey that is held by a number of very astute observers is that both major parties, the People's Party and the Justice Party, are now largely in the hands of local vested interests. Thus, one has the worst of all worlds, bitter strife between parties that have been captured by one limited segment of the population coupled with lack of urgently needed basic social reforms.

remain middle leaders for only about one or two full sessions of the legislature, after which they either rise to top leader level or else fall back to backbench status and possibly even out of politics completely. Fractious movements within the parliamentary party group most frequently erupt among this middle leader element.

3. Almost every group consciously engaged in recruiting new members does so in terms of a roughly ordered and transitive set of criteria. The less valued attributes from this hierarchy make only a slight difference in the selection and behavior of most recruits. But there are frequently marginal members not meeting the main criteria for whom these less valued attributes have highly magnified importance. Thus, the marginal recruitment decisions may often revolve about considerations that are hardly noticed in most selections. Knowing this and reacting to it, the marginal members may well prove to be operating under rather different situational estimates and pressures from most of their colleagues, and one cannot well understand the political behavior of the marginal legislator without taking this altered perspective into account.

4. Political systems differ appreciably and significantly from one another in the location of the *watershed of social background divergence* between political leaders and the general populace. In Turkey, this watershed of deviation seems to be quite far from the general adult populace. Turkey's deputies are, in most essential social background characteristics, quite different from all Turkish adults, all males, all household heads, all urban Turks, and so on. The first broader population segment that seems strongly to resemble the body of deputies would be that of all intellectuals (*münevverler* or *aydınlar*), that is, the university-educated, though even here the professional and official substrata of this group have been decisively overrepresented. In other societies where, for example, a military junta rules, the location of the watershed is probably still closer to the political elite — the officers' corps of the army in our example. In still other cases, though the parliament may not resemble the adult population in social background, it may fairly accurately reflect the urban adults, or the rural adults, or some other subgroup that is socially farther out from the elite and not too many steps removed from the general adult population. Presumably, location of the watershed (or watersheds) of social background divergence, if any, may provide a clue to the most relevant power-wielding public in the society.

5. One matter that I have not been able to investigate, but that seems to be of keen importance, is the relationship between similarities of social background, ease of communication, and decisional styles. There seems to be little doubt that similarity of social background among politicians many times acts to facilitate clear and rapid com-

munication. Similarly reared, trained, and occupied, the politicians possess a common language and shared set of referents that facilitate discourse and minimize conflict and tension. Karpat has recognized that this was in some respects true even for the People's Party and Democrats in Turkey.[7] And one can recall instances, such as when Clydeside Labour M.P.'s first stormed into the precincts of the House of Commons, when extreme differences in social background stacked great barriers in front of political communication. It should also be recognized that similarity in social background may foster continuity in policy and smooth the transfer of power from one group or party to another.

Against these possibly very real beneficial consequences of similarity in social background we must weigh evidence which indicates that lack of diversity can lead to rigidity, narrowness, clubbiness, and vested interest. How diverse does a legislature have to become in social background before communication is impaired and conflict and tension rise to destructive levels? How similar do social backgrounds have to be before the body becomes ingrown, cliquish, and out of touch with its environment? Such questions appear to be realistic and important, though to answer them we require attitudinal and behavioral information not easily obtained to blend with our existing stock of social background information.

6. Still more limited hypotheses of the following types can be offered. Legislators with professional occupational backgrounds tend to speak more in the parliament, regardless of party, than do legislators from other occupations. The changes in social characteristics of new legislators portend and highlight basic changes in the characteristics of all legislators. It takes a given cohort of legislators approximately two reelections to reach maximal formal power in the legislature. The rise in formal power of new or minority social *groups* recapitulates the process of rise in formal power of the successful majority-group *individual*. Internal opposition within political parties of the legislature springs most frequently from the younger and more inexperienced members.

These are just a few examples of the sorts of lower-order hypotheses and generalizations that the present analysis suggests. Hopefully, additional social background research will permit the falsifica-

---

[7] Karpat, *Turkey's Politics, op. cit.,* p. 336, n. 25: "The friendly relations between Republicans and Democrats were determined partly by their common social background and their past associations." What was common, as we have shown, at the time to which Karpat refers (the Eighth Assembly) was mainly level of education. Actually, the main political party leaders are more similar now in social background than they were then.

tion, partial confirmation, or more fruitful formulation of propositions of this type. Moreover, once such a yield is assembled and critically compared, connective and interstitial propositions should be forthcoming to link previously unrelated low generalizations into a more comprehensive structure.

POWER AND PRESTIGE

"The truth is, that the vulgarity will not choose men from among themselves; they never do so when left perfectly free to choose." So said, not Marie Antoinette, Nietzsche, or Carlyle, but Francis Place, the Westminster tailor, after years of organizing the working classes of London.[8] Political analysts have repeatedly made the same discovery, to their delight or dismay, over the ensuing years since Place politicked in Westminster. Most recently, Mattei Dogan, comparing the social backgrounds of politicians in France, Great Britain, the United States, Germany, Italy, Sweden, and Holland, has observed that "To the extent that political parties do not form their own cadres, they chiefly recruit their representatives and their leaders from the social elite. . . ."[9]

Modern social background analysis permits us to refine this generalization and elaborate what is one of the most widespread and striking regularities of politics. Recall that Turkish national legislators differed from the bulk of the Turkish population primarily by being better educated and more often engaged in official and professional occupations. The cabinet was found to differ from the Assembly as a whole along exactly the same social background lines as the Assembly differed from the population. Moreover, when we divided the Assembly still more precisely according to levels of formal power or authority (a type of power), we discovered that each level of authority differed from the next lower level in having a greater proportion of members with high education and official or professional occupation.

If we also recall that education and occupation are two of the prime indicators of a man's social prestige in his society, we can formulate the observed relationship in a more interesting and general way. *Within a political system or subsystem, the higher the level of formal authority of the concrete unit selected for examination, the greater the incidence of personnel of high social prestige among the members of that unit.* Using information about the level of formal authority of a political unit (a cabinet, legislature, party group, com-

[8] Graham Wallas, *The Life of Francis Place* (London: Allen & Unwin, 1925), p. 155.
[9] Dogan, *op. cit.*, p. 68.

mittee, office, etc.) and independent indicators of the social prestige of its component personnel (prior occupation, education, income, residence, etc.), one regularly tends to find that within a given system, the units of higher authority have a larger proportion of incumbents with high social prestige. Furthermore, if one starts at the bottom of a relatively clearly delineated structure of formal authority and moves, step by step, up to the apex of that structure, he discovers in a preponderance of cases that the prestige levels of the personnel involved rise in exactly the same step-by-step fashion. The formal authority of a political organ and the incidence of prestigious members of that organ are strongly and positively associated.

Others have previously noted this relationship.[10] My present purpose, however, is to call attention to its regularity and extent, to urge that it has been rather neglected, and to suggest a basic hypothesis partially to explain it.

If one examines the relationship between the social status of cabinet members and ordinary legislators in the several dozen nations for which data are available, one finds, invariably, the same thing. The occupational and educational prestige of ministers surpasses that of backbenchers — in India, France, Japan, the United Kingdom, New Zealand, West Germany, Canada, and other countries. On a slightly different tack, inspection of this phenomenon through comparison of state and provincial bodies with their national counterparts produces the same result. The national politicians are almost without exception of higher occupational and educational status. If one contrasts upper and lower houses of bicameral legislatures, national or state, where the upper house has greater formal authority, one unearths the same finding. If one compares legislative committee chairmen with ordinary committee members, the result is the same. Even if one moves into the realm of the appointive bureaucracy or into business organizations and trade unions, similar results appear.

In one of the few vertical studies of the representation of one constituency (New York City) at all important levels of formal governmental authority, Gabriel Almond long ago found the steplike pattern I have described.[11] The occupants of municipal council seats had less prior vocational and educational prestige than those in the lower house of the state legislature; these, in turn, ranked below State Senators, who were below U.S. Congressmen. The typical U.S. Senator from

---

[10] See, e.g., William Miller, *Men in Business* (Cambridge: Harvard University Press, 1952), p. 298; Donald Matthews, *The Social Background of Political Decision-Makers* (New York: Doubleday, 1954), p. 56; Matthews, "U.S. Senators and the Class Structure," *Public Opinion Quarterly*, XVIII (1954), p. 191; Lasswell, Lerner, and Rothwell, *op. cit.*, p. 10.

[11] Gabriel Almond, *Plutocracy and Politics in New York City* (unpublished doctoral dissertation, University of Chicago, 1938).

New York City possessed more antecedent occupational and educational prestige than the Congressman, and federal cabinet officials tended to surpass both national legislators. This general relationship was maintained over many years in the face of a secular democratization of recruitment that sharply reduced the over-all level of direct political participation of the privileged.[12] Though alterations in the pool of available talent may occur, within the limits set by that available pool a clear-cut tendency for relatively prestigious individuals to occupy more than their share of the seats of higher formal authority is almost always found.

Noting the great regularity and extension of this authority-prestige association, I shall consider a few alleged reasons for dismissing the findings as obvious or insignificant and then conclude with an explanatory hypothesis. First of all, it could be argued that the underlying fact is simply that the prestigious differentially *prefer* to occupy positions of higher formal authority. With greater resources at their disposal they can usually obtain their desires; this would explain their disproportionate presence. This argument refers, of course, to one indubitably important aspect of a complex phenomenon. However, the ubiquity of the finding — its occurrence in small groups, bureaucracies, labor unions, ethnic organizations, and highly democratic political systems with open elections under which expenses are either controlled or readily available to large numbers of people — tends to cast doubt on the adequacy of such an explanation. Wealth or prestige cannot automatically commandeer office in many of these environments. While undoubtedly true and a significant element contributing to the prestige-authority relationship, the cited factor would hardly seem to account for more than a limited portion of that relationship.

Another common explanation that we should reject on largely the same grounds contends that the augmented presence of the prestigious in posts of higher formal authority is merely the result of a recognized or unrecognized *rational calculation* of their greater worth. The prestige that places one in an authoritative position is said to be an earned reflection of excellence. Others rationally desire to place capable people in authority to get certain valued jobs done. While again perhaps partially true, this explanation seems to be insufficient. For example, both explanations apply only to one side of the association. They can explain only why the already prestigious are disproportionately granted positions of high formal authority. But an equally important aspect of this phenomenon is that those in positions of great formal authority who do not enter with high prestige are *accorded* that prestige after their accession to office. Not only does

[12] These statements are based upon my calculations using Almond's original data.

prestige produce power, but power produces prestige. The prestigious are differentially given power, and the powerful are differentially given prestige.

In fact, the last point calls to mind a third explanation for the authority-prestige association. It is argued, "Of course there is this relationship between formal authority and prestige. Authority is the basis of prestige." Such a contention, like the rest, is clearly true in part. But it is inadequate as a full explanation of both sides of this relationship in which either element can be the dynamic factor. While authority is one basis of prestige, most of the types of prestige to which I have referred — primarily nonpolitical occupational and educational prestige — would seem to *antedate* the acquisition of formal authority by the individual. It can be maintained that various occupational and educational experiences have prestige because it is recognized that they tend to *lead* to positions of formal authority; once again, however, to explain a phenomenon of the magnitude and scope of the observed relation on these tenuous grounds alone seems highly improbable. The authority-prestige association is a relationship in which either element can be the dynamic factor. An explanation which allows for this fact would seem to be more satisfactory than a collection of hypotheses explaining only one or the other side of the relationship.

The hypothesis I should like to suggest arises from much research on power relations as well as from social background analysis. Put most succinctly, it is that *recognition of the fact that another individual holds power over oneself tends to be psychologically repugnant to an individual.* It is generally regarded as being somehow restrictive and ego-humbling. Of course, there are wide cultural and personal variations in this reaction, and the mapping and explanation of these variations is another challenging task. The United States would appear to have a culture in which this negative reaction to the perception of self as influencee is particularly strong, while in Turkish culture, vis-à-vis other Turks, it seems to be rather mild.[13]

In any event, the self-perceived influencee tends to react to this recognition in three basic ways. The initial reaction is probably to try to *terminate the relation* — to "leave the field" in Lewinian terms.

---

[13] Thus we have a strong clue to the often rigid American insistence on a "government of laws, not of men" even when this idea is patently naive. Thus we comprehend the near-mandatory public reluctance of candidates for all sorts of office in American society; reluctance is a device for minimizing the fact that one is going to have power over others. If one does not want power, one will probably not be inclined to use it. Even the authoritarian who submits readily to power illustrates the point, for the price of that "authoritarian submission" is a counterpart "authoritarian aggression," presumably engendered by the strain of the power submission.

Ordinarily, however, such termination is impossible for the influencee, since it would require the sacrifice of many other values that the individual is satisfying through the relationship or would involve him in certain punishments or sanctions. Therefore, the second reaction of the influencee is most likely to be an attempt to *limit the scope* of the influence exerted over him as best he can.

The adjustment to the perception of self as influencee that can be made by removing or reducing the power of the influencer is usually quite limited. The objective power situation is often not susceptible to alteration without drastic and even less desirable consequences than the awareness of one's influencee status. But the influencee still has a third major adaptation at his command. If he cannot alter the relationship itself, he can *alter the way he perceives it*. He resorts to mechanisms to make recognition of the relationship psychologically more palatable.

One very common device for achieving this end is to perceive the power wielder as possessing qualities of special worth that justify his superior position. A greatly facilitating factor in the perception of worth in the influencer is the known attribution of worth to him by others — which is another way of referring to his prestige. The more generally society ascribes worth to an individual, the easier it is to admit the fact that he wields disproportionate power over oneself. The prestigious person is not granted authority only because it is believed that he actually *can* get the job done more effectively than another. He is granted authority *because he is prestigious*; his attributed special worth makes his recognized exercise of power less grating than the exercise of power by a nonprestigious individual since it can be *rationalized* in terms of his presumed ability to get the job done, his presumed moral fiber, or his presumed purity of lineage, to cite a few examples. It is less ego-humbling and restrictive to be influenced by a socially established, clear status-superior than by a peer.

Again, should the nonprestigious individual arrive at a position of power, my hypothesis would predict a tendency on the part of the self-perceived influencee to *re*perceive that individual — that is, to alter his view of such a person in the direction of according him more prestige, so long as the influencee feels he cannot escape from or drastically reduce the scope of the relationship. Authority and prestige tend to move toward one another, and either can be the dynamic element. We have seen in Turkey that the most profound change in occupational status that occurred during the First Republic was the acute rise in the prestige of the professionals, a rise that very neatly paralleled their rise in formal authority. Though we have less evidence, the same phenomenon would seem to have operated within the professional group, at least for engineers and probably for lawyers.

In this connection one point should be emphasized. I am not saying that the absolutely most prestigious will always have the most power, or vice versa. I am speaking of relative levels of prestige and power. Incumbents at higher levels of authority will have higher prestige than incumbents at lower levels. But for various reasons there may be groups in the system, outside the organs of formal authority, that have greater prestige than those represented in the organs of authority. However, according to my hypothesis, these groups would be particularly likely to chafe under the rule of those they recognize as powerful over them but less prestigious.

As I have said, formal authority is a form of power. "Authority" I shall define as the legitimate power of one role over another. Formal authority is that authority which is officially enunciated or proclaimed within a given political system. Hence, it is quite apparent that formally authoritative relationships are perhaps the most obvious, the most easily recognized, of all power relationships. Therefore, the association between formal authority and prestige should tend to be stronger than the association between most other forms of power and prestige. Certainly, if one looks about for flagrant examples of power without prestige, one is primarily directed to criminal and possibly para-military types who are notorious for clandestine operations and for not personally possessing formal authority, even though they find it useful — in keeping with my hypothesis — to control that authority. As the level of formal authority of a political unit rises, the *visibility* of its power also seems to rise. Thus, the recruitment of previously prestigious figures to its offices would also tend inordinately to rise.

The proffered hypothesis is attractive because it explains, at least in part, both sides of the authority-prestige relationship — including the accordance of prestige to the authoritative, a fact that most other explanations have to handle separately. Both the disproportionate recruitment of the previously prestigious to formal authority and the grant of prestige to those who happen to obtain formal authority without it are to be seen as manifestations of the same underlying psychological process.

Naturally, what I have presented is an unverified and rather gross hypothesis, albeit a most important and interesting one, I contend. Moreover, the hypothesis is subject to verification through experiments and field observations that seem to offer no abnormal difficulty. Indeed, it seems to accord well with evidence from diverse fields. For example, there is the suggestion that the central element in occupational prestige-awarding is itself the relative "independence" (freedom from the influence of others) felt to exist for members of the occupation. There is also, as I indicated, the view taken of authoritarianism as an extreme reaction to the repugnance of a particularly helpless, early influence position, in response to which the individual tends completely to surrender to a potent influencer and to demand complete surrender from his own subordinates, being unable to handle power relationships with more subtlety.[14]

In any event, I want to emphasize the ubiquity of the authority-prestige relationship as uncovered through social background analysis and to stress the great potential interest of this finding for the contemporary discipline of political science. It is my hope that the present work will contribute to additional efforts to glean more from the rather wasted harvest of previous social background research and that it will support further refinements in technique and added acquisitions of data.

Some Stages of Political Development

Talking about "stages of political development" can be tricky, yet such talk seems necessary. It is difficult to scan the array of so-called "developing nations" around the world and not get some sense that many of them are travelers along the same road, some a little behind and some a little ahead. In fact, we in the West, far from being statically "developed," are only travelers on that road, merely further ahead in many respects, but also moving. One intriguing problem for social scientists is the relative rate of acceleration of the developed and underdeveloped nations and the consequences of gross differences in these rates. We operate under the implicit assumption that the acceleration of the developed nations cannot much longer exceed that of the underdeveloped nations without producing an explosive political situation. Making explicit the hypotheses behind such reasoning would seem to be important to the policy maker as well as to the social theorist.

When I mentioned the word "stages" and used the road analogy, those who had already been alerted to the dire dangers of "historicism," "social Darwinism," "the Whig interpretation of history," and other "onward and upward" views were probably certain that I myself was off the right track. Let me hasten to explain both the word "stage" as I now employ it and the analogy used.

I do not speak of *inevitable* stages through which all emerging nations must somehow pass. Nor shall I contend that the stages of

[14] See Ann Roe, *The Psychology of Occupations* (New York: John Wiley, 1956), pp. 8, 38, and especially 307, where she summarizes her observations and those of Caplow to the effect that "the most important determinant of [occupational] prestige is the subject's degree of control of other people's behavior and the degree to which his behavior is controlled by others." Cf. also Donald Super, *The Psychology of Careers* (New York: Harper and Brothers, 1957), pp. 5, 38.

political development or change that I suggest are the only stages theoretically possible or actually found. All I shall contend is that *there seem to be regularities in the sequence of political changes actually observed in many of the new nations over the world.*[15] The stages of political development I have in mind merely describe these regularities. There is no *necessary* passage from one stage to the next, even though an appreciable number of new nations do seem to be following a rather visible sequence. Any particular nation can retrogress or come to a standstill at a given point. Again, there are other conceivable stages into which some nations, with infinite ingenuity, manage to propel themselves. In short, the road to which I refer has many turnoffs and diversionary paths, occasional detours, and resting places. However, all this does not mean that the analyst with a proper bird's-eye view cannot note some general traffic patterns and fruitfully infer, simply from the struggles and activities of those who are furthest in a given direction, the travail and tests that await those behind but also traveling along that route. This is the nature of my "stages" and road.

Another criticism, generally valid, of the stages of political development or change that I shall discuss is that they are *ex post* and almost purely descriptive. What we really want to know is the location of a given nation at a given time, whither, in our scheme, that nation will move next, and why. To chart this course for a long period in the future seems to be impossible, as Popper has well indicated.[16] But there is no reason to believe that essentially accurate prediction of the next major movement is not possible in many cases, and I shall supply some previously mentioned crude observations which help in making such a prediction. Though our present "stages" are largely descriptive, they are viewed as mere way stations in progress to more analytic and predictive stages.

So much by way of preface. Let us now proceed to the description of the actual stages suggested by reflection on the Turkish experience and on the experiences of several other developing nations in various parts of the world, particularly in Asia. I shall discuss six stages of political development, though it must be realized that I am arbitrarily cutting into a continuing process at one point and again arbitrarily taking leave of that same process at another point. Moreover, I shall

---

[15] By political change I mean an alteration in the allocation and distribution of power in a social unit. By political development I mean change toward a greater distribution and reciprocity, or mutuality, of power among the elements in the social unit. For some further discussion, see F. W. Frey, "Political Development, Power and Communications in Turkey," in Pye (ed.), *Communications and Political Development, op. cit.*

[16] Cf. K. R. Popper, *The Poverty of Historicism* (London: Routledge & Kegan Paul, 1957).

deal more intensively with the last four of the six stages than with the first two simply because other writers have already distinguished the first two and portrayed them in able fashion. The six stages, several of which have internal phases, are as follows:

Concentrative Stages:

1. Formation and organizational embodiment of a sense of national identity.
2. Struggle for national independence.
3. Postindependence realignment.
4. Establishment of a tutelary regime.

Dispersive Stages:

5. Initial democratization: opening up the tutelary regime.
6. Opposition rule: consolidation of democracy.

The first four stages involve, as indicated, a concentration of power among the elements in the political system, while the last two stages involve a dispersion of power.[17] There is another dimension of this political development that can cut across either of the last two dispersive stages but whose sequential timing is rather unpredictable, so I have not included it in the paradigm. This dimension is the sharing of power with mass elements in the society as opposed to sharing it with elite elements, defined in terms of prestige. I reiterate that at every stage there are common and uncommon deviations from the depicted pattern.

The Formation and Organizational Embodiment of a Sense of National Identity

Though in some countries nationhood has been virtually inflicted on the inhabitants, most nations are in large measure the result of ef-

---

[17] Thus, technically, according to my own definition, only the last two stages can be called political development. Some will find this result awkward. My view is that a completely satisfactory conception of political development is a chimera, since it involves either verbal awkwardness of this type if one insists on an empirical and descriptive conception, or it involves vagueness, circularity, or dissensus, if one insists on the normative and ethical connotations of the word "development." A clear descriptive conception of wide applicability always produces a situation in which one can cogently say, "Yes, that is development, and it is bad or unfortunate." A normative conception is either vague and metaphysical ("the greatest good for the greatest number," "a more equitable distribution of income") or else subject to important disagreement. Personally, for reasons of this type, I prefer to talk about the relationships in various societies, new or old, of more standard variables, such as power, prestige, tolerance of nonconformity, and fatalism, rather than about "development." The stages of political development outlined above are really stages in the distribution of power and formation of political attitudes in new nations.

forts at national unity on the part of at least a portion of the affected population. One of the first steps in this process has been the formation of a sense of national identity, the awakening of national consciousness. I have indicated that in Turkey this national consciousness initially arose among those who represented the state in its dealings, diplomatic or military, with other states. Historically, the same would seem generally to have been true in European history as well as in Japan, the developed nation of Asia. It is, on the whole, very true of the currently emerging nations of Asia, Africa, and Latin America. Four crucial factors leading a group to an early sense of national identity appear to be: (1) strong involvement (positive or negative) with the governing agency of the existing polity, be it the chief, the dynasty, or the government; (2) dissatisfaction focused on the perceived performance of the traditional system; (3) relatively great exposure to nationalistic external communications; and (4) relatively good internal communications with similarly situated persons in one's own polity. Thus, for example, the military man is usually strongly involved with the state, engages in the most challenging of all interactions (mortal combat) with military men from other polities, and usually has excellent communications with other military men in his own polity. National identification has frequently sprung from the military. The same essentially holds for bureaucrats, journalists, and students, who are also seen as carriers of national self-awareness.

The fourth point above is rather critical. Ordinarily, the mere formation of a sense of national consciousness on the part of a few diverse souls has been of scant import. For national consciousness to grow rapidly and extensively it needs organizational embodiment. Power multiplies power; up to a rather remote point, the more effective the internal power structure of a group, the more potent that group will be vis-à-vis other groups in the broader environment. National identification has been spread most frequently and most rapidly through organized effort. Thus, in most developing societies we can trace rather clearly the growth of what is commonly called "the nationalist movement." The first stirrings of a sense of national identity can be observed in most developing nations to have occurred among those who were involved with the governing agency of their polity and engaged in competitive interaction with role counterparts from other polities. These stirrings have then become truly potent when they have been focused in an effective organization usually labeled a nationalist movement.

The Struggle for National Independence

If nature abhors a vacuum, so do the great powers of the world. The relative weakness of the underdeveloped nations created a political vacuum into which the sundry great powers surged on a worldwide basis. The resulting presence or pressure of nationalistic foreigners not only helped prompt the sense of national identity among the inhabitants of the underdeveloped land, but it also meant that for such national consciousness to be fully realized a struggle for independence from foreign occupation or influence had to be waged. The nationalist movement has generally assumed as its paramount goal the expulsion of the foreigner and has dedicated all its energies to that task. For our purposes, the salient features of the struggle for national independence — so common to developing nations — are twofold: first, that it tends to throw up a charismatic leader, sometimes almost inflicting charisma on some very improbable persons, and second, that the nationalist movement of the independence struggle tends to have an ephemeral and largely negative unity revolving about the elimination of foreign influences. Many highly disparate elements are able to cooperate temporarily under a "throw the foreigners out" banner. But the unity is self-terminating; when the foreigners are apparently evicted at last, such a shibboleth can no longer integrate the diverse components of the nationalist movement. Both these facts help set the scene for the third stage of political development — the postindependence realignment.

The Postindependence Realignment

With independence secured, at least for the time being, the developing nation abruptly encounters the Augean problems of what has aptly been called "nation-building." Former insurgent leaders, revolutionaries, militants, and passive resisters now must shoulder the quite different responsibilities of being not the levelers of an enemy's power but the architects of a new state. Decisions are now required regarding how to govern a compatriot, not how to get rid of a foreigner. Vested interests, sacred traditions, and dreams of cherished reforms that had lain dormant during the exigencies of the independence struggle now rush to the surface of political discussion and dispute. The unity of the nationalist movement is at least momentarily ruptured by the question, "What is to be done?"

In this postindependence crisis we frequently find arrayed against one another, on one side, the charismatic leader and many of his loyal followers, whom I have christened the "ardent nationalists," and, opposed to them, many of the erstwhile lieutenants of the charismatic leader in the national struggle together with their followers, a group that we can label the "postindependence conservatives." The ardent nationalists appear to include a disproportionately large number of individuals who have been deeply affected by the felt disrespect accorded their nation and their people by the more developed countries.

Consequently, they tend to desire above all else a program of national growth or revitalization. They believe that the only solution to the problem of how to realize such national goals or, more specifically, how to end the debility and disunity of the postindependence crisis lies in the concentration of power in the hands of the government or some other single institution that they control. They favor the creation of a tutelary regime of concentrated power.

The "postindependence conservatives," on the other hand, frequently are led by individuals who were prominent in the preindependence society and who gained even more eminence during the independence struggle. Though in most cases they can hardly be called "democrats," they do for many reasons, some venal and some principled, oppose the concentration of power advocated by the ardent nationalists. In a relatively clear-cut situation, as in Turkey, the postindependence crisis consists essentially of the contest between these two groups.

More often than not recently, the ardent nationalists seem to win — no doubt partly as a result of their greater unity and discipline, the carry-over of some of the momentum of the independence struggle, their control over the nationalist organization, and their initial strategic location in the army and government. Many times, however, and under conditions that the political scientist has yet adequately to spell out, either the "postindependence conservatives" win or else victory is denied either side and an uneasy compromise or stalemate ensues. Stalemate tends to produce political weakness, intrigue, and stagnation, which sooner or later tend in turn to yield another crisis and, frequently, a still more severely authoritarian regime. Some nations, often because of the complex and fragmented distribution of power within the elite, seem to have been quite unable to resolve this postindependence crisis over a considerable period, so that constant jockeying for advantage among contending elite elements occurs, and scant secular development is seen. It also sometimes seems that the more clear-cut and disciplined the independence struggle has been, the better the chances for a clear-cut and decisively resolved postindependence crisis.

Establishment of a Tutelary Regime

Though several possible outcomes of the postindependence realignment are found, let us consider perhaps the most striking and momentous outcome, victory by the ardent nationalists. What then is likely to occur, based on past experience? To answer that question we must inspect the political situation in the new nation as it is and as it appears from the ardent nationalists' perspective.

A schematic representation, greatly oversimplified, of what political development as we have defined it involves is presented in Figure 13.2. At the time of the postindependence crisis the "traditional" underdeveloped nation usually has a power structure bearing a considerable resemblance to that of Subfigure I. Two important aspects of this structure stand out. First, there is an appreciable amount of mutual or reciprocal influence within the elite sector of the society. No single elite member dominates the rest of the elite. Nearly all elite elements can influence some other elite elements, and no element can unilaterally compel unified elite action. Thus, considerable elite consensus on a policy requiring elite coordination is required. In the absence of that consensus, the opportunities for a dissident elite element to frustrate positive action are ample. Since that consensus has ordinarily been missing, stagnation, lack of development, and the absence of reform have been the rule.

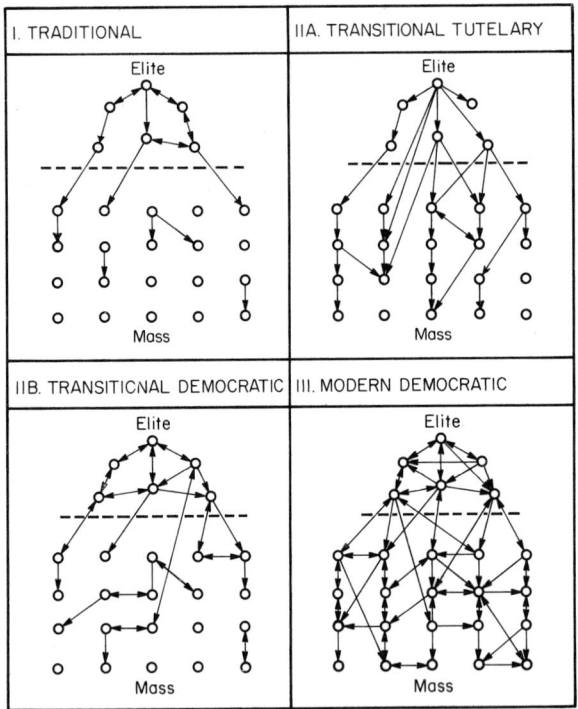

Figure 13.2. Four characteristic power structures during the process of political development

The second crucial aspect of the "traditional" power structure is its incompleteness — the low over-all level of power. Particularly among the masses, great sectors of the society are largely outside the power domain of the dominant elite. Through special efforts any single village or other mass element could probably be strongly influenced by a united elite, but the linkages are not regularly in the structure so as to permit all or nearly all such mass elements to be influenced at a given time. Goals demanding extensive or full mobilization of the society — coordination of the behavior of most elements in the nation — simply cannot be achieved, save in the exceptional case when such great consensus exists that all elements in the system are induced to coordinate their behavior spontaneously. Needless to say, such moments are rarer than rare.

The postindependence crisis essentially consists in an intraelite struggle, as I have suggested. A victory by the ardent nationalists in that struggle has generally meant an attempt by the ardent nationalists to consolidate their power over all other elite elements by *eliminating the reciprocity in the system,* that is, by eliminating the reverse flow of influence and making the structure unilateral. Then, the ardent nationalists attempt to coordinate, integrate, or mobilize the behavior of other elements in the system by *creating new power linkages,* still unilateral, where virtually no linkages of any sort previously existed in the system. In other words, a concentration and then an extension of power occur, and the basic motivation for this policy is the urgent, intense desire to achieve certain substantive goals that demand concerting the behavior of large numbers of people throughout the society — for example, raising and equipping a modern mass army; installing a nationwide system of education; lacing the country together with roads and new media of communication; embarking on national health and sanitary campaigns. With many elements in the society unprepared voluntarily to adopt these same goals, the ardent nationalist feels that the only way to ensure their achievement is through the establishment and effective use of a concentrated and extensive structure of power. This centralized approach and these changes have been labeled the "tutelary" road to development.

Though the difference between the tutelary approach and that which I have, for want of a better name, christened the "transitional democratic" approach is one of degree, with many intermediate positions admissible and found, a glance toward the other end of the power spectrum is rewarding. Subfigure IIB of Figure 13.2 gives a representation of the "transitional democratic" power structure. In this system approximately as many or more new power linkages as in the tutelary system have been created; the over-all level of power in the system has gone up by approximately the same factor. But the distribution of power is obviously quite different. Instead of the elimination of reciprocal linkages in the elite sector, those linkages have been maintained or even increased. Instead of vertical and unilateral linkages being extended to almost all mass elements, reciprocal and horizontal linkages have appeared in that sector. Clearly, no one dominates or dictates to the elements of the total polity in tutelary fashion. But what are the prospects for reform — for the achievement of goals demanding extensive coordination of behavior? They are only about as good as the degree of goal consensus in the polity. To be content with such an arrangement one must either have a relatively low and flexible level of demand for such goals, or else such goals must be achieved primarily through means other than the widespread exertion of influence — that is, through that sharing or extensive compatibility of values and cognitive outlooks called consensus. In most developing societies in which the ardent nationalists have managed to dominate the postindependence realignment, such consensus is conspicuously lacking, and the ardent nationalists have a high and often rigid demand for their goals. Not surprisingly, we find under these conditions a strong tendency for them to opt for the tutelary pattern.

Initial Democratization: The Opening Up of the Tutelary System

The "politically developed," "modern democratic" power structure is represented by Subfigure III of Figure 13.2. It differs from the tutelary structure primarily in containing many more reciprocal power relations. It differs from the transitional democratic structure primarily in its completeness; the entire system can be mobilized through the exertion of influence, provided that those with reciprocal power over the strategic power-holders choose not to halt that mobilization by exerting their reciprocal power. Like the tutelary system, the modern democratic system can be relatively fully mobilized through the use of influence. Like the transitional democratic system, it permits mutual, reverse flows of influence. But most important of all, for present purposes, while the modern democratic system is less dependent on consensus than the transitional democratic system (where mobilization can be achieved only by consensus), it is still able to achieve extensive coordination of behavior only if crucial elements at least abstain from using their reciprocal power to block action. This abstention is ordinarily achieved in two ways: (1) widespread goal agreement and/or relatively low goal intensity presumably aided by high standards of living, and (2) pervasive emphasis on and consensus regarding the legitimate means of political action, so that if an opposed goal cannot be stopped by certain broadly accepted means, other dangerous and rear-guard power attempts will not be made.

Perhaps the most significant question of all, for policy makers and for political theorists, is that of the conditions under which a successful passage from a tutelary structure to a modern democratic structure is most likely.[18] I wish to stress again that there are numerous deviations from the basic pattern of stages of political development here described. For instance, the struggle for national independence may be diffuse, protracted, and long indecisive in its outcome. Iran is a good case in point. For this reason I have generally avoided the term "crisis," which other writers have employed. But the deviations at each stage from the described pattern themselves often cluster into a few fundamental types of change. This is rarely clearer than in the late tutelary stage. Two main deviations from passage from the tutelary to the defined modern democratic structure seem to be found. First of all, one common occurrence is for the tutelary leaders to be seduced by the headiness of power and to try to perpetuate their domination indefinitely. Thus, the transitional tutelary system may well congeal into a hardened and entrenched dictatorship. As I suggested earlier, two valuable indicators of the likelihood of movement in this direction are (1) whether an ideology justifying totalitarianism is developed and (2) whether under the tutelary system there is created a political infrastructure that encourages reciprocal flows of influence.

The second and possibly more common deviation from the tutelary to modern democratic movement is passage from a tutelary system into a transitional democratic system rather than into a modern one. This would seem to be especially likely if the tutelary structure was incomplete or faulty in various ways when the transition to modern democracy was attempted. Such was perhaps the case in Turkey. What has seemingly happened there is that, prior to the full elaboration of the power structure and prior to the development of the necessary goal consensus, especially among the elite, reciprocal linkages more akin to those of the traditional system than to those of the modern democratic system were reestablished. A resurrection of virulent intraelite conflict resulted which has produced stagnation and instability. I do not argue that the tutelary period could have been or should have been prolonged. What my analysis has indicated, however, is that the tutelary regime absorbed various elements in the expanding elite too slowly. Moreover, various mass elements now on the rise though not formally present in the halls of authority, like the peasants and the workers, were hardly recognized at all. Smoldering

[18] In this connection, the European experience should be taken into account. Though the time span was much more extensive, the same basic sequence of political change seems to have prevailed in many European countries: first the concentrative stages, generally seen as the centralization of power under a king, such as Henry VIII or Louis XI; then the dispersive stages, basically in the nineteenth century, though with earlier antecedents within the elite. The general analytic comparison between European political development and change in the currently emerging nations urgently needs attention.

hostility was thus provoked among the slighted elite elements, and no consensus was reached with regard to what was to be done for the peasant and worker. When power was finally granted to the slighted elite and to the peasants under these conditions, there was a strong tendency for it to be used in a vindictive or irresponsible fashion. Under such conditions, greater reciprocity has simply produced weakness and an inability to achieve broad goals.

Though the Iranian tutelary development never accomplished as much as the Turkish, which was its sometime model, and though it foundered earlier, it, too, seemed to pass into that frequently frustrating form poorly labeled transitional democracy. Egypt is in the midst of its tutelary phase; which way it will turn remains to be seen. As has been said, a propitious sign is the absence of a totalitarian ideology; but a distressing omen is the difficulty Nasser has had in elaborating a potentially democratic, mediating, political infrastructure. Many other emerging nations all over the world can clearly and profitably be examined from this same perspective.

In the initial opening up of the tutelary regime — that is, the sharing of power through creation of numerous reciprocal and horizontal power relations in the previously unilateral and vertical structure — at least three internal phases can be distinguished. Sometimes these phases are compressed and dealt with in a single action, but they are analytically distinct. First, the tutelary regime generally permits opposition to *organize*; second, it makes whatever adjustments are necessary in the formal structure of power to give that opposition a *chance to obtain authoritative control*, usually by amending the electoral laws; and third, it *turns over formal power* to an organized opposition that has legally won authoritative control. Decisions to take each of these actions are usually turning points in the career of a tutelary regime, and deviation from the path to modern democracy can occur at any phase. Opposition may never be vouchsafed the chance visibly and legally to organize. An organized opposition may never be given the chance to enter a free election. Though capable of entering a free election, an organized opposition may never win such an election so that the tutelary leaders are never confronted with the acid test of surrendering power to their opponents. When such opposition victory does occur, the tutelary leaders may decide to deny that victory by force. Each of these decisions tends to be another milestone on the road to a modern democratic system and a possible point of deviation.

Opposition Rule: The Consolidation of Democracy

If and when the opposition does come to formal power, it, in turn, encounters the same frequently wracking set of decisions that the tutelary leaders confronted. If that opposition-come-to-power is infected with fear and revanchist sentiment as a result of felt sufferings under the tutelary regime, it may well begin to close the political system again by tampering with the electoral laws and restricting the right of the opposition to organize. This tendency may be spurred on by the discomfort and vehemence of the former governing group now in opposition. Such is exactly what happened in Turkey. However, the reciprocal linkages built into the former tutelary power structure during the move toward democracy enable the opposition of this stage to wage a rather effective battle against the antidemocratic encroachments of the new government. An internecine political struggle may ensue that can frequently lead to at least temporary discredit of democratic processes and a reversion to dictatorship, this time of a much more extreme type.

In such a situation, if stagnation, which also produces extremism, is to be avoided and the movement toward a modern democratic structure is to be continued, then some means for mollifying or resolving the intra-elite conflict would seem to be essential. Rapid economic development might contribute to such an end, but it is hardly likely under these very unsettled conditions.

However, the recognition of the perilous nature of their course by the more responsible and dedicated political leaders in the various contending elite groups is a more probable remedy. But the difficulty here would seem to be that such recognition and restraint is necessary on *all* major sides. If only one side perceives the danger and restrains itself, the disintegration may be temporarily reduced; but in such a charged atmosphere that actor tends to lose power to his rivals, and if the infighting persists over a very long time, the party of restraint may suffer complete collapse.

Of course, such a grim development is not the only possibility. The opposition-come-to-power and the tutelary-government-fallen-to-opposition may behave admirably. The new government may serve its term in office and then itself relinquish the scepter of authority to its duly elected opponents. With each successive and successful transfer of power, trust in the political decency and minimal competence of one's opponents grows, and the probable viability of the democratic structure increases.

In time, however, and perhaps quite quickly if the society is unfortunate, a crisis may arise whose solution clearly demands temporary return to a much greater concentration of power — a crisis such as a war or a severe oscillation of the economy. When this situation occurs, we perceive another vital aspect of the durable modern democratic political system, indeed, of any durable system — the need for *power flexibility*.

Each political system consists of actors (individuals and groups) with goals or values that they try to realize. These goals are desired with different intensities and demand different degrees of behavioral coordination from the members of the polity. When goals which demand great and extensive behavioral coordination are intensely desired by many or by especially powerful actors, then a relatively concentrated power structure is usually required to achieve those goals. If the system cannot be restructured to yield such concentration of power, high dissatisfaction can result which may do permanent damage, depending on the power and actions of the dissatisfied. For example, the war effort may be lost or jeopardized. Riot and revolution may erupt if the recession or unemployment is not ended, and so on. Thus, even the strongest democracies have formal plans for alteration of their political systems to yield a more concentrated power structure. These arrangements are frequently called "constitutional dictatorship," "state of siege," "crisis government," "martial law," etc. Informal mechanisms to secure the same end are still more numerous. But after the crisis is over, when the intensity of motivations dies down and the yoke of power begins to bind and irritate, then the democratic political system must be able to disperse power again — must be able to revert to its normal state. The conscious ability readily to make these alterations in the concentration and dispersion of power to meet shifting popular demands I call "power flexibility." The politically developing nations would seem to acquire it with difficulty. Smooth and ordered adjustment of the power structure of the society to altered environmental conditions and altered motivations on the part of its members, difficult even for the most experienced polities, is especially hard for the new and inexperienced nation.

Finally, the politically developing nation moving from the transitional tutelary stage to the modern democratic state ultimately faces the problem of granting power not only to other elite elements, whom the tutelary governors fear but respect and communicate with, but also to mass elements, whom they similarly fear but do not respect and do not regularly encounter. In Turkey, both grants of power were undertaken at roughly the same time. Perhaps that fact alone tremendously complicated the problem. However, it is difficult to see how it could have been arranged otherwise, save for a somewhat earlier and smoother co-optation of excluded elite elements; and it is even more difficult to see how other emerging nations, more victimized by the compression of political time than Turkey, will be able to avoid confronting these two profound transformations almost simultaneously. That is one reason why the Turkish experience, still unresolved and capable of going in any of several directions, is so fascinating. If the Turks, with their deep resources of political realism and self-sacrifice, can work their way clear of their present swamp of troubles and continue on their exemplary path to political freedom and effectiveness, then they will have served not only themselves, but truly the entire world.

Appendices

APPENDIX A

Formal Requirements for Deputies

The Electoral System

The roots of the Turkish electoral laws in force between 1920 and 1957 can be traced back to the first Turkish constitution, the *Fundamental Law* of the Ottoman Empire, dated May 1, 1877. This constitution set up an Ottoman Chamber of Deputies and a Senate. The popular house, the Chamber of Deputies, excluded the following classes of persons from membership: all those who were not Ottoman subjects; those in the service of a foreign state; those not knowing Turkish; those less than thirty years of age; those in personal slavery; those who were insolvent and condemned for bankruptcy; those in bad repute; those who had lost their legal rights; those who were wards of courts, etc.; and those who claimed foreign nationality (Article 68). Moreover, a person could not maintain a deputyship and another official governmental post simultaneously (Article 67). The constitution took pains to specify the Burkean view that each deputy was "the representative of all Ottomans and not the separate deputy of the constituency which elected him" (Article 71).[1]

[1] This information and all subsequent material on Ottoman and Turkish electoral laws through 1946 comes from the valuable compilation of the texts of such laws that was put out by the Turkish government to aid in the discussions prior to the Electoral Law of 1950. It is entitled *Türkiyede ve Yabancı Memleketlerde Seçim Mevzuatı* (*Electoral Topics in Turkey and Foreign Countries*), (Ankara: Başbakanlık Devlet Matbaası, 1949). For short surveys of national elections in the Ottoman Empire and Turkish Republic, see Tarık Z. Tunaya and Reşit Ülker, *Milletvekilleri Seçimi Kanunu ve Ilgili Mevzuat* (*The*

APPENDIX A

Supplementary legislation concerning the qualifications and mode of election of Ottoman deputies amplified the meager constitutional stipulations. The *Provisional Instructions* of 1877 specified in their third article that a deputy must *own some property,* slight or great, *in his native region,* and also that the deputy be at least twenty-five years of age, which is rather surprising in view of the constitutional requirement of thirty years. For this earliest, short-lived Ottoman Assembly, a two-stage electoral process was used whereunder the members of elected Provincial Councils in turn chose the deputies to the Chamber of Deputies (Article 2).

The next Ottoman parliament was not seen until the Young Turk Revolution of 1908 overcame Abdülhamid II, the "Red Sultan," who had abolished the Assembly of 1877 some thirty years before. Again a two-stage, indirect electoral process was specified by the *Temporary Electoral Law* of September 20, 1908. The basic constituency was the province *(sancak).* Ottoman males over twenty-five years, possessed of their civil rights and not subject to the usual disabilities from foreign service or foreign citizenship, slavery, bankruptcy, conviction of a felony, etc., could vote. One year's local residence was also required, and the elector was barred if he paid no *direct* tax (property tax). There was one secondary elector for up to 750 registered primary electors, and one additional secondary elector for up to each additional 500 primary electors. In the same fashion, each *sancak* got one deputy for up to 75,000 population, and an additional deputy for up to each additional 50,000 population. The aforementioned qualifications for being a deputy found in Articles 67, 68, and 69 of the 1877 constitution were restated.

In 1912 a provisional law denied electoral rights to commanders, officers, noncommissioned officers, gendarmes, and members of the armed forces.

The First Grand National Assembly was elected partly under these Ottoman electoral provisions. Actually, two distinct electoral paths to this Assembly existed. First, those who were elected to the last Ottoman Chamber of Deputies under the above provisions, and who managed to escape Allied clutches, were accepted in the First Assembly. Ninety-two deputies came to the First Assembly directly from the last Ottoman Chamber of Deputies, though at least 102 had previous experience in one or more of the four Ottoman Assemblies between 1908 and 1920.[2]

Deputies' Electoral Law and Associated Topics), (Istanbul: Ismail Akgün Matbaası, 1954), pp. 1–8, and Tarık Z. Tunaya, "Elections in Turkish History," *Middle Eastern Affairs,* V (April 1954), pp. 116–119.

[2] For the names of these 92 deputies, cf. *T.B.M.M. Isim Defteri, Devre* I (Ankara: T.B.M.M. Matbaası, 1943), pp. 19–21.

APPENDIX A 425

The majority of the remaining 349 deputies elected were chosen according to the method indicated by Mustafa Kemal in telegrams to the provinces (*Vilayetler*), to the autonomous districts (*müstakil Livalar*), and to Army Corps commanders. The essence of the electoral scheme was as follows. The *Liva* was the basic electoral constituency with five deputies to be elected from each *Liva*. The customary two-stage, indirect system of primary and secondary electors was used, though the qualifications of the secondary electors varied somewhat: "in the same manner that each party, group and union [could] choose candidates for this Assembly, so every one individual [had] the right in his constituency independently to put forward his candidature...." The elections were to be conducted by the highest official in each town, by secret ballot, and by a "clear majority." [3] Apparently there were few restrictions on candidacy and membership for those deputies to the G.N.A. not coming from the Istanbul Chamber of Deputies. It is certainly true that several of these persons did not meet the Ottoman requirements previously enumerated. For example, several of the deputies were less than thirty years old.

These elections to the First Assembly seem to have been relatively open and honest. For example, Halide Edib Adıvar, Turkey's most famous woman of letters and an intelligent if not unbiased participant observer of these events, states that "the elections took place in absolute freedom all over the country. I do not remember any election which had been so free, with the posible exception of the one in 1908." [4]

On April 3, 1923, a law was passed (No. 320) that amended some provisions of the existing Ottoman electoral laws that were tacitly deemed to have continued in force. The franchise was extended to all males over eighteen years of age, the taxpaying requirement for first and second electors was lifted, and the ratios for computing the numbers of deputies and numbers of secondary electors were reduced. Government and military officials were precluded from being elected deputies from their government service locales if they had not resigned two months prior to the election of secondary electors (instead of merely being forced to choose one post or another if elected).

The Turkish Constitution of April 20, 1924, which I have mentioned before, declared that "Every male Turk over thirty years of age can be elected a deputy" (Article 11). It then went on, in Article 12, to add that the following persons were not eligible to be elected deputy: persons in the service of a foreign state; those sentenced for theft, fraud, swindling, abuse of confidence, fraudulent bankruptcy,

[3] Cf. Atatürk, *Nutuk, op. cit.*, pp. 301–302; English version, *Speech...*, *op. cit.*, pp. 365–366.
[4] Halide Edib (Adıvar), *The Turkish Ordeal, op. cit.*, p. 48, n. 15.

or other defamatory offense; those under guardianship; those claiming foreign citizenship; those deprived of their civil rights; and those who were unable to read and write Turkish (not those who did not "know" Turkish, as before). It can be seen that these provisions are very similar to the Ottoman requirements. With regard to voting qualifications, the same observation holds. The new constitution stipulated that every male Turk over eighteen years of age could vote in elections to the G.N.A., either as a primary or secondary elector. Within this framework, the older regulations still applied.

In June 1927 and March 1931 trivial changes in the national electoral laws were made. But in early 1934 a basic alteration occurred. In February of that year a law altered the conditions of franchise by making a significant one-word omission — the word "male" was dropped from the necessary qualifications of both electors and deputies. Thus, women, who gained voting rights in municipal elections in 1930, also became eligible to be national primary and secondary electors and deputies. In the same law (No. 2598) the minimum voting age, which had been eighteen years, was raised to twenty-two years, and the population bases for the allocation of deputies were set at one deputy for up to 55,000 population, and one additional deputy for up to each 40,000 thereafter. Law No. 2631 of December 1934 then changed the ratio of secondary electors to be one such elector for up to 600 population and one additional secondary elector for up to each added 400 persons. The Fifth Assembly, elected in 1935, was the first to have female deputies; there were eighteen.

A major codification of the various valid electoral laws and provisions occurred in 1942, when, in mid-January, Law No. 4320 was passed by the G.N.A. and promulgated. This law once more declared that the province (*vilayet* or *il*) was the basic electoral constituency and repeated the prior formulas for the allocation of deputies to the provinces and the determination of secondary electors. It detailed the technical procedures of preparing the voting lists, administering the elections, etc., and it reiterated the qualifications for being a first or second elector. Moreover, it restated the existing disqualifications which barred one from becoming a deputy: being in the official service of a foreign state; being condemned for a major crime or some form of fraud; being under legal interdiction; claiming citizenship in a foreign state; being barred from public service (that is, already holding official posts); not knowing how to read and write Turkish; and being under thirty years of age.

One particularly significant provision of the 1942 codification was that which concerned the manner in which a desirous citizen had his name added to the lists of certified candidates which were now used. There were three requirements: the citizen must have had his name presented to the Provincial Inspection Committee chairman by "*the political party*"; he must have presented a petition for his candidacy signed by 300 electors of the constituency; and he must have requested, formally and personally as a qualified citizen, that his name be placed on the list (Article 43).

Since there was only one legal political party operating in the national elections of the Turkish Republic up to the election of 1946, the first of these three requirements gave that party, the Republican People's Party, control over the nomination of all candidates for the Grand National Assembly. In point of fact, this was merely the legal expression of a situation which existed in reality at least from 1927 on, with some minor exceptions.

In June 1946, Law No. 4918 superseded the 1942 law just described (No. 4320). Most of the provisions regarding the qualifications of electors and deputies remained the same, but there were two most important alterations. First of all, the electoral system was changed to a direct, single-stage mechanism. The secondary electors were abandoned.[5] Old procedures for the allocation of deputies and voting were retained, but the indirect, intermediate, secondary stage was dropped. Henceforth, the general electorate voted directly for lists of candidates. Those candidates, up to the provincial quota, who received the greatest numbers of votes were elected. Since straight party lists were usually supported, this meant that a sort of "unit rule" actually operated — that one party usually garnered all the deputyships of a province.

The second vital change of the 1946 law was that, in keeping with the recent opening up of political life in Turkey and the legal formation of new political parties, as opposed to the previous dominance of a single party, the old provision covering the nomination of candidates was changed. Under the 1946 law (Article 33), the requirement for a candidate to have his name placed validly on a list was that he must offer *either* nomination by *a* political party *or* a petition signed by 300 electors, as opposed to the mandatory nomination by *the* political party found in the previously discussed 1942 law.[6]

Another major electoral law, that which basically governed the elections to the Ninth and Tenth Assemblies (Law No. 5545), was passed on February 16, 1950, and promulgated on February 21, 1950. It was the basis for the second and third admittedly open and free

---

[5] Actually, this step had been formally accepted by the National Congress of the People's Party as early as 1931, when female voting was also accepted. Cf. Tunaya, *Türkiyede Siyasî Partiler, op. cit.*, p. 569.

[6] As stated in note 1, the texts of all electoral provisions referred to in the previous discussion are to be found in *Türkiyede ve Yabancı Memleketlerde Seçim Mevzuatı, op. cit.*

elections of the period, those of 1950 and 1954 (the first, it will be recalled, was that of 1920, though the election of 1946, with the exception of some skulduggery in Istanbul, seems to have been basically honest in most of the rest of the county).[7]

The major reforms of the 1950 electoral law were in the area of electoral administration. The qualifications demanded of deputies and voters changed little. Article 33 repeated the requirement that a deputy be at least thirty years of age. Article 34 repeated that those who were under legal interdiction, who could not read and write Turkish, who claimed foreign citizenship, who were in the official service of a foreign state, who had committed various serious crimes, and who were already in the public service were barred from being deputies.

Article 35 specified that a candidate on the list of one party could not simultaneously be on the list of another political party for another constituency without his written consent.[8] Similarly, an independent candidate could not be added to the list of any party without his written consent. The general headquarters of the political parties were to announce the party candidates to ensure that the required number in each province was not exceeded. Any qualified citizen could become a candidate by obtaining and presenting an officially certified petition containing the signatures of at least fifty electors together with a written request for candidacy. The county and provincial Election Board chairmen and the chairman and members of the Supreme Election Board could not become candidates, and various governmental and military officials were required to have resigned their official posts two months prior to a regularly scheduled

[7] This is, I must add, a moot point. Cf. Kemal H. Karpat, *Turkey's Politics*, *op. cit.*, pp. 160–165, and the references cited there. However, comparing electoral returns with the known organization of the Democratic Party at the time, I find it difficult to agree with any representations of large-scale electoral fraud outside of Istanbul. Cf. George Harris, *A Political History of Turkey, 1945–1950* (unpublished Ph.D. dissertation submitted to the Department of History, Harvard University, 1956).

[8] The Democratic Party changed this provision for the 1957 election so as to prevent alliances between the opposition parties. Obviously, such alliances, formed by agreeing to put the same candidates on two or more separate party lists, were possible, with the written consent of the candidates, under the old system. On July 7, 1957, prior to the election in late October of that year, the Democrats altered Article 35 by Law No. 6428 to state that a candidate put on the list of one political party could not be put on the list of any other party or even run also as an independent, nor would joint lists by groups of parties be allowed. Two months later, on September 13, 1957, Law 7053 made this even more rigid by applying the same restrictions to those who *applied to parties* for candidacy. Moreover, anyone who had resigned from a political party less than six months before the election could not be a candidate for a different political party (Law 7053). For these and other modifications in the basic 1950 law (No. 5545), see Tunaya and Ülker, *op. cit.*, addendum of 1957.

election or no more than seven days after the announcement of irregularly scheduled elections and at least one month before such elections. A candidate could be nominated from at most two constituencies. If elected from both, he was required to select one, and a by-election was to be held in the other to select a replacement (Article 36).[9]

In Ottoman and Turkish history, then, there were seventeen general elections prior to the *coup d'état* of May 27, 1960. The dates of these elections were: 1876–1877 (two elections), 1908, 1912, 1914, 1919, 1920 (the first G.N.A. election and perhaps not really "general"), 1923, 1927, 1931, 1935, 1939, 1943, 1946, 1950, 1954, and 1957. With regard to the electoral laws under which these elections were conducted, the essential picture can be drawn by indicating that: (1) the 1876–1877 elections were administered under the *Provisional Instructions (Talimatı Muvakkate)*; (2) the elections from 1908 through 1942 were under the basic electoral law passed by the 1908–1912 Ottoman Assembly called the *Law for the Election of Deputies (Intihab-i Mebusan Kanunu)*, with the subsequent modifications which have been described; (3) the 1943, 1946, and 1950 elections were administered according to new and separate electoral laws for each; and (4) the 1954 and 1957 elections took place under the basic 1950 law with the indicated amendments.[10]

Of the more modern elections, however, Dr. Tarık Tunaya maintains that only those of 1908, 1912, 1919, 1931, 1946, 1950, 1954, and 1957 featured at least some party or group competition.[11] To these we should add the election of 1920. The other elections (1914, 1923, 1927, 1935, 1939, 1943) occurred under what was fundamentally a single-party regime, and they had the co-optative aspect previously mentioned, rather than a competitive atmosphere. Moreover,

[9] Tarık Z. Tunaya, *Milletvekilleri Seçimi Kanunu (Law for the Election of National Deputies)*, (Ankara: Ulus Basimevı, 1950); also, Tunaya and Ülker, *op. cit.*, pp. 9–84. Portions of the 1950 Electoral Law are found in English in Eleanor Bisbee, *The New Turks, op. cit.*, App. E, pp. 275–280, though there are some inaccuracies. A complete English text is found in Helen Clarkson Davis, *Constitutions, Electoral Laws, Treaties of States in the Near and Middle East* (Durham: Duke University Press, 2nd ed., 1953), pp. 467–485. The first edition of the same work (1947) contains the English text of the 1942 Electoral Law, pp. 358–369.

[10] Cf. Tunaya and Ülker, *op. cit.*, p. 2; Tunaya, *Türkiyede Siyasî Partiler, op. cit.*, p. 546.

[11] Tunaya and Ülker, *op. cit.*, p. 3, and, Tunaya, *Türkiyede Siyasî Partiler, op. cit.*, p. 547, where he states: "Up to the year 1950, with the exception of the 1946 election, elections [of G.N.A. deputies in the Turkish Republic] always took place under the influence of the People's Republican Party and were featured by the confrontation of the electorate generally with a single set of candidates and by an indifferent public opinion; from this point of view, for a long while elections had no educational function."

the election of 1931 displayed more of the nature of intraparty rivalry than interparty competition, as we have seen. For these reasons, some examination of the relevant political party regulations and practices regarding membership and nominations for deputyship seems also to be required.

Political Party Membership and Candidate Nomination

Because of the chaotic condition of the country and the inchoate state of the Defense of Rights organization, it seems that there was less organizational control over the nominations of candidates in the election of 1920 than in any other election of our period. Though Dankwart Rustow rightly suggests that there was "vigorous and skillful electioneering by the Defense of Rights Societies, often supported by local army commanders," which produced a nationalist majority in the First Assembly, inspection of the backgrounds of the candidates elected suggests the not incompatible fact that very mixed and local forces affected the *nominating* processes in many areas.[12] A most heterogeneous, cantankerous, and divided body resulted.

The second election to the G.N.A. in 1923 was a different affair. After the difficulties of riding herd on the unruly First Assembly, Mustafa Kemal and his close advisors apparently decided that a more united and tractable Assembly was necessary. Difficult years of social reform lay ahead, perhaps involving greater strains than those involved in the negative task of ridding the country of direct foreign presence, which confronted the First Assembly. Greater legislative consensus seemed required for the unpopular measures which were to be forthcoming against established religion and old traditions. As a result, Mustafa Kemal seems personally to have supervised the nomination of candidates for the Defense of Rights Association in 1923 (the Republican People's Party, which was then the newly formed successor party to this organization, was effectively launched after the elections to the Second Assembly). The Gazi also took a most active part in the campaign. Out of 118 listed members of the opposition "Second Group" in the First Assembly, only 3 per cent were reelected, as opposed to 58 per cent reelected from the 197 "First Group" members.[13] Though some intervention in the election by troops and gendarmes was claimed, a Turkish writer summarizes the situation well when he says: "In the country, the elections resulted in the experience that, unconditionally, no organization or group or person would be able to win

[12] Dankwart A. Rustow, "The Army and the Founding of the Turkish Republic," *op. cit.*, p. 544.

[13] Many writers, like Halide Edib Adıvar, Geoffrey Lewis, and others, mistakenly list the "Second Group" as being only forty strong.

out against the 'Chief' [Mustafa Kemal]." The candidates who were proclaimed by the Gazi were all elected.[14]

For most of the period, membership in and nominations by the People's Party were formally regulated by provisions like those accepted at the Party Congress of 1927. Membership in the party was open to every Turkish citizen who was at least eighteen years of age, not of bad repute, had not been convicted of serious crime or dishonorable offense, had not worked against the National Movement, and did not have a "negative political psychology." The prospective member also had entirely to accept Turkish culture and all the goals of the party.[15] Every entering member must have been recommended to the local party unit (*Ocak*, hearth) by two party members, and was required to give a written undertaking that he would abide by the party's regulations and principles.[16]

With regard to candidacies, Article 23 of these *1927 People's Party Regulations* stated that the Council of the General-Presidency (*Umumi Riyaset Divanı*) was to establish the party's candidates for deputyships and manage the electoral campaign. The list of candidates was to be announced by the General-President of the party — its top leader. This Council of the General-Presidency was composed of the General-President, the General-Vice-President (whom the General-President appointed), and the General-Secretary (whom the General-President appointed from the members of the General Executive Committee).[17]

Actually, as these formal arrangements suggest, basic power over

---

[14] Neşet Halil (Atay), *Büyük Meclis ve Inkilap*, *op. cit.*, p. 173. This is a rather valuable little book covering the period 1920–1933. Chapter V, on "Methods of Operation in the Grand National Assembly," gives a most useful brief sketch. Chapter VI contains information on the composition of the Council of Ministers and Council of the Presidency of the Assembly for Assemblies I–III (complete) and IV (partial). Chapter VII, on "Political Life in the Assembly", is also quite useful, as are some of the speeches and statistics in other parts of the work.

For another indication of the Gazi's part in this election, see Cebesoy, *Gl. Ali Fuat Cebesoy'un Siyasî Hatıraları, op. cit.*, pp. 316–319.

The claim of the use of force against the adherents of the "Second Group" in the 1923 election is made, for example, by M. Sadık Yiğitbaş in his book *Kiği* (the name of a town and county in the East), (Istanbul: Cemal Azmi Matbaası, 1950), where he describes the supposed experiences of the "Second Group" leader, Hüseyin Avni (Ulaş), a favorite son of Kiği: "Actually, the election began. But, in this election, which was run with army and gendarmerie forces and was stormy as a whirlwind, those connected with the Second Group, Hüseyin Avni Ulaş and Sülyman Necati Güneri, were unable to be elected deputies." (p. 242).

[15] *Cumhuriyet Halk Fırkası Nizamnamesi, 1927, op cit.*, Article 8, p. 6.
[16] *Ibid.*, Article 9, p. 6.
[17] *Ibid.*, Articles 21 and 23, pp. 12–13.

the designation of party candidates for deputyships lay with the General-President of the party — Mustafa Kemal. This is reflected in the tone of the statement of the Gazi with which he announced the candidate lists in 1927:

> My fellow citizens: I submit to you the list of persons whom I have chosen in the entire country in the name of the Republican People's Party as candidates for deputyship to the Grand National Assembly of Turkey.
>
> I have judged it useful that each citizen have before his eyes the complete list of comrades with whom I propose to work during the entire legislature.
>
> I present to you separately, under my signature, the candidates whom I have chosen on this list for each electoral constituency.[18]

Vakit (Time), the Istanbul daily, went so far as to say, on July 10, 1927, that "... the designation of new candidates for the People's Party is a right which belongs directly to the Gazi, just as there belongs to him also, in conjunction with Ismet Pasha (Inönü) and Saffet Bey (Arıkan) [the R.P.P. General-Vice-President and General-Secretary, respectively], the direction of elections." [19] There seems to be some formal confusion, partly engendered by the vagueness of the regulations themselves, as to whether the triumvirate of the General-President, General-Vice-President, and General-Secretary designated the nominees or whether the General-President did it alone. Certainly, after 1927, the three officials *formally* did the nominating, even though the General-President alone announced the results. In the 1927 election itself — the only case of any uncertainty — *Milliyet,* the semi-official paper, on July 28, 1927, attempted to stifle a rumor that the party's candidates had already been chosen by pointing out that the President (Mustafa Kemal) was in Istanbul, the Vice-President (Ismet Pasha) was in Bursa, and the Secretary (Saffet Bey) was in Ankara. Therefore, the candidates could not be nominated until such time as all three got together.[20] Again, on August 28, 1927, the same paper reported that Saffet Bey, the General-Secretary, was going over the lists of persons desirous of becoming candidates and said that the final selection depended on the three officials.[21]

---

[18] *Bulletin de Presse Hebdomadaire, op. cit.,* VI, No. 109, p. 6. These bulletins are typewritten weekly summaries of the Turkish press, done with great care and consequently quite valuable, prepared by the French Embassy (?) in Istanbul. Since the author does not yet read Turkish in the Arabic script used up to 1928, these reports were doubly useful.

[19] *Ibid.,* No. 101, p. 8.

[20] *Ibid.,* No. 104, pp. 3–4.

[21] *Ibid.,* No. 108, p. 3. Cf. also Alfred Lybyer, "Political Changes in the Moslem World," *American Political Science Review,* XVIII (August 1924), p. 518.

The most accurate assessment is probably that nomination was formally in the hands of the President, Vice-President, and Secretary of the party, but that the President, who alone *announced* the results, was dominant, especially when that person was Mustafa Kemal.[22]

The People's Party regulations on deputy nominations remained essentially the same for the following twenty years. The President of the party made the ultimate decisions. The Vice-President and the General-Secretary also had formal authority. And, in fact, other important officials had significant influence in particular cases. Judged from the social composition of the constituency delegations, local factors were definitely not ignored, as has been shown. But the direction was overwhelmingly central, even to the extent that on occasion completely unsuspecting persons whom the party authorities had decided to co-opt found themselves nominated without consultation.

The People's Party *Regulations,* adopted by the Fourth Party Congress in May 1935, essentially repeated the 1927 provisions which I have discussed. Article 9 of these *Regulations* contains the same membership qualifications as before, save that the requirement of "speaking Turkish regularly" is added. The Council of the General-Presidency retains the same formal composition and selection procedure, that is, the President together with the Vice-President and General-Secretary, who are appointed by the President (Article 24). This Council, as before, decides on the People's Party's candidates for the Grand National Assembly and manages the election. Candidates are to be proclaimed by the General-President, and a proviso is added that the Council may consult the Assembly Group's Executive Committee on the choice of candidates if it so wishes (Article 26). Another article (No. 28) emphasized that "all decisions made by the Council of the General-Presidency are obeyed by party members without condition or reservation." [23]

Up to the end of the Second World War, the main deviation from

---

[22] On this topic it is also interesting to note the following statement by Ali Fuat Cebesoy: "On the 16th of April (1923), in an announcement made by the Presidency of the Defense of Rights Association concerning deputyship candidacies, the name of the People's Party was first brought out. It said that 'Those who aspire to be candidates of the Defense of Rights Group and the People's Party, together with indicating this to the central organization, are at the same time free to place their candidacies in the constituencies which they desire. However, the candidates of the Association and the party, after an examination which will be made by the central organization and consultation with the localities, are designated and then proclaimed by the central organization.'" (Ali Fuat Cebesoy, *op. cit.,* p. 315)

[23] For a detailed summary in English of these *Regulations* (*Cumhuriyet Halk Partisi Tüzüğü, 1935*), (Ankara: Ulus Basimevı, 1935), cf. Webster, *The Turkey of Atatürk, op. cit.,* pp. 173–177.

this system occurred in the nominating procedures used by the People's Party in the 1931 national election. After the disbanding of the Republican Liberal Party (*Serbest Cumhuriyet Fırkası*) in November 1930, Mustafa Kemal and the People's Party leaders decided to open up the party's nominations for deputyship to a certain degree. Names of prospective nominees were solicited from all parts of the country. To fill 287 deputyships, the party received (and published in its official organ, *Hâkimiyeti Milliye*) 1,176 suggested nominees. From these names, then, the responsible leaders presumably selected the 287 final party nominees. Moreover, besides these 287 persons, another thirty deputyships (making the official total of 317) were deliberately left vacant by the party so that the voters could elect whomever they chose. The electorate, unaccustomed to such a process, seems hardly to have made enthusiastic use of its new discretion. It gave votes to independent candidates only in twenty of the thirty cases, and the People's Party ended up by having to fill the vacancies with ten of its own numbers after all.[24]

With the partial democratization of Turkish political life after World War II, we find basic changes in the structure of the People's Party, especially with regard to the designation of G.N.A. candidates. Provisions which suited a *parti unique* proved ill adapted to the position of a mass party competing for popular support in a multi-party environment. However, change took time. The new *Regulations*, adopted by the National Congress of the Republican People's Party (*Cumhuriyet Halk Partisi*) in 1947, basically reiterated the earlier membership provisions. The only real difference from the 1927 stipulations was that the age requirement was now hitched to the Law of Associations of 1938, which demanded that all members of political associations be at least twenty-two years of age, though only eighteen

---

[24] The information comes from the *T.B.M.M. Yıllığı, op. cit., Devre* IV, *Fevkalâde İçtima*, pp. 307 ff. The twenty-two favored provinces from which the thirty independent deputies were to come were:

Adana	1	Burdur	1	Kocaeli	2
Afyon Karahisar	1	Bursa	1	Konya	1
Aksaray	1	Istanbul	4	Kütahya	2
Antalya	1	Izmir	2	Manisa	1
Aydın	1	Isparta	1	Niğde	1
Balıkesir	1	Kastamonu	1	Samsun	2
Bolu	1	Kayseri	2	Sinop	1
				Tekirdağ	1

It is significant to note that these twenty-two provinces were entirely from the western, west central, and Black Sea regions of Turkey. Not one was an eastern province, or east central province — with important Kurdish population or not.

years was required for other associations (Article 3 of Law of Association). However, the procedures for the selection of candidates for deputyships became much more democratic and more involved than heretofore. Article 148 of the new *Regulations* stated that the party's candidates were to be selected by secret vote, 70 per cent of them by the provincial organizations and 30 per cent by the Party Council (*Parti Divanı*). This Party Council consisted (according to Article 62) of forty members elected by the National Congress and the following ex officio members: the G.N.A. President (if the party was not in power, then one of its members from the Assembly President's Council), the Prime Minister (if the party was in power), the Vice-Chairmen of the party's Assembly Group, the General-President, General-Vice-President, and General-Secretary of the party. All members of the *Parti Divanı* did not have to be deputies. The provincially chosen deputies were selected by examining committees as set forth in a directive prepared by the General Executive Committee and approved by the Party Council (Article 148).[25] No new limitations on the characteristics of the prospective deputies were involved in this.

The People's Party *Regulations* of 1950 stayed basically the same as those of 1947, except that the Party Council was reduced to thirty members. But in 1954 further important changes were introduced. Membership provisions were altered in part. The "not in bad repute" stipulation was abandoned, as was the requirement of support for a membership application from two party members of at least one year's standing. As we have observed, in a competitive, multi-party system, soliciting new members, this characteristic of the old elite party had become anachronistic. Now, merely a written pledge to accept the party's aims, program, and regulations and a verbal promise to carry out one's duties as a party member were sufficient.

With regard to candidate designation, the previous arrangement of 70 per cent provincial and 30 per cent central now became 100 per cent provincial. Party candidates, according to Article 55, were totally selected by examining committees formed from party members in their respective provinces, the examining committees for each province designating that province's People's Party candidates.[26] An important factor in this further transfer of formal power from the central to the provincial organizations was the confiscation by the Democratic Party government in 1953 of all the property (especially the central records, resources, funds, and printing plant) of the People's Party. Having less to offer — less power of purse, printing, and services — the influence of the central organization declined, and

---

[25] This material is from the *C.H.P. Program ve Tüzüğü, 1947, op. cit.*
[26] See *C.H.P. Tüzüğü, 1954* (Ankara: Güzel Istanbul Matbaası, 1954).

the provincial organizations have rather jealously guarded their new prerogatives ever since, even though central authority has increased somewhat from the nadir of 1954–1955.

The provincial examining committees for the selection of provincial candidates for deputyships were constituted, after 1954, according to a directive prepared by the central organization of the party and approved by the National Congress.[27] The essential procedure is that committees of party officials, notables, and prominent supporters are convened in the province as a whole and in its counties (*kaza* or *ilçe*). These committees vote secretly on the prospective candidates, who are listed and described through brief biographies provided by the General-Secretary. The voting results of all committees are then tabulated, with equal weight, and the prospective candidates with the most votes, in accordance with the number of deputyships available to the province, become the party's nominees in that province. Prospective candidates cannot appear before or be present at the meetings of these examining committees. The General Executive Committee of the party can propose candidates for consideration along with the others by the provincial examining committees, but that is all. The local and provincial units also propose candidates for consideration. The final list of all party candidates for all provinces is formally announced by the General-President of the party.

The *Regulations* of the other major political party in Turkey in the last three Assemblies, the Democratic Party, were very similar to those of the People's Party — rather naturally, since they influenced each other in this respect. Article 3 of the party's *1951 Regulations* specified that every male and female Turk who was not found in movements against the National Struggle, who did not support antidemocratic principles or aim at the destruction of Turkish unity and independence, who had not been convicted of major crime or dishonor, who was not of bad repute or had not lost his civil rights, who accepted Turkish culture and the party's principles, who had not previously been expelled from the party, and who had attained the age (twenty-two) required by the Law of Association, was eligible to join the party. The support of two party members and written acceptance of the party's program and regulations were necessary (Article 4).

All candidates for deputyship had to have been party members for at least six months, excepting eligible government officials (Article 96). Those requesting candidacy were required to notify the General or Provincial Executive Committee of the party, which immediately was

---

[27] This directive is the *C.H.P. Milletvekilliği Adaylık Yönetmeliği* (*Republican People's Party Deputyship Candidacy Directive*), in *C.H.P. 'nin el Kitabı* (*Republican People's Party Handbook*), op. cit., pp. 84–96.

to give this information to the examining committees. Provincial examining committees, similar to those of the People's Party but narrower in their representation of party officials and leaders, nominated 80 per cent of all candidates, and the party's General Executive Committee added the other 20 per cent as "central candidates," though all nominees ran in particular provinces, of course (Article 92). The final, official party lists were announced by the General Executive Committee.[28]

---

[28] Cf. *Demokrat Parti Tüzük ve Programı, 1951,* op. cit.

APPENDIX B

Official Number of Deputyships and Actual Number of Deputies by Region and Province

1. REGION:[a]

Region	ASSEMBLY										
	I	II	III	IV	V	VI	VII	VIII	IX	X	XI
I. North Central	62–63	41–48	44–46	47–55	59–70	62–70	65–71	67–71	69–70	80–80	88–83
II. Aegean	63–65	45–52	55–57	55–60	67–72	70–77	74–80	74–77	79–79	87–86	95–94
III. Marmara	32–30	33–44	42–43	43–45	48–54	52–57	61–69	60–69	65–65	72–71	86–84
IV. Mediterranean	43–48	24–25	26–29	25–26	32–37	39–43	42–45	43–44	45–45	52–52	62–62
V. Northeast	31–32	15–18	20–21	20–20	32–38	29–34	29–29	32–36	33–33	36–36	41–41
VI. Southeast	71–74	32–40	22–24	19–22	32–35	34–38	33–35	34–40	35–36	40–40	52–52
VII. Black Sea	44–48	45–50	52–55	52–57	58–62	66–72	70–75	73–77	75–79	80–79	84–84
VIII. East Central	43–46	25–28	26–28	26–29	34–37	40–41	42–45	42–45	43–44	48–48	49–49
IX. South Central	31–31	27–28	29–32	30–34	37–39	37–38	39–43	40–40	43–43	46–45	53–53
Deputyships	420–	287–	316–	317–	399–	429–	455–	465–	487–	541–	610–
Deputies	437	333	335[b]	348	444	470	492	499	494	537	602

[a] The map in the frontispiece indicates the boundaries of the nine regions. The official number of deputyships appears in each cell of the table, followed by a dash and the actual number of deputies.
[b] The true total of different individuals was 333, since two men were each elected twice — once each from two different constituencies for each man.

2. PROVINCE

Region	Province	I	II	III	IV	V	VI	VII	VIII	IX	X	XI	Code
IV	1. Adana (Seyhan)	5-7	3-3	4-4	4-4	—	—	—	—	—	—	16-16	AD
VI	2. Adıyaman (Malatya)	—	—	—	—	—	—	—	—	—	—	5-5	AI
IX	3. Afyon Karahisar (Karahisarı Sahip)	—	6-6	6-6	6-7	7-7	7-8	8-8	8-8	9-9	9-9	10-10	AF
V	4. Ağrı (Bayazıt)	—	—	—	—	—	3-4	3-3	3-3	3-3	4-4	5-5	AG
IX	5. Aksaray (Niğde)	—	3-3	3-3	4-4	—	—	—	—	—	—	—	AK
VIII	6. Amasya	7-7	3-4	3-3	3-3	3-3	3-3	4-4	4-4	4-4	5-5	6-6	AM
I	7. Ankara	9-9	6-7	8-8	9-11	13-15	14-16	15-15	17-18	18-18	21-21	27-22	AN
IV	8. Antalya	6-6	4-4	5-5	5-5	7-8	7-8	7-8	7-7	7-7	8-8	9-9	AT
V	9. Ardahan (Kars) (Çoruh)	2-2	2-3	—	—	—	—	—	—	—	—	—	AR
V	10. Artvin (Çoruh)	—	1-1	2-2	2-2	—	—	—	—	—	—	5-5	AV
II	11. Aydın	8-7	4-6	5-5	5-6	6-7	7-8	7-7	7-8	7-7	9-8	11-10	AY
II	12. Balkesir (Karesi)	—	—	10-10	10-10	12-12	12-12	13-13	13-14	13-13	14-14	15-15	BK
V	13. Batum	5-5	—	—	—	—	—	—	—	—	—	—	BM
V	14. Bayazıt (Ağrı)	5-5	2-2	3-3	3-3	3-4	—	—	—	—	—	—	BY
II	15. Biga (Çanakkale)	5-3	3-3	—	—	—	—	—	—	—	—	—	BG
I	16. Bilecik (Ertuğrul)	—	—	3-4	3-3	3-3	3-5	4-5	3-3	4-4	4-4	4-4	BC
VI	17. Bingöl (Genç) (Tunceli)	—	1-2	3-3	—	—	2-2	2-2	2-2	2-2	3-3	3-3	BN
VI	18. Bitlis	7-7	5-5	5-6	6-6	7-10	7-8	7-8	2-3	2-3	2-2	3-3	BT
I	19. Bolu	8-8	4-4	—	—	—	—	—	7-8	7-7	8-8	8-8	BL
I	20. Bozok (Yozgat)	—	2-2	2-2	2-2	3-4	3-3	3-4	—	—	—	—	BZ
II	21. Burdur	8-8	5-6	9-9	9-9	11-12	11-12	12-12	3-3	3-3	4-4	4-4	BD
III	22. Bursa	7-7	3-3	—	—	—	—	—	12-13	12-12	14-13	15-14	BS
VII	23. Canık	6-6	—	—	—	—	—	—	—	—	—	—	CN
IV	24. Cebelibereket (Kozan, Adana)	3-3	2-2	3-5	3-3	—	—	—	—	—	—	—	CB

APPENDIX B   439

440 APPENDIX B

| Region | Province | \multicolumn{11}{c}{Assembly} | Code |
		I	II	III	IV	V	VI	VII	VIII	IX	X	XI	
II	25. Çanakkale (Biga) (Gelibolu)	—	—	4-4	4-5	5-5	6-6	6-6	6-6	8-8	8-8	8-8	ÇK
I	26. Çankırı (Kangırı)	7-7	4-4	4-4	4-4	5-8	5-6	5-6	5-5	5-5	6-6	6-6	ÇN
III	27. Çatalca (Istanbul)	—	1-1	—	—	—	—	—	—	—	5-5	—	ÇT
V	28. Çoruh (Artvin)	—	—	—	—	8-10	4-4	4-4	5-5	5-5	5-5	—	ÇH
I	29. Çorum	7-7	5-6	5-5	6-6	7-7	8-8	8-9	8-8	8-8	9-9	10-10	ÇM
II	30. Denizli	6-6	5-5	6-6	6-6	8-8	7-9	8-10	8-8	8-8	9-9	9-9	DZ
VIII	31. Dersim (Tunceli)	6-6	2-2	—	—	—	—	—	—	7-7	—	—	DM
VI	32. Diyarbakır	7-7	5-7	4-6	4-4	7-8	7-8	6-6	7-7	7-7	8-8	9-9	DY
III	33. Edirne	5-5	3-3	4-4	4-4	4-4	5-6	5-5	5-5	5-5	6-6	6-6	ED
VIII	34. Elazığ (Elaziz)	7-7	5-6	5-7	5-7	5-6	5-5	5-5	5-5	5-5	5-5	6-6	EL
VI	35. Ergani (Diyarbakır) (Elaziz)	8-11	3-3	—	—	—	—	—	—	—	—	—	EG
I	36. Ertuğrul (Bilecik)	5-5	5-5	—	—	—	—	—	—	—	—	—	ET
V	37. Erzincan	5-5	2-3	3-3	3-3	4-4	5-7	5-5	5-7	5-5	5-5	6-6	EC
V	38. Erzurum	9-10	6-7	7-7	7-7	10-12	9-9	9-9	10-11	10-10	12-12	13-13	ER
I	39. Eskişehir	7-7	3-4	4-4	4-4	5-5	5-5	5-5	6-7	6-7	7-7	8-8	ES
IV	40. Gaziantep	6-6	5-5	6-6	4-5	7-10	7-7	8-8	7-7	7-7	8-8	10-10	GZ
II	41. Gelibolu (Çanakkale)	1-1	1-1	—	—	—	—	—	—	—	—	—	GL
VI	42. Genç (Bingöl)	6-6	1-2	—	—	—	—	—	—	—	—	—	GÇ
VII	43. Giresun (Şarkı Karahisar)	—	5-5	5-5	5-5	7-7	7-7	8-9	8-9	8-8	8-8	8-8	GR
VII	44. Gümüşane	6-6	3-4	4-5	3-3	5-5	5-5	5-5	6-6	6-7	6-6	6-6	GM
VI	45. Hakkâri	6-6	2-2	1-1	1-1	—	1-1	1-1	1-1	1-1	1-1	1-1	HK
IV	46. Hatay	—	—	—	—	—	5-5	6-6	6-6	6-6	8-8	9-9	HT
IV	47. İçel (Mersin)	6-6	2-2	2-2	2-2	5-5	6-7	7-8	7-8	7-7	8-8	9-9	IÇ
II	48. Isparta	6-6	3-3	4-4	4-4	4-4	4-5	5-5	5-5	5-5	5-5	5-5	IP
III	49. Istanbul	13-12	15-23	16-17	16-18	17-20	17-19	23-28	23-30	27-29	29-29	39-39	IS
II	50. Izmir	8-8	9-11	11-12	11-12	13-14	14-15	15-17	16-16	17-17	20-20	22-22	IZ

APPENDIX B   441

Region	Province	\multicolumn{11}{c}{ASSEMBLY}	Code
		I	II	III	IV	V	VI	VII	VIII	IX	X	XI	
III	51. İzmit (Kocaeli)	7-6	—	—	—	—	—	—	—	—	—	—	IT
IX	52. Karahisarı Sahip (Afyon Karahisar)	8-8	—	—	—	—	—	—	—	—	—	—	KS
II	53. Karesi (Balıkesir)	7-6	8-8	—	—	—	—	—	—	—	—	—	KA
V	54. Kars	3-3	2-2	5-6	5-5	7-8	8-10	8-8	9-10	10-10	10-10	12-12	KR
VII	55. Kastamonu	8-8	7-8	6-6	7-8	9-9	9-11	9-9	9-11	10-11	10-10	10-10	KT
IX	56. Kayseri	7-7	4-5	5-6	5-5	8-10	8-8	9-10	9-9	9-9	10-9	11-11	KY
III	57. Kırklareli	—	2-3	3-3	3-3	3-3	5-5	5-5	5-5	5-5	5-5	6-6	KK
I	58. Kırşehir	6-7	3-5	3-3	3-3	4-4	4-5	4-4	4-4	4-4	5-5	4-4	KŞ
III	59. Kocaeli (İzmit) (Sakarya: 12/1/54)	—	5-6	7-7	7-7	8-10	9-10	10-13	10-10	11-11	12-12	6-5	KC
IX	60. Konya	10-10	10-10	11-13	11-14	15-15	15-15	15-17	16-16	17-17	19-19	21-21	KN
IV	61. Kozan (Adana) (Seyhan)	5-5	2-2	4-5	4-4	5-6	5-5	5-5	6-6	7-7	7-7	9-9	KZ
I	62. Kütahya (Uşak: 7/5/53)	6-6	6-8	7-7	7-12	9-11	9-10	10-12	7-10	7-7	7-7	8-8	KÜ
VII	63. Lazistan (Rize)	6-6	—	—	—	—	—	—	—	—	—	—	LZ
VIII	64. Malatya (Adıyaman: 12/1/54)	10-11	5-5	6-6	6-6	9-9	10-10	11-11	11-12	11-11	12-12	9-9	ML
II	65. Manisa (Saruhan)	—	—	9-10	9-11	11-12	12-13	12-12	11-12	12-12	12-12	14-14	MN
IV	66. Maraş	6-8	4-5	4-5	4-4	5-6	5-5	5-5	6-6	7-7	7-7	9-9	MŞ
VI	67. Mardin	6-6	5-6	5-5	3-3	7-7	7-8	7-7	7-10	7-7	7-7	8-8	MD
II	68. Menteşe (Muğla)	6-11	3-3	—	—	—	—	—	—	—	—	—	MT
IV	69. Mersin (İçel)	6-7	2-2	2-2	3-3	—	—	—	—	—	—	—	MR
II	70. Muğla (Menteşe)	—	—	4-4	4-4	5-6	5-6	5-6	5-5	6-6	6-6	7-7	MG
VI	71. Muş	7-7	3-3	—	3-4	4-4	2-2	2-2	2-3	2-2	3-3	4-4	MU
IX	72. Nevşehir	—	—	—	—	—	—	—	—	—	—	4-4	NV
IX	73. Niğde (Nevşehir: 12/1/54)	6-6	4-4	4-4	4-4	7-7	7-7	7-8	7-7	8-8	8-8	7-7	NG
V	74. Olti (Erzurum)	2-2	—	—	—	—	—	—	—	—	—	—	OL

APPENDIX B

Region	Province	\	\	\	\	\	ASSEMBLY \	\	\	\	\	\	Code
		I	II	III	IV	V	VI	VII	VIII	IX	X	XI	
VII	75. Ordu (Canik)	—	5-5	5-6	5-6	7-7	8-8	8-8	8-9	8-8	9-9	10-10	OR
VII	76. Rize (Lazistan) (Çoruh)	—	5-6	6-6	6-6	—	6-6	6-6	6-6	6-6	6-6	6-6	RZ
III	77. Sakarya (İzmit, Kocaeli)	—	—	—	—	—	—	—	—	—	—	8-8	SY
VII	78. Samsun (Canik)	—	—	6-6	6-7	8-9	8-9	9-11	10-10	10-10	12-12	14-14	SM
II	79. Saruhan (Manisa)	8-9	7-10	—	—	—	—	9-10	10-10	11-11	13-13	—	SR
IV	80. Seyhan (Adana)	—	—	—	—	8-8	9-11	9-10	10-10	11-11	13-13	—	SH
VI	81. Siirt	6-6	2-2	2-2	2-2	4-6	4-5	4-5	4-4	4-4	4-4	5-5	SI
VII	82. Sinop	6-6	3-4	3-3	4-4	5-6	5-5	5-5	5-5	5-6	6-6	6-6	SP
VIII	83. Sivas	8-8	6-7	7-7	7-7	10-11	11-11	12-15	12-12	12-13	14-14	15-15	SV
VI	84. Siverek (Urfa)	6-6	3-4	—	—	—	—	—	—	—	—	—	SK
VII	85. Şarkı Karahisarı (Şebin Karahisar) (Giresun)	5-5	3-4	3-3	3-3	—	—	—	—	—	—	—	ŞK
III	86. Tekirdağ (Tekfürdağı)	—	2-2	3-3	4-4	5-5	5-5	6-6	5-6	5-5	6-6	6-6	TE
VIII	87. Tokat	5-7	4-4	5-5	5-6	7-8	8-9	8-8	8-10	9-9	9-9	10-10	TO
VII	88. Trabzon	7-11	7-7	8-8	7-9	9-9	10-11	11-11	12-12	12-12	12-12	12-12	TB
VIII	89. Tunceli (Dersim)	—	—	—	—	—	3-3	2-2	2-2	2-2	3-3	3-3	TU
VI	90. Urfa	5-5	4-6	5-5	4-6	7-7	6-7	6-6	6-7	7-7	8-8	9-9	UF
I	91. Uşak (Kütahya: 7/15/53)	—	—	—	—	—	—	—	—	—	4-4	4-4	Uş
VI	92. Van	7-7	3-3	2-2	2-2	3-3	3-3	3-4	3-3	3-3	4-4	5-5	VN
I	93. Yozgat (Bozok)	7-7	—	5-5	5-6	6-7	7-7	7-7	7-8	7-7	8-8	9-9	YZ
VII	94. Zonguldak	—	4-4	6-7	6-6	8-10	8-10	9-11	9-9	10-11	11-10	12-12	ZG
	Total Provinces	66	72	63	63	57	63	63	63	63	64	67	
	Total Deputyships	420	287	316	317	399	429	455	465	487	541	610	
	Total Deputies	437	333	333[a] (335)	348	444	470	492	499	494	537	602	

[a] Mehmet Sabri (Toprak) represented Manisa and then Cebelibereket. Mithat represented Diyarbakır and then Manisa. Thus the true total was 333 persons.

APPENDIX C

Analysis of Judges' Ratings of Assembly Posts and Committees: 1920-1957

1. POSTS:
    a. Range of means of rank order correlation coefficients of all judges. The rank order of each individual judge's ratings was compared with the rank order of the average scores of all judges. Range = .300 (.648 to .948).
    b. Mean rank order correlation coefficient for all judges and the entire period: .847, standard deviation = .051.
    c. Mean rank order correlation coefficient and standard deviation for each subperiod:

    I. (Period 1920–1923) $r = .824$, $s = .109$ $N = 31$
    II. (Period 1923–1939) $r = .858$, $s = .041$ $N = 37$
    III. (Period 1939–1950) $r = .871$, $s = .061$ $N = 43$
    IV. (Period 1950–1957) $r = .833$, $s = .086$ $N = 49$

2. COMMITTEES:
    a. Range of means of rank order correlation coefficients of all judges. The rank order of each individual judge's ratings was compared with the rank order of the average scores of all judges. Range = .168 (.682 to .850).
    b. Mean rank order correlation coefficient for all judges and the entire period: .783, standard deviation = .045.
    c. Mean rank order correlation coefficient and standard deviation for each subperiod:

    I. (Period 1920–1923) $r = .743$, $s = .052$ $N = 24$
    II. (Period 1923–1939) $r = .802$, $s = .056$ $N = 17$

III. (Period 1939–1950) $r = .797$, $s = .077$ $N = 20$
IV. (Period 1950–1957) $r = .785$, $s = .083$ $N = 20$

3. ACTUAL RANK ORDER CORRELATION COEFFICIENTS FOR EACH JUDGE:

	Posts					Committees				
Judges	I	II	III	IV	Mean	I	II	III	IV	Mean
#1	.648	.880	.909	.850	.822	.693	.858	.882	—	.881
#2	.649	.818	.765	.773	.751	.697	.822	.808	.870	.799
#3	.856	.873	.937	.929	.899	.796	—	—	.742	.769
#4	.948	.888	.924	.707	.867	.714	.871	.680	.709	.744
#5	.908	.935	.905	.937	.921	.780	.816	.916	.887	.850
#6	.813	.810	.790	.885	.825	.808	.721	.826	.834	.797
#7	.849	.830	.896	—	.858	.790	.804	.753	—	.782
#8	.920	.826	.785	.706	.809	.666	.720	.700	.642	.682
#9	—	—	.932	.873	.902	—	—	.814	.809	.812
$N =$	(31)	(37)	(43)	(49)		(24)	(17)	(20)	(20)	

APPENDIX D

Committee Rankings

I. PERIOD 1920–1923   *Score* *Index*

		Score	Index
Müdafaai Milliye	National Defense	84	
Muvazenei Maliye	Budget	83	1.0
Kanunu Esasi	Fundamental Law (Constitution)	79	
Adliye	Justice	73	
Dahiliye	Interior	70	.8
Hariciye	Foreign Affairs	68	
Encümeni Mahsus	Special Committee	59	
Şeriye ve Evkaf	Religious Law and Pious Foundations	59	
Kavanini Maliye	Finance	58	.6
Divanı Haysiyet	Discipline	56	
Maarif	Education	53	
Nizamnamei Dahilî	Internal (Assembly) Regulations	53	
Lâyiha	Bills	49	
Iktisat	Economy	48	
Irşat	Public Morality	48	
Nafia	Public Works	46	
Defteri Hakanî	Civil List	45	.4
Sıhhiye ve Muaveneti Içtimaiye	Health and Social Welfare	44	
Tetkiki Mezabıt Birinci	Minutes	43	
Posta ve Telgraf	Post and Telegraph	42	
Tetkiki Hesabat	Accounts	41	
Istida	Petitions	41	
Orman ve Maadin	Forests and Minerals	40	
Kütüpane	Library	31	.2

Mean score = 55, range = 53.   24 Committees.   Median score = 51.

APPENDIX D

Score Index

II. PERIOD 1923–1939

		Score	Index
Bütçe	Budget	88	1.0
Adliye	Justice	81	
Dahiliye	Interior	80	
Hariciye	Foreign Affairs	77	.8
Millî Müdafaa	National Defense	76	
Maarif	Education	73	
Maliye	Finance	70	
Teşkilatı Esasiye	Constitution	66	
Arzuhal	Petitions	65	
Nafia	Public Works	63	.6
Sıhhiye ve Içtimai Muavenet	Health and Social Welfare	61	
Ziraat	Agriculture	60	
Iktisat	Economy	57	
Divanı Muhasebat	Accounts	54	.4
Gümrük ve Inhisarlar	Customs and Monopolies	53	
Meclis Hesaplarının Tetkiki	Assembly Accounts	46	
Meclis Kütüphanesi	Library	41	.2

Mean score = 65, range = 47. 17 Committees. Median score = 65.

III. PERIOD 1939–1950

		Score	Index
Bütçe	Budget	93	1.0
Adalet	Justice	82	
Dışişleri	Foreign Affairs	79	
Millî Savunma	National Defense	78	.8
Içişleri	Interior	75	
Anayasa	Constitution	71	
Millî Eğitim	Education	69	
Dilekçe	Petitions	66	
Maliye	Finance	65	
Ekonomi	Economy	63	
Bayındırlık	Public Works	62	.6
Çalışma	Labor	60	
Sağlık ve Sosyal Yardım	Health and Social Welfare	59	
Tarım	Agriculture	58	

		Score	Index
Ulaştırma	Transport and Communications	54	
Ticaret	Trade	51	.4
Gümrük ve Tekel	Customs and Monopolies	51	
Sayıştay	Accounts	47	
Meclis Hesaplarını Inceleme	Assembly Accounts	38	.2
Meclis Kitaplığı	Library	31	

Mean score = 65, range = 62. 20 Committees. Median score = 62.5.

IV. PERIOD 1950–1957[a]

		Score	Index
Bütçe	Budget	93	1.0
Adliye	Justice	79	
Anayasa	Constitution	68	
Dilekçe	Petitions	68	
Dahiliye	Interior	67	.8
Maliye	Finance	66	
Maarif	Education	66	
Millî Müdafaa	National Defense	64	
Hariciye	Foreign Affairs	63	
Bayındırlık	Works	59	
Ziraat	Agriculture	59	
Çalışma	Labor	58	.6
Ticaret	Trade	57	
Ekonomi	Economy	56	
Ulaştırma	Transport and Communications	52	
Gümrük ve Tekel	Customs and Monopolies	51	.4
Sayıştay	Accounts	44	
Meclis Hesaplarını Inceleme	Assembly Accounts	39	.2
Meclis Kitaplığı	Library	37	

Mean score = 60, range = 56. 20 Committees. Median score = 61.

[a] The Health and Social Welfare Committee was omitted, but rated .6.

APPENDIX E

The Number of Times Selected Prominent Deputies Spoke on the Floor of the Parliament during the First Assembly, by Faction

(Based on a 10 per cent sample of the pages of the *Parliamentary Debates* for the period from April 23, 1920, to April 4, 1922.) [a]

I. NOT SPEAKING:

A. First Group: Bekir Sami, Halil Hulki (Aydın), Mustafa Fehmi (Gerçeker), Ali (Çetinkaya), Mehmet (Şahin), Ibrahim Süreyya (Yiğit), Tahsin (Uzer), Şakir (Kınacı), Ziya (Esen), Hamdi (Ülkümen), Ali Saip (Ursavaş), Ali (Kılıç), Kâzım Karabekir, Ali Fuat (Cebesoy), Cevat Abbas (Gürer).

B. Second Group: (No *prominent* figures not speaking.)

C. Unaffiliated (but excluding the totally inactive): Fahrettin (Altay), Ziyaettin (Başara), Eyüp Sabri (Akgöl), Hakkı Behiç (Behiç-Beyiç).

[a] Some of the deputies listed held Assembly offices and were called upon to speak as part of their official duties. For example, Mustafa Kemal was President of the Assembly and entered into the discussions as presiding officer. All such official comments have been excluded from the present tabulation. Only personal utterances as an individual deputy have been considered.

In computations of this sort one encounters the problem of interruptions and of recording the rapid cross-fire of parliamentary debate. If a deputy was speaking, then was clearly interrupted, and then resumed speaking again after the interruption, I have counted this as one speaking turn for that deputy. On the other hand, if a deputy made a speech, sat down, was met with counter-arguments, and then spoke again to answer those arguments, I have classed such a situation as two speaking turns for that deputy. Naturally, there were a few situations in which a rather arbitrary decision was necessary to categorize a verbal exchange.

APPENDIX E 449

II. SPEAKING FROM ONE TO TWENTY TIMES:

A. First Group: Emin (Sazak), Mustafa (Cantekin), Faik (Öztrak), Zamir (Arıkoğlu), Rauf (Orbay), Kâzım (Özalp), Celâl Nuri (Ileri), Abdülhalim Çelebi.

B. Second Group: Neşet (Akkor), Süleyman Necati (Güneri), Mehmet Akif (Ersoy), Cemal (Mersinli).

C. Unaffiliated: (No prominent figures.)

III. SPEAKING TWENTY OR MORE TIMES (emphasis is on those speaking more than one hundred times):

A. First Group: Ahmet Ferit (Tek) — 637, Tunalı Hilmi — 459, Mehmet Vehbi — 426, Mustafa Kemal (Atatürk) — 417, Refik Şevket (Ince) — 384, Sırrı (Içöz) — 333, Hasan Fehmi (Ataç) — 230, Mazhar Müfit (Kansu) — 219, Hamdullah Suphi (Tanrıöver) — 204, Hasan (Saka) — 179, Mahmut Celâl (Bayar) — 172, Yahya Galip (Kargı) — 157, Refik (Koraltan) — 151, Besim (Atalay) — 135, Fevzi (Çakmak) — 97, Ismet (Inönü) — 80, Ali Fethi (Okyar) — 50.

B. Second Group: Mehmet Şükrü — 395, Hasan Basri (Çantay) — 363, Müfit — 327, Hamdi Namık — 298, Hüseyin Avni (Ulaş) — 239, Abdülkadir Kemali (Öğütçü) — 225, Ismail Suphi (Soysallıoğlu?) — 209, Ali Şükrü — 200, Operatör Emin — 178, Mehmet Salih — 164, Ömer Lutfi (Yasan) — 162, Ömer Lutfi (Argeşo) — 162, Nafiz — 153, Hakkı Hami — 146, Celalettin Arif — 131.

C. Unaffiliated: Ömer Vehbi — 209, Yusuf Izzet — 59, Ismail Fazıl — 50, Refet (Bele) — 44.

Select Bibliography

Books and Pamphlets

Abadan, Yavuz. *Inkilâp Tarihine Giriş (Introduction to the History of the Revolution)*. Ankara: Ajans Türk Matbaası, 1960.
Adıvar, Halide Edib. *Ateşten Gömlek (Shirt of Flame)*. Istanbul: Ahmet Halit Yaşaroğlu, 1957.
———. *The Clown and His Daughter*. London: George Allen & Unwin, 1935.
———. *Conflict of East and West in Turkey*. Lahore: Ashraf, 1935.
———. *Memoirs of Halidé Edib*. New York: Century, 1926.
———. *Shirt of Flame*. New York: Duffield, 1924.
———. *Sinekli Bakkal* (literally, *The Fly-Filled Grocery*; though actually appearing as *The Clown and His Daughter*). Istanbul: Ahmet Halit Yaşaroğlu, 1957.
———. *Turkey Faces West*. New Haven: Yale University Press, 1930.
———. *Turkish Ordeal*. New York: Century, 1928.
Afetinan. *Atatürk Hakkında Hâtıralar Ve Belgeler (Reminiscences and Documents Concerning Atatürk)*. Ankara: Türk Tarih Kurumu Basımevi, 1959.
———. *Kemâl Atatürk'ü Anarken (Recalling Kemal Atatürk)*. Ankara: Güzel Sanatlar Matbaası, 1956.
Ağaoğlu, Ahmet. *Serbest Fırka Hatıraları (Liberal Party Memories)*. Istanbul: Nebioğlu Yayınları, 1950.
Ağaoğlu, Samet. *Babamın Arkadaşları (Friends of My Father)*. Istanbul: Nebioğlu Yayınevi, 1958.
Akkerman, Naki Cevat. *Demokrasi ve Türkiye'de Siyasî Partiler Hakkında Kisa Notlar (Brief Notes on Democracy and Political Parties in Turkey)*. Ankara: Ulus Basımevi, 1950.

Aksoy, Muammer. *Partizan Radyo ve D.P. (Partisan Radio and the D.P.).* Forum Yayınları Seri I; Ankara: Ayyıldız Matbaası, 1960.
Allen, Henry Elisha. *The Turkish Transformation: A Study in Social and Religious Development.* Chicago: University of Chicago Press, 1935.
Almond, Gabriel. *Plutocracy and Politics in New York City.* Unpublished Ph.D. dissertation, Political Science Department, University of Chicago, 1938.
Altın, Mehmet. *Türkiye'de Siyasî Hareketleri Ve Sosyal Yapı (Political Movements and Social Structure in Turkey).* Ankara: Doğus Ltd. Şirketi Matbaası, 1961.
Amca, Hasan. *Doğmayan Hürriyet (Freedom Unborn).* Istanbul: Akim Yayınları, 1958.
Arar, Asım. *Son Günlerinde Atatürk (The Last Days of Atatürk).* Istanbul: Selek Yayınları, 1958.
Arıburnu, Kemal. *Millî Mücadelede Istanbul Mitingleri (Istanbul Meetings in the National Struggle).* Ankara: Yeni Matbaa, 1951.
Arık, Remzi Oğuz. *Türk Inkilâbı Milliyetçiliğimiz (Our Nationalism in the Turkish Revolution).* Ankara: Ayyıldız Matbaası, 1958.
Armaoğlu, Fahir, and Birkhead, Guthrie S. *Graduates of the Faculty of Political Sciences, University of Ankara, 1946-1955.* Ankara: Public Administration Institute for Turkey and the Middle East, 1957 — English.
Armstrong, Harold C. *Grey Wolf.* London: Arthur Barker, 1932.
———. *Turkey in Travail.* London: John Lane, 1925.
Armstrong, John A. *The Soviet Bureaucratic Elite: A Case Study of the Ukrainian Apparatus.* New York: Praeger, 1959.
Arnold, Thomas W. *The Caliphate.* Oxford: Oxford University Press, 1924.
Aşkun, Vehbi Cem. *Sivas Kongresi (The Sivas Congress).* Sivas: Kâmil Matbaası, 1945.
Atatürk, Mustafa Kemal. *Atatürk'ün Askerliğe Dair Eserleri (Atatürk's Works on Military Matters).* Ankara: Doğuş Ltd. Sirketi Matbaası, 1959.
———. *Atatürk'ün Söylev Ve Demeçleri (Atatürk's Sayings and Speeches).* Vol. I: *T.B.M. Meclisinde ve C.H.P. Kurultaylarında (1919-1938).* Istanbul: Maarif Matbaası, 1945. Vol. II: *(1906-1938).* Ankara: Türk Tarih Kurumu Basımevi, 1952. Vol. III: *(1918-1937).* Ankara: Türk Tarih Kurumu Basımevi, 1954.
———. *Nutuk (Speech).* Istanbul: Devlet Basımevi, 1938.
———. *Nutuk (Speech).* Vol. I: *1919.* Vol. II: *1920-1927.* Vol. III: *Vesikalar (Documents).* Istanbul: Milli Egitim Basımevi, 1950-1961.
———. *A Speech Delivered by Ghazi Mustapha Kemal.* Leipzig: K. F. Koehler, 1929.
———. *Zâbit Ve Kumandan Ile Hasbıhal (Chat with the Officer and Commander).* Ankara: Türk Tarih Kurumu Basımevi, 1956.

"Atatürk," *Islâm Ansiklopedisi*. 10 Cuz. Istanbul: Millî Eğitim Basımevi, 1949.
Atay, Falih Rıfkı. *Bana Atatürk'ün Anlatiklari (What Atatürk Explained to Me)*. Istanbul: Sel Yayınları, 1955.
———. *Çankaya: Atatürk Devri Hatıralari (Çankaya: Memories of the Atatürk Era)*. Vol. 2. Istanbul: Dünya Yayınları, n.d.
———. *19 Mayıs (May 19)*. Ankara: Ulus Basımevi, 1944.
Bailey, F. E. *British Policy and the Turkish Reform Movement*. Cambridge, Mass.: Harvard University Press, 1942.
Barss, Lawrence W. *Political Change and Economic Growth: A Methodology Applied to Japan, Turkey and India*. Cambridge, Mass.: M.I.T. Center for International Studies, 1961. Mimeographed.
Başar, Ahmed Hamdi. *Atatürk'le Üç Ay ve 1930'dan Sonra Türkiye (Three Months with Atatürk and Turkey after 1930)*. Istanbul: Tan Matbaası, 1945.
———. *Yaşadığımız Devrin Içyüzü (The Inside Story of Our Era)*. Ankara: Amerikan Neşriyat Burosu, 1960.
Bayur, Yusuf Hikmet. *Türk Inkilâbı Tarihi (History of the Turkish Revolution)*. 3 vols. Istanbul, Ankara: Maarif Matbaası, Türk Tarih Kurumu Basımevi, 1940–1957.
Bekata, Hıfzı Oğuz. *Birinci Cumhuriyet Biterken (Ending the First Republic)*. Ankara: Çiğir Yayınları, 1960.
Bekman, Muzaffer. *Veteriner Hekimliğimizin Büyükleri (Our Great Veterinarians)*. Istanbul: Maarifet Basımevi, 1945.
Belen, Fahri. *Demokrasimiz Nereye Gidiyor? (Where Is Our Democracy Going?)*. Istanbul: Özyurt Basımevi, 1959.
Bell, Wendell; Hill, Richard, J.; and Wright, Charles, R. *Public Leadership*. San Francisco: Chandler, 1961.
Bengül, Necat. *Problems of Economic Development in Turkey, 1948–1955*. Cambridge: Center for International Studies, M.I.T., 1957. Typescript.
Benoist-Méchin, J. *Mustapha Kémal*. Paris: Éditions Albin Michel, 1954.
Berkes, Niyazi. *Bazı Ankara Köyleri Üzerinde Bir Araştırma (An Investigation of Some Ankara Villages)*. Ankara: Ankara University, 1942.
Berksan, Nazim. *Başvekil (Prime Minister)*. Istanbul: Ismail Akgün Matbaası, 1957.
Bilge, Necip. *Bakanların Görev Ve Sorumları (The Duties and Responsibilities of Ministers)*. Ankara: Yeni Desen Matbaası, 1956.
Birge, John Kingsley. *The Bektashi Order of Dervishes*. London: Luzac, 1937.
———. *A Guide to Turkish Area Study*. Washington: The American Council of Learned Societies, Committee on Near Eastern Studies, 1949.
Bisbee, Eleanor. *The New Turks: Pioneers of the Republic, 1920–1950*. Philadelphia: University of Pennsylvania Press, 1951.
Bıyıklıoğlu, Tevfik. *Atatürk Anadolu'da (1919–1921) (Atatürk in Anatolia, 1919–1921)*. Ankara: Türk Tarih Kurumu Basımevi, 1959.

———. *Trakya'da Millî Mücadele* (*The National Struggle in Thrace*). 2 vols. Ankara: Türk Tarih Kurumu Basımevi, 1955, 1956.
Borak, Sadi (ed.). *Atatürk'ün Özel Mektupları* (*Atatürk's Private Letters*). Istanbul: Varlık Yayınevi, 1961.
Brock, Ray. *Ghost on Horseback*. New York: Duell, Sloan & Pearce, 1954.
Campbell, Angus, *et al*. *The American Voter*. New York: John Wiley, 1960.
Campion, Sir Gilbert. *An Introduction to the Procedure of the House of Commons*. London: Macmillan & Co., 1950.
Canlı Tarihler (*Living Histories*). 6 vols. Istanbul: Türkiye Yayınevi, 1944-1947.
Cebesoy, Ali Fuat. *Gl. Ali Fuat Cebesoy'un Siyasî Hatıraları* (*General Ali Fuat Cebesoy's Political Memoirs*). Istanbul: Vatan Neşriyatı, 1957.
———. *Millî Mücadele Hatıraları* (*Memories of the National Struggle*). 3 vols. Istanbul: Vatan Matbaası, 1953-1957.
Clerget, Marcel. *La Turquie Passé et Présent*. Paris: Armand Colin, 1947.
Conker, Mehmet Nuri. *Zâbit Ve Kumandan* (*Officer and Commander*). Ankara: Doğuş Ltd. Şirketi Matbaası, 1959.
Conker, Orhan, and Witmeur, Emile. *Rédressement Économique et Industrialisation de la Nouvelle Turquie*. Paris: Recueil Sirey, 1937.
Cumhuriyet Halk Fırkası. *C.H.F. Intihap Yoklama Talimatnamesi* (*R.P.P. Election Examination Instructions*). Ankara: Hakimiyeti Milliye Matbaası, 1934.
———. *Cumhuriyet Halk Fırkası Nizamnamesi* (*Republican People's Party Regulations*). Ankara: Zelliç Biraderler Matbaası, 1929.
———. *C.H.P. Programı* (*R.P.P. Program*). Ankara: Ulus Basımevi, 1953.
———. *C.H.P. Program ve Tüzüğü*. Ankara: n.p., 1947.
———. *C.H.P. Tüzüğü* (*R.P.P. Regulations*). Ankara: Güzel Istanbul Matbaası, 1959.
———. *C.H.P. Tüzüğü*. Ankara: n.p., 1950.
———. *C.H.P. Tüzüğü*. Ankara: Güzel Istanbul Matbaası, 1954.
———. *C.H.P., 25 Yıl: 1923-1948* (*R.P.P., 25 Years: 1923-1948*). Ankara: Ulus Basımevi, 1948.
———. *Seçim Neticeleri Üzerinde Bir İnceleme* (*An Examination of Election Results*). C.H.P. Araştırma Bürosu Yayın No. 7; Ankara: Güven Matbaası, 1959.
———. *Turquie 1938*. Ankara: Parti Républicain du Peuple, 1938.
Cumhuriyet Halk Partisi Beyoğlu Ilçesi Evliyaçelebi Ocağı. *C.H.P.' nin el Kitabı* (*R.P.P. Handbook*). Istanbul: Şevket Unal Matbaası, 1958.
C.H.P. Istanbul Il Gençlik Kolu. *C.H.P., 36 Yıl* (*R.P.P., 36 Years*). Istanbul: Gün Matbaası, 1958.
Çankaya, Ali (Mücellitoğlu). *Mülkiye Târihi Ve Mülkiyeliler, 1859-1949* (*History of the Political Science School and Its Graduates, 1859-1949*). 3 vols. Ankara: Örnek Matbaası, 1954.
Çark, Y. G. *Türk Devleti Hizmetinde Ermeniler, 1453-1953* (*Armenians

in the Service of the Turkish State, 1453–1953). Ankara: Yeni Matbaa, 1953.

Davis, Helen Clarkson. *Constitutions, Electoral Laws, Treaties of States in the Near and Middle East.* Cambridge, England: Cambridge University Press, 1947.

Deliorman, Altan. *Mustafa Kemal Balkanlarda* (*Mustafa Kemal in the Balkans*). Istanbul: Türkiye Yayınevi, 1959.

Demiray, Tahsin (ed.). *Canlı Tarihler* (*Living Histories*). 6 vols. Istanbul: Türkiye Yayınevi, 1944–1947.

Demokrat Parti. *Demokrat Parti Tüzük Ve Programı* (*Democratic Party Regulations and Program*). Ankara: Güneş Matbaacılık, 1952 and 1957.

———. *Vilayet Ve Kazalar Itibarile Seçimler Mükayesesi 1950–1953* (*Electoral Comparisons for Provinces and Counties*). Ankara: D.P. Genel Idare Kurulu Arşivi, 1953.

The Development of Manufacturing Industry in Egypt, Israel and Turkey. New York: United Nations Department of Economic and Social Affairs, 1958.

Dressen, Robert B. *The Democrat Party of Turkey, 1946–1954.* Unpublished senior thesis, Princeton University, 1955.

Dursunoğlu, Cevat. *Millî Mücadele'de Erzurum* (*Erzurum in the National Struggle*). Ankara: T. C. Ziraat Bankası Matbaası, 1946.

Durusoy, M. Orhan, and Gökman, M. Muzaffer. *Atatürk Ve Devrimleri Bibliyografyası* (*Bibliography for Atatürk and His Times*). Ankara: Türk Tarih Kurumu Basımevi, 1957.

Duteil, Henri-Jean. *Loin dans la Turquie.* Paris: La Table Ronde, 1958.

Duverger, Maurice. *Les Partis Politiques.* Paris: Armand Colin, 1951.

———. *The Political Role of Women.* Paris: UNESCO, 1955.

Economic Developments in the Middle East 1958–1959. Supplement to *World Economic Survey, 1959.* New York: United Nations Department of Economic and Social Affairs, 1960.

Economic and Social Aspects of Farm Mechanization in Turkey. Ankara: Ankara University Political Science Faculty, 1954.

Ediboğlu, Baki Suha (ed.). *Falih Rıfkı Atay Konuşuyor* (*Falih Rıfkı Atay Speaking*). Ankara: Berkalp Kitabevi, 1945.

Ekrem, Selma. *Turkey, Old and New.* New York: Charles Scribner's Sons, 1947.

———. *Unveiled: The Autobiography of a Turkish Girl.* New York: Ives Washburn, 1942.

Elevli, Avni. *Hürriyet İçin: 27 Mayıs 1960 Devrimi* (*For Freedom: The Revolution of May 27, 1960*). Ankara: Yeni Desen Matbaası, 1960.

Elman, Ahmet Şevket. *Dr. Reşit Galip 1892–1934.* Ankara: Akay Kitabevi ve Berkalp Kitabevi, 1955.

Engin, Arin. *Atatürkçülük'te Dil Ve Din* (*Language and Religion in Atatürkism*). Istanbul: Atatürkkent, 1955.

Erdemir, Sabahat. *Muhalefet'de Ismet Inönü* (*Ismet Inönü in Opposition*). Istanbul: M. Sıralar Matbaası, 1956.

Erden, Ali Fuat. *Ismet Inönü*. Istanbul: Burhaneddin Erenler Matbaası, 1952.
Erden, Fethi. *Türk Hekimleri Biyografisi (Biographies of Turkish Doctors)*. Istanbul: Çituri Biraderler Basımevi, 1948.
Ergin, Osman. *Türkiye Maarif Tarihi (History of Turkish Education)*. 5 vols. Istanbul: Osmanbey Matbaası, 1939-1943.
Erk, Hasan Basri. *Meşhur Türk Hukukçuları (Famous Turkish Jurists)*. Adana: Hasan Basri Erk, 1958.
Eseniş, Adnan. *Education for Democracy in Turkey*. Ankara: Millî Eğitim Basımevi, 1950.
Evrenol, H. Malik. *Revolutionary Turkey*. Ankara and Istanbul: Librairie Hachette, 1936.
Falk, André. *Turquie*. Paris: Georges Lang, 1956.
Feyzioğlu, Turhan. *Demokrasiye ve Diktatörlüğe Dair (On Democracy and Dictatorship)*. Istanbul: Matbaacılık, 1957.
Fındıkoğlu, Ziyaeddin Fahri. *Ziya Gökalp: Sa Vie et Sa Sociologie*. Paris: Éditions Berger-Levrault, 1936.
Fisher, Sydney Nettleton (ed.). *Social Forces in the Middle East*. Ithaca: Cornell University Press, 1955.
Foreign Labor Information: Labor in Turkey. Washington, D.C.: Bureau of Labor Statistics, U.S. Department of Labor, February, 1959.
Froembgen, Hanns. *Kemal Atatürk*. New York: Hillman-Curl, 1937.
Frye, Richard N. *Islam and the West*. 's-Gravenhage: Mouton & Co., 1957.
Galloway, George B. *The Legislative Process in Congress*. New York: Thomas Y. Crowell, 1953.
General Directorate of Statistics, Republic of Turkey. *Small Statistical Abstract of Turkey, 1948*. No. 291. Ankara: n.p., n.d.
———. *Small Statistical Abstract of Turkey, 1949*. No. 314. Ankara: n.p., n.d.
Georges-Gaulis, Berthe. *Angora, Constantinople, Londres*. Paris: Armand Colin, 1922.
———. *La Nouvelle Turquie*. Paris: Armand Colin, 1924.
Gibb, H. A. R., and Bowen, Harold. *Islamic Society and the West*. Vol. I: *Islamic Society in the Eighteenth Century*. London: Oxford University Press, Part I, 1950; Part II, 1957.
Giritli, Ismet. *27 Mayıstan Ikinci Cumhuriyete (From the 27th of May to the Second Republic)*. Gençlik Yayınları No. 1. Istanbul: Turkiye Millî Gençlik Teşkilâtı, 1961.
Gorvine, Albert. *An Outline of Turkish Provincial and Local Government*. Ankara: Yeni Matbaa, 1956.
——— and Barber, Laurence L., Jr. *Organization and Functions of Turkish Ministries*. Ankara: Ajans-Türk Matbaası, 1957.
Gough, Mary. *The Plain and the Rough Places*. London: Chatto & Windus, 1954.
Göğem, Ziya. *Daday'lı Halit Beğ Akmansü*. 2 vols. Istanbul: Halk Basımevi, 1954.
Gökalp, Ziya. (Translated and edited by Niyazi Berkes). *Turkish Na-*

tionalism and Western Civilization. New York: Columbia University Press, 1959.

Gökbilgin, M. Tayyib. *Millî Mücadele Başlarken: Mondros Mütarekesinden Sivas Kongresine (Beginning the National Struggle: From the Mudros Armistice to the Sivas Congress)*. Ankara: Türk Tarih Kurumu Basımevi, 1959.

Göreli, Ismail Hakkı. *Devlet Şurası (The Council of State)*. Ankara Üniversitesi Siyasal Bilgiler Fakültesi Yayınları No. 36-18. Ankara: Yeni Matbaa, 1953.

Gövsa, Ibrahim Alâettin. *Türk Meşhurları Ansiklopedisi (Encyclopedia of Famous Turks)*. Istanbul: Yedigün Neşriyatı, 1946.

Gözübüyük, A. Şeref, and Kili, Suna (eds.). *Türk Anayasa Metinleri (Turkish Constitutional Texts)*. Ankara University Political Sciences Faculty, Administrative Sciences Institute Publication No. 2; Ankara: Ajans-Türk Matbaası, 1957.

Gözübüyük, A. Şeref, and Sezgin, Zekai (eds.). *1924 Anayasası Hakkındaki Meclis Görüşmeleri (Assembly Discussions Concerning the 1924 Constitution)*. Ankara Üniversitesi Siyasal Bilgiler Fakültesi Idari Ilimler Enstitüsü Yayın No. 3; Ankara: Balkanoğlu Matbaacılık, 1957.

Graves, Philip Perceval. *Briton and Turk*. London: Hutchinson, 1941.

Günaltay, Şemsettin. *Hürriyet Mücadeleleri (Struggles for Freedom)*. Istanbul: Gün Matbaası, 1958.

Güngör, Selâhaddin. *Atatürk'e Kafa Tutanlar (Those Who Defied Atatürk)*. Istanbul: Hadise Yayınevi, 1955.

Güntekin, Reşat Nuri. *Afternoon Sun (Akşam Güneşi)*. London: Heinemann, 1951.

———. (Translation by Sir Wyndham Deedes.) *The Autobiography of a Turkish Girl*. London: Allen & Unwin, 1949.

Güralp, Şerif. *Istiklâl Savaşının Içyüzü (Inside Story of the Independence Struggle)*. Istanbul: Ahmet Halit Yaşaroğlu, 1958.

Habib, Ismail (ed.). *Atatürk Için (For Atatürk)*. Istanbul: Cumhuriyet Matbaası, 1939.

Halil (Atay), Neşet. See Neşet Halil (Atay).

Hanson, A. H., *et al*. (eds.). *Studies in Turkish Local Government*. Ankara: Yeni Matbaa, 1955.

Harris, George. *A Political History of Turkey, 1945-1950*. Unpublished Ph.D. dissertation submitted to the Department of History, Harvard University, 1956.

Hazey, S. *Tory M.P.* London: Gollancz, 1939.

Helling, Barbara and George. *Rural Turkey: A New Socio-Statistical Appraisal. Istanbul:* Fakülteler Matbaası, 1958.

Hershlag, Zvi Yehuda. *Turkey: An Economy in Transition*. The Hague: Uitgeverij Van Keulen, 1958.

Heyd, Uriel. *Foundations of Turkish Nationalism*. London: Luzac and Harvill Press, 1950.

Histoire de la République Turque. Istanbul: Devlet Basımevi, 1935.

Howard, Harry N. *The Partition of Turkey: A Diplomatic History, 1913-*

1923. Norman, Oklahoma: University of Oklahoma Press, 1931.
Hürriyet Partisi. *Hürriyet Partisi Ana Nizamnamesi Ve Programı (Fundamental Regulations and Program of the Freedom Party)*. Ankara: Örnek Matbaası, 1956.
Ilmen, Süreyya. *Dört Ay Yaşamış Olan Zavallı Serbest Fırka (The Unfortunate Liberal Party Which Lasted Four Months)*. Istanbul: Muallim Fuad Gücüyener Yayınevi, 1951.
Inal, Mahmud Kemal. *Osmanlı Devrinde Son Sadrazamlar (The Last Grand Viziers of the Ottoman Period)*. Istanbul: Millî Eğitim Basımevi, 1940–1953.
L'Instruction Publique en Turquie Républicaine. Ankara: Matbaat Umum Müdürlüğü, 1936.
International Bank for Reconstruction and Development. *The Economy of Turkey*. Washington, D.C.: International Bank, 1951.
International Labor Organization. *Labor Problems in Turkey*. Geneva: International Labor Office, 1950.
Investment in Turkey. Washington, D.C.: U.S. Department of Commerce, 1956.
Iskora, Korgl. M. Mazlum. *Erkâniharbiye Tarihçesi (History of the General Staff)*. Ankara: Harp Akademisi Matbaası, 1944.
Iz, Fahir. *The Role of Education in the Westernization of Turkey*. 25th Annual Sir John Adams Lecture, University of California, Los Angeles, March 25, 1959.
Jackh, Ernest. *The Rising Crescent*. New York: Farrar & Rinehart, 1944.
Jäschke, Gotthard. *Die Türkei Seit Dem Weltkriege III (1930)*. Berlin: Deutsche Gesellschaft für Islamkunde, 1931.
———. *Die Türkei Seit Dem Weltkriege IV (1931–1932)*. Reprinted from *Die Welt Des Islams*.
———. *Die Türkei in Den Jahren 1933 und 1934*. Berlin: Walter de Gruyter, 1936.
———. *Die Türkei in Den Jahren 1935–1941*. Leipzig: Otto Harrassowitz, 1943.
———. *Die Türkei in Den Jahren 1942–1951*. Wiesbaden: Otto Harrassowitz, 1955.
———, and Pritsch, Erich. *Die Türkei Seit Dem Weltkriege (1918–1928)*. Berlin: Reichdruckerei, 1929.
Kandemir, Feridun. *Atatürk'e Izmir Suikastinden Ayrı 11 Suikast (Eleven Plots Against Ataturk Apart from the Izmir Plot)*. Istanbul: Ekicigil Basımevi, 1955.
———. *Atatürk-Inönü, Inönü-Mareşal Dargınlığı (The Atatürk-Inönü, Inönü-Marshal Disputes)*. Istanbul: Ekicigil Matbaası, 1956.
———. *Cumhuriyet Devrinde Siyasî Cinayetler (Political Crimes in the Republican Period)*. Istanbul: Ekicigil Matbaası, 1955.
———. *Izmir Suikastinin Içyüzü (Inside Story of the Izmir Plot)*. 2 vols. Istanbul: Ekicigil Matbaası, 1955.
———. *Karabekir'in Kitabı Niçin Ve Nasıl Yakıldı (How and Why the Karabekir Book Was Burned)*. Istanbul: Ekicigil Matbaası, 1956.
———. *Serbest Fırka: Nasıl Kuruldu — Nasıl Kapatıldı (The Liberal*

Party: How It Was Founded and Closed). Istanbul: Ekicigil Matbaası, 1955.
Kandemir, Feridun. *Siyasî Dargınlıklar (Political Controversies)*. 3 vols. Istanbul: Ekicigil Matbaası, 1955.
(Kansu), Nafi Atuf. *Türkiye Maarif Tarihi (History of Turkish Education)*. Istanbul: Milliyet Matbaası, 1932.
Karabekir, Kâzım. *Istiklâl Harbimizin Esasları (Essentials of Our War for Independence)*. Istanbul: Sinan Matbaası Neşriyat Evi, 1951.
Karacan, Ali Naci. *Lozan Konferansı Ve Ismet Pasa (The Lausanne Conference and Ismet Pasha)*. Istanbul: Maarif Matbaası, 1943.
Karal, Enver Ziya. *Turkiye Cumhuriyeti Tarihi (1918–1944) (History of the Turkish Republic, 1918–1944)*. Istanbul: Millî Eğitim Basımevi, 1945.
Karaosmanoğlu, Yakup Kadri. *Atatürk*. Istanbul: Remzi Kitabevi, 1938.
———. *Vatan Yolunda: Millî Mücadele Hatıraları (On the Fatherland Road: Recollections of the National Struggle)*. Istanbul: Selek Yayınevi, 1958.
———. *Yaban (Wilderness)*. Istanbul: Remzi Kitabevi, 1960.
———. *Zoraki Diplomat (Involuntary Diplomat)*. Istanbul: Inkilâp Kitabevi, 1955.
Kardeş, Sırrı. *Heyet-i Temsiliye ve Mustafa Kemal Kırşehirde (The Representative Committee and Mustafa Kemal in Kırşehir)*. Ankara: Ulus Basımevi, 1950.
Karpat, Kemal H. *Turkey's Politics: The Transition to a Multi-Party System*. Princeton: Princeton University Press, 1959.
Kaza Ve Vilâyet Idaresi Üzerinde Bir Araştırma (An Investigation of County and Provincial Administration). Ankara Üniversitesi Siyasal Bilgiler Fakültesi Yayın No. 77-59; Ankara: Ajans-Türk Matbaası, 1957.
Kılıç, Ali. *Atatürk'ün Son Günleri (Atatürk's Last Days)*. Istanbul: Sel Yayınları, 1955.
———. *Kılıç Ali Hatıraların Anlatıyor (Kılıç Ali Presents His Memoirs)*. Istanbul: Sel Yayınları, 1955.
Kılıç, Altemur. *Turkey and the World*. Washington, D.C.: Public Affairs Press, 1959.
Kingsley, J. Donald. *Representative Bureaucracy*. Yellow Springs, Ohio: Antioch Press, 1944.
Kral, August Ritter von. *See* Von Kral.
Krüger, Karl. *Kemalist Turkey and the Middle East*. London: George Allen & Unwin, 1932.
Kuran, Ahmed Bedevî. *Inkilâp Tarihimiz ve Ittihad ve Terakki (Our Revolutionary History and Union and Progress)*. Istanbul: Tan Matbaası, 1948.
———. *Inkilâp Tarihimiz ve "Jön Türkler" (Our Revolutionary History and the "Young Turks")*. Istanbul: Tan Matbaası, 1945.
———. *Osmanlı Imparatörluğunda Inkilâp Hareketleri Ve Millî Mücadele (Revolutionary Movements in the Ottoman Empire and the National Struggle)*. Istanbul: Baha Matbaası, 1956.

Kurnow, Ernest. *The Turkish Budgetary Process.* Ankara: Yeni Matbaa, 1956.
Kutay, Cemal. *Cumhuriyet Devrinde Suiistimaller: Divani Âliler Meclis Tahkikati (Maladministration in the Republican Period: High Court Assembly Investigations).* Istanbul: Mahmut Yurter, 1958.
———. *Halit Paşa, Ali Çetinkaya Vuruşması (The Halit Pasha – Ali Cetinkaya Fight).* Istanbul: Sabri Özakar, 1955.
———. *Ismet Paşa, Çerkes Ethem Çekişmesi (The Ismet Pasha – Çerkes Ethem Quarrel).* Istanbul: Ercan Matbaası, 1956.
———. *150'likler Faciası (The Tragedy of the 150).* Istanbul: Sabri Özakar, 1955.
Külçe, Süleyman. *Mareşal Fevzi Çakmak.* 2 vols. Istanbul: Cumhuriyet Matbaası, 1953.
Ladas, Stephan. *The Exchange of Minorities — Bulgaria, Greece and Turkey.* New York: Macmillan, 1932.
Lasswell, Harold D.; Lerner, Daniel; and Rothwell, C. Easton. *The Comparative Study of Elites.* Hoover Institute Studies, Series B, Elites, No. 1; Stanford: Stanford University Press, 1952.
Lenczowski, George. *The Middle East in World Affairs.* Ithaca: Cornell University Press, second edition, 1956.
Lengyel, Emil. *Turkey.* New York: Random House, 1941.
Lerner, Daniel. *The Passing of Traditional Society: Modernizing the Middle East.* Glencoe, Ill.: The Free Press, 1958.
Leuthy, Herbert. *France Against Herself.* New York; Praeger, 1955.
Levonian, Lutfy. *The Turkish Press, 1925–1932.* Athens: School of Religion, 1932.
———. *The Turkish Press, 1932–1936.* Beirut: n.p., 1937.
Lewis, Bernard. *The Emergence of Modern Turkey.* London: Oxford University Press, 1961.
Lewis, Geoffrey. *Turkey.* London: Benn, 1955.
Lindzey, Gardner (ed.). *Handbook of Social Psychology.* Vol. II. Cambridge, Mass.: Addison-Wesley, 1954.
Linke, Lilo. *Allah Dethroned.* London: Constable, 1937.
Lipset, Seymour Martin. *Agrarian Socialism.* Berkeley: University of California Press, 1950.
Luke, Harry (Sir). *The Old Turkey and the New: From Byzantium to Ankara.* London: Geoffrey Bles, revised ed., 1955.
Lybyer, Albert Howe. *The Government of the Ottoman Empire in the Time of Suleiman the Magnificent.* Cambridge, Mass.: Harvard University Press, 1913.
Makal, Mahmut. (Translated by Sir Wyndham Deedes). *A Village in Anatolia.* London: Vallentine, Mitchell, 1954.
———. *17 Nisan (April 17th).* Istanbul: Yeditepe Yayınları, 1959.
Marvick, Dwaine (ed.). *Political Decision-Makers.* New York: The Free Press of Glencoe, 1961.
Matthews, A. T. J. *Emergent Turkish Administrators.* Ankara: Faculty of Political Sciences, Ankara University Press, 1955.

Matthews, Donald R. *The Social Background of Political Decision-Makers.* New York: Doubleday, 1954.

———. *United States Senators: A Study of the Recruitment of Political Leaders.* Unpublished Ph.D. dissertation, Department of Politics, Princeton University, 1952.

———. *U.S. Senators and Their World.* Chapel Hill: University of North Carolina Press, 1960.

Maynard, Richard E. *The Lise and Its Curriculum in the Turkish Educational System.* Unpublished Ph.D. dissertation, Department of Education, University of Chicago, 1961.

Mears, Eliot Grinnel (ed.). *Modern Turkey.* New York: Macmillan, 1924.

Melzig, Herbert. *Kamâl Atatürk.* Frankfurt A.M.: Societäts-Verlag, 1937.

Mercanligil, Muharrem Doğdu. *Atatürk ve Devrim Kitapları Kataloğu (Catalogue of Books on Atatürk and the Revolution).* Ankara: Yeni Matbaa, 1953.

Meyer, A. J. *Middle Eastern Capitalism: Nine Essays.* Cambridge, Mass.: Harvard University Press, 1959.

Mikusch, Dagobert von. See Von Mikusch.

Miller, Barnette. *The Palace School of Muhammad the Conqueror.* Cambridge, Mass.: Harvard University Press, Harvard Historical Monograph XVII, 1941.

Miller, William (ed.). *Men in Business.* Cambridge, Mass.: Harvard University Press, 1952.

Mills, C. Wright. *The Power Elite.* New York: Oxford University Press, 1956.

Moorehead, Alan. *Gallipoli.* New York: Harper, 1956.

Morris-Jones, W. H. *Parliament in India.* Philadelphia: University of Pennsylvania Press, 1957.

Morrison, John A. *Alişar: A Unit of Land Occupancy.* Unpublished Ph.D. dissertation, University of Chicago, 1939.

Nadi, Yunus. *Ankaranın Ilk Günleri (Ankara's First Days).* Istanbul: Sel Yayınları, 1955.

———. *Birinci Büyük Millet Meclisi (The First Grand National Assembly).* Istanbul: Sel Yayınları, 1955.

———. *Çerkes Ethem Küvvetlerinin Ihaneti (The Treason of Çerkes Ethem's Forces).* Istanbul: Sel Yayınları, 1955.

———. *Mustafa Kemal Paşa Samsunda (Mustafa Kemal Pasha in Samsun).* Istanbul: Sel Yayınları, 1955.

Nebioğlu, Osman. *Kim Kimdir Ansiklopedisi. (Who's Who Encyclopedia).* 2 vols. Istanbul: Nebioğlu Yayınevi, 1961–1962.

Neşet Halil (Atay). *Büyük Meclis Ve Inkılâp (The Grand Assembly and the Revolution).* Ankara: T.B.M.M. Matbaası, 1933.

Oğuzkan, Turhan. *Adult Education in Turkey.* Paris: UNESCO Education Clearing House, 1955.

Oktay, Afşin. *Who's Who in Turkey.* Ankara: Kültür Matbaası, 1958.

———, and Bağlum, Kemal. *Biyoğrafiler Ansiklopedisi 1959 (Biographical Encyclopedia 1959).* Ankara: Afşin Oktay, 1959.

Orga, Irfan. *The Caravan Moves On.* London: Secker & Warburg, 1958.

Orga, Irfan. *Phoenix Ascendant*. London: Robert Hale, 1958.
———. *Portrait of a Turkish Family*. New York: Macmillan, 1950.
Ostrorog, Count Léon. *Angora Reform*. London: University of London Press, 1927.
———. *The Turkish Problem*. London: Chatto & Windus, 1919.
Ökte, Faik. *Varlık Vergisi Faciası (The Capital Levy Tragedy)*. Istanbul: Nebioğlu Yayınevi, 1951.
Örik, Nahid Sırrı. *150 Yılın Meşhurları Ansiklopedisi (Encyclopedia of Notables of 150 Years)*. Istanbul: Ekicigil Yayınevi, 1953.
Paneth, Philip. *Turkey, Decadence and Rebirth*. London: Alliance Press, 1943.
Parker, John, and Smith, C. *Modern Turkey*. London: George Routledge, 1940.
Parsadan, Sabahattin; Hunca, Cemalettin; and Göktürk, Ismail (eds.). *Adnan Menderes: Siyasî Hayatı ve Nutukları (Adnan Menderes: His Political Life and Speeches)*. Ankara: Ekspres Matbaası, 1955.
Patmore, Derek. *The Star and the Crescent*. London: Constable, 1946.
Patrick, Mary Mills. *Under Five Sultans*. New York: Century, 1929.
Popper, Karl R. *The Poverty of Historicism*. London: Routledge & Kegan Paul, 1957.
The Press in Turkey. Washington: Library of Congress, European Affairs Division, November, 1949.
Presthus, Robert V., with Erem, Sevda. *Statistical Analysis in Comparative Administration: The Turkish Conseil d'Etat*. Ithaca: Cornell University Press, 1958.
Price, Clair. *The Rebirth of Turkey*. New York: Thomas Seltzer, 1923.
Price, M. Philips. *A History of Turkey*. London: George Allen & Unwin, 1956.
Ramsaur, Ernest E., Jr. *The Young Turks: Prelude to the Revolution of 1908*. Princeton: Princeton University Press, 1957.
Redden, Kenneth. *Legal Education in Turkey*. Istanbul: Fakülteler Matbaası, 1957.
République Turque, Office Centrale de Statistique. *Population de la Turquie, 28 Octobre 1928*. Angora: Imprimerie Turk-Odjak, 1928.
Resimli Türk Ve Dünya Meşhurları Ansiklopedisi (Illustrated Encyclopedia of Turkish and World Notables). Istanbul: Altın Kitaplar [Şehir Matbaası], 1957–1958.
Rivinus, E. *Social Stratification in Modern Turkey and Its Significance in the Light of United States Policies*. Washington, D.C.: Foreign Service Institute, 1950. Mimeographed.
Robinson, Richard D. *Developments Respecting Turkey*. Vol. 1: *July 1953 – October 1954*. Vol. 2: *October 1954 – September 1955*. Vol. 3: *September 1955 – August 1956*. Vol. 4: *September 1956 – September 1957*. New York: American Universities Field Staff, 1954, 1955, 1956, 1957.
———. *The First Turkish Republic*. Cambridge, Mass.: Harvard University Press, 1963.

Robinson, Richard D. *Letters.* Institute of Current World Affairs, 1948–1954. Mimeographed.

———. *Village Economics.* New York: Institute of Current World Affairs, 1949.

Roe, Ann. *The Psychology of Occupations.* New York: Wiley, 1956.

Ross, J. F. S. *Parliamentary Representation.* New Haven: Yale University Press, 1944.

Roux, Jean-Paul. *La Turquie: Géographie, Économie, Histoire, Civilisation et Culture.* Paris: Payot, 1953.

Rustow, Dankwart A. *Politics and Westernization in the Near East.* Princeton: Center of International Studies, 1956.

Safa, Peyami. *Türk Inkilâbina Bakışlar (Views of the Turkish Revolution).* Istanbul: Inkilâp Kitabevi, n.d.

Sassani, Abul H. K. *Education in Turkey.* Washington, D.C.: Office of Education (Department of Health, Education and Welfare), 1952.

Schueller, George K. *The Politburo.* Hoover Institute Studies, Series B, Elites, No. 2; Stanford: Stanford University Press, 1951.

Selznick, Philip. *T.V.A. and the Grass Roots.* Berkeley: University of California Press, 1949.

Sevgen, Nazmi. *Celâl Bayar Diyorki: 1920–1950 (Celâl Bayar Speaks: 1920–1950).* Istanbul: Tan Matbaası, 1951.

Sherif, Muzaffer and Carolyn W. *An Outline of Social Psychology.* New York: Harper, 1956.

Sherrill, Charles H. *A Year's Embassy to Mustafa Kemal.* New York: Charles Scribner's Sons, 1934.

Shotwell, James T., and Deák, Francis. *Turkey at the Straits.* New York: Macmillan, 1941.

Smith, Elaine D. *Turkey: Origins of the Kemalist Movement and the Government of the Grand National Assembly (1919–1923).* Washington, D.C.: Judd & Detweiler, 1959.

Smith, Wilfred Cantwell. *Islam in Modern History.* Princeton: Princeton University Press, 1957.

Soku, Ziya Şakir. *Celâl Bayar — Hayatı Ve Eserleri (Celâl Bayar — His Life and Works).* Istanbul: Ismail Akgün Matbaası, 1952.

———. *Ismet Inönü: Hususî, Askerî, Siyasî Hayatı (Ismet Inönü: His Private, Military and Political Life).* Istanbul: Ülkü Basımevi, 1939.

Söylemezoğlu, Galip Kemalî. *Yok Edilmek Istenen Millet (The Nation They Wanted to Destroy).* Istanbul: Selek Neşriyatı, 1957.

Sperco, Willy. *Moustapha Kemal Ataturk: Créateur de la Turquie Moderne, 1882–1938.* Paris: Nouvelles Éditions Latines, 1958.

Stirling, Paul. *The Social Structure of Turkish Peasant Communities.* Unpublished doctoral dissertation, Oxford University, 1951.

Sturm, Albert L., and Mıhçıoğlu, Cemal. *Türk Âmme Idaresi Bibliyografyası (Bibliography on Turkish Public Administration).* Ankara Üniversitesi Siyasal Bilgiler Fakültesi Idari Ilimler Enstitüsü Yayın No. 5; Ankara: Ajans Türk Matbaası, 1959.

Su, Mükerrem Kâmil, and Su, Kâmil. *Türkiye Cumhuriyeti Tarihi (History of the Turkish Republic).* Istanbul: Kanaat Yayınları, 1958.

Summary of the Labor Situation in Turkey. Washington, D.C.: U.S. Department of Labor, Bureau of Labor Statistics, May 1956.
Super, Donald. *The Psychology of Careers*. New York: Harper, 1957.
Szyliowicz, Joseph S. *Erdemli: A Case Study in the Political Integration of the Turkish Villager*. Unpublished Ph.D. dissertation submitted to the Deparment of Public Law and Government, Columbia University, 1961.
Şahingıray, Özel. *Atatürk'ün Nöbet Defteri 1931–1938 (The Log-book of Atatürk's Guard, 1931–1938)*. Ankara: Türk Tarih Kurumu Basımevi, 1955.
Şakir, Ziya. *Yakın Tarihin Üç Büyük Adamı: Cemâl, Talât, Enver Paşalar (Three Great Men of Recent History: Cemâl, Talât and Enver Pashas)*. Istanbul: Fuat Gücüyener, 1944.
(Sapolyo), Enver Behnan. *Inkilâp Ötkünçleri, Millî Mücadele Hatıraları (Revolutionary Tales, Memories of the National Struggle)*. Istanbul: Devlet Matbaası, 1934.
———. *Kemâl Atatürk ve Millî Mücadele Tarihi (Kemal Atatürk and the History of the National Struggle)*. Istanbul: Rafet Zaimler Yayınevi, 1958.
———. *Kuvayı Milliye Tarihi (History of the National Forces)*. Ankara: Ayyıldız Matbaası, 1957.
———. *Ziya Gökalp: Ittihadi Terakki Ve Meşrutiyet Tarihi (Ziya Gökalp: Union and Progress and Constitutional History)*. Istanbul: Güven Basımevi, 1943.
T.(uran) G.(üneş)?: *S.B.F. Hâdisesi Ve Ilim Hürriyeti (The Political Science Faculty Incident and Academic Freedom)*. Ankara: Yıldız Matbaası, n.d.
Thomas, Lewis V., and Frye, Richard N. *The United States and Turkey and Iran*. Cambridge, Mass.: Harvard University Press, 1952.
Thornburg, Max Weston; Spry, Graham; and Soule, George. *Turkey: An Economic Appraisal*. New York: The Twentieth Century Fund, 1949.
Tobin, Chester M. *Turkey, Key to the East*. New York: G. P. Putnam's Sons, 1944.
Tomlin, E. W. F. *Life in Modern Turkey*. London: Thomas Nelson & Sons, 1946.
Tongas, Gérard. *Atatürk et le Vrai Visage de la Turquie Moderne*. Paris: Librairie Orientaliste Paul Geuthner, 1937.
Topçu, Nurettin. *Türkiyenin Maarif Dâvası (Turkey's Educational Problem)*. Istanbul: Çeltüt Matbaası, 1960.
Toros, Taha. *Türk Hatipleri (Turkish Orators)*. N.p.: Kültür, Basım Ve Yayım Kooperatifi, n.d.
Toynbee, Arnold. *Turkey: A Past and a Future*. New York: George H. Doran, 1917.
———. *The Western Question in Greece and Turkey*. Boston: Houghton Mifflin, 1922.
———, and Kirkwood, Kenneth P. *Turkey*. New York: Scribner's, 1922.

Tunaya, Tarık Z. *Hürriyetin İlânı (The Proclamation of Freedom)*. Siyaset Ilmi Serisi No. 1. Istanbul: Baha Matbaası 1959.

———. *Türkiyede Siyasî Partiler (Political Parties in Turkey)*. Istanbul: Doğan Kardeş, 1952.

———. *Türkiyenin Siyasî Hayatında Batılılaşma Hareketleri (Westernizing Movements in Turkish Political Life)*. Siyaset Ilmi Serisi No. 8. Istanbul: Yedigün Matbaası, 1960.

———, and Ülker, Reşit. *Milletvekilleri Seçimi Kanunu ve Ilgili Mevzuat (The Electoral Law for Deputies and Related Topics)*. Istanbul: Ismail Akgün Matbaası, 1954.

Turkish Information Office. *Education in the New Turkey*. New York: Turkish Information Office, Turkey Today Series No. 5, 1949.

———. *Education in Turkey*. New York: Turkish Information Office, Turkey Today Series No. 2, n.d.

———. *Facts on Turkey, 1923–1954*. New York: Turkish Information Office, n.d.

———. *Facts on Turkey, 1960*. New York: Turkish Information Office, n.d.

———. *Government in Turkey*. New York: Turkish Information Office, n.d.

———. *New Turkey*. New York: Turkish Information Office, n.d.

———. *Progress Report from Turkey, 1952*. Turkey Today, No. 16. New York: Turkish Information Office, n.d.

———. *Progress Report from Turkey, 1954*. Turkey Today, No. 20. New York: Turkish Information Office, n.d.

———. *Self-Government in Turkey*. New York: Turkish Information Office, n.d. [1956].

———. *The Turkish Constitution*. Turkey Today, No. 11. New York: Turkish Information Office, n.d.

———. *Turkish Elections of 1950 and United States Reaction*. New York: Turkish Information Office, 1950.

———. *Turkish Literature*. New York: Turkish Information Office, n.d.

———. *Turkish Women*. Turkey Today, No. 6. New York: Turkish Information Office, n.d.

———. *Women in Modern Turkey*. Turkey Today, No. 7. New York: Turkish Information Office, 1949.

Turkish National Commission on Education. *Report of the Turkish National Commission on Education*. Istanbul: American Board Publication Department, 1961.

Tülbentçi, Feridun Fazıl: *Cumhuriyet Nasıl Kuruldu? (How Was the Republic Founded?)*. Istanbul: Sel Yayınları, 1955.

Türkgeldi, Ali Fuad. *Görüp Işittiklerim (What I Saw and Heard)*. Ankara: Türk Tarih Kurumu Basımevi, 1951.

Türkiye Büyük Millet Meclisi (T.B.M.M.). *Türkiye Büyük Millet Meclisinin 25'nci Yıl Dönümünü Anış Albüm: Dönem 1. (The 25th Anniversary Commemorative Album of the Grand National Assembly of Turkey: Assembly 1)*. Ankara: T.B.M.M. Basımevi, 1945.

———. *T.B.M.M. Albümü (G.N.A. Album)*. Devre: V, İçtima: 3 (1937). Devre: VII, İçtima: 1 (1943). Devre: VIII, İçtima: 1 (1946). Devre: VIII, İçtima: 2 (1947). Devre: VIII, İçtima: 4 (1950). Devre: IX, İçtima: Olg. (1950). Devre: X, İçtima: F.ve 1 (1954). Devre: X, İçtima: 2 (1955). Devre: XI, İçtima: 1 (1958). Ankara: T.B.M.M. Matbaası, 1937-1958.

———. *T.B.M.M. Isim Defteri. (G.N.A. Name List)*. Ankara: T.B.M.M. Matbaası, 1943-1957. Devre: I-X (1920-1957).

———. *T.B.M.M. Teşkilâtı Esasiye Kanunu Ve Dahilî Nizamname (G.N.A. Law of Fundamental Organization and Internal Regulations)*. Ankara: T.B.M.M. Matbaası, 1954-1958.

———. *T.B.M.M. Yıllığı (G.N.A. Annual)*. Devre: III, İçtima: 1 (1928), İçtima: 2 (1929), İçtima: 3 (1930), İçtima: 4 (1931). Devre IV, İçtima: F. (1931), Ictima: 1 (1934). Devre: V, İçtima: F. (1936), İçtima: 1 (1937), İçtima: 2 (1938), İçtima: 3 (1939), İçtima: 4 (1939). Devre: VI, İçtima: F. (1940), İçtima: 1 (1941), İçtima: 2 (1942), İçtima: 3 (1943), İçtima: 4 (1943). Devre: VII, İçtima: F. (1944), İçtima: 1 (1945), İçtima: 2 (1945), İçtima: 3 (1947). Devre: VIII, İçtima: F. (1948), İçtima: 1 (1948), İçtima: 2 (1950). Devre: IX, İçtima: F-4 (1955). Devre: X, İçtima: F-3 (1958). Ankara: T.B.M.M. Matbaası, 1928-1958.

———. *T.B.M.M. Zabıt Ceridesi (Tutanak Dergisi) (G.N.A. Debates)*. Ankara: T.B.M.M. Matbaası, 1920-1960. Devre I-XI (1920-1960).

Türkiye Cumhuriyeti Başbakanlık İstatistik Genel Müdürlüğü. *21 Ekim 1945 Genel Nüfus Sayımı (General Population Census, October 21, 1945)*. Yayın No. 286. Ankara: n.p., 1950.

T.C. Başvekâlet İstatistik Umum Müdürlüğü. *22 Ekim 1950 Umumî Nüfus Sayımı (General Population Census, October 22, 1950)*. Nesriyat No. 359, Ankara: n.p., n.d.

———. *1955 Genel Nüfus Sayımı (1955 General Population Census)*. (10% Örnekleme Usulûile), Yayın No. 372. Ankara: n.p., 1961.

———. *23 Ekim 1955 Genel Nüfus Sayımı (General Population Census, October 23, 1955)*. Yayın No. 412. Ankara: n.p., 1961.

———. *Istatistik Yıllığı 1951 (Statistical Annual 1951)*. Yayın No. 332. Ankara: n.p., 1952.

———. *Memurlar Istatistiği 1938 (Statistics Concerning Government Officials 1938)*. Ankara: n.p., 1939.

———. *Nüfus Sayımları 1927-1950 (Population Censuses, 1927-1950)*. Ankara: n.p., 1953.

T.C. Emniyet Genel Müdürlüğü. *Türkiye'de Siyasî Dernekler (Political Associations in Turkey)*. Ankara: Başbakanlık Devlet Matbaası, 1958.

T.C. İçişleri Vekâleti. *Idare Taksimatı 1953 (Administrative Divisions, 1953)*. Ankara: Karınca Matbaası, 1953.

Türkiye Cumhuriyeti Maarifi, 1923-1943 (Education in the Turkish Republic, 1923-1943). Ankara: Maarif Matbaası, 1944.

Türkiye ve Yabancı Memleketlerde Seçim Mevzuatı (Electoral Topics in

Turkey and Foreign Countries). Ankara: Başbakanlık Devlet Matbaası, 1949.
Ulaş, Mehmet. *Hüseyin Avni Ulaş'ın Son Yılları* (*The Last Years of Hüseyin Avni Ulaş*). Istanbul: Berksoy Basımevi, 1952.
Unat, Faik Reşit. *Tarih Atlası* (*Historical Atlas*). Istanbul: Kanaat Yayınları, n.d.
Uran, Hilmi. *Hatıralarım* (*Memoirs*). Ankara: Ayyıldız Matbaası, 1959.
Ünaydın, Ruşen Eşref. *Atatürk'ü Özleyiş Hatıralar* (*Longing Memories of Atatürk*). Ankara: Türk Tarih Kurumu Basımevi, 1957.
———. *Atatürk'ün Hastalığı* (*Atatürk's Illness*). Ankara: Türk Tarih Kurumu Basımevi, 1959.
Ünver, Hakkı Şinasi. *Yeni Seçim Mevzuatı* (*New Electoral Topics*). Ankara: Hazine Yayınları, 1961.
Vere-Hodge, Edward R. *Turkish Foreign Policy, 1918–1948.* Ambilly–Annemasse: Imp. Franco-Suisse, 1950.
Von Kral, August Ritter. *Kamâl Atatürk's Land.* Wien: Wilhelm Braumüller, 1938.
Von Mikusch, Dagobert. (Translated by John Linton.) *Mustapha Kemal: Between Europe and Asia.* Garden City, N.Y.: Doubleday, Doran, 1931.
Von Sanders, Liman. *Five Years in Turkey.* Annapolis, Md.: U.S. Naval Institute, 1927.
Wallas, Graham. *The Life of Francis Place.* London: George Allen & Unwin, revised edition, 1918.
Ward, Barbara. *Turkey.* London: Oxford University Press, 1942.
Ward, Norman. *The Canadian House of Commons: Representation.* Toronto: University of Toronto Press, 1950.
Ward, Robert E., and Rustow, Dankwart A. (eds.). *Political Modernization in Japan and Turkey.* Princeton: Princeton University Press, 1964.
Webb, L. C. *Government in New Zealand.* Wellington, 1940.
Webster, Donald Everett. *The Turkey of Atatürk: Social Process in the Turkish Reformation.* Philadelphia: The American Academy of Political and Social Science, 1939.
Weiker, Walter F. *The Free Party of 1930 in Turkey.* Unpublished Ph.D. dissertation submitted to the Department of Politics, Princeton University, 1962.
———. *The Turkish Revolution 1960–1961.* Washington: The Brookings Institution, 1963.
Werfel, Franz. *The Forty Days of Musa Dagh.* New York: Modern Library, 1934.
Wittlin, Alma. *Abdul Hamid: The Shadow of God.* London: John Lane, 1940.
Woodsmall, Ruth Frances. *Moslem Women Enter a New World.* New York: Round Table Press, 1936.
Wortham, H. E. *Mustapha Kemal of Turkey.* Boston: Little, Brown, 1931.
Yakınlarından Hatıralar (Atatürk). (*Memories by Those Close to Him*). Istanbul: Sel Yayınları, 1955.

Yalman, Ahmet Emin. *Development of Modern Turkey as Measured by Its Press.* New York: Columbia Studies in History, Economics and Public Law, 1914.
―――. *Turkey in My Time.* Norman: University of Oklahoma Press, 1956.
―――. *Turkey in the World War.* New Haven: Yale University Press, 1930.
Yasa, Ibrahim. *Hasanoğlan.* Ankara: Yeni Matbaa, 1957.
Yiğitbaşı, M. Sadık. *Kiğı.* Istanbul: Cemal Asmi Matbaası, 1950.
Young, T. Cuyler (ed.). *Near Eastern Culture and Society.* Princeton: Princeton University Press, 1951.
Yücebaş, Hilmi. *Aka Gündüz.* Istanbul: Ahmet Halit Yaşaroğlu, 1959.
Yücel, Hasan Âli. *Hürriyet Gene Hürriyet (Freedom, Again Freedom).* Ankara: Türk Tarih Karumu Basımevi, 1960.

Articles

Abadan, Nermin. "Türkiye'de Ordu Ve Siyaset" ("The Army and Politics in Turkey"). *Forum,* XIV (August 1961, September 1961), pp. 6–7, 6–8.
Adıvar, Abdülhak Adnan. "The Interaction of Islamic and Western Thought in Turkey." In T. Cuyler Young (ed.), *Near Eastern Culture and Society* (Princeton: Princeton University Press, 1951), pp. 119–129.
Agger, Robert E. "Power Attributions in the Local Community: Theoretical and Research Considerations." *Social Forces,* XXXIV (May 1956), pp. 322–331.
Alexander, Alec P. "Industrial Entrepreneurship in Turkey: Origins and Growth." *Economic Development and Cultural Change,* VIII (July 1960), pp. 349–365.
―――. "Turkish Economic Development." In Irma Adelman and Adam Pepelassis (eds.), *Economic Development* (New York: Harper, 1960).
Altay, Fahrettin. "Millî Mücadele Hatıralarım" ("My Recollections of the National Struggle"). *Hayat* (1959).
Aray, Suat. "Bir Galatasaraylının Hatıraları" ("Memories of a Galatasaray Student"). *Hayat* (Winter 1958–1959).
Ataöv, Türkkaya. "The Faculty of Political Sciences of Turkey." *Middle East Journal,* XIV (Spring 1960), pp. 243–245.
Bellah, Robert N. "Religious Aspects of Modernization in Turkey and Japan." *American Journal of Sociology,* LXIV (July 1958), pp. 1–5.
Bentwich, Norman. "The Turkish Constitutions, 1876–1942." *Contemporary Review,* CLXII (November 1942), pp. 273–278.
―――. "Village Life in Turkey." *Contemporary Review,* CLXXV (March 1955), pp. 174–177.
Berkes, Niyazi. "Sociology in Turkey." *American Journal of Sociology,* XLII (September 1936), pp. 238–246.

Berkes, Niyazi. "Ziya Gökalp: His Contribution to Turkish Nationalism." *Middle East Journal,* VIII (Autumn 1954), pp. 375-390.
Bing, Edward J. "Progress of Women in New Turkey." *Current History,* XVIII (May 1923), pp. 305-311.
Birge, John K. "Islam in Modern Turkey." In Dorothea S. Franck (ed.), *Islam in the Modern World* (Washington, D.C.: Middle East Institute, 1951), pp. 41-46.
———. "Turkey Between Two World Wars." *Foreign Policy Reports,* XX (November 1944), pp. 194-207.
Bisbee, Eleanor. "The Test of Democracy in Turkey." *Middle East Journal,* IV (April 1950), pp. 170-182.
Careless, J. M. S. "Frontierism, Metropolitanism, and Canadian History." *Canadian Historical Review,* XXXV (March 1954).
Cebesoy, Ali Fuat. "Mustafa Kemal—Millî Lider" ("Mustafa Kemal—National Leader"). *Belleten,* XX (October 1956), pp. 549-555.
Coşar, Ömer Sâmi, and Ipekçi, Abdi. "Ihtilâlin Içyüzü" ("The Inside Story of the Revolution"). *Milliyet* (May 27, 1962, to July 10, 1962).
Dahl, Robert A. "The Concept of Power." *Behavioral Science,* II (July 1957), pp. 201-215.
Davison, Roderic H. "Turkish Diplomacy from Mudros to Lausanne." In Gordon A. Craig and Felix Gilbert (eds.), *The Diplomats, 1919–1939* (Princeton: Princeton University Press, 1953), pp. 172-209.
———. "Westernized Education in Ottoman Turkey." *Middle East Journal,* XV (Summer 1961), pp. 289-301.
Day, Langston. "Women King's Counsel in Britain." *American Bar Association Journal,* XXXV, No. 11 (November 1949).
Deny, Jean. "Zia Goek Alp." *Revue du Monde Musulman,* LXI (1925), pp. 1-41.
De Planhol, Xavier. "Geography, Politics and Nomadism in Anatolia." *International Social Science Journal,* XI (1959), pp. 525-531.
De Salve, M. "Education in Turkey." In *Circulars of Information of the Bureau of Education: No. 3–1875* (Washington, D.C.: Government Printing Office, 1875), pp. 237-252.
Dogan, Mattei. "Political Ascent in a Class Society: French Deputies 1870-1958." In Dwaine Marvick (ed.), *Political Decision-Makers* (New York: The Free Press of Glencoe, 1961), pp. 57-90.
Eberhard, Wolfram. "Nomads and Farmers in Southeastern Turkey." *Oriens,* VI (1953), pp. 32-49.
Ellis, Ellen D. "Turkish Nationalism in the Postwar World." *Current History,* XXXVI (February 1959), pp. 86-91.
Evan, William M. "Cohort Analysis of Survey Data: A Procedure for Studying Long-Term Opinion Change." *Public Opinion Quarterly,* XXIII (Spring 1959), pp. 63-72.
Feyzioğlu, Turhan. "Les Partis Politiques en Turquie: Du Parti Unique à la Democratie." *Revue Française de Science Politique,* IV (January-March, 1954).
Fischer, A. J. "Turkey After the First Free Elections." *World Affairs Quarterly* (October 1946), pp. 220-230.

Fotos, Evan. "An Appreciation of Turkish University Life." *Middle Eastern Affairs*, VI (August–September 1955), pp. 248–258.

Frey, Frederick W. "Arms and the Man in Turkish Politics." *Land Reborn*, XI (August 1960), pp. 3–14.

———. "The Atlantic Report: Turkey." *The Atlantic*, CCVI (August 1960), pp. 14–20 (with David Hapgood).

———. "Education and Politics in Turkey." In Robert E. Ward and Dankwart A. Rustow (eds.). *Political Modernization in Japan and Turkey* (Princeton: Princeton University Press, 1964), pp. 205–235.

———. "Political Development, Power, and Communications in Turkey." In Lucian W. Pye (ed.), *Communications and Political Development* (Princeton: Princeton University Press, 1963), pp. 298–326.

———. "Surveying Peasant Attitudes in Turkey." *Public Opinion Quarterly*, XXVII (1963), pp. 335–355.

———. "Turkey's 'War.' " *The Nation*, CXC (May 1960), pp. 419–420.

———, and Payaslıoğlu, Arif. "Babaların Mensup Oldukları Meslek Gurupları Bakımından Siyasal Bilgiler Fakültesi Talebeleri Üzerinde Bir İnceleme." *Ankara Üniversitesi Siyasal Bilgiler Fakültesi Dergisi*, XIII (September 1958), pp. 225–243.

Gerth, Hans. "The Nazi Party: Its Leadership and Composition." *American Journal of Sociology*, XLV (January 1940), pp. 517–541.

Gibb, Cecil A. "Leadership." In Gardner Lindzey, (ed.), *Handbook of Social Psychology* (Cambridge, Mass.: Addison-Wesley, 1954), Vol. II, pp. 877–917.

Gilead, Baruch. "Political Parties in Turkey." *Middle Eastern Affairs*, IX (March 1958), pp. 101–107.

Gordon, Leland J. "Turkish-American Treaty Relations." *American Political Science Review*, XXII (August 1928), pp. 711-721

Gorvine, Albert, and Payaslıoğlu, Arif. "The Administrative Career Service in Turkish Provincial Government." *International Review of Administrative Sciences*, XXIII (1957), pp. 467-474.

Gören, Leyla. "Turkish Women of Today." *American-Turkish Topics* (May 1958), pp. 5, 7.

Guttsman, W. L. "Aristocracy and the Middle Class in the British Political Elite, 1886–1916." *British Journal of Sciology*, V (March 1954), pp 12–32.

Gülek, Kasım. "Democracy Takes Root in Turkey." *Foreign Affairs*, XXX (October 1951), pp. 135-144.

Hanson, A. H. "Democracy Transplanted: Reflections on a Turkish Election." *Parliamentary Affairs*, IX (Winter 1955- 1956), pp. 65–74.

Herz, John H. "The Problem of Successorship in Dictatorial Regimes: A Study in Comparative Law and Institutions." *Journal of Politics*, XIV (February 1952), pp. 19–40.

Heyd, Uriel. "Islam in Modern Turkey." *Royal Central Asian Journal*, XXXIV (July–October 1947), pp. 299–308.

Hyman, Herbert H.; Payaslıoğlu, Arif; and Frey, Frederick W. "The

Values of Turkish College Youth." *Public Opinion Quarterly,* XXII, (Fall 1958), pp. 275–291.
Jäschke, Gotthard. "Die Grösseren Verwaltungsbezirke der Türkei Seit 1918." *Mitteilungen des Seminars für Orientalische Sprachen zu Berlin, Ostasiatische Studien,* XXXVIII (1935), pp. 81–142.
Jameson, Samuel H. "Social Mutation in Turkey." *Social Forces,* XIV (May 1936), pp. 482–496.
Jones, D. D., and Johnson, Henry. "Mustapha Kemal and Peter the Great: A Study in Parallelism." *Sociology and Social Research,* XXII (January 1938), pp. 212–222.
"Kahraman Yuvası" ("Nest of Heroes"). *Akis* (June 1960), pp. 22–23.
Karpat, Kemal H. "Social Effects of Farm Mechanization in Turkish Villages." *Social Research,* XXVII (Spring 1960), pp. 83–103.
———. "Social Themes in Contemporary Turkish Literature." *Middle East Journal,* XIV (Winter 1960), pp. 29–44 (Part I), *Middle East Journal,* XIV (Spring 1960), pp. 153–168 (Part II).
———. "The Turkish Elections of 1957." *Western Political Quarterly,* XIV (June 1961), pp. 436–459.
Kerwin, Robert. "Private Enterprise in Turkish Industrial Development." *Middle East Journal,* V (Winter 1951), pp. 21–38.
Key, Kerim Kâmi. "The Origins of Turkish Political Parties." *World Affairs Interpreter,* XXVI (Spring 1955), pp. 49-60.
———. "Trends in Modern Turkish Literature." *Muslim World,* XLVII (October 1957), pp. 318–328.
Kircheimer, Otto. "The Composition of the German Bundestag, 1950." *Western Political Quarterly,* III (December 1950), pp. 590–601.
Kostanick, Huey Louis. "Turkish Resettlement of Refugees from Bulgaria, 1950–1953." *Middle East Journal,* IX (Winter 1955), pp. 41–52.
Kurat, Akdes Nimet, and Reed, Howard A. "A Century and a Half of Turkish-American Relations." *American-Turkish Topics* (May 1958), pp. 6–7.
Laski, Harold J. "The Personnel of the English Cabinet, 1901–1924." *American Political Science Review,* XXII (February 1928), pp. 12–31.
Lerner, Daniel, and Riesman, David. "Self and Society: Reflections on Some Turks in Transition." *Explorations,* XX (1955), pp. 67–80.
Lerner, Daniel, and Robinson, Richard D. "Swords and Ploughshares: The Turkish Army as a Modernizing Force." *World Politics,* XIII (October 1960), pp. 19–44.
Lewis, Bernard. "Democracy in Turkey." *Middle Eastern Affairs,* X (February 1959), pp. 55–72.
———. "History-Writing and National Revival in Turkey." *Middle Eastern Affairs,* IV (June–July 1953), pp. 218–227.
———. "The Impact of the French Revolution on Turkey." *Cahiers d'Histoire Mondiale,* I (July 1953), pp. 105–125.
———. "Islamic Revival in Turkey." *International Affairs,* XXVIII (January 1952), pp. 38–48.

———. "Recent Developments in Turkey." *International Affairs*, XXVII (July 1951), pp. 320–331.
———. "Turkey: History." *The Middle East*. London: Europa Publications, 1957.
———. "Turkey: Westernisation." In Gustave von Grunebaum (ed.), *Unity and Variety in Western Civilization* (Chicago: University of Chicago Press, 1955), pp. 311–331.
Lewis, Geoffrey. "Turkey: The Thorny Road to Democracy." *The World Today*, XVIII (May 1962), pp. 182–191.
Lybyer, Albert Howe. "Recent Political Changes in the Moslem World." *American Political Science Review*, XVIII (August 1924), pp. 513–527.
McCally, Sarah P. "Party Government in Turkey." *Journal of Politics*, XVIII (May 1956), pp. 297–323.
McKinney, Madge M. "Personnel of the 77th Congress." *American Political Science Review*, XXXVI (February 1942), pp. 67–75.
Malleterre, Col. "L'Armeé Jeune—Turque." *Revue des Sciences Politique*, XXVI (September 1911), pp. 734–755.
March, James G. "Group Norms and the Active Minority." *American Sociological Review*, XIX (1954), pp. 733–741.
———. "An Introduction to the Theory and Measurement of Influence." *American Political Science Review*, XLIX (June 1955), pp. 431–451.
Matthews, Donald R. "U.S. Senators and the Class Structure." *Public Opinion Quarterly*, XVIII (Spring 1954), pp. 5–22.
"26 Mayıs Gecesi Harp Okulunun İçi" ("The Night of May 26 Inside the War School"). *Akis* (October 3, 1960).
Meyer, A. J. "Turkish Land Reform: An Experiment in Moderation." In A. J. Meyer, *Middle Eastern Capitalism: Nine Essays* (Cambridge, Mass.: Harvard University Press, 1959), pp. 65–79.
Michaelis, Alfred. "The Economy of Turkey." *Middle Eastern Affairs*, IV (August–September 1953), pp. 278–289.
Miller, A. "Turkey's Path of Development." *PROD Translations*, III (June 1960), pp. 21–28.
Okyar, Osman. "Economic Framework for Industrialization: Turkish Experiences in Retrospect." *Middle Eastern Affairs*, IX (August–September 1958), pp. 261–267.
———. "Industrialization in Turkey." *Middle Eastern Affairs*, IV (June–July 1953), pp. 209–217.
———. "The Turkish Stabilization Experiment—Before and After." *Middle Eastern Affairs*, XI (August–September 1960), pp. 238–246.
Onar, Sıddık Sami. "Les Transformations de la Structure Administrative et Juridique de la Turquie et Son État Actuel." *Revue Internationale des Sciences Administratives*, XXI (1955), pp. 741–786.
Östen, Necmi. "Administrative Organization of Turkey: Historical Summary and Present Day Administration." *Asiatic Review*, XXXVIII (October 1942), pp. 407–413.

Perlmann, Moshe. "Upheaval in Turkey." *Middle Eastern Affairs*, XI (June–July 1960), pp. 174–179.
"The Press in Turkey." Supplement to *The European Press Today*. Washington D.C.: Library of Congress, European Affairs Division, 1949.
Price, M. Philips. "The Parliaments of Turkey and Persia." *Parliamentary Affairs*, I (Summer 1948), pp 43–50.
Psomiades, Harry J. "Turkey: Progress and Problems." *Middle Eastern Affairs*, VIII (March 1957), pp. 90–96.
"Rahmetli Başvekil Dr. Refik Saydam'ın Hayatı" ("The Life of the Late Prime Minister Dr. Refik Saydam"). *Siyasî Ilimler Mecmuası*, CXXXVII (August 1942), pp. 161–164.
"The Reception of Foreign Law in Turkey." *International Bulletin of Social Sciences*, IX (1957).
Reed, Howard A. "The Faculty of Divinity at Ankara. I, II" *The Muslim World*, XLVI (October 1956), pp. 295–312; *The Muslim World*, XLVII (January 1957), pp. 22–35.
———. "A New Force at Work in Democratic Turkey." *Middle East Journal*, VII (Winter 1953), pp. 33–44.
———. "The Religious Life of Modern Turkish Muslims." In Richard N. Frye (ed.), *Islam and the West* ('s-Gravenhage: Mouton, 1957), pp. 108–148.
———. "Revival of Islam in Secular Turkey." *Middle East Journal*, VIII (Summer 1954), pp. 267–282.
———. "Secularism and Islam in Turkish Politics." *Current History*, XXXII (June 1957), pp. 333–338.
———. "Turkish Democracy at Crossroads." *Foreign Policy Bulletin*, XXXIV (March 1955), pp. 97–98, 104.
Robinson, Richard D. "Tractors in the Village—A Study in Turkey." *Journal of Farm Economics*, XXXIV (November 1952), pp. 451–462.
———. "Turkey's Agrarian Revolution and the Problem of Urbanization." *Public Opinion Quarterly*, XXII (Fall 1958), pp. 397–405.
Ross, Irwin. "From Atatürk to Gürsel: What Went Wrong in Turkey." *The New Leader*, XLIII (December 1960), pp. 14-18.
Ross, J. F. S. "Women and Parliamentary Elections." *British Journal of Sociology*, IV (March 1953), pp. 14–24.
Rossi, Peter H. "Community Decision-Making." *Administrative Science Quarterly*, I (March 1957), pp. 415–443.
Rustow, Dankwart A. "The Army and the Founding of the Turkish Republic." *World Politics*, XI (July 1959), pp. 513–552.
———. "Foreign Policy of the Turkish Republic." In Roy Macridis (ed.), *Foreign Policy in World Politics* (Englewood Cliffs, N.J.: Prentice-Hall, 1958), pp. 295–322.
———. "Politics and Islam in Turkey, 1920–1955." In R. N. Frye (ed.), *Islam and the West* ('s-Gravenhage: Mouton, 1957), pp. 69–107.
———. "The Politics of the Near East." In Gabriel A. Almond and James S. Coleman (eds.), *The Politics of the Developing Areas*

(Princeton: Princeton University Press, 1960), pp. 369–454.
Sadak, Necmeddin. "Turkey Faces the Soviets." *Foreign Affairs*, XXVII (April 1949), pp. 449–461.
Sarç, Ömer Celal. "Changes in the Urban-Rural Distribution of the Population." *Revue de la Faculté des Sciences Économiques de l'Université d'Istanbul*, IX (October 1947–January 1948).
―――. "Economic Policy of the New Turkey." *Middle East Journal*, II (October 1948), pp. 430–446.
Savcı, Bahri. "Ara Secimleri Üzerinde Tartışmalar" ("Discussions Concerning By-Elections"). *Ankara Üniversitesi Siyasal Bilgiler Fakültesi Dergisi*, XIII (September, 1958), pp. 244–252.
―――. "Hukûmet Üyesi Kimin Vekilidir?" ("The Government Member Is Whose Deputy?"). *Ankara Üniversitesi Siyasal Bilgiler Fakültesi Dergisi*, XIII (September 1958), pp. 255–256.
―――. "Mecliste Başkanlık Divanı Meseleleri" ("Problems of the Council of the Presidency in the Assembly"). *Ankara Üniversitesi Siyasal Bilgiler Fakültesi Dergisi*, XIII (September 1958), pp. 256–258.
―――. "Partilerimizde Tabakalaşmanın Gerçek Mahiyeti Ve Sosyal Muhtevali Politika Meyli." ("The True Character of Stratification in Our Parties and the Social Aspect of Political Orientation"). *Ankara Üniversitesi Siyasal Bilgiler Fakültesi Dergisi*, XIII (March, 1958), pp. 42–80.
Shils, Edward. "The Intellectuals in the Political Development of the New States." *World Politics*, XII (April 1960), pp. 329–368.
Smith, Edward C. "Debates on the Turkish Constitution of 1924." *Ankara Üniversitesi Siyasal Bilgiler Fakültesi Dergisi*, XIII (September 1958), pp. 82–105.
Smith, Wilfred Cantwell. "Modern Turkey: Islamic Reformation?" *Islamic Culture*, XXV (January 1951), pp. 155–186.
Stirling, Paul. "Religious Change in Republican Turkey." *Middle East Journal*, XII (Autumn 1958), pp. 395–408.
―――. "Social Ranking in a Turkish Village." *British Journal of Sociology*, IV (March 1953), pp. 31–44.
Tachau, Frank. "The Face of Turkish Nationalism as Reflected in the Cyprus Dispute." *Middle East Journal*, XIII (Summer 1959), pp. 262–272.
Tahsin, Orhan. "Vekiller Okulu" ("Ministers' School"). *Hayat* (June 19, 1959), pp. 6–7.
Thomas, Lewis V. "The National and International Relations of Turkey." In T. Cuyler Young (ed.), *Near Eastern Culture and Society* (Princeton: Princeton University Press, 1951), pp. 167–187.
―――. "Recent Developments in Turkish Islam." *Middle East Journal*, VI (Winter 1952), pp. 22–40.
―――. "Turkish Islam." *Muslim World*, XLIV (July 1954), pp. 181–185.
Thornburg, Max Weston. "Turkey, Aid for What?" *Fortune*, XXXVI (October 1947), pp. 106–107, 171–172, 174, 176, 178, 181.

Tokar, Feyyaz. "Ali Rıza Türel'in Cevapları" ("The Answers of Ali Rıza Türel"). *Cumhuriyet* (December 7, 1959).
Tunaya, Tarık Z. "Elections in Turkish History." *Middle Eastern Affairs,* V (April 1954), pp. 116–119.
Von Vorys, Karl. "The Legislator in Underdeveloped Countries." *PROD,* III (November 1959), pp. 23–26.
Waugh, A. Telford. "Nine Years of Republic in Turkey." *Journal of the Royal Central Asian Society,* XX (January 1933), pp. 52–69.
Webster, Donald E. "State Control of Social Change in Republican Turkey." *American Sociological Review,* IV (April 1939), pp. 247–256.
Wolfinger, Raymond. "Reputation and Reality in the Study of 'Community Power.'" *American Sociological Review,* XXV (October 1960), pp. 636–644.
Wright, Walter Livingstone, Jr. "Truths about Turkey." *Foreign Affairs,* XXVI (January 1948), pp. 349–359.
Yalman, Ahmet Emin. "The Struggle for Multi-party Government in Turkey." *Middle East Journal,* I (January 1947). pp. 46–58.

Index

Abadan, Nermin, 162n
Abadan, Yavuz, 84n, 112n, 167n
Abalıoğlu, Yunus Nadi, 85
Abdülhamit II, Sultan, 33, 48, 424
Adalan, Şevket, 296
Adato, Salamon, 146n
Adıvar, Dr. Adnan, 114, 325
(Adıvar), Halide Edib, 29n, 36n, 38n, 48n, 85, 91, 114n, 128, 136, 150n, 151, 153n, 306n, 328n, 337, 425
Adnan, see Adıvar, Dr. Adnan
Aegean Region, 189, 190–191, 192, 195, 221, 267, 273–276, 298
Afetinan, Dr., 154n, 336n
Ağaoğlu, Ahmet, 91, 339n
Ağaoğlu, Samet, 92, 297, 314n, 340
Age
    of legislators in selected countries, 171, 394
    significance in Turkey, 168–169
Age of Turkish deputies, 168–171, 194
    carryovers, 200–202, 222
    at first election, 58–60, 71, 88, 130, 172–173, 221, 249–250
    First Group, 308
    leadership groups, 249–251
    newly elected, 200–202, 222
    Ninth and Tenth Assemblies, 356–357
    Second Group, 308
Agger, Robert E., 226n
Ağralı, Fuat, 289
Agricultural deputies, 124–125, 133, 183
Agriculture, Ministers of, 286, 295
Akaygen, Enis, 352n
Akçura, Yusuf, 91
Akgöl, Eyüp Sabri, 102n
Akkerman, Naki, 114
(Akmansü), Halit Beğ, 324n, 330
Aksal, Ismail Rüştü, 355
Aktan, Tahir, 158n
Aktaş, Basri, 18n
Alataş, Hulusi, 295
Aldoğan, Sadık, 352n
Alexander, Alec P., 123n

Alevi (or Shiites), 147
Ali Fuat (Pasha), see (Cebesoy), Ali Fuat
Allen, Henry E., 67n, 69n, 108n, 109n, 114n, 144n
Almond, Gabriel, 100, 401–402
Alphabet, adoption of Roman, 41
Altay, Fahrettin, 102n
Alternative elite, 349, 388
American College, 106
Anatolian Club (*Anadolu Kulübü*), 99
Angell, G. W., Jr., 124n, 136n
Ankara, 94, 103–104
Ankara University, 20, 33, 61
Apaydın, Zekâi, 102n, 291
Arabic language, 109, 119
Aras, Tevfik Rüştü, 290
Araslı, Asım Vasfı, 309
"Ardent nationalists," 327–329, 378, 410–411, 413
Arif, Colonel, 48
Arıkan, Saffet (Bey), 102n, 145n, 292, 432
Armstrong, H. C., 145n, 324n
Armstrong, John A., 148n
Artunkal, Ali Rıza, 291
Ataç, Hasan Fehmi, 288
Ataman, Sebati, 167n
Atatürk, Mustafa Kemal, 5, 7n, 32n, 39n, 40n, 41n, 47–48, 61, 69n, 76, 89, 92n, 103, 106, 121n, 137, 161, 165, 166, 167, 169, 179, 183, 187–188, 206, 219, 225, 227, 230, 232, 271, 287, 288, 302n, 306–307, 309–310, 314, 317–318, 324, 325, 326n, 331, 334–339, 343n, 389, 425, 430–432, 434, 448, 449
Atatürk Revolution, 33, 38, 40–42, 70, 151
Atay, Falih Rıfkı, 85, 303–304
(Atay), Neşet Halil, 121n, 242n, 324n, 431n
Ath, Âşir, 102n
Authoritarianism, return to, 162
Authority, formal, see Formal authority

475

Authority-prestige relationship, 403–405
Avni, Hüseyin, *see* (Ulaş), Hüseyin Avni
Aydın, Halil Hulki, 126n
Aykurt, Izzet Ulvi, 102n

Backbenchers, 243–248, 266
Baǧlüm, Kemal, 19n
Baldwin, Stanley, 35
Balfour, Arthur J., 35
Balta, Tahsin Bekir, 108n
Bankers as deputies, 125–126
Barutçu, Faik Ahmet, 297
Batur, Suphi, 352n
Bayar, A. V., 146n
Bayar, Mahmut Celâl, 125–126, 162, 173, 225, 271n, 273, 275, 278, 287, 288, 293, 355, 369n, 370
Bayazıt, Kemali, 347
Bayur, Yusuf Hikmet, 34n, 344n, 369n
Bekata, Hıfzı Oǧuz, 347
Bekir Sami Bey, 91, 92
(Bele), Refet, 151, 330
Bell, Wendell, 394n
Bellah, Robert N., 126n
Berkan, Abdürrahman Münip, 167n
Berkes, Niyazi, 39n, 126n
Beyatlı, Yahya Kemal, 102n
Birgen, Muhittin, 167n
Birsel, Münir, 290
Birthplace *(memleket)*, importance to Turks, 90–92
Birthplace of Turkish deputies, 89–98, 103, 104, 131, 184–192, 195
 cabinet, 273–275
 cohort group, 221–222
 First Group, 308–310
 leadership groups, 251
 newly elected, 202–206, 222
 Ninth and Tenth Assemblies, 357
 Second Group, 308–310
Bisbee, Eleanor, 36n, 48n, 136, 150n, 429n
Bıyıklıoǧlu, Tevfik, 337n
Bodrumlu, Avram Gâlanti, 146n
Bölükbaşı, Osman, 167n
Bowen, Harold, 32n
Bozkurt, Mahmut Esat, 69, 291
Budget Committee of G.N.A., 10–11, 241, 242, 266
Bureaucrats, higher education of, 115–119
By-elections of deputies, 60–61, 71, 105–106, 165–166, 193

Cabinet, 269–300
 education of, 278–282
 localism of, 275–278
 occupation of, 281
 reelection of, 273
 regional origin of, 273–275
 size and stability of, 269–273
(Çakmak), Fevzi, 335
Calendar, adoption of Western, 40
Caliphate, abolition of, 40
Campbell, Angus, 148n

Campion, Sir Gilbert, 10n
Canada, 103, 148, 394, 401
Çankaya, Ali, 19n
Capillary recruitment, 282–284, 299, 393
Capital levy, 144, 349
Caplow, Theodore, 406n
Careless, J. M. S., 103n
Çavuşoǧlu, Muammer, 294
(Cebesoy), Ali Fuat, 48, 102n, 137, 325, 330, 334, 433n
Çelikbaş, Fethi, 356
Cemal (Pasha), 137
Cenani, Ali, 293
CENTO, 3
Cevat (Pasha), 335
Cilli, Ahmet, 294
Civil Service School, *see* Political Science Faculty
Cohort group analysis, 25, 199–200, 212–222
Consensus and conflict, 328–329
Constituency continuity, 100–103
 of cohort group, 219, 220, 223
 of newly elected deputies, 223
Constitution, Turkish (1924), 7, 9, 49n, 425
Constitutional Act of 1921, *see* Law of Fundamental Organization
Constitutional Committee of G.N.A., 241, 266, 302n
Co-optative policy, *see* Recruitment in G.N.A.
Coşkun, Tahsin, 167n
"Cosmopolitanism," 396–397
Council of Ministers, 9
 see also Cabinet
Coup d'état (May 27, 1960), 7, 9, 38, 61, 169, 227, 261, 371, 389, 390
Customs and Monopolies, Ministers of, 286, 296

Dahl, Robert A., 226n
Davis, Helen Clarkson, 429n
Day, Langston, 147n
Death of deputies, 164, 165
Defense, National
 Committee (G.N.A.), 241, 266
 Ministry of, 228–231, 234, 235, 238, 239, 241, 265, 286, 290–291, 300
Defense of Rights of Anatolia and Rumelia, Association for, 7, 11, 48, 230, 301n, 306–307, 309, 376, 430, 433n
 Erzurum Congress of, 7, 8n, 77
 Sivas Congress of, 7
Defense of Rights Associations, 229
Demiralay, Ibrahim, 126n
Democracy in Turkey, 334–339
Democratic Party, 12, 102, 162, 167, 168, 173, 180, 183, 196, 197, 201, 206, 222, 275, 282, 303n, 340, 350–353, 356, 370–375, 380–382, 391–392, 399, 428n, 435, 436
 formal power ratings of, 237–241

INDEX 477

Dentists as deputies, 65, 68, 80, 84–88, 93, 96, 103, 107, 113–114, 132, 182
Deputies to G.N.A., *passim*
 formal qualifications of, 12–15, 423–429
 marginal status of, 118
 from Ottoman Chamber, 424n
 party candidacy of, 13–15
De Salve, M., 33n, 34n, 36n, 150, 151n
Dinç, Raif, 102, 126n
Doctors as deputies, 62–67, 68, 84, 85–88, 93, 96, 103, 107, 112–114, 132, 182, 259
Dogan, Mattei, 103n, 171n, 394n, 400
Dursunoğlu, Cevat, 8n, 20n, 48n, 77, 169n
Duverger, Maurice, 148n, 155n, 338n

Economics and Trade, Ministers of, 286, 293
Edib, Halide, *see* (Adıvar), Halide Edib
Education (Turkey)
 bifurcation in, 29–31, 37–39, 41, 70, 75
 of cabinet, 278–282, 298
 higher, 33, 62
 level of, 43–46
 medrese schools, 32, 34, 38, 50–52, 176
 military schools, 32, 37
 Minister of, 231, 233, 235, 238, 286, 292
 primary, 34–35
 private, 50–51
 public, 34, 45
 School Law of 1869, 34
 secondary, 34–37
 and social prestige, 400
 system of, 44
Education of Turkish deputies, 43–46, 175–176, 179, 194, 389
 bureaucrats, 115–119
 cohort group, 220–221
 foreign, 67–70, 72
 higher, 87
 lag in, 179
 leadership groups, 252–254
 level, 43–46, 175–176, 194, 389
 newly elected, 208, 222
 Ninth and Tenth Assemblies, 358–359
 and political experience, 65
 and political longevity, 132
 political significance of differences in, 46–49
 reelection and, 50–52
Educators as deputies, 121–122, 183, 262
Egypt, 416
Ekrem, Selma, 124n, 148, 149n
Election rates of deputies, 25
Elections, general, dates of, 429
Electoral Law (Turkish)
 of 1934, 426
 of 1942 (No. 4320), 426
 of 1946 (No. 4918), 427
 of 1950 (No. 5545), 427–429
Electoral system (Turkey)
 in First Assembly, 424–426
 in Ottoman parliaments, 423–424
 during period 1920–1957, 423–429
Elman, Ahmet Şevket, 314n
Engineers as deputies, 182
England, 92, 109, 147, 394, 401
 British Conservative Party, 326n
 House of Commons, 6, 399
 M.P.'s tenure, 394, 395
English language, 179
Enver (Pasha), 39, 69n, 106, 137
Erden, Fethi, 19n
Ergin, Osman, 33n, 121n
Erim, Nihat, 297, 356
Erk, Hasan Basri, 19n
Erkmen, Hayrettin, 295
Erkmen, Muhlis, 295
Erkut, Selâmi, 18n
Ersoy, Mehmet Akif, 114
Erzurum Military School, 37
Erzurumlu, Nasuhi, 167n
Esen, Ali Rıza, 369n
Eseniş, Adnan, 33n
Eton, 35
Evan, William, 200n
Evrenol, H. Malik, 34n, 76n, 112n

Faik, of Ordu, 330n
Fakaçelli, Nikola, 146n
Family, importance in Turkey, 137
Fathers of deputies
 and occupational mobility, 136–143
 occupations of, 135–143
Fevzi, Marshal, *see* (Çakmak), Fevzi
Feyzioğlu, Turhan, 10n, 18n, 144n, 344n, 349n, 355
Finance Minister, 231, 233–235, 237, 238, 265, 286, 288–289
Fındıkoğlu, L. F., 69n
First Constitutional Period, 12
First Group (Defense of Rights Group), 305, 307, 325, 376–377, 430
First Turkish Republic, 7, 11, 166, 196
Fisher, S. N., 70n
Foreign Affairs, Minister of, 228, 230, 234, 235, 237, 238, 241, 265, 286, 289–290
Foreign languages of deputies, 52–57, 71, 86–88, 106–110, 118–119, 132, 177, 178–180, 194, 358–359
 of cabinet, 278–279, 298–299
 of leadership groups, 254–255
 and reelection, 54
Formal authority and social prestige, 400–403, 405
Formal power rating
 analysis of, by judges, 434–444
 in Atatürk Era (1923–1939), 231–235
 for cohort groups, 399
 of committee rankings, 445–447
 in Democratic Party Era (1950–1957), 237–241
 in First Assembly subperiod (1920–1923), 227–230
 in İnönü Era (1939–1950), 235–237

478 INDEX

Formal power rating *(continued)*
  rating scale explained, 226–227
  selection of judges for, 225–226
Formal requirements of deputies, 423–429
Fotos, Evan, 90n, 121n
"The Fourteen" (Committee of National Union), 169
France, 69, 92, 103, 108, 148, 394, 401
  Assembly in, 6, 103n, 299
  average tenure of deputies in, 394, 395
  and Radical Socialist Party, 326n
  reelection rates of deputies in, 394–395
Free professions, *see* Professions, free
Freedom Party, 357n, 359–360, 381
French-speaking deputies, 179
Frey, Frederick W., 33n, 62n, 81n, 124n, 127n, 136n, 153n, 162n, 328n, 334n, 407n
Frye, Richard N., 7n, 39n, 41n, 42n
Fuat, Ali (Pasha), *see* (Cebesoy), Ali Fuat
Fundamental Law (1877), 423

Galatasaray Lycée *(Mektebi Sultani)*, 36, 128n, 280
Galip, Dr. Reşit, 314n
Galloway, George, 10n
Gazi, *see* Atatürk, Mustafa Kemal
Gazi Pedagogical Institute, 33
Gedik, Namık, 289
Gedik, Süleyman Sırrı, 126n
General Staff, Chief of the, 229
Generation, new political, 354–356
Geographical representation of deputies, 308–310, 438–442
Gerçeker, Mustafa Fehmi, 126n
Gerede, Hüsrev, 102n
Germany, 69, 109, 148, 394, 395, 401
Gibb, Cecil, 23
Gibb, H. A. R., 32n
Göğem, Ziya, 314n, 324n, 331n
Gökalp, Ziya, 29n, 39, 76, 106, 114
Göle, Münir Hüsrev, 289
Gorvine, Albert, 117n
Gough, Mary, 30, 74–75
Gövsa, İbrahim Alaettin, 19n, 102n
Grand National Assembly (G.N.A.), 6–15
  Council of Presidency of, 10
  Deputy President of, 230
  early history of, 6–11
  electoral system of, 12
  First, 306
  Internal Regulations, 17
  officers of, 9–10
  organization of, 224
  permanent committees of, 10–11, 17
  political position of, 6–7
  Secretariat of, 17, 20
Great Britain, *see* England
Gülek, Kasım, 106, 137, 167n, 349n, 355
Günaltay, Şemsettin, 271, 288
Güneri, Sülyman Necati, 431n
Güneş, Turan, 356

Güntekin, Reşat Nuri, 128n, 144n
Guttsman, W. L., 36n

Hacopulos, Aleksandros, 146n
Halide Edib, *see* (Adıvar), Halide Edib
Halit Beğ (Akmansü), *see* (Akmansü), Halit Beğ
Hanson, A. H., 158n
Harris, George, 162n, 240n, 348n, 428n
Harrow, 35
Hatipoğlu, Şevket Raşit, 295
Hayirlioğlu, Eyüp Sabri, 90n
Hazey, S., 35n
Health, Ministers of, 286, 295
Helling, George and Barbara, 189n
Herz, John H., 5n
Heyd, Uriel, 76n, 91n
Hill, Richard, 394n
Hilmi, Tunalı, 317
Hyman, Herbert H., 62n

Içöz, Ş. Sırrı, 369n
Ikdam (Effort), newspaper, 89
Ileri, Tevfik, 292
Ilmen, Süreyya, 339n
Inan, Atıf, 278, 293
Ince, R. Ş., 369n
Independent Democratic Party, 351n
India, 394, 401
Influencee's adjustment to power, 403–404
Influencee's perception of influence, 403
Initial democratization (in stages of political development), 414–416
Inönü, Ismet, 5, 21, 102n, 106, 126, 161–162, 169, 233, 271, 275, 287, 288, 325, 330, 389, 392n, 432
Intellectuals, 31, 38
Interior, Ministry of, 117–119, 132, 231, 235, 238, 241, 265, 286, 289
International Bank for Reconstruction and Development, 123n, 124n, 158n
International Press Institute, Zurich, 127n
Intraelite conflict, 391–392, 413, 417
Iran, 303n, 415, 416
Ismet (Pasha), *see* Inönü, Ismet
Istanbul, 8, 94
  metropolitanism, 103–105, 131–132, 186–187
Istanbul Erkek Lisesi, 37, 128n, 280
Istanbul riots, 144n
Istanbul Technical University, 33
Istanbul University, 33, 61, 90
Italy, 92
Iz, Fahir, 29n, 32
Izbudak, Velet, 126n
Izmir, 7, 94

Jäschke, Gotthard, 349n
Japan, 3, 401, 409
Journalism in Turkey, 127–129
Journalists as deputies, 127–129, 133, 183
Justice, Minister of, 231, 233, 235, 238, 241, 286, 291

INDEX 479

Justice Party, 303n, 340, 397n

Kalafat, Emin, 273
Kansu, Mazhar Müfit, 102n
Kansu, Nafi Atuf, 33n, 102n
Kaplan, Rasih, 126n
Karabekir, Kâzım, 76, 325, 330, 334
Karaosmanoğlu, Yakup Kadri, 92n, 336n
Karpat, Kemal, 29n, 39n, 78n, 91n, 92n, 108n, 109n, 123n, 127n, 136, 152, 303n, 339n, 344n, 348n, 352n, 354n, 399n, 428n
Kaya, Şükrü, 289
Kemal, Mustafa, see Atatürk, Mustafa Kemal
Kemalism, democratic tendencies of, 349–350
Kemalists, 158, 166, 169, 183, 189, 191, 194, 204, 212, 216–217, 219, 221, 232, 234, 303–304
Kesebir, Şakir, 102n
Key, Kerim Kami, 349n
Khadduri, Majid, 169n
Kılıç, Ali, 306
Kingsley, J. Donald, 36n
Kircheimer, Otto, 171n
Kirdar, Lütfi, 102n
Kitabcı, Hüsnü, 369n
Köken, Rahmi, 293
Konus, Vasil, 146n
Köprülü, Fuat, 137, 162, 273, 290, 297, 369n
Koraltan, Refik, 90n, 162, 352n, 369n
Kostanick, H. L., 145n
Kral, (August) Ritter von, 145n, 343n
Kubalı, H. N., 29n
Külçe, Süleyman, 164n
Kuleli Military School, 37
Kurdish deputies, 147n
Kurdish language, 109–110
Kurdish Rebellion, 335
Kurtbek, Seyfi, 290
Kutay, Cemal, 324n, 326n, 330n
Kuyucak, Hazım Atıf, 369n

Labor, Ministers of, 286, 295–296
Laborers as deputies, 123–124
Land Reform Bill, 78
Laski, Harold J., 35n
Lasswell, Harold, 377, 396, 401n
Lausanne Treaty negotiations, 325
Law of Association (1938), 434, 435, 436
Law of Fundamental Organization (1921), 8, 336n
Law School (Istanbul), founding in 1888, 33
Lawyers
  as legislators in selected countries, 395–396
  as Turkish deputies, 62, 63–67, 68, 80, 84, 85–88, 93, 96, 103, 107, 111–112, 129, 132, 180–182, 195, 259, 388

Leadership groups, 243–264
  cohorts, 248–249
  First Group, 313
  Second Group, 313
Lenczowski, George, 5n, 121n
Lerner, Daniel, 31, 75, 162n, 396n, 401n
Leuthy Herbert, 103n
Lewis, Bernard, 7n, 36n, 76n, 91n, 92n, 100n, 108n, 121n, 126n, 127n, 138n, 143n, 144n, 145n, 158n, 302n, 338n, 348n, 354n
Lewis, Geoffrey, 7n, 39, 40n, 147n, 152n, 354n
Liberal Party, see Liberal Republican Party
Liberal Republican Party, 11, 75n, 212, 233, 378–379, 434
  background characteristics contrasted with R. P. P., 341–343
  chronology and character of, 336n, 339–341
Library of Congress, European Affairs Division, 127n
Lipset, Seymour Martin, 103n
Lipstein, K., 69n
Lloyd George, David, 92
"Local elites," growth in Turkey, 397
Local government experience, elective, 98–99
Local leader versus national elite, see National elite
Localism of deputies, 89–98, 119, 130, 131, 173, 187–192, 195, 196–197, 397
  in cabinet, 275–278, 298
  in cohort group, 217, 218–219, 223
  compared with whole population, 94
  and election rates, 95–98
  in First Group, 310
  in leadership groups, 263–264
  newly elected, 206–207, 222
  in Ninth and Tenth Assemblies, 357–358
  in Second Group, 310
Longevity (length of service) of cohort group, 215–217
Luke, Sir Harry, 75n, 143n
Lybyer, Alfred, 432n

McKinney, Madge M., 171n
Makal, Mahmut, 75n, 152n
Makbule (Atatürk's sister), 340
Malta, 8
Manastir Military Secondary School, 37, 47
Mansur, Fatma, 158n
March, James, 57n, 226n
Mardom Party (Iran), 303n
Marginal status of deputies, 118
Marital status of deputies, 173–175, 194
  leadership groups, 251
Marmara Region, 185–187, 190–191, 192, 195, 202–205, 221, 267, 273–276, 298

Marmaralı, Abravaya, 146n
Marvick, Dwaine, 171n, 394n
Masses, transfer of power to, 418–419
Matthews, A. T. J., 137, 164n
Matthews, Donald, 99n, 142n, 171n, 401n
Maynard, Richard E., 33n
Mears, Eliot G., 33n, 104n, 127n, 145n, 306n
Medrese schools, *see under* Education
Mehmet VI, Sultan (Vahdeddin), 8, 161
Melliun Party (Iran), 303n
Memleket, see Birthplace
Menderes, Adnan, 21, 100, 102n, 106, 137, 162, 173, 225, 273, 275, 281, 288, 341, 355, 369n, 370
Menderes-Bayar regime, 90, 196, 374–375
Menderes, Ethem, 273, 289, 290
"Menemen Incident," 75n
Mercan Idadisi, 37, 128n, 280
Metropolitanism, 103–105, 131–132, 186–187
  dominance of Istanbul, 103–105
Meyer, A. J., 40n
Middle leadership group, 244–248, 266, 397–398
Mikusch, Dagobert von, 324n
Military men as deputies, 119–121, 132, 182, 260–262, 300, 390
Military tradition of political neutrality, 162
Miller, A., 42n
Miller, Barnette, 32n
Miller, William, 401n
Millet system, 143
Mills, C. Wright, 35, 36n
Ministries, formal power ratings explained, 284–287
Mithat (Pasha), 34n, 39
"Modern democratic approach," 414–418
Modernization, regional differences in, 189–191
Modernizing cadre, 5, 70, 157–158
Monroe, Paul, 33n, 34, 35n
Moorehead, Alan, 69n, 106n
Morkaya, Burhan Cahit, 167n
Morris-Jones, W. H., 171n
Moshos, Ahilya, 146n
Muhtar, Ahmet, 318
Multi-party system, 162, 166, 188, 349, 380, 389, 390, 396
Muş, Ilyas Sami, 102n
Mustafa Kemal, *see* Atatürk, Mustafa Kemal

Names denoting birthplace, 90
Nasser, Gamal Abdel, 416
NATO, 3
Nation (Ulus), newspaper, 19
Nation Party, 239, 241, 351n, 357n
National elite
  components changed, 349
  versus local leaders, 117, 118, 132–134, 157, 196–197, 388, 397

National Front Party (Iran), 303n
National identity (stage of political development), 408–409
National independence struggle (stage of political development), 409–410
National Recovery Party, 350n
National Sovereignty (Hâkimiyeti Milliye), 19, 343
"National Struggle," 161, 164, 169, 325, 354, 436
National Union, Committee of, 169, 371
Nationalist movement (First Congress), 309
Naval War Academy, 120
Naval War College, 120
Nebioğlu, Osman, 19n
New Zealand, 148, 394, 401
Non-Muslim deputies, 144–146
Non-Muslims in Turkey, 143–145

Ocaklar (party cells), 375
Occupational mobility of deputies, 136–143
Occupational prestige, 405–406
Occupations
  of all males over fifteen years, 81
  of household heads, 83
  political significance of, 75–78
  of population and deputies, 79–84
  social significance of, 73–75, 400
Occupations of Turkish deputies, 63–67, 180–184
  as bankers, 125–126
  and birthplace, 93–98
  as bureaucrats, 114–119, 130
  in cabinet, 281, 283, 299
  change of, 395–396
  in economic group, 123–126, 130
  as educators, 121–122
  and first election at by-election, 86
  in First Group, 310–312
  as journalists, 127–129, 133
  in leadership groups, 255–263
  as military men, 119–121, 132
  in newly elected group, 208–212, 222–223
  in Ninth and Tenth Assemblies, 359
  and overrepresentation, 63, 72
  in professional group, 404
  profile of, 78–86
  and reelection, 84
  in religious profession, 126
  in Second Group, 310–312
  in trade group, 123–124
Oğuz, Ahmet, 352n
Oğuzkan, Turhan, 30, 77n, 136, 138n
Oktay, Afşin, 19n
Ökte, Faik, 144n
Öktem, Haydar Rüştü, 102n
Okyar, Ali Fethi, 233, 288, 339
Okyar, Osman, 18n, 102n, 123n
Onaran, Halit, 102n
Onat, Naim Hazım, 126n
Opposition movements, 304–305

Opposition party, development of, 371–372
Opposition rule (stage of political development), 416–417
(Orbay), Rauf, 102n, 325, 326, 330
Orga, Irfan, 148, 149n
Örgeevren, Süreyya, 102n
Ottoman Assembly, 8
Ottoman Empire, 7–8
Özalp, Kâzım, 291
Özdamar, Hüseyin Hüsnü, 126n, 146n

Parental status of deputies, 175
Parliamentary experience of deputies, 53, 163, 164–168
 of cabinet 272–273, 297
 and educational level, 51
 of leadership groups, 247–248
 for Ninth and Tenth Assemblies, 358
 and publication, 58
Party membership and candidate nominations, 430–437
Party role in Turkish politics, 301–305, 375–376
Patrick, Mary Mills, 149n
Payaslıoğlu, Arif, 62n, 81n, 117n
Peasant Party, 239, 241, 357n
Peker, Recep, 271, 353, 369n
People's House *(Halkevi)*, 74
People's Party, *see* Republican People's Party
Perlmann, Moshe, 29n
Persian language, 109
"Pinnacle post," 229, 232, 237, 240, 265, 271, 302
Place, Francis, 400
Polatkan, Hasan, 289
Political development, stages of, 406, 407–419
Political infrastructure, 234
Political Science Faculty *(Mülkiye)*, 19, 33, 62, 115, 119, 132, 139, 288, 290
Popper, K. R., 407n
Populism, 337, 338
Postindependence conservatives, 329–330, 378, 411
Postindependence realignment (stage of political development), 327–328, 378, 410–411
Power, granted to masses, 418–419
"Power flexibility," 417–418
Power rating, *see* Formal power rating
President of Republic, 9, 197, 239–240, 265, 271, 286–288
Press Law, 48–49
Price, M. Philips, 40n, 124n, 145n
Prime Minister (Premier), 9, 230–232, 238, 239, 265, 286–288
Princes Islands, 99
Professional men, and amount of speaking in G.N.A., 399
Professional schools, 62
Professions, free, 111–114

Progressive Republican Party, 11, 231, 233–234, 377–378, 390
 background characteristics contrasted with R.P.P., 332–335
 chronology and character of, 330-331
 genesis of, 324-327
 manifesto and program of, 331
Psomiades, Harry J., 143n
Public Works, Ministers of, 286, 294
Publication by deputies, 57–58, 87

Ramsaur, Ernest E., 61n
Rauf, *see* (Orbay)
Recruitment in G.N.A.
 co-optative policy of, 23
 criteria for, 268, 277, 398
Red Crescent *(Kızılay)*, 100
Reed, Howard, 29n, 34n, 126n, 148, 150n
Reelection of deputies, 164, 167–168, 194, 394–395
 in cabinet, 272–273, 297
 in First Group, 312–313
 in Ninth and Tenth Assemblies, 358
 in Second Group, 312–313
Refet (Pasha), *see* (Bele), Refet
Regional origin of cabinet, 273–275, 298
"Release process" of political systems, 392–393
Religion in Turkey, 143–145
Religious group as deputies, 126, 183, 388
Religious institutions abolished, 40
Removal of deputies, 166–167
Renda, Mustafa Abdülhalik, 289
Representation, Burkean conception of, 13, 89, 423
Representative Assembly *(Temsilciler Meclisi)*, 76
Republic (Cumhuriyet), newspaper, 19
Republican People's Party, 11–15, 69n, 78, 102, 121, 162, 166, 167, 169, 173, 177, 180, 183, 187, 191–192, 196, 197, 201, 202, 204, 217, 219, 222, 232, 236–241, 271, 299, 303n, 304–305, 325, 330, 344, 349, 350–353, 356, 380–382, 393, 397n, 399, 427, 430, 431–435, 437n
 Council of Presidency, 14
 creation of, 40
 General Executive Committee, 14
 General-President, 14, 234, 235, 238
 General-Secretary, 14, 231, 233–234, 237, 238, 265
 General-Vice-President, 14, 232, 238
 Independent Group of, 343–347, 379–380
 occupational representation in, 76
 Research Bureau, 18n, 20
Requirements of deputies, *see* Formal requirements of deputies
Residency requirements for deputies, 89–90
Resignation of deputies, 163–165, 193

INDEX

Revolution of 1908, 33
Robert College, 33
Robinson, Richard D., 3n, 90n, 147n, 162n, 169n, 348n
Roe, Ann, 406n
Ross, J. F. S., 147n, 171n, 394n, 396n
Rossi, Peter H., 226n
Rothwell, C. Easton, 396n, 401n
Russell, Bertrand, 35n
Russia, 92, 148, 349
Rustow, D. A., 33n, 52n, 79n, 91n, 92n, 126n, 127n, 162n, 169n, 271n, 312n, 324n, 339

Saka, Hasan, 271, 288, 289, 293
Salonika Military Middle School, 47
Salve, M. de, see De Salve, M.
Sami, Bekir, see Bekir Sami Bey
Sanay, A. Ş., 124n, 136n
Saracoğlu, Şükrü, 137, 271n, 288, 291
Sassani, Abul H. K., 152n
Savcı, Basri, 10n, 84n
Saydam, Refik, 271n, 288, 295
Sazak, Emin, 369n
Scandinavia, 148
Schueller, George, 148n
Second Constitutional Period, 12, 301
Second Group (Defense of Rights Group), 11, 305, 307, 326, 331, 376–377, 430, 431n
Selznick, Philip, 284n
Shiites, see Alevi
Shils, Edward, 31
Single-party system, 375–376
Sirmen, Fuat, 293, 346
Sırrı, Süleyman, 294
"Six Arrows," People's Party Program, 76
Smith, Edward C., 9n
Smith, Wilfred Cantwell, 29n, 70n
Social backgrounds of deputies, 157–158, 196, 387–394, 398–400
  research methods used for, 22–25
  sources of information on, 16–20
Social mobility in Turkey, 135–138
Social prestige, relation to formal authority, 400–403
Society for Protection of Children (Çocuk Esirgeme Kurumu), 100
Soriano, Hanri, 146n
Soule, George, 38n
Soviet Union, see Russia
Soyak, Hasan Rıza, 337n
Speaking patterns of deputies
  in First Assembly, 313–323, 448–449
  in First Group, 313–323
  in Second Group, 313–323
Sporel, Zeki Rıza, 167n
Spry, Graham, 38n
State, Ministers of, 286, 296–297
Stirling, Paul, 12n, 152n, 168n
Süleyman, Sultan (the Magnificent), 32
Sultanate, termination of, 40
Super, Donald, 406n
Supreme Court, Turkish, 197

Switzerland, 69
Szyliowicz, Joseph, 158n

Tachau, Frank, 29n
Tahsin, Orhan, 37n
Tahtakılıç, Ahmet, 352n
Talat (Pasha), 137
Tankut, Hasan Reşit, 102n
Tanrıöver, Hamdullah Suphi, 102n, 292
Tanzimat (Reform) Era, 34, 39
Taptas, 146n
Tarhan, Ali Rana, 278, 296, 344
Tarver, Zakar, 146n
Tayyar, Cafer, 335
Teachers in Turkey, 138n
Tek, Ahmet Ferit, 317
"Thirty five," faction of R.P.P., 169, 353–356, 370, 380–381
Thomas, Lewis V., 7n, 29n, 41, 42n, 126n
Thornburg, Max W., 38n
Tomlin, E. W. F., 114n
Top leaders of G. N. A., 244–248, 266
Totalitarian ideology, development of, 338–339
Trade group as deputies, 123–124, 183, 388
Tunca, Cemal, 102n
Türel, Ali Rıza, 14
Tokar, Feyyaz, 14n
Toynbee, Arnold, 29n, 91n
"Transitional democratic" approach, 413–414, 415
Transportation and Communication, Ministers of, 286, 296
Tunaya, Tarık Z., 8n, 11n, 38n, 75n, 77n, 100n, 306n, 312n, 324n, 326n, 330n, 331n, 336n, 339n, 340n, 342, 344n, 348n, 350n, 353n, 354, 423n, 424n, 427n, 428n, 429n
Türk Ocağı (Turkish Hearth), 38n, 61, 91, 150, 192
Türk Yurdu, 91
Türker, Berç (Bedros Keresteciyan), 146n
Turkey
  General Directorate of Statistics, 94n
  political significance of, 3–6
  social background research on, 394
Turkish Information Office, 33n, 48n, 150n, 152n
Turkish National Commission on Education, 33n
Turkish Republic, First, see First Turkish Republic
Turkish revolution, second stage of, 42–43
Tutelary approach in political development, 4–5, 134, 158, 161, 196, 329, 376, 388, 390–391, 393, 396, 411–414, 415–416
  definition of, 413

(Ulaş), Hüseyin Avni, 307n, 431n
Ulema, 39
Ülker, Resit, 423n, 428n, 429n

INDEX 483

Ulus (Nation), newspaper, 19
Ulusan, Mustafa, 126n
Union and Progress Association, 301
United Nations, 349
United States, 103, 108, 349, 395
   social backgrounds of public leaders in, 393–394
Uran, Hilmi, 344n, 345n, 349n
Us, Hakkı Tarık, 369n
U.S.S.R., *see* Russia
Uybadın, Cemil, 289
Uzer, Tahsin, 102n

Varlık Vergisi (capital levy), *see* Capital levy
Vefa Idadisi (school), 37, 128n, 280
Vehbi, Mehmet, 317
Veterinarians as deputies, 114
Voluntary association membership, 99–100
Von Kral, *see* Kral, (August) Ritter von
Von Mikusch, *see* Mikusch, Dagobert von, 324n
Von Vorys, Karl, 171n
Voting behavior of deputies (First to Tenth Assembly), 360–375, 382–383

Wallas, Graham, 400n
War Academy *(Harb Akademisi)*, 66n, 120, 133, 288, 290
War College or School *(Harbiye* or *Harb Okulu)*, 33, 47, 48, 61, 66n, 120, 133
War for Independence, 5, 78, 150–151
Ward, Barbara, 39, 40n, 150n
Ward, Norman, 171n
Ward, Robert E., 33n
Watershed of social background divergence, 22, 82–84, 398
Webb, L. C., 171n
Webster, Donald, 30, 76n, 106n, 123n, 136, 137, 144n, 153n, 343n, 433n
Weiker, Walter, 11n, 339n
Werfel, Franz, 143
Wolfinger, Raymond, 226n
Women
   as deputies to G.N.A., 147–155, 192–193, 195–196, 426
   emancipation of, in Turkey, 148–151
   in G.N.A. leadership, 251–252
   in professions, 151–152
   social position of, 151–153
World War I, 7
World War II, 348
Wright, Charles, 394n

Yalçın, Hüseyin Cahit, 102n
Yalman, Ahmet Emin, 46n, 76n, 91n, 102n, 127n, 150n, 348n
Yardımcı, Celâl, 273, 297
Yasa, Ibrahim, 152n, 158n, 168, 169n, 340
Yiğitbaş, M. Sadık, 307n, 431n
Yılmaz, Kenan, 290
Young, T. Cuyler, 42n
Young Turks, 33, 34, 38, 100, 424
Yücel, Hasan Ali, 292
Yurdakul, Mehmet Emin, 102n

Zafer (Victory), newspaper, 19
Zeytinoğlu, Kemal, 294
Ziya (Bey), 163n
Zorlu, Fatin Rüştü, 273, 297

WITHDRAWN